Education for INCLUSION AND DIVERSITY

Third edition

Education for INCLUSION AND DIVERSITY

Third edition

Edited by Adrian Ashman and John Elkins

Pearson Education Australia
Unit 4, Level 3
14 Aquatic Drive
Frenchs Forest NSW 2086

www.pearsoned.com.au

Senior Acquisitions Editor: Alison Green
Senior Project Editor: Katie Millar
Editorial Coordinator: Jessica Sykes
Production Coordinator: Chris Richardson
Copy Editor: Bree DeRoche
Proofreader: Felicity McKenzie
Copyright and Pictures Editor: Emma Gaulton
Cover and internal design by Natalie Bowra
Cover illustration from Getty Images
Typeset by Midland Typesetters, Australia

Printed in Malaysia (CTP - PA)

1 2 3 4 5 13 12 11 10 09

National Library of Australia
Cataloguing-in-Publication Data

Author:	Ashman, Adrian F. (Adrian Frederick)
Title:	Education for inclusion and diversity/authors, Adrian Ashman; John Elkins
Edition:	3rd ed.
Publisher:	Frenchs Forest, N.S.W.: Pearson Education Australia, 2008
ISBN:	9781442502048 (pbk)
Notes:	Previous ed.: 2005 Includes index
Subjects:	Special education Inclusive education Children with disabilities — Education
Other Authors/Contributors:	Elkins, John
Dewey Number:	371.9

An imprint of Pearson Education Australia (a division of Pearson Australia Group Pty Ltd)

Brief contents

Contents

About this book

Over the past four or five years, we have watched developments in Australian education systems with considerable interest. In all Australian states and territories, education departments and non-government sectors have continued to evolve and reconstruct themselves and inclusive education has been high on the agenda. Despite the widespread appeal of inclusion as a social justice ideal, its success in improving the educational outcomes of students with diverse learning needs has not been fully explored or reported.

For even longer than these few years, we have advocated strongly for equity in educational provisions for students with special learning needs and this led to the release of the first edition of this textbook in 1990. Back then it was called *Educating children with special needs*. At that time, it was the first comprehensive Australian text in the area and it has maintained this status since then.

The changes in school education over these two decades have been substantial. Sections or divisions within the various state education authorities with the label 'Special Education' no longer exist. The responsibility for supporting students with diverse learning needs now typically falls under the curriculum sections from which state-wide and territory-wide services are managed.

Over the same period, preservice teacher education programs have been largely static. There is no consistent requirement across Australian states and territories for students studying to be teachers to take specific courses or subjects dealing with student diversity and inclusive education practices. Certainly, in some states there is a requirement for special needs education to be included in the suite of courses comprising the preservice teacher education. This means that many young (and not so young) newly qualified teachers enter the service without much knowledge of the diversity of student characteristics that will be found in their first classroom and all later ones.

It is inevitable that newly qualified teachers will be challenged by the huge variations in their students' skills, knowledge, motivation, and capabilities. In a submission to the Senate Employment, Workplace Relations and Education Committee, school principal Peter Symons said:

> *Recently I spoke to a group of exit students at a university and asked 30 of them, "How many of you expect to be teaching a student with a disability next year?" and no one put their hand up. I informed them that they would not only have one student with a disability but five or six. The fact that the institution had not even moved in that area to provide those skills was going to cause those teachers frustration. (Commonwealth of Australia, 2002, p. 79)*

The purpose of this book, therefore, is to work toward overcoming the situation to which Mr Symons

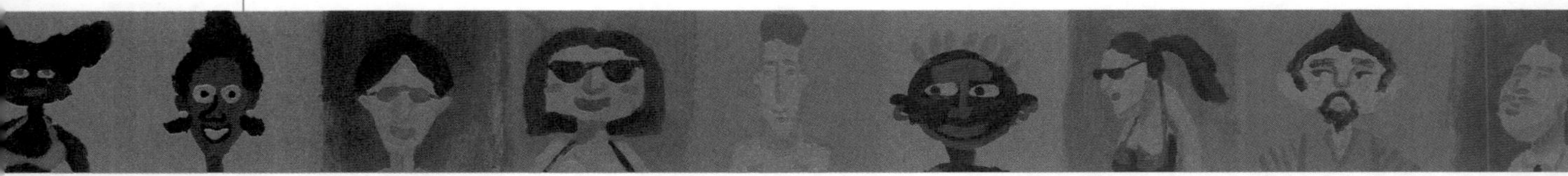

referred. Our approach has been to focus on educational policies and practices that teachers can implement in their classrooms to assist all students achieve positive learning outcomes.

Here, we have adopted an approach that is common to the authors who have contributed to this book. That is, we recognise that there are teaching principles that apply across all teaching and learning contexts and that these are appropriate regardless of age and capability. We all accept that having a diagnosis or a label as a person with a specific impairment or disability tells little about how that person will respond in a learning situation at preschool, primary, middle school, or high school and beyond. But it is folly to think that the conditions experienced by a person with a particular physical, sensory, or intellectual condition have no bearing on teaching and learning events. In this book, we have endeavoured to address both influences.

We have approached this task by generating a source book that will provide the reader with a foundation on which professional practice can be securely based. It should stimulate your search for knowledge and provide a mental map to guide your further research and studies.

Let's have a quick look though the book. You can see from the Contents pages that it is divided into four sections:

- Section 1 Inclusive Societies;
- Section 2 Inclusive Schools;
- Section 3 Inclusive Practices; and
- Section 4 Inclusive Outcomes.

There is also a CD inside the back cover where readers will find information about specific disabilities and impairment that is not contained in the text. This information will provide a useful starting point for a search of the literature and basic reference material.

Section 1 deals with general issues that relate to all learning and every learning situation.

Section 2 considers essential school-based characteristics that include system supports, managing student behaviour, and the use of technology.

Section 3 introduces teaching principles that are applicable generally and also specifically to the various phases of schooling.

Section 4 looks at outcomes. Ideally, a comprehensive education provides opportunities for young people to become valuable members of society. This is a whole-of-community responsibility that involves the home, the school, and the wider community.

As you will see as you page through the book, each chapter is written according to the same template:

- The 'Case studies' section appears at the beginning of each chapter, and provides two examples. These are intended to orient the reader to a number of issues that teachers experience each day.
- 'Teaching–learning context' is the next section. It provides a general background to the chapter content.
- 'Issues and challenges' then draws attention to some of the key topics that confront education systems, schools, teachers, students, and parents.
- 'Teaching essentials' deals with teaching strategies that are relevant to all students generally, plus specific practices that address the needs of students with particular learning needs.
- 'Learning essentials' focuses on students' responses to teaching, including developmental issues and transitions.
- 'Using this chapter in schools' draws attention to the key issues raised in the chapter and gives suggestions about how a newly qualified (or

experienced) teacher might apply the knowledge gained in their specific teaching situation.

- The 'Practical activities' section directs the reader to short projects or assignments that will augment their knowledge gained in the context of a university course, and also activities that can be undertaken while the reader is on a practicum placement or working in a school.

As editors, we are delighted to have such a distinguished group of contributors to this book. As you will see in the 'About the authors' section, all are eminent scholars with decades of experience working in their own specialist fields. They represent the breadth of senior Australian academics, and they are not ivory tower professionals. All are regular visitors to schools and understand the issues and the challenges that teaching presents to newcomers to the profession. All have careers that span many years.

Readers of this book are most likely to be undergraduate students who are intending to become teachers, or students taking a postgraduate program to gain their teaching credentials. Readers from other disciplines such as speech pathology, physiotherapy, occupational therapy, nursing, psychology, or adult and human services will also find much in this book of value. All will benefit from knowing about education, how to expand the learning opportunities for all young people, and how educators and supporting professionals can best serve students' needs and interests.

We hope that you find this book as stimulating to read as we have when preparing it for you. As a last point, we want to acknowledge several people who have helped immeasurably in the editing process. Rob Allen has been an inspiration and constant source of support throughout the entire project. He has proof-read chapters and generated a number of the graphics. Annette and Geoff Hilton, Margaret Ballinger and Kathy Allen are also to be thanked for giving their time generously to proofread material. Finally, we are indebted to Alison Green (Pearson Education Australia) who has given us tremendous support at every stage of the process. Thanks to all.

ADRIAN ASHMAN AND JOHN ELKINS

REFERENCE

Commonwealth of Australia (2002). *Education of students with disabilities*. Report of the Senate Employment, Workplace Relations and Education Committee (ISBN 0 642 71205 0). Canberra: Author.

About the authors

ADRIAN ASHMAN

Adrian Ashman is Professor of Education at the University of Queensland. He has a 30-year history of research and publication in the fields of education and psychology with a particular interest in students' learning problems and inclusive education policy and practices. He is a Fellow of the American Psychological Association and of the International Association for the Scientific Study of Intellectual Disability.

DOUG BRIDGE

Dr Doug Bridge has worked in the field of education for over 30 years, initially as a classroom teacher, then in the area of special education. Doug was principal of several special schools in Tasmania before moving into administrative roles with the Tasmanian Department of Education. Doug has a PhD through Curtin University of Technology that explores the inclusive schooling as practised in a range of settings and countries. He has been involved in research related to literacy teaching and learning and into homophobia in schools. Recently Doug has completed a period of work at the University of Tasmania in the Institute for Inclusive Learning Communities.

SUZANNE CARRINGTON

Suzanne Carrington is Professor and Head of School of Learning and Professional Studies, Faculty of Education, Queensland University of Technology. She has 10 years of experience in early childhood, primary, special, and secondary schools, and she was the Foundation Director and Manager of the Staff College, Inclusive Education in Education Queensland (2002–2004). In this position, she directed professional development of Education Queensland teachers to progress a more inclusive approach to curriculum and pedagogy. She has conducted research and published in international journals in the areas of inclusive culture, policy and practice, learning support, Autistic Spectrum Disorder, teaching/professional development, and service learning.

ROD CHADBOURNE

For much of the 1960s, Rod Chadbourne taught in secondary schools in Western Australia, New Zealand, Canada and England. While in London he completed an MA in comparative education. He began tertiary teaching at Adelaide Teachers College in 1971 and moved to Edith Cowan University (ECU) in 1973. From 1975 to 1980 he studied on a part-time basis for his doctorate in sociology at Murdoch University. For the past six years at ECU he has been teaching, researching, and publishing in the field of middle schooling. Rod is Associate Professor in the Faculty of Education and the Arts.

BOB CONWAY

Professor Robert Conway is the Dean of Education at Flinders University in Adelaide. He has a background as both a regular education and a special education teacher, and has worked extensively with

schools and educational jurisdictions across Australia and internationally. He has a particular teaching and research interest in students with emotional and behaviour problems and the ways in which systems respond to the management needs of these students. He has also conducted a number of reviews of behaviour and special education services both nationally and abroad.

RUTH CROSER

Ruth Croser has qualifications in professional education from the Universities of Tasmania, Newcastle, and South Australia, and also from Flinders University. She was employed in the South Australian education system as a computer access specialist following a career as an occupational therapist. Since 2003 she has been employed in the State Support Service and Inclusive Learning Support Service, and in the Tasmanian Department of Education. Ruth has a particular interest in the application of electronic aids in daily living.

SUSAN DANBY

Susan Danby is Professor of Education and senior researcher in the Early Years program at Queensland University of Technology. She publishes in the area of adult–child interaction and children's peer interactions. Her current Australian Research Council study investigates talk and interaction on help-lines and twin children's social worlds in the early years.

JOHN ELKINS

John Elkins is Emeritus Professor of Education at the University of Queensland and has been Professor of Literacy Education at Griffith University since 2003. He chairs the Queensland Minister's Advisory Committee on Students with Disabilities. His interests include policy and practice in inclusive education.

ROBYN GILLIES

Robyn Gillies PhD is a Professor of Education at the University of Queensland. She has worked extensively in primary, middle, and high schools to help teachers embed cooperative learning pedagogical practices into their classroom curricula, and more recently has researched teacher and student discourses in the cooperative classroom. In 2007 she published *Cooperative learning: Integrating theory and practice*, a textbook designed to present evidence-based practices that teachers can use in classrooms to promote socialisation and learning.

IAN HAY

Ian Hay is Dean of Education at the University of Tasmania. He has authored some 200 publications for international and national peer-reviewed journals, chapters in books, and conference proceedings. His main research interests relate to students with special education needs, students' literacy development, and the interactions between students' psychosocial development and their academic achievement. Ian has had academic

appointments at the University of Queensland and Griffith University. He is a Fellow of the International Academy of Research into Learning Disabilities, and is both a registered teacher and a Member of the Australian Psychological Society.

HEATHER JENKINS

Heather Jenkins is Associate Professor of Special Education at Curtin University of Technology, and has been lecturing and researching in inclusive and special education since 1995. She was the president of the WA Chapter of the Australian Association of Special Education from 2002 to 2004, and is the academic representative on the WA Department of Education and Training's Building Inclusive Schools steering committee. Her current Australian Research Council grants are investigating the early detection of children at risk of developing learning and attentional problems, and the impact of the new nonstimulant medication on the development of children with Attention Deficit Hyperactivity Disorder.

PETER MERROTSY

Peter Merrotsy is a lecturer in Gifted and Talented Education at the University of New England. Previously, he enjoyed 18 years' experience as a teacher of mathematics and head teacher in rural New South Wales, during which time he completed his doctorate on curriculum for gifted students. His current research is focused on gifted children and youth from backgrounds of disadvantage such as rural and isolated contexts, low-socioeconomic status, and cultural-minority status. He is involved in professional training and development of teachers and in community-based workshops all over Australia. He is Editor of the journal *TalentEd*, and Co-editor of the journal *Gifted and Talented International*.

KAREN MONI

Dr Karen Moni is a senior lecturer in English and literacy education at the University of Queensland. She is the Executive Director of Latch-On (Literacy and Technology-Hands On), a post-school literacy program for young adults with intellectual disabilities. Her research interests include teaching and learning in higher education, literacy and young adults with intellectual disabilities, and teacher education. Karen is also the Editor of the peer-reviewed journal *English in Australia* and past president of the English Teachers' Association of Queensland.

JOHN MUNRO

John Munro is Associate Professor in the Faculty of Education at the University of Melbourne. John has been involved in special needs education almost since he began his career as a teacher. He has experience in the state education authority in Victoria, and has particular interest in the development of inclusive schools, inclusive practices, and professional learning.

PAUL PAGLIANO

Paul Pagliano is Associate Professor of Education at James Cook University. He has more than 30 years' experience working in inclusive education in Australia, North America, Europe, and Asia. His PhD focused on parents living with a child with a disability and his particular research interest is in the role of sensory stimulation in education and therapy. Paul is on the editorial boards of the *Australasian Journal of Special Education*, *Australian Education Researcher*, *Journal of Intellectual and Developmental Disability*, the *British Journal of Visual Impairment*, and the *Journal of the South Pacific Educators in Vision Impairment.*

DONNA PENDERGAST

Donna Pendergast is Associate Professor of Education at the University of Queensland. She has expertise in teaching and education for the middle years, providing ministerial advice, and conducting research and professional development in the field. She also has an international profile in Family and Consumer Studies. She has researched and published widely, including her recent books: *Teaching middle years: Rethinking curriculum, pedagogy and assessment*, which was selected as a *Choice* Outstanding Academic Title; and *The millennial adolescent*, which focuses on teaching Generation Y students.

CHRISTINA VAN KRAAYENOORD

Christina van Kraayenoord is an Associate Professor of Education at the University of Queensland. She teaches courses in literacy, and diversity and education. Her research and publications are in the areas of: literacy, related to reading, writing, metacognition and motivation, learning difficulties, and inclusive education, especially Universal Design for Learning and differentiated instruction. She is a Fellow of the International Academy for Research in Learning Disabilities and is the Editor of the *International Journal of Disability, Development and Education*.

Acknowledgements

The publisher would like to thank the following academics for their invaluable feedback and advice:

Lorraine Hammond	Edith Cowan University
Andrea Rosewarne	RMIT
Anne Petriwskyi	Queensland University of Technology
Karen Edwards	Charles Sturt University
Lucie Zundans	Queensland University of Technology
Emma Little	RMIT
Julie Lancaster	Charles Sturt University
Ingrid Harrington	University of New England
Mervyn Hyde	Griffith University
Marilyn Kell	University of Western Sydney
Jill Burgess	Australian Catholic University

I

Inclusive Societies

Inclusive Societies

Just over one hundred years ago, the first manned aircraft lifted off the beach at Kitty Hawk in North Carolina. *The Flyer* was not much more sophisticated than a timber and wire frame covered with fabric. It weighed 860 pounds, had a wingspan of 40 feet, and was powered by an 18-horsepower engine. It carried Wilbur Wright into the annals of aviation history. At the same time, the most rapid form of mass communication was the radio set around which families crowded when important announcements of national or international significance were expected.

Twenty-five years ago, the largest passenger airliner weighed over 860,000 pounds, had a wingspan of more than 200 feet, and its engines could produce more than 56,000 pounds of thrust. Three Americans had already left a zigzag of foot and tyre prints on the moon. Today, many millions of people log onto the world wide web or send SMSs to friends in the next room, across the street, or on the other side of the world.

It is amazing how much the world has changed in 100 years.

It is also amazing how little has changed. There is hardly a day when there is no news of local, national, and international conflicts; or when some group has claimed responsibility for another atrocity against fellow humans. There are still disputes between neighbours, within families, and between total strangers. And despite the technological advances, there remain huge differences between the lifestyles of people living in Third- and Fourth-World countries and those in what we call "advanced" societies.

Of course, there is little benefit to be gained from cataloguing everything that is wrong with the world and its societies. Detailing the woes leads nowhere. Recognising what some of those woes might be and planning and implementing strategies to redress them *can* make a difference. This is what this book is about: making changes wherever and whenever we can within our own spheres of influence. For most readers, this is likely to be within the field of education and within the classroom.

The first section of this book deals with the context in which teaching and learning occurs. We step back from particular education events to examine, first, the landscape and the many factors that affect what, how, and where we learn. Because we are concerned about making every educational environment accessible to all students, this volume is intended as a "first reader". In a book like this, it is impossible to deal with every permutation and combination of factors that might affect the learning experiences of every person. There are, of course, some general principles and each of the authors has set these out in a consistent way.

In books on diversity and inclusive education, there is an almost unavoidable emphasis on learners who have traditionally been excluded from regular schools or regular classrooms. These days there is a belief that regular schools must change if they are to meet the needs of all students. There is an imperative to take into account ethnicity, gender equity, and poverty. By developing a curriculum that is relevant to the needs of every student (generally called an "inclusive" curriculum), teachers can attend to the educational necessities rather than pay heed to labels that provide scant information about how to provide an education that maximises academic and social development.

In this first section, we consider some of the fundamental issues concerning the education of all students. In Chapter 1, Adrian Ashman begins with a look at the global context which includes the social and cultural aspects of education. In Chapter 2, John Elkins draws attention to the legislative and policy matters that frame the delivery of educational services within the various Australian authorities, systems, and schools. In Chapter 3, Adrian Ashman and Peter Merrotsy focus on the individual learner in context, setting the stage on which each of the later contributors will appear.

Adrian Ashman

1

CONTEMPORARY CULTURES AND EDUCATION

What you will learn in this chapter

This chapter is an orientation to the context in which teaching and learning occur. Everyone is subject to social and cultural influences, but each of us deals with these influences in a variety of ways. Our cultural background, our social situation, and family circumstances also affect how we think and learn.

In this chapter you will learn:

- how society and culture are defined;
- how important society and culture are in the lives of most young people;
- about different family types and how these may affect children's education;
- about the importance of recognising and valuing difference;
- how school communities can accommodate diversity and difference; and
- how school professionals can bring society and culture into the foreground when considering how to deal with learners from very different backgrounds.

CASE STUDIES

These two case studies are examples of situations that teachers might encounter in the course of their professional lives. They draw attention to a range of issues including a clash of cultures, contact between the school and parents, the appropriateness of the curricula, and student behaviour that teachers are sometimes required to manage. As you read, keep in mind your own attitudes and beliefs about culture and individual differences and think about how you might respond to the situations in which these two teachers found themselves.

individual differences

The various personal qualities (intellectual, personality, social-emotional) that constitute the differences between individuals.

CAMROSE PARKLAND STATE SCHOOL

Kevin Atkinson grew up in Melbourne until he was 10 years old, then moved to Queensland with his parents and spent his teenage years attending a well-known college. By the time he finished Year 11, Kevin still hadn't made up his mind about what career he wanted to pursue, and at the end of Year 12 was not much further along in that decision-making process. He took a gap year (when gap years weren't quite as popular as they are now) and worked his way around the United Kingdom and Ireland until his parents lost all enthusiasm for topping up his almost permanently drained bank and credit card accounts. He returned home and decided that a career in education was possibly the least unattractive option. Four years later he was a primary teacher and was offered a job in an area of the city renowned for its social disadvantage.

Camrose Parkland State School has an enrolment of just over 500 students. It was built in the 1960s. The campus looks a bit tired but is reasonably well maintained and the staff is a mixture of "old hands" who have been at the school for more than 10 years and some newcomers who are in their first three to five years of teaching. Camrose is located in a neighbourhood with many social and cultural complexities, including significant Indigenous and Pacific Islander communities, single-parent families, and many long-term welfare households.

Autism Spectrum Disorder (ASD)

The symptoms and characteristics of autism can present themselves in a wide variety of combinations, from mild to severe. Although autism is defined by a certain set of behaviors, children and adults can exhibit any combination of the behaviors in any degree of severity. This is characterised by impairments in social interaction, communication, and stereotyped behaviours, interests, and activities.

Kevin did relatively well at university and thought that he was about as prepared as he could be for his first year out. Before Christmas, after his graduation, he was offered a Year 4 class following the unexpected resignation of one of the school's more experienced teachers. Kevin didn't give his new appointment much thought because a vacation from the pressures of university meant exactly that: surfing, fishing, parties.

His orientation to Camrose Parkland came shortly after the beginning of the school year. His class—AK4, as it would be known—was not what Kevin expected. He had two students who were verified as having Autism Spectrum Disorder and he realised from the first day that they were going to be difficult to manage. There were also five students who seemed to have abilities beyond the curriculum expectations for a beginning Year 4 class.

skill

An acquired aptitude or learned act (e.g., reading, riding a bicycle).

In his first few days, he did his best to learn the students' names and get to know something about them. He was surprised to discover that many lived in single-parent homes in which there were many brothers and sisters. Most of the mums stayed at home to look after the preschool-aged children and there was a scattering of "uncles" and "dads" who shared the homes for short or long periods. Most of the students had language skills below Year 4, some below Year 2, and a brief conversation with the school counsellor confirmed that half of the students in Kevin's class

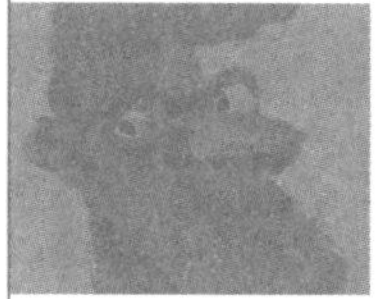

lived in near-poverty situations. Brothers and sisters often had different fathers and there were a few mothers who weren't exactly sure of their children's birthdays.

The first six months in the school were very difficult for Kevin. All of the expectations he had about having fun with his students and watching them blossom under his guidance slowly evaporated.

I was a bit like St John seeing God on the road to wherever he was going—knowing that what I learned at uni hadn't prepared me for what I had to deal with. You know, it was a big deal just working on reading and writing and I couldn't say, "When you get home, ask your mum to help you with your spelling list" because Mum couldn't spell as well as Jamie or Trag. The great thing, though, was the counsellor told me that all the kids needed was TLC and they'd respond, and you know what? They did. The kids'd gather around me during lunch and playtime, which was nice but a bit much when I needed a break.

At the end of his first year, Kevin seriously considered leaving teaching.

I thought about trying the hospitality industry but when I talked to my friends who'd been given schools in some of the middle-class areas, I figured my year was full of experiences they couldn't even dream of. The boss's moving me up to Year 5 with the same kids next year and I'm stoked about that. I've got to know some of the parents—some are really weird—I never imagined people living like that. I'm back at Cammie Park next year. For how long, I don't know, but it's certain for next year.

ST ROSE'S COLLEGE

Melanie Tiffin has been teaching for eight years. She completed an Arts degree at a regional university and then a diploma of education. She supply-taught for two years in a state high school and then was offered a one-year contract. When her husband was transferred and they moved cities, she got a continuing appointment at a church-run girls college. Rosie's—how its "old girls" affectionately refer to the school—offers high-quality educational experiences but is not as academically selective as some other private colleges. The children of old girls have admission priority and this means that the mix of student abilities is rich across the primary and secondary years.

Melanie teaches English to Years 10, 11, and 12 students.

It's interesting that you ask about cultural and social issues that teachers should think about. When I came to Rosie's it was a bit of a shock. I was expecting the focus to be on the academics and getting as many of the girls as possible into things like medicine and dentistry at uni. And there is a focus on that, but we have a lot of girls who'll never get into the university programs they want, or even to university.

Melanie's previous teaching year was in a state high school in a regional industrial city. The school drew its enrolments from a lower socioeconomic area in which there was a significant Indigenous community.

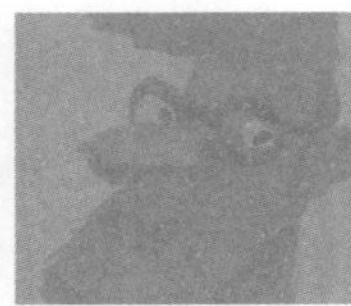

You really had to work hard with those kids because many of them came from tough families and there wasn't much interest in school or studying. At first I used to set homework like I was supposed to, but only four or five of the kids would do it—the rest never bothered—so I soon gave that idea away and set homework assignments like getting the kids to use a new word at home each week. It was kinda fun, actually, because we'd talk in class about new words the kids had read or I'd told them about, and we'd work out how many of their family members were likely to know the words. Then we'd pick a day for their new words to be taken home and discussed and how the kids would teach their parents what their words meant. I figured out a secret acronym for the process they'd use and, not surprisingly, the kids remembered it pretty well. SEXT: Say, Explain, ConteXt, RepeaT. I used to giggle when I heard people talking about modifying the curriculum. Anyway, it worked. The next lesson we'd talk about how it went. At the end of the year I got them to do a test and you wouldn't believe how well they did. It was brilliant.

curriculum

Structured content of schooling, often used to include all planned experiences of students.

Melanie's Year 10, 11, and 12 classes at St Rose's College include some very bright students and a few who are struggling.

At Rosie's it's really interesting because some of the tricks I learned at my last school work just as well here, but the girls don't have to deal with the same social problems at home. But there are some parallels. Like, at the high school, the parents didn't really care too much about whether their kids got jobs or not. At Rosie's, I think the parents care but most of the girls live in families in which both parents work and they just don't have time to be interested in what's happening at school. The parents at the high school could never help their kids with homework, and many of the Rosie's parents don't have time.

TEACHING–LEARNING CONTEXT

This book deals with two concepts in tension: inclusion and diversity. On the one hand, inclusion is about belonging, about being rightly placed within a group of people, and having the rights and qualities that characterise members of that particular group. On the other hand, diversity is all about difference and variety. How is it then that education systems have come to advocate policies and practices that seek to bring all students together as one? As you read through this chapter and those that follow, it is hoped that the tensions will become apparent and that you will see ways in which we can value and appreciate difference and variety as a positive attribute in all educational and social environments. Most important is the focus on how each member of a school community can contribute to good teaching and learning practices that benefit all students.

In this chapter, I lay the foundations that will set the context for the contributions that follow. That context is the culture and society in which learning occurs.

When teachers talk about essential classroom strategies, culture and society are often overlooked, or at least thought to be irrelevant to how knowledge is accumulated or how teaching is done in schools. This is surprising when you think that education is both a process and a consequence of the experiences that occur throughout the course of each person's life. What we learn and how we learn is governed by the culture and the society in which we live, and our responses to them. And education is not limited

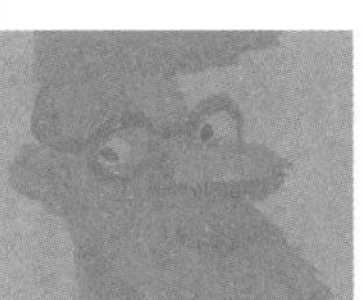

to what happens within the compulsory years of schooling. Arguably, our education begins when we are first able to detect causes and consequences, and it continues until we are no longer able to gather and store knowledge about ourselves and the world around us.

So, let us turn our attention first to these very important issues.

Culture and society

Culture is the warehouse of human or national values and has a historical sense that relates to the meaning of all forms of activity (Mulhern, 2000). Culture includes the norms, values, beliefs, languages, traditions, symbols, activities, achievements, and possessions that characterise a group of people. It also includes the social relationships and interactions that communicate the features of that culture.

In Australia, as in other Western countries such as the United States, Britain, Canada, and many European countries, there has been a broadening of cultural influences that is often called the cultural mosaic. This has come about as those who have immigrated maintain many of their homeland traditions while embracing, to a greater or lesser extent, the new norms, values, and practices of the adopted country. Multiculturalism is the recognition and promotion of the cultural mosaic and this is reflected in community acceptance of some, although not necessarily all, of the traditions and practices of those coming from other nations. The extent to which multiculturalism is part of Australia's present and future can be gauged by Australian Bureau of Statistics (2003a; 2003b) reports that show that around 25% of Australians were born in other countries, nearly half the population has direct links with relatives born overseas, and over 2.5 million people speak a language other than English at home. A more basic appreciation of the impact of Asian, Indian, Middle Eastern and even North American food can be made by walking the aisles of any supermarket or visiting restaurant precincts.

A society is a collection of people who live together in a more or less ordered community. A society has a distinctive culture, a shared history or background, interests, customs, and behaviour that define it. Of importance are the social institutions that make and preserve the characteristics of a society. These institutions establish and influence customs and traditions (such as marriage, the family, religion), they look after peace and order (such as government and the judiciary), and they are concerned with imparting knowledge about society, its history, and culture (such as schools, universities, and museums).

Education, therefore, is not simply the process of giving and receiving systematic instruction but it also has an important role to play in socialisation. Consider, for example, that children attend school from about 5 to 16+ years of age despite their willingness or otherwise to do so. Parents are required by law to ensure that their children attend school or receive an education through an acceptable alternative (such as home schooling) and penalties can be imposed if parents fail to comply. Some writers have drawn attention to the way in which schools require students to conform by wearing a school uniform, observe school rules, and respond in prescribed ways to bells and timetables. They argue that this is evidence that there is also a social control aspect to schooling.

The socialisation aspects of schooling are nowhere more obvious than in school discipline policies that commonly include the following expectations and requirements:

socialisation

The process of learning the behaviours, beliefs, values, and norms of a culture.

- lawful, ethical, and responsible behaviour;
- prohibition of illegal drugs, alcohol, tobacco, and weapons;
- recognition of the rights of others;
- demonstration of respect for themselves and others in the school community and the environment;
- adherence to the predetermined standards of dress; and
- obedience to requests from persons in positions of authority.

But education is not solely the responsibility of teachers, schools, and education systems. The family also plays a major role in passing down conventions and traditions from one generation to the next. In the same school discipline policies you will often find reference to what is expected of parents. These include:

- showing an active interest in their child's schooling;
- working with the school to accomplish positive learning outcomes for their child;
- cooperating with school staff to maintain a safe and respectful learning environment; and
- engaging in constructive communication about their child's welfare, learning, and behaviour.

So, let us turn our attention to the nature of contemporary families and ways in which families can affect children's educational outcomes.

Families and education

The family is a cornerstone of society. Indeed, satisfying the basic needs of family units may have been the only consideration when humans banded together to form the earliest communities. But changes have occurred over the millennia and in contemporary societies we might argue that the survival of the collective is more important than the survival of any part of it.

The family has the earliest and most enduring effect on the growth and development of children. This influence extends beyond the reproduction and nurturing of offspring to the physical, economic, emotional, and psychological domains. Ideally, the family provides a secure environment and the context in which children develop a disposition toward learning and problem-solving.

While satisfying children's physical needs is fundamental, the educational experiences that occur within the family cannot be underestimated. The very early years of a child's life are arguably the most

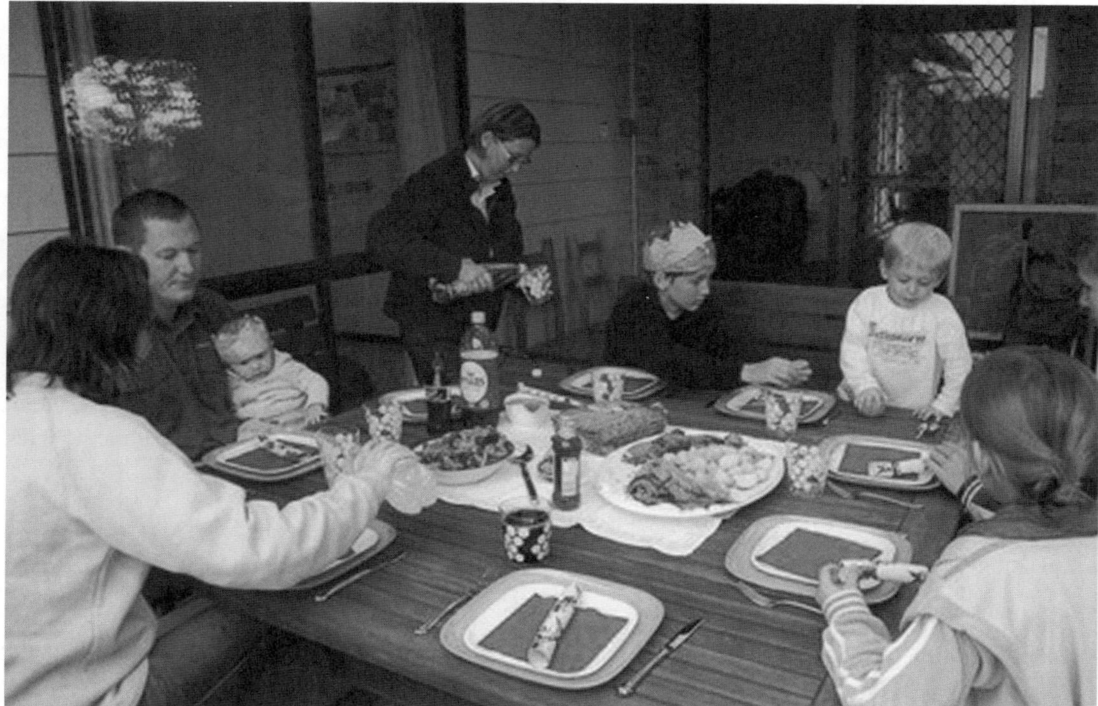

Consider the wonderful family dynamics occurring in this family

important for establishing the basic intellectual and emotional aspects of learning, such as meaning making, persistence, and curiosity. Children also learn to manipulate their surroundings and those within it. For example, a howl after a clumsy trip and fall will often lead to a wooing cuddle and a sweet treat designed to divert attention from a hardly visible graze on the knee.

As children grow and develop, parents can contribute handsomely to their education, perhaps more significantly in childhood than during the teenage years. Visits to museums, art galleries, exhibitions, parks, zoos, and vacation destinations provide children with experiences that expand their knowledge and interests and expose them to what some writers have called cultural capital (e.g., Wacquant, 2005).

The influence of the family is strengthened or modified through contact with others. Toddlers learn family conventions about right and wrong, and when they begin school, their values, beliefs, and attitudes are extended further and, in some cases, realigned to correspond with those of the wider society. In the teenage years, life within the family moves to a new dimension. The language skills of today's teenager sometimes leave much to be desired, with "Huh?" and "Wa?" often being the primary means of expression following requests to undertake simple domestic tasks, like emptying the dishwasher or putting their dirty clothes in the laundry basket. Such communication skills seem grossly inconsistent with teenagers' mobile phone, SMS, and internet capabilities.

Parents' involvement in their children's education is not always expansive. A critical factor that determines parental involvement seems to be the parents' perceptions of school, often formed during their own school days. Some parents' participation is limited to a monitoring role in respect of their children's accomplishment ("What did you learn at school today?" "Have you finished your homework?" "How could you have got a D in social studies?"). And the only direct contact between the parents and the school—other than the occasional parent–teacher night—may come after a summons to the principal's office where the wrongdoings of the offspring are elaborated in indignant detail and when parents are asked to offer any compelling argument why the child should continue attending the school.

For others, the school and family work cooperatively to provide their children with the widest range of educational opportunities regardless of their capabilities. Middle-class families seem to form more positive relationships with schools than those who are less socially advantaged (see e.g., Mills & Gale, 2004). Many prosperous parents, for example, are inclined to send their children to private schools or, at least, to schools that have a reputation for high-quality programs and teachers. Such a commitment to their children's education often makes the pathway from school to tertiary education to full-time employment of choice relatively easy, unless some unforeseen disaster is encountered along the way.

The need for parents to be involved in their children's education has, however, been a matter for debate. Parenthetically, I do not remember my working-class parents being especially concerned with my day-to-day schooling, although there were always moans and gasps of disbelief, gnashing of teeth, and rending of garments when my end-of-term reports appeared and my truly mediocre performance was exposed. My friends' parents did not seem to take much more interest in their children's education either, although most performed at a more respectable standard than I did.

These days, when family arrangements do not necessarily conform to the traditional structure (e.g., when both parents work or when there is only a single parent in the home), it is more difficult for parents to be involved in their children's education on a daily basis. As a result, many parents do not engage with the school community once their children have passed beyond preschool, and many have little understanding of the school curriculum, how their children are taught, or even their rights and legal obligations as parents.

The impact of culture and society on young people's educational outcomes is perhaps most serious in families that live on the fringe of society, or lack social acceptance or political or economic power. These include:

- families in which there are racial or ethnic considerations (e.g., refugees; multi-racial backgrounds; Indigenous backgrounds);
- disadvantaged families (e.g., through poverty; unemployment);
- families in which there is physical or sexual abuse;
- disrupted or re-formed families (e.g., through death; divorce; criminal activity);
- families in which there is a member with a serious health problem (e.g., terminal illness; mental illness; substance abuse; severe impairment or disability); and
- families with atypical arrangements (e.g., foster-care parents; a single parent; gay, lesbian or transgender parents).

Of course, not every child who lives in a family that might be included in the list above will necessarily be at risk. Many families are highly resilient and able to deal with difficult and frustrating circumstances as well as, or better than, intact traditional families, so there are dangers in generalising, as you will see from the cases presented in Boxes 1.1, 1.2, and 1.3 a little later. Notwithstanding this, at least some children's school progress is limited by factors that stem from disadvantaged circumstances. For example, some children find textbooks difficult to read, the curriculum and assessment demands alien, teachers unhelpful, and situations in their home and friendship environments that erode motivation. Certainly, students who experience learning difficulties, who have medical, sensory, or physical complications, or who fall beyond the boundaries of the dominant culture, are in jeopardy of having less-than-fulfilling school experiences.

learning difficulties

Term used in Australia and New Zealand to describe individuals who experience marked difficulties with achieving in school. These problems, however, may continue in adolescence and adulthood.

The effects of socioeconomic status on students' educational outcomes have been shown in research data from literacy and numeracy surveys conducted from 1975 to 1998, and these differences in educational outcomes across social groups have remained constant for the past 25 years (see e.g., Rothman, 2002). Similar concerns were raised in a report entitled "The future of Australian schools" (Council for the Australian Federation, 2007). The report stated that differences in students' educational outcomes are greatly affected by their social backgrounds and by the company they keep in school. For example, there are benefits to students from advantaged backgrounds because they keep company with similarly advantaged peers, but the opposite is the case for students from a range of disadvantaged backgrounds, including those from Indigenous groups.

socioeconomic status (SES)

An individual's standing in society, generally related to occupation. High SES is generally attributed to professional occupations, with low SES being attributed to semi- and unskilled jobs.

Indigenous people

In recent times, there have been substantial changes in the way in which Australians perceive Indigenous cultures and there is considerably more attention being given to providing relevant educational opportunities to Indigenous young people. In Indigenous cultures, education is an all-of-life experience that is mediated by the relationships that exist within a community. Young people learn from the older members and elders who provide educational opportunities and experiences. Indigenous knowledge is a living knowledge that has local and contextual aspects and it is deeply rooted in the individual's perceptions of the world and the sharing of these perceptions.

The First Australians taught their young about the ways of life, their laws, social organisation, and customs largely through legends, song-cycles, and oral histories. These provided accounts of geological changes that occurred over millennia and social events that significantly influenced their cultures; not the least of these, we might suggest with hindsight, was the coming of the Europeans to Terra Australis.

For many years, Indigenous people were largely excluded from the English-speaking society. It was only in the 1870s that Aboriginal children were enrolled in state schools, sometimes on reserves to avoid any adverse influence on White children. And it was not until the early 1970s that school principals in New South Wales lost the right to refuse or defer the enrolment of an Indigenous child if there was community opposition to the presence of that child in the school (Lovitt, 1992).

Today, there is still a marked disparity between the educational outcomes of students from Indigenous and non-Indigenous families. For example, the Human Rights and Equal Opportunity Commission (2003) reported that only 17% of Indigenous students over 15 years of age complete Year 12 (or its equivalent) compared with 39% of non-Indigenous students. Only 36% of Indigenous young people continue to Year 12 and less than 2% go on to undertake tertiary studies.

Many of the teaching and learning strategies used in schools are said to be incongruent with Indigenous ways. In Western countries, the imperative to learn exists within a clearly hierarchical structure. Many Indigenous students see no connection between the way in which learning is delivered in school and the way in which it occurs within their families and communities. For many, a curriculum based in the Western—largely British/North American—history provides little connection with their languages, traditions, and values and largely ignores the treatment of Indigenous people by early European settlers. As a result, many become passive or even reluctant learners and there is little contact between parents and the school.

Indigenous students who either excel or have a learning difficulty that is independent of cultural influence (e.g., a sensory impairment or developmental disability) require special mention. In the first case, it is important to reassure students that they can maintain their place within their family and community and achieve excellence at school at the same time. In the second case, it is essential to prevent the onset of a failure spiral for a non-performing student through their loss of confidence and self-esteem, which in turn leads to further low achievement and school avoidance.

sensory impairment

The loss or degradation or absence of a sense organ (e.g., vision, hearing), which leads to a learning problem.

developmental disability

A disability that arises or is manifested early in a person's life and that persists (most often refers to an intellectual disability).

Indigenous students of high school age who live in rural or remote communities often face an additional challenge associated with the necessity of leaving home to attend senior secondary school. While it is common for teenagers who grow up on remote cattle stations to attend boarding school, it has a particular impact on Indigenous students who are required to leave not only their families but their culture as well. Separation from their family and culture is one of the major reasons why some young people fail to complete their secondary school studies. A few even work actively to be expelled so that they will be sent home to their community.

Considerable challenges confront Indigenous students associated with the mismatch of cultures and traditions. And while these are significant for Aboriginal and Torres Strait Islander youths (see Ministerial Advisory Committee for Educational Renewal, 2004), they are not altogether different from those faced by other students with diverse abilities and from culturally and linguistically different backgrounds. Indeed, the threats to achievement are much the same for all students but can be minimised when appropriate attention is given to a number of issues. These include:

- identifying physical or medical problems that may affect learning, such as vision and hearing (see Australian Institute of Health and Welfare, 2007);
- improving English-language skills;
- raising low self-perception and increasing learning independence, through recognition of the young person's positive attributes and encouraging discovery learning;
- improving motivation for educational achievement, through encouragement and support;
- appreciating the importance of cultural diversity, such as values, traditions, lifestyles, and kinship structures;

self-perception

A general term that refers to how we view ourselves in terms of the way we think others see us or how we appear to others. That is, it is our view of other people's evaluation of us and our internal positive or negative reaction to it.

- providing career or vocational guidance; and
- developing partnerships and two-way exchanges between the school and local communities.

These matters can become important when a child and the family are stressed by cultural, linguistic, interpersonal, or financial circumstances.

Families with limited financial means

For some people, living on a very meagre income might be inconvenient but not a terrible burden. For instance, many older people whose income is a full single-person Centrelink pension only (around $460 per fortnight at the time of writing) can live comfortably—but certainly not in luxury—if they own their home, have no major debts, and have modest day-to-day living expenses. For others (e.g., those with several dependent children), the likelihood of any Centrelink pension lasting for two weeks might be little more than a great idea.

The term *poverty* is based on an index of per capita household disposable income. Whether a person lives in poverty (that is, below the poverty line) depends upon the type of income unit (i.e., family groups, including people who live alone). For a single person without any dependants and including housing, the poverty line at the time of writing is about $352 per week. For a family of two adults (one of whom is working) and two children, the figure is about $661 per week (Melbourne Institute of Applied Economic and Social Research, 2007).

Determining how many Australians live at, or below, the poverty line is an exercise in inference. More than 1 million households (families and single persons living alone) exist near or below the poverty line, that is, between 12% and 15% of the population. Many of these are older people receiving a pension only, but there are also many children living in families with an income below the poverty line. Additionally, there are thousands of homeless young people who receive no government support at all. They live in a variety of locations from youth shelters to squats under bridges, derelict buildings, caves, and a hundred other locations around our cities. For one reason or another, they may not be included in national census data.

Living in a low-income household has a substantial effect on children and adolescents. Children living in a low-income household are at risk of receiving inadequate health care due to parental oversights or inattention. There are also risks of malnutrition due to the family's inability to provide adequate nourishment, or providing the wrong type (e.g., having only a diet cola drink for breakfast). Hungry children find it difficult to concentrate at school and often display behaviour problems in the classroom (see e.g., Pascoe, Shaikh, Forbis, & Etzel, 2007). Chronic malnutrition can eventually lead to brain damage.

There are some discrepancies in research findings on the detrimental effects of poverty due to the different methodologies employed by investigators, but there are some consistent results. Overall, these children have a higher incidence of health problems and intellectual, emotional disorder/disturbance, and behaviour disorders. They are also more likely to be expelled from school and to repeat grades than other children living in more favourable circumstances (see Brooks-Gunn, Britto, & Brady, 1999).

emotional disorder/disturbance
A condition where emotional reactions are inappropriate or deficient. Emotional disturbance has often referred to extreme acting out or withdrawn behaviour. It is now being replaced by the term "severe behaviour disorders".

behaviour disorders
Although there is no agreed definition of behaviour disorders, most educators agree that behaviours that disrupt other students and teachers to a marked degree are disordered. Students with severe behaviour disorders have often been called emotionally disturbed.

In general, poverty appears to have a greater effect on school achievement than emotional or behaviour problems, although its influence declines during adolescence. Of concern is the co-occurrence of poverty with other social or cultural factors that also affect performance at school, such as the family structure and parenting behaviour, race or ethnicity, and violence or abuse within the home.

Disrupted families

The constitution of the family unit has been changing in Australia over the past two decades. There has been a decrease in marriage rates and an increase in divorce rates. In addition, there has been an increase in the number of babies being born outside marriages and an increase in cohabitation (Parker,

2005). This means that the traditional family of mother, father, and one or more children is becoming less common. About 55% of Australia's population aged 15 years and over is in a registered marriage. The Australian Bureau of Statistics (2007) also reported that between 2004 and 2006 there were on average 486,000 one-parent families with children less than 15 years of age, that is, 22% of all families with children in that age group. These figures suggest that more children than ever are being raised in non-traditional family units. Several researchers have reported how children respond to these changes in their lives, and draw attention to the need for special attention or consideration at school. For example, when there is a marriage breakdown, the effect on educational progress is less harmful for younger than older children, but about the same for boys and girls.

Parents' remarrying after divorce can also have a negative effect on the children. Again, the impact is less for younger than older children. Children often resent the intrusion of the step-parent (girls are more resentful than boys) and many choose to isolate themselves from the family and spend little time at home or involved in family activities, with the ensuing risk of delinquency, and antisocial and self-destructive behaviour.

The influence of family life, however, goes well beyond the divorced or single-parent households and includes step-families, adoptive families, grandparent-headed families, intergenerational and multi-racial families, and families that are headed by lesbian or gay parents, or by a parent who has never been married. In the same way that special attention—or simply a watchful eye—is given to children when their family is in crisis, consideration must also be given to children who experience child-rearing practices that are not the norm within society.

Multi-racial and adoptive families

Children in multi-racial families are often confronted by the issue of identity, that is, how to define themselves racially. This is affected by a range of realities, including their physical appearance, the language that might be used only in the home, values and customs with which they may or may not agree, and whether or not they live in an area where there are others from the same racial background. Occasionally, children from mixed-race families experience ridicule that can lead to the loss of established friendships and difficulty making new friends.

Society also needs to define these children in some way and this is much easier if they are seen to be more of one racial group than another (see an example of this in Box 1.1). If children are defined on the basis of colour or facial characteristics, they need to know about identity and how to exist safely with it (see McLeod & Yates, 2003). At school, there may be pressure on the multi-racial child to take on a mono-racial identity, for example to identify as Malaysian or Vietnamese despite the fact that they and their parents—and perhaps their grandparents—were born in Australia.

Parents who adopt children (including children from another ethnic/racial background) also face a number of challenges and there is a small body of literature about the adoption of children, including those from other racial backgrounds or who have a physical impairment or intellectual disability. There is no consensus about the level of disruption to families when the children have any of these characteristics. Some researchers report a range of problems, including disruptive and aggressive behaviour of the adopted child or their new siblings, while others have found no significant disturbance. In some cases, both parents and children derive considerable satisfaction from the new family configuration.

Families with same-sex attracted parents

In Australia, anti-discrimination legislation has been proclaimed in each state and territory to reflect evolving values of tolerance and acceptance of diversity due to race, colour, religious beliefs, sexual

BOX 1.1

Looks can be deceptive

Gary Tan grew up in a mixed-race family. His father is Chinese and his mother, German. The parents met while Gary's father was training to be a chef in London. Physically, Brigit Tan is quintessentially German—blond hair, blue eyes, striking features—and Harry Tan has features that clearly establish his racial origin. Gary and his brother were born in Australia and both inherited their father's racial features to the apparent almost total exclusion of any genetic material from Brigit. Cantonese and German were never heard in the family home. English was the only language spoken at home and both boys grew up with familiar Australian accents.

Gary never thought of himself as Chinese or German. He is Australian, and there were regular jokes made by his close friends that when Gary looked in the mirror in the morning he saw a Caucasian smiling back at him.

When he returned from a holiday in China, Gary joked about being in a shop, in a restaurant, or on the street and having people come up to him speaking in rapid Cantonese or Mandarin, expecting him to respond in kind ("It could have been either language, or it could have been Icelandic, as far as I'd know," he said. "And they always looked at me as though I was stupid. And then would turn away mumbling something I'm sure meant that I was the rudest person in the world").

One afternoon, Gary and one of his closest friends were riding an escalator in a shopping centre. He looked up and with a big grin on his face called out, "Hello, Mum!" as they neared the upper level. The friend, who had never met Brigit, looked around for the Asian face in the crowd and saw none. When Gary stepped off the escalator, he threw his arms around the blonde haired, blue-eyed Brigit, to the complete amazement of the friend.

identity, and sexual preference. The passage of legislation, however, is one step only in the process of moderating social and community attitudes toward minority groups. Despite legislation and the rhetoric surrounding it, many individuals continue to experience prejudice and injustice because they do not align with the views, dispositions, or characteristics of the dominant social or cultural group.

Same-sex attracted individuals have confronted antagonistic responses from sectors of society for hundreds (if not thousands) of years. Most learn to minimise their exposure to threats by the time they reach adulthood and live within communities and neighbourhoods in much the same way as everyone else, many as parents. There is a growing literature on families in which the sole parent is gay or lesbian, or in which both parents are of the same sex. There is also a developing literature about gay and lesbian couples who wish to have a child through surrogate parenting, in vitro fertilisation programs, or a formal adoption process.

An issue occasionally raised is the extent to which growing up in a gay or lesbian family adversely affects a child's psychosexual development. It is assumed that the parents exert significant influences on the children that are different, in important ways, to those imposed by heterosexual parents. Research dealing with these matters over 20 years, and across samples that are representative of the

wider population, has revealed no substantive differences in child-rearing practices. The children grow up no different from peers in their mental health, sexual identity, social relationships, career interests, future employment decisions, job stability, or recreation and leisure pursuits. The key issue that is significantly associated with children's adjustment during the developmental period for the children of same-sex parents (as it is in most families) is the quality of child–parent relationships rather than family composition (Patterson, 2006; Wainright & Patterson, 2006).

The positive finding about parenting does not mean that same-sex parent households are tension free or that the children face no complications outside of the family. Professional attitudes toward gay and lesbian parents are generally positive, as an American study by Choi, Thul, Berenhaut, Suerken, and Norris (2006) has shown. In an Australian study, however, Ray and Gregory (2001) found that just under half of their school-aged sample of children of gay or lesbian parents had been teased and/or bullied about their parents' homosexuality by other students. Of much greater concern, they found that teachers either did not intervene to stop the harassment or they joined in with homophobic retorts along with the students.

In Box 1.2 is an account written by a father about some of the joys and challenges he faced when raising his daughter.

BOX 1.2

Our lives with Catherine

My name is Sean. I married Tracy when I was 20, the same year I graduated as a high school teacher. Catherine was born two years later.

When Catherine was two, I came to a point in my life where I had to accept the growing reality that I wasn't heterosexual. It wasn't easy to leave my wife and child to begin a new life as a relatively young, unattached, gay male, but I did. I never intended to abandon Tracy and Catherine and, in truth, I never did. I could never have done that, and I contributed much more than the Family Court order required in child support to make sure that they could live comfortably and Catherine could get the best education possible. For quite some time, Tracy wasn't keen to let me see Catherine and I had to return to the Court to make sure I wasn't being cut out. In time, Tracy and I became closer and she allowed me access to Catherine whenever I wanted it.

I met Peter about a year after the end of the marriage and we've been together for almost 26 years. That's longer than many marriages last. A couple of years after that, Tracy remarried and she and Catherine moved in with the new husband and his two girls. Catherine hated her stepfather and the stepsisters, they fought constantly, and the only sensible option to avoid the constant tension was for Catherine to move in with Peter and me.

I had a lot to do with Catherine's schooling, as you'd expect, and Peter (who's also a teacher) took at least as much interest as I did. He was terrific with Catherine, although there were times—early in our relationship—when there were also stresses because Peter thought that I was giving all of my attention to her. We talked it through and worked out how I could share my time and affection equally between the two of them.

Catherine's education through primary school and early high school was uneventful. She was an average student—maybe a bit above average—and had lots of friends. I remember well, however, the night I was marking assignments and she came into my study and asked me about my relationship with Peter. She was 11.

"One of my friends says you're a faggot. I know what that means. Are you?"

I know I blushed. I sat her down, told her that I didn't especially like the word faggot but, yes, I was gay and Uncle Peter was my partner. I explained that I loved him and I loved her, but in a different way, and then—this blew me off the planet—she said, "Okay, I can understand that. Goodnight, Dad." She kissed me and skipped off to bed. And that was it.

Over the years Cath has always brought her friends home. Tracy visits and phones regularly and is always involved in family celebrations.

Cath has had a few boyfriends. One lasted a couple of years. I didn't like him but would have coped if they'd eventually got married. As it happened, he cheated on her and she broke it off, totally devastated, of course, as only a teenage girl can be. We spent a lot of time after that talking about relationships. I'm as much an expert on that topic as anyone and I shared some of my life experiences as a young gay man and how it hurt like hell when I was dumped. That was the first time we'd ever spoken candidly about that part of my life, how I feel about Peter, and what's special about our lives together. I think we came out of that stronger than ever.

She's had several boyfriends since the break-up and, fortunately, that didn't affect her Year 12 performance. She's now in her second year at uni doing Law, and going really well.

I know people think that kids who live with gay and lesbian parents turn out weird or queer but that's just not true. Cath is as heterosexual as any young lady could be and more sensible and emotionally stable than many of her friends, as far as I can tell. If growing up with Peter and me has had any detrimental effect on Cath's life, I'd really like someone to tell me what it is.

1.2

ISSUES AND CHALLENGES

So far in this chapter, I have not mentioned disability or impairment. What I have drawn out of the first few pages are the cultural, social, and community imperatives that daily affect our lives. By that, I mean that there are expectations about shared values, beliefs, and behaviours linked with membership of a particular society. Some educational sociologists have argued that there has been a fusion of cultures and that the time has passed when each cultural minority is a distinct entity (see, e.g., McCarthy, 1998). While this may be true in part, in Australia and in most other Western countries, the notion of a cultural mosaic remains firmly entrenched. In these societies where there is a conversation between cultures and an interdependence, there are still significant differences between in-groups and out-groups, those in the mainstream and others who are marginalised. It has only been in recent times, for example, that there has been a productive social dialogue between Indigenous peoples and the descendants of those who came to populate Australia at the end of the 18th century (see Hart, 2003).

mainstream
An early US term that referred to the general education stream in which students with special needs may be placed. Mainstreaming is the US term for integration of students with special needs into the ordinary education system.

In short, humans do not "do difference" well, as should be painfully obvious if you watch world—or even local—news. Those who are clearly (or believed to be) different are viewed as being outside of the mainstream, and this has its complications.

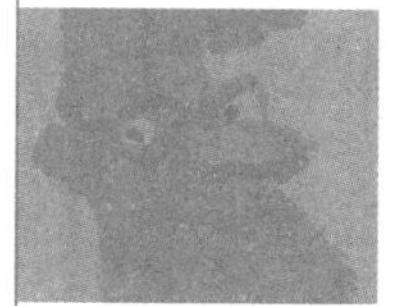

When we consider the issue of the inclusion of marginalised individuals or groups into a community or a school, we confront additional impediments, namely the way in which, and the extent to which, a society or community can adapt and accommodate difference and diversity, especially in educational settings. Let me turn now to a cultural phenomenon that is having an increasing effect on teaching and learning in schools.

Generational change and adaptation

Data from the Australian Bureau of Statistics (2003c) clearly show the reversal in the age distribution of Australian teachers over the past two decades. The median age of teachers (i.e., the midpoint of the frequency distribution) went from 34 to 43 years over the period 1986 to 2001. The number of teachers aged 45 years and older went from 17% to 44%. Thus, almost half of the teachers in schools today are Baby Boomers, that is, were born immediately after the Second World War up to about 1965. A significant number are also members of Generation X, that is, were born between 1960 and roughly 1980.

The Baby Boomers and the Generation Xs grew up in quite different social periods. The end of the Second World War brought a stability that re-established traditional family values and led to an upsurge in births, the expansion of cities through housing developments, and new economic growth. Technology and industry also expanded, although the economic progress was slowed by a recession in the late 1950s. There were international tensions associated with the Cold War and widespread unrest linked to Australia's involvement in the unpopular Vietnam War. The years of Generation X post-Vietnam have seen a steady change in social and cultural diversity, along with relatively consistent world economic growth.

"Generation X" as a pejorative term was brought into popular use through Coupland's (1991) novel, *Generation X: Tales for an accelerated culture*. This group was said to have grown up without affection for the cultural beliefs and values of their parents, associated notably with an antagonism toward accumulating wealth and social status. There were also views expressed about Generation X's cynicism and disenfranchisement, their hostility toward religion, and their over-education but also underachievement. Of course, like all generalisations, the characteristics of the Baby Boomers and Generation Xs are far from uniform. There is no doubt, however, that those who grew up in those periods have had quite different social, cultural, and economic experiences to those attending school today.

Today's students are Generation Y, a term that implies the transition from X. Those in Generation Y have been born into the Information Age, a period of rapid change, significant wealth, and great social and cultural diversity. Heath (2006) argued that in current education environments it is crucial to recognise the characteristics of the present generation and develop appropriate strategies for the next. Generation Ys are said to be street smart, informal, lifestyle centred, gratification seekers, technologically competent, practical, sceptical, ambitious, and impatient (see e.g., Goldgehn, 2004; Sheahan, 2005).

The characteristics of the present generation of youth are no more apparent that in the use of technology. School communities have reacted swiftly to the age of mobile phones and the short message service (SMS) by banning the use of phones during school hours, but this is often a difficult policy to police. And while multiculturalism is a familiar reality and diversity generally accepted, the new phenomenon of bullying and victimisation through SMSs and racial and cultural slurs sent via email are far from being eliminated.

The implications for the school classroom relate to the generalisations that characterise Generation Y, especially their scepticism, practicality, informality, social awareness, and technological sophistication (see Moore, 2007). While generational differences may not necessarily cause complications, there are many teachers who prefer chalk-and-talk lessons to more loosely organised classes; who perceive

themselves as being technological incompetents; and who expect students to be self-motivating and self-sufficient, and learners for the sake of learning. Orienting lessons toward contemporary students might be achieved by emphasising:

- social interactions to improve knowledge (e.g., group work; free discussions; consultation);
- time-saving classroom procedures and processes (e.g., imbedded use of electronic and technological resources);
- teacher expectations and standards (e.g., focusing on explicit goal-oriented lessons and activities);
- task relevance (e.g., future-orientation, practical and/or career relevance); and
- the provision of timely and relevant feedback (e.g., simple; performance and outcomes related).

With these points in mind, I move on to consider the factors that influence teaching procedures and practices in contemporary schools.

TEACHING ESSENTIALS

Difference is based on society's standards of normality and being different is something that many of us cherish as adults. Being unconventional by choice can be fun and we express our unique character through the clothes we wear, our hairstyle, body piercing and tattoos, the toys we own, and even the foods we prefer to eat. There are conventional ways of being different. For example, we admire people who challenge nature's physical and climatic extremes and how many of us have not secretly wished that we were on the Olympic podium awaiting the presentation of a gold medal, flashing a smile that would stop traffic?

There are also unconventional ways of being different. For example, there are leather-clad members of society who have a singular fascination with a particular brand of noisy motorcycle, and those who choose to live without the possessions that many others believe are essential, and still others who dress in ways that are inconsistent with local customs or conventions.

It is one thing to be different by choice; there are quite different implications and consequences if a person is different by accident. It is important to recognise that we often look, or see, no further than the characteristic that defines difference, overlooking many other traits and qualities that are similar to those of other members of the community and society. It is useful, therefore, to consider why we often see only the differences that distinguish us from others.

Values, attitudes, and prejudices

Being identified as different from members of the dominant culture or group is a common stimulus for intolerance and discrimination. We forget that in many ways each of us will be a member of an out-group from time to time. For example, there have been several occasions when I was the only male at a well-attended professional workshop, the only person who knew no one at the party other than the host, and the only one wearing jeans and a very casual short-sleeved shirt at an unexpectedly formal conference dinner. There are also times when we apply our cultural norms in places where those norms are inconsistent with local customs. And, curiously, we are sometimes oblivious to our own cultural contradictions and impose our values and standards without appreciating that others may not share them.

values
The principles or standards of behaviour that reflect judgements about what is held to be important in life. They are affected by cultural influences and personal preferences and beliefs.

I remember, for example, eating dinner with friends in America and noticing their sly looks at my highly developed knife and fork skills, the essence of the very best of Australian table manners instilled deeply into my subconscious by my mother when I was a child. And I recall sniggering when an American visitor was eating at my parents' dining table and my father leaned over toward him with a wicked grin on his face and asked loudly, "Why don't you eat like everyone else?"

When we travel overseas, most people are aware of the need to respect the prevailing local customs. We also expect that others do likewise when they are in our country. This might mean complying with the appropriate social distance when talking to others, removing a hat (or wearing one) when we enter a place of worship, and saying "Please" and "Thank you" as a courtesy when purchasing items in a shop. And when we see others contravening the standards we believe should apply, our reaction is often one of disapproval.

Some writers have expressed concern about the pervasiveness of negative reactions to difference and, in particular, the development and persistence of prejudice. There are several commonly accepted roots of prejudice. They include economic competition, sexual apprehensions, cultural styles, the social history of racism, and family characteristics. There is also a common belief that parents influence the development of prejudice in their children, although the evidence for this is less apparent than generally thought. Prejudice has its foundation in the tensions that exist across economic, political, and personal boundaries and is rooted in the emotional link that a person has with the group with which he or she identifies (see e.g., Dovidio, Gaertner, & Pearson, 2005; Smith, Seger, & Mackie, 2007).

prejudice

An opinion or belief that is not based on accurate knowledge, actual experience, or logical reasoning.

Values, attitudes, and prejudices develop early in our lives. Children combine their experiences and knowledge with existing assumptions and beliefs about the world, and as their understanding of human nature evolves, the assumptions they hold grow in number and are modified and simplified. Grouping by similarity and difference is a human attribute (perhaps genetically wired) that helps to reduce complexity and the associated cognitive demands. But there is also a danger in this. Classifying people by common characteristics can lead to stereotyping, often based on illogical beliefs, negative judgments, and undesirability, depending upon how much a person deviates from the features of the in-group. Age, size, appearance, disability, or impairment, and membership of an ethnic or sexual minority group are common bases for prejudice and discrimination.

attitudes

Learned predispositions to react consistently in a particular way toward certain persons, events, objects, or concepts. Attitudes have cognitive, emotional, and behavioural components.

discrimination

The unfair treatment of a person or group of people on the basis of prejudice to the extent that the person or group is disadvantaged because of, for example, age, colour, handicap, marital status, national origin, race, religion, sex, or sexual preference.

One way of overcoming prejudice is to provide an alternative way of viewing relationships with others to remove the basis of difference (such as race, age, or impairment) and substitute an inclusive identity. This can be achieved by looking for shared features or characteristics. This could be as broad as nationality or as narrow as belonging to a specific neighbourhood, or a classroom group.

Identifying shared characteristics is the principle feature of the Common In-Group Identity Model developed by Dovidio, Gaertner, and their colleagues (see Dovidio, Gaertner, Hudson, Houlette, & Johnson, 2005). The model aims to subtly redirect attention away from difference and the reason for exclusion and help people focus on the issues that exemplify membership of a specific group. In a classroom, for example, these attributes might include wearing the same uniform, everyone being 11 years of age, living in the same suburb, using the same tuckshop, going to the same shopping centre, and having the same teacher (Mrs Thompson). Dovidio et al. claimed that focusing on shared experiences and purposes leads to positive inter-group attitudes, promotes inclusion, encourages justice and fairness, and supports positive and trusting behaviours such as helping and personal disclosure.

attributes

Qualities or characteristics that are either fundamental or inherent parts of someone or something.

Trying to break down the barriers that are erected because of difference is very important in the context of education, as most school campuses are rich with in-group/out-group politics. There are friendship groups, cliques, and gangs that establish themselves separate from others and individuals who are isolated because of socially undesirable characteristics, such as behaving in ways that are offensive, or liking school or chess. While school discipline policies proscribe actions that infringe the rights of, or show disrespect for, others in the school community, there are many breaches that still occur within the school day. At least some of these are implicitly condoned by the lack of response from teachers and other school staff, such as bullying and victimisation and the more subtle forms of

harassment via email and SMS messages. Those who are targeted are affected in many ways that can lead to stress and an aversion to school, with a resulting serious impact on academic performance.

The school community is an important context in which to promote positive social and cultural attitudes and values, and when considered within the framework of inclusive education, the implicit message is that "All children belong." This means that the teaching essentials include sensitivities to any attitudinal, architectural, and instructional barriers that might hinder a student's progress through the school years. Teachers and other members of the school community must engage in the shared responsibility of creating an environment that welcomes all students, including those who are different, for a wide range of reasons. The goal should be to make difference ordinary. Hence, teaching essentials include:

- embedding social justice topics into the curriculum (e.g., including an assignment on anti-discrimination in studies of society and environment—SOSE); using a mathematics lesson on graphing to focus attention on infant mortality in African countries or on languages spoken by students at the school);
- designing and adapting the curriculum to suit a particular student's learning needs (e.g., using interest inventories can focus the teacher's attention on students' interests and allow them to look into the students' worlds);
- projecting values and attitudes inside and outside the classroom that affirm diversity and inclusion (e.g., listening attentively to what children have to say);
- designing and adapting assessment tasks that enable all students to demonstrate skills and knowledge (e.g., taking the reading or writing aspect out of a task for a student who has difficulty reading or writing);
- accommodating differences in students' learning styles, talents, and abilities (e.g., setting up the classroom that has work stations for group work and for individual discovery; gathering resources that tap different skill levels on the same topic or curriculum area);
- promoting equal treatment and opportunities for learning (e.g., using cooperative learning activities that are effective in bringing students with various skills and talents—including students with learning difficulties—together to work on a specific task or project);
- focusing on students' strengths and the contributions that each makes to the school community (e.g., talking about abilities rather than disabilities, skills rather than impairments, and unique contributions rather than being strange); and
- recognising and rewarding personal achievements (e.g., praising a student who has learned a new concept successfully; giving an award at the school assembly to a students who has struggled, and achieved).

talent
Distinctly above-average performance on systematically developed skills in a field of human endeavour, such as academic, technical, artistic, interpersonal, and athletic.

When difference is made ordinary, there is genuine acceptance of, and respect for:

- cultural differences (e.g., religious and ethnic practices);
- values and beliefs that we may not share (e.g., political views);
- lifestyles that may be unfamiliar or incomprehensible to us (e.g., homelessness, same-sex attraction, ostentatious wealth);
- tragic life experiences (e.g., sexual abuse, inter-racial violence, persecution); and
- intellectual and physical capabilities (e.g., attention deficits, sensory impairments).

We may not necessarily agree with the views, dispositions, attitudes, or values of others when they are at odds with our own, but it is important to hear and understand the basis of those viewpoints.

LEARNING ESSENTIALS

The announcement "I haven't learned anything today" is almost inevitably untrue. Learning is something that humans find very hard to avoid or prevent. Certainly, there is knowledge that might not be acquired at a particular time and this can be a source of some frustration to teachers, parents, and students.

Learning involves a partnership between the learner and others involved in any teaching–learning event. These relationships might include peers, parents, teachers, instructors or trainers, the creator of a website or instructional CD or DVD, and even the authors of a book like this.

What we learn and how we learn is established very early in life, and the environment in which we live facilitates or limits exposure to learning events and experiences. In the first five years of life, for example, children gain much from the intimate relationship with their parents, especially mothers, when early language and intellectual and emotional developments are emerging. Household routines provide examples of schedules, plans, and problem-solving. Sensible and reasoned discipline is also important for establishing boundaries, the nature of relationships, a sense of what is right and wrong, and the rudiments of an identity that allows children to position themselves in relation to others. Interactions with parents, siblings, and peers assist by exposing the young person to opportunities and events that can encourage positive attitudes toward reading, numeracy, and a range of values about the importance (or otherwise) of learning and discovery.

As years progress, the young person's world expands to include the preschool and school, the wider community, and the world through television, the internet, and the world wide web. Social contacts extend beyond the family to include other children and adults in the neighbourhood. Access to libraries, museums, art galleries, shopping centres, parks, and recreation and leisure facilities further expands the learning and socialisation opportunities. If the child lives in a situation where there are few chances to learn about the world and interact with it successfully, or is not exposed to positive models of learning, the childhood and adolescent years may be characterised by intellectual, social, or emotional isolation.

Experience is the essential prerequisite for success because it is the primary source of the individual's storehouse of knowledge. Even some unacceptable behaviour can lead to positive results. For example, children play with fire, cut school, mix with undesirable companions, take things that are not theirs, and disobey rules imposed by parents, schools, and society. While these activities are often annoying or worrying, they can provide valuable lessons and life experiences, most often without long-term physical or emotional damage, or contact with the juvenile justice system.

While defiance of law and order cannot be ignored, opportunities to test independence and the consequences of actions are essential to the development of problem-solving skills, initiative taking, and self-determination. For some young people (such as those with an intellectual disability or limited mobility), the opportunities to take risks are fewer than typically available to their able-bodied peers because of intended or inadvertent constraints imposed by parents or carers. For example, they may not have the opportunity to post a letter, or to use the telephone or common household appliances. They may have meals or snacks prepared for them, travel with a chaperone or support worker, and have their shopping and banking done by someone else. Other skills that are important to day-to-day living include short- and long-term life planning in matters of personal care, health, recreation, and even personal safety and self-defence. Box 1.3 gives a vivid picture of the limitations experienced by one young man as a result of physical impairment.

BOX 1.3 The mundane things in life

I met Alan several years ago. He volunteered to participate in a research project in which I was involved dealing with the early learning experiences of people with physical and sensory impairments. I knew Alan was 31 years old at the time but that was about all I knew, apart from the address of the law firm where we would meet. As I waited for our appointment I chatted to the receptionist who told me that Alan was quickly making himself an enviable reputation as a sensitive and insightful lawyer.

I was surprised when he appeared in a wheelchair, introduced himself, and nearly broke four of my fingers as we shook hands. He led the way to a small meeting room where there was already tea and coffee waiting on the table.

I talked with Alan for about an hour, about his early education experiences, what his teachers were like, how the school accommodated his physical impairment, what adjustments were made for him, about his friends and family, and his decision to go to university and study Law.

Toward the end of our session, I asked what he thought were the most limiting aspects of his childhood and adolescent years. He frowned for about half a minute, looking out through the window across the city. Then he turned and looked straight into my eyes.

> *You know, I never got to do really mundane things. I'll give you an example. When my friends were young they'd be bundled into the family car and taken off to the corner shop or the shopping centre. I rarely got to do that. Think about it. For my Mum to take me with her to the corner shop to buy a carton of milk she had to go through the most amazing routine. She had to make sure I was presentable, then wheel me out of the house to the car. Go back and lock up. Bundle me into the passenger's seat, take the wheelchair around and pack it into the boot, then climb in and drive the 30 seconds to the shop, jump out, unpack my chair, wheel it around and manhandle me into it, push me into the shop, buy the milk and reverse the whole procedure to get me home. What'd take another mother and child two minutes would take my Mum half an hour. So, the quick trips to the shop, and a lot of other really commonplace experiences, rarely happened in my life.*

We talked some more about what it meant to miss those everyday routines.

> *I used to get really angry at my Mum for not taking me places, but now I know how unreasonable that was. And I remember crying in her arms like a baby one afternoon because I was so frustrated at my stupid body, and she held me really tightly until I settled. I suppose I was lucky in many ways because I loved to read and I learned about things through books that I could never hope to experience in real life. Having said that, I was 16 before I knew what a butcher's shop smelt like. Funny thing. I never found a scratch-and-sniff book about a butcher's shop.*

Maximising students' learning opportunities is the motto of most contemporary educators, and guided (or mediated) experiences ensure that students acquire relevant knowledge and life skills. In Australia, the British tradition of education has placed emphasis on learning in structured settings, like schools and tertiary institutions, and there has been an unspoken belief that what a student learns in the classroom and from textbooks is the most important knowledge one can acquire. Certainly, there are times when didactic instruction may be the most efficient way to transmit specialist knowledge and facts, like learning physical laws and equations, algebra, calculus, or philosophical propositions. Despite this, there is much that children learn outside of the classroom and even more that we learn on the job and during recreation and leisure pursuits.

didactic instruction
Teaching approaches that are in lecture form designed to tell in contrast to other approaches that promote discovery or shared learning.

The culture we experience and the society in which we live provide almost unlimited opportunities to learn in both formal and informal settings. What many of us might overlook, however, are the limitations that many young, and older, people experience because the culture and the society adversely affect their lives. These are the individuals that we commonly bring together under the heading of students at risk.

Accommodating their skills, knowledge, and life experiences requires an understanding and a harnessing of their aptitudes and capabilities. For some, such as those with:

aptitude
A capacity or potential ability to perform an as yet unlearned skill or task.

- exceptional gifts or talents;
- intellectual disability or acquired brain injury;
- multiple physical/sense/intellectual impairments;
- serious academic learning problems in, for example, literacy or numeracy;
- severe behaviour disorders such as attention deficits;
- non-English-speaking backgrounds; and
- a traditional Indigenous upbringing;

the focus of attention may be the curriculum and the way in which teaching occurs. As you will realise, there is little common ground among the specific circumstances and needs of these students. The application of generic teaching strategies alone is unlikely to maximise their learning outcomes.

teaching strategies
Any of the numerous ways in which a teacher can present curriculum content or information to students.

Other students need additional specialist materials, physical resources, and advice from health care professionals (e.g., occupational, physical, and speech therapists, specialist medical consultation) because of their particular learning needs. These include young people with:

- sensory impairments such as vision or hearing;
- physical impairments such as cerebral palsy;
- serious medical conditions (e.g., due to epilepsy, diabetes, or muscular dystrophy); and
- multiple impairments (e.g., a vision *and* hearing impairment).

cerebral palsy
A general term for a group of diseases that cause physical disability in human development by affecting areas of the brain. Cerebral palsy damages the motor control centres of a developing brain and this can occur during pregnancy, childbirth, or after birth up to about age three.

There are also students whose educational needs might ordinarily be met by the standard curriculum but whose cultural, social, and emotional needs affect their ability to take full advantage of that curriculum. These young people often require assistance and support from guidance or counselling staff, or social work or mental health professionals. These include young people who:

- have been neglected or abused;
- live outside a family unit (e.g., homeless, or in detention);
- have a serious psychiatric disorder;
- are substance abusers;
- live with a family member who has a serious medical or psychiatric illness;
- live in poverty or a welfare household;

- live in single-parent families;
- live in foster care arrangements;
- live in very traditional or culturally severe family units;
- are gay, lesbian, bisexual, or transgender;
- have experienced significant personal losses (e.g., death of a parent or sibling); and
- become pregnant during the school years.

All of these young people will be at risk of delayed or impeded school progress, although this may never eventuate. Of importance, there is no single response that will adequately deal with the problems that any faces. And for most, the answer is not found solely in adapting the curriculum or changing one's teaching style or approach. As might be expected, when factors combine the effect may be even more significant, with the purpose of learning lost or obscured. It is not unreasonable, therefore, that motivation and effort will wane and this is especially so for students who have a history of learning problems. In many cases, it is the culture and environment that imposes limitations on their school progress and holistic approaches are required to facilitate learning. In Box 1.4 is an example of the responses needed when dealing with students who come from non-English-speaking backgrounds.

BOX 1.4 English as a second language

Multiculturalism in education was introduced in the late 1970s as a federal government initiative intended to make all levels in the education system responsive to the cultures represented within the Australian population. There was an emphasis on the removal of barriers that would increase access to community and educational support services.

While schools and teachers generally focus on language issues, these are subordinate to:

- cultural background assumptions (i.e., both specific knowledges and more general cultural knowledges and assumptions); and
- educational context issues that relate to expectations about what education is, and how language is delivered.

These issues are in evidence in many curriculum initiatives that focus on the development of English as a Second Language (ESL), such as the new *English for ESL Learners* under trial in Queensland and a major curriculum project on culture in language teaching by Tony Liddicoat of the University of South Australia.

There are a number of issues that relate to ESL students and those from certain cultural backgrounds, such as the following:

- Students may bring different learning styles to the classroom, which were appropriate to their culture or former educational system. This might include top-down knowledge transmission when important knowledge is given rather than discovered, with the resulting over-dependence on support or "spoon feeding." This might require teachers to support and encourage new ways of autonomous learning.

- Students may bring different cultural norms and ways of dealing with texts such as different perceptions of the authority of teachers and texts. This may require the development of a specific language for academic learning, for example, research skills, writing styles and skills, speaking and listening skills.
- Students may bring different cultural understandings about the nature of the world. They want to learn about the host culture and cultural canon but initially need to do this through experiences and texts that have universal (Western) themes, before moving to more locally grounded work.
- Students may not have been exposed to materials that are critical of cultural contexts (e.g., issue-based fiction; feminist perspectives) and this may require the learning of critical reading and analysis skills.
- It is important to recognise that ways of writing and speaking, including specific expressions and usages, are more culturally loaded and may need paraphrasing or explanation (e.g., "We need to get a couple of chooks for dinner tonight").
- It is important to value the language and cultural skills that students have already acquired and to see these as additive rather than subtractive.

Thanks to Professor Richard Baldauf, School of Education, University of Queensland for these ideas.

1.4

The goal for teachers—and education systems in general—is to engage students' imaginations, the skills that each has developed over the course of a lifetime, and explore ways in which the content of the school curriculum can dovetail with their personal characteristics and learning style. Importantly, there is a clear need for teachers to recognise the learning opportunities that are readily accessible outside the classroom (e.g., plays, movies, exhibitions, public events such as Anzac Day marches, and Indigenous cultural displays), to seek ways of integrating the curriculum into alternative learning environments, and to draw on the resources available inside and outside the school to promote the acquisition of knowledge and skills.

Boys and girls

More than a decade ago, attention was being given to ways of delivering education in schools to ensure that girls were not disadvantaged in the traditionally male curriculum areas such as mathematics and science. Then, not quite 10 years ago, came a reaction, "What about the boys?" It was argued that boys learned in ways different to girls and that the methods and practices of teaching (i.e., pedagogy) had shifted ground so that it subtly advantaged girls and disadvantaged boys (see e.g., Biddulph, 1997; see also Martino & Meyenn, 2001, for a critique of this position). There was also debate over the difference between the terms *sex* (the biological distinction between the male and female of a species), *gender* (the social formation of roles that society imposes on males and females), and *masculinity/femininity* (the character, qualities, and appearance traditionally associated with being male or female).

Nationwide, attention turned to boys' education through projects such as the Boys' Lighthouse Schools Project (Department of Education, Science and Training, 2003) and there was even a

parliamentary inquiry into boys' education (House of Representatives Standing Committee on Education and Training, 2002). Considerable resources were directed toward the examination of the curriculum and the generation of teaching policies and strategies to ensure that boys' ways of thinking and learning were not overlooked.

The issues surrounding education outcomes for boys and girls are not as clearly defined as one might want. For example, socioeconomic status is of more importance than one's sex in determining education attainments. While boys generally perform below girls on tests of literacy, boys and girls from working-class backgrounds are equally at risk. Poverty and racial background are further confounding variables. The question then arose, "Which boys and which girls are disadvantaged by contemporary pedagogies?" And this, in turn, has drawn attention to the nature of gender politics in education, that is, the influence of social roles, power, and the influence of gender identify.

In recent times, the issues about boys' education have gathered around the concept of masculinities (i.e., how boys project themselves as males) and developing ways in which boys can be introduced to a range of masculine identities through male role models, masculine teaching styles, authoritarian disciplinary strategies, and even advocacy for single- rather than mixed-sex classes. Keddie (2005), however, argued that those strategies can be counterproductive because they do not necessarily lead to more liberal views of what it is to be a young male, and they often reinforce a conventional white, middle-class, heterosexual view of masculinity. She believes that teachers should expand their knowledge of what it means to be a male and a boy in today's world, and to help young males to achieve the same understanding.

To this end, there have been claims that teachers should aim to provide opportunities for boys to be physical during learning activities, that is, to have hands-on experiences with concrete resources and materials. Keddie (2005) again stated that many gender inequities are a result of social practice and it is important for teachers to blur the masculine/feminine distinction (i.e., the gender binary) by providing boys with opportunities to draw on what are often considered to be feminine ways of expression, for example, through drama and dance, and to explore ways in which popular youth culture represents gender in, for example, video games, magazines, and toys.

Keddie and Mills (2007) continued these themes in a recent book. However, they also raise the issue of the importance of taking into account difference among boys and among girls and difference between them, which makes it difficult to propose generic teaching and learning strategies that are appropriate for all boys. Keddie and Mills proposed changes in practice that support greater democracy in the classroom based upon respect for differences in socioeconomic status, gender, sexual identity, race and ethnicity, and other limiting conditions and circumstances. They argued that democratic behaviour doesn't just happen, it needs to be taught. They also detail practices employed by teachers in classrooms that have had a positive impact on the educational experiences of boys without sacrificing the needs of girls. Their suggestions primarily focus on developing lessons that promote discussions about social justice topics within the context of any curriculum area. These include:

- "How can we make our community a better place to live?" This might involve scans of newspaper stories, conducting surveys, and interviews from a variety of sources such as parents, student, agencies, and sporting groups.
- "What are some of the key issues affecting our school?" These might raise topics such as under-achievement, retention, special needs, homophobia, and bullying. Questions to prompt students' responses include, "Why do some students underachieve?" "What would cause a young person to leave school early?" "Why are some students bullies?" "What kind of offences are boys suspended for?" "Are some areas of the school more dangerous than others?"

- "What is a nice girl/boy?" "Why?" "Is being nice good?" These questions might prompt issues about gender and social justice.
- "Is there a hierarchy of students in the school?" "If so, what is it?" "Is this a positive or negative phenomenon?" "What are the consequences of hierarchies?"

Schools and social order

Students are helped or hindered in the pursuit of learning and knowledge by a range of personal and family characteristics that includes attitudes, personality, motivation, gender, ethnic or racial background, family circumstances, and even geographical location. For those who live in advantageous situations, schooling can help to secure a successful career and future. For those who are less fortunate, positive experiences at school can help overcome the adverse effects of past circumstances or events and build a solid base for further intellectual and social development. However, a school's ability to support all students can be limited because it is part of a wider community. Teachers are generally members of the dominant cultural group and are influenced by the norms, rules, and imperatives of society.

While it is easy to be critical of schools and teachers, they cannot be blamed for all social ills. There may be some justification for holding an education system responsible for the lack of opportunities when there are less than adequate resources or untrained staff. In some countries, schools are held accountable for failing to overcome all the pre-existing differences between students, and teachers—individually and collectively—are blamed for students' failure to meet minimum education standards (especially in literacy and mathematics).

Some writers have suggested that schools implicitly endorse social stratification and inequality to the extent that the needs of the least advantaged are rarely high on the agenda of educational priorities. Sometimes, it appears as though school systems overlook the fact that there are "haves" and "have nots" in our community, and even in their schools. For example, there are families in which a computer (or computers) is as familiar as the television, while in others, making a telephone call requires a walk up the street to where the payphone may or may not work depending on the level of vandalism that week. There are also families totally unaffected by any hardship and others in which there is a person with an intellectual, sensory, medical, or physical handicap or one who displays behaviour that is completely socially unacceptable. There are some schools with the most advanced technological equipment and facilities and others where a working computer is a novelty.

Dealing with such cultural, social, and system differences should not be beyond the capacity of the school, especially in providing appropriate levels of support and education opportunities to all students. But there are still many students who fail to make progress across the years of compulsory schooling and for whom the notion of difference and sense of belonging is so intense as to be almost physical.

USING THIS CHAPTER IN SCHOOLS

It can be quite a terrifying experience to teach your first lesson. I remember my own situation many years ago as though it were only last week. I'd prepared, over-prepared, reviewed, refined, and prepared again. And yet there was nothing I could do to calm the flight of butterflies in my stomach as I walked to my first classroom. And when I entered the room, looking as bold as I could, there were eager, and not-so-eager, faces looking up, wondering—I'm sure—what this strange-looking adult was about to do to them.

This chapter is about matters that I should have considered before I stepped into that classroom, but didn't. It is about knowing yourself as a teacher, knowing the environment in which you will participate, and knowing about the young people with whom you will interact.

So, what are the important points raised in this chapter?

The teacher

Culture and society play a huge but often unappreciated part in educational outcomes. Success in any learning environment is a product of a constellation of influences—some positive, some negative—and success is rarely the result of a simple cause–effect relationship.

Newly qualified teachers, and even some old hands, often overlook the importance of experience and background in the teaching–learning equation. Experience and background come from our own acculturation, that is, what we have learned about our culture and society and what we hold to be important and essential. Most teachers have middle-class values and ethics, have language skills commensurate with their university qualifications, and may not realise how their values and expectations may be at odds with those of their students. This has a considerable impact if a teacher is working in a low-socioeconomic area.

These dispositions are communicated to our peers and students by the way in which we teach. For example, in all school systems and across the primary and secondary years there is an imperative to teach the curriculum and sometimes there is an implicit (or even obvious) competition between teachers as to whose students perform best on the system-wide examinations. Such an emphasis means that many students are left behind because they are incapable of dealing with the stream of content.

The more effective you can be in accommodating social and cultural differences, the higher will be the proportion of your students who will be favourably placed to learn, and to achieve vocational and career success. As a teacher, you also need to consider the conflict between the view that school is where social order and conformity are endorsed, and school as a place where equality and social justice prevail, where the importance of difference is minimised, and where diversity and variation are promoted as positive aspects of society.

The student's environment

In this chapter, I have dealt mostly with families and parents. Certainly, it is important for you as teachers to consider yourself as an expert (an education professional) but not to the detriment of learning how you might improve the quality of your students' learning experiences. Arguably, parents know their children better than anyone and that knowledge can be invaluable when you're looking for the right way to communicate the curriculum to a young person in your early childhood centre, or in a primary, middle years, or secondary classroom. How you gain this knowledge is the key issue.

Some parents do not manage very well in school communities. They may not know how to communicate effectively with school staff about their children's home life and their education and this is often a result of their lack of contact with the school. In an early study, Leitch and Tangri (1988) reported that teachers perceived that only 1% of parents ever initiate contact with the school and only 5% make contact after they receive a notice concerning a child's poor academic performance. It is unlikely that much has changed over the past 20 years. And while some teachers claim that it is the parents, themselves, who avoid contact with the school, many parents see themselves as unwelcome visitors and have few opportunities to learn about the school and its operation. How can you change this?

One answer is through parent and teacher education sessions, and the school can be a useful venue for this activity. On the one hand, encouraging your parents to use the school as a resource can lead to greater involvement in the school community and develop a strong collaboration ethic within the school. Some schools host parent information evenings, often using the library as the venue. Guest speakers provide input on teaching innovations or topics of general interest, and informal interactions and discussions between staff and parents are encouraged. On the other hand, teachers and parents can learn about their own culture and the cultures and customs of others in school-sponsored cultural

awareness days. Many schools hold these special events when the students can taste food from other countries, learn about their traditions, and even learn folk dances. These can be readily extended to parents and others.

The criticisms of proposals like these include such arguments as:

- It is not the role of the school to educate adults.
- Parents do not have the time to attend such school activities.
- Those who need it most are the least likely to attend.
- The resources needed are too costly.

These points might be valid, but if a school is a place where the acceptance of difference is a guiding principle, you (the teacher) must take the initiative. Of course, collaboration and cultural awareness activities are not magic wands that will make everything better, or solve all the problems that confront your students, your colleagues, the school, and the school system. If there is a solution, it may come as a result of understanding the needs of each student (the way in which a student does or does not learn, their family and cultural backgrounds), taking steps to redress inequity, and providing support and services where they are needed. There can also be unexpected benefits when you contact parents to tell them something positive about their child, such as being the most improved student in mathematics or arithmetic, or producing the most informative project on rainforests.

More than a decade ago, Bruner (1996) argued that culture lies at the core of education. He stated that education cannot simply be reduced to a description of how students process information, learn, and solve problems, because it relates to the more general notion of meaning-making that encompasses ways of perceiving, thinking, feeling, and carrying out discourse. To be truly educated, young people need to know about their culture because it shapes the intellect and provides the building blocks that enable us to construct our world and understand our place in it. You, as their teacher, will play a crucial role in your student's cultural and social development.

discourse

Units of language above single sentences. Includes conversation and storytelling (narrative).

Matches and mismatches

Many of the difficulties that stem from cultural and social disadvantage exist because of at least three important areas of mismatch:

- personal mismatches—when the values, beliefs, and attitudes of the student do not align with those of the teacher or a student's peers, for example through a lack of cultural knowledge or sensitivity;
- school mismatches—when the expectations of the school and its administration overlook the realities of children living in disadvantaged circumstances, for example when school rules about dress standards and wearing school uniforms cannot be accommodated by parents who have very low or limited incomes, or when the language use in the home is different to that required at school (and here I'm not only talking about languages other than English but also the English expression and usage);
- system mismatches—when parents' and school expectations are not aligned, for example if parents are advocating for teaching resources for a child with very high support needs that the school does not believe it could, or should, provide.

The key to successful collaborations is communication, although few of us are skilled communicators regardless of our background or professional credentials. Preservice teacher education programs rarely include specific subjects, units, or modules in communication skills and processes that characterise collaborative activities (such as how to talk to a parent during a parent–teacher interview). Some teacher educators talk about team-teaching, and some students may observe or

participate in cooperative teaching lessons or classrooms in which two teachers work together. All things taken into consideration, this chapter is about the influences that affect any student in your class or classes. The practical exercises that follow will continue to focus your attention on ways in which you can learn about yourself, your culture, and the backgrounds and experiences of the young people with whom you will work.

PRACTICAL ACTIVITIES

The practical activities in this book have been divided into two sets. The first, called *Uni-work*, involves activities that can be undertaken at your tertiary institution, via the world wide web, through access to libraries and other resources, or even by sitting by yourself and thinking about them, or discussing and doing them with your friends and colleagues. You can work on the second set, called *School-work*, in a school setting during a practicum placement or when you are working in your own school or education setting. The activities can be undertaken in any setting at any level, preschool through senior secondary. All you need to do is adapt them to suit your specialisation.

Uni-work

1 Get together with your study friends and make a list of all the characteristics of education that reflect the society in which you live. This would include, for example, being able to read, kids being driven to school, using a computer at home, using a mobile phone to take pictures, going on an excursion to a museum, using a digital camera to add "life" to a project, and so on. (Your list could be huge.) Consider the circumstances of young people who live in an African country (like Chad) or in a South American country (like Ecuador) in respect of your list. You might start with a web search to find out a bit about the country you choose before you begin the exercise. How does education fare in those countries?

2 Visit a community library and the library at your tertiary institution. Locate resources about Indigenous cultures. Read through them to look for material that relates to the way in which education occurs in those cultures. Make a list of the important issues and list some ways in which you might use these in your own teaching situation.

3 Choose one of the family situations discussed in the section of this chapter entitled "Culture and society" (e.g., disrupted families, adoptive and multi-racial families, and so on). Take a cruise through the world wide web and generate a resource to inform teacher colleagues about the circumstances affecting the family and how those circumstances would influence students' behaviour in school, especially those factors that might contribute to diminished school performance.

School-work

School policies vary in regard to contact with parents and the use of students' records or other information for projects outside the usual teaching and learning events that occur as part of any school day or school calendar. Before beginning any of the following activities, speak to your supervising teacher or a member of the school administration to confirm that you can undertake the activity within existing school guidelines and policies.

4 Make time to talk to three or four of your teacher colleagues. Choose them so that you get a range of experiences, for example one that has been at the school for a long time, another who is a relative newcomer, like you, someone you respect, and maybe one of the administrators. Talk to them about the socioeconomic characteristics of the students who attend the "school" (if you

work in a preschool setting, this exercise applies to you as well). Try to get a picture of the number of ethnic/cultural backgrounds that are represented by the young people and their families, the languages that might be spoken by the children at home or by their parents, the extent to which parents are involved in the school/preschool activities, the extent to which parents volunteer. Turn your interview data into a cultural profile of the school. If you do this on a prac placement, you might even turn it into a PowerPoint presentation for one of your classes.

5 Check with your supervising teacher about the school protocol for parent–teacher meetings about academic progress. In collaboration with your supervising teacher, focus your attention on one student in your class or group who is known to have a learning problem. Make an appointment to meet with one or both of the student's parents/guardians. Find out how the young person fits in at home, what his or her interests are, and what keeps him or her engaged. Find out the extent to which the parents are involved in their child's education and whether there are siblings who might help out with the young person's learning at home. Talk to the parents/guardians about how they might help generalise the new learning that will occur in the classroom or the centre. The idea of this exercise is to get to know the student from all angles and the family's role in the young person's education. Then, work out a learning strategy for that student. You don't have to spend a lot of time on this. Making the effort will be reward in itself.

6 Over the course of a few weeks keep a social/cultural diary. This might be a small Spirax notebook, or a dedicated section of your lesson plan or log. Make at least one entry each day that records ways in which your students reflect their culture (or cultures) and the dominant society. For example, you might list the typical slang used in the class or learning setting, or how the students subtly (or not-so-subtly) project themselves in dress, perhaps despite the requirement to wear a uniform? What cliques or in-groups/out-groups exist and who comprises these groups, and why? How technologically sophisticated are the students, and who are the "haves" and the "have-nots" and why? Are there any isolated students and why?

After a couple of weeks, bring your ideas together as a collection. You can do this in your notebook or wherever will be convenient. Look for themes and trends. What is dominant and obvious, what is subtle? Then think about your own life experiences. How different do you operate to your students? For example, what are your favourite expressions and what do they convey or communicate to others? What is your fashion? How closely are you aligned culturally with your students? Now, the tough part. Where is the interface between your cultural and social characteristics and your students? What do you need to know or take into consideration? Can you change? Can they?

SUGGESTED READING AND RESOURCES

Books

Alexander, R. (2000). *Culture and pedagogy: International comparisons in primary education*. Oxford, UK: Blackwell Publishers.

Banks, J. A. (2006). *Race, culture, and education: The selected works of James A. Banks*. London: Routledge.

Brisk, M. E. (Ed.) (2007). *Language, culture, and community in teacher education*. Boca Raton, FL: Taylor & Francis.

Bruner, J. S. (1996). *The culture of education*. Cambridge, MA: Harvard University Press.

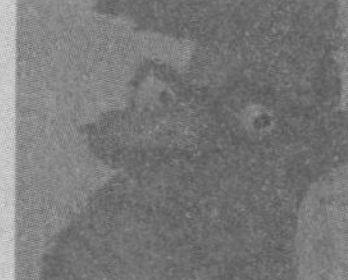

Clarke-Stewart, A. & Dunn, J. (2006). *Families count: Effects on child and adolescent development.* Cambridge: Cambridge University Press.

Harrison, N. (2004). *Indigenous education and the adventure of insight: Learning and teaching in indigenous classrooms*. Flaxton, Qld: Post Pressed.

Hope, A. & Oliver, P. (Eds) (2005). *Race, education, and culture.* Aldershot, Hants: Ashgate.

Lamb, M. E. (Ed.) (1999). *Parenting and child development in "nontraditional" families*. Mahwah, NJ: Erlbaum.

Leicester, M. (2000). *Systems of education: Theories, policies, and implicit values*. London: Falmer.

Ogletree, B. T., Fischer, M. A., & Schulz, J. B. (Eds) (1999). *Bridging the family–professional gap: Facilitating interdisciplinary services for children with disabilities*. Springfield, IL: Charles C. Thomas.

Journals

Australian Journal of Communication

Australian Journal of Education

Australian Journal of Indigenous Education, The

Social Alternatives

Unicorn

REFERENCES

Australian Bureau of Statistics (2003a). *Australian social trends: Population—National summary tables* <www.abs.gov.au/ausstats>. Canberra, ACT: Author.

Australian Bureau of Statistics (2003b). *Australian social trends: Population—Population characteristics: Ancestry of Australia's population* <www.abs.gov.au/ausstats>. Canberra, ACT: Author.

Australian Bureau of Statistics (2003c). *Australian social trends 2003*. Canberra, ACT: Author.

Australian Bureau of Statistics (2007). *Australian social trends, 2007: One-parent families*. Canberra, ACT: Author. <http://144.53.252.30/AUSSTATS/abs@.nsf/Latestproducts/F4B15709EC89CB1ECA25732C00 2079B2?opendocument>, accessed 10 October 2007.

Australian Institute of Health and Welfare (2007). Intellectual disability in Australia's Aboriginal and Torres Strait Islander peoples. *Journal of Intellectual and Developmental Disabilities*, *32*, 222–225.

Biddulph, S. (1997). *Raising boys*. Sydney: Finch.

Brooks-Gunn, J., Britto, P. R., & Brady, C. (1999). Struggling to make ends meet. In M. E. Lamb (Ed.), *Parenting and child development in "nontraditional" families* (pp. 273–304). Mahwah, NJ: Erlbaum.

Bruner, J. S. (1996). *The culture of education*. Cambridge, MA: Harvard University Press.

Choi, H-s., Thul, C. A., Berenhaut, K. S., Suerken, C. K., & Norris, J. (2006). Survey of school psychologists' attitudes, feelings, and exposure to gay and lesbian parents and their children. *Journal of Applied School Psychology*, *22*, 87–107.

Council for the Australian Federation (2007). *Federalist Paper 2: The future of Australian schools* (Rev. ed.). Melbourne, Vic: Victorian Department of Premier and Cabinet.

Coupland, D. (1991). *Generation X: Tales for an accelerated culture.* New York: St Martin's Press.

Department of Education, Science and Training (2003). *Meeting the challenge: Guiding principles for success from the Boys' Education Lighthouse Programme Stage One 2003*. Canberra, ACT: Author.

Dovidio, J. F., Gaertner, S. L., & Pearson, A. R. (2005). The nature of prejudice: The psychological foundations of hate. In R. J. Sternberg (Ed.), *The psychology of hate* (pp. 211–234). Washington, DC: American Psychological Association.

Dovidio, J. F., Gaertner, S. L., Hudson, G., Houlette, M. A., & Johnson, K. M. (2005). Social inclusion and exclusion: Recategorization and the perception of intergroup boundaries. In D. Abrams, M. A. Hogg, & J. M. Marques (Eds.), *The social psychology of inclusion and exclusion* (pp. 245–264). New York: Psychology Press.

Goldgehn, L. (2004). Generation who, what, Y? What you need to know about Generation Y. *International Journal of Educational Advancement*, *5*, 24–34.

Hart, V. (2003). Teaching black and teaching back. *Social Alternatives*, *22*(3), 12–16.

Heath, R. (2006). *Please just F*off it's our turn now*. Melbourne: Pluto Press.

House of Representatives Standing Committee on Education and Training (2002). *Boys' education: Getting it right.* Canberra, ACT: Australian Government.

Human Rights and Equal Opportunity Commission (2003). *Face the facts: Aboriginal and Torres Strait Islander People*. <www.humanrights.gov.au/racial_discrimination/face_facts/index.html>, retrieved 6 February 2008.

Keddie, A. (2005). A framework for "best practice" in boys' education: Key requisite knowledges and productive pedagogies. *Pedagogy, Culture and Society*, *13*, 59–74.

Keddie, A., & Mills, M. (2007). *Teaching boys: Classroom practices that work*, Allen & Unwin: Sydney.

Leitch, M. L., & Tangri, S. S. (1988). Barriers to home–school collaboration. *Educational Horizons*, *66*, 70–74.

Lovitt, T. J. (1992). *Sociology for teachers*. Wentworth Falls, NSW: Social Science Press.

Martino, W. & Meyenn, B. (2001). *What about the boys? Issues of masculinity and schooling.* Buckingham, UK: Open University Press.

McCarthy, C. (1998). *The uses of culture: Education and the limits of ethnic affiliation*. New York: Routledge.

McLeod, J., & Yates, L. (2003). Who is "Us"? Students negotiating discourses of racism and national identification in Australia. *Race, Ethnicity and Education*, *16*, 29–50.

Melbourne Institute of Applied Economic and Social Research (2007). *Poverty lines, Australia, June Quarter, 2007.* Melbourne, Vic: Author. <www.melbourneinstitute.com/labour/inequality/poverty/default.html>, accessed 17 October 2007.

Mills, C. & Gale, T. (2004). Parent participation in disadvantaged schools: Moving beyond attributions of blame. *Australian Journal of Education*, *48*, 268–281.

Ministerial Advisory Committee for Educational Renewal (2004). Report on Indigenous education, recommendations to the Minister for Education and the Minister for the Arts. Brisbane, Queensland: Department of Education and the Arts.

Moore, A. (2007). They've never taken a swim and thought about Jaws: Understanding the millennial generation. *College and University*, *82*, 41–48.

Mulhern, F. (2000). *Culture/metaculture*. London: Routledge.

Parker, R. (2005). Perspectives on the future of marriage. *Family Matters*, *72*, 78–82.

Pascoe, J. M., Shaikh, U., Forbis, S. G., & Etzel, R. A. (2007). Health and nutrition as a foundation for success in school. In Robert C. Pianta, Martha J. Cox, & Kyle L. Snow (Eds), *School readiness and the transition to kindergarten in the era of accountability* (pp. 99–120). Baltimore, MD: Paul H Brookes Publishing.

Patterson, C. J. (2006). Children of lesbian and gay parents. *Current Directions in Psychological Science*, *15*, 241–244.

Rothman, S. (2002). *Achievement in literacy and numeracy by Australian 14-year-olds, 1975–1998.* Melbourne: Australian Council for Educational Research.

Sheahan, P. (2005). *Generation Y: Thriving and surviving with Generation Y at work.* Prahran, Vic: Hardie Grant Books.

Smith, E. R., Seger, C. R., & Mackie, D. M. (2007). Can emotions be truly group level? Evidence regarding four conceptual criteria. *Journal of Personality and Social Psychology*, *93*, 431–446.

Wacquant, L. J. D. (2005). *Bourdieu reader*. Oxford: Polity Press.

Wainright, J. L. & Patterson, C. P. (2006). Delinquency, victimization, and substance use among adolescents with female same-sex parents. *Journal of Family Psychology*, *20*, 526–530.

John Elkins

2

LEGISLATION, POLICIES, AND PRINCIPLES

What you will learn in this chapter

This chapter deals with the social movement toward the inclusion of people with disabilities and other movements such as civil rights that have led to students with special education needs being accepted with their peers into regular schools and particularly regular classes. As you are already aware, inclusion relates to the provision of appropriate educational experiences to meet the needs of all students, including those who are exceptionally gifted or talented, and those who have high support needs. This chapter focuses attention on changes to schools and educational practices as a consequence of the adoption of legislation and policies of inclusion in states and territories in Australia.

In this chapter you will learn about:

- the meaning of the terms *inclusion* and *inclusive education*;
- the legal environment in which schools operate, especially anti-discrimination;
- the development of policies of inclusive education, particularly for students with disabilities;
- enacting policies for inclusive education;
- educational adjustments and supports; and
- how changes might occur in schools to assist the inclusion of students with diverse abilities in regular classes.

CASE STUDIES

MARCELLE

Marcelle is 17 years old and attends a secondary school near her home. Her education has been markedly different from that of other young women in her neighbourhood. Until last year she attended a special class located in a secondary school several suburbs away. She was taught to use public transport and was no longer taken to school by taxi. At the special class she learned functional daily living skills, including personal hygiene and some basic cooking. She also learned to recognise survival words such as "drink" and "toilet".

Specialist teachers and other professionals have provided hands-on services to Marcelle on a one-on-one or two-on-one basis whenever possible. She never had homework, and had few friends outside her special class, and none in her own suburb. As concern grew in society about discrimination against various disadvantaged people and groups, legislation and education policies indicated that education such as that offered to Marcelle was discriminatory. Thus, educators accepted a request from Marcelle's parents that she attend her local secondary school and participate in a range of classes—all of which contained mostly students who did not have a major disability.

Although teachers were apprehensive about the change, with guidance from a consultant they soon learned how to involve Marcelle in one of two ways. Sometimes, she achieved progress toward a reduced set of learning outcomes that were consistent with those of the class when they were working on mathematics or English activities. At other times, she learned how to perform tasks unique to her needs while participating in small group activities pertinent to the class lesson. For example, if there was a science lesson, Marcelle participated in the small work groups and, with support and considerable patience from her classmates, was able to participate in the experiments.

Overall, Marcelle, her family, and the school community have grown through the experience of her inclusion. According to her parents, she has become a new person. She looks forward to school each day, is much easier to manage at home, has significantly improved her vocabulary, and is paying much more attention to her personal care.

CONSTANCE McGREGOR

Now that community attitudes are much more positive about people with disability and impairment than in past decades—can you remember the 2000 Paralympic Games in Sydney?—it is likely that a primary school principal would be the first person to be approached to discuss the enrolment of a child with a disability. This is what happened to Constance McGregor toward the end of the school year.

speech therapy
The diagnosis and treatment of speech and language problems by a trained professional. Speech therapists work in schools, hospitals, and other settings where children and adults may attend or be referred.

Mrs Edakis, the mother of a Year 2 student named Tony, phoned to discuss her son's attending Endeavour School. She brought Tony to the appointment and he seemed interested in the school environment. Mrs Edakis explained that Tony had been seriously ill as a toddler and that his previously normal development had been compromised, with delayed language, mild autistic tendencies, and a fascination with electric torches and ladders. Tony had received weekly speech therapy for the past two years, and attended both a regular kindergarten and an early-intervention program each week.

Ms McGregor was aware of the many factors that would need consideration. Mrs Edakis did not reject the option of a special class or school for Tony. She simply wanted him to have the best school experience possible. Of course, having Tony attend the same school as his sister was a plus, but she knew how valuable the specialist input had been to Tony's development since his illness. Mrs Edakis asked whether Tony could receive ongoing speech therapy. Fortunately, this was a possibility, but the length of the waiting list would need to be checked. At the same time, Constance would enquire about teacher's aide time. These services, she knew, would be contingent on an assessment and the preparation of an individual education plan (IEP) that would set goals and expectations for Tony's education.

individual education plan (IEP)

A written document that is intended to aid in the provision of educational programs for students with special needs. It includes a statement of the student's present performance, instructional objectives and goals (sometimes called the individual education plan), services required by the student, and evaluation procedures to be used.

The review team would face the challenge of developing a feasible plan that would work for Tony in a regular classroom. Constance knew that experienced special educators often constructed IEPs as if the student was in a special setting. It would be imperative to involve the class teacher right from the start. But did she have a teacher in the reception classes who could take on the challenge of providing an excellent education for Tony? There was at least one experienced early-childhood teacher who could handle the challenge and several others who would be willing to do so in future years to ensure Tony's inclusion was successful.

Constance knew that provision of resources would be essential to overcome any opposition from school staff to Tony's placement. She also knew that entanglement in antidiscrimination litigation was something to be avoided. An overarching consideration was her belief that inclusion should be attempted and, as the principal, it was her responsibility to set up the attitudinal and resource context for Tony's enrolment.

TEACHING–LEARNING CONTEXT

Schools today are much more complex than in previous generations. Those who completed school in the past decade may find subtle changes in the ways that schools operate. If you are one of the many student teachers who have years of experience in the workforce and/or in caring for your children, then the schools in which you will work are likely to be very different from those you attended. Governments are increasing the accountability demands on schools, especially for literacy and numeracy achievement, and we may expect that students will be required to take national achievement tests every few years, as well as regular school and classroom assessments.

Increasing pressure for a highly productive workforce will result in curriculum revision and greater national standardisation. Teachers will need to interpret these pressures to produce the best outcomes for their students, including those who may experience difficulties in what could be a rigid learning environment.

Students in the schools of the next decade will be more competent in digital communication than many, if not most, of their teachers and parents. Just as time spent by students in watching television was a concern in previous generations, today's students often spend many hours playing computer games, some of which do not involve much literacy or numeracy. There is some concern expressed in the media that students are not spending sufficient time in traditional leisure pursuits, such as reading novels, and that text-messaging may be responsible for poor written expression and spelling. Whether these concerns have substance is uncertain, but teachers may find ways to move beyond stereotypes to motivate students and help them achieve personal goals as well as meet societal expectations.

ISSUES AND CHALLENGES

Normalisation in society and education

The concept of normalisation for people with disabilities arose in the Scandinavian countries. Bank-Mikkelsen (1969) argued against an overly protective approach to services for children and adults with disabilities, and asserted that they should enjoy a lifestyle as close as possible to that of society in general. Nirje (1985) added that the achievement of such outcomes needed to be based on methods that were culturally normative. These ideas were adopted by Wolfensberger (1972) who became prominent for his views that emphasised the *valuing* of people. Later preferring the term *social role valorisation*, Wolfensberger took the emphasis away from the mechanical application of rules, and reasserted that the valuing of people in society is paramount (Wolfensberger, 1988).

normalisation
A belief that people with a disability or impairment should enjoy the same rights, privileges, opportunities, and access to services and facilities as those who do not have a disability or impairment.

social role valorisation
A re-formulation of the normalisation principle.

This suggests that it is inappropriate to expect administrative action alone to produce successful outcomes. If children with disabilities and others who may be marginalised are to be educated successfully, much effort needs to be expended on preparing other children, teachers, and the wider community to understand and accept the philosophy of inclusion (Thomas, 2001) that has emerged from the idea of normalisation.

The past 50 years have seen several changes in society that have had the effect of gaining more equal conditions for particular groups, though earlier changes such as the abolition of slavery in the United States and the restriction of child labour were important precursors of what become known as the civil rights movement. In the United States the struggle for equal opportunity of, and compensatory treatment for, ethnic minorities served as an example for social activism and legislative changes. Other groups who struggled and in large part succeeded in bringing about social change were women and gays and lesbians. While Australians like to think of themselves as egalitarian and value mateship and a fair go, many examples of unfair practices and prejudice persist.

Education of All Handicapped Children Act (PL 94-142)
This is the US legislation that prescribes education for all children. The legislation contains a mandatory provision that states that school systems must provide free public education for every child 3–21 years of age, regardless of disability, unless state laws do not provide for education between ages 3 and 5 years, or over 18 years. A supplementary law (PL 99-457) extended PL 94-142 to remove the exception clause (for children aged 3–5 years) and to encourage early intervention incentives.

Vigorous advocacy for the inclusion of virtually all students has been increasing as evidence has accumulated about numerous successful programs for students with substantial disabilities (see Armstrong & Moore, 2004; Giangreco, 1989, 1993, 1996, 2003; Giangreco & Doyle, 2007; Loreman, Deppeler, & Harvey, 2005). Here the evidence was not about comparative effectiveness of inclusion (versus separate programs) but about inclusion actually providing the academic and social benefits desired—the students were receiving an education as close to the norm of society as possible.

Deliberate government action in regard to increased equity in education owes much to two examples from the United States. One was the attempt to achieve balanced ethnic enrolment in public schools, which involved the busing of students to schools away from their local area. This attempt at school desegregation had mixed success, and points, among other things, to the difficulty of using laws to modify traditional patterns of education. The other example was the *Education of all Handicapped Children Act* of 1975. Later renamed as the *Individuals with Disabilities Education Act* and in 2005 as the *Individuals with Disabilities Education Improvement Act* (Weber, 2007), this legislation has influenced other governments around the world to introduce similar legislation aimed at improving education for students with disabilities, especially through the mandating of practices such as the Individualised Education Plan, Child Find, and its use of the concept of the least restrictive environment. Some of the consequences of the US legislation have been controversial, and the regulations appear to be excessively bureaucratic. Nevertheless, this American legislation has stimulated teachers and parents in many countries to strive for better education for students with disabilities.

The legislation that applies

Teachers today need to understand that both government and non-government schools are required to meet the requirements of various laws. Some are specifically about education, while others are more widespread in their application, such as judicial review and copyright. Many education Acts distinguish between students generally and students with disabilities. Thus, while the parents of all students are required to ensure that they attend school (apart from those who provide approved home schooling), some schools may be established for students with disabilities, and sometimes for students with one particular type of disability, such as very high support needs.

least restrictive environment

The educational setting in which a child with a disability or impairment can succeed and which is as close as possible to the regular classroom (which is considered to be the ideal).

Under some education Acts, regulations may be approved that restrict the attendance of students with disabilities at certain schools that have specialist staff or facilities. Specific legislation varies across jurisdictions such as states and territories, while regulations and policies differ also within sectors such as state and non-state schools. As an example of the legislation that may apply, the Queensland Department of Education and the Arts <http://education.qld.gov.au/strategic/eppr/curriculum/crppr009> lists various state and Commonwealth Anti-Discrimination Acts, Child Protection, Disability Services, and Privacy legislation. Also, there are more general Acts, such as the *Human Rights and Equal Opportunity Act* and the *Queensland Education Act*.

A very important aspect of the *Commonwealth Disability Discrimination Act* is the regulations known as the Disability Standards for Education <www.dest.gov.au/NR/rdonlyres/482C1E4B-9848-4CC3-B395-067D79853095/15406/DisabilityStandards_004_screen.pdf>. Another important consequence of the past decade of legislative reform is that all aspects of educational policy development need to take into account the rights of students with disabilities. Other states and territories have legislative and regulatory constraints that are broadly similar, though differing in detail. If problems arise with the education of students with disabilities, sometimes the student or parents may use the provisions of anti-discrimination legislation (Box 2.1).

Disability Standards for Education

The *Disability Discrimination Act 1992* (Cth) has an extra condition that applies to disability, that is, discrimination may be allowed if not to discriminate would constitute an unreasonable hardship. Thus, when cases concerning inclusive education are brought before the Human Rights and Equal Opportunity Commission, the point at issue is usually whether an unreasonable hardship results for the school, the teacher or for other students. Bringing cases for resolution is expensive and time-consuming, and therefore the Commonwealth Government authorised the *Disability Standards for Education 2005* in an attempt to clarify expectations and legal obligations under disability discrimination legislation. In effect, if schools and teachers act in accordance with the Standards, then they will not contravene the *Disability Discrimination Act 1992* (Cth). The Standards cover the following areas:

- enrolment;
- participation;
- curriculum development, accreditation and delivery;
- student support services; and
- elimination of harassment and victimisation. (p. 6)

Guidance Notes are provided to assist in interpretation. "Disability" has a specific meaning that may differ from common understandings, from the way that disability is used elsewhere in this book or in the past policies and practices of schools. For example, it means *inter alia*, "the presence of organisms

BOX 2.1

Using anti-discrimination legislation

In a provincial city, a primary school had accepted the enrolment of a girl who had a severe hearing impairment. The school was willing to support Amy to enable her to gain her education, and part-time input was provided by a teacher trained in the area of hearing impairment. However, the approach to teaching students like Amy that had been used in state schools included augmentation of hearing and Signed English, an approach that used manual signing to interpret English language. However, the adult Deaf community does not sign using Signed English and Amy's parents wanted her to be supported in school by an interpreter fluent in Auslan, the sign language used by profoundly deaf adults.

Amy's parents sought to persuade the state education department that Amy should be afforded the support of in-class Auslan. When this request was denied, they sought redress through the Anti-Discrimination Commission, which was successful. After some time, the state education department decided to cease the use of Signed English and, instead, required teachers to use Auslan when teaching students who needed signing communication. The state education department accepted the responsibility of ensuring that Auslan would be available in schools where a student might need this medium. The challenge of ensuring sufficient staff fluent in Auslan was taken up by a university.

Deaf community
It is characterised by its own language (sign language) and its own pattern of beliefs, values, customs, arts, institutions, social forms, and knowledges.

Auslan
See *Australian Sign Language.*

capable of causing disease or illness" (p. 8), such as hepatitis C. It also includes what are commonly called emotional disorders.

The Standards apply from preschool to post-compulsory education and training, universities, and other adult education. A key concept is that of adjustments, which are measures or actions taken to assist a student with a disability. Adjustments are "an aid, a facility or a service that the student requires because of his or her disability" (p. 13). Unlike standards for buildings, the issue of whether adjustments are reasonable may not be straightforward, and thus the student or parent must be consulted about whether the adjustment proposed is reasonable, whether it would be effective and whether another adjustment would be less disruptive yet no less beneficial.

Sometimes courses of study involve elements in which a student cannot participate, and it is expected that he or she will be offered another activity or content that fits within overall course aims. As far as possible, where activities take place outside the school, they should be chosen or designed to include the student. Curriculum and opportunities to learn might also involve adjustments, which can challenge teachers as they strive to retain essential elements of the curriculum. Recent research on Universal Design for Learning (Rose & Meyer, 2002), though not mentioned in the Standards, provides guidance for designing curriculum and teaching, which minimises the need for adjustments.

What this means for schools

Students with disabilities have developmental needs that must be addressed by schools and school systems working in partnerships with parents. Prior to the final quarter of the 20th century, most of these students were not enrolled in regular schools and classes but were educated through a special education system. In recent years, much debate has occurred about whether special schools and classes

were the most appropriate ways of educating these students. While either or both special schools and classes are still used in state and territory education systems, they enroll from 0.5% to 1.0% of all students, with some parents choosing these services. Other parents are strongly in favour of their children being enrolled in local schools or the schools attended by siblings, and education systems have developed policies to respond to these choices.

Just as this book is broader in scope than its major emphasis, students with disabilities, policies on inclusive education are tending to address student diversity ranging across language, ethnicity, gender issues, poverty as well as disability. To illustrate this, let us look at the policy on inclusive education adopted by Education Queensland in 2005 <http://education.qld.gov.au/studentservices/learning/docs/inclusedstatement2005.pdf>. The first notable point is the way in which the policy describes the way educational experiences should be for all students. It states that it:

- fosters a learning community that questions disadvantage and challenges social injustice;
- maximises the educational and social outcomes of all students through the identification and reduction of barriers to learning, especially for those who are vulnerable to marginalisation and exclusion; and
- ensures all students understand and value diversity so that they have the knowledge and skills for positive participation in a just, equitable, and democratic global society. (p. 1)

Inclusion implies the complete acceptance of a student with a disability or other marginalised students in a regular class, with appropriate changes being made to ensure that the student is fully involved in all class activities. Thus, inclusion is characterised by the redesign of regular schools, both physically and in curriculum, to provide for the complete education of all students who seek to attend. Inclusive education has relevance to more than just students with disabilities. Gender, ethnicity, sexual orientation, and language background are student variables that also need to be addressed, as you will recall from Chapter 1. As stated in its policy on inclusive education, Education Queensland:

- responds optimistically and constructively to the needs of educationally disadvantaged/marginalised students;
- uses diversity as a rich resource for building a connected and intellectually challenging curriculum in the classroom;
- ensures that students, teachers and community members from diverse groups feel safe and free from discrimination, bias and harassment;
- respects student voice and ensures that all students learn through democratic processes;
- promotes locally negotiated responses to student, family and community needs through effective community engagement processes and cross-agency collaboration; and
- ensures that all Education Queensland policies and initiatives recognise the centrality of inclusive education practices to quality education. (p. 2)

The mission to provide appropriately for all students applies not only to public schools but also to independent schools and those operated by religious denominations. It is clear that inclusive education exists in a growing number of schools throughout Australia. There is also growing recognition in government policy statements that schools should strive to be inclusive of all students who wish to enrol.

There are variations with respect to inclusion among the standard categories of disability. Most students with vision impairment, and those with hearing impairment who do not use a sign language, are well supported in regular classes. However, any additional staff or resources required to meet a student's educational needs would have been provided by sources outside the school's regular budget.

student voice
The thoughts as expressed by students; the concept urges the reception of these ideas by the teacher.

sign language
A language in its own right. It has its own grammar, morphology, syntax, location, semantics, and pragmatics. Meaning is achieved through the combination of hand shape, location, movement pattern, and intensity, as well as facial and bodily expression. In both Australia and New Zealand, the language of the Deaf community is recognised as a legitimate national language.

This can reduce the extent to which students with disabilities are thought to belong to the regular school community. However, governments are striving to find ways of improving the necessary supports for these students.

Students whose disabilities do not require a high level of resources are commonly enrolled in regular classes. Under current arrangements, in which schools compete vigorously for students with high academic potential, and there is government pressure for high standards, students with disabilities may not be especially valued. Despite this, the movement of students out of special classes and special schools has continued over the past three decades and only those who satisfy rigid enrolment criteria are retained in special schools.

It appears that few educators or members of the public see this situation as inappropriate. Parents themselves are polarised. Some parents are ardent advocates for inclusion, whereas others prefer to support traditional segregated special education services. It is understandable that parents might wish to have a choice, allowing them to change the school enrolment if there are problems at their child's existing school.

Another facet of change has been the increased prominence within education of the political concept of social justice. Social justice seeks to maximise educational outcomes for all students. As indicated earlier, this has been supported by the passage of anti-discrimination legislation and there has been considerable discussion about providing education fairly to all students, including those with disabilities.

social justice
The concept of a society in which justice is achieved in every aspect, in which individuals and groups receive fair treatment and an impartial share of the benefits of society.

In addition, the likelihood of parents rejecting segregated settings as being discriminatory has increased. Various North American and British advocates of the inclusion of children with severe disabilities in regular classes have visited the Antipodes to challenge parents and school staff to be more assertive in dealing with educational bureaucracies. In New Zealand, and to varying extents in Australian states and territories, parents and local communities have considerable control over schools, and some aspects of the advocacy role have shifted from central bureaucracies to local school councils, or boards.

Even if schools have provided an appropriate program, an understanding of the full meaning of inclusion can be lacking. Examples such as holding a high school dance at an inaccessible venue, and arranging a school excursion that was inaccessible to students using wheelchairs, illustrate that schools need to be vigilant in thinking about how all aspects of school life can be inclusive of all students. Judging by newspaper columns and letters to the editor, many people remain unappreciative of what such practices indicate about how certain students are valued. This need for sensitivity extends to all students likely to be marginalised.

It is important to recognise that regular schools already provide varied educational experiences for students, and all students in a class are not "working on the same page at the same time". Rather, teachers offer individual students or small groups curriculum and materials that maximise engagement and learning. Meeting the needs of those who have disabilities or other special needs is often a simple extension of such practices. In primary schools, curriculum differentiation (i.e., varying the objectives of lessons and units of work) occurs mostly through classroom teachers' use of informal grouping and varied forms of assessment. In secondary schools, the curriculum is highly differentiated in response to student choice and need within the constraints of, for example, tertiary entrance requirements.

curriculum differentiation
The need to arrange teaching–learning environments and practices so that they are appropriate for the different learning styles and characteristics of different students. This might involve deleting already mastered material from the curriculum, adding content, processes, or expectations, extending existing curriculum through enrichment activities, providing work for able students at an earlier age than typical, and including new units or courses that meet the needs of specific students.

Schools also need to work in partnership with parents. In most cases, parents are best placed to know how a school can tailor its services to the needs of their child. Mutual information flow between the home and the family is imperative.

TEACHING ESSENTIALS

Enacting policy for students with disabilities

Berry, Andrews, and Elkins (1977) raised criticisms of special schools in Australia three decades ago. At that time, special schools were usually situated away from neighbourhood facilities, thereby restricting the social integration that students might enjoy. Examples of improvements that have occurred in special schools include high-quality programs that secure effective transition to adult life, including work. Strategies used include:

- forming links with technical and further education (TAFE) colleges;
- mobilising the community to increase the acceptance by employers of students in their workforce;
- careful prevocational programming such as the operation of enclaves in local factories; and
- maintaining interest in support for students for up to a year after graduation.

As the percentage of all students who are enrolled in special schools has dropped to less than 1%, many of the skills and understandings developed in special schools have been adopted, or adapted, to support students with disabilities in regular schools. However, useful as this knowledge was, it ignored the power of the peer group and regular teaching strategies to produce desired learning. Gradually, teaching approaches have developed that reflect practices that originated in regular class teaching and in special schools.

We have relatively little data from the follow-up of students with disabilities after they have finished their schooling, although transition programs for adolescents with disabilities are common in secondary schools and special schools. If students who have been educated in the inclusive education settings are not able to pursue adult activities in the community and, instead, find themselves working in supported environments or living relatively unproductive lives in protective residential facilities, then arguments favouring inclusion lose some force. Unfortunately, employment for young adults with disabilities is too often unattained, even for those who complete secondary schooling or tertiary studies. However, employment services to assist young people with disabilities to enter the workforce are available, and, together with transition programs in secondary schools, contribute to positive employment prospects.

Some people question whether all students can be included. The answer depends on what we take inclusion to mean. Some evidence comes from settings in which segregation is not possible. For example, in isolated rural areas children with disabilities perforce must be educated along with their peers. Although this does not always produce successful outcomes, it does suggest that if teacher expertise and essential resources can be provided the local community might well be accepting and supportive of a child with disabilities (Armstrong, Armstrong, & Barton, 2006). Where a special class or special school is at hand, as is often the case in provincial towns and cities, community cohesion is often less than in rural areas, and it is easier for teachers and parents to expect that others (i.e., specialists) should provide services for students who have special needs. So, in some contexts there are strong influences against regular school placement for at least some students with severe disabilities. Nevertheless, it has been asked whether it is possible to eliminate all segregated special education, and some believe that it is, while most teachers doubt this.

Some groups, especially parent organisations, have claimed that this is both possible and desirable. A practical example is the professional development materials for teachers that were produced by the parents of children with Down syndrome (Down Syndrome Association of Queensland, 2003). In the United States, organisations such as The Association for Severe Handicap (known as TASH) advocate inclusion more strongly than the Council for Exceptional Children, which reflects the perspectives of teachers already working in special education service delivery.

Down syndrome

A condition resulting from a chromosomal abnormality. There are three types: Trisomy 21, mosaicism, and translocation.

School systems continue to wrestle with the pattern of services for students with disabilities. Teachers also recognise that inclusive education represents challenges to their professional learning. Funded by teachers and parents, the Vinson Report in New South Wales provided ideas on special education. It has chapters on behaviour and students with disabilities. Further details can be found at the Public Education Inquiry NSW website <www.pub-ed-inquiry.org/reports/final_reports>.

Inclusion has been widely adopted for students with physical and sensory impairments. In most cases, students whose main need is the use of low vision or hearing aids will enrol in the school of choice. Some specific support will be given, as supplementary instruction to the student or as advice for the teachers, using staff who have specialist knowledge and experience. Where students rely on alternative communication methods, and a specialist teacher is needed to instruct them in Braille or sign language, they are likely to be enrolled in small numbers in a school where such support is made available. A bilingual/bicultural model is sometimes used for deaf children, which involves their enrolment in classes with hearing children, and both a regular teacher and a signing teacher/interpreter are in the classroom. It is anticipated that many students and staff will learn sufficient sign language to increase communication among hearing and deaf children.

Braille

A tactual language system based on a cell of six potential raised dot positions, arranged in two columns and three rows. Various combinations of these six dots then form the basis for all Braille symbols.

The proportion of the total student population currently educated in segregated facilities is at an all-time low, but this situation conceals two important issues. The first is that services to students in regular school classrooms may result in increased stress among teachers (Box 2.2).

BOX 2.2 Teacher stress

Darien is a teacher who has had the usual range of successes and problems in his short teaching career. In the past, Darien taught in a middle-class district in a school that was well staffed with experienced teachers.

Then he moved to a school in a low socioeconomic suburb in which there are many students from Polynesia. This has presented him with a new set of challenges, especially understanding issues relevant to that culture. He believes that he needs help to manage student behaviour, and to motivate the boys to do homework.

Some weeks after the start of the year, a new student who has a diagnosis of Attention Deficit Hyperactivity Disorder (ADHD) joined Darien's class. With classroom management skills that he knew already needed upgrading, Darien found that he began to feel very tired and frustrated by his limited ability to manage the new constellation of challenges within his classroom. Teaching was no longer something that he enjoyed, and feeling stressed meant that he lacked the spark that teachers need to inspire their students. He found it difficult to share his concerns with more experienced colleagues, and after some months began to contemplate leaving the teaching profession.

Fortunately, professional development opportunities became available that gave Darien some new ideas about how to manage the classroom as a whole and to establish processes to provide effective education for the new student with ADHD. Aware that Darien had been experiencing stress at his new school, the administration team were able to provide support that helped him regain his feelings of competence as a teacher.

The second is the continuing high support needs of those students who remain in special schools. Thus, equitable mechanisms for providing these students with support is required if they are to be included in regular classrooms. In recent years education systems have changed funding procedures from level of disability to the profile of educational adjustments that are needed. These efforts have been directed toward determining the needs of students with disabilities and allocating funding for support (both material and personnel) with mixed success (Box 2.3).

BOX 2.3

Support through consideration of education adjustments

Education Queensland designed an instrument to identify the various ways in which teachers adjust their teaching to help children learn. The initial intention was to provide a way of supporting students with disabilities in a more equitable way and in line with inclusive education principles and policies than the earlier ascertainment process. The Education Adjustment Program Profile (EAP) asks teachers and other school professionals involved with a particular child to identify how, and how often, the school is currently making adjustments to assist children's learning. The EAP accommodates students with disabilities and impairment, language, medical, and behavioural complications. It records adjustments in the following domains:

- curriculum;
- communication;
- social participation/emotional wellbeing;
- health and personal care;
- safety; and
- learning environment/access.

Items in all domains include consideration of adjustments to curriculum content and teaching strategies. In addition, the *Curriculum* domain includes items on consultations and curriculum planning, and assessment. *Communication* includes items on consultation and planning for communication (such as teacher consultations with a speech and language pathologist), and the use of assistive technology (such as hearing aids). *Social participation* and *emotional wellbeing* deal with planning and school-wide student management. *Health and personal care* and *Safety* include monitoring and specific health care procedures. *Learning environment* and *access* include planning about learning environments and the use of assistive technology.

While the EAP profile is used within the Queensland education systems as a funding mechanism, it could be usefully employed as a way of considering what is already being done, and what can be done, for students who need support, including students identified as gifted and talented.

For greater details and to see the EAP profile, go to the Queensland Department of Education, Training and the Arts website <http://education.qld.gov.au/students/disabilities/adjustment>.

Perhaps in the longer term it will be more productive to provide block grants to schools or clusters of schools to support the majority of students with special learning needs, and to minimise the number of students for whom funding allocation is made based on individual needs. Another issue is that the prevalence of students labelled as Autism Spectrum Disorder is increasing.

LEARNING ESSENTIALS

While the legislative framework discussed earlier has emphasised the education of students in regular schools, the historical practice of enrolling some students in special schools continues. In most special schools, the students are those who have high support needs, and the teachers and other staff have specialist skills. Although contexts differ in their receptivity to students with special needs, there is also variability in the extent to which parents and their children seek regular education settings. In the first place, if parents have initially obtained a regular school placement—often at preschool level—there is a natural tendency to expect the school to maintain appropriate education for the child. Thus, a move to a special school occurs only if the regular school proves unsatisfactory, or if the school rejects the child's continued enrolment. Of importance here are the criteria that might determine continuing enrolment or exclusion. From the parents' perspective, the most important issue is likely to be the child's happiness and general social development. Failure to make academic gains can also feature, particularly if this has a negative influence on the child's self-concept and behaviour.

Three issues constitute the main points of resistance from regular schools to the inclusion of students with disabilities. The first is the provision of physical access for students who use wheelchairs or have other constraints on their mobility. Although new buildings generally conform to standards set down in building codes, the majority of older schools present access problems, and most education authorities resist making expensive modifications to enable one student to attend the school of their choice.

Second, a teacher must be able to manage student behaviour. Problems typically cited are toileting, aggression toward others, lack of intelligible speech, and making uncontrolled noises that disturb other students. If an aide or other support is provided, inclusion is more likely to occur. From the teacher's perspective, aggressive or non-compliant behaviour is the major reason for seeking to exclude or transfer a child.

A third cause of concern to many teachers occurs when the student's achievement level is substantially below that of low-achieving students in the class. The teacher may try to develop a separate program for the child (which is often impractical) or find ways to include the student in common classroom activities that provide useful learning opportunities. However, classroom organisation that assumes that students will differ in how they can engage in curriculum is likely to make the challenge of accommodating students with disabilities seem, and be, more manageable.

Limitations in learning are important only when the gap between the child's needs and the main class curriculum becomes too great. It seems likely that teachers who are more flexible in how they teach find it easier to manage a child with major learning problems. Thus, the major concerns for teachers are behaviour and rate of learning. If children have physical or sense impairments, a relatively modest investment of consultant time and the provision of appropriate aids can often enable a regular class teacher to manage without undue strain.

Inclusion and the curriculum

If continued progress toward greater inclusion in Australia is to be made, several issues need to be addressed by education authorities. These include the modification of the curriculum to include the

Attention Deficit Hyperactivity Disorder (ADHD)
Excessive motor activity and restlessness. Frequently associated with poor attention and chronic distractability.

ascertainment
The process of determining the most suitable educational placement for a student with a disability or impairment.

assistive technology
Any item, piece of equipment, or product system that is used to increase, maintain, or improve functional capabilities of individuals with disabilities.

prevalence
The number of cases existing within the population at any given time (e.g., the percentage of the total school population having a learning difficulty).

self-concept
The perception or image that people have of themselves.

needs of children with disabilities, the development of positive attitudes to disability, the role of school policies, and having regular classroom teachers assume major responsibility for educating children with special needs.

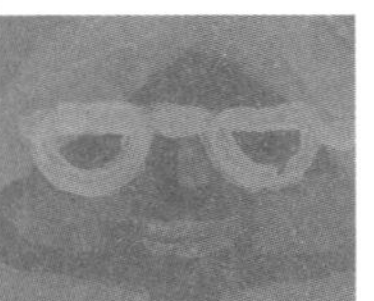

Curriculum in primary schools and up to Year 10 is structured by reference to Key Learning Areas (KLAs). These have covered English, health/physical education, languages other than English (LOTE), mathematics, science, study of society and the environment (SOSE), technology, and the arts. However, some KLAs have been given more or less emphasis in public debate. For example, the emphasis on literacy and numeracy indicates that English and mathematics are of central importance. Concern about increasing obesity in children and youth has emphasised the importance of health and physical education. It has been claimed that Australian history has been neglected, and that SOSE should be replaced by traditional disciplinary treatment of history. Some are not convinced that languages other than English are essential for all students. Some attention is paid in syllabuses and support materials to students with special needs (see, for example, the Education Queensland website: <www.qsa.qld.edu.au/yrs1to10/special-needs/index.html>.

Key Learning Areas (KLAs)

The main subject areas identified by the Australian Education Council, and developed by the Australian Education Council's Curriculum and Assessment Committee in response to a formal initiative to develop national collaborative curriculum projects. The KLAs are the Arts, English, Health and physical education, Languages other than English, Mathematics, Science, Studies of society and environment, and Technology. Various Australian states use slightly different labels for their KLAs.

It is vital, as we consider the curriculum for students with special needs, that we first recognise that these students all have capabilities, and it is these capabilities that are the starting point for learning. Another fundamental orientation is to regard teaching as assisting learners to perform some physical or mental action that lies just beyond their present capabilities.

There are many facets to curriculum, which in its broadest sense has to do with teaching and learning activities across many domains (knowledge, skills, values and attitudes), and especially with the scope and nature of student experiences as set out generally by society and specifically by education authorities, principals, and teachers. The dominant form of curriculum is devised by education authorities with reference to the age of students (or the number of years they have attended school), often with no regard to the diversity of student achievements at any particular age or grade level. In some cases, the curriculum is formulated as little more than a syllabus (or list of topics to be taught), whereas in others the curriculum takes the form of broad guidelines that are to be interpreted by teachers in the light of local circumstances and the characteristics of particular students.

Over the past three decades or so there has been a move away from syllabus statements toward guidelines for content and process in which teacher autonomy is accepted. However, there has been some move back to central control through either national or state prescription, or as a response to industry demands for vocational relevance and competency in the curriculum.

Whatever the level of specificity and central control, there are some things that children learn in school that lie outside most formal curriculum documents. If students attend schools in which no students with disabilities are enrolled, nondisabled students might well lack knowledge, skills, values and attitudes that would assist them to interact successfully with people with disabilities. They might also learn, through the absence of students with disabilities in their school, that discrimination is acceptable.

A key feature of successful inclusion is the relevance of the regular school curriculum for all students. In recent years the term *inclusive curriculum* has been used to emphasise the point that schools need to be sufficiently flexible to accommodate the characteristics of all students who are enrolled. There are several aspects that must be considered. The major issue for some students, particularly those with physical or sensory impairments, is access to the curriculum that is provided for other students. Ramps, toilets, aids, brailled and taped text materials, and FM transmitters and receivers might be necessary to enable them to gain physical access to the curriculum.

FM transmitters and receivers

A hearing aid that uses FM radio waves to broadcast directly to a hearing aid from a miniature transmitter worn by a teacher. Also known as a radio aid.

For other students, although ultimately sharing the same curricular goals as their peers, additional opportunities to learn are required because they have not developed the knowledge base that is required

of students at a particular grade level. They need to be taught material that school staff members assume is learned incidentally outside school. For other students, existing skills are well above their peers. Figure 2.1 indicates how the special education curriculum explicitly addresses such issues.

Current Australian curricula have been influenced at the upper age levels by governments seeking to have schooling better prepare youth for a complex, changing, and multi-skilled workplace. Influences from the business and manufacturing sectors have brought attempts to unify curriculum across Australia and to introduce competencies thought to be relevant by industry. At a time of high employment and skills shortages, increased use of achievement testing has been introduced in the hope that standards in literacy, numeracy and work skills will result. Although some attention has been paid to these changes by special educators, relatively little consideration has been given by those centrally involved in curriculum reform as to what changes might mean for students who have special learning needs.

Little attention has been given to the appropriateness of newer competency-based curricula or to the accompanying profile assessments for students with disabilities. However, special education has developed its own competency-based approach in the Individual Education Plan (IEP) <www.ltag.education.tas.gov.au/focus/inclusiveprac/IEPguidelines.htm>.

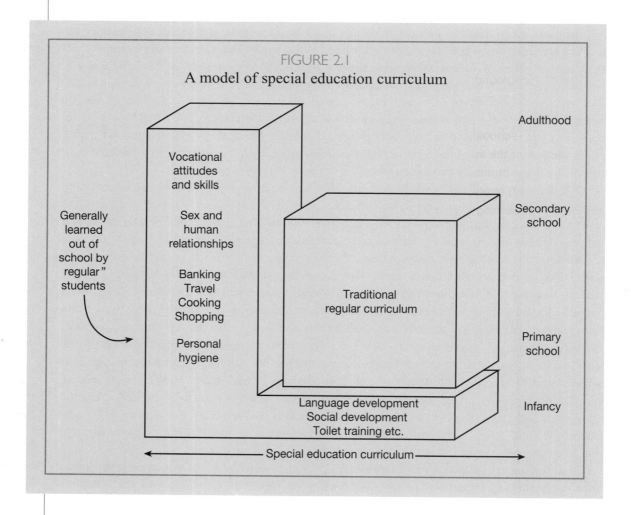

FIGURE 2.1
A model of special education curriculum

Adulthood
Vocational attitudes and skills
Sex and human relationships
Banking Travel Cooking Shopping
Personal hygiene
Secondary school
Generally learned out of school by regular" students
Traditional regular curriculum
Primary school
Language development
Social development
Toilet training etc.
Infancy
Special education curriculum

The IEP is a process designed to bring parents, teachers and other professionals, and sometimes the student together to plan and review the instructional goals and methods required for optimal progress. The IEP process may incorporate:

- gathering information;
- meeting of participants to share perspectives;
- designing/modifying the IEP;
- using the IEP; and
- regularly evaluating the IEP.

Box 2.4 illustrates the basic components of an IEP. (See <www.edu.gov.mb.ca/k12/specedu/iep/paul.html> for additional detail.) In regular classrooms, we might expect teachers to bring the IEP and competency approaches into rough alignment. This might not be easy, since the mainstream curriculum often has not been designed for students with diverse learning needs. Many assumptions are made about student competencies in terms of knowledge, skills, values, and attitudes. Yet these assumptions probably do not apply well to students with disabilities, and teachers must design activities that enable participation in the class program.

BOX 2.4

An example of an IEP framework

Background:

- information on student's impairment;
- other information; and
- schooling.

For each of the Intended Outcomes:

- relevant curriculum statements;
- teaching strategies;
- extra teaching resources; and
- who does what and by when.

The daily teaching plan

There are two basic models of classroom activity for included students. In one, the goals are similar for all students, with an expectation that outcomes differ in degree. In the other, participation has different goals for students with very different learning needs. In practice, both models might apply in different areas of the curriculum. These models can be called *multilevel instruction* and *curriculum overlapping*.

In *multilevel instruction*, students have different expectations for breadth and sophistication of outcomes in the same content area, and heterogeneous groups are frequently used so that support is extended to the less proficient learners. In contrast, *curriculum overlapping* has qualitatively different goals for a student with certain support needs (e.g., social skills) although they might participate in lessons with their peers who have advanced cognitive learning goals. In a science class, relevant activities—such as fetching equipment, or counting events or objects—might be integral to the lesson in which others are learning about scientific principles through experimentation.

social skills

Skills that relate to human interactions (e.g., waiting for a turn, asking questions politely, responding when spoken to, shaking hands when appropriate).

Matching the curriculum to students with special needs has not been easy, as evidence from Australia, New Zealand, and other countries has shown. Attempts have been made to standardise curriculum in different countries, but few of these have taken the needs of all students into account. Where this has been done, as with the National Curriculum in the United Kingdom, many significant problems have been encountered. These standard curricula often constrain teachers and make it difficult to meet individual needs.

National Curriculum
Movement within the UK that has been emulated in Australia seeking to standardise curricula and monitor student progress using achievement tests.

A different idea is contained in the concept of *inclusive curriculum* that is sensitive to such matters as gender, race, and poverty in deciding both content and method. In the area of disability, there are two aspects of importance: the obvious one is the creation of curriculum relevant to the needs of the students, and the other is a recognition that knowledge about, and attitudes to, disability are necessary prerequisites for working with students with special needs.

It is an indictment on past curricula that disability was never mentioned, so much so that widespread ignorance and prejudice have hampered the efforts of people with a disability to participate fully in society. There are many examples in literature, science, history, art, citizenship, and physical education in which knowledge, skills, values and attitudes can include the topic of disability. Refashioning curricula to include the needs of all students cannot proceed on the assumption that mainstream content and teaching methods are ideal. Thus, there are increasing calls for the inclusion of all students to become the reformation of regular education.

Interestingly, calls for inclusion are strongest from parents of students with major support needs, whereas parents of those with mild educational problems might argue for at least part-time segregated instruction. This suggests that school reform is, indeed, the heart of the matter. The common conception of regular schooling is of relatively common instructional methods and content in any classroom, even though the range of student achievement is quite large, perhaps equivalent to several year levels.

If regular schools can offer greater flexibility of curriculum content for all students, then the concerns of both groups might be met. Some schools achieve this through flexible grouping, the use of collaborative teaching situations and cooperative learning, and by ensuring that all students are valued and their achievements recognised.

cooperative learning
A form of peer-mediated learning that involves children working together in small groups to accomplish shared goals. In cooperative learning, each student is not only required to complete a task but is also required to ensure that those with whom s/he is working do likewise; in other words students are dependent on one another.

Primary schools probably find that the biggest challenge is to break down the isolation experienced by the teacher working alone in a single classroom—by requiring the entire staff to help solve problems faced by individual teachers. In contrast, secondary schools have plenty of flexibility, but often large enrolments and a mix of teachers present other challenges in delivering effective curriculum to all students. There are many ways in which schools are restructuring to meet the needs of a diverse enrolment, and to create a more satisfying working environment for staff. Box 2.5 illustrates one school's innovative efforts.

Another factor influencing the ability of schools to respond to the challenge of full inclusion is the presence of other stressors, including increasing accountability measures (such as reporting of student achievement), socioeconomic disadvantage, increased prevalence of behaviour problems, and increased class sizes. Clearly, there is no justification for inclusion that is inadequately resourced, in either materials or, probably more importantly, inservice support. It is relatively easy for teachers to modify some aspects of their teaching to meet the needs of some students. Examples include having a choice of textbooks with different readability levels, and setting assignments with graduated tasks that enable the more able students to be challenged while the less able accomplish the easier tasks.

Caution should be observed when adjusting readability by shortening sentences or substituting vocabulary. Often the coherence of a text is damaged by such changes. It might be better to annotate the text with brief explanations of difficult vocabulary, to underline major ideas, ask preliminary

BOX 2.5

Maifield Primary School

Maifield is a government school in a provincial city. The principal has taken an innovative approach to inclusion by sharing the specialist skills of teachers with other staff through the use of pairs of teachers in double teaching spaces. The pairs consist of a teacher with special education experience and another with less knowledge and experience. Not only does this permit the sharing of expertise through on-the-job training, but it also makes the management of student behaviour more straightforward.

While there is a special education unit in the school, this is not apparent to a visitor, since the students with disabilities and their allocated teachers and aides are distributed throughout the buildings. This organisational pattern is accompanied by flexible grouping and an increased age spread in the double classes. This alters the teaching approaches to meet the individual needs of all students.

While this school's views about inclusive education were formed to meets the needs of students with disabilities, it also increases the sensitivity of students, teachers, other staff, and the school community to the unmet needs of all students. Thus, several gifted students are supported through the same pattern of team teaching, multi-age grouping, and mutual support.

Unfortunately, some other schools in the city continue to regard meeting the needs of students in regular classrooms as too hard, for there is a suggestion that parents of difficult students are advised to try Maifield. The most important message of the experiences of Maifield in educating students with disabilities in regular classes is that inclusion is best approached at the whole-school level, rather than by fitting in individual children without considering the nature of the educational experience offered to each and every student.

questions, or use alternative (non-text) media with limited reading or writing demands (e.g., video or computer). Another approach is to use group-introduced methods that encourage students to help each other, as in reciprocal teaching (Palincsar & Klenk, 1992), which is discussed more fully in Chapter 7.

The Commonwealth Government has placed increasing emphasis on all students meeting benchmarks for literacy and numeracy. Although schools do not expect many students with intellectual disabilities to reach the benchmarks for specific ages, there is a general recognition that literacy and numeracy achievements are important goals for all students, regardless of their varying education and personal histories.

As a final comment, it is important that curriculum developments in regular education be examined for their implications for educating the greatest diversity of students. This means that teachers need to be familiar with, and sometimes critical of, the curricula they may be required to implement. Even more important is to participate in the creation of curricula that are inclusive. Reid and Thomson (2003) have edited a stimulating collection of papers on curriculum in public education, which points to the need to engage students through personally relevant content.

The New Basics project (Education Queensland, 2000) has already been the source of innovative action by schools that have recognised that students with disabilities can benefit when teachers are

reciprocal teaching

A teaching approach that was designed to teach students to use the strategies that successful readers use to understand text. There are four main strategies: previewing, monitoring reading and learning, focusing on the main idea, and summarising.

intellectual disabilities

See developmental disability.

encouraged to think and plan and teach creatively (Weir, 2003). Not only must curriculum essentials reflect the foreseeable needs for living in a technologically sophisticated world, but they should also be synthesised rather than presented in separate content domains.

Technology

You will find that technology is mentioned in many chapters of this book, not only in Chapter 6, which is devoted entirely to that topic. Commentary about technology is included because many aspects of curriculum are amenable to support and extension through technology. Here, I simply want to draw attention to the range of technologies available so that you can consider these as you work your way through the following chapters.

With the advent of the internet, world wide web, and CD-ROMs there are opportunities for the use of multimedia in education in ways that enhance the content and learning modes available to all students, including those with special needs. Early examples of technology-supported learning were developed at Vanderbilt University in Nashville, Tennessee, by Bransford et al. (1996). Using the acronym MOST (Multimedia Environments that Organize and Support Text), they have developed dynamic visual support for comprehension that can accelerate linguistic and conceptual development that is primarily language-based. Highly motivating video presentations provide structure and enable participation—for example by the student recording a verbal soundtrack to go with the video. Print books can be produced with stills from the video and transcription of the student-supplied soundtrack. Thus, students can learn to identify text structures (e.g., story grammars and contextual schemata) that enable them to comprehend written text.

Hence, technology provides opportunities to support the learning of students who experience difficulties, regardless of the cause of the disability. Basic curriculum areas—such as reading, writing, mathematics, and spelling—and generic information-gathering have received attention. Although some applications of technology have been transitory, word processors have become invaluable tools for increasing the volume and quality of created writing. The availability of word processors at home and at school is unlikely to increase the amount of revision students do but, if teachers and parents plan carefully, students can improve their writing at every level from overall cohesion to spelling and punctuation.

Among other sources of information on technology applications are the Center for Applied Special Technology (CAST) <www.cast.org/index.html> and the *Journal of Special Education Technology* <http://jset.unlv.edu>.

USING THIS CHAPTER IN SCHOOLS

Since we wrote the first edition of this book, one major change in Australia has been the overt role of legislation in the process of schooling. Through much of the 20th century, if students presented with little knowledge of English, it was presumed that they would learn it informally. If students exhibited unacceptable behaviour, they were expelled and parents were expected to find another school willing to accept them. If students had impairments, especially those with intellectual limitations, they might be advised strongly to attend a special school. Much of this control of schooling was informal, or based on regulations approved by the Minister, and few parents challenged decisions.

Over the past few years, schools have become very conscious of various pieces of legislation, particularly those that are concerned with discrimination. However, child abuse is a major concern in society, and teachers are at the frontline of detection and reporting.

The teacher

As a teacher in Australia, you can expect to have a deep understanding of discriminatory behaviour and, of course, how to prevent it. The school community of which you will be part has an important role in ensuring that education is available equitably to all students. You will not only need to play your part, but you will also be helping produce a new generation of citizens who are more likely to promote acceptance of difference in Australian society.

Also, as a teacher, you will need to plan and implement lessons that benefit all students. While we do not know everything we would like to know about how to teach all students, we do know that most students learn in broadly similar ways, and that improving the quality of your teaching will usually benefit most of the students in your class. Nevertheless, students do have different preferences and abilities, and you must strive to increase the tailoring of your planning to what you learn about your students across the school year. This means trying to learn more about the use of technology in teaching. One aspect is that technology may help increase the access of students to the curriculum. Another is that it may enable you to plan lessons that anticipate the needs of your students.

The students in the school context

In recent years, the notion of inclusive education has highlighted similarities among several groups of students. Using the notion of social justice, participation in education should not involve discrimination against females, ethnic or other social minorities, Indigenous groups, and those with diverse learning needs. This has made education an issue of equity.

A second aspect is the need for schools to be organised with individual differences among students in mind. Schools must differentiate among students to offer them equal access to common educational goals.

A third feature is the incorporation into the curriculum of knowledge and values that are pertinent to each group of students. Gender, ethnicity, and disability are topics that occur in the language, social studies, and science curricula. If all students have a more informed basis for attitudes and actions, instead of stereotypes derived from ignorance, a short-term benefit of this approach should be a more cooperative school climate than might currently exist. Much work is needed to develop fully the concept of inclusive curriculum—there is a danger that the potential of the concept of inclusive curriculum might be lost if inclusion becomes merely a synonym for integration or mainstreaming.

integration
The process of moving children from special education settings into regular classrooms where they undertake most, if not all, of their schooling.

The practical activities that follow will help you to gain an understanding of policies and practices that operate in your state or territory, and in the particular jurisdiction in which you hope to find work, or in which you are already working.

PRACTICAL ACTIVITIES

Uni-work

1 Look at Education Department (or Catholic Education) websites for two states or territories and compare their policies on inclusive education. It can be useful to draw up a chart in which you will list the various issues/statements and see how both state policies align. Why do you think there is overlap, and how can you explain the absence of overlap in some areas? What are the implications for the lack of overlap in some areas?

2 Visit a weekend sporting activity for people with disabilities (e.g., blind cricket, wheelchair basketball, horse riding) and compare this with other community recreational activities for people who do not have a disability of impairment. Look around. How many people attend each type of

activity and who are they? Are there other characteristics that distinguish the two events? Can you design a game or physical activity that would suit students who have disabilities and is challenging and satisfying for all to play?

3 As a group effort, collect the various pieces of legislation such as Anti-Discrimination Acts, Disability Acts, and Education Acts for the Commonwealth, state and territories. Many can be downloaded from the web. Divide up the areas and summarise the main issues in each. In Education Acts, for example, look for indications about teachers' responsibilities and duty of care. Note that there may be differences across government and non-government sectors. Plan a presentation and handout that summarises your collective findings that could be made available to student colleagues.

School-work

Remember that school policies may apply that restrict your ability to undertake one or more of the activities suggested below. Before beginning, speak to your supervising teacher or a member of the school administration to confirm that you will not breach existing school guidelines and policies.

4 Check around your school for documentation that deals with equity and anti-discrimination issues. You might look around the staff room, or in public areas. Ask some of your colleagues if they have seen any such documents and where you might locate relevant material. Based on what you find, look for any information on the school's website that relates to the legislative framework that applies in your state/territory and how this may have influenced school policies.

5 Do a web or library search for information on normalisation and social role valorisation (discussed early in the chapter). Get a sense of what these concepts are and how they are applied. Then, while observing a class or other activities around the school, look for examples of normalisation or social role valorisation (or the lack of it). What can you do in your role in the school to change the environment that would increase the school community's response to disability and impairment. Remember that diversity includes students with learning and behaviour problems as well as those who have exceptional talents.

6 Take a lesson plan you have developed and modify it as if there were a student in the class who has either: (a) a sensory disability, or (b) an intellectual impairment. Could you have designed the lesson originally so that it would have suited most students with disabilities or other special needs?

SUGGESTED READING AND RESOURCES

Books

Capper, C. A., Frattura, E., & Keyes, M. W. (2000). *Meeting the needs of students of all abilities: How leaders go beyond inclusion*. Thousand Oaks, CA: Corwin Press.

Culatta, R. A., Tompkins, J. R., & Werts, M. G. (2003). *Fundamentals of special education: What every teacher needs to know* (2nd ed.). Upper Saddle River, NJ: Merrill.

Friend, M. & Bursuck, W. D. (2002). *Including students with special needs: A practical guide for classroom teachers* (3rd ed.). Boston: Allyn & Bacon.

Giangreco, M. F. & Ruelle, K. (2007). *Absurdities and realities of special education: The complete digital set.* Minnetonka, MN: Peytral Publishers.

Janney, R. & Snell, M. E. (2000). *Behavioral support*. Baltimore, MD: Paul H. Brookes.

Loreman, T., Deppeler, J., & Harvey, D. (2005). *Inclusive education: A practical guide to supporting diversity in the classroom.* Crows Nest, NSW: Allen & Unwin.

Mittler, P. (2000). *Working toward inclusive education: Social contexts.* London: David Fulton.

O'Hanlon, C. (2003). *Educational inclusion as action research: An interpretive discourse.* Maidenhead, UK: Open University Press.

Thomas, G. & Vaughan, M. (2004). *Inclusive education: Readings and reflections.* Maidenhead, UK: Open University Press.

Journals

International Journal of Inclusive Education

International Journal of Special Education

Websites

Education authority—websites in each state and territory.

<www.hreoc.gov.au>—Human Rights and Equal Opportunity Commission.

REFERENCES

Armstrong, F. & Moore, M. (Eds) (2004). *Action research for inclusive education: Changing places, changing practice, changing minds.* London: RoutledgeFalmer.

Armstrong, F., Armstrong, D., & Barton, D. (Eds) (2000). *Inclusive education: Policy, contexts and comparative perspectives.* London: David Fulton.

Ashman, A. F. & Elkins, J. (1996). School and integration. In B. Stratford & P. Gunn (Eds), *New approaches to Down syndrome* (pp. 341–357). London: Cassell.

Bank-Mikkelsen, N. (1969). A metropolitan area in Denmark: Copenhagen. In R. Kugel & W. Wolfensberger (Eds), *Changing patterns in residential services for the mentally retarded* (pp. 227–254). Washington, DC: President's Committee on Mental Retardation.

Berry, P. B., Andrews, R. J., & Elkins, J. (1977). *An evaluative study of educational, vocational and residential programs for the moderately to severely mentally handicapped in three states.* St Lucia, Qld: Fred and Eleanor Schonell Educational Research Centre.

Bransford, J. D., Miller Sharp, D., Vye, N. J., Goldman, S. R., Hasselbring, T. S., Goin, L., O'Banion, K., Livernois, J., Saul, E., & The Cognition and Technology Group at Vanderbilt (1996). MOST environments for accelerating literacy development. In S. Vosniadou, E. de Coste, R. Glaser, & H. Mandl (Eds), *International perspectives on the design of technology-supported learning environments* (pp. 223–255). Mahwah, NJ: Lawrence Erlbaum Associates.

Brown, L., Long, E., Udvari-Solner, A., Davis, L., Vandeventer, P., Ahlgren, C., Johnson, F., Gruenewald, L., & Jorgensen, J. (1991). How much time should students with severe intellectual disabilities spend in regular education classrooms and elsewhere? *Journal of the Association for Persons with Severe Handicaps*, *16*, 39–47.

Down Syndrome Association of Queensland (2000). *Where do we go from here? Information and ideas for regular primary schools about including a child with Down syndrome.* Brisbane: Author.

Down Syndrome Association of Queensland (2003). *Where else but here? Including students with Down syndrome in secondary schools: Information for teachers.* Stafford, Qld: Author.

Education Queensland (2000). New Basics project. <http://education.qld.gov.au/corporate/newbasics>, accessed 15 March 2004.

Giangreco, M. F. (1989). Facilitating integration of students with severe disabilities: Implication of "planned change" for teacher preparation programs. *Teacher Education and Special Education*, *12*, 139–147.

Giangreco, M. F. (1993). Using creative problem-solving methods to include students with severe disabilities in general education classroom activities. *Journal of Educational and Psychological Consultations*, *6*, 113–135.

Giangreco, M. F. (1996). What do I do now? A teacher's guide to including students with disabilities. *Educational Leadership, 53*, 56–59.

Giangreco, M. F. (2003). Moving toward inclusive education. In W. L. Heward (Ed.), *Exceptional children: An introduction to special education* (7th ed.) (pp. 78–79). Englewood Cliffs, NJ: Merrill, an imprint of Prentice Hall. Available in Full Text PDF. Posted with permission of Prentice Hall.

Giangreco, M. F. & Doyle, M. B. (Eds) (2007). *Quick-Guides to Inclusion: Ideas for educating students with disabilities* (2nd ed.). Baltimore: Paul H. Brookes.

Hart, S. (Ed.) (1996). *Differentiation and the secondary curriculum: Debates and dilemmas*. London: Routledge.

Loreman, T., Deppeler, J., & Harvey, D. (2005). *Inclusive education: A practical guide to supporting diversity in the classroom.* Crows Nest, NSW: Allen & Unwin.

Nirje, B. (1985). Setting the record straight: A critique of some frequent misconceptions of the normalisation principle. *Australia and New Zealand Journal of Developmental Disabilities*, *11*, 69–74.

Palincsar, A. S. T. & Klenk, L. (1992). Entering literacy learning in supportive contexts. *Journal of Hearing Disabilities*, *25*, 211–225, 229.

Reid, A. & Thomson, P. (Eds) (2003). *Toward a public curriculum*. Flaxton, Qld: Post Pressed.

Rose, D. H. & Meyer, A. (2002). *Teaching every student in the digital age: Universal design for learning.* Alexandria, VA: ASCD.

Thomas, G. (2001). *Deconstructing special education and constructing inclusion*. Philadelphia, PA: Open University.

Weber, M.C. (2007). Inclusive education in the United States and internationally: Challenges and response. *The Review of Disability Studies: An International Journal*, *3*, 19–33.

Weir, K. (2003). A critical semiotic analysis of the Rich Tasks. In J. A. Vaneboncoeur & S. Rawolle (Eds), *Educational imagining: On the play of texts and contexts.* Brisbane: Australian Academic Press.

Wolfensberger, W. (1972). *The principle of normalization in human services*. Toronto: National Institute on Mental Retardation.

Wolfensberger, W. (1988). Common assets of mentally retarded people that are commonly not acknowledged. *Mental Retardation*, *26*, 63–70.

Credit

Adrian Ashman and Peter Merrotsy

3

DIVERSITY AND EDUCATIONAL ENVIRONMENTS

What you will learn in this chapter

As you can see from the title, this chapter is about the environments in which teaching and learning occur. Where we are today in terms of the delivery of education is at least partly the result of historical developments and government responses to the needs of young people and reactions to political pressures. The previous chapter provided a background to these influences. Here, we explore the context and the factors that lead to successful learning and problem-solving.

In this chapter you will learn about:

- some of the historical place-markers in the treatment and education of people with diverse learning needs;
- how disability is defined;
- the place of giftedness and talent in the presentation of diversity;
- the importance of self-perception and identity in school achievement;
- the range of educational placement options available in school systems around Australia; and
- the teaching–learning ecology that governs successful learning outcomes.

CASE STUDIES

ELISE

Elise grew up in an old weatherboard house in a quiet back street of a small rural town. She learnt to read when she was three years old. At primary school, she spent a lot of class time teaching other children to read, and while at home she was reading Dickens and other adult literature. Her parents and teachers often noticed that Elise had difficulty relating with other children and she threw temper tantrums at school.

Elise didn't cope well when she went to high school. She was frightened to cross a street, felt intimidated by the other students, was socially isolated, and felt unchallenged by her schoolwork. She made friends with two girls, one of whom had cerebral palsy and spent the day in a wheelchair, and the other had few friends because of her family's religion. They called themselves *The Outcasts*. In class, Elise was harassed, which included name-calling and being spat upon. She escaped the boredom and torment of school by thoroughly immersing herself in her piano music and by reading 18th century European history.

Eventually, during Year 9, she forced her teachers to do something to help her. Literally "bored to tears", she pleaded that she be accelerated one year in mathematics. A teacher gained her confidence and became her mentor. After school, they began working on a special program of problem-solving, and he introduced her to some classic works in philosophy.

At home, Elise was also emotionally and physically abused. Her mother suffered from recurrent mental health problems and the mentor eventually found respite accommodation for Elise, which was used during times of crisis. Elise, too, was clearly experiencing her own mental health problems. Professional help was sought and she was diagnosed with Asperger's syndrome. She experienced severe discomfort in many social situations, had very poor verbal and nonverbal communication skills, and her behaviour was best described as eccentric. It was suggested that Elise be classified as emotionally disturbed, but she declined the classification because she didn't want to have such a diagnostic label placed upon her.

Asperger's syndrome
A form of Autism Spectrum Disorder (ASD) characterised by difficulties in social interaction, and by restricted, stereotyped interests and activities. People with Asperger's syndrome generally have no delays in language or cognitive development.

The school made provision for Elise to study in a variety of ways and her senior curriculum was completed largely through independent learning, which she negotiated and which suited her well. Most of her teachers were very understanding even though most were not completely aware of her situation. Some teachers expressed concern about her independent learning style and didn't like the fact that Elise seldom came to class. She summarised this tersely by commenting, "A few teachers don't like acceleration."

For Elise, the alternative approaches to her learning were very important. She felt much happier and more comfortable because she was doing more interesting and more challenging things than she would have been doing in class, and she could progress when she was ready. Her program vastly expanded her study choices, gave her access to higher-level courses that closely matched her academic ability, gave access to tertiary-level courses while she was still at school, and brought many opportunities and invaluable experiences that she would not have had otherwise.

Elise believes that she would not have done well academically if she had not had a program that met her personal needs. She is sure that she would have dropped out of school before completing Year 10. She said:

It is important to study something that interests you and is at an appropriate, stimulating level for you. If you're at school and you want to be studying and you actually like it, and are interested in things, and you're not given that opportunity, then people are going to underachieve.

Before leaving school, Elise completed 19 HSC units, AMEB Grade 8 Piano, and first-year university courses in philosophy and mathematics.

THE FEEL GOOD STORY

Alex is 16 years old and has had an intellectual disability since birth. When he was 12 months old, his parents noticed that he wasn't as alert as his older brother had been at the same age and was not responding normally to affection and eye-contact. Something was wrong. They took Alex to a paediatrician and were devastated when told that it would be unlikely that Alex would develop intellectually beyond what might be expected of a five-year-old.

It took many months for the sense of loss to fade. Sometimes his parents, Jim and Caroline, blamed themselves for Alex's disability and at other times they blamed him and resented the trauma that had come into their lives. Tim, Alex's older brother, didn't react quite the same way. He was just five years old when Alex was born and was fascinated by his baby brother. He cuddled Alex a lot and used to talk to him almost continuously when they were alone together.

As the years passed, Jim and Caroline lost their anguish and started to work as hard as they could to give Alex the best start in life possible. They got him to preschool, supported the teachers, and made sure that the learning experiences that were introduced in the preschool flowed into the family home. It worked. Alex responded well and by age 10 had developed solid, although not especially sophisticated, language skills. Jim, Caroline, and Tim taught Alex to count, schooled him in the times tables, taught him about money, and did everything they could to reinforce what Alex was learning at school.

Alex attended a regular primary school and was "included". Some of the teachers weren't especially supportive of inclusion and two were often irritated by Jim and Caroline's insistence that Alex *could* learn like the other students in the classes if he was given the right opportunities and if the learning environment was supportive. There was absolutely no thought in their minds about Alex attending a special school or even a special class.

After primary school, Alex was enrolled in the local state secondary school. There were lengthy discussions with the principal, then the year coordinator, then the learning support teacher, who was brilliant. He spent several hours out of school time talking to Jim and Caroline about how Alex got on at home, what he could do easily, what took effort, and what was well beyond his capability. He also talked to the learning support teacher at Alex's former primary school and then developed a profile of Alex that he turned into an individual learning support plan. He "sold" the plan to Alex's teachers based upon the idea of flexible assessment, which included student reflections, self- and peer-assessment, and as much feedback as was sensible and possible. He developed and adapted some learning resources, worked out progress markers, and set out exactly how Alex's progress would be assessed.

Three years of solid work has seen Alex make remarkable gains. Most, but by no means all, of his classmates accept him and interact easily in class, in sport, and on the playground. The

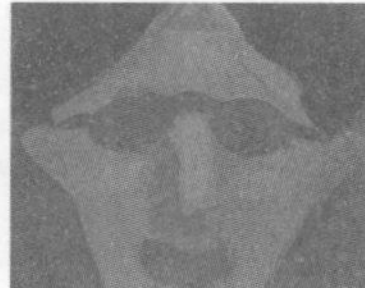

concentration on academic outcomes rather than on functional life skills only has meant that the teachers' efforts have paid off handsomely. Alex is a very pleasant and good-humoured young man who sees a future for himself in the food industry. Jim and Caroline have slightly higher expectations, but time will tell what the future holds for Alex.

TEACHING–LEARNING CONTEXT

Chapter 1 introduced the concept of diversity and variation, and talked about the many ways in which people are different and the impact of those differences in the eyes of the dominant group within society. In this chapter, we move closer to the discussion of ways in which educational responses support and promote diversity and difference.

As you know, being different has its complications and these are no more apparent than for those who have a disability or an impairment that limits the opportunities they have to progress through school at the same rate as their peers who experience no impediments. At this point, therefore, it will be useful for us to consider what a disability is.

It may not be so obvious, but being different can also have complications for those who have very high ability. For many gifted students, school can be a very lonely and frustrating experience. Advanced intellectual ability, for example, is often not appreciated by others, and can result in rejection by age peers. An unchallenging curriculum can also lead to underachievement. Both make school an unhappy place to be.

To understand the education systems of today, it is useful to reflect on the past. So, in the following section, we take you on a very brief historical tour.

The legacy of history

The history of exceptionality is different to the history of educating students with special learning needs, although the two are closely related. Arguably, the former began with social and cultural responses to difference as long ago as the beginning of society. Much of that history is speculative, although historical records reveal that humans, in general, have not been very tolerant of those who differed from the society's view of normality at the time. In the early years of recorded human history, many people who today would be labelled as having a disability were viewed with considerable suspicion. Many were subject to scorn, rejection, isolation, and cruelty (see e.g., Winzer, 1993).

Few verified facts are known of the circumstances of people with disability until about the 1600s when education pioneers gave brief accounts about their students, their teaching methods, and their successes. And it was not until the European Age of Enlightenment in the mid-1700s that there were early attempts at systematic instruction for people who had diverse learning needs. For example, it was then that a Spaniard, Francisco Lucal of Saragossa, carved letters on wooden tablets to assist blind people to read, and also when an Italian, Girolamo Cardano, developed a device to assist reading and writing through touch using a method similar to modern Braille.

The history of special education then began during the 18th century. Special schools were opened for children with profound vision and hearing impairments, such as those in Paris, de l'Epée's School for the Deaf and Valentin Haüy's Institution for Blind Children. It was in Haüy's Institution where Louis Braille (who had a vision impairment) later invented the six-dot system of reading and writing which bears his name.

The closing years of the 18th century are often considered to be the starting point in the modern history of special education. Prominent in almost any text on special education or inclusive education is the work of Jean-Marc Itard who accepted the challenge to work with the renowned wild boy of

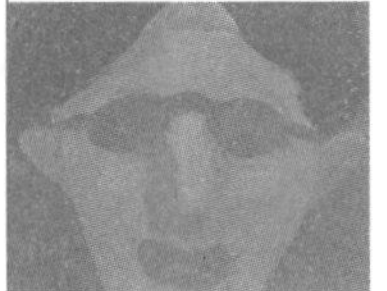

Aveyron, an 11- or 12-year-old who was thought to have survived alone in the desolate countryside in the French department of Aveyron (about midway between Marseilles and Bordeaux). Feral children were not unknown at the time and Victor, as the boy was known, was taken to Paris in 1801 where the supremely confident Itard set about delivering his education.

Humphreys, the first translator of Itard's book dealing with the boy's education, claimed that Victor's social and emotional development was impressive under the ever-attentive Itard. At the end of his training, Victor was clean, affectionate, able to read a few words and capable of understanding much of what was said to him. Sadly, the story of the wild boy did not have a happy ending. Victor disappeared into obscurity to live out his life in custodial care (Kenner, 1964). The story is unlikely to vanish from the education history books given the continuing attention that writers (including ourselves) pay to it, and there are even novels recounting Itard's efforts and the impact that the boy had on the Parisian society of the time (one of these is Dawson, 2003).

Australia has its own history of special education, beginning at almost the same time as Itard was working with Victor. The first public institution for people with an intellectual disability was established in New Norfolk (outside Hobart) in a precinct that became part of the Royal Derwent Hospital. It appears that the first systematic attempt at schooling for underprivileged youth occurred at Point Puer, part of the Port Arthur penal colony near Hobart. About 10% of all convicts sent to New South Wales were boys, some as young as nine years of age. Most of the boys at Point Puer had few educational skills, not surprising since 41% of the English population at the time were illiterate. Their lessons included reading, writing, and learning the simple rules of spelling and arithmetic. Despite attempts to raise their educational standards, many of the boys made little progress except in reading (see Hooper, 1967).

From these very humble beginnings, a major education industry emerged in Australia in much the same way as in other Western countries. The *National Education Act* of 1848 set the stage for critical developments, and compulsory education was legislated as a state responsibility near the turn of the 20th century. Readers keen to learn more about the history can find sources in early editions of Ashman and Elkins (1990, 2002).

In Australia, as in other Western countries, education has been provided in class size groups, which up to a half-century ago often contained 40, 50, or even 60 students, all of whom were competing for limited resources and teacher attention. Allocation to a class was made on the basis of age and, sometimes, achievement. The top students would be assigned to the "A" class, the average students to the "B" class, and the students having difficulty with the regular curriculum were relegated to the "C" or lower class depending upon the size of the school. Assigning students to "A", "B", and "C" seemed like a good idea because it allowed the teacher to aim instruction at the middle ground of each ability group—the "average" student—more effectively than would have been the case if students were assigned to classes randomly.

Of course, regardless of how well students might be streamed, "A", "B", and "C" classes are still far from homogeneous in terms of skills, abilities, motivation, and the 30 some ways of viewing the world, one for each person in the class. In other words, there is no average student. (Average is a statistical concept that represents a central tendency, a balancing point among a set of scores.) Everyone has a different set of learning experiences and a different way of reacting to any teaching–learning situation. Most students with a mild sensory or motor disorder received prosthetics (e.g., spectacles, hearing aid, crutches) and were then left to cope with regular class activities, sometimes with little encouragement. Most teachers were accustomed to controlled and quiet classrooms and were less than enthusiastic about noisy equipment, like the early mechanical braillers.

It became common to group students who presented with the same physical, sensory, or intellectual impairment in special schools and special classes, most of them set well away from the regular

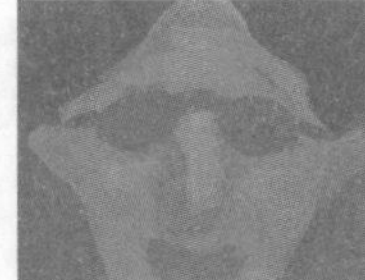

education classes and students. Then, in the mid-1960s a negative reaction to segregated settings began in the United States as school administrators, policy-makers, and researchers began to concede that students were gaining few benefits from special education. Arguments were mounted for reintegration of these students into regular classes in which they could benefit from contact with non-disabled peers.

Gifted and talented students in Australia have fared little better than students with learning difficulties. Some have been assisted by streaming into "A" classes and enrolment at selective secondary schools (the first of these came into existence in 1883). The earliest classes specifically for gifted and talented students were established in 1932. There were called OC classes (O for opportunity, C because there were already As and Bs). During the 1970s, there was a growing recognition among educators and parents of the need for more appropriate educational opportunities for gifted and talented students as there was a clear recognition that education systems were not responding enthusiastically to the demand. Organisations to support gifted children were formed to provide accurate information about giftedness, facilitate networks for teachers, parents, and children, and advocate for gifted children at a political level. This movement led to the foundation of state associations for gifted children and the establishment of a national body, the Australian Association for the Education of the Gifted and Talented, in 1985. Since then there have been a number of reports about the inadequacy of the education of gifted children by, for example, the Commonwealth Schools Commission and two reports by Senate Select Committees.

Despite some fine programs for gifted students throughout Australia, it is also fair to say that there is much more that can be done. This statement echoes one in the report by the Senate Employment, Workplace Relations, Small Business and Education References Committee (Commonwealth of Australia, 2001) that gifted students have special needs in the education system. The needs of many are not being met and many suffer underachievement, boredom, frustration, and psychological distress as a result.

Let us turn now to the issue of how disability is defined.

Defining disability

Some years ago, the World Health Organization made the distinction between impairment (defined as the loss of some capacity), disability (a restriction resulting from an impairment), and a handicap (a disadvantage resulting from an impairment or disability). The main purpose of these definitions was to establish a standard language and framework for the description of health-related matters. In 2001, however, the World Health Assembly endorsed an *International Classification of Functioning, Disability and Health* (ICF). The Assembly acknowledged that any individual can experience a decrease in health that can lead to some degree of disability, including the social aspects of disability.

Of significance, the ICF does away with the medical orientation that was implied by the earlier classification. It now focuses attention on human variation while at the same time recognising that the status of a bodily function or bodily structure can affect what a person *could do* in a usual environment (i.e., their capacity to act) and what they *actually do* (i.e., their performance).

The ICF is graphically shown in Figure 3.1. A person's ability to act is a function of their health condition and the context in which an act is to occur.

One's health condition is mediated by the operation of body structures (i.e., organs, limbs, and their components) and body functions (i.e., physiological functions of the body system such as the senses, cardiovascular, respiratory and digestive systems, and psychological/mental systems). Depending upon the interaction of these, one can be healthy or affected by disease, disorders, or injury.

The interaction of health condition and context that leads to one's functional performance is, therefore, affected by biological, personal, and social influences. In other words, disability comes as a

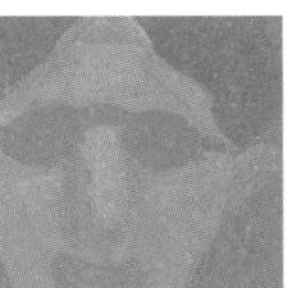

FIGURE 3.1

A graphic representation of the components of the International Classification of Functioning

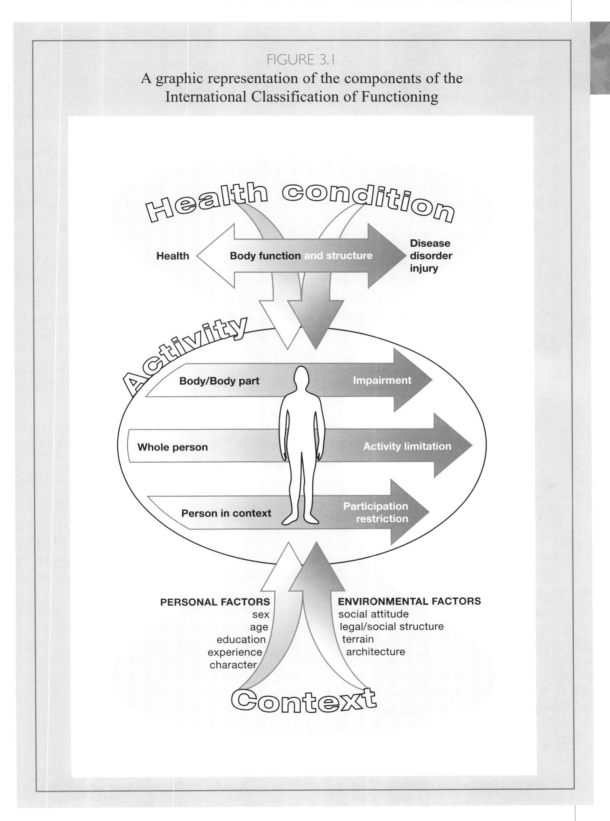

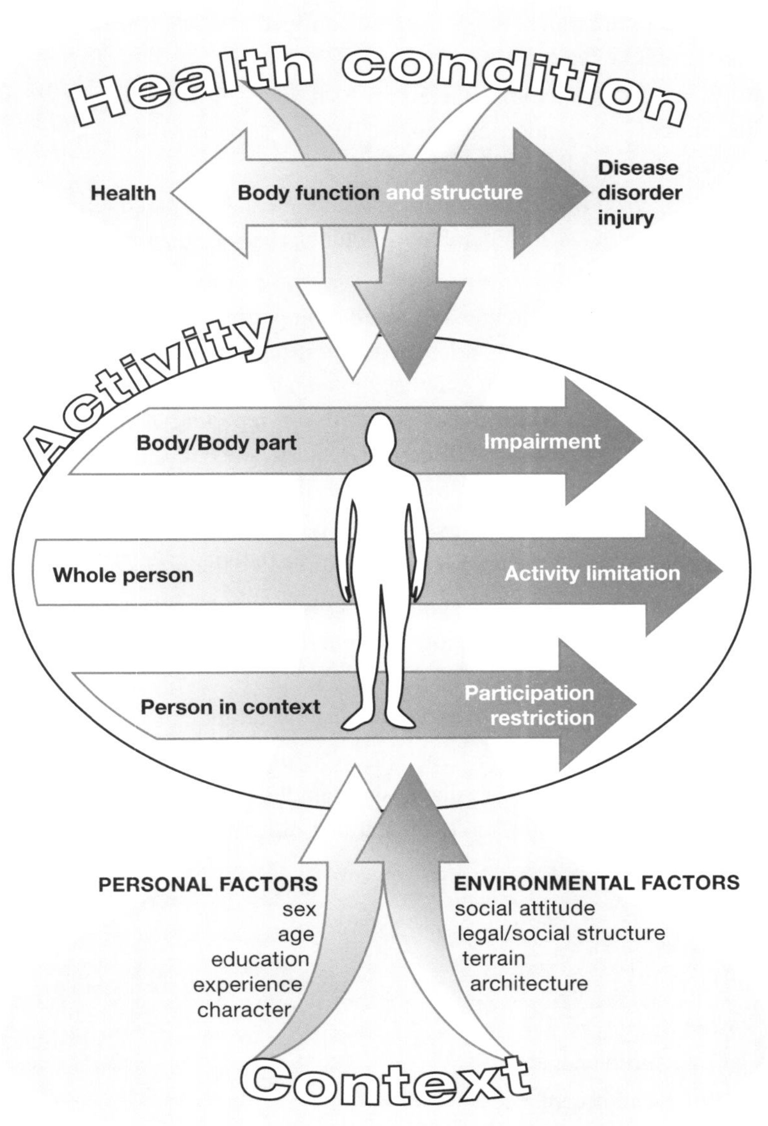

Health condition

Health

Body function and structure

Disease
disorder
injury

Activity

Body/Body part

Impairment

Whole person

Activity limitation

Person in context

Participation
restriction

PERSONAL FACTORS
sex
age
education
experience
character

ENVIRONMENTAL FACTORS
social attitude
legal/social structure
terrain
architecture

Context

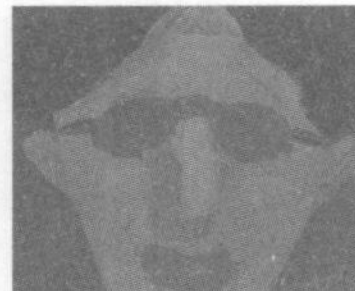

result of complications arising from the interactions between health conditions (such as diseases, injuries, and disorders) and the context in which the person lives, including the environment and personal factors. Contextual factors relate to the environment in which a person lives (e.g., legal structures, terrain, architecture, social and cultural conventions) and individual or personal factors (e.g., sex, age, education, experiences, learning styles).

So, how a person acts and what they can do is the result of the interaction between these multiple sources of influence. Here are three examples:

- If the person is compromised by a body function or part, the context in which the person operates may then lead to an impairment (e.g., a person confined to a wheelchair cannot climb a set of stairs, but this might be the only impairment).
- If the whole person is affected then there may be limitations in what a person might do (e.g., a person with cerebral palsy may need assistive devices or personal assistance to undertake activities of daily living, like showering).
- If the issue is the person in context, a person with a mental health condition might be able to live alone successfully, but have considerable difficulties sharing accommodation with others or interacting with others effectively.

Disability, therefore, is defined no longer as a result of impairment but encompasses limitations that are imposed by a loss or significant deviation in body structure or function, by difficulties executing activities, or by problems that a person may have in engaging in life situations.

The ICF was developed as the global standard for reporting and classifying diseases, health-related conditions, and external causes of disease and injury. The ICF screening tool allows the collection of information about an individual across four domains that comprise major elements of the model:

- body functions (e.g., mental functions such as memory and intellectual growth, voice and speech functions, functions of the skin, and related structures like the protection capabilities and quality);
- body structures (e.g., nervous, cardiovascular, immunological, and respiratory systems);
- activities and participation (e.g., learning and applying knowledge, mobility, self-care, community social and civic life); and
- environmental factors (e.g., supports and relationships, attitudes).

The implications of the ICF are far reaching, well beyond the earlier definitions of impairment, disability, and handicap. It confirms that a diagnosis of an illness or medical condition (e.g., cerebral palsy, spina bifida) or a psychological condition (e.g., learning difficulty, Autism Spectrum Disorder) *does not predict*:

spina bifida

A group of congenital defects in which one or a number of spinal vertebrae do not fuse, leaving a gap. In some instances, the spinal cord or its surrounding membrane may protrude through the gap.

- the service needs;
- the level of care required;
- the adjustments needed to facilitate access to the community or its resources;
- progress at school;
- an individual's performance; and
- the likelihood of social acceptance.

As the ICF is quite extensive, it would be useful for you to browse the various aspects of it at the ICF website <www.who.int/classification/icf/site/icftemplate.cfm>.

It is curious that the language of impairment usually reflects disability and handicap, rather than celebrating the ability of the person. It will be valuable for us to consider briefly those individuals who do not have a physical, sensory, or intellectual disability, but instead have advanced capabilities.

Gifts and talents

It is interesting that disability is often presented as simply the opposite to high ability. For example, some models (including a forum on the World Health Organization website) equate "mentally retarded" (*sic*) with an intelligence quotient (IQ) of less than 70 points (with the average IQ being 100 points) and contrast this with another group called "gifted" who have an IQ over 130 points.

The distribution of IQ in the population is said to conform to a bell-shaped curve (called the *normal curve*) that is reproduced in Figure 3.2. You can see that the highlighted groups are equally distant from the fictitious typical student who has an IQ of 100. If a young person attending school is located in one of the shaded sections and has learning needs that are not met by the standard curriculum (e.g., a person with an intellectual disability), it can be deduced that a member of the group at the other end of the continuum may also have difficulty gaining access to a curriculum that meets their cognitive and affective needs. In other words, individuals at both ends of the IQ continuum could have particular learning needs requiring assistance.

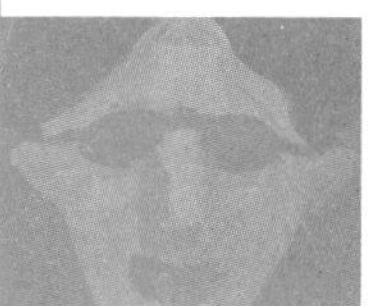

IQ

A figure determined as a results of the administration of one of the many tests of intelligence. The IQ represents the position of a person relative to others of similar age on the same test. An IQ of 100 is the convention that represents the average score of those taking the test. If an individual is given two different tests of intelligence, two different IQs are likely to result.

FIGURE 3.2
The normal curve showing the putative proportions of people in the total population who are thought to be gifted and those who have an intellectual disability

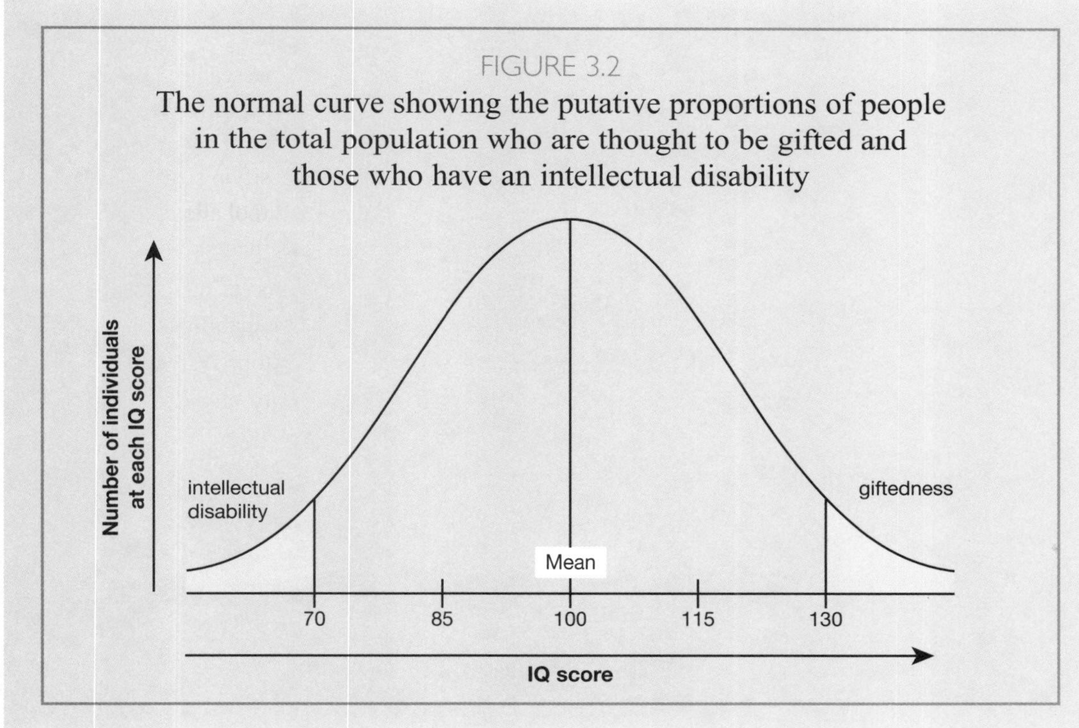

Many educational authorities around the world have accepted this logic. That is, a diagnosis of giftedness can imply special learning needs. As with a diagnosis of a medical or a psychological condition, this does not predict:

- the level of support needed;
- the educational adjustments required to ensure continuity of access to curriculum at a level and pace commensurate with the student's ability and progress;
- the individual's performance; and
- the likelihood of social acceptance.

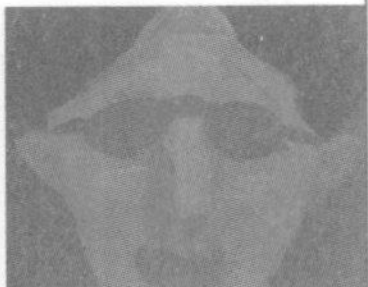

Therefore, it seems appropriate to adopt terms outside of the language of special education. In Australia, however, education systems have been slow to accept the notion that giftedness implies special learning needs. While most teacher education institutions (i.e., faculties and schools of education in universities), and the Australian Bureau of Statistics, recognise gifted education as part of

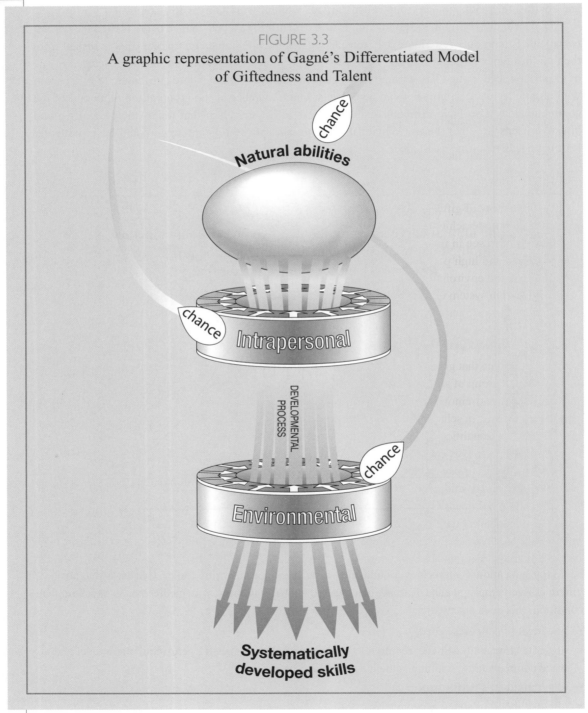

FIGURE 3.3
A graphic representation of Gagné's Differentiated Model of Giftedness and Talent

special education, state departments of education have not yet fully embraced this belief, perhaps fearing the responsibility and resource implications that it entails.

To this point, we have been coy about the meaning of the word "gifted".

In the literature, many terms are used to refer to gifted individuals. There are also many competing definitions and models of giftedness. Each term, definition, or model is accompanied by a political agenda with implications for teaching and learning. A model widely adopted by education systems in Australia is Gagné's (2000) Differentiated Model of Giftedness and Talent (see Figure 3.3).

Gagné distinguished natural abilities (or aptitudes) and systematically developed abilities or skills. Giftedness refers to competence that is distinctly above average in one or more domains of *human natural abilities* (such as intellectual, creative, socio-affective, and sensorimotor). Talent is reflected in distinctly above-average performance on *systematically developed skills* in one or more fields of human endeavour, such as academic, technical, artistic, interpersonal, or athletic.

How one achieves talent is a result of the interaction between intrapersonal and environmental factors. Intrapersonal factors include one's physical characteristics, motivation, willpower and persistence, and personality. Environmental factors include one's culture, society, family, teachers, available programs and activities, and events and achievements.

The dichotomy of giftedness and talent allows for an expanded model that is inclusive of the gifted student who is underachieving, and also recognises the role that chance can play in the life of a gifted child, as you can see in the Figure 3.3. It is a model that describes the dynamic relationship between high potential and high performance. Gifts are developed into talents through the interaction between intrapersonal and environmental catalysts.

An education system that adopts Gagné's model accepts responsibility for the identification of high potential in students, and of providing appropriately for their education.

Dual exceptionalities

We tend to assume that gifted children do not experience difficulties with their learning. However, there is a significant group of students who are gifted and have disabilities, which include learning, developmental, social, and emotional disabilities, and in one way or another, they are often overlooked in education systems, in schools, and in classrooms. These students are said to be twice exceptional or to have dual exceptionalities. Such students may underachieve because of the barriers to perform to their cognitive potential. This can lead to frustration, which at times may be inappropriately expressed.

Some problems of psycho-social maladjustment may arise or may be exacerbated when educational provision for gifted students is inappropriate. For example, there is a risk of depression when the person's emotional needs and needs for knowledge and expression are obstructed. This is clearly and carefully documented by Gross (2004), who emphasises that such afflictions arise not because of the exceptional intellectual ability but rather as a result of others' responses to them. At the same time, pathological disorders may be slow to manifest themselves, usually becoming apparent after puberty, but with signs often exhibited much earlier. In the first case study, Elise's emotional behaviour disorder and possible Asperger's syndrome were not diagnosed until halfway through her secondary schooling.

Gifted students may be disadvantaged in any of the following ways, through:

- special learning difficulties, such as verbal (e.g., dyslexia), nonverbal (e.g., attention deficit hyperactivity disorder—ADHD), and developmental delays in motor coordination and speech acquisition;
- physical, sensory, and medical difficulties, such as hearing impairment, vision impairment, or cerebral palsy;

dyslexia

An impairment of the ability to read. This is a controversial term more often used by medical practitioners.

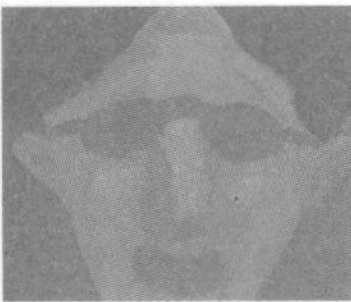

- social, emotional, and behavioural difficulties such as attention seeking, personal isolation, school phobia, truancy, oppositional-defiant disorder, conduct disorder, emotional behaviour disorder, anxiety, eating disorder, depression, mood disorder, personality disorder, and dissociative disorder; and
- particular diagnoses such as Asperger's syndrome, obsessive-compulsive disorder, bipolar disorder, and schizophrenia.

It is significant that by focusing on the individual in context, the ICF implicitly includes giftedness and talent as equivalent variables to those that affect people with a disability. Importantly, when attention is drawn away from any specific condition or circumstance and toward an understanding of the person in a living context, it also draws attention to the way in which individuals perceive themselves. This relates to the way in which each of us establishes our identity and how this affects ability to function within society and within educational settings. Let us briefly consider identity as the projection of individuality.

school phobia
A symptom of a childhood anxiety disorder similar to separation anxiety. Children who develop school phobia become terrified and try every tactic possible to stay away from school.

oppositional-defiant disorder
An ongoing pattern of disobedience, hostility, and defiance directed toward authority figures.

dissociative disorder
Problems with memory, awareness, perception, and may include aspects of identity.

self-system
The dynamic interaction between self-awareness and self-regulation (metacognition), intellectual and academic performance (cognition), and a positive feeling state about learning (motivation).

self-efficacy
The developing sense of personal effectiveness as a learner, and an enhanced awareness of one's own capacity to learn and perform tasks.

self-esteem
The value that people place on the data of their self-concept. It refers to the positive and negative judgements of the characteristics people attribute to themselves.

Perceptions of self

Self-perception is a general term that relates to a person's self-system. This incorporates other terms such as self-concept, self-efficacy, self-attribution, self-image, self-esteem, and self-acceptance, many of which have overlapping definitions (see e.g., Wigfield, Lutz, & Wagner, 2005). Self-concept is perhaps the most commonly used term. It refers to our appraisal or evaluation based upon our perceptions and awareness of ourselves, especially in regard to self-worth, personal values, and aspirations, often made in comparison to others around us. This regard we have for ourselves was once thought to be a single dimension, that is, it was the sum total of every aspect of our being (physical, psychological, social). These days, researchers view self-concept as a multi-dimensional concept, meaning that we have one view of, for example, our mathematical self, another of our physical self, and so on.

Researchers also believe that we are not born with a specific self-concept. It develops over time and is shaped and reshaped as a consequence of our interactions with others and through the totality of our experiences. How others react to our behaviour and our performance become the tools that shape and reshape. In other words, our self-concept is learned over a long period and is hard to change once we have consolidated that view of ourself, in positive or negative terms.

For many years, educators and other helping professionals have been interested in the relationship between self-concept, a person's motivation to learn, and its influence on school performance. There has also been interest in the formation of self-concept in boys and girls and the effect on achievement, although the research results have been equivocal. There has been a popular belief that low self-concept explains learning difficulties, although the research findings are again equivocal.

There is no doubt that self-concept is a factor in educational outcomes, but it is more likely to be an effect rather than a cause. Perhaps more closely related to causation is the notion of self-efficacy (i.e., our perceptions of how well we produce a desired result), which is intimately linked to our identity.

Identity

Identity is established within a social context and involves transitions and transformations across time and the social interactions that one has with others. At a basic level, identity can involve the adoption of dress conventions and behaviour that emulates the conduct standards of one's subgroup or the circle of friends with whom one seeks affiliation. Put another way, seeking identity involves consciously employing strategies that enhance personal and social power and is very important during childhood and adolescence (see e.g., Lindholm, 2007).

Establishing identity leads to tensions between perceptions of self-sufficiency and independence and the support that we gain from others. During childhood and early adulthood, the family provides

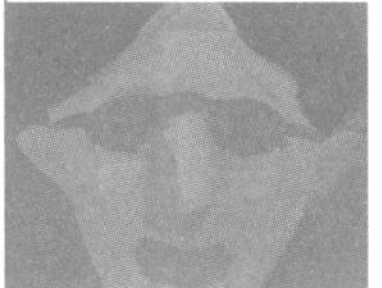

the foundations that are adjusted as young people develop friendship networks during and outside the school hours. Self-assurance develops through social interactions and peer support networks and also from young people's successes in formal and informal learning situations and, in the adolescent years, through romantic relationships.

Not too surprisingly, we all tend to do things that provide satisfaction and reinforce our sense of self-worth, and we shy away from things that denigrate our identity. Bandura (2003) raised this point in regard to self-efficacy. He argued that if we believe that we cannot achieve a desired outcome from actions, then we have little or no motivation to act, or to continue to act when faced with adversity. This is the case whether or not our beliefs are justified. Self-efficacy, therefore, is closely related to the ability to plan and achieve the desired outcomes. It influences choice of task, how much effort is made, how persistent one might be, and what is actually achieved. Bandura believed that behaviour can be

BOX 3.1

Tips on raising self-efficacy of students who are underachieving

Apply effective pedagogy:

- teach the learning strategies needed to complete a task (e.g., when a new concept is introduced, start with concrete examples and encourage the student to make generalisations, model how the concept is applied in a range of examples in class and group work, and then support the student to use the concept in an individual task);
- link new work to recent achievements (e.g., know what concepts and skills the student has mastered and build them into some activities in the coming weeks);
- progress at first in small steps with scaffolding (e.g., if the level of difficulty is too far beyond the student's ability to achieve success with support, then the student will not be able to accomplish the task);
- develop metacognitive skills (e.g., brainstorming, and there are many ideas in Edward de Bono's *Six Hats* and *CoRT*); and
- give appropriate performance feedback (e.g., it is better not to praise the student after every question or activity is successfully completed; rather, encourage them to apply the concept on a slightly harder problem, and then give praise).

Establish students' mastery of each step:

- give class work at the instructional level of the student (e.g., cater to a range of abilities in the classroom by using Bloom's Taxonomy of Cognitive Abilities—the revision by Anderson and Krathwohl, 2001—is highly recommended) (see page 218);
- set homework that is challenging but that the student is able to complete independently (e.g., apply concepts learnt in class to solve problems of interest to the student that can be presented in a range of media);
- ensure success in tasks that the student expects to fail (e.g., scaffold the learning activity and support them to achieve success in tasks such as mathematics for which they may have low self-efficacy); and
- progress when ready; attribute success to the hard work and ability of the student (e.g., success in a task is not due to luck but is due to the good thinking and hard work).

Model success:

- provide positive vicarious experiences (e.g., provide opportunities for the student to meet successful adults from the same cultural or social background);
- make opportunities for the student to relate to like-minded peers from a similar background; construct achievable short-term life plans (e.g., help the student to set several goals to achieve over a period of three weeks);
- change the student's language so that there are no self-putdowns, negative language, or verbal aggression used as a defence mechanism (e.g., if the student says "I can't do it", you say, "I can't do it yet"); and
- maintain a positive attitude about the student's ability and express high expectations about what they can achieve (e.g., make sure that your body language is positive and accepting of the student; know what the student is capable of achieving and prompt them to improve on that in the next activity).

3.1

scaffolding

A term that refers to the gradual withdrawal of teacher support given during an educational intervention as the learner become more capable and is, thus, able to work independently. In language development, scaffolding refers to the way a competent communicator builds conversation using the less adequate utterances of a partner.

predicted by determining self-efficacy for a particular task. Note that behaviour may not necessarily reflect actual capabilities due to the potency of perceived self-efficacy.

According to Bandura (2003), students with high self-efficacy for particular tasks will participate more readily in those tasks, will engage with the activities, will work harder, will tackle the challenges, and will persist when difficulties are encountered. On the other hand, students with low self-efficacy will resist engaging because they believe that, no matter how hard they try, they will not succeed. Some tips for overcoming low self-efficacy are given in Box 3.1.

Self-efficacy, therefore, is central to identity and of particular importance to disadvantaged and marginalised young people who perceive a lack of support that is sometimes experienced as victimisation and vilification. How an individual reacts to these extreme indications of ingroup/outgroup difference depends upon their individual circumstances.

For some young people, formal education settings can be very unrewarding and lead to extreme learner resistance. Some young (and even older) people react negatively to formal learning experiences by actively refusing to engage in the process. They choose to resist learning and restrict their educational experiences. This phenomenon was introduced by Kohl (1994) who used the term *non-learners* to describe those who aggressively refuse to pay attention, act dim-witted, scramble their thoughts, and override curiosity. It distinguishes them from others who do not learn because of specific intellectual limitations. Kohl's notion of non-learning was generated within the domain of cultural and social oppression, his examples being largely taken from black American and other underprivileged communities in New York. However, the principles apply more generally than to those specific groups.

The reactions of non-learners in culturally disadvantaged circumstances are similar to the experiences of many other young people who engage in battles of will or authority with teachers who are intent on coercing or seducing them to learn. While the young persons' motives may be different, the behaviour of these non-learning students has much in common. In many cases, active non-learners do not believe that they are failures or inferior to others who are succeeding at school. Their intent is distinctly different from other students who want to learn but cannot.

Kohl argued that non-learning occurred when disadvantaged young people have to deal with unavoidable challenges to their integrity, cultural loyalties, or identity when there is no middle ground to which they can retreat. Their choice is either to agree to learn from a stranger who does not respect them—thereby causing a major compromise to identity—or reject the stranger's advance and refuse instruction.

Non-learners often see little value in learning that occurs in formal education settings. They draw their knowledge and identity from the interactions and the considerable amount of learning and problem-solving that occurs beyond the school grounds. Those who are not deliberate non-learners, but who have difficulty learning, also develop a picture of themselves in relation to others.

Bloom's Taxonomy of Cognitive Abilities

Developed by Benjamin Bloom and colleagues in the mid-1950s as one of three education domains (the other two are affective and psychomotor). The cognitive domain involves knowledge and the development of intellectual skills such as the recall or recognition of specific facts, patterns, and concepts that serve in the development of intellectual abilities and skills. There are six major categories (knowledge, comprehension, application, analysis, synthesis, and evaluation) starting from the simplest behaviour to the most complex. The categories progress in difficulty requiring the first one to be mastered before the next, and so on.

creativity

A process in which a person creates a new idea (thinking) or a new product (outcome), or changes existing ideas or outcomes, which results in something new for the individual.

Identity and giftedness

As indicated previously, we cannot overlook the needs of students who have exceptional gifts or talents when we are considering the influences that affect successful learning outcomes. Mahoney (1998) introduced a model called the Gifted Identity Formation Model in which four primary forces shape and influence the identity of a gifted person:

- validation—the acknowledgement by others or one's self that the person is gifted;
- affirmation—the further acknowledgement and reinforcement of ability by supportive individuals interacting with the person;
- affiliation—the formation of relationships with others of similar ability and intensity, and who share similar interests and passions; and
- affinity—the attraction toward people who spark the imagination and ignite creativity, and toward activities that maintain the fire of the self, the calling that gives a sense of purpose in life.

These four notions contribute to the development of giftedness by interacting with 12 systems: self, living companions, biological family, culture, vocation, environment, education, society, psychology, politics, organic-physiology, and development. The interaction defines the way in which a gifted person perceives and feels about himself or herself as they grow from childhood to adulthood and are at their greatest intensity during adolescence.

The concerns about gifted young people draw attention to two important ideas. The first is asynchronous development. This refers to the marked difference between chronological age (or typical development), intellectual development (some people call this mental age), and affective development (some call this emotional age) of the gifted person. Precocious affective development can be seen particularly in emotional sensitivity, advanced moral reasoning, an advanced sense of justice and fairness, a capacity to empathise and feel compassion, and advanced awareness of philosophical, ethical and existential issues, and is apparent in some gifted children at a very young age (Gross, 2004).

The second concept is what Gross (2004) terms the forced-choice dilemma. This refers to the choice that gifted young people often have to make between excelling in an area of talent that is not valued by the peer culture, and being accepted by that peer culture. If there is a primary need to form or maintain relationships with age-peers, the intellectual potential or interests will retreat behind a talent mask so that the person can conform to a value system that may be markedly at odds with their asynchronous development.

Identity formation for a gifted person can be very complex and challenging. These affective issues can be a heavy burden for the gifted child or adolescent to bear. The website Supporting Needs of the Gifted <http://sengifted.org> gives teachers, counsellors, and parents access to resources that can help build environments in which a young, gifted person's identity is understood and valued, and its development nurtured and supported.

We have written a little about historical developments, for example the transition between the previous and current WHO definitions of disability, and hinted at research developments in self-concept and identity. Here, there is some value in very briefly drawing attention to some of the more substantive

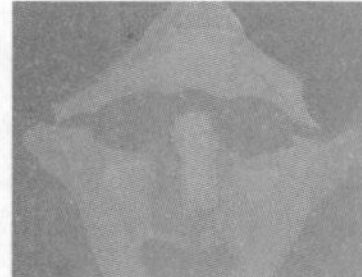

historical events that have led to the way in which we presently view diversity in our culture and society and the way in which educational environments have evolved to deal with that diversity.

ISSUES AND CHALLENGES

It has been 50 years since the introduction of the view that students with particular learning needs could be educated successfully in regular classrooms. Learning needs in this context generally meant students with severe intellectual or learning disability, or serious physical or sensory impairment.

Success for some

Mainstreaming, as the movement was called initially, came about as a response to the recognition of the social injustice that kept students with special needs separated from their peers who were progressing according to age norms and expectations. At that time, mainstreaming involved not much more than forming class groups that contained one or more students with a disability or impairment, but there were few adaptations made to either the curriculum or teaching practices that might have produced educational benefits for those mainstreamed students. In other words, teacher and schools made few adaptations to accommodate the apparent differences between students.

Parents of mainstreamed students soon realised that their children were getting little, if any, instruction that was relevant or appropriate to their needs. They applied political pressure to improve the resources available to their children in regular classes and advocated professional development for teachers in the hope that this would advantage their children socially and scholastically. With this development came the demise of the term *mainstreaming* and its replacement by *integration* and, later, by *inclusion*.

Along with political and administrative directions and mandates came many recommendations for ways in which teaching and learning might occur across education settings to benefit the largest number of students. Curriculum content and classroom practices were examined with a view toward accommodating all learners, and any search of a university library catalogue or database will reveal a vast collection of books designed to help teachers adapt their teaching methods and the curriculum to support students with special learning needs. Teachers were offered professional development designed to improve their knowledge of disabling conditions and teaching skills, although there was usually no requirement to attend. Again, in reality few significant changes were made to classroom teaching practices or administrative procedures in most schools worldwide.

Research on inclusive education should be punctuated with work on innovative teaching strategies and approaches that enhance students' learning experiences regardless of ability or impairment. And while any wide-ranging review of literature using "inclusive education" or "inclusion" in, for example, the ERIC database, will show a huge range of initiatives, the conclusion that one might reach from close examination is that inclusive education generally has fallen well short of the target. Evidence of positive outcomes in both social and academic areas is far from expansive, despite the claims of many writers who advocate inclusive education.

While rarely reported in the professional literature, there has been considerable opposition to mainstreaming, integration, and inclusion. Teachers have complained that they were not trained to deal with low-functioning students, those presenting very challenging behaviour, or students with severe physical or sensory impairments. Many have argued that regular classrooms are not places for very demanding students—when compared with their peers—because this reduces the amount of one-to-one teaching that can be given to any student in a class. Parents of students achieving according to age expectations have complained that their children were being disadvantaged, while parents of students with special learning needs also protest that their children receive significantly less attention and fewer learning

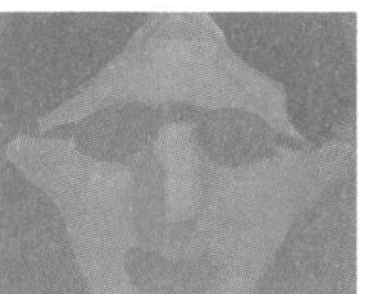

opportunities than are available in special education settings. Jenkinson (1997) presented perhaps the most balanced discussion of the arguments.

By the late 1990s, inclusion had become the accepted educational policy, with associated rhetoric, in most Western countries. Despite this, special education classes and schools continue to exist, as mentioned in the previous chapter. Included students who attend regular classes more often than not are those with learning difficulties, mild intellectual disability, uncomplicated medical conditions, speech and language difficulties, vision impairment, and those identified as gifted and talented.

Several writers argued that inclusion is a moral imperative that does not require, and cannot wait for, empirical justification (see Stainback, Stainback, & Ayres, 1996) while others many years ago warned about a rush headlong into inclusion because of the lack of support provided by administrators and others responsible for its implementation (e.g., Kauffman, Gerber, & Semel, 1988). It is curious that the number of empirical studies about the success of inclusive education relative to the vastness of the literature is small and, of these, few focus specifically on innovative teaching approaches (e.g., co-teaching, strategy instruction, peer-mediated learning) aimed at improving academic outcomes. These will be considered in later chapters of this book.

Having made these comments above, we are not advocating a return to two separate education systems that existed two decades ago (regular, special). Inclusive education is the ideal that should be pursued vigorously, but a question immediately comes to mind: Why has inclusion not been as effective as initially expected? There is no simple answer to the question but a starting point for addressing the answer can be found by looking at the way in which societies and communities deal with difference and variation. We need to look at the assumptions that are made about individuals who do not look, act, or think the way the majority does, because these are precisely the characteristics of many young people in our education systems. Let us follow this thought by considering the circumstances of students who excel.

Access for all

Inclusion tends to be interpreted in a narrow way: it is often taken to mean integration in a mainstream class of age peers who progress through school in a lock-step manner. Ironically, often due to a lack of understanding of the nature of giftedness, the teachers of these classes may consider that gifted young people are included. Hence, for many students, such a placement may not provide an appropriate education in the least restrictive environment. Gross (2006, p. 123) carefully argued for a reconsideration of the meaning of inclusion for gifted students.

> *If it is true that learning is a developmental and sequential process, that there are striking differences in developmental rates among individuals of the same age, and that effective teaching must be grounded where the learner is, then how do we justify an educational system that ignores competence (what pupils are able to do) and achievement (what they have already mastered) and utilises chronological age as the primary, or only, factor in pupil placement?*

In Chapter 1, it was stated that inclusion is about belonging, about being rightly placed within a group of people and having the rights and qualities that characterise members of that particular group. For gifted students, belonging will be reflected in participation and engagement in new and challenging learning, the right placement should imply flexibility and choice, and the group of people may well be eclectic and will include intellectual peers and peers with similar interests.

The current reality is that we have to make such a modified curriculum accessible in the regular classroom for, rightly or wrongly, that is the context in which most gifted students are to be found. This is possible to do, but only if the teacher allows the student to learn at an appropriate pace and to

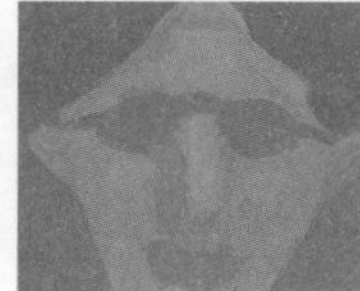

progress when ready, to develop critical and creative thinking skills, to pursue areas of special interest, to express their knowledge and creativity in a variety of ways, and to relate to intellectual peers. Of course, this is a big ask for any teacher. Later in this chapter we will expand a little on John Elkins' comments about curriculum differentiation, which is an important tool in any teacher's toolkit to meet the learning needs of all students within the classroom. To support the teacher to achieve this goal it can be helpful to place such an approach within the conceptual framework of multi-grade teaching. You can find a useful discussion of this in Cornish (2006).

These days, class sizes have largely stabilised in the mid- to high-20s and teachers and parents have taken some heart in the belief that smaller classes provide greater learning opportunities. However, the question of how to provide the most appropriate instruction has remained largely unanswered. In many classrooms, instruction might still be aimed at a commonly accepted middle ground, whether through expediency or design. This means that brighter students are often left to survive as best they can, and lower ability students must put in greater personal effort to stay up with the teacher's relentless progress through the curriculum, or fall further behind. Teachers can certainly provide personal attention to students and this goes some way toward ensuring that everyone in the class will master the content at an acceptable standard.

Today, education is a huge industry. State education budgets run into the billions of dollars and this is not surprising when you consider that there are over 3.3 million school-age students in Australia. The Australian Bureau of Statistics (ABS) prepares a school census report each year that includes information on children in government and non-government schools. The 2002 document, Schools (Australian Bureau of Statistics, 2006), reported that there were 9,612 schools in Australia. Of these, government departments of education ran 6,902 (71.8%). There were 158,194 full-time equivalent teachers in government schools and 81,445 in non-government schools. The number of teachers in government schools grew by 9.8% over the previous 10 years compared with a 35.7% increase in non-government schools. Two-thirds (66.8%) of the students attend government schools. While the actual number of students in public schools is stable, the number of enrolments in independent schools is increasing at about 7% per year.

Since 1990, the Australian Bureau of Statistics has not separated students according to regular or special education or teachers who teach in each setting, these students and teachers being allocated to either primary or secondary levels of school education.

Statistics on disability

In 2003, the Australian Bureau of Statistics published its most recent *Survey of Disability, Ageing and Carers*. The data show that about 20% of people in Australia reported a disability divided evenly between males and females. The Bureau defines a disability as any limitation, restriction or impairment that endures beyond six months and restricts everyday activity. This result is much the same as for the previous reporting period that ended in 1998.

Disability rates for school and early adult years were reported as:

- 4.3% of approximately 1.24 million for children aged birth to 4 years;
- 10% of approximately 2.66 million for those aged 5 to 14 years; and
- 9.0% of approximately 2.81 million of those aged 15 to 24 years.

Of significance, about 7.5% of the 4 to 14 year olds reported a restriction in relation to schooling, as did 5.8% for the 15 to 24 years group for schooling or employment.

The incidences of most debilitating conditions have been known for decades. These are just a few examples:

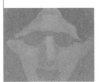

- about 1 in 100 persons has an intellectual disability;
- about 2 in 1,000 children have a sensorineural hearing loss;
- about 1 in 3,500 boys is affected by Duchenne muscular dystrophy; and
- about 1 in every 10,000–15,000 girls is affected by Rett syndrome (a childhood neurodevelopmental disorder that generally affects females, characterised by loss of hand capabilities, slowed brain and head growth, gait abnormalities, seizures, and intellectual disability).

The incidence of some conditions varies depending upon certain factors. For example, Down syndrome occurs more frequently as the age of the mother increases, from about 1 in 1,923 live births when the mother is 20 years old to 1 per 12 live births at 49 years of age.

As with any classification of disability, incidence tells us little about the level of educational support that is needed by an individual with any condition, and even less about how we might provide appropriate educational experiences to children. For example, while about 30% of children have vision impairment, in only two cases in every 1,000 are the circumstances sufficient to warrant adaptations in the education environment beyond correction provided by spectacles. And while Down syndrome affects intellectual ability, its impact on any individual can vary considerably, from extremely debilitating to very mild.

Bureau data have commonly shown differences between boys and girls in terms of their schooling limitations. The difference between the sexes is particularly pronounced in the case of Attention Deficit Disorder (ADD) and Attention Deficit Hyperactivity Disorder (ADHD). Of children with a disability, nearly one in five boys is diagnosed with these conditions, compared with one in 14 girls. Although ADD and ADHD represent only a small number of children overall, it is a condition that has been diagnosed more frequently during the past 10 years along with Autism Spectrum Disorder (ASD), and in a recent Western Australian study of over 9,500 young people aged 2 to 17 years, it was found that 2.8 times as many males as females (about 75% versus 25%) were prescribed stimulant medication for ADHD (Calver, Preen, Bulsara, & Sanfilippo, 2007).

Medically related problems become more common with increasing age, but children are at-risk because of conditions present at birth and as a consequence of environmental factors such as accidents. A number of conditions occur more frequently in the younger age groups, such as asthma, ADD/ADHD, intellectual and developmental disorders, and hearing or speech loss. Asthma is the most common persistent health condition for young people, affecting more than 310,000 children. However, unlike other conditions, there is a low level of restriction associated with that condition. For example, about three-quarters of those with asthma live normal or near-normal lives.

at-risk

This refers to children who have been identified by school personnel as being vulnerable to an educational or learning difficulty. The cause may be social, behavioural, intellectual or medical.

BOX 3.2

Statistics on giftedness

The Australian Bureau of Statistics (2006) includes gifted students in the category of students with special needs. In that document the Bureau defined a special needs teacher as a person who teaches academic and living skills to school students with particular learning difficulties using various techniques, and there is an additional note referring to teachers of gifted students.

The only available statistical information on giftedness comes from definitions of giftedness that rely on IQ scores, or refer to a strict percentage of students or to levels of giftedness (see, e.g., Gross, 2004). Caution is needed when applying such concepts, for four reasons. First, strict percentages may well exclude gifted students who most need special provision to realise their potential. Second, models of levels of giftedness usually rely on IQ scores, which for many gifted students may not draw an accurate picture of their giftedness. In other words, it does not take into account their cognitive abilities and learning needs. Third, the distribution of measured IQ scores does not actually fit onto a normal curve and so incorrect assumptions might be drawn about how many gifted students there are. Finally, gifted students from backgrounds of disadvantage (e.g., low socioeconomic status, cultural minority status) notoriously underperform on IQ tests.

The key idea from levels of giftedness is the greater the measured IQ, the greater the asynchronous development is, and the greater the learning needs and the social and emotional needs of the student are. Conceptions of giftedness that refer to IQ scores strongly suggest that advanced learning needs begin at an IQ of about 115 or 120 (Gagné's model refers to 10% of students being gifted). The table below indicates the proportion of students expected to be found at each of the typical levels of giftedness.

Before a teacher dismisses such figures, saying that this does not apply to their classroom, it is important to remember that giftedness has no respect for social or cultural background, or for sex. That is, gifted children are found in all walks of life, in each cultural group, in each social group, at all economic levels of society, in metropolitan, regional and rural areas, and equally in both boys and girls. Therefore, a teacher should expect to find gifted children in their classroom.

Level of giftedness	IQ	Percentile	Expected number	Proportion
Mildy gifted	115 +	84	16 per 100	1:6.3
'Top 10%'	120 +	90	10 per 100	1:10
Moderately gifted	130 +	97.7	23 per 1,000	1:44
Highly gifted	145 +	99.87	13 per 10,000	1:740
Exceptionally gifted	160 +	99.9968	32 per 1,000,000	1:31,250

A percentile refers to the division of a population into 100 groups of equal size. So, if a person is at the 84th percentile, his or her score is at or above 84% of the population.

BOX 3.2

Just to keep these matters in perspective, in Box 3.2 you will find a short note about statistics relating to gifted and talented individuals.

Educators around the world have tried to resolve the dilemma of how to provide the most appropriate instructional settings and teaching strategies that will accommodate the learning needs of most children. The word *appropriate* is the weak element in the argument because what might be

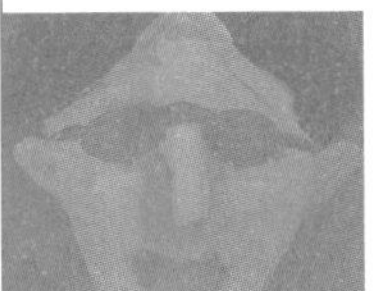

appropriate for one child might be inappropriate for another. The adaptation of a curriculum in a certain way might assist one child but it might be detrimental to another who appears to have the same medical circumstances or even the same learning needs, as in the case of gifted and talented young people. How teachers and school systems have addressed these issues differs from place to place. In South-East Asia, and the Asia–Pacific region especially, there have been major efforts to move toward inclusive policies and practices, but there appear to be few definite answers (see, e.g., Forlin, 2007; Wu, Ashman, & Kim, 2008).

We turn now to begin the consideration of how teachers might develop a suite of strategies from which they can draw to move toward individualising instruction to the greatest extent possible. As this chapter is about diversity and environments, our attention will focus on setting up the context in which teaching and learning occurs.

TEACHING ESSENTIALS

Accommodating the diverse range of students' skills, abilities, and backgrounds in today's schools and classrooms provides many challenges. To a large extent, the focus of the compulsory years of schooling is the transmission of knowledge set out in the curriculum, with literacy and numeracy being the fundamental building blocks. Along with the ideals of inclusive education came the precept that the regular classroom was the most suitable context in which learning can occur. Exactly how this belief became established is likely a matter that can only be unravelled by a close examination of history. Class groupings seem to have been used for centuries if not millennia. It is likely that they evolved in the formal schooling of ancient Greece, and were consolidated in the monasteries of the Middle Ages when monks brought children of wealthy families together to teach them reading and writing. And so class groups continued down through the ages.

In early 19th century England, Joseph Lancaster popularised schools in which students were taught by peers using a monitorial approach; that is, one master taught a select group of older pupils (monitors), and these in turn taught the classes. Lancaster's approach proved highly successful and the number of schools grew quickly, with the idea leap-frogging the Atlantic to spread across the Americas.

Class groups, however, are unlikely to be the ideal learning environment for all students and, indeed, could be highly punishing places for some. While some students prefer to work alone, others work more effectively in small groups, some in structured settings, and a small number prefer practical hands-on in informal contexts. For some students, one-to-one or small group settings provide the most effective way for the teacher to guide and overcome particular learning obstacles or provide enrichment activities.

Maynard Reynolds (1962) proposed the idea of a range of teaching–learning environments that might meet different student needs at different times. Evelyn Deno (1970) and others revisited his service delivery system through the presentation of a cascade of services model, which became the multi-tiered approach that is the basis of the least restrictive environment (LRE) that is an integral component of inclusive education practices. Our view of contemporary services is more along the lines of an array of alternative places and this is graphically shown in Figure 3.4.

service delivery
The provision of an educational, training, therapeutic, medical, vocational, or other program or treatment to an individual, group, or organisation.

cascade of services model
A concept, introduced by Deno, that ranked educational placements from least to most integrated. Also referred to as a continuum of services from least to most restrictive.

An array of alternative placements

A general principle guiding the development of educational programs for students with special support needs is the provision of instruction in an environment that is as near to normal as possible, being mindful of the student's ability and the limitations imposed by any particular circumstance or condition. In general, the regular classroom is accepted as that norm; in other words, it is the most suitable location for students because it provides age-appropriate role models and curriculum, and regular interactions

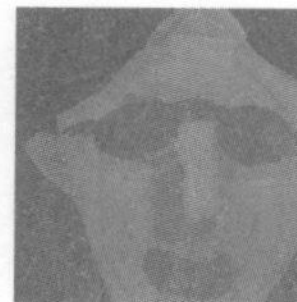

FIGURE 3.4

A schematic representation of the array of educational placements

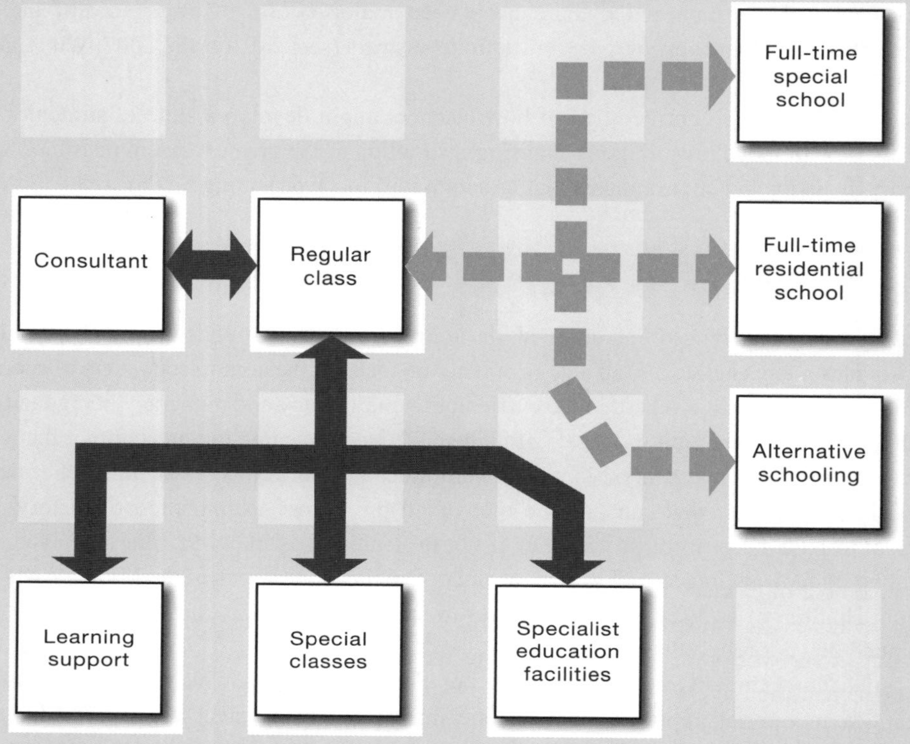

Consultant
Regular class
Full-time special school
Full-time residential school
Alternative schooling
Learning support
Special classes
Specialist education facilities

with other students. The widely held assumption that the regular classroom is the least restrictive education setting is more historical than conceptual. It is arguably more appropriate to fit the context to the student than the student to the context, and this is the way it is depicted in Figure 3.4.

We have chosen the term *array of alternative placements* to ensure that there is no hierarchy implied across these teaching–learning settings. In the ideal education world, support would be provided to teachers and students as needed, and students would move between settings depending upon their particular learning needs and any restrictions that might exist for any number of reasons. One can draw a parallel here to the array of activities provided in any classroom, ranging from didactic whole-of-class teaching to small group work, individual discovery via library or the world wide web, peer tutoring, and one-on-one lessons with a teacher.

peer tutoring
A method of teaching whereby one individual in a pair takes on the role of the teacher while the other individual is the learner.

Below are the settings that can be found in most education systems. We start with the regular classroom and move through the range of education options.

THE REGULAR CLASSROOM

Classrooms have changed quite a lot over the years. At one time students sat in ordered rows of desks, the configuration changing only when the cleaning staff came in to polish the floor at the end of term. These days, classrooms reflect the range of available information and communication technology, and many primary school classrooms have break-out areas for group work and even small resource centres.

The regular classroom is the context thought to accommodate most students' social and intellectual requirements. It is a place where there are familiar peer role models and established standards of behaviour. Typically, one teacher aims to provide most of the academic input but, in some cases, additional equipment and resources are available for students with special support needs, such as large print books or Braille-writing equipment for students with vision impairment, or hearing assistive technology for a student with a hearing impairment, such as an audio-loop system or personal amplifier.

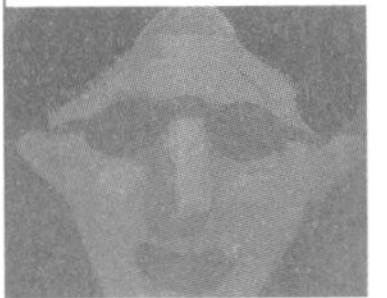

information and communication technology

Refers to the range of technologies that are being integrated into school environments as part of the infrastructure for learning. This definition encompasses the broad range of technologies used for accessing, gathering, manipulation, and presentation or communication of information.

CLASSROOM WITH CONSULTANT SUPPORT

In this configuration, young people with particular learning needs remain as full-time members of the regular classes but gain benefit by support that is provided to the teacher by specialist consultants (e.g., consultants in reading, mathematics, art, primary or secondary special education, behaviour, or gifted and talented education). Consultants work with classroom teachers to consider how the curriculum might be adapted to support a student who is having difficulty with reading or mathematics, or to design new resources that might help a child who is hard of hearing. Most consultants have a very heavy caseload, so it is really important to use their time as efficiently as possible.

CLASSROOM WITH LEARNING SUPPORT

There are times when a student might need assistance with an ongoing learning difficulty, such as reading, that is hard for the classroom teacher to address in the course of the teaching day. Alternatively, students with exceptional academic skills may need opportunities to work alone or in small groups with a learning support teacher, or a parent or community volunteer on enrichment activities, or a project that crosses a number of curriculum areas.

Learning centres exist in most schools (in government and non-government sectors) and may have one or more teachers who have specialist training in, for example, learning difficulties or gifted education. Some years ago, these centres were called Special Education Centres, or Learning Support or Remedial Centres, names that stigmatised the students who were withdrawn from the regular classroom to get "fixed". It is not surprising that many young people were less than enthusiastic about attending the remedial centre. These days, students attend learning centres to engage in a range of activities over a number of periods each week. These might include an intensive program to address an area of academic weakness, or provide opportunities for small groups to investigate special topics. Sometimes a learning centre teacher might go to a regular classroom to provide support to a particular child. The crucial point about learning centres is the lack of a label that implies a problem.

Some students perceive that the learning centre is used by particular groups of students and many draw their own conclusions about its purpose. If they don't identify with the other students there, they may refuse to go. For example, gifted and talented students typically don't want to be seen as "special needs".

SPECIAL CLASS PLACEMENT

There are times when a young person requires more intensive support than might be available through participation in learning centre activities. A student with a mild intellectual disability, for example, might benefit greatly from a short-term adapted program in literacy or numeracy that might not be easily delivered or monitored successfully in the regular classroom or in a learning centre. Such a student might work alongside others with similar learning needs. The ratio between regular class work and special class work can be adjusted according to the availability of resources and the needs of the student. In other words, the student might attend the special class part-time, depending upon the configuration in any particular school.

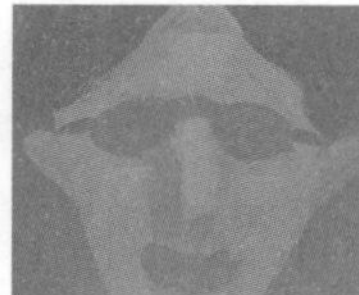

In some schools there are several classes, for example in a secondary school that caters for students who have similar learning constraints. These class sets are sometimes called Special Education Units and are staffed by teachers with skills in a particular area such as hearing impairment, vision impairment, intellectual disability, or Autism Spectrum Disorder.

SPECIALIST EDUCATION FACILITIES

Some facilities are designed for relatively short-term placement of children, with the extent of instruction provided depending largely upon the purpose of the facility. Such specialist facilities include those for young people awaiting court appearances, or for the treatment of critical incidents, such as a severe emotional disturbance.

Young people who are in-patients in hospital for short- or long-term medical treatment may also attend a special facility called a "hospital school". These schools may include students who are school phobic and have been hospitalised to break the pattern of non-school attendance. An intensive period of in-patient admission will combine therapy and schoolwork. Teachers working with these children liaise with the young person's regular teachers and work toward a supported re-entry of the student to their home school.

FULL-TIME SPECIAL SCHOOL

Enrolment in a special school or a special class might be recommended if a young person is in need of support that is not readily available in a regular school. This can include intensive therapy or other services provided by personnel not usually located in preschool, primary, or secondary schools, such as occupational and physical therapists.

In state education sectors, gaining enrolment in a special school might require fulfilling certain criteria, for example a diagnosis of intellectual disability. In other words, a student with very severe Autism might not be eligible for enrolment unless he or she has an intellectual disability diagnosis as well. This can create significant hardships for the student who would benefit greatly from specialist teachers who are trained to work with young people with such high support needs, and also hardships for teachers in regular schools who do not have the skills or resources available to support that young person properly. Special schools are found in both government and non-government education sectors, with those in the latter often targeting students with demanding behaviour problems such as Autism, or very antisocial behaviour.

ALTERNATIVE SCHOOLING

There are many education facilities now that do not look, or act, like regular schools. These include alternative schools for students who have dropped out of school for one reason or another or have been excluded. These education settings are often based on greater levels of student democracy than exist in most schools. There are also schools for Indigenous students that use teaching–learning approaches that foreground Indigenous cultures and learning styles. Distance education is another schooling alternative, originally developed to cater for students living in rural and remote areas. These days, however, there are many students enrolled in distance education because they have been excluded from regular schools for antisocial or severe challenging behaviours.

Some parents do not wish their children to attend regular schools and prefer to educate their children themselves at home. It has been estimated that there are over 25,000 young people being homeschooled in Australia. While this number is rubbery, this group of students is significant nationwide. You can find out more about homeschooling by typing "homeschooling Australia" into your favourite web browser.

FULL-TIME RESIDENTIAL SCHOOLS

Typically, these are isolated learning situations for children who are in need of both structured and intensive training or care. Two groups of children for whom this environment might be chosen are students who have a profound intellectual disability or extremely serious intellectual or multiple disabilities, and those who have a serious emotional disorder. There are also schools attached to juvenile detention centres where residents continue their education with the support of very capable primary- and secondary-trained teachers.

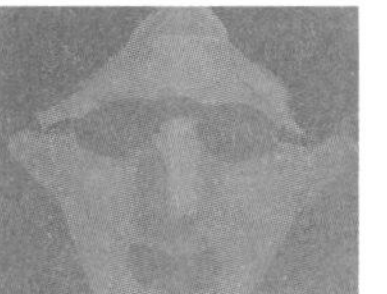

multiple disabilities
Usually refers to more than two disabilities.

In the literature on inclusive education, the least restrictive environment (LRE) means that students who have a disability should have the opportunity of an education with students who are achieving according to the age-grade average. They should have access to the regular curriculum and extracurricular activities and programs, as do all other peers. The cascade of services model implies that when specialist support or a specialist learning environment are needed to achieve certain teaching and learning objectives, such additional support should be as brief as necessary to improve their skills or behaviour, and then the student should return to options as close as possible to the regular class.

One issue that is not often addressed when considering special support is the view of parents. In some cases, parents are very enthusiastic about having their children educated in regular school settings. Others fight to have their children enrolled in special schools and settings. Indeed, it is not only parents who advocate for special school placement. There are many counsellors and teachers who argue for such enrolments for students with highly challenging behaviour and students with severe Autism Spectrum Disorder who, under less restrictive system enrolment criteria, would be very appropriately placed in a special school. If it is a matter of choice, at least some parents have found their only recourse to be litigation under anti-discrimination legislation, as you will have discovered in the previous chapter.

LEARNING ESSENTIALS

Learning can be hard work. It demands that many factors come together to provide the right environment and conditions for a person to link what is already known with what is being presented. We refer to the right environment and conditions as the teaching–learning ecology.

Teaching–learning ecology

Ashman and Conway (1997) extended ideas originally proposed by Doyle and Ponder (1975) to show the influences of four important contributors to successful learning and problem-solving. At the most general level, learning involves a series of inputs, the employment of teaching and learning processes and procedures, and a series of outputs. Looking more closely, every student regardless of age, ability, or any other personal or cultural characteristic is subject to influences that affect what, and how, they learn. Four factors—the learner, the teacher or instructor, the setting, and the curriculum—interact as shown in Figure 3.5 and are described below.

THE LEARNER

Each learner in every teaching–learning setting is unique. Each has a singular learning history comprising knowledge, a mental and emotional disposition toward learning, and a set of strategies that are commonly used to learn.

Knowledge includes specific detail, such as arithmetic or historical facts, and information about how to perform mental and physical tasks, such as how to remember a friend's birthday, read, how to get home from work, or how to fill the car with petrol. It is the accumulated total of all this knowledge that forms the foundation on which the learner operates.

Successful learning outcomes, however, are not just about knowing things. The student's emotional reaction to learning and the learning situation is also important because it predisposes the student to become, or not to become, involved. Motivation is one of the more important emotional elements that

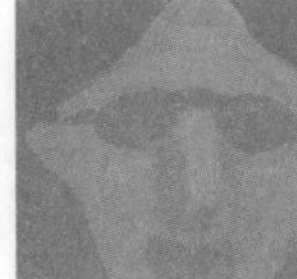

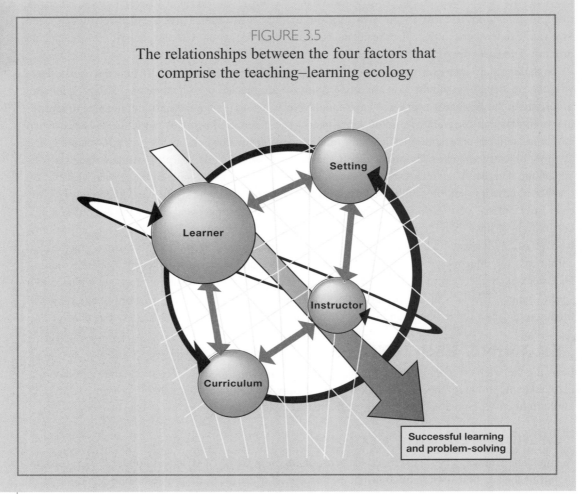

FIGURE 3.5
The relationships between the four factors that comprise the teaching–learning ecology

Setting
Learner
Instructor
Curriculum
Successful learning and problem-solving

is linked to past experiences and to the willingness to attempt new tasks or activities. When learners experience success, the likelihood that they will be prepared to engage in similar or new learning activities increases. The reverse is true when there is repeated failure.

In the course of our lifetime, we develop a constellation of strategies that enables us to learn and solve problems, and to adapt to new and novel learning experiences. These strategies include setting priorities, making decisions, and planning with a particular outcome in mind. These organisational skills are vital to effective and efficient learning. When students can develop plans, set priorities, and make decisions, their ability to work independently is increased and their reliance on teacher direction is reduced.

So, there is an intimate connection between knowledge, personality and affective variables (such as motivation), and superordinate mental capabilities (such as planning and priority setting).

THE TEACHER

The person usually responsible for the implementation of a curriculum is the teacher or instructor. The teacher decides what will be learned and how learning will occur. Even in those situations in which the teacher passes control of some or all aspects of learning to the student, the underlying operational control remains with the teacher.

Teachers operate according to the same intellectual and emotional dimensions as their students (i.e., knowledge, emotions, organisational skills). Teachers can determine the quantity and quality of students' learning by the way in which they interact with their students. For example, when a teacher is confident, supportive, and enthusiastic, those characteristics are communicated to the students and the learning experience and the outcomes are generally positive. When the teacher fails to motivate the students or provide learning experiences that are aimed at satisfying their learning needs, comparatively little productive learning may occur. Thus, teachers play a pivotal role in the teaching–learning process because they manage themselves and others involved in the learning environment.

Peers, family and friends, machines, and even educational media can assume the teaching role. This is especially the case in informal learning contexts such as the home, playground, museum, art gallery or even at the beach.

THE SETTING

The physical environment has a major impact on the way in which we learn. Optimum levels of noise, light and temperature, and comfortable and accessible physical facilities are necessary to maximise concentration and minimise distraction. Suitable resources, teaching materials, time and space are also important elements in the environment.

While teachers and learners can adapt or habituate to adverse conditions, some naturally occurring and man-made phenomena can seriously hinder their capacity to do so. For example, extremes of heat or cold can reduce the students' ability and willingness to learn because their attention is focused on maintaining comfort rather than on the task. Less extreme conditions can also affect teachers' and students' performance. For example, many teachers will confirm that students' behaviour becomes significantly more disruptive on wet and windy days.

Social factors, including the cultural and socioeconomic circumstances in which the learner lives and the ethos of learning and respect that exists within the school, also play important roles in learning. For example, when the language of instruction differs from the students' home language, difficulties can arise not only in the actual process of instruction but also in communicating with family and friends, and in the support for education that is available within the home.

THE CURRICULUM

Finally, what is to be taught and learned and how this information is conveyed determine learning outcomes. The term *curriculum* can have a number of meanings. It can refer to all learning regardless of the age or ability level of the students (i.e., everything students are to learn in school), to a systemic curriculum (e.g., as defined by the Key Learning Areas), or to the content that a teacher might develop for a specific student.

The curriculum is not just the body of specifics that a student is to learn but also a mosaic of strategies and learning skills that are part of the teaching–learning process. Teaching the curriculum might also be facilitated by an individual education plan or program (IEP) that is developed for students who have high support needs. It is a management tool that sets out the student's present level of education performance, how the student's disability influences participation and progress through the general curriculum, and measurable annual goals (for a more expansive description of IEPs, see Smith, 2006).

The four components (learner, instructor, setting, curriculum) must be in balance if a successful learning outcome is to be achieved. Success can be measured in a number of ways, for example by a prize for outstanding achievement received at the end-of-year speech night, entrance into a preferred university program, or the gleeful squeal that a young person with severe mobility impairment makes after being able to walk a half dozen steps unaided. Whatever the measure of success might be, each

achievement, or lack of it, influences the way in which the learner perceives himself or herself. How we learn, how we feel about ourselves as learners, and how we react to learning situations contributes to the formation of our identity.

USING THIS CHAPTER IN SCHOOLS

In this chapter, we have sketched out a framework for teaching and learning that includes all students in any educational environment, from preschool through the compulsory years of schooling, and on into adulthood and career training. We firstly emphasised aspects of the individual that affect learning, including the self-system and identity. We then drew attention to the environments where learning occurs and the levels of support that are currently provided in an array of educational contexts from the regular classroom through to settings specifically designed for students who require the most intensive support. The same dynamic and influences operate in every learning context.

Every personal and environmental factor affects learning outcomes. The challenge for teachers and instructors (and the authors of the chapters in this book) is to set up the conditions that facilitate the transfer of knowledge and skills.

Perhaps the most important information raised in this chapter that will guide you in your professional life is given in Figure 3.4, the teaching–learning ecology. You will recall that this involves an interaction between the learner, the teacher, the setting, and the curriculum. Your job as a teacher is to bring each of these elements into play to maximise the learning outcomes of your group or class.

Adjustments to teaching and learning

To finish this chapter, we want to provide some practical ideas that will help you put this chapter into the context of your own teaching setting. We want to do this in the context of curriculum differentiation, which you will also read about in several later chapters. So, what is this curriculum differentiation?

Curriculum differentiation refers to a flexible approach to teaching that addresses the different learning rates, styles, and interests of students in any learning setting. Very broadly speaking, the curriculum can target several outcomes by focusing on three areas of mastery:

- content mastery—in which the student learns ideas and skills;
- concept mastery—in which the student understands and appreciates systems of knowledge through an exposure to key concepts, themes, and principles; and
- process mastery—in which the student learns investigatory and information management skills that support learning and decision-making.

It is important for you to think of these outcomes when preparing lesson plans that are appropriate for all members of your class or group. Curriculum differentiation requires slightly more effort than simply presenting the syllabus in hierarchically arranged chunks. We can put curriculum differentiation in the context of the teaching-ecology.

Maker (1982) and VanTassel-Baska (1998) can help us here. They have suggested that, when differentiating the curriculum, the teacher needs to consider the learners' characteristics, the present skill/knowledge levels, the pace of presentation, the complexity of the information, and the depth of learning that is required. The level must be sufficient to interest and challenge each student. The pace must be adjusted to accommodate students who learn at a faster or slower rate. The complexity should reflect the extent to which the learner can engage in simultaneous rather than linear processing of ideas. The depth should allow students to continue exploring an area of special interest to the level of an expert if they wish.

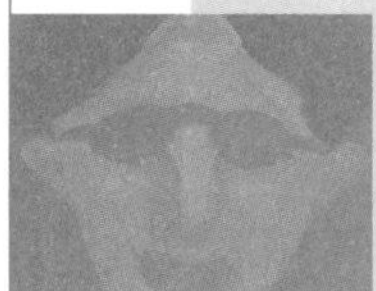

Adjusting student outcomes

So, the prerequisite knowledge you need before considering curriculum differentiation is about the learners, your students. You will get to know some young people better than others because of their enthusiasm, or lack of it. Remember, most students don't want you as a friend; they want you to be a competent and fair teacher. Here are three questions you might ask yourself:

- How can I get to know my students and their learning needs?
- What are the characteristics and traits that affect their learning?
- How might I deal with a mismatch involving me and one of my students?

One of the most effective ways of dealing with student differences is to think about the outcome *you* want to achieve, and what you want *your students* to achieve. Negotiating the products with students will typically increase their interest and lead toward autonomous learning and problem-solving. The students will, of course, need to be supported by realistic planning and time management.

Many students these days are interested in solutions to real problems so you will have to think carefully about appropriate forms of evaluation (and student's self-evaluation) and feedback. The aim is to give your students opportunities for each of them to produce a body of work that reflects their interests, skills, and potential.

Adjusting the context

The learning environment should be student-centred, open, and accepting, and should encourage independence. Here are three questions that might help you consider the need for a rich variety of resources, technology and media, activities, and ideas.

- What do you want your work space to look like? This depends upon the phase of schooling in which you work. At the preschool level, your "classroom" might have several activity areas where young people will work alone or with one or two others; in senior secondary school you might need to consider safety issues in, for example, a laboratory or workshop.
- Do you want your students to work alone, in small groups, or independently as a member of a whole class? How you set up your classroom should take into consideration the preferences that some students have to work autonomously or as a member of a group. Remember also that peers can assist students who have learning problems when the work groups are supportive and cooperative.
- Are there physical conditions that need consideration? Space limitations, climate, noise, and resources are all part of the setting.

In some activities you might want to encourage movement in and out of groups within the classroom, between classes, between year levels, and, if possible, across schools. The aim is to create a safe and flexible learning environment that will engage students at all times and will encourage them to take learning risks.

Adjusting the teacher

Chapter 1 drew attention to attitudes, beliefs, and values that influence the way in which teachers (and, indeed, everyone else in society) respond to others, especially those who are different in noticeable ways. As a teacher, you need to be aware or your own dispositions and behaviour. There is no doubt that some days you will feel excited and enthusiastic, while on some other days the world could stop revolving and you wouldn't notice it. You will be susceptible to the same personal factors that influence the behaviour of your students.

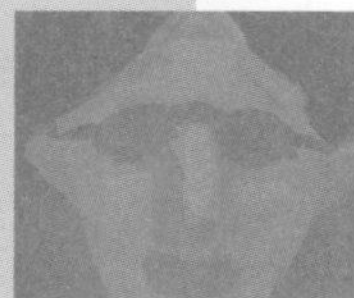

One of the tricks to teaching is flexibility. Your teaching style and approach need to respond to your students' cognitive ability and skills. This means being receptive to new ways of involving students in the teaching–learning process by providing them with freedom of choice and working in groups of varying sizes. Look for innovative and practical ways of presenting concepts, perhaps through interdisciplinary activities (i.e., across KLAs). This will encourage students to see learning as an open-ended process where paradox, analogy, tolerance for ambiguity, intuition, proof, reasoning, and critical appraisal are common elements.

Flexibility in teaching accommodates difference and diversity and extends students' thinking beyond remembering, comprehension, and application to tap the more cognitively demanding skills of analysis, synthesis and evaluation. Each of these six processes needs to include four kinds of knowledge: factual knowledge, conceptual knowledge, procedural knowledge, and metacognitive knowledge (i.e., knowledge that relates to an awareness and understanding of one's own thought processes).

So, a few questions that you might ask are:

- What are my views on inclusion? Almost assuredly you will have students in your classes with learning difficulties that will require extra effort on your part to ensure positive learning outcomes and progress.
- Am I prepared to learn as I go when I meet new challenges? Every young person with whom you work over your career as a teacher will be unique. Facilitating their intellectual, emotional, social, and physical development will involve a process of continual learning.
- Am I prepared to take the intellectual risks associated with flexibility?

Adjusting the curriculum

The points made in the last sub-section relate to this topic as well but are primarily aimed at the teacher. As mentioned in the previous chapter, in its broadest sense the curriculum has to do with teaching and learning activities across several domains: knowledge, skills, values, and attitudes. It is not only about what we teach but also how we teach it.

Generally, the curriculum content is hierarchically arranged so that there is the laying of foundations with concrete activities and the progressive addition of abstract notions and ideas. Not all students can accommodate what is to be learned at the same rate/pace or depth. You need, therefore, to think carefully about moving ahead at an appropriate pace to enable all students to gather facts and to understand definitions, generalisations, concepts, and relationships between concepts. In general terms, your aim is to match student aptitudes to curriculum offerings by recognising students' prior learning and by building upon the basics.

PRACTICAL ACTIVITIES

As you will already know, the activities below are divided into two sets, those that can be undertaken alone and those to be done as group activities in your study context. The second set is designed to be undertaken in a teaching–learning setting, depending upon your area of expertise: preschool, primary, middle school, or secondary school.

Uni-work

1 In this chapter, we have foregrounded gifted and talented students to emphasise that these students do not always breeze through school. Bright and gifted students require special consideration if their needs are to be met. Establish a small work group with your student

colleagues and undertake a literature search. Assign one member of the group to each of the following areas:

- social-emotional development;
- community programs for bright and gifted students (your university might provide some of these); and
- school-based learning enhancement strategies (e.g., acceleration, enrichment) and myths about giftedness and exceptional talent.

2 Each group member should prepare a short report (perhaps as notes or bullet points) that focuses on teaching strategies and classroom responses for these students.

3 Undertake a library search on self-perception and its affect on learning outcomes. Keep notes on the recommendations given. What teaching adaptations are suggested? What, if any, of these are relevant to students from non-dominant cultural backgrounds?

School-work

School policies vary in regard to contact with parents and the use of students' records or other information for projects outside the usual teaching and learning events that occur as part of any school day or school calendar. Before beginning any of the following activities, speak to your supervising teacher or a member of the school administration to confirm that you can undertake the activity within existing school guidelines and policies.

4 In your own classroom, identify two students, one who appears to be having difficulty with learning, and another who seems to be progressing very rapidly. Pay attention to the ways in which they participate in their education program (this might be at any schooling phase). Look particularly at how they:

- interact with their peers;
- respond to the way in which you teach;
- complete assigned work;
- persist when the activity is difficult;
- respond to encouragement; and
- seek, receive, and give feedback to others.

Keep track of these issues over a couple of weeks by noting your observations in a day book or diary. At the end of that time, analyse where the similarities and differences exist. What does this mean for your teaching and the presentation of the curriculum?

5 Check out your classroom in terms of the influence of the setting on students' learning. Make a list of all the positive and negative aspects. Against each of your points, jot down some notes about how supportive or restrictive each aspect is. How can you best use each aspect and how can you change those that are restrictive?

6 Starting with this chapter, explore the literature and the internet to find ways in which "inclusion" is described and understood. Make a collection of the ones that stand out most for you, and the ones that best challenge you to meet the needs of each of your students. For example, the Canadian Child Care Federation says "Inclusion means Belonging" and "Inclusion means Happiness". In a paragraph or in one page, write down what "inclusion" means for you. Summarise this in two or three succinct statements, "Inclusion means …". Use these statements to make a series of posters to promote diversity and inclusion in your classroom.

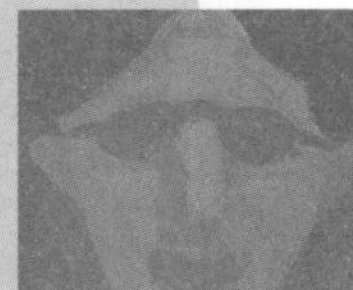

SUGGESTED READING AND RESOURCES

Websites of each state association for gifted and talented children provide many examples of models for differentiating the curriculum, along with lesson plans and ideas. You can gain access to them via the website for the Australian Association for the Education of the Gifted and Talented: <www.aaegt.net.au/eddept-links.html>.

The Australian Science and Mathematics School, Adelaide: <www.asms.sa.edu.au/Pages/default.aspx>. This website provides an excellent example of an integrated approach to curriculum differentiation using Problem Based Learning.

Cornish, L. (Ed.) (2006). Reaching EFA through multi-grade teaching: Issues, contexts and practices. Armidale, NSW: Kardoorair Press. Education For All [a Millennium Development Goal]. Cornish draws a rich picture of the strengths of multi-grade teaching for the inclusive classroom. Multi-grade teaching makes good pedagogical sense because it is founded on an approach to learning that is focused on each individual and their particular learning needs.

REFERENCES

Anderson, L. & Krathwohl (Eds) (2001). *A taxonomy for learning, teaching, and assessing: A revision of Bloom's taxonomy of educational objectives*. New York: Longman.

Ashman, A. F. & Conway, R. N. F. (1997). *An introduction to cognitive education*. London: Routledge.

Ashman, A. & Elkins, J. (Eds) (1990). *Educating children with special needs*. Sydney: Prentice Hall.

Ashman, A. & Elkins, J. (Eds) (2002). *Educating children with diverse abilities*. Sydney: Pearson Education Australia.

Australian Bureau of Statistics (2003). *Survey of disability, ageing and carers; Summary of findings, Australia*, No. 4430.0. Canberra, ACT: Author.

Australian Bureau of Statistics (2006). *Schools, Australia*, No. 4221.0. Canberra, ACT: Author.

Bandura, A. (2003). *Self-efficacy: The exercise of control*. New York: W.H. Freeman and Company.

Calver, J., Preen, D., Bulsara, M., & Sanfilippo, F. (2007). Stimulant prescribing for the treatment of ADHD in Western Australia: Socioeconomic and remoteness differences. *Medical Journal of Australia*, *186*, 124–127.

Commonwealth of Australia (2001). *The education of gifted and talented children*. Report of the Senate Employment, Workplace Relations, Small Business and Education References Committee, 2 October. Canberra: Parliament of Australia. Available on the internet <www.aph.gov.au/senate/committee/eet_ctte/gifted/report/>, accessed 6 November 2007.

Cornish, L. (Ed.) (2006). Reaching EFA* through multi-grade teaching: Issues, contexts and practices. Armidale, NSW: Kardoorair Press.

Dawson, J. (2003). *Wild boy*. London: Septre.

Deno, E. (1970). Special education as developmental capital. *Exceptional Children*, 37, 229–237.

Doyle, W. & Ponder, G. A. (1975). Classroom ecology: Some concerns about a neglected dimension of research on teaching. *Contemporary Education*, 46, 183–190.

Forlin, C. (2007). A collaborative, collegial and more cohesive approach to supporting educational reform for inclusion in Hong Kong. *Asia Pacific Education Review*, *8*, 1–11.

Gagné, F. (2000). Understanding the complex choreography of talent development through DMGT-based analysis. In K. Heller, F. Mönks, R. Sternberg, & R. Subotnik (Eds), *International handbook of giftedness and talent* (2nd ed.) (pp. 67–79). Amsterdam: Elsevier.

Gross, M. (2004). *Exceptionally gifted children* (2nd ed.). London: Routledge Falmer.

Gross, M. (2006). To group or not to group: Is that the question? In C. Smith (Ed.), *Including the gifted and talented: Making inclusion work for more gifted and able learners* (pp. 119–137). London: Routledge.

Gross, M., MacLeod, B., & Pretorius, M. (2001). *Gifted students in secondary schools: Differentiating the curriculum*. Sydney: GERRIC, UNSW.

Gross, M., MacLeod, B., Drummond D., & Merrick, C. (1999). *Gifted students in primary schools: Differentiating the curriculum.* Sydney: GERRIC, UNSW.

Jenkinson, J. C. (1997). *Mainstream or special? Educating students with disabilities.* London: Routledge.

Kauffman, J. M., Gerber, M. M., & Semmel, M. I. (1988). Arguable assumptions underlying the Regular Education Initiative. *Journal of Learning Disabilities*, *21*, 6–12.

Kohl, H. (1994). *I won't learn from you: and other thoughts on creative maladjustment.* New York: The New Press.

Lambros, A. (2004). *Problem-based learning in middle and high school classrooms: A teacher's guide to implementation*. Thousand Oaks: Corwin Press. (This book provides a good introduction to the potential of Problem Based Learning.)

Lindholm, C. (2007). *Culture and identity*. Oxford: Oneworld Publications.

MacLeod, B. (2004). *Curriculum differentiation for gifted students. Gifted and talented education professional development package for teachers: Module 5*. Sydney: GERRIC, UNSW.

Mahoney, A. (1998). The Gifted Identity Formation Model: In search of the gifted identity, from abstract concept to workable counselling constructs. *Roeper Review*, *20*, 222–226.

Maker, J. (1982). *Curriculum development for the gifted*. Rockville, MD: Aspen.

Merrotsy, P. (2003). Acceleration: Two case studies of access to tertiary courses while still at school. *TalentEd*, *21*(2), 10–24.

Montgomery, D. (2006). Double exceptionality: Gifted children with special educational needs—what ordinary schools can do to promote inclusion. In C. Smith (Ed.), *Including the gifted and talented: Making inclusion work for more gifted and able learners* (pp. 176–191). London: Routledge.

NSW Department of Education and Training (2004). *Curriculum differentiation. Policy and implementation strategies for the education of gifted and talented students. Support package*. Sydney: Curriculum K–12 Directorate.

Reynolds, M. C. (1962). A framework for considering some issues in special education. *Exceptional children*, *28*, 367–370.

Smith, D. D. (2006). *Introduction to special education: Teaching in an age of opportunity*. Boston: Pearson Education.

Stainback, S., Stainback, W., & Ayres, B. (1996). Schools as inclusive communities. In W. Stainback & S. Stainback (Eds), *Controversial issues confronting special education: Divergent perspectives* (2nd ed.). Boston: Allyn & Bacon, 31–43.

VanTassel-Baska, J. (1998). *Excellence in educating gifted and talented learners.* Denver, CO: Love.

Wigfield, A., Lutz, S. L., & Wagner, A. L. (2005). Early adolescents' development across the middle school years: Implications for school counsellors. *Professional School Counseling*, *9*, 112–120.

Winzer, M. A. (1993). *A history of special education: From isolation to integration*. Washington, DC: Gallaudet University Press.

Wu, W-T, Ashman, A., & Kim, Y-w (in press). Educational reforms in special education. In C. Forlin & M-G. J. Lian (Eds), *Reform, inclusion and teacher education: Towards a new era of special and inclusive education in Asia-Pacific regions*. London: Routledge.

SECTION

2

Inclusive Schools

Inclusive Schools 2

Regular schools have always enrolled students whose responses to learning has been reason for concern. In most cases, teachers have coped with the range of students' skills and abilities although not always in a manner that promoted a passion for learning. These days, there is an imperative that education systems, schools, and teachers move toward the use of strategies and procedures that accommodate the needs of all students who attend school.

In the first section, we considered the foundations on which inclusive teaching and learning are based. In this section, the contributors build on that foundation.

Specifically, inclusive schools bring together the human, physical, technological, and education resources that provide opportunities that enable all students to achieve positive learning outcomes commensurate with their capabilities. As you will see as you read the following chapters, achieving this goal is the mission of most education systems (public and private) and most have comprehensive resource and service capabilities to support schools and teachers. John Munro opens this section with a discussion of the services that are available in most states and territories to support students with a range of learning needs.

To make any progress toward inclusive education, a school needs to operate as a supportive and cooperative entity where the rights of every member of the community are respected. It will come as little surprise that we focus first on student behaviour and its management. Students who exhibit inappropriate behaviour generally gain their education in regular classes with classroom teachers doing whatever is possible to direct their energies appropriately and minimise disturbances to other class members. These children are fewer in number than those identified as having a learning problem, and once the behaviour is socially appropriate the student should not demand much attention from teachers.

Bob Conway's chapter is lengthy and practical. The ideas presented there should equip newly qualified teachers with the necessary knowledge to move comfortably into their teaching roles.

Having said that whole school policies and collaboration among all members of the school community are essential elements in addressing the needs of students with learning difficulties and/or behaviour problems, the success generally rests on individual teacher capabilities. Being a teacher these days is like being a jack-of-all-trades (and master of some). Teachers need to know about behaviour management principles and practices, but also how to use technology that will support and encourage all members of a class and facilitate learning where specialist support is required. The chapter by Doug Bridge and Ruth Croser will deal with general principles that guide the choice of commonly available technologies and also augmentative communication devices.

John Munro

4

EDUCATION SYSTEMS AND SERVICES

What you will learn in this chapter

This chapter examines how education systems help teachers and schools to support students with particular learning needs in regular classrooms.

In this chapter you will learn:

- about the characteristics of an inclusive teaching–learning context;
- how barriers to inclusive learning can arise at the classroom and school levels;
- how systems assist with curriculum provision and teaching support for inclusive practice, and assist schools and teachers to develop teaching–learning plans;
- how systems support schools to monitor and review inclusive teaching practices;
- how systems help teachers to provide a safe classroom learning environment and climate for exceptional learning students;
- about the procedures systems use to distribute resources to support inclusive practice;
- about school-level support and guidance for inclusive education;
- about how educational systems assist teachers to identify the learning needs of individual students and exceptional student learning profiles; and
- the programs that systems provide to support exceptional students in regular schools.

CASE STUDIES

The two case studies below are examples of situations in which inclusive teaching practice might be influenced by education systems.

JAN

Jan returned to teaching after an 18-year break pursuing another career, and inherited a Year 5 class halfway through the school year. The school was in an area of Melbourne known for its social disadvantage and was under pressure to improve its students' literacy and numeracy outcomes.

Almost immediately, Jan became aware of the diverse nature of her class. It included five students from Africa who had never been to school, four Indigenous students, three students who had intellectual disabilities and received a Program for Students with Disabilities, a gifted student who also had an anaphylactic allergy, and two students who were medicated for Attention Deficit Hyperactivity Disorder (ADHD).

Jan received little initial briefing from the school's leadership team. When she raised the range of student abilities and characteristics in her classroom with her coordinator, she was told that her class was generally representative of others in the school and that she should do the best she could. No reference was made to supporting resources, either within the school or beyond. When she raised the issue, somewhat tentatively, with her new colleagues, they added little. As long as she kept her students in their classroom during the school day and prevented fighting when on playground duty, she would be fulfilling her role as a teacher.

In her earlier work in business, Jan had learnt the importance of trying to imagine what the solution would look like, clarifying what was in place at the beginning, and having a plan that involved taking one very small step at a time. She had also learnt the importance of recognising positive aspects of a situation and giving clear feedback.

During the first few weeks she tried to apply these to her class. She had the students work on one small task at a time. As well, she made small changes in classroom management progressively. Some of the students needed a high level of support to complete the assigned tasks but she continued to work on this. She used feedback strategically to recognise what they knew and made a point of having the students regularly and briefly review what they had learnt and share it with the group. She encouraged them all to see themselves learning.

Jan realised that she needed to focus on literacy. She planned a range of small tasks that covered various aspects in comparative professional isolation, as did the other teachers.

Coincidentally, she met a colleague with whom she had worked many years earlier. The colleague, hearing about Jan's situation, alerted her to a number of resources that might support her and the school more generally. These were largely services and programs provided by the education system of which her school was a member.

Her phone call to the regional school improvement officer informed her of the programs that were being implemented in neighbouring schools that had similar student populations. The consultant provided her with contact names, emailed her the list of programs and teaching modifications being run at each grade level, and offered to facilitate visits.

Jan also learnt about the teacher self-support group that met monthly at another school in the local cluster and was offered recent resources developed by the group. A consultant explained

the resources provided by the regional office and how support services for individual students could be obtained. She provided a list of future relevant professional education offerings.

Jan was fired up to gain access to this veritable treasure trove of support options. When she raised them with her colleagues she found that some had a vague knowledge but had never used them. No one else thought they would be useful. "What would regional desk pilots know about students like ours?" she was told, or "It wouldn't work here."

The school leadership team didn't know how to gain access to the services: "We've never been successful in the past" and "It's not worth the trouble, there'll be a long waiting list." One team member remarked: "We don't want outsiders coming in upsetting our routines and telling us how to suck eggs."

Only one colleague showed any interest in pursuing it further, and she and Jan began to develop a resource plan.

TIM

Tim was brand new to teaching. In the first few weeks of his career he found that his Years 7 and 8 English and humanities students didn't behave in similar ways to the students he'd taught during his school experience practice the year before. In the class in which he taught three subjects, the four most disruptive students had exceptional learning needs; two were diagnosed as having Autism Spectrum Disorder (ASD) and two had severe language disorders. They seemed to play off each other, and some lessons would go by without these students doing any work at all. Other students in the class, meanwhile, were asking him to ignore these students or remove them from the class.

Senior staff soon became aware of Tim's predicament and began to provide support. First, although the school had received additional funding for the four students, it had not found its way into Tim's class. This was rectified and a teacher's aide was made available.

Second, the need for individual teaching–learning plans for each student was recognised and these were developed. A consultant from the regional office guided this process. The consultant explained to Tim how these students went about learning. Tim mentioned the topics he planned to teach and the consultant gave detailed recommendations about how to design appropriate learning activities for the students.

A guidance officer from the regional office suggested ways in which Tim might interact with the students, how to use feedback strategically, and how to guide and direct the students' learning. This consultant also helped Tim to understand how these students could feel more engaged in the classroom. Together, the consultant and Tim developed a teaching plan that involved the gradual modification of his teaching practices over two terms and then the consultant reviewed this with Tim each month.

The school received resources from the system to provide a small group support program for students who had severe language disorders and Tim's students were included in that program. The topics developed in the small group contexts were those that Tim would teach in a few weeks.

The four students became increasingly more engaged in class. Not only was their learning more successful but also their peers began to value them and became more accepting of their ways of learning. As Tim felt his competence as a teacher improving, so did his self-confidence as an inclusive teacher.

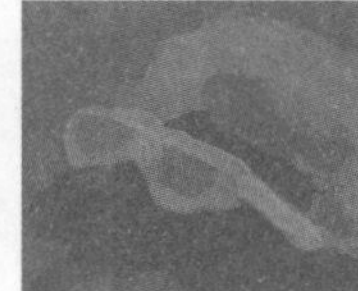

TEACHING–LEARNING CONTEXT

There are quite a few websites listed in this chapter. Some will be of particular interest because they relate to the phase of learning in which you intend to teach or in which you are already teaching. Others might be relevant because they relate to your curriculum area or areas. Still others might be useful general references.

It's easy to "misplace" practical URLs so I suggest that you have a marker pen or pencil with you as you read and highlight those that you think will be of use later. If you don't want to mark your book, have a note pad handy and jot down the item and the textbook page number.

Let's begin.

How does an education system support students with particular learning needs? You will have read about Australian legislation to mandate inclusive educational practice. Educational systems have produced broad policies that enable the legislation to be implemented. The policies outline the broad goals and outcomes to be achieved and teachers and schools implement them.

The policies developed by systems are unlikely, by themselves, to lead to schools implementing inclusive practices. For this to happen, schools and teachers need to interpret the policies in the context of their own cultures (Whitehurst, 2004). How can an educational system assist a school to do this?

The teaching–learning context is the interface between the learner and learning opportunities. It is where the policies become teaching practice and also where the quality of a school's inclusive practice is evaluated. Schools vary in how they implement inclusive policies. This is because they differ in the extent to which their teaching–learning contexts facilitate inclusive teaching practice.

As the focus of this chapter is how education systems help or hinder schools to develop inclusive teaching–learning contexts, a useful place to start is to examine the characteristics of a teaching–learning context that facilitates effective inclusive practice.

The characteristics of inclusive teaching–learning contexts

Index for Inclusion

A resource designed to support schools in a process of inclusive school development. It was developed in the United Kingdom at the Centre for Studies in Inclusive Education.

What does an inclusive teaching–learning context look like? We can begin to answer this question by looking at the *Index for Inclusion* (Booth & Ainscow, 2002). The *Index* was developed in the United Kingdom in the late 1990s by a team representing teachers, parents, school administrators, and disability groups. It identifies three key characteristics of the teaching–learning context, in other words, the extent to which the environment:

- operates as an inclusive culture;
- facilitates inclusive policies; and
- permits inclusive practices in its core work of teaching.

Inclusive practices are more likely when the school operates as an inclusive learning culture, that is, when its characteristics include the following:

- students learn collaboratively, share their knowledge, and help each other;
- staff and students treat one another with respect;
- staff and parents/guardians develop cooperative partnerships that show mutual respect for and value each other's knowledge;
- staff, school leaders, and community members cooperate to achieve the core work of the school; and
- each participant is valued for the unique knowledge and perspectives they contribute.

Staff members can work to lower or remove barriers to learning, to minimise discriminatory practices, and to maximise participation in all aspects of school life. So, how well does the teaching–learning context operate as an inclusive learning culture? A teacher can determine this by examining the extent to which it displays the attributes through the decisions made, the dialogue in which staff engage, and the actions used by members of the school community to do its core work.

The second area relates to school policies that foster and provide inclusive education. Policies should focus on what the school would see as the ideal context for achieving inclusive education. An inclusive school policy:

- acknowledges that educational provision is for all students—for example, a policy that states that the school seeks to admit all students from its locality and makes its buildings physically accessible to all people;
- aims to provide a context that is optimally accessible to staff and students—for example, the policy that classroom organisation takes account of how all students learn; and
- indicates how the school will resource its commitment to supporting diversity—for example, by referring to the removal of physical obstacles and by minimising barriers caused by staff and student knowledge gaps.

The policy statements framed by a school reflect a response to system policies. They show what the system policy will look like in the school's teaching–learning context. They may also indicate the level of knowledge about the inclusive policies and the commitment that the school has toward them. You can gain an insight into the ways in which a school interprets inclusive education and is committed to it by noting what the policy statement says and what it omits.

The third area looks at what the school actually does to achieve an inclusive education, through teaching and resources. There are two aspects here:

1 How teaching is implemented. To what extent do teachers:
    - take account of the range of student characteristics and aptitudes (i.e., learning profiles) in the classroom in their teaching and respect diversity and difference? Planning lessons so that they take account of the language backgrounds of students in the class, or their earlier experiences, is an example of this.
    - encourage the active involvement of all students in the teaching–learning context? Teaching that looks for and invites responses and feedback from all students in the class is an example. This teaching says to every child, "I want to see/hear what you have learnt."
    - use assessment practices that target the achievements of all students? This might be illustrated by giving students alternative ways of showing what they have learnt, for example by saying what they know as an alternative to writing.
    - encourage mutual respect. An example is teaching that invites students to comment on the support they believe they need and to evaluate the quality of the lessons and that builds on them.

2 How resources facilitate learning. To implement inclusive practices, schools need a range of resources that they need to use strategically.

Schools need to recognise the range of resources they have, the additional resources they need to enhance their inclusive practice, and how they can gain access to them. They need to recognise the knowledge held by their staff and the expertise that resides in their community. They also need to know how to build staff knowledge about inclusion by providing and supporting relevant professional learning opportunities and staff collaboration to develop student-learning resources. They also need to know how to distribute resources equitably to support inclusion.

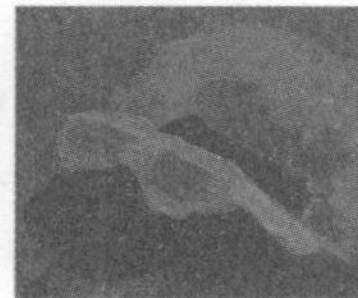

The *Index for Inclusion* provides a means for putting a system's policy about inclusive education into practice in a school. First, it helps staff members see where they are in terms of inclusive practice. Second, it helps schools see ways in which their inclusive practice could be improved. The *Index* provides a set of tools that schools may use for evaluating and improving inclusive practices.

The *Index* is considered a little more comprehensively in the final chapter of this book. However, the issues considered here will help you to begin to understand how schools and teachers can introduce and maintain the process of inclusive school renewal.

ISSUES AND CHALLENGES

A key challenge for many schools is how to maximise their accommodation of students with diverse learning needs. What do schools and teachers need to know and do to lower or remove the barriers to participation in mainstream activities for students who have a variety of learning needs?

Inclusion is limited when obstacles or barriers within a school restrict access to effective learning opportunities. To understand how well a school implements inclusive practices, and how these practices can be improved, we need to look first at these obstacles or barriers.

Barriers at the classroom level

Some of these were introduced in the previous chapter and include the teaching procedures and content, the classroom climate, and the physical context (e.g., where students are sitting in relation to key information sources such as whiteboards or display screens). Barriers to optimal participation in classroom learning can arise in any of these areas.

Many obstacles are due to a mismatch between the teacher's assumptions about how students learn, and how they actually do learn. Whenever we teach we assume that our students can think about the teaching information and can use it in particular ways. Some students may not learn in the ways we assume they can. When in a lesson we mention concepts we taught in an earlier lesson, for example, we assume that all of the students recall them. When we ask students to learn an idea by observing particular actions being done, we assume that all can tell themselves what they saw and remember the action sequence.

These assumptions may be invalid for some students and, as a result, the teaching won't work for them. Teachers who are attuned to inclusive practices recognise and deal with these less obvious barriers. When you understand how different students learn, you can make better decisions about how to teach them. This is illustrated in the scenario in Box 4.1.

Barriers due to teachers' concerns about inclusion

In some situations, barriers are caused by the context. The teaching procedures used, for example, may not take account of how particular students learn. While a classroom may have a heavy reliance on oral communication, some students may learn better via imagery or through motor activity. In these cases the barriers arise because the teaching doesn't take account of how the students learn. They are due to either the teacher's lack of knowledge about how some students learn and how to modify their teaching to accommodate them or the teacher's attitude to particular students.

oral communication

A method to teach deaf children where the emphasis is placed on student talk using amplification, speech reading, cued speech, auditory training, and state-of-the-art technological aids to assist with auditory, tactile, and visual information input.

In addition, some teachers have concerns or anxiety about teaching in an inclusive classroom. They may have negative or ambivalent attitudes to inclusive practice, believe they lack the necessary knowledge or skills to cater for a range of learning profiles, or lack self-confidence. These teachers may need to reflect on various fundamental principles such as:

BOX 4.1

Teaching knowledge can create barriers

Ted Brown saw himself as a good literacy teacher. Many of his students made great progress and achieved high-level outcomes. Each year, however, there was a small group of students in the class who didn't progress as he expected. Ted noted, "These students don't get involved or stay focused. They just didn't seem to be interested. I guess there will always be low achievers. Not everyone can learn to read." His observations were accurate. In his classes, these children didn't get involve or stay focused, weren't interested, and remained low achievers.

A replacement teacher, Sally Green, taught Ted's class for a term. She talked with the underachieving readers and noticed that they had rich imagery knowledge of the topics they discussed but often needed time to put their images into words. She helped them practise doing this. Before they began to read a narrative, she had them do this. Sally also had them talk in sentences about the pictures in the narratives and to recall vocabulary.

The students began to achieve as readers using their existing knowledge to read and to anticipate the ideas in a text. They learnt to paraphrase and visualise as they read, and to review each paragraph.

Ted came back to school from long-service leave and noticed that the small group of students had improved in their reading. Because he did not understand the conditions under which they had improved, he was unable to scaffold their learning. Soon some of the students plateaued in their reading and Ted was sure that this was, again, because of their lack of interest.

- the right to mainstream access as a human rights issue;
- what inclusive education looks like in practice; and
- the benefits that students derive from inclusive education.

Barriers at the whole-of-school level

These barriers might arise because the staff as a whole know little about how to implement inclusive practice or may not see it as school policy despite the fact that it is a system-wide policy. This was Jan's experience in the first case study. They might also arise because the school doesn't collect data or feedback that would tell them that some students are effectively excluded from the teaching.

Schools need clear guidelines to deal with this. Useful activities include the school collecting regular feedback from parents and students, particularly from those who have diverse learning needs. They might also engage in ongoing professional development that assists teachers to improve their knowledge and skills in inclusive teaching.

Effective communication about inclusive issues

One indicator of how well a school operates as an inclusive learning community is how these issues are raised and discussed among staff. To evaluate the communication network, you can look at the following, which are the purposes for which members are encouraged to communicate about inclusive education issues. Questions such as the following can promote useful discussion among colleagues:

narrative
A monologue, either fictitious or a recounting of real events. (See also discourse.)

human rights
A convention prescribing opportunities for all individuals to gain access to the social, educational, vocational, legal, and political structures of the society. In Australia, there is no legal basis to guarantee human rights or access to the services provided in the community.

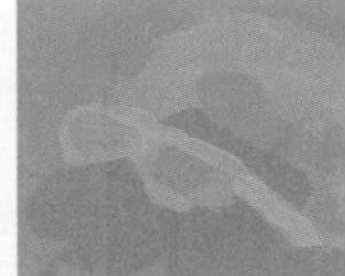

- To what extent does the dialogue focus on the learning pathways and progress of individual students and groups?
- To what extent is this dialogue reactive, that is, responding to issues that have arisen rather than focusing on future strategic activity?
- Is the dialogue used more to tell, to share, or support?
- How effectively is information about students and student groups communicated to and used by teachers to inform teaching?
- Do you know how to get assistance and guidance with problems and issues?
- What is the level of mutual respect and valuing that is shown in the information that is shared?
- Is information about student learning and progress communicated sensitively and effectively?
- Are you comfortable about discussing problems in your work?

Supporting professional learning

As noted earlier, teachers need ongoing professional learning opportunities inside and outside the school to maintain effective inclusive teaching practice. This professional learning can assist in:

- improving a teacher's knowledge about teaching effectiveness;
- solving problems and issues in teaching practice; and
- planning and reviewing the curriculum so that all students have ready access to the curriculum.

TEACHING ESSENTIALS

When we look at a class of students, we often see it as an entity in its own right. We forget that it is similar in many ways to other classes around the state and across the country. This is because each classroom is part of a sector, a state, and a national education system. The systems determine in part what is done in individual classrooms. As well, what occurs in individual classrooms can indirectly determine what is done in the system. A system usually determines the educational policies and goals, it determines key aspects of what we teach and sometimes how we teach, and it allocates resources to particular aspects of school's work.

Educational systems support inclusive practices in a number of ways. They provide programs and procedures that are aimed at assisting students to participate and optimise their learning outcomes in regular classes. In the following section we examine how educational systems:

- provide teaching support and the opportunity for staff to learn additional teaching procedures;
- develop and recommend curriculum frameworks and teaching options;
- assist teachers to develop classroom learning plans for individual students; and
- specify assessment and reporting processes that schools and teachers can use.

Teaching support

I noted earlier that optimising learning opportunities is a key aspect of successful inclusive practice. Educational systems respond to the need to enhance teachers' knowledge about effective teaching procedures in various ways. These include:

- providing in-school consultancy support;
- providing professional development opportunities; and
- developing and providing resources to support inclusive teaching.

IN-SCHOOL CONSULTANCY SUPPORT

Most educational systems provide in-school or on-site consultancy support for teachers of students with disabilities in their regular classes. Specially trained staff can guide classroom teachers to modify the teaching and learning for students so that they meet their specific learning needs. As well, they frequently coordinate the development, implementation, monitoring, and evaluation of learning support plans.

Systems differ in how they implement this consultancy. In South Australia, for example, it is referred to as Support Teacher Learning Assistance (STLAs) and is intended to assist students experiencing difficulties in basic areas of learning in regular classes. STLAs are allocated to primary and secondary schools based on the literacy, language, and numeracy needs.

In Western Australia, Student Services teams provides individual, group, and whole school/ professional learning support to assist schools to maintain learning environments that maximise students' educational and psycho-social outcomes.

The focus here is on assisting the classroom teacher, in the context of the regular classroom, to implement procedures and structures to support the teaching of students who have diverse learning needs. The consultancy staff work with class teachers to plan, develop, implement, monitor and evaluate programs for students experiencing difficulties in learning. They can offer individualised assessment and curriculum planning and adjustments to assist students who are at risk of underachieving or disengaging, or who would benefit from individualised curriculum planning. They can provide consultancy assistance through a range of avenues such as:

- team teaching;
- professional support and advice;
- support for peer tutoring and other learning assistance programs;
- withdrawal of students for assessment or short-term intensive instruction; and
- consultation services for parents/carers.

Sometimes the assistance is provided on the basis of the particular category or type of disability, for example assistance provided by a speech and language pathologist for a student who has communication difficulties. Recent examples of effective inclusive teaching activities for secondary level students who have visual impairments have been provided by Tomasik (2007) and for students who have moderate and severe disabilities by Kleinert, Miracle, & Sheppard-Jones (2007).

School counsellors or guidance officers can direct and assist teachers to modify classroom practices to deal with issues that affect educational progress and adjustment, including learning difficulties, behaviour management, social skills, family and peer relationships, and personal development.

The Department of Education and Training of Western Australia employs specialist teachers in the role of Visiting Teacher (Inclusive Education). These teachers guide schools to develop inclusive cultures and practices. They provide information about the education of students with disabilities and assist schools to develop programs and structures that support an inclusive school community. The Department also employs consultants in a Classroom Management Strategies (CMS) Program who implement the CMS professional learning program in schools.

You would need to make enquiries about the consultancy services provided in your school district through an official school request if you thought one or more of these would be beneficial in your teaching circumstances. In some states, each school has an allocated time provision for Support Teacher services. In other states access to specialised staff is based on demand.

You may have already made a connection between the services described here and the array of education placements shown in Figure 3.4. In most cases, you will need to provide a rationale for

requiring the service. This will include a clear description of the student's exceptional learning profile and the obstacles that restrict the student's learning.

PROFESSIONAL DEVELOPMENT OPPORTUNITIES

In addition to the consultancy assistance described above, education systems provide formal professional development opportunities on inclusive education. The activities that systems typically support include the following:

- One-off professional development activities conducted off the school site, as well as online professional development courses. These are sometimes developed around one or more categories of exceptional learning, for example Indigenous learners, gifted education, or mild to moderate intellectual disability with additional special needs. On other occasions they focus on a challenge or an issue, such as strategies to improve literacy or boys' education.

  These activities may help you learn more about learning issues and problems that arise in inclusive classrooms, particular learning needs, and teaching options for inclusive provision. Teachers generally need to make a commitment to explore ways in which they can change their teaching practice for them to be successful and to develop an implementation strategy.
- Professional development activities conducted off the school site, which encourage teachers to trial and evaluate particular teaching procedures between sessions. Sharing the outcomes with the group on subsequent occasions allows participants to broaden their teaching options further.
- Professional development activities which encourage teachers to learn new teaching approaches and provide coaching in how to use them, initially under supervision. These activities assist the teacher to convert new approaches into teaching actions and to have them evaluated.
- On-site professional development activities, which also allow teachers to work in collegiate teams to learn more about how to understand and to accommodate students who have diverse learning needs. The team develops and collates group knowledge about how to implement an inclusive teaching practice that is appropriate to the particular teaching–learning context.

These activities allow a group of staff to take control of their professional learning, support each other in improving their teaching, learn from each other, and develop a positive school approach. Staff can also collaborate in developing learning units for particular students or groups and engage in peer coaching to refine their teaching practice, and these help to build capacity for implementing inclusive education. This is where Jan, in the first case study, was keen to move her school. Her group was initially a pair.

Each of these activities has its own values in enhancing teaching practice. Teachers and school leaders can identify the professional development needs of staff for inclusive education at any time and decide which one or more of these options might suit their needs. Dialogue with system administrators can also assist in selecting the most appropriate activities to meet staff and school needs at any time. Useful questions that can guide their professional learning include:

- What are the issues that affect inclusive practices in my classroom?
- What does the progress of students with diverse learning needs tell me?
- What are the problems that specifically affect these students?
- Which problem/issue will I target first/second …?
- How well are all students adjusting to learning in an inclusive classroom?
- What does the feedback from students and parents tell me?

It is also useful to include parents/carers and members of the broader community in professional learning activities. In addition, collaboration between schools can build effective partnerships and a broader community capacity for inclusive education.

RESOURCES TO SUPPORT INCLUSIVE TEACHING

Most education systems, agencies, and organisations have developed resources to support teachers and schools to deliver inclusive education. In recent years, many have become available on the internet. Visit the URLs listed as you read this chapter. It will help to emphasise many of the points made and will break up the reading process into sensible chunks.

Internet-based resources need to be evaluated judiciously and strategically. They vary in the reliability and complexity of the information they provide, the purposes for which they were written, and their relevance to education in Australia. Given these caveats, some useful sources include:

- The materials provided by educational institutions and agencies. These include tool kits for teaching students who have exceptional learning needs, curriculum frameworks that specify how student knowledge in particular subject areas gradually changes, and extensive teaching programs such as the Language Support Program produced by Victoria's Department of Education and Early Childhood Development. These materials are examples of those provided by the education systems and are described in more detail in later sections of this chapter.
- Databases related to inclusive teaching. For example, the Australian Disability Clearinghouse on Education and Training (ADCET) <www.adcet.edu.au/default.aspx> provides information about inclusive teaching, learning and assessment strategies, and support services for people with disabilities in post secondary education and training.
- The LD OnLine site <www.ldonline.org> provides a range of articles and resources for educators interested in inclusion and students with diverse learning needs in regular classrooms: ADHD, behaviour and social skills, early identification, gifted students, individual education plans, processing deficits, dyslexia, special education, speech and language.
- Esmerel's Collection of Disability Resources <www.esmerel.org> is another site that provides links to disability-related resources relevant to inclusive education, such as adaptive technology, visual and hearing impairments, English as a Second Language, genetic disorders, rehabilitation, special education, speech and communication disabilities, and specific disability resources.
- Many agencies that target particular categories of exceptional learning provide information online. These include sites by the Autism Association of Western Australia, Indigenous education, or Down Syndrome of Victoria.
- Another example of an online resource is the Curriculum Toolkit *Including students with disabilities: A curriculum toolkit for schools and teachers* <www.sofweb.vic.edu.au/wellbeing/disabil/curriculum.htm> prepared by Melbourne's Royal Children's Hospital Education Institute. The toolkit provides information, strategies, and tools intended to assist school leadership teams and teachers to enhance learning and teaching practices for all students including those with disabilities. It comprises five components:
  1 student-centred planning;
  2 setting curriculum-based goals;
  3 teaching and learning strategies;
  4 maximising human resources; and
  5 positive behaviour support.

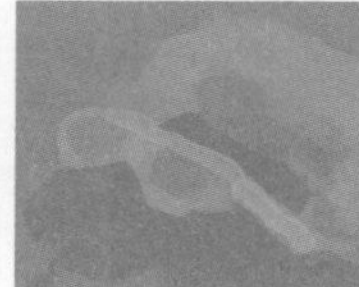

Each component is described in terms of its purpose. All five components are necessary to improve inclusive curriculum practice. Together they establish a benchmark of exemplary practice. Schools can also use the audit tool provided for each key component to match their practice with the exemplary procedures outlined in the resource.

- Yet another example of an online resource is the Education Queensland's Framework for Gifted Education. This site provides a framework for identifying key stakeholder needs in the education of students who are gifted and guidelines for acceleration within the compulsory years. A range of teaching resources are available at the Learning Place <www.learningplace.com.au/default_suborg.asp?orgid=23&suborgid=158>.

Curriculum frameworks and teaching guidelines

PROVISION OF CURRICULUM FRAMEWORKS

Educational systems provide curriculum frameworks that are intended to be accessible to all students. As well, they recommend providing all students with the teaching and learning opportunities necessary for success in school. The teaching needs to take account of diverse learning profiles. It needs to be intellectually challenging and build on students' background knowledge and cultural understanding.

The South Australian Curriculum Standards and Accountability Framework reflects this criterion of accessibility for all. Entitled *Curriculum Justice is Everybody's Business*, it ". . . reaffirms a long-held belief that education is central to the making of a fairer society. The flexibility of the SACSA Framework enables programs to be devised which do not privilege or exclude particular groups, and which encourage all learners to reach their potential and achieve success" (SACSA Framework, General Introduction, p. 7). It acknowledges the need for an inclusive curriculum framework to provide a teaching methodology and content that reflects the diversity of views and experiences. It recognises that some groups of learners need specific plans and programs to support their access to learning.

The SACSA Framework identifies various principles of equity that underpin curriculum justice. These can guide and scaffold the work of all educators. It recognises learner diversity as a foundation for curriculum and interprets this in terms of influences such as gender, socioeconomic status, Aboriginality, cultural and linguistic backgrounds, rural/urban location, ability, and sexuality. It acknowledges how these are associated with advantage and disadvantage.

As you will have read in Chapter 1, these influences exist in most Australian classrooms. They are likely to be more pronounced in inclusive learning contexts. Inclusive teaching practice needs to recognise them explicitly to optimise learning opportunities for all students. The Framework also identifies the need for effective partnerships between classrooms, families, the community, and other organisations.

MODIFIED CURRICULUM FRAMEWORKS FOR PARTICULAR LEARNING PROFILES

The curriculum frameworks provided by some state curriculum authorities have been modified to take account of particular categories of exceptional learning. These are examined in this section because of their implications for teaching practice.

Modifications to state curricula have been developed for students from Indigenous cultures, students who have English as their second language, gifted and talented students, and students with disabilities or learning difficulties such as intellectual or developmental delays. An example of this modification is the *English as a Second Language (ESL) Companion* to the Victorian Essential Learning Standards for English <http://vels.vcaa.vic.edu.au/support/esl/esl.html>. Have a look at this site before you read on.

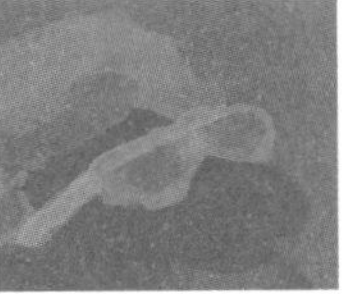

This modification is based on the idea that students who have English as their second language do not comprise a homogeneous group as they come from differing first-language backgrounds, with varying periods of education in their first language, and with varying levels of English competence.

The modifications are focused on these students pursuing the same goals in learning English as other students, but via different learning pathways and, therefore, they require alternative programs. The teaching alterations include explicit English language teaching, additional time, support, and exposure to English. The teaching alterations are seen as necessary before the English Standards can be appropriate for ESL students. The modifications are described using the same dimensions as the English standards.

There are 11 stages of ESL learning. As the students move through the stages, it is assumed that the English standards become more appropriate for their English knowledge, and when this approximates the levels of their peers, the English standards are used instead of the ESL standards. However, it is accepted that these students are still likely to need focused ESL teaching support.

Similar approaches to modifying curriculum frameworks have been developed by other education systems. They provide valuable tools for teaching in inclusive classrooms, both for understanding the learning of particular categories of exceptional students in inclusive classrooms and for developing teaching–learning pathways. You can investigate how this has been done by the system that has designed your school's curriculum framework.

BOX 4.2

Teaching strategies

The South Australian Curriculum Standards and Accountability Framework identifies a range of teaching strategies for educators that will be applicable to all education jurisdictions. These include recommending that teachers:

- Have high expectations and give high support for learners.
- Have stimulating and rewarding learning programs with regular diagnostic feedback on progress, processes and products, and opportunities for learners to take responsibility and exercise judgment.
- Draw on stories of hope and inspiration from a diverse range of perspectives.
- Use topics and context that are relevant to the learners' world and teach the knowledge, skills, and understandings that support their academic and social learning outcomes and the formation of a just society.
- Plan for flexible curriculum delivery and learning opportunities at school and in the wider community (i.e., moving in and out of school to undertake further studies and training).
- Promote the importance of mathematics and ICT for girls as well as boys in relation to their post-school aspirations, and the importance of the humanities for boys as well as girls in relation to civil and social life.
- Assist learners to participate in a range of school subjects, to enhance their opportunities to develop their full human, social, and cultural capital.
- Recognise and respect the diversity within and between groups of learners.

- Work with the understanding that language is neither neutral nor free of its context and plays a major role in including or excluding learners.
- Challenge narrow gender identities and peer groups that constrain rather than enable educational choice and flexibility.
- Create specific groupings (e.g., girls groups, boys groups) for some tasks or topics.
- Assist learners with the skills and understandings to build positive and flexible identities, which means they develop positive relations and get on well with others, both like them and unlike them.
- Structure specific activities to consciously promote better working relationships and understandings between girls and boys.
- Develop a school culture that is characterised by a welcoming environment in which students and their families are valued, and where there is active elimination of harassment, violence, and bias.
- Ensure anti-discrimination legislation is enacted in the classroom even in seemingly insignificant occurrences.
- Incorporate equity and just futures perspectives across curriculum, teaching, and learning.

These bullet points illustrate how a system perceives good teaching practice in inclusive classrooms. Can you imagine what each of these would look like in your teaching?

4.2

INDIVIDUAL LEARNING AND TEACHING PLANS

Most education systems require teachers and schools to design and use detailed teaching–learning plans for students with particular learning needs. They are included in the teaching essentials section because they relate directly to how the student will be taught in the classroom.

Individual learning pathways can take various forms. They include individualised learning plans, individualised education plans (IEPs) and individualised assessment plans. One version of this planning is the Negotiated Education Planning process developed by the Department of Education and Children's Services in South Australia.

These plans provide pathways for students whose learning profiles suggest that they would benefit from specific provisions beyond those currently offered within their classroom. They indicate what support is required for student participation and achievement and specify procedures for modifying the curriculum, teaching practices, and learning outcomes for these students. They set out the background information, ability, performance, strengths, and needs of the student and the learning goals.

To develop the plan for any student, some key questions teachers may ask include:

- How do I set outcome targets and specific goals for the individual student?
- What are the steps involved in moving toward each goal?
- What teaching, materials, and resources will be necessary?
- How do I establish the entry skills?
- How will I monitor student progress?

These sets of questions will help you to become an effective teacher. For these questions to be useful, you will need to stop and consider the questions and generate some answers before you read on. Don't just read on without thinking about the questions and writing some answers. The pathways are most effective if the teaching draws on what learners know. A negotiated education plan, for example, includes the following:

- the purpose of the plan;
- a statement about who is responsible for the process;
- eligibility criteria;
- legislation/policy information;
- the teaching and learning plan;
- a parent brochure;
- a list of support services that are available to the student; and
- referral forms.

The plan for any student is developed collaboratively with ongoing input from teachers, parents/carers, other relevant professionals, support agencies, and students. Teachers and schools should note that, while parent participation is a key aspect of the planning, their perspectives are often not understood or used in the decision-making process (Yssel, Engelbrecht, Oswald, Eloff, & Swart, 2007).

The plan is negotiated, reviewed, and updated on a regular basis. Education systems frequently provide guidance in doing this. The Negotiated Education Planning process, for example, is based on the South Australian Curriculum Standards Accountability framework and the needs of the learner.

Plans can be developed for gifted students, those who have a learning difficulty, and those who require formal assessments of their learning needs and specialist support, such as Language Pathology services. They are also useful for students with a disability who require high frequency adjustments to gain access to curriculum and specialist support staff in areas of intellectual delay, global developmental delay, vision, hearing, or physical disability, as well as Autism Spectrum Disorders and Asperger's syndrome. Students for whom English is a second language also benefit from a plan that specifies access to ESL support.

It is important to recognise that school contexts may differ in the ease with which individualised education programs can be implemented. Nolan (1994), for example, compared the development and implementation of IEPs for students with mild intellectual disabilities in primary and secondary schools. Primary school teachers were more able than their secondary colleagues to do this.

The results may be related to organisational and teaching–learning differences between the two contexts, and suggest the need for preservice and inservice training that assists secondary teachers to implement IEPs in their context.

Once the plan has been specified, the education system frequently evaluates the extent of additional support needed by the student to participate in a broad and balanced education. A level of resourcing is allocated to each student and is provided to the school to be used to support teaching strategies and goals.

Monitoring and reviewing

MONITORING AND REPORTING

Effective inclusive classrooms have clear, explicit procedures for monitoring students' learning outcomes. Education systems provide various way of doing this, in particular through:

- developmental curricula that describe progress in student knowledge; and
- assessment procedures for monitoring and interpreting student knowledge at any time.

Both tools are valuable in describing student learning progress in inclusive classrooms.

Most curriculum frameworks specify increments in student knowledge on continua. An example is the English Developmental Continuum P–10 for the English Domain of the Victorian Essential Learning Standards <www.education.vic.gov.au/studentlearning/teachingresources/english/englishcontinuum/reading/default.htm>. The continuum provides six-monthly indicators of progress in reading, speaking and listening, and writing. With the modified versions of the continua to take account of diverse learning needs, the progress of individual students is easy to monitor. It also assists teachers to identify and describe the range of English knowledge and skills in a class.

Statewide testing in specific subject areas is increasingly being modified to describe the progress of particular categories of students. An example of this is the data available to schools from the Achievement Improvement Monitor (AIM) English assessment program conducted in Victoria <www.vcaa.vic.edu.au/prep10/aim/testing/index.html>. The data permit teachers and schools to describe the reading and writing profiles of individual students in terms of the particular literacy strategies they use. These data permit effective follow-up teaching based on how the students learn.

Systems can collate group data that they can use to analyse performance trends in classrooms and to set benchmarks for particular groups of students, including those who may be at risk of educational disadvantage. They provide the collated data to schools, where it can be used to interpret the learning of individual students and groups. When teachers are aware of the learning profiles in their classes, they can use the matching system-level achievement trends to monitor the corresponding students in their class.

Systems usually require teachers who work in an inclusive classroom to monitor the learning progress of students and the effectiveness of the teaching as the students move through the learning plans described in the earlier section. The questions that systems recommend teachers use to guide them to do this include the following:

- How can I rate the overall progress of individual students?
- What would be evidence of progress?
- What processes can I use to collect this evidence?
- How do I identify when the student has achieved particular steps toward the goals?
- What would be indicators of reaching intermediate steps on the learning path?
- How will I measure between intermediate steps?
- How do I establish the entry skills?
- How will I report and measure student progress?

Teachers can meet the system's requirements for monitoring student learning by responding to these questions. They can also use the questions to modify individual teaching–learning programs to optimise students' progress.

REVIEWING PROGRAMS

Most education systems have processes for reviewing how well programs are implemented for students with particular learning needs. They require a formal In-School Review for all students having access to a special education service. The review is based on a formal meeting to discuss progress and make recommendations for the next phase of inclusive education. Review meetings are held each year. Teachers and school administrators can use the reviews to monitor the impact of policies and programs

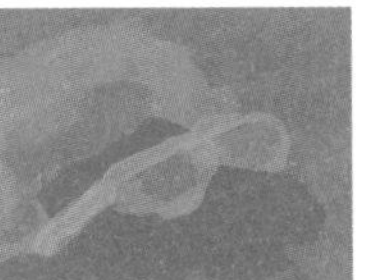

in their classrooms. They can analyse the educational progress of all students and those who are, or have been, educationally disadvantaged.

Take a few minutes to see how systems can inform the ongoing monitoring of program provision by examining the approach described in *Measuring academic progress against each KLA: Students with disabilities*. This publication, by Victoria's Department of Education and Early Childhood Development <www.eduweb.vic.gov.au/edulibrary/public/stuman/wellbeing/daiprogress.pdf>, highlights issues and problems commonly associated with monitoring programs for students with diverse learning needs.

A key issue for any inclusive program and for the system implementing it is how the various aspects are integrated over time. This can be described in terms of student learning progress, monitoring over time how well the planning for students works, how progress is reported, and how teaching and the curriculum are modified. Weilenmann (2003) described the integration for the inclusion model implemented in a public school system in the District of Columbia, USA. The performance patterns and program placement for a group of 75 special education students were monitored over a five-year period from kindergarten to second grade.

While the outcomes of the study are relevant to its location and time, the framework used to monitor progress of students would be value to any school and educational system. The factors in the framework include:

- the reason for a student being referred to special education services, that is, the exceptional learning profiles of students;
- changes in a student's learning profile, as indicated in their IEP;
- changes in students' access to special education services, for example in terms of the time involved;
- the extent and level of classroom modifications and accommodations needed as the student progressed;
- the extent to which the progress reporting procedures (such as report cards) needed to be modified as students progressed through the grades; and
- the extent to which individual students achieved the IEP goals.

A school can use these factors to describe the progress of students involved in inclusive programs and to examine, from a school perspective, how the programs are progressing, and where modifications can be made. Classroom teachers would obviously need to develop procedures for collecting and collating these data in an ongoing way. The data collection could include portfolios of student achievements.

Safe classrooms

Providing a safe learning environment and climate is an important issue in every school. Students with particular learning needs can be threatened in various ways. First, they may be more likely to experience physical threats to their safety because they do not have well-developed perceptual motor or sensory-perceptual skills that allow them to detect or remove themselves from physical danger, for example when playing games, using equipment such as scissors, or crossing a road. Education systems provide advice for making inclusive contexts safer. They recommend, for instance, how to improve the safety on excursions, when students are engaging in sport activities such as swimming, and when taking these students on school camps.

Second, students may also experience (or perceive) emotional threats such as teasing or bullying. Students may perceive instances of discrimination, non-inclusion, and/or harassment. These can affect a student's ability to participate fully in schooling and lower their sense of wellbeing. This issue is dealt with more fully in Chapter 5.

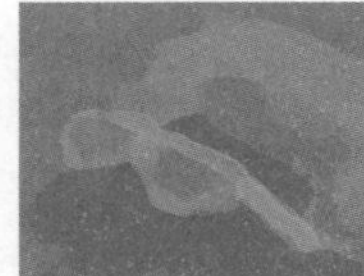

Education systems also provide advice on fostering and supporting student wellbeing. The Inclusive Education Standards Directorate of Department of Education and Training of Western Australia, for example, runs programs and strategies to assist teachers and schools with effective social skills, a healthy lifestyle, and resilience. These include identification, prevention, and intervention processes.

Third, the diverse learning profiles of some students may restrict effective decision making in some situations. As a result, the students may be less able to recognise or to extricate themselves from potentially threatening or dangerous situations. These students benefit from being taught health practices that maintain and promote their good health. Education systems provide advice and support to teachers and schools in the area of student health, for example, through the implementation of the *Student Health Care* policy in Western Australia.

You can get an insight into resilience from *Developing Resiliency in Young People K–12*, available at <www.who.int/school_youth_health/media/en/92.pdf>. This resource unpacks the concept of resilience, and shows how it affects student wellbeing and educational outcomes. It links educational risk with various social-emotional factors and disengagement from school, unacceptable behaviour, and a decline in personal health and wellbeing. It shows how the key to developing social competence in children and adolescents is to foster a sense of belonging to one's family and school. It recommends a range of strategies for promoting resiliency in students and creating resiliency-building schools.

Students involved in inclusive education programs may also require a level of protection not necessary for other students. System resources assist teachers and schools to protect the safety and welfare of students in many ways, for example through the implementation of a Child Protection policy and procedures. In some states, all school staff complete professional development programs, for instance the *Child Protection Professional Learning Program* in Western Australia. The Department of Education and Children's Services in South Australia also provides a link to 'Protecting Children & Young People with Disabilities', a useful resource relating to critical child protection issues.

Teachers must be aware of these possible threatening situations, recognise them when they occur, and take steps to deal with them. The system support and guidance provided assist the school leadership to develop school strategies and programs and assist the teachers to use classroom-based procedures for responding to issues such as victimisation and harassment and reducing their incidence.

School-level support and guidance

Systems provide an indication of what classroom teachers might reasonably expect of their school leadership in terms of support and guidance for implementing inclusive education policy and practices. Most suggest that it is the responsibility of the school leadership teams to:

school culture
A term used to describe the beliefs, values, habits, and assumed ways of doing things in a school community.

- foster and develop a school culture that reflects high expectations for all students and that treats all students with dignity so they can enjoy the benefits of education and the same general rights and opportunities through enrolment, participation, access to curriculum, and achievement;
- embed across the school an inclusive approach to curriculum development, teaching, learning, and resource selection;
- identify and resolve barriers to student access through consultation and collaboration;
- build a school-wide capacity to support all students by collaborating and networking with other service providers;
- establish open and positive relationships with parents/carers and the wider community to improve access to programs, facilities, information, and expertise; and
- implement school-based data collection on student achievement, retention, and participation to evaluate progress and identify priorities for school improvement.

The position taken by most systems on the importance of the school leadership team is supported by research (Bovalino, 2007; Ingram, 1994). Bovalino, for example, showed that inclusive education is more likely to be successful in education systems in which school leaders implement distributed leadership, encourage professional development, and share their vision of inclusion in the regular classrooms in an ongoing way. Ubben and Hughes (1992) noted that the school leader is increasingly seen as the key agent in establishing a climate for inclusion.

distributed leadership

A situation in which all staff members are considered experts in their own right with important sources of knowledge and experience. All staff members are considered to be responsible and accountable for leadership within their areas, and everyone feels free to develop and share ideas.

In the first case study, for example, Jan found little guidance or leadership from the leadership team in her school. This was based largely on little knowledge of what was possible and a lack of commitment. Over the subsequent months she was able to use a list similar to the above to seek support from the leadership team.

System influences

Most of the issues referred to above are relevant to all levels of education. There are some systemic issues, however, that relate to particular levels. You can generally locate these through a web search. I'll mention just two here.

First, in some jurisdictions there has been recent recognition of the importance of early intervention for preschool students who have diverse learning needs. The goal is to assist them to acquire the knowledge necessary for effective learning in regular contexts. These include Early Intervention Units for younger children who have particular learning needs. A key focus of these has been on speech and language development.

early intervention

A program provided for young children with a disability or impairment to optimise their chances of enrolment in regular education programs. Typically, early interventions focus on management of bodily functions and on preacademic skills, such as concept development.

Factors that contribute to the success of these programs have been noted by Purcell, Horn, and Palmer (2007) and by Rasowsky (2007). They include a shared vision, strategies for using key staff effectively, and developing a clear structure for implementing each program.

Second, education systems have also recognised the need to assist the transition of students with learning difficulties into further education. In most education systems there are retention and transition programs to support 15–17 year olds through Individual Pathway Plans that focus on suitable education/training, work, and/or employment options.

LEARNING ESSENTIALS

This section examines how state and other education systems approach the practicalities of inclusion from the learner's perspective. How do educational systems help teachers to:

- understand the learning profiles of students?
- identify the learning needs of individual students?
- implement appraisal procedures to allow equitable allocation of resources for students with disabilities?
- provide programs for students with particular learning profiles?

Student learning profiles

Effective teaching takes account of what students know and how they learn. To do this, teachers and other school personnel need a set of tools to describe a range of learning profiles.

Classification systems are in place in every Australian education system. This seems contrary to inclusive education philosophies but they are useful to identify what is usual or typical ways of thinking and behaving in the culture in which the student has grown up. While it is misleading to think in terms of generalised learning profiles and stereotypes of learners (e.g., student with ASD or Down syndrome), each category within a classification system can be a helpful starting point from which to consider a

student's unique cluster of learning characteristics. This will help begin the process of understanding how any student might learn.

You can get more information about how each cluster learns by exploring the relevant websites provided by the systems operating in your region. There are, in addition, many specialist sites that describe the generic issues faced by students in each category.

Identifying the learning needs of individual students

A second way in which the systems assist teachers and schools to get information about how individual students learn is through specialist learning diagnostic services. As noted in the *Teaching essentials* section, the education systems provide diagnosticians to guide teachers and schools to implement effective teaching and to develop learning pathways and plans for students. A range of professional services is usually available for this assessment.

Teachers trained in learning difficulties, for example, can assess a student's academic attainment and the learning capacities in these areas. Speech and language pathologists assess a student's use of speech and language and the student's linguistic readiness for literacy and for interacting socially. Audiologists assess a student's hearing capacities. Education psychologists (or guidance officers) assess the student's reasoning abilities, learning competence, emotional development, management of challenging behaviours, and self-confidence. Other professionals such as paediatricians, opthamologists, and occupational therapists can also contribute.

audiologist

A non-medical practitioner who evaluates the degree of hearing impairment and prescribes hearing aids.

occupational therapist

A paramedicist or rehabilitation professional who works to improve the patient's muscular control, often through the use of handicrafts or other creative art activities. Occupational therapists are most commonly employed in hospitals and facilities for aged people and for those with an intellectual disability.

Equitable allocation of resources

All education systems in Australia have procedures in place to ascertain an equitable level of resourcing necessary to educate the student in a regular classroom. While they may differ in the detail, they follow an essentially similar set of procedures. As an example, the approach used in South Australia is described here.

Resourcing in South Australia is provided through the Disability Support Program administered by the Department of Education and Children's Services. To be eligible for support, a student must be verified, through formal assessment procedures, as having a disability in one of the following categories:

- intellectual;
- global developmental delay;
- speech and/or language;
- vision and/or hearing;
- ASD/Asperger syndrome; and
- physical capabilities.

There is a set of eligibility criteria for each category. Explore these at <www.decs.sa.gov.au/svpst/files/links/DE705_Elig_Crit_booklet_1_2.pdf>. The criteria are matched against the assessment and general disability information gathered by a Guidance Officer/Psychologist (Early Childhood) and/or Speech Pathologist. Eligibility criteria like the South Australian version are similar in all states and territories.

Once a student is verified as being eligible for the program, a district disability coordinator works with the school to describe the educational needs of the student and match these against a level of support. The coordinator uses the school's knowledge of the student, learning assessment results and the Level of Support guidelines below to allocate the appropriate level of support, based on the

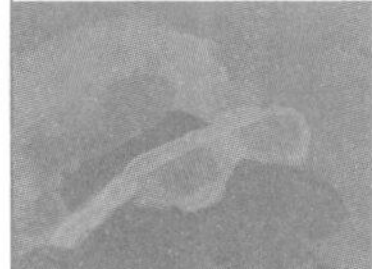

TABLE 4.1 LEVEL OF SUPPORT CATEGORIES

<table>
<tr><th>Level of support</th><th colspan="2">Type of support</th></tr>
<tr><td>Review</td><td colspan="2">District Support Services staff monitor the student's progress. A Negotiated Education Plan (NEP) will set out goals for the student.</td></tr>
<tr><td>Consultation</td><td colspan="2">District Support Services staff provide support to the student or his/her teacher.</td></tr>
<tr><td>Additional</td><td>Level of Support one</td><td rowspan="3">Funding is allocated to the school to support the achievement of learning goals and to make the necessary adjustments to enable the student to participate in the curriculum.</td></tr>
<tr><td>Direct</td><td>Level of Support two</td></tr>
<tr><td>Intensive</td><td>Level of Support three</td></tr>
<tr><td>High sustained level</td><td>Vision and hearing loss</td><td>Central funding approval</td></tr>
<tr><td>Very high sustained level</td><td></td><td></td></tr>
<tr><td>Severe and multiple disabilities</td><td></td><td></td></tr>
</table>

learner's needs. A state panel application process is required for Intensive (I), High sustained (H) and Very high sustained (V) levels of support.

The level of support categories are shown in Table 4.1.

A Negotiated Education Planning process, described earlier, is developed in partnership with parents, relevant support services and agencies, and the schools.

If you work in an inclusive classroom, it is useful to be aware of the criteria used by your school system to allocate resources to particular levels of learning need. For state schools in Victoria, for example, the *Program for Students with Disabilities Guidelines* is available at <www.sofweb.vic.edu.au/wellbeing/disabil/psdhandbook.htm>.

You can note:

- the categories of learning that are resourced;
- the formal assessment procedures used;
- the eligibility criteria for each category; and
- the means by which the level of support is ascertained.

In this way you can ensure that you and your students have the resources necessary for effective learning and teaching in your class. It also allows you to collect relevant data for ascertaining the level of support appropriate for a student.

PROGRAMS FOR EXCEPTIONAL STUDENTS IN REGULAR SCHOOLS

All education systems provide various programs for students who have exceptional learning profiles. They are usually based on categories and cater for particular age ranges. Their goal is usually to

enhance the students' competence to learn in regular classrooms. Some of these programs involve temporary withdrawal from the regular contexts.

Knowledge of these programs can enhance your work as an inclusive education teacher in several ways. First, it may stimulate you to investigate the support programs available to you and to students with exceptional learning needs in your classroom. Second, you may want to learn more about the nature of the teaching approaches used in these programs. Third, the programs are likely to broaden your understanding of exceptional learning needs.

In this section, I will deal briefly with programs offered by systems for three categories of exceptional learning only:

- Indigenous students;
- students who are diagnosed with ASD; and
- students who have learning difficulties.

SUPPORTING INDIGENOUS STUDENTS

Most education systems provide a range of programs and strategies to improve Indigenous students' access to, and participation in, all levels of education. Obstacles frequently arise in relation to successful literacy and numeracy learning and in relation to seeing school education as a pathway to future options. They also arise because non-Indigenous teachers are often less able to incorporate aspects of Indigenous cultures and ways of thinking into the classroom.

Regular classroom and school provision needs to be modified to deal with these barriers. The education systems provide programs in these areas. Examples of system provision in this area are the *School Programs for Aboriginal Students* provided by the Department of Education in New South Wales <www.aboriginaleducation.nsw.edu.au/school_programs/index.html> and the Western Australia Department of Education and Training website for Aboriginal Education and Training, Participation and Achievement Standards Directorate <www.det.wa.edu.au/education/Abled/index.html>.

Inclusive education opportunities for Indigenous students are facilitated by the education systems in several ways. They provide programs to improve literacy and numeracy outcomes for students, particularly in years K–2. One cause of low literacy achievement is a middle-ear infection (such as otitis media or gluey ear). A second relates to the transition of these students from home to school, with fewer students attending preschools. Strategies recognise these and provide programs for Indigenous students and their families and for training professional staff to assist classroom teachers in these areas.

otitis media
An inflammation of the middle ear and one cause of conductive hearing loss.

Many systems also provide strategies aimed at improving the participation of Indigenous students in school leadership positions. An increased participation rate helps these students to see a pathway through education for realistic career and futures planning. It also provides ongoing opportunities for them to display their knowledge and to receive positive feedback. Seeing peers perform leadership roles and responsibilities provides other Indigenous students with successful models.

Classroom practice is more likely to be inclusive when students can perceive aspects of their cultural experiences in the classroom environment and when they can see their culture is understood and valued. School systems provide specially trained teaching staff, including aides to guide and support the learning of Indigenous students in inclusive classrooms. These staff members also work with classroom teachers, parents, and community members to improve the access and participation of Indigenous students at all levels of schooling.

They also provide, through professional development, opportunities for teachers to learn more about Indigenous cultures and the beliefs and ways of thinking that underpin them. This knowledge is particularly valuable to teachers who have Indigenous students in their classroom or school. The

program *What Works. The Work Program* <www.whatworks.edu.au> provides such guidance. It is based in part on research from the Australian Government Indigenous Education Strategic Initiatives Programme's Strategic Results Projects. It is web-based and interactive.

Inclusive learning programs assist Indigenous students to make the transition to employment. Vocational Education and Training (VET) programs are provided through TAFE in the various states. Staff from Indigenous backgrounds are usually available both for teaching and for individual student support and guidance.

STUDENTS WHO HAVE AUTISM SPECTRUM DISORDER

Autism Spectrum Disorder (ASD) can seriously restrict students' ability to participate in inclusive classrooms. Education systems are aware of this. An example of a system's response to this issue is the *Autism State Plan* <www.sofweb.vic.edu.au/wellbeing/disabil/index.htm#H2N40010F> developed by the Student Wellbeing Branch of Victoria's Department of Education and Early Childhood Development. The plan is developed in partnership with Autism Victoria. A key goal is to support students with Autism Spectrum Disorders in all government schools.

To accommodate students with ASD in an inclusive setting, teachers need to be aware of the characteristic learning profiles of these students and how to improve their access to the curriculum. Briefly, these students have difficulty learning in inclusive classrooms because of communication difficulties, impaired social skills, behavioural responses, and their unique learning styles.

A more complete description can be found in Bob Conway's chapter and you can obtain more in-depth information about this profile by contacting organisations that support young people and families in which there is a person with ASD.

Most education systems provide a suite of programs and strategies to support these students with access to, and participation in, all levels of education. They provide:

- teacher consultancy, school support, and professional learning programs aimed at increasing awareness of the impact of ASD on teaching and learning and effective practices; and
- assessment and diagnostic support that is used to identify students who have ASD and how they go about learning and interacting—these data are mapped onto a learning plan for each student, which usually involves school psychological and other specialist input.

In some cases, these students have significant difficulties adjusting to mainstream schooling. They need temporary access to alternative programs that help them learn how to learn effectively in regular classrooms. These programs are usually intensive and short-term and offer support to students with the greatest needs. They usually work collaboratively with schools, parents/carers, and community agencies.

An example of this type of system response is the provision of intervention services by the ACT Department of Education and Training <www.decs.act.gov.au/services/SpecEdServices.htm>. Children in the preschool years who are identified as having ASD can attend a small group intervention unit within a regular preschool environment. School-age students can attend a small group setting that is again located within a regular school environment. Each school can develop its own model of delivery, which includes a balanced program comprising individual and small group instruction as well as supported inclusion into regular classes as appropriate.

STUDENTS WITH LEARNING DIFFICULTIES

Approximately 16% of students in regular classrooms have difficulty with literacy and numeracy (*Building Inclusive Schools, Department of Education and Training*, 2004). To accommodate these students, teachers need to be aware of their learning profiles. The difficulty may be due to causes

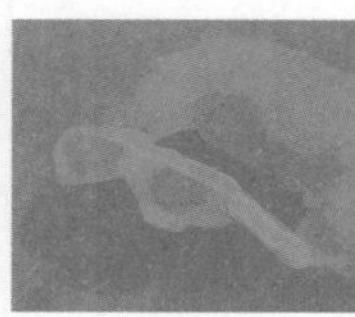

ranging from cultural–environmental factors to sensory–perceptual difficulties, such as visual difficulties. Some students don't use the cognitive or psycholinguistic processes necessary for learning, such as recognising and forming sound patterns or learning visual symbols such as letter patterns, despite having general reasoning and intellectual ability within the normal range.

Most education systems provide a range of programs and strategies to support students who have learning difficulties. These include:

- teacher consultancy and professional learning opportunities similar to those provided for students with ASD, but specifically targeting numeracy and literacy;
- assessment and diagnostic support usually completed by staff trained in learning difficulties, including assessment by speech pathologists and psychologists; and
- programs implemented by specifically trained teachers, such as Reading Recovery, that has been used extensively in primary schools throughout Australia (for further commentary about Reading Recovery, see Chapter 8).

Reading Recovery

Developed in New Zealand by Professor Marie Clay, this program selects the children at age six who have the poorest performance in reading and writing and tries to bring them to average levels of performance. Tuition is individualised and lasts about 12–20 weeks.

Education systems in Australia are increasingly recognising the importance of early language competence for later learning and as a means of reducing the incidence of learning difficulties. Enhancing oral language competence early may reduce the incidence or severity of learning difficulties later. The Language Support Program produced by Victoria's Department of Education and Early Childhood Development in 2005 exemplifies this position. The initiative began with the development of teacher professional learning materials to help teachers to implement teaching that fostered language. The materials are available at <www.eduweb.vic.gov.au/edulibrary/public/stuman/wellbeing/DRAFT_LDP_Workbook_v1.pdf>. Staff from each region were trained to implement the program and it was launched as a statewide initiative. Regional implementation included teacher consultancy and development, the development of class-level teaching and learning materials, and small group student teaching sessions for students who had difficulty accessing classroom teaching.

USING THIS CHAPTER IN SCHOOLS

When you first begin to teach, your focus is on your classroom. It is on the students and how you will work with them. You see individual faces and also a group. You have the teaching activities you have prepared, and knowledge and procedures to help you communicate the curriculum to your students. In addition, you will have learnt about managing behaviour and how to guide your students to maintain a positive and supportive learning environment.

Your focus is also very much in the present. It is only after a while that you begin to see how the learning and behaviours of individual students change over time and across settings. You also see how some students differ from others in many ways.

This chapter is about matters that are beyond the here and now of the classroom that you see. First, it is about your classroom being one of many hundreds within a system, all with a similar cross-section of students. It is also about how the system can help you, and the teachers in other classrooms, to deal with these differences so that all students make optimal progress. The more you know about how your school system can do this, the better you will be able to seek and use the assistance they provide, such as information sources and support services.

Teaching

How can you be assisted in your teaching by the system in which you work? You can investigate the possibility of both in-school consultancy support and various professional development opportunities.

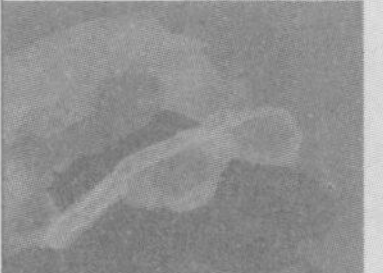

As you learn more about the individual learning profiles of students in your class, you will get a better impression of where assistance would be of most help. You can also learn from your school about the forms of assistance that are available and how you can gain access to them.

To use a range of available resources, you need to be clear on the particular problems or issues you want to solve. Otherwise, you might spend a good deal of time pursuing interesting but irrelevant information sources.

The following questions can assist you to focus on how you might use the available resources to broaden your teaching capabilities to accommodate the diverse ways in which students learn. To what extent do you need to:

- modify how you organise the curriculum content you will teach to capture the interest of learners and increase their learning success? You may need to use familiar contexts or multiple formats. Individual consultancy and professional learning activities provided by your school system may assist here.
- modify how you teach so that you can guide the learning of these students? Some students need additional assistance to interpret the curriculum content and stay focused and to review, consolidate, and demonstrate what they have learnt. You can examine the curriculum frameworks and teaching guidelines provided by your system.
- modify and extend how you use students' learning pathways to implement the teaching? The earlier discussion relating to development and use of individual and classroom curriculum plans can assist here.
- modify how you monitor the learning outcomes of these students and provide feedback? You can investigate the ways in which your system assists with procedures to monitor and review inclusive teaching and the range of assessment and reporting processes used in inclusive teaching.
- modify the classroom management procedures you use with these students?
- modify your classroom organisation, such as seating, learning spaces, assistive technology?

To influence your students' learning outcomes, you need to put the new knowledge you gain from professional development or online research into practice. This means reflecting on what you have learned, what it means for your teaching situation, and how you can apply that information for your students' benefit. Remember to look for the general principles rather than for specific examples or specific teaching–learning events. Examples that are given in early childhood or senior secondary levels have underlying principles that apply across all levels. Coaching and guidance from experienced colleagues or from consultants can be of great help here.

You also need to know what is reasonable to expect of your school leadership in terms of support and guidance. As well, you need to evaluate the quality of your working relationship with parents/carers of your students, and with the broader community. It may be useful to reflect on how you could enhance this collaboration. You will read more about this in Chapter 12.

Learning

In the *Learning essentials* section, it was noted how educational systems could assist you to understand students' learning profiles. A place to start is to observe the students who you believe are displaying exceptional learning characteristics and for whom adjustments or modifications to regular classroom practice seem necessary. Noting the needs of these students, the contexts and conditions under which they do and don't learn well, and the exceptional or unusual behaviours they show will be invaluable information when constructing learning profiles for such students.

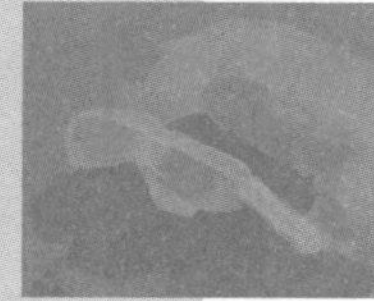

To assist with this, you can use the checklist for collating a student's learning capacity profile shown in Box 4.3. At the same time you can familiarise yourself with how the system describes various categories of exceptional learning and see if you can recognise these in the students in your classroom. This will help you to fill in some details that relate specifically to those individuals. Remember that characteristics that might be common in young people who have a particular diagnosis are not all represented in every individual. You will need to modify or fine tune the profiles for your own student and match your teaching to those.

BOX 4.3 Learning capacity profile

Name: ______________________________ Date: ________

Rate the frequency with which the student has differed from her/his peers on each of the following criteria. Each criterion is rated as "1" or never if the student never differs in this way, 2 if the student on a few occasions has differed in this way, 3 if the student has sometimes differed in this way, 4 if the student often differs in this way, and 5 if the student always differs in this way.

To what extent does the student differ from peers in their ability to:

	1	2	3	4	5
use the visual information to learn?					
hear and interpret the auditory information used in teaching?					
use the fine motor and dexterity skills needed for classroom learning?					
link what they need to do with what they see or hear in order to learn?					
understand concepts about space and time in the required ways?					
cope with changes in their physical environments?					
use language to learn new ways of thinking?					
maintain on-task attention and persevere with tasks?					
retain information they hear or see as part of teaching and learning?					
use language effectively to manage their actions?					
communicate effectively in social situations to achieve their goals?					

	1	2	3	4	5
learn various areas of knowledge and skills incidentally and spontaneously?					
use the corrective feedback they receive?					
store new knowledge in memory and recall it easily?					

BOX 4.3

A second step involves being aware of how you can obtain additional information about how individual students learn. Specialist diagnostic services may help and this is particularly valuable when combined with your own observational data. Most diagnosticians describe the outcomes of their assessments in written reports. Ask the diagnostician to explain what the assessment outcomes mean for the student learning in your classroom and how the teaching needs to be modified. One common criticism of such reports is their separation from classroom practices. Raise questions with specialists about how the student's learning can be supported, what are reasonable expectations, how well the student can learn independently, and how the student might interact with peers.

fine and gross motor skills
Those skills associated with the use of small muscles (e.g., finger movement) and large muscles (e.g., arms, legs, trunk).

There are two important outcomes of specialist assessments. The first provides the basis for an explicit teaching–learning plan for the target student. The second provides an idea of the level of resourcing necessary to educate the student in a regular classroom. You may want to investigate how the educational system in which you work achieves these two goals.

PRACTICAL ACTIVITIES

Uni-work

1 All education systems in Australia, state and private, have procedures in place to ascertain the level of resourcing necessary to educate the student in a regular classroom. While they differ in the detail they use to make these decisions, they follow an essentially similar set of procedures. Do a web search of four education systems. You might want to expand your search to at least one system in another country. Note their similarities and differences in:
   - the categories they use to describe exceptional learning;
   - the set of eligibility criteria the system uses for each category;
   - the assessment information that is collected to ascertain eligibility;
   - procedures followed to determine the appropriate level of support; and
   - the use of the information to develop a learning plan.

   Write up some comments about the implications of the differences for student learning opportunities. Decide whether there is evidence to support or refute an Australia-wide approach to ascertaining the level of resourcing.

2 All students involved in inclusive classrooms are expected to learn literacy and numeracy knowledge and skills. Select four categories of exceptional learning. Investigate how the typical learning profiles of each group might influence their capacity to learn and the teaching procedures that are most effective for the group. Investigate the particular programs used in your

state or territory to assist each category of learner to learn literacy and numeracy in regular classrooms.

3 What are the tools provided by educational systems to teachers and schools to monitor the effectiveness of inclusive teaching practice? Select an educational system and research the means by which it makes these resources available to teachers and schools. You may need to approach someone in the education system to complete this activity, rather than expecting to find all the answers on the web.

School-work

Before beginning any of the following activities, check with your supervising teacher or a member of the school administration to confirm that you can undertake the activity within existing school guidelines and policies.

4 Implementing an inclusive classroom involves removing barriers to learning. A key source of obstacles is the mismatch between how a student learns and the learning demands made by the teaching. Find three examples of this mismatch in your class or in a class in which you have participated. How can teachers become aware of this type of obstacle? How can they go about modifying their teaching to remove or reduce this obstacle? What opportunities are provided by your education system to assist teachers and schools to become aware of this type of obstacle and how to deal with it?

5 Effective teaching–learning plans are key aspects of inclusive classrooms. Locate and evaluate two teaching–learning plans. What are their key features? How are they used? How could they be used more effectively? Investigate what your system recommends about designing such plans. In what ways would you recommend they be modified to improve their usefulness?

6 Discuss with other teachers in your school the effectiveness of recent professional development activities in which they have participated. Under what circumstances did the activities lead to the teachers modifying their teaching so that it was now more inclusive? What do the teachers see as barriers in the school to implementing more inclusive teaching practice?

SUGGESTED READING AND RESOURCES

Most systems communicate with schools and teachers using the internet. They provide a range of online resources that are regularly updated. The suggested reading and resources here are websites together with a brief description of what they contain.

Department of Education and Children's Services (2006). South Australian Curriculum Standards and Accountability Framework *Curriculum Justice is Everybody's Business*—Revised. Adelaide: DE&CS <www.sacsa.sa.edu.au/index_fsrc.asp?t=LL>. This website exemplifies the response of a system to the challenge of providing an inclusive curriculum for all students. It includes principles of equity on which teaching can be based, planning and programming, teaching strategies, strategies for data collection, policies, and frameworks, and provides links to curriculum provision for particular groups of learners.

Department of Education and Children's Services (2006). Disability Support Program 2007 Eligibility Criteria. Adelaide: DE&CS. <www.decs.sa.gov.au/svpst/files/links/DE705_Elig_Crit_booklet_1_2.pdf>. This document illustrates clearly how systems determine whether individual students are eligible for additional resources to support their inclusion in regular classrooms.

Department of Education, Employment and Training (2005). Language Support Program. Melbourne: DEET <www.eduweb.vic.gov.au/edulibrary/public/stuman/wellbeing/DRAFT_LDP_Workbook_v1.pdf>. Many students

involved in inclusive education programs have particular language learning needs. This set of resources, part of the Program for Students with Disabilities, provides teachers with a range of strategies for assisting students to improve their oral language communication in regular classroom contexts.

Department of Education, Science and Training (2005). What Works. The Work Program. Canberra: DEST <www.whatworks.edu.au>. This interactive website provides a range of relevant materials for the education of Indigenous students in regular classrooms.

LD OnLine <www.ldonline.org/educators>. This website provides articles that relate to a range of issues to do with inclusive teaching, It includes recommendations for teaching students with learning difficulties or ADHD, for designing differentiating instruction in literacy and numeracy, assessment and evaluation procedures, for using technology in the classroom, for teaching behaviour and social skills, for classroom management strategies, for achieving inclusion criteria and requirements and for working with parents.

Royal Children's Hospital Education Institute (not dated). Curriculum Toolkit including students with disabilities: A curriculum toolkit for schools and teachers <www.sofweb.vic.edu.au/wellbeing/disabil/curriculum.htm>.

REFERENCES

ACT Department of Education and Training <www.decs.act.gov.au/services/SpecEdServices.htm>.

Australian Disability Clearinghouse on Education and Training (ADCET) <www.adcet.edu.au/default.aspx>.

Autism Association of Western Australia <www.autism.org.au>.

Booth, T. & Ainscow, M. (2002). *Index for inclusion: Developing learning and participation in schools.* Bristol, England: Centre for Studies on Inclusive Education.

Bovalino, J. W. (2007). The role of the principal in the change process: The road to inclusion. Unpublished doctoral dissertation, University of Pittsburgh (Dissertation DAI-A 68/06, AAT 3270099).

Department of Education. *School Programs for Aboriginal Students* <www.aboriginaleducation.nsw.edu.au/school_programs/index.html>.

Department of Education and Children's Services. Disability Support Program <www.decs.sa.gov.au/svpst/files/links/DE705_Elig_Crit_booklet_1_2.pd>.

Department of Education and Children's Services (2006). South Australian Curriculum Standards and Accountability Framework *Curriculum Justice Is Everybody's Business—Revised.* Adelaide: DE&CS <www.sacsa.sa.edu.au/index_fsrc.asp?t=Home>.

Department of Education and Early Childhood Development (2007a). *Program for Students with Disabilities Guidelines.* Melbourne: DE&ECD <www.sofweb.vic.edu.au/wellbeing/disabil/psdhandbook.htm>.

Department of Education and Early Childhood Development (2007b). *Autism State Plan* <www.sofweb.vic.edu.au/wellbeing/disabil/index.htm#H2N40010F>.

Department of Education and Early Childhood Development (2007c). The English Developmental Continuum P–10 for the English Domain of the Victorian Essential Learning Standards <www.education.vic.gov.au/studentlearning/teachingresources/english/englishcontinuum/reading/default.htm>.

Department of Education, Employment and Training, (2000). *Measuring academic progress against each KLA: Students with disabilities*. Melbourne: DEET <www.eduweb.vic.gov.au/edulibrary/public/stuman/wellbeing/daiprogress.pdf>.

Department of Education, Employment and Training (2005). *Language support program.* Melbourne: DEET.

Department of Education and Training (not dated). Aboriginal Education and Training, Participation and Achievement Standards Directorate <www.det.wa.edu.au/education/Abled/index.html>.

Department of Education and Training (undated). Discussion Paper #1: *Intervening in the Early Years of Schooling for Students with Disabilities and Additional Learning Needs* <www.eduweb.vic.gov.au/edulibrary/public/stuman/wellbeing/Discussion_Paper_1-v1.0-2000612.pdf>.

Department of Education and Training (2004). *Building Inclusive Schools* <http://ies.det.wa.edu.au/content/themes/providing-statewide-specialist-services/centre-for-inclusive-schooling>.

Department of Education, Science and Training (2005). *What works: The work program.* Canberra, ACT: Author <www.whatworks.edu.au>.

Education Department of Western Australia (2000). *Developing Resiliency in Young People K–12.* East Perth, WA: Author <www.eduweb.vic.gov.au/edulibrary/public/stuman/wellbeing/DRAFT_LDP_Workbook_v1.pdf>.

Esmerel's Collection of Disability Resources <www.esmerel.org> (1994). A study of leadership behaviors of principals in schools which educate students with moderate and severe disabilities in regular education classrooms. Unpublished doctoral dissertation, Western Michigan University (DAI-A 55/06, p. 1436, Dec 1994 AAT 9426889).

Kleinert, H., Miracle, S., & Sheppard-Jones, K. (2007). Including students with moderate and severe disabilities in extracurricular and community recreation activities: Steps to success. *Teaching Exceptional Children, 39*, 33–38.

Komasik, M. (2007). Effective inclusion activities for high school students with multiple disabilities. *Journal of Visual Impairment & Blindness, 101*, 10, 657–658.

LD OnLine site <www.ldonline.org>.

Learning Place/Professional Communities Home. <www.learningplace.com.au/default_suborg.asp?orgid=23&suborgid=158>.

Nolan, J. M. S. (1994). The involvement of general educators in the development and implementation of individualized education programs of students with mild disabilities. Unpublished doctoral dissertation. University of Alabama (DAI-A 56/03, p. 891, Sep 1995, AAT 9522437).

Purcell, M., Horn, E., & Palmer, S. (2007). A qualitative study of the initiation and contribution of preschool inclusion programs. *Exceptional Children, 74*, 85–99.

Rasowsky, Carol (2007). Indicators of quality in a full-time inclusive preschool program. Unpublished doctoral dissertation. State University of New York at Albany (DAI-A 68/06, Dec 2007, AAT 3270273).

Royal Children's Hospital Education Institute (undated). Curriculum Toolkit *Including students with disabilities: A curriculum toolkit for schools and teachers* <www.sofweb.vic.edu.au/wellbeing/disabil/curriculum.htm>.

Ubben, G., & Hughes, L. (1992). *The principal: Creative leadership for effective schools.* Meedham Heights, MA: Allyn and Bacon.

Victorian Curriculum and Assessment Authority (2007). *English as a Second Language (ESL) Companion* to the Victorian Essential Learning Standards for English <http://vels.vcaa.vic.edu.au/support/esl/esl.html>.

Weilenmann, P. R. (2003). *A descriptive study of a public school system's inclusion model: A post hoc study of K–12 program placement and performance patterns of children previously identified as eligible for preschool special education.* George Washington University, 2003, 202 pages; DAI-A 64/03, p. 861, Sep 2003 AAT 3083814.

Whitehurst, C. (2004). *A case study of the patterns of practice used to provide access to the general curriculum for secondary students with disabilities.* (Doctoral dissertation, Virginia Polytechnic Institute and State University, DAI-A 68/03, Sep 2007, AAT 3255293).

Yssel, N., Engelbrecht, P., Oswald, M., Eloff, I., & Swart, E. (2007). Views of inclusion: A comparative study of parents' perceptions in South Africa and the United States. *Remedial and Special Education, 28*, 356–365.

Robert Conway

5

BEHAVIOUR SUPPORT AND MANAGEMENT

What you will learn in this chapter

This chapter addresses an area that causes most concern to both beginning and more experienced teachers: how to manage students' behaviour across the broad range of teaching–learning contexts. These include the yard/playground, corridors, bus and train lines, the canteen/tuckshop, in fact all areas associated with the school. As you will see, teachers often believe that the behaviour problems that students display in school come from the home and, not surprisingly, parents believe that behaviour problems at home come from the management strategies used at school.

In this chapter you will learn:

- what factors influence behaviour problems in classrooms, schools, and the wider community;
- how students with special behavioural needs are identified and assessed;
- teaching strategies that can be used in the classroom and more generally to assist students with behaviour problems and their teachers;
- preventative and remedial strategies for students with specific behavioural needs;
- learning strategies for students with specific behaviour needs; and
- alternative full-time and part-time placement options that exist outside of the regular school for students with severe behaviour problems.

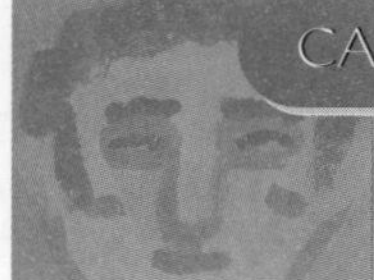

CASE STUDIES

LUKE

Luke came to high school with a history of truanting and community issues including being associated with a group that was cautioned for graffiti and harassing older people at bus stops. In primary school, he struggled with the academic content as he moved into the senior years. His approach was to truant to avoid difficult tasks, and he was always absent during assessment times. His primary school was quietly pleased to see him depart, as he was beginning to intimidate some of the younger children, demanding money or food. His family are now concerned about his involvement with older boys, as he is attracted to their daring and bravado. He has many friends in the older, difficult group of the school and seeks out their company.

Luke is often away Monday and Thursday as he has English, language, and mathematics lessons on those days. He is always late to school and is failing in all his subjects. Tests conducted by the Learning Difficulties teacher and the school counsellor revealed that he is reading at a Year 4 level and makes little effort to attempt any written activities. He is happy to participate in oral discussions and group activities, provided he isn't asked to record any information.

He has a lot of attachment to various objects in his bag and often takes them out through class. When requested to put them away his behaviour escalates quickly and violently and results in removal from class. Luke frequently speaks to his year coordinator about his hate of certain teachers. He sometimes targets students on the playground and will threaten, intimidate, and sometimes physically harm them. He had his first long suspension at secondary level because of violence toward other students and has gained status among the older adolescent problem group for his suspension.

To address his problems, the Year Advisor/Coordinator asked the specialist behaviour disorders teacher to undertake a Functional Behaviour Assessment (FBA), which has involved Luke, all of his teachers, and his parents. The outcomes of the FBA have indicated a need for Luke to receive support for his learning difficulties, which will be combined with social skills content. This will focus on his anger management, as well as developing positive relationship skills to encourage him to spend his time in positive activities with his peers rather than with older students who have problem behaviours. All Luke's class teachers have agreed to work together in supporting his academic and behaviour program through providing consistent management strategies (not an easy task in secondary schools), and through adapting curriculum and teaching strategies to support his learning difficulties. The Year Advisor/Coordinator will also provide the coordinating role supported by the School Counsellor and the Behaviour Support Teacher when specialist advice is needed.

Functional Behaviour Assessment (FBA)

A problem-solving process for addressing student problem behaviour. It aims to identify the purposes of targeted behaviour and to assist teachers and other school personnel to develop interventions to address the behaviour. It focuses on identifying pupil-specific social, emotional, cognitive, and environmental factors that might contribute to the occurrence and non-occurrence of the targeted behaviour.

The principal and deputy principal have also been informed of the new strategy so that they can be supportive of both Luke and the staff's efforts. It is expected that over the next two years, with consistent support, Luke will develop the academic and social skills needed to maintain his enrolment in the school without the need for further suspensions.

TANYA

Tanya is in Year 1. She has few friends because she irritates and even alienates other students in the classroom and the playground. She tries to make friends but becomes intrusive and over-

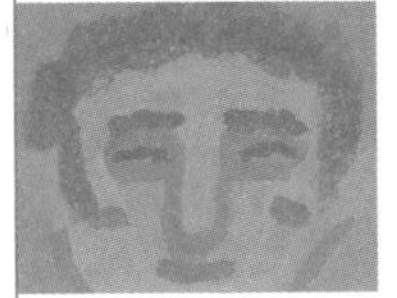

bearing. She frequently leaves her seat and rarely finishes any set work. She responds well to positive reinforcement and likes rewards. Tanya touches other students while sitting on the floor during reading time so no one wants to sit near her. Her desk area and tub/tote tray are always disorganised and her handwriting is very messy. As she is frequently distracted by what is in the room, the teacher constantly needs to keep her on task.

Although Tanya doesn't have a formal diagnosis of Attention Deficit Hyperactivity Disorder (ADHD), she demonstrates many of the symptoms, such as high levels of physical activity, including physical contact with other children, distraction from tasks, impulsive behaviours, and disorganisation of personal materials. Tanya also demonstrates poor social skills, particularly in approaching others to join in activities and sharing. As Tanya doesn't gain reinforcement for positive behaviours, she rewards herself by stealing stickers from the teacher's desk.

The class teacher firstly asked the school counsellor to assess Tanya's behaviours to see whether she thought that the behaviours were consistent with a diagnosis of ADHD, not because that would excuse Tanya's behaviours but because it would give the teacher some ideas on how to manage them. The school counsellor also spoke to Tanya's parents, who were concerned about their daughter's behaviours as her father had similar difficulties at school, but was working exceptionally hard in a demanding job.

The teacher's focus has been on teaching social skills to the whole class with an emphasis on recognising diversity in skills and interests, rather than working with Tanya in isolation. She has also focused on group work activities in which she has used a wide variety of groups work structures. She has used interest groups, ability groups, mixed ability groups, and random allocation to groups. She has also used a variety of strategies within the groups, including jigsaw and allocating specific tasks to students to ensure that all students over time play each of the group roles (e.g., leader, recorder, reporter).

The class teacher has also developed a personal plan with Tanya so that Tanya can ensure she has her desk clear of items other than the ones she needs for the lesson. She has bought a stress-ball that Tanya can keep on her desk and squeeze as she works so that she doesn't disrupt others, and it also keeps her hands busy. Tanya earns stickers now because the teacher has ensured that the rewards for positive activities in class are recognised. In the playground, the class teacher has asked her colleagues to keep an eye on Tanya's social interactions and has asked them to reward her when positive behaviours occur and to provide a reminder of the appropriate social skill when she forgets.

The class teacher keeps in closer contact with the parents now so that they are kept informed about the positive things Tanya does and so the parents can reinforce the progress as well.

TEACHING–LEARNING CONTEXT

All students display a wide range of positive and negative behaviours. Whether a specific behaviour is considered appropriate or not depends on many factors, such as the age of the student, the setting, the duration, the frequency, the intensity of the behaviour, as well as home and cultural factors. The appropriateness of behaviour is in the eye of the beholder. Frequently, behaviours are labelled as problem or unacceptable because they annoy, disrupt, or negatively affect the lives of others. In schools, teachers

commonly identify behaviours as unacceptable because they disrupt their teaching. Yet sometimes it is the teaching and the curriculum that cause the students to misbehave because the learning environment is boring.

The statistics in some states and territories show that over 40% of beginning teachers leave the profession in the first five years. Many of them identify student behaviour as a prime reason for leaving. While this is a key issue, there are other matters that lie behind the behaviour of students, including the quality and engagement of the curriculum, the ability of the teacher to engage the students in learning, and, at a broader level, the support of parents and the community for teaching as a profession.

The response of educational systems to increasing levels of behaviour problems in schools has been inconsistent. Dictums requiring principals to be strong on the use of suspensions and in-school management processes have often been followed by requests to reduce suspension levels as local and aggregated systems data show unacceptable levels of suspensions, which have associated political implications. While many educational jurisdictions have opted for keeping students in mainstream settings, others have chosen the path of multiple layers of alternative settings, many of which are of questionable success in meeting student needs.

For an increasing number of students, inappropriate classroom behaviour (e.g., disrupting the class, refusal to complete work), physical aggression (e.g., throwing things at other children, punching and kicking), verbal aggression, stealing food by aggressive means, and difficulties in following directions are common. Most of these behaviours are very visible and easily identified because they are directed at the teacher and/or students, and are designed to attract maximum attention, or to maximise disruption to the teaching and learning in the class. Other externalising behaviours can be difficult to detect, particularly if they occur outside the teacher's view, like bullying.

Of increasing concern in schools is the level of students with internalising behaviour problems. These include withdrawn behaviours, depression, obsessive-compulsive disorders (OCD), and self-injurious behaviours. Australian data show that adolescents now identify depression as their greatest concern (Sawyers et al., 2000). Indeed, the World Health Organization (WHO) has claimed that depression will be the world's major health issue by 2020.

obsessive-compulsive disorder (OCD)

A psychiatric disorder most commonly characterised by anxiety, and by obsessive, distressing, and intrusive thoughts that lead to compulsions or rituals designed to neutralise the obsessions.

The differences between internalising and externalising behaviour problems is easily seen in Table 5.1 (Algozzine, Serena, & Patton, 2001), which identifies a wide range of the behaviours we may see in students.

Students who exhibit behaviour problems often have associated learning difficulties. These fall into three main categories:

1 those that relate to a specific academic skill (e.g., reading and mathematics);
2 those that relate to thinking skills (such as following directions); and
3 those that relate to awareness and understanding of thought processes (i.e., metacognition) such as recognising inappropriate behaviours and correcting them.

Studies in the United States have shown that students with behaviour disorders have the lowest grade point average of any group of students with special learning needs and have the highest levels of truancy, which exacerbates their low academic performance.

It is difficult to change behaviour in isolation. Behaviour change needs to take place where the behaviour problem occurs. For example, if the problem relates to the classroom, then that should be the focus of the behaviour change. If the problems relate to the playground, then the issues need to be addressed in that setting. Because behaviour cannot be changed in a vacuum, it must be addressed in the environment in which it occurs.

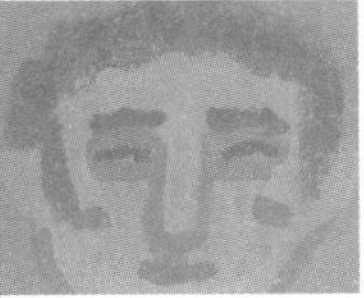

TABLE 5.1 CATEGORISING EMOTIONAL AND BEHAVIOURAL DISORDERS

Externalising behaviours	Internalising behaviours
Aggression toward people and objects	Withdrawn
Defiant	Apathetic, restricted activity levels
Disobedient	Fixated on certain thoughts
Noncompliant	Avoids social situations
Argumentative	Fearful, anxious
Destructive	Inferiority
Temper tantrums	Sad, moody, depressed
Jealous	Self-conscious, overly sensitive
Distrustful, blames others	Irritable
Patterns of lying and stealing	Inappropriate crying
Lack of self-control	

Source: Drawn from Algozzine, Serena, & Patton (2001).

What is a behaviour disorder?

Defining behaviour disorders is difficult because they can occur in many forms and can be identified as being serious only when someone makes a social judgment about their occurrence in a specific context. Unlike intellectual disability and sensory impairments, for which there are generally accepted definitions, behaviour disorders have no such agreed definition. Terms that have been in common use in Australia include "behaviour of serious concern", "disruptive, disturbed, and alienated behaviours", "emotional disturbance", "emotional problems", "behaviour problems", "social/emotional handicaps", "behavioural disability", and "socially unacceptable behaviours". This range of terms and associated definitions makes it difficult to reach consensus.

The problem of definition is further exacerbated by the lack of distinction between students with mild behaviour problems in regular classes and those attending special settings for more severe behaviour disorders. In some states and territories a distinction is made between behaviour disorders, behaviour problems, and emotional disturbance. Students displaying severe emotional disturbance have a specific diagnosis and generally attend a specific educational setting in which they receive services jointly from education and health professionals. They might also be supported in regular classes through outreach services and do not necessarily attend special schools on a full-time basis.

Funding for students with a behaviour disorder, when it is as part of a mental health diagnosis, is provided through Commonwealth Inclusion Funding and can be used to support these students in regular education. In practice, this means that students with a mental health disability are entitled to the same funding opportunities as those with an intellectual, physical, or sensory disability.

For a student to be defined as having a severe emotional disturbance, one or more of the following characteristics must be exhibited to a marked extent, and occur over time:

- an inability to learn that cannot be explained by intellectual, sensory, or general health factors;
- an inability to build or maintain satisfactory interpersonal relationships with peers and teachers;
- inappropriate behaviours or feelings under normal conditions;
- a general pervasive mood of unhappiness or depression; and
- a tendency to develop physical symptoms, pains, or fears associated with personal or school problems.

This definition alerts us to some constraints of defining behaviour disorders. These include:

- rate, duration, topography, and magnitude of occurrence;
- range and variability; and
- relationships to other disabling conditions.

topography of behaviour

The patterns of the behaviour including when it occurs, where it occurs, how it presents, and its consequences. It is a mapping of the behaviour as would occur through a Functional Behaviour Assessment (FBA).

The issues related to the definition of behaviour are best summed up as follows: what makes a behaviour disordered is its appearance in the wrong place, at the wrong time, in the presence of the wrong people, and to an inappropriate extent.

When is behaviour unacceptable?

We all display behaviours at times that can be considered disordered or unacceptable, depending on location, frequency, intensity, duration, socioeconomic and cultural influences, and age appropriateness of the behaviour.

Location is important. A drama or physical education teacher, for example, might see active behaviour as being appropriate, whereas another teacher (e.g., of mathematics) might see the same activity as inappropriate. On a basketball court, aggressive team behaviour is valued, whereas in a mathematics class withdrawn silent work on individual tasks may be expected. The difficulty for some students is making the distinctions between acceptable behaviour patterns in different locations.

The *frequency* of the behaviour is also important because a behaviour that occurs once is unlikely to be a problem, whereas if it continues it can be a problem. If the intensity is such that a teacher takes offence immediately (e.g., swearing), the behaviour might be seen as a problem based on one event. Each teacher will have a different tolerance level, so duration may be variously defined. This is most common with attention-seekers who, initially, might entertain both other students and the teacher but who eventually wear out the teacher's patience.

The *socioeconomic status* of the family is another consideration because many students with specific behaviour problems come from socially disadvantaged backgrounds.

Students from low socioeconomic situations and single-parent family backgrounds are over-represented in Australian studies of students with specific behaviour disorders and in studies of truancy. Earlier Australian studies have indicated that significantly more students attending schools in lower socioeconomic areas were identified as having a behaviour disorder.

Cultural factors are reflected in the different emphases that cultural groups place on behaviour. While some teachers might have certain expectations of students, families from different cultural

backgrounds might not share these expectations, or expect their children to share them either. For example, some parents may actively discourage this child from participating in group or team activities, preferring them to work and study alone as a way of increasing their academic results. We know from the literature on resilience and protective social factors that involvement in positive group activities such as sporting teams is an essential component of social development.

Indigenous children can also be at risk because of the concurrence of a cultural minority status and a socioeconomic disadvantage. Participation by Indigenous children in education is very low at all levels of the education system, and is worst in rural and remote communities (Aboriginal and Torres Strait Islander Commission, 2004). Many Aboriginal children have low literacy levels, many display major behaviour problems at school, and many leave school early to become the most arrested, most imprisoned, and most convicted group in Australian society (Carroll, Hattie, Houghton, & Durkin, 2001). In the Northern Territory, Indigenous Australians constitute 72% of public order offence court appearances and 81% of all imprisonments (Conway, 2006).

Although Indigenous students present a major challenge for our education systems, the same is true for children from some other cultural minority groups. However, the supporting evidence about these groups is more anecdotal than published.

Incidence and prevalence of behaviour problems

A study dealing with the inclusion of students with a variety of disabilities was recently conducted in South Australia and New South Wales. Westwood and Graham (2003) reported that teachers in both states saw students with emotional and behaviour problems as the most challenging of any disability group in the regular class. They represented the single largest cohort of students with special needs in each state.

The tendency to interchange the terms we use to define students with behaviour problems also adds to the difficulty of providing clear incidence rates. In some cases, political or interest groups can inflate prevalence figures by arguing for the inclusion of students with specific diagnostic labels such as ADHD. In addition, children with other primary disabilities (e.g., severe intellectual disability or Autism Spectrum Disorder, ASD) often exhibit behaviour disorders but are not included in behaviour disorders figures. One diagnostic label that is becoming increasingly common in schools is Asperger's syndrome—considered by some to be a higher-functioning type of autism. Given the prominence of diagnoses of ADHD, ASD, and Asperger's syndrome, a section later in this chapter (*Specific behaviour problems in regular schools*) addresses these topics.

Prevalence figures are based on widely differing samples and terminology. In comparison with overseas figures, Australian prevalence rates are at the lower end of a range that extends from 1% to an abnormally high figure of 30%, depending on the criteria used for diagnosis. Boys are more frequently labelled as having a behaviour disorder than girls. The ratio often quoted in the literature is 4:1 (Ryan & Lindgren, 1999) although in Australia it is closer to 2.1 boys to 1 girl. This is consistent with figures reported by teachers of primary-aged students in Sydney where the ratio was 2.5 boys to 1 girl (Stephenson, Linfoot, & Martin, 2000).

As indicated by enrolment grade, age generally does not appear to be a major influence on the prevalence of behaviour disorders. Earlier studies in Queensland and Victoria suggest that primary and secondary levels are relatively consistent. In Queensland, the figures were 3.6% for primary levels and 4.4% for secondary; in Victoria, the corresponding figures were 4.2% and 3.1%. An early study in Western Australia (Sugai & Evans, 1997) found a consistency across early education and primary grades of 2%.

Models of identifying and explaining behaviour problems

A model is a way of describing the relationship between the causes of a condition and the nature of that condition. A model defines the condition and prescribes how to treat it. Two categories of models have been used to identify behaviour problems: medical models and conceptual models.

MEDICAL MODELS

Before the emergence of a framework of educational services for children with behaviour disorders, medical diagnosis provided the classification system for all of these, from the mildest to the most severe. The emphasis of medical or mental health models was primarily on severe or abnormal behaviours, and on identifying collections of symptoms (syndromes), rather than on classifying behaviour based on classroom factors.

The Diagnostic and Statistical Manual for Mental Disorders (DSM-IV), developed by the American Psychiatric Association (2000), is the primary medical classification system, providing categories of disorders from infancy to adulthood. While it does not enjoy universal support in terms of its application to students, particularly in educational settings, it does provide clinical diagnoses for specific behaviour problems such as ADHD, Conduct Disorder (CD), and Oppositional Defiant Disorder (ODD), all of which are used by medical staff to identify the need for medication. The presence of medical treatment can influence the choice of educational intervention. Professional training largely influences which causal factors are used to explain behaviour disorders.

As we will see in the following section, the medical model remains as a powerful influence on the diagnosis and treatment of behaviour disorders, particularly through the use of medication to treat behaviour problems such as ADHD, Depression and Obsessive Compulsive Disorders (OCD).

CONCEPTUAL MODELS

Conceptual models have been seen as reflecting the professional views of those working with students with behaviour problems. While each of the models has a distinct approach to both identification and treatment, the classroom teacher must address the behaviour problems in an educational context, regardless of the other professional approaches being used concurrently. Figure 5.1 shows the relationship between the differing models. The three behaviours forming the triangle represent the physical (biological), emotional (psychodynamic), and behavioural aspects of the individual. The two circles around the triangle represent the external influences that affect the student, most closely the ecological factors and then the sociological factors of the schools and society. The models within the triangle represent the importance of the thinking and planning skills of the individual as both the cause of behaviour problems and the methods of finding solutions.

Early conceptual models of behaviour disorders locate the causes within the student, describing the causes as being genetic or biomedical (biological model), or stemming from imbalances in the personality structure of the student (psychodynamic model). In neither case was the educational environment seen as a causal factor. Some writers have argued that the cause lay partially within the child and partially within the student's personality and emotional reactions to the school environment (psychoeducational model).

Overall, the behavioural model has been seen as the most relevant approach to take in educational settings, and this is the most widely accepted by teachers. The relatively simple emphasis on observable behaviours, rather than on underlying physiological or psychological causes, can be related easily to the classroom and does not require the involvement of other professions to identify, assess, or remediate

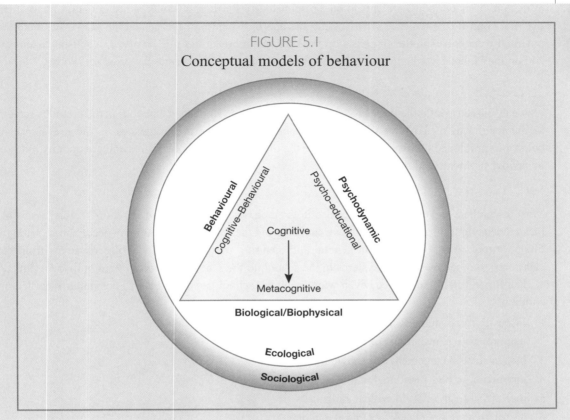

FIGURE 5.1
Conceptual models of behaviour

Behavioural
Cognitive–Behavioural
Psycho-educational
Psychodynamic
Cognitive
Metacognitive
Biological/Biophysical
Ecological
Sociological

specific disordered behaviours. Although many studies on the effectiveness of behavioural approaches have been reported, concern has been expressed that these studies have often been conducted in rigorous conditions not normally replicable in the average classroom (see Alberto & Troutman, 2006; Porter, 2007).

The ecological model focuses on the classroom ecosystem (shown in Figure 5.2 below) and reflects interactions among the four groups of variables in the classroom: the physical environment; teacher characteristics; the curriculum and how it is taught, including the resources used; and a multitude of student variables. These four groups interact continuously within the class and constitute the teaching–learning environment. Behaviour problems can result from any one of the four components but are most likely to occur from the interaction between components. At a broader level, the ecological approach recognises that the school operates as an ecosystem and that the home and community are other ecosystems in which the student operates. The sociological model recognises that the school operates as a society bound by the rules and structures of the school. Where students do no comply with the rules, the school restricts their rights and may punish the behaviour by placing the student in detention, or on short or long suspension. In this model, schools operate as a microcosm of the broader society, enforcing rules.

More recent models have reflected an eclectic approach, moving away from an emphasis on behaviour alone in diagnosis and treatment to awareness of the importance of thinking and planning skills (Ashman & Conway, 1997). The cognitive behavioural model emphasises observable behaviours and other skills such as self-monitoring, planning, and decision-making. This approach has the added

attraction of encouraging students to take responsibility for their behaviours rather than relying on an external control (the teacher) for assessing the appropriateness of the behaviour. However, there are potential weaknesses in the emphasis on the student's motivation to be involved in self-management, and on the higher-level language skills that are required to work through the program (Porter, 2007).

ISSUES AND CHALLENGES

I have discussed briefly the three broad areas of influence on students' behaviour in the previous section as the focus was on how we identify behaviour problems and the influences on the prevalence of behaviour problems. In this section, I explore the influences the school, home, and community have on behaviour problems and their solution.

School factors

Most researchers and educational administrators emphasise the importance of school factors in school-located behaviour disorders, although we cannot avoid the reality that behaviours occur across settings. First, we look at school factors in general and then at a progression of school ecosystems from the classroom to other specific ecosystems in the school, to the school as an ecosystem in its own right.

Kauffman (2005) suggested seven ways in which school can contribute to behaviour disorders in children:

1 insensitivity to students' individuality;
2 inappropriate expectations of students;
3 inconsistent management of behaviour;
4 instruction in non-functional and irrelevant skills;
5 ineffective instruction in critical skills;
6 destructive contingencies of reinforcement; and
7 undesirable models of school conduct.

This list of contributing factors highlights the interrelatedness of factors, particularly between academic failure and behaviour problems. The failure trap that commences with inability to succeed on an academic task can lead to an avoidance of schoolwork, which can then lead to behaviour problems, with a cycle of failure being established. An associated factor is the level of academic task presented by the teacher. Many students with a behaviour disorder are unable to cope with regular curriculum topics, particularly in secondary schools. The combination of low student ability, year level, and high teacher expectations provides an environment for classroom disruption (Kauffman, 2005).

TEACHER ATTITUDE AND TOLERANCE

Teacher attitude and tolerance are important contributing school factors and are critical in the identification of students as having a behaviour disorder. This is seen most clearly in secondary schools where some teachers can have considerable difficulty with a particular student while others have no difficulty at all.

Teachers experiencing difficulties are more likely to see the behaviour disorder as lying within the student, and more likely to ignore the reality that it is the outcome of interactions between teachers and students, and that this behaviour cannot be dismissed as the responsibility of the student alone. Where teachers deliberately use the same management techniques for students with behaviour problems and regular students, they are setting up themselves and the students to fail. As teachers, we need to examine our approaches to teaching and our responses to individual students as well as to the students as a class group.

THE CLASSROOM

As discussed in Chapter 3, the classroom contains four main factors that determine the cause of behaviour problems as well as the solution to replacing negative behaviours with more positive behaviours (shown graphically in Figure 3.2):

1 students;
2 teachers;
3 curriculum and teaching strategies; and
4 physical setting.

Students are commonly identified as having behaviour problems when they disrupt classroom teaching. In his study of teachers in NSW, Vinson (2002) found that the behaviours of students of most concern to teachers were:

- clowning;
- swearing;
- disobedience;
- refusal to cooperate; and
- disruption of the teaching and learning process.

The final behaviour makes us realise that, for many teachers, teaching is a process that involves the giving of knowledge from the person who holds the knowledge (teacher) to those who need to acquire it (students). In this model, the role of the student is to be passive and receptive. It is also interesting that the list includes only externalising or disturbing behaviours and no internalising behaviours are listed (see Table 5.1 earlier), although students themselves see depression as a key concern in their education.

Teachers also contribute to behaviour problems in the classroom when they are not thoroughly prepared, know their work, and can put it across in an interesting and motivating way. Studies of student beliefs about Australian teachers' discipline styles by Lewis and colleagues (Lewis, 2001; 2006) found two broad categories of teachers:

1 coercive (aggressive reaction and punishing of misbehaviours); and
2 relation-based discipline (discussion and reasoning about inappropriate behaviour, hints on positive behaviour and rewarding of positive behaviour).

Primary teachers were perceived as using more relations-based discipline and less aggression. It is interesting that confrontational behaviour by teachers will likely result in more severe behaviour by problem students (Salend & Sylvestre, 2005). Where students have special needs there is a greater need to ensure that positive behaviours from teachers model desired behaviour rather than confrontational behaviour (Babkie, 2006).

One of the difficulties experienced by beginning teachers in particular is the management of whole classrooms and the concern that by being too harsh in their management students will not like them. Lewis (2006) showed that students have a greater respect for teachers who know their content, who can put the content across in interesting and motivating ways, and who have good management skills. Being liked by students is not a quality of particular importance to students.

Curriculum and resource factors are a major stumbling block in addressing behaviour in classrooms. Where a teacher seeks to implement the curriculum content without regard to student learning needs, the potential for behaviour problems increases.

At a broader level than an individual classroom, what we teach and how we teach it are critical issues. The link between behaviour problems and learning difficulties has been clearly established.

Among the features of schooling that contribute to behaviour problems are irrelevant curricula, inflexible and alienating instructional structures, and rejection or neglect of underachievers. One issue being addressed in some states and territories is curriculum irrelevancy, a major risk factor in adolescent behaviour problems such as boredom, class disruption, and truancy.

Students will not engage in the learning process when their frustration level is exceeded by the presentation of curriculum content that is beyond their comprehension, and when teaching material and the teaching methods are incompatible with their learning style. Some educational jurisdictions have moved away from the use of Key Learning Areas to focus on essential learning skills rather than curriculum content. The South Australian curriculum (South Australian Curriculum Standards and Accountability Framework, 2007) has a strong blend of Essential Learnings (Identity, Interdependence, Communication, Thinking, Futures) and Key Learning Areas (KLAs). Other jurisdictions are also moving away from formal key secondary academic assessments (e.g., Queensland, ACT, South Australia, Northern Territory), freeing schools to make curriculum decisions based on school needs rather than external examination and curriculum authorities.

Physical setting factors are important in addressing positive and negative behaviours. Where classrooms are poorly maintained, with no stimulating features, they do not create an environment in which students are encouraged to learn. Other classrooms can be so stimulating that students are constantly distracted by the many objects around them. For specific behaviour needs (such as ADHD) the classroom may exacerbate inattentive or distractible behaviours. The difficulty is to balance the needs of the student who is distracted by over-stimulating classrooms with the needs of other students for whom the room provides a stimulating and exciting place to learn.

The layout of the room also has an effect on the management of student behaviour. Some teachers prefer desks to be in rows, with minimum contact between students. This is more frequently used in secondary classes. In contrast, many primary classrooms are arranged with groups of desks and work areas for different subjects as students are in the room for the majority of the day. Both layouts have advantages for classroom management. Rows of single desks may reduce behaviour disruptions and increase on-task time for both primary and secondary students. If, however, the aim is to promote discussion and increase cooperative work skills, small groups of desks may be more appropriate. This is the case for Tanya in the second case study where the need was for her to develop positive social skills through being involved in different groups.

Teaching and learning involve a constantly changing combination of all four factors at all times. They are critically important in determining what may exacerbate the behaviour problem(s) and how they may be addressed. Focusing only on the student as the cause of the behaviour problem avoids the reality that the other three factors may contribute more to the problem through poor teacher preparation, and using inappropriate teaching and learning strategies to implement a curriculum that isn't related to the student interests in an unstimulating classroom. In that case, the teacher-defined inappropriate behaviours of the students may simply be their way of filling in the academically unengaged time. Where students also have a special need, the issue of combining academic and social skills becomes more important and often requires addressing the four factors over extended periods of time, and, in the case of students with ASD or Asperger's syndrome, perhaps even years (see e.g., Bullard, 2004).

WHOLE-SCHOOL ENVIRONMENT

The management of student behaviours requires considerations beyond the classroom. School locations such as the playground and corridors are areas of the school that require management of student

behaviour. For students with special needs, inclusion in playground activities is a particular area of concern as they may be subjected to bullying or may not have the social support they have in the classroom. Particularly in larger schools, playground support for students with special needs or students with behaviour problems requires cooperation across the school. We saw this in the case studies of both Luke and Tanya.

A MODEL FOR SCHOOL-WIDE BEHAVIOUR SUPPORT

Most students with behaviour problems are part of the regular school and need their behaviour managed by teachers as part of the regular educational process. Most students remain in the regular school with assistance and are not placed in a specialist setting. Within the regular school setting, students can receive assistance according to a continuum of positive behaviour support, as shown in the effective behaviour support (EBS) model of Lewis and Sugai (1999) (see Figure 5.2). The model proposes three levels of implementation that are consistent with the approach used in many Australasian schools.

FIGURE 5.2
Effective behaviour support model

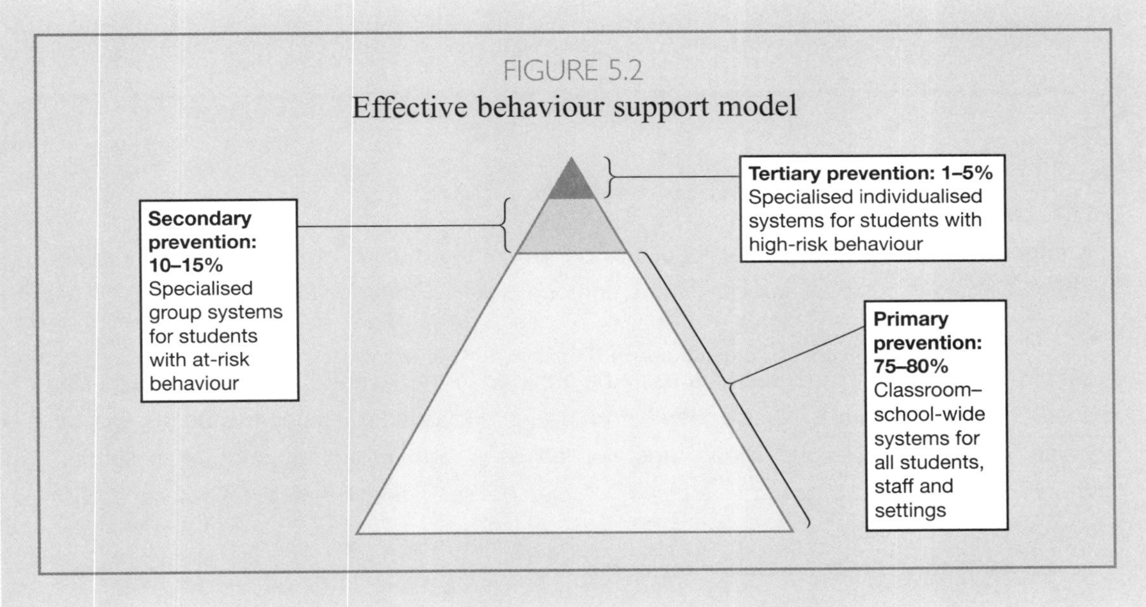

At the first level, the school develops universal school-wide management strategies to meet the needs of all students. The strategies should be implemented consistently and efficiently across all school settings, with specific strategies dealing with the areas of classrooms, corridors, and playgrounds. Importantly, students must be reinforced for the positive behaviours they demonstrate. If students are playing cooperatively in the playground, reinforce this by a positive comment.

At the next level are secondary support interventions to assist targeted individuals and groups who are at risk, and who require repeated practice and environmental modifications to increase academic and social success. This is perhaps the most critical group in the school as these students can either learn the positive behaviours that will enable them to return to the bottom of the triangle or proceed to the top if their problem behaviours are ignored or reinforced. If a student spends detention time learning new social skills that he or she can use in the classroom, that reinforces positive behaviour. Alternatively, writing out lines only reinforces a dislike of writing lines and/or a

dislike of the person requiring them to do so. There are no positive new behaviour skills learned in writing out lines.

At the third (or tertiary) level of support are targeted and highly specialised strategies for those few students (1–7%) who engage in serious challenging behaviours and who do not respond to the first or second levels of support. These students have made a clear choice to operate outside the school's behaviour standards and need to be managed within the school discipline policies.

Although the approach is very similar to some previous and existing approaches to managing behaviours in schools, the key difference is the development and implementation of a process that comes from within the school rather than from any individual (e.g., the principal) or an external source. Real behaviour change comes from within and cannot be imposed. Hence, in reading the total-school approach in Box 5.1, note that the school community develops the approach and a team (principal, staff, students, and parents), implements and monitors it.

The successful supervision of students with behaviour and emotional problems relies heavily on the administration of the whole-school discipline and management policy. If teachers know that they are supported it is much easier to run a classroom efficiently. Nevertheless, the control of behaviour within the class still presents a major challenge to individual teachers.

BOX 5.1 Effective school-wide behaviour support

STATEMENT OF PURPOSE

It is important to develop a brief and positive statement that outlines what the school stands for (e.g., *Our school values: respect for one another; positive attitudes to work*).

RULES OR EXPECTATIONS

A list of positive behaviour expectations can be grouped to form a set of school rules (e.g., *be respectful*, *be cooperative*, *be safe*, *be kind to others*). However, rules need to be applied to specific locations across the school and not left as a general set of amorphous school statements. Hence *be respectful*, *be cooperative*, *be safe*, and *be kind to others* in the playground could mean:

- keep game rules the same during the game; and
- line up when the whistle blows.

The same school rule in assemblies could mean:

- not touching others.

PROCEDURES FOR TEACHING SCHOOL-WIDE EXPECTATIONS

Schools should *explain* to students what is expected, *practise* the skill through role-play and real-life situations across all school settings, particularly with younger students and those with special needs, and *reinforce* positive behaviours.

CONTINUUM OF PROCEDURES FOR ENCOURAGING SCHOOL-WIDE EXPECTATIONS

Positive reinforcement of pro-social skills is needed to ensure that rules are followed. It should be a genuine acknowledgment of the student's positive involvement. Name the rule when giving the earned reward and remember to reinforce across the year and not just at the beginning when new rules are being established.

CONTINUUM OF PROCEDURES FOR DISCOURAGING PROBLEM BEHAVIOURS

The school must develop a clear consequence for each problem behaviour. Consequences for not complying with school rules need to be clear and consistently applied. Schools need to ensure that there is a range of consequences at classroom, playground, and school levels. This avoids classroom behaviour problems having to be handled by the school executive, rather than in the classroom where the problem behaviour occurs.

PROCEDURES FOR MONITORING THE IMPACT OF THE SCHOOL-WIDE BEHAVIOUR PROGRAMS

Keeping student behaviour data allows schools to better manage school-wide programs. For example, knowing how often a student is referred to the school executive helps to develop positive behaviour plans that meet the specific needs of the student and the school. Data can also show when and where common problem behaviour problems occur.

Source: Based on Lewis, T. J. & Sugai, G. (1999). 'Effective behavior support: A systems approach to proactive schoolwide management'. *Focus on Exceptional Children*, *31*, 1–24.

5.1

The need for discipline policies in schools and the attraction of teacher-managed options has led schools to adopt other schools' approaches without due consideration of the needs of their own school. As a result, schools implement a discipline policy that has no staff or student involvement in its development, and hence no ownership or commitment. A possible positive solution might lie in approaches such as the effective behaviour support model, which aims at securing and maintaining student and teacher confidence in cooperatively developing teaching and learning strategies, and in which discipline becomes an educational issue rather than a teacher-imposed management issue.

Beyond the school

Beyond the school are four factors that influence school behaviour issues: family; socioeconomics; culture, religion and race; and sociopolitics (see Figure 5.3).

FAMILY FACTORS

The nuclear family of two parents and children no longer reflects the average family in many areas of Australia, as you will have discovered in Chapter 1. There is an increasing incidence of single-parent families and blended families as a result of remarriage, and a shift in values held by the community about what is appropriate behaviour for young people. In contrast, some cultural groups have a very strongly developed extended family model in which support for students with behaviour problems can be either a positive or a negative depending on the beliefs held by that cultural group toward education and, particularly, teacher authority. This can be exacerbated by the reality that females comprise the majority of teachers. These factors have ramifications for the role of the family as an agent of socialisation.

In the case of students with mental health needs, there is a clear link between their mental health needs and the home situation. The National Health and Wellbeing Survey (Sawyer et al., 2000) focused on a number of key family variables:

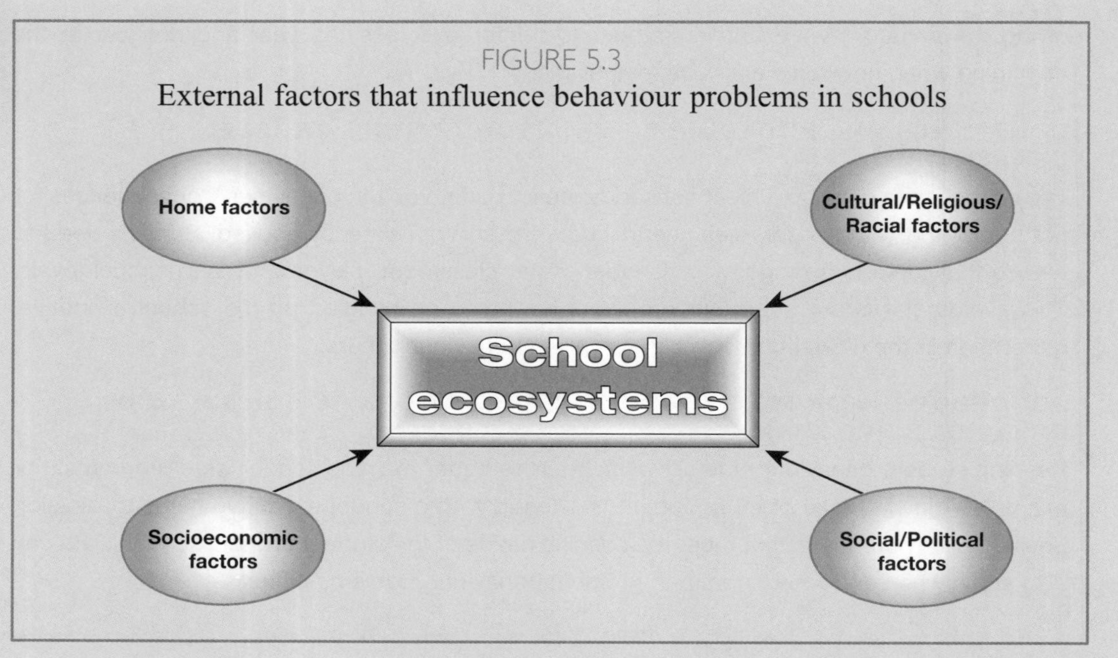

FIGURE 5.3
External factors that influence behaviour problems in schools

- unstable relationships with parents or carers;
- death of a parent;
- inadequate parenting skills;
- family discord, violence, separation, or family breakdown; and
- parents with serious mental health problems, or alcohol/drug problems that affect parenting.

Weatherburn (2003) identified a clear relationship between data on household poverty and juveniles convicted of violent crimes. He found that "economic and social stress influence crime by exerting corrosive effects on the parenting process" (p. 21). The combination of high rates of family dissolution, inadequate parenting, and delinquent peers results in a much greater likelihood of a young person becoming involved in delinquent behaviour. Weatherburn identified other issues including the adolescent's completion of school and the transition from school to employment.

Although schools cannot be responsible for events that occur within the home, teachers and other personnel need to be sensitive to the difficulties that some students face within dysfunctional families. Educators and educational administrators need to be aware that any solution to behaviour problems in schools depends on addressing the whole problem, not just one aspect of it. In the case of suspected abuse of students, teachers must report abuse to the relevant authority.

SOCIOECONOMIC FACTORS

Areas of high unemployment and low socioeconomic areas have a higher proportion of students with behaviour problems. Often this can arise from a lack of community resources and a lack of opportunities for positive social interactions, such as sporting groups and clubs that are part of resilience-building in children and youth. A higher police presence in low socioeconomic areas also builds negative, rather than positive, relationships with authority figures. This can translate into negative relationships with teachers, the vast majority of whom do not live in the local area.

CULTURAL, RACIAL, AND RELIGIOUS FACTORS

Cultural and racial minority groups have often been identified as having higher levels of emotional and behavioural problems in countries such as the USA (Bullock & Gable, 2006) and the UK (Cooper, 2006). Often these problems emerge from large concentrations of cultural and racial groups in suburbs of large cities and the difficulties of integration of these communities within the educational system. Behaviours developed and expected in some neighbourhoods, child-rearing practices in some cultural groups, and the impact of certain religious beliefs on daily lives are all relevant influences.

POLITICAL FACTORS

Education has always been a political issue. Law and order issues affect school systems because educators and parents alike are concerned about the impact of students with behaviour problems on the education of students without behaviour problems. School principals have commonly called for the removal of students with severe behaviour problems from their schools and have them placed in segregated settings in the belief that removal of problem students will result in a school that is manageable under a single set of school rules. Such a hope is simply that. Some governments have responded to pressure to develop alternative placements for students with behaviour problems and establish multiple alternative setting. The result is that these fill quickly, resulting in the need to establish more settings.

The complex pathway of risk

The factors within the school and outside combine to form a path toward long-term negative outcomes for students. Walker and Sprauge (1999) developed a model that represents the combinations of home, school, community and peer factors that result in negative outcomes for student. The pathway represents the cumulative effects of personal, school, home, and community factors. Often it is left to the school to address the issues without other supports (see Figure 5.4).

Submissions from across Australia to the House of Representatives Standing Committee on Education, Employment and Training (1996) identified recurrent themes in truancy and these represent the combination of factors that affect the lives of students with emotional and behavioural problems. These were:

- family conflict;
- poverty;
- single parent;
- blended families;
- neglect of physical and psychological wellbeing;
- lack of supportive care and concern;
- lack of communication;
- alcohol and substance abuse;
- emotional, physical, and sexual abuse;
- stress; and
- damaged relationships.

While education cannot address all issues that affect the lives of students with behavioural difficulties, schools can provide a stable and encouraging environment in which to develop the resilience and protective skills that will assist students. In the following sections, teaching and learning issues are addressed.

FIGURE 5.4

The path to long-term negative outcomes for children and youth who are at risk for school failure, delinquency, and violence.

Leads to development of maladaptive behaviours
Defiance of adults
Lack of school readiness
Coercive interactive styles
Aggression toward peers
Lack of problem-solving skills

Produces negative short-term outcomes
Truancy
Peer and teacher rejection
Low academic achievement
High number of school discipline referrals
Attending a large number of schools
Early involvement with drugs and alcohol
Early age of first arrest (under 12 years)

Negative, destructive long-term outcomes
School failure and dropout
Delinquency
Drug and alcohol use
Gang membership
Violent acts
Adult criminology
Lifelong dependence on welfare system
Higher death and injury rate

Source: Based on Walker, H. M. & Sprague, J. R. (1999). "The path to school failure, delinquency, and violence: Causal factors and some potential solutions". *Intervention in School and Clinic*, *37*, 67. Copyright 1999 by Sage Publications, Inc. Reproduced with permission from Sage Publications, Inc. Journals in the format Textbook via Copyright Clearance Center.

TEACHING ESSENTIALS

Before considering the types of behaviour problems that occur in the classroom and how to support those students it is useful to remember that:

- children with a label of behaviour disorder or problem do not have a monopoly on problem behaviours;
- problem behaviours considered indicative of disorders are common among most normal children; and
- the problem behaviours displayed by children who are not thought to have a persisting difficulty are often not different in kind from those shown by disturbed children, but are different in frequency of occurrence, degree of severity, duration, and clustering.

Students who are referred for behaviour support might present a variety of behaviours. These include:

- constant wandering around the classroom;
- leaving the classroom or school without permission;
- frequent shouting in class;
- fighting with peers;
- teasing;
- frequent swearing;
- throwing equipment or furniture in a rage;
- threatening students and teachers;
- vandalism;
- non-compliance intended to disrupt;
- withdrawal, total silence, or no eye-contact;
- persistent compulsive lying;
- stealing; and
- self-mutilation.

In a 2003 study, I identified the characteristics of students who have behaviour disorders or who are discipline problems in regular schools (Conway, 2003a). Differences emerged among preschools, primary schools, and secondary schools. Teachers of children from five to eight years of age in western Sydney were most concerned about distraction, problems with listening, physical aggression, demands for teacher attention, inability to remain on task, and disruption of others (see also Stephenson et al., 2000). It is of interest that I found that 7% of the students in the class had behaviours that were severe enough to warrant intervention. This is in contrast to a study of primary teachers in inner-Sydney schools in which 15% of the students were reported by Beaman and Wheldall (1997) as needing support. Hence, there is a wide variety of behaviour needs, and assessment procedures need to address this variety within a common set of procedures.

Assessment procedures and practices

Assessing the reasons for, and causes of, behaviour problems is an important start to setting up appropriate interventions. Functional Behaviour Assessment (FBA), described below, is not the only method of assessment that can be used but is a framework in which to identify behaviour problems. There is also a range of general assessment resources that contain sections specifically addressing student behaviour (see, e.g., McLoughlin & Lewis, 2005; Rosenberg, Wilson, Maheady, & Sindelar, 2004a).

FUNCTIONAL BEHAVIOUR ASSESSMENT (FBA)

Functional assessment has its roots in the analysis of students' challenging behaviours. FBA identifies its application to students for whom the prime cause of concern is their behaviour. (Note that *behavior* assessment and *behavioral* assessment are used in the North American literature.) For most students, the regular classroom, the school rules, and standard management practices are sufficient to maintain acceptable behaviour. If the student's behaviour is seriously affecting his or her learning, or that of others, functional assessment might be appropriate.

As the rapidly expanding literature on FBA is almost entirely American, the references in the following sections are US-based rather than Australasian. A thorough overview and training program, both for FBA and for the development of behaviour intervention plans, has been developed by the Center for Effective Collaboration and Practice (CECP). The materials can be downloaded free of charge at <http://cecp.air.org> (click on 'Functional Behavior Assessment' to go to the manuals).

Manual 2 (CECP, 1998) provides coverage of Functional Behaviour Assessment and Manual 3 (CECP, 2000) provides coverage of positive behaviour plans. Another excellent resource is by Crone and Horner (2003). There are additional references in the suggested reading and resources section at the end of this chapter.

FBA is the process of gathering data to understand the student's behaviour and to determine likely purposes of the behaviour. Two principles underlie student behaviour. First, almost all behaviour serves a purpose—to get something that is desired, to avoid something undesirable, or to communicate a message or need. Second, behaviour occurs in a context, that is, under certain conditions and not at other times.

If a student refuses to complete a task set by the teacher and is sent out of the room, the function of the behaviour can serve one or a combination of getting, avoiding, and communicating, and these can be internal or external. Table 5.2 provides an example of how this may happen. Notice that the teacher should be picking up the message that the student is unable to do the task, and without assistance and support will likely not be able to do the task in the future. If that's the case, the student's behaviour may escalate as he or she learns that refusal is the best way of addressing low academic performance.

TABLE 5.2 **POSSIBLE FUNCTIONS OF A BEHAVIOUR**

	Internally	Externally
Get	Refusing to do the task gets personal satisfaction	Peer approval for "standing up to" a teacher request
Avoid	Having to attempt a task that he or she most likely can't do	Peers seeing that he or she can't do the task
Communicate	I can avoid tasks by refusing to do them but I still can't do the task and will not be able to do it without assistance	*Should* be communicating to the teacher that he or she can't do the task and hence needs assistance not removal

A key feature of FBA is the identification of the relationship between the problem behaviours and the events before and after that make the behaviours more likely to occur again. This is often referred to as ABC.

- **A**ntecedents—what happens before the behaviour?
- **B**ehaviour—the actual observable and measurable action.
- **C**onsequences—what happens after the behaviour?

Environmental conditions, or the ecological factors, are also examined. These include the layout of the classroom or other teaching space and distractions to learning.

FBA provides an objective method of identifying behaviours to target for intervention.

If the teacher manipulates events after the behaviour has occurred, there is no opportunity to understand why it occurred in the first place. In an FBA approach, students can be taught to replace problem behaviours with more socially acceptable ones that still meet their needs.

The six steps in conducting an FBA are described below. Notice that it is not essential to complete all activities in all steps, and a full assessment would only be conducted if the behaviours were of very serious concern.

Step 1: The seriousness of the problem

Through discussion with a specialist behaviour teacher or a colleague, the class teacher determines as accurately as possible the exact behaviour of concern (e.g., Tom is punching other students in the classroom). A colleague then observes the classroom to verify the behaviours and see whether the behaviours are demonstrated by other students as well, which might mean that the classroom procedures need to be changed rather than a specific program set up for one student only. These classroom observations are also an opportunity to see whether the behaviours are being triggered by any other factors in the classroom setting, such as teacher behaviour or expectations. If the teacher can alter unrealistic academic or social expectations, there might be no need for a behaviour intervention for the student.

If, after discussing the outcomes of the observations and considering any cultural issues, the teacher and colleague believe that a functional behaviour assessment is appropriate, they proceed through the following steps.

Step 2: Definition of the problem behaviour

A succinct definition of each behaviour is essential before data are collected. Hence, an appropriate definition of a specific behaviour might be "Closed-fist hitting other students to the body and head" rather than a non-specific description of "Being aggressive". It is also important to collect data in all possible settings. The information required is:

- when the behaviour occurs;
- the location of the behaviour;
- conditions under which the behaviour occurs and does not occur;
- who is present when the behaviour occurs;
- events or conditions that typically occur before the behaviour;
- events or conditions that typically occur after the behaviour;
- common environmental (setting) events; and
- any other behaviours that are associated with the behaviour in question.

As a result of collecting this information, some behaviours might be grouped (e.g., in-seat and on-task), although there is always the option to return to specific behaviours later if the grouped-behaviour approach does not work.

Step 3: Possible functions of the problem behaviour

It is important to collect information from a range of sources. This might include the completion of a checklist and/or rating scales by classroom teachers, parents, and the student (if appropriate), as well as interviews with teachers, parents, and psychologists, and, most importantly, direct observation in multiple settings on multiple occasions. Often these approaches to data collection are divided into direct assessment (e.g., observation) and indirect assessment (e.g., checklists, rating scales, and interviews).

Direct observations in the classroom provide a clearer indication of the student's behaviour than do teacher checklists and rating scales, which are open to teacher bias and tolerance. Observation can provide valuable assessment and program information for that setting. Direct observation of the behaviour might include any of the following dimensions:

- rate (how often per unit of time it occurs);
- duration (how long it lasts);
- force (how intense it is);
- topography (what the behaviour looks like);
- locus (where it occurs); and
- latency (the length of time before the behaviour occurs).

Scatterplots, graphs, and Antecedent-Behaviour-Consequences (ABC) charts, or combinations of these, are commonly used to collect data. (See Alberto & Troutman, 2003; Rosenberg et al., 2004b, for specific methods and charting.)

Checklists and rating scales are also useful tools. Of the rating scales, the Achenbach Child Behavior Checklist (Achenbach, 2001) is the most widely used in Australian schools as it has the advantage of using both parent and teacher ratings together with computer marking and analysis based on Australian norms. The teacher report form also provides the opportunity to gather data on academic performance. There is also a youth self-report form for children and adolescents aged between 11 and 18 years.

Interviews can assist in verifying information gathered through checklists, rating scales, or direct observations. However, there is no suitable substitute for direct observation of behaviour, particularly in the area of attention deficit disorders in which medical diagnosis is often based on isolated clinical interviews with the child and parents, with no input from educators.

It is important to ensure that there is a breadth of data gathered for assessment and that as many opportunities and methods as possible are used to gather data and as many relevant players as possible are involved. An example of gathering data from multiple sources is the use of a collaborative management approach that includes input from all relevant professionals, as proposed in *Talk time teamwork*, a publication of the NSW Department of School Education (1995). In this model, using blank forms provided in the document, documentation and observational data are gathered from schools and medical practitioners at initial referral and throughout the monitoring of intervention approaches.

Step 4: Triangulation and/or problem pathway analysis

Having collected data, it is time to analyse the information to determine which social, affective, and environmental conditions are associated with the problem behaviours. Triangulation of data is very important, and a triangulation chart listing the data from each source can assist in visually comparing the data.

The aim is to identify possible patterns of behaviour, triggering events, consequences that trigger or maintain the behaviour, and the likely functions of the behaviour. It is also possible to develop pathways for the behaviour—from the setting events, to the antecedents, to the behaviour, to the consequences that maintain the behaviour. This is termed *problem pathway analysis*.

Step 5: Generate a hypothesis on the probable purpose of the problem

The statement of probable function is a concise summary of the information collected during the assessment phase so that the behaviour intervention plan can be written. It allows the person or team writing the plan to know that when X occurs the student does Y to achieve Z.

Step 6: Test the hypothesis statement

It is important that the intervention plan is not developed until the prediction is tested. If there are any environmental changes that can be made, such as changing the curriculum content or its presentation,

so that the behaviour changes, there is no need to proceed with developing a behavioural plan. For example, if the student was annoying others during a worksheet activity and the teacher produced worksheets that the student could complete unassisted and without disruption, then a behavioural plan for the student to work unassisted would not be needed.

Five to seven lessons are used to test the hypothesis statement and to assess whether changes can be made without a formal plan. In other cases, such as aggressive or other serious behaviours, it might be appropriate to proceed with the behavioural plan more quickly.

The most important outcome of the FBA is behavioural change. This can be either in the form of manipulation of environmental events (e.g., curriculum, teaching and learning strategies, or the layout of the classroom or playground) or the development of a behaviour intervention plan.

Following the completion of the FBA process, a positive behaviour improvement plan can be developed and implemented if required. This process is discussed later in this chapter.

Changing the way we teach in the regular school

The minimum requirement for managing all students is a total and consistent commitment to a positive school environment in which agreed behavioural expectations are: (a) developed, (b) known, (c) applied consistently and fairly, (d) supported at all levels within the school community, and (e) supported by district and systems authorities.

Maintaining a positive, well-disciplined class in a supportive school community relies on the cooperation of all staff members who work to ensure that they are all involved in developing a consistent discipline and welfare policy and in applying that policy persistently. In this section I consider ways in which this can be achieved, both at the total school level and in the individual classroom.

THE IMPORTANCE OF EARLY INTERVENTION

Early intervention is essential for students with behaviour problems. Today, many students are identified in early childhood settings, and interventions are put in place at that stage. Within school-aged placements there is, again, strong emphasis on early intervention. Although some behaviour problems do not appear in the early years, the vast majority do and, without early attention, students and teachers can expect a worsening of the behaviour patterns, particularly in cases of conduct disorder. It has been argued that if antisocial behaviour is not addressed and changed by the end of Year 3, it must be treated as a chronic condition much like diabetes. It may not be cured but can be managed with appropriate supports and continuing intervention. This does not mean that we abandon help for students with behaviour problems in the later years of school, but it emphasises that intervention should occur as soon as the behaviour is identified, whether that is in preschool, primary, or secondary school, or at the tertiary level.

REGULAR CLASS MANAGEMENT

The individual classroom is where most teachers have greatest difficulty with students with behaviour problems. And, of course, there is great variety of behaviours that can disrupt classroom learning. A key feature of regular classrooms for any student, particularly those classrooms that include students with behaviour problems, is the presence of a positive classroom environment. This is a setting that meets the physical, psychological, social, and educational needs of all students. There are three dimensions in a positive classroom: conditions, curriculum, and consequences.

Conditions in a positive classroom include:

- physical and psychological safety for teachers and students, that is, no ridicule or humiliation by any person;

- knowledgeable, skilled, charismatic, and courageous staff with a strong background in behaviour management, a positive self-concept and a clear understanding of the educational needs of students with behaviour problems;
- attainable goals and objectives for each student with a behaviour problem that are individualised, developmental, measurable, and achievable;
- relevant curriculum providing experiences related to the lives, problems, and needs of the students;
- positive instructional techniques providing instruction that ensures success according to the student's individual goals and objectives;
- opportunities for socialisation that provide students with behaviour problems opportunities to communicate in a natural (group) setting under supervision;
- instruction in social skills, including peer instruction and cooperative learning; links to and among the students' worlds (i.e., school, peers, family linkages through socialising, communicating and collaborating, and community participation);
- classrooms that are highly structured in terms of expectations, routines, rules and schedules and, as an essential, an explicit behaviour management system;
- classroom rules that are few, fair, clearly displayed, taught, and consistently enforced with no loopholes for challenges; and
- prohibition of violence and abuse, that is, there must be non-physical aversive consequences for any acts of aggression, abusive language, or put-downs (otherwise the student might see these behaviours as being acceptable).

Curriculum in a positive classroom is a critical issue as students with behaviour problems may have missed many experiences that occur naturally in families due to their non-acceptance by families, peers, and community members. Hence, curriculum needs to include the following:

- effective, motivating, and therapeutic experiences to meet the most basic of learning needs—it becomes therapeutic as it ameliorates the problems that have contributed to the student being identified as having behaviour problems;
- thematic units that provide an integrated learning experience and have been shown to be very effective in both regular and special education;
- careful selection of instructional materials that are relevant to the student's life, related to what he or she knows, and relevant to the student's neighbourhood and community;
- concrete, manipulable materials;
- age-appropriate materials to teach basic skills;
- positive materials that show people and society in a positive light;
- social skills that are modelled all day, every day and in teachable moments to reinforce social skills, including anger management, assertiveness, aggression replacement; and
- materials that encourage interactions in which students learn (under supervision) to communicate without arguments, fights, or put-downs.

Consequences in the positive classroom include:

- those that are positive, natural, and logical;
- those that are primary or concrete rewards in conjunction with social rewards;
- token rewards that cannot be counterfeited;
- the most desirable reinforcer, particularly for adolescents, the avoidance of work; and

- the achievement of less desired activities *before* more desirable activities (this is called the Premack Principle).

INDIVIDUAL CLASSROOM MANAGEMENT STRATEGIES

Lewis and Sugai (1999) identified a number of important points. These include:

- Provide advance organisers or precorrections. Students must be reminded beforehand of the correct behaviour to increase the likelihood of its occurring in that setting. For example, before they go into the classroom, "Remember to have your books and pens on the desk ready to start." Teachers can also model the desired behaviours.
- Keep students engaged. The best way to keep students on task is to ensure that the lesson content and presentation, and the reinforcement given, keep students motivated, and that alternative inappropriate sources of reinforcement or attention are not available. Short monitored tasks and varying the lesson style through activities can be very effective.
- Provide a positive focus. Commonly, teacher interactions are frequent, short, and negative. One strategy is to have at least four positive interactions to each negative one. The teacher should also ensure that a positive classroom climate exists, rather than one of confrontation.
- Consistently enforce school and class rules. Stated simply, if it is worth having an "If … then" approach to classroom rules for students with behaviour problems, it is worth ensuring that they are respected and followed by all students. Similarly, reinforcing school rules is an important part of ensuring a positive school behaviour plan.
- Correct rule violations and social behaviour errors proactively. Correction needs to be applied consistently and, if possible, without drawing attention to the student and the problem behaviour. There is also a need to ensure that the teacher does not become involved in a power struggle with the student. If the behaviour persists, consideration should be given to moving to a specific behaviour intervention plan.

REDUCING BEHAVIOUR PROBLEMS

A critical aspect of maintaining students with behaviour problems in an inclusive classroom is the recognition of the learning difficulties that students face (Mooney, Epstein, Reid, & Nelson, 2003). Teachers must adapt their teaching styles and the curriculum to ensure that students do not fail, as this often results in behaviour problems and failure to cope in the regular classroom. When this occurs, the student is trapped in a failure cycle. The challenge for students and teachers alike is to make changes such that classrooms work effectively, rather than relying on the student to change unassisted.

Some possible questions for teachers to consider when determining ways to change curriculum presentation and to reduce behaviour problems include:

- Is the curriculum relevant to the students' life?
- Is there an alternative that is more relevant and functional?
- How can I vary the teaching and learning activities?
- Do I provide opportunities for students to respond to academic tasks in differing ways?
- How actively engaged are students in the learning?

While changing the teaching–learning environment will not solve all behaviour problems, such changes might avoid the need to embark on specific management programs. In summary, the most useful strategies include:

- being well prepared;
- giving short-term tasks;
- providing clear academic and behaviour expectations;
- monitoring activities frequently; and
- encouraging cooperative learning.

Teaching social skills

Social skills are complex and include overt, observable behaviours as well as problem-solving behaviours. These are considered in other chapters (especially Chapter 11) so I won't deal with them extensively here. Social skills include:

- *Peer friendship-making*—such as introducing yourself, joining in, asking a favour, offering to help, giving and accepting compliments, and apologising.
- *Teacher-pleasing*—including following directions, working consistently, and listening to the teacher.
- *Self-management skills*—allow a student to assess a social situation, select an appropriate skill, and determine its effectiveness; self-related behaviours include following through, dealing with stress, understanding feelings, and controlling anger.
- *Assertiveness skills*—allow students to convey their needs without resorting to aggression.
- *Communication with peers and adults*—skills that include asking for information, listener responsiveness, turn-taking, maintaining conversational attention, and giving the speaker feedback.

A social skills difficulty can occur at one of three levels.

1 *Skills deficit*—that is, the student doesn't have the social skill and needs to learn that skill.
2 *Performance deficit*—that is, the student may have the skill but either doesn't know when to use it or chooses not to use it and hence needs to learn to use the skill without a request or prompt.
3 *Fluency deficit*—that is, the student uses the skill but only in certain situations and needs to learn to maintain and generalise the skill so that it occurs in other situations without a request or prompt.

Social skills training programs range from the teaching of specific behaviours (such as eye-contact and facial expressions) to broader, more complex social skills (such as making friends). Although social skills were once taught in isolation, and then generalised to social settings in the classroom, more recently there has been a move to teach clusters of social skills, as well as incorporating cognitive and environmental influences in programs.

Many teachers prefer not to use packaged programs for social skills training but use ideas from a variety of sources and develop a program that meets their own needs. An excellent American website with practical ideas for teaching social skills is <www.cccoe.net/social>, which provides access to many teaching ideas.

Self-efficacy and self-management skills

Self-efficacy is the belief we have that we can do a task successfully. As many students with behaviour problems have had negative social experiences in classrooms, their self-efficacy might be lowered and they are, therefore, unwilling to persevere if obstacles or rejection occur. Positive teaching and an emphasis on supporting the student through graded learning tasks can also enhance self-esteem as success builds on success.

Self-management skills include monitoring, recording, and reinforcing performance. Importantly, self-management skills incorporate the use of thinking strategies such as taking responsibility for initiating learning through the acquisition of problem-solving skills. Students can work quietly as a group provided they understand the part they play in maintaining a positive classroom environment.

A critical component for the student with a behaviour problem is monitoring, because the ability to use feedback to assess the effects of their own actions is a critical variable missing from the student's repertoire. It is also the critical variable missing from traditional behaviour management programs, in which the assessor and reinforcer of behaviour is the teacher.

Developing and implementing behaviour plans

If the student has such significant emotional or behaviour problems that they cannot function within the class and school system, individualised instruction might be necessary. To develop an intervention plan, a functional behaviour assessment will have been completed. The plan comprises part of the total individual education plan, or individual learning plan, which provides the overall educational program for the student. The behaviour intervention plan can be developed, implemented, and monitored through a four-step procedure that continues on from the sixth step of the functional behaviour assessment discussed earlier.

The steps in the development of the Behaviour Improvement Plan (BIP) are designed to develop a positive intervention that will develop appropriate behaviours while reducing or eliminating the challenging behaviours that prevent successful learning in the class. Following on from the six steps in the FBA, the steps in a BIP are as follows.

Step 7: Develop the plan

The same team that conducted the FBA should develop the plan. It should have specific behaviour expectations to meet the skills or performance deficits of the student, be built on the experiences of previous interventions and of course be positive in focus. The plan will contain both long- and short-term goals.

Step 8: Monitor the plan's implementation

The monitoring provides a check on the consistency and accuracy of the plan's implementation by the staff. This is often done through a checklist completed by team members at the BIP team meeting.

Step 9: Evaluate the effectiveness of the plan

Comparing the baseline data collected in the FBA with BIP performance data provides a demonstration of behaviour change. It also provides a measure of the movement through short-term goals toward the long-term goal.

Step 10: Modify the plan

The plan is considered to be complete when the long-term goal is met or, in the case of the goal not being met, the plan is no longer appropriate. Data from Steps 8 and 9 will provide the evidence for decisions in Step 10. If the behaviour has not changed in the desired direction, it may be necessary to conduct a new FBA based on the new data and develop a further plan or a revised plan.

An excellent model of a behaviour plan is the Individual Positive Behaviour Plan developed by the Catholic Education Office, Catholic Archdiocese of Sydney (2006). This plan (Figure 5.5) provides all of the content needed to implement an individual plan as it links:

- the outcomes of FBA (Identified behaviours of concern);
- the positive replacement behaviour (Desired outcome);

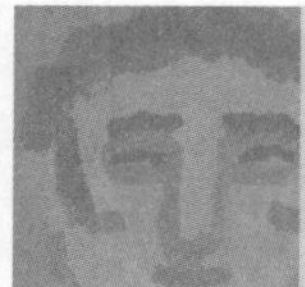

FIGURE 5.5
Individual Positive Behaviour Plan

Individual Positive Behaviour Plan (IPBP)

STUDENT NAME: ______________________________ DOB: __________

**The following table should be completed with reference to the Risk Assessment.

Identified behaviours of concern	Desired outcome	Agreed management strategies	Strategies to be undertaken by	Monitoring comments

Source: Catholic Education Office, Archdiocese of Sydney (2006). Individual Positive Behaviour Plan. Sydney: Author.

- what the team has decided will be done (Agreed management strategies);
- who will do it (who will apply the strategies); and
- how it will be assessed, by whom and when (Monitoring comments).

The final plan is really a series of interventions that address these needs. As the plan consists of multiple intervention strategies, CECP suggests a number of techniques that might be useful (CECP, 2000). Rosenberg et al. (2004a; b) is another useful source of intervention strategies, including the following:

- Teach more acceptable replacement behaviours that have the same function as the inappropriate behaviour, or use conflict resolution skills, or use alternative strategies such as self-management or coping.
- Teach how to deal with the physical location such as the layout of the classroom or places that are safe to play in the playground. Often this is referred to as changing the setting events.
- Manipulate the things that happen before the behaviour (antecedents), such as changing the teaching materials or teacher instructions.
- Manipulate what happens after the misbehaviour (consequences), such as how you react. Think about reinforcing an incompatible behaviour instead.
- Change the teaching–learning ecology of the classroom—what you teach, and how you teach it.

The use of a chart can demonstrate which behaviours the student uses to obtain something, and which behaviours are used to avoid something. Remember, the behaviours of each student may be different for the same desired outcomes. This is why each student who is causing a severe behavioural disruption in the class will need a specific behaviour assessment and intervention plan.

Specialist behaviour services

Although students, support personnel, and executive staff expect that teachers will handle most behaviour problems within the regular classroom by themselves, there are some students whose behaviour requires specialist assistance. If the student is causing a problem in other classes or in other places (such as the playground), it might be appropriate to seek specialist assistance. Working with behaviour support services can enhance the learning and social environment for all students in the class. Help can be provided in the class or through short-term intensive withdrawal. Guidance officers and educational psychologists can also provide assistance with assessment, referrals, and additional support and advice.

The main focus of specialist services is the provision of assistance to teachers and students in managing behaviour disorders so that students can remain within the regular school. Education departments in the various states and territories have different provisions for services, and even within states variations occur in the operation of a particular service.

In New South Wales, the Support Teacher (Behaviour), or ST-B, model is a good example of a specialist advisory service for teachers of students with behaviour disorders. Although it operates slightly differently in each education district in New South Wales, the ST-B model is designed to provide services to teachers of students who:

- present continuing behaviour and adjustment difficulties (e.g., they fail to respond to the usual range of management strategies employed by the regular school); and
- are likely to benefit by maintenance in their regular class with provision of specialist support to the classroom teacher(s).

Although the ST-B might provide individual or small-group assistance in some circumstances, the role is essentially to consult and team-teach. Teacher referrals are usually made through the school counsellor to a district behaviour team leader, with each ST-B serving a cluster of schools. The ST-B role involves considerable skill in balancing the needs of difficult students and their teachers across a number of schools. Specialist teachers focus more on professional learning by teachers, giving them additional skills to manage behaviours.

Integration teachers also provide assistance to students who are emotionally disturbed but who are able to cope with full-time or part-time mainstream placements. Support is also provided to the teachers of these students.

For the 1–7% of students with more severe behaviour problems who are beyond school-based services and those provided at the small-group level in the Effective Behaviour Support model, there is the possibility of limited short-term withdrawal by a specialist behaviour disorder teacher or integration teacher. In some states, large schools might have a special needs support unit within the school to meet a wide range of special needs, including behaviour disorders. Within regular schools, specialist teachers can conduct small-group withdrawal sessions on social skills training and can establish behaviour programs.

In some schools, program funding has been provided to combat bullying or to support general anti-violence measures. Some schools pool funds to run a program to meet local needs. Examples of these are discussed in the following section. They are specialist programs often operated in alternative settings such as police-citizens clubs.

A number of jurisdictions have a clear focus on not providing formal alternative behaviour services, preferring to focus on supporting students in the mainstream classes or within school-based programs. The Tasmanian Department of Education model, called *Maintaining and Retaining Students in Secondary Schools*, provides schools with additional staffing based on the Educational Needs Index, which identifies the socioeconomic needs of the school. Funding is also used to develop curriculum-based tasks such as farming, horticulture, and mechanics that integrate academic and social skills training (Conway, 2003b). The ACT Department of Education and Training has adopted a similar approach to maintaining students in mainstream schools rather than in specialist placements, having identified that alternative settings do not address the fundamental underlying problems of meeting the educational needs of students within their community school (Conway, 2003c).

Considering that the focus is on the provision of services rather than on specific programs, most special placements follow one of two approaches. They are:

1 regular curricula with strong emphasis on social and personal development skills to assist the student to return to the regular class; and
2 alternative programs aimed at social skills development and preparation for post-school options such as employment or further job training programs.

Special classes and units

Special classes and units constitute one of the largest and most diverse ranges of service for children and adolescents with behaviour problems. Full-time and part-time special classes and units are provided in many Australian states, although the terminology, function, and operational definition of services differ within and among jurisdictions.

One of the major difficulties confronting secondary conduct disorder units has been meeting the needs of adolescents who were unable, or unwilling, to comply with the discipline and academic constraints of the school. Secondary conduct units have provided a transition to the post-school world through work experience programs, access to job training courses, and leisure activities. This has worked well for many students aged 14–15 years. However, the increasing number of referrals of students in the first year of high school, or directly from primary schools, has placed increasing demands on these services because the younger students are ineligible for work experience placements. Consequently, the focus for this group is more commonly on academic skills with the aim of reintegration into mainstream secondary programs.

There is no universal support for the development of separate programs. It has been argued that such centres are unlikely to change teacher behaviour or school environments that contribute to disruptive behaviours. Off-site centres might reduce the likelihood of regular schools attempting to alter their approach because they could send their troublesome students to another location. Not having access to off-site units places the responsibility for catering for students with disruptive behaviours back on regular classrooms and schools, and thus encourages the development of more effective whole-school policies.

To overcome the problems of reintegrating students from special classes, many programs now offer half-day attendance at the class (with the remainder of the day in the student's regular class), or four days at the special class and one day in the regular class. These have distinct advantages because they avoid the need for students to leave their home school and they enable the special-class teacher to integrate social and academic programs with those of the class in which the behaviour disorder was demonstrated. In addition, part-time placement avoids the need to arrange reintegration of students into schools in which the staff might otherwise have perceived that the problem student had been successfully removed. A

potential advantage in part-time placement is the occasional need to separate the students from the home-school environment. This gives the students, teachers, and peers relief from continued confrontation.

Residential schools and shared facilities

Residential schools for students with behaviour disorders are provided:

- as specialist private schools; and
- as facilities operated by education departments on premises belonging to departments of health, community welfare, or juvenile justice.

In all Australian states and territories, residential facilities are provided for young offenders and educational services exist on-site for school-aged residents. Behavioural disorders of young offenders are a major concern because, while they are in detention, they are costly to maintain.

The issue of reintegration

One of the prime concerns of placements at all levels is the goal of reintegration of students with behaviour problems into regular school settings, or the maintenance of such students in the regular classroom. Studies in Australian schools and abroad (see Westwood & Graham, 2003) have shown that students with behaviour problems are among the least acceptable of students with special needs for reintegration.

In the case of adolescents with a history of prior behaviour problems, there is a strong reluctance on the part of secondary school staff to accept them back in their home schools, and even a reluctance to accept out-of-area placements. Hence, meeting the needs of these students involves not only providing specialist programs but also having them accepted back into the regular school. For many secondary students, the aim of specialist conduct disorder settings is not to reintegrate students but to look for alternative, non-school placements—such as technical and further education (TAFE) colleges or employment—and help in acquiring personal and social skills for post-school settings.

One method of ensuring this is to maintain the student in the regular school throughout the specialist intervention, or to secure a post-intervention placement prior to accepting the student. Where full-time withdrawal occurs, academic and social skills training in special classes and schools (in preparation for re-entry into mainstream education) must be accompanied by preparation of the teacher(s) and students in the regular class before the student is readmitted.

LEARNING ESSENTIALS

In this section, I look at specific behaviour problems that we face in mainstream classroom setting. Four behaviours that teachers find difficult to deal with are:

1. Attention Deficit Hyperactivity Disorder (ADHD);
2. bullying;
3. Autism Spectrum Disorder (ASD); and
4. Asperger's syndrome.

Attention Deficit Hyperactivity Disorder

ADHD was previously included with disruption, inattention, impulsivity, and hyperactivity as a group. All students display these behaviours at some time. They become behaviour problems only when they are more frequent or more severe than usual for that age. Today, ADHD has two main types: predominantly hyperactive and predominantly inattentive.

We know that there is a strong genetic component to ADHD. Students with ADHD might have trouble with:

- remaining seated;
- following instructions;
- concentrating on one task;
- taking turns;
- finishing work;
- understanding and following rules;
- organising tasks; and
- working and playing in groups.

Although the student is likely to have a formal diagnosis by a paediatrician and might be on medication, there are a number of strategies that can be implemented. And it needs to be remembered that medication does not replace the need for effective teaching. The following positive teaching strategies are based on the NSW resource document (*Talk time teamwork*, NSW Department of School Education, 1995).

LEARNING ENVIRONMENT

- Provide a structured environment (at home, in class, in the playground).
- Request and supervise an uncluttered desk space.
- Provide consistent routines for transition between activities and lessons (e.g., tell the student the lesson is about to end. At the end tell the student what's needed for the next lesson).

MANAGING BEHAVIOURS

- Teach all new behaviours rather than expecting them to occur (e.g., teach having a clear desk, don't just demand it).
- Teach how to organise time and work tasks (e.g., have a visual timetable on the student's desk).
- Seat the student appropriately in the learning environment with supportive peers.
- Clearly communicate rules and expectations and reinforce with frequent feedback on progress (i.e., state the rule and the expected behaviour and reinforce as soon as it occurs).
- Increase the frequency of reinforcers (e.g., at first, reinforce often).
- Use consequences that are relevant (i.e., ensure the student understands why the consequences are applied).
- Use positive statements rather than negative ones (positive statements reflect what you want, negative ones don't).

TEACHING

- Design and communicate academic tasks clearly so that the student knows exactly what is expected (e.g., "Do questions one and two and then stop").
- Provide step-by-step instructions both orally and visually (e.g., use a visual plan).
- Use interactive teaching strategies (e.g., work with the student and check progress rather than leaving him or her to work alone).
- Consistently use one instructional method or strategy rather than constantly changing (e.g., ask a question and come back for the response, because standing and waiting for a response adds to the pressure).

- Allow for slower speed of response.
- Allow the student to see progress on short tasks.
- Structure the workload into manageable sections or mini-assignments.
- Ensure coordination between home and school (i.e., talk with parents or use a communication book to maintain contact).

There is also a need for the teacher to work with parents and medical personnel if a young person is on medication, particularly if the teacher is involved in the administration of medication. School systems have set procedures for the management of medications in schools, including those for students with specific behavioural needs. Given the move toward slow release medication, the need to administer medication during school time is reducing. Teachers are also able to provide medical personnel with information on the effects of the medication during school time.

Bullying

Many students are affected by bullying at some time during their schooling: as a bully, as a victim, or as an observer. In some cases students are involved in more than one role. Bullying in schools affects more than 15% of students (Rigby, 2003). Bullying can occur at any age, affects boys and girls of all cultures and socioeconomic groups, and is a major issue for many schools in Australasia.

Bullying is based on a power imbalance between the bully and the victim. The bully is generally bigger, stronger, or more powerful (but not necessarily older) than the victim. Bullying occurs when the incidents are repeated occurrences, not one-off, and the incidents are designed to injure. For some students, being bullied is an ongoing problem that can lead to depression and (potentially) suicide.

Bullying has many forms: verbal, physical, extortion, damage to property, isolation, gestures, intimidation and, most critical now, psychological bullying through technology. We used to think bullying frequently occurred out of teachers' sight, often in the playground. Today, bullying is a 24-hour-a-day, seven-days-a-week problem for students. Cyber-bullying occurs through email bullying, and messages on MSN Messenger, MySpace, YouTube, and other internet formats. Cyber-bullying through videos of teachers and other students can be circulated to a level that previous bullying methods could never have been imagined by earlier researchers.

Although students do not like bullying, they commonly do not expose the bullies, and not to their teachers if they do. Hence, studies of bullying in schools often reveal levels that surprise school staff. The consequences of bullying for the victim include physical injury, loss of confidence and self-esteem, school avoidance, and loss of friends (as they can be despised by others). Bullies can become more aggressive, more demanding, more brazen over time, and can attract students who seek association with powerful students in the school.

The signs can be hard to see but among the common ones identified in the Australian Government (Commonwealth of Australia, 2000) information for parents are:

- unexplained bruises, scratches and cuts;
- torn or damaged clothes;
- headaches, stomach aches, and other pains;
- unexplained tears, temper, depression;
- not wanting to go to school or play with friends;
- changing the route to school and/or home;
- failing schoolwork; and
- needing extra money without offering a reason.

Dealing with bullying requires a whole-school approach that includes teachers, students, and parents. Seven aspects of the school need to be addressed in a total approach: victim, bully, school environment, role modelling, administration, curriculum, and teaching. Before tackling the specific problems, the school needs to know the actual extent of bullying, the types of bullying, its frequency and severity, where it occurs, who is involved and why. This can be achieved through surveys of students, checks of the playground, record keeping, and an examination of the school discipline and administrative procedures. Once the extent and nature of the problem are known, a policy can be put in place. To do this, all staff members, students, and parents need to be involved in implementing and maintaining the zero tolerance policy. Providing alternative positive options, such as an emphasis on acceptance of diversity and difference, are also important.

Autism Spectrum Disorder

Autism Spectrum Disorder is a developmental disability that affects communication skills and interpersonal relationships. In the past 15 years there has been an epidemic growth in the number of students identified with ASD in the United States, and students with ASD now comprise the largest group of litigation cases in special education (Baird, 1999).

As this chapter focuses on all aspects of behaviour and not on developmental disabilities, the following information is a guide only and not a complete discussion on ASD or Asperger's syndrome. Readers are referred to specialist texts for further information.

ASD is identified as a lifelong disorder that is usually diagnosed before the age of three years. It has no accepted known cause or cure and is more common in boys than girls. The three main characteristics are:

1. a disturbance in the development of language concepts and in the ability to communicate verbally or non-verbally;
2. disturbances and impairments in the ability to relate to, and interact with, people; and
3. limited imagination and restricted interests.

A number of other characteristics may also be present, including:

- inability to cope with changes in routine;
- stereotypic and repetitive movements such as rocking, hand flapping, or finger flicking;
- actions, behaviours, or interests that are repetitive, obsessive, and ritualistic; and
- high sensitivity in a sensory area.

In the past, students with severe ASD were very unlikely to be in regular classes, but more students are now at least beginning their schooling in regular classes. The body of literature on interventions for ASD has grown enormously in the past 20 years. Lovannone, Dunlap, Huber, and Kincaid (2003) identified six key variables in effective teaching programs for students with ASD. Each is briefly explored below.

INDIVIDUALISED SERVICES

There is no one approach that has been endorsed as better than any other. Hence, the approach adopted for each student should meet that student's needs and interests. Any individual education program developed should draw from the breadth of educational opportunities, from minor adaptations of the curriculum to an individual functional academic program. In developing the program, three criteria of successful services should be considered: family preferences, student preferences and interests, and the student's strengths and weaknesses.

SYSTEMATIC INSTRUCTION

Specific education programs and goals, together with systematic planning, teaching, and evaluation, are critical. Strategies based on Applied Behaviour Analysis (see Alberto & Troutman, 2006) provide this framework, with an emphasis on skills acquisition and planned teaching to allow the student to maintain and generalise the skills. This may place considerable demands on the class teacher and the support of a teacher's aide or integration aide is important during the implementation of the teacher's curriculum and when making instruction decisions.

COMPREHENSIVE/STRUCTURED LEARNING ENVIRONMENTS

The literature supports flexibility and adaptation in the following activities: organising the teaching setting; providing a schedule of activities; careful planning of options that require making choices; providing behaviour support; defining specific working areas of the school and classroom; and assisting in transitions. The aim is to provide support that allows the student to build competencies and to move beyond the confines that exist.

SPECIFIC CURRICULUM CONTENT

The main curriculum areas of need are communication and social interaction. Specialised curriculum instruction in these areas is essential but should be based on individual student needs and parent preferences. Social skills areas, such as initiating and responding to social cues, and recreational and leisure skills, are important. The use of augmentative and alternative communication (AAC) systems and adaptive technology will increase communication skills, which in turn support the possible development of social skills. Language/communication skills and social skills together enhance the ability of the child with ASD to be part of the school community.

A FUNCTIONAL APPROACH TO PROBLEM BEHAVIOUR

Management of students' behavioural needs through a model of developing positive behaviours has replaced earlier approaches that may have used punishment for inappropriate behaviours. The strategies discussed earlier in this chapter on the use of Functional Behaviour Assessment and the development of Positive Behaviour Plans are important for students with ASD. As with all students with behaviour difficulties, the systematic stages of this model support positive behaviour change and provide clear guidelines for home–school support.

FAMILY INVOLVEMENT

Parents play a key role in the educational decisions for their child as programs must operate across home and school settings. Cooperation of parents in the development of program content and implementation of behaviour and curriculum strategies helps to provide a consistent set of expectations and reinforcers. While students with ASD provide a considerable challenge for teachers of regular classes, help from specialist teachers and assistants, together with strong parental support, can assist their retention in the class and school.

Asperger's syndrome

In broad terms, Asperger's syndrome is a neurological disorder in which social relationships are impaired, difficult, and not age-appropriate. Both verbal and nonverbal communication are affected. The student has restricted interests, and repetitive behaviours are common. It is important to realise that a student with Asperger's syndrome does not have the same learning and behavioural profile as a student with classic ASD (Attwood, 2003).

Specific behavioural criteria were developed as diagnostic criteria (see Garnett & Attwood, 1994). They include:

- Social impairment (extreme egocentricity) with at least two of the following dispositions: inability to interact with peers; lack of desire to interact with peers; lack of appreciation of social cues; socially and emotionally inappropriate behaviour.
- Narrow interest to the extent of at least one of the following: exclusion of other activities; repetitive adherence.
- Repetitive routines including at least one related to self or to others. Speech and language peculiarities displaying at least three of the following: delayed development; superficially perfect expressive language; formal pedantic language; odd patterns of rhythm or sounds (prosody); peculiar voice characteristics; impairment of comprehension, including misinterpretations of literal and implied meanings.
- Nonverbal communication problems with at least one of the following: limited use of gesture; clumsy or gauche body language; limited facial expression; inappropriate expression; peculiar stiff gaze.
- Motor clumsiness (poor performance on neurodevelopmental examination).

Ehlers, Gillberg, and Wing (1999) modified the original diagnostic criteria to form a school-aged screening questionnaire. There is also an Australian scale for Asperger's syndrome (Attwood, 2004) that includes a discussion on assessment, interview procedures, and how to assess children and adults.

There are four emerging educational issues for students with Asperger's syndrome: screening and assessment, placement, educational support, and social skills instruction. The first issue is addressed in the screening methods discussed above. The issues of educational placement and support are confused, because the student is not actually disturbed, and does not have an intellectual disability that is severe enough to warrant either specialist psychiatric or developmental disability services. Hence, the student is most often placed in the regular classroom. In many ways, this is the most appropriate placement, as other students may provide models of appropriate social behaviour. In some regular schools, specialist assistance might be available. For example, in New South Wales there is specific training for specialist behaviour teachers to provide assistance to schools, and Queensland has specialist advisory visiting teachers.

Attwood (2000) identified a number of teacher characteristics that are important for helping students with Asperger's syndrome. He suggested that teachers should have a calm disposition, be predictable in their emotional reactions, be flexible in teaching style and curriculum presentation to accommodate the child, and recognise the child's positive aspects. A sense of humour helps, as the child can change from one emotional state to another within seconds.

As change is a critical issue for the student, a quiet, stable classroom is important. A supportive, calm regular teacher in a small well-ordered room is preferable. Changes in school, particularly in the transition phase from early education to primary, and from primary to secondary, are critical times, and multiple orientation sessions are important. Having teacher and student buddies is also helpful. Secondary schools can be very difficult due to the academic structure of schooling, combined with the difficulties of adolescence. In these circumstances, the chance of negative social interactions increases dramatically as the stability of the primary school is replaced by constant change.

In secondary school, there is a risk that students with Asperger's syndrome will develop an anxiety disorder, an obsessive-compulsive disorder, depression, or aggression in response to the attitudes of teachers and students. Some will end up being expelled as a result of their unusual behaviour patterns, and parents might seek alternative placements for their children, often in specialist settings comprising other students with the same needs.

Students with Asperger's syndrome vary greatly in their performance from day to day. One day they concentrate, conform, socialise, and learn fairly well, while on other days the reverse is true. Attwood (2000) identified this as a series of internal waves or tides in the student that affects performance. On the positive tides, it is time to learn, but on the off tide, revision is a better approach.

Social skills training has been identified as the fourth area of need. Attwood (2000) recommended that one-to-one training might be provided by either a specialist behaviour teacher or a trained teacher's aide. Specific aspects of support include:

- encouragement to be sociable, flexible, and cooperative when playing or working with other children;
- help for the child to recognise social cues and learn the codes of social conduct;
- personal tuition in understanding and managing emotions;
- tuition and practice to improve friendship and teamwork skills;
- help for the student to develop special interests as a means of improving motivation, talent, and knowledge;
- a program to improve gross and fine motor skills;
- encouragement to take the perspectives of others; and
- encouragement to develop conversation skills.

Any social skills program needs to include cognitive, linguistic, and sensory abilities.

USING THIS CHAPTER IN SCHOOLS

Managing student behaviour in classrooms is one of the greatest concerns that beginning teachers face, as well as being one of the concerns teachers mention throughout their careers. At the end of their careers, it is often one of the aspects of teaching they will report as being the least satisfying aspects of their careers, and the one thing they will not miss in their retirement or in their new careers. It is certainly one of the key issues that cause, as previously mentioned, up to 40% of beginning teachers not to continue beyond the first few years of a teaching career. There are numerous textbooks on classroom management, but many of these books often present classroom behaviour and management of classrooms as separate from the learning and teaching that occurs in those classrooms. This is one of the critical aspects of classroom management. Teaching, learning, and management are inextricably linked.

The teacher

As a teacher, you will be a critical factor in the management of your classroom and your students' behaviour. As discussed above, this comes about because you have the critical role of selecting the content to be taught as well as how that content will be taught, the resources that will be used, and the learning strategies that your students will use. Where this selection does not match student abilities, the chance of the learning being successful is diminished, and student engaged time can be reduced from the ideal of >85% to, in some cases, <40%. Students who are engaged less than 40% of the time have over 60% of their time to engage in other activities in the classroom, many of which teachers will see as off-task or disturbing the learning of other students. More critically for teachers, it is seen as disrupting their teaching.

Management of student behaviour needs a consistent approach: one that recognises that student behaviour is, in part, a reflection of their engagement in the teaching and learning in the classroom. We saw this in the case study of Tanya. Tanya's class teacher worked on altering the activities and ensuring that reinforcement was provided to Tanya to encourage her to continue to perform.

Management also recognises that any classroom is part of the wider school, and you will be part of a consistent school-wide management of behaviour. As we saw in Luke's case study, the role of the principal and executive is critical in ensuring that management is effectively implemented across all settings in the school including corridors, playground, and canteen, and on buses, trams, or trains. If you are working in a secondary school, you will need to team up with your colleagues to manage difficult behaviours of the 1–5% of students in the top section of the school behaviour triangle. It is also important for you to balance management of these students with the need to reinforce the positive behaviours of those students at the base of the triangle so they continue to be supportive of the school management practices and remain in that group. Focused positive behaviour training of students at risk (10–15%) remains a priority to ensure these students don't reach the top group and, hence, take considerably more time to manage their behaviours.

The students' environment

The above discussions about your contribution to the classroom and school environment apply to students as well. The two issues are very closely linked. In classrooms, your students respond best when you are fair in your interactions with them, and when you present the curriculum content in interesting ways. Students also respond well to positive, clear expectations.

The school provides many challenges for students with externalising behaviour problems but also spends considerable time responding to them. Students with internalising behaviours such as withdrawn behaviours, depression, obsessive-compulsive behaviours, and behaviours that reflect potential self-harm (such as suicide), receive much less attention. As we know from the literature, this group of students constitutes an increasing cohort in schools and there is a need to address their issues through resilience and social skills training.

As we saw in Figure 5.4, life experiences outside the school are also critically important in addressing the social and behaviour needs of students at school. Students can come from families that are not supportive of the school either because they are antagonistic toward the school or because they do not have the skills or interests to be supportive of their child's learning. We know from the literature that students with behaviour problems are more likely to be male, to demonstrate externalising behaviours, and to come from lower socioeconomic and more dysfunctional families. While this is a generalisation, it reflects the lack of positive links between the home and the school that were raised in Chapter 1. It also says that addressing the behavioural needs of your students requires a sustained and positive relationship with their parents. This is often best established by parent-training programs conducted by professionals who work with parents in a location other than the school. Other family issues include the need for students to come to school with an adequate diet, including breakfast, to ensure that learning time is productive and that students have the opportunity to take part in the full range of school activities. That's why so many schools now are providing breakfast programs, have clothing pools, and have funding reserves to pay for additional activities where the parents are unable to pay.

Influences such as the peer group are also important as they can provide a pathway to delinquent behaviours, as we saw could happen in the case of Luke. School programs that provide positive social experiences such as sporting and cultural activities provide the resilience skills that students need in order to thrive in and out of schools. These include positive social interactions with peers and teachers, sharing, turn-taking, and working as a team rather than as an individual.

You will have a critical role in enhancing the learning and behaviour outcomes for all of your students, by reinforcing the positive behaviours of the majority and supporting behaviour change in those with internalising behaviour needs as well as those with externalising behaviours that challenge us as teachers.

Summary

You need to be prepared both in content and classroom management skill areas. This means:

- know your curriculum area thoroughly in terms of content, skills, and vocabulary;
- have a range of teaching strategies to provide variety for your students; and
- have a range of learning strategies to ensure that differing learning styles of students are catered for—students with learning and/or behaviour problems often learn best with tactile and kinaesthetic strategies.

You will also need to have clear classroom management strategies. This means:

- establish clear classroom rules with your students;
- be consistent and persistent in implementing classroom management practices; and
- know the school's discipline policy and its requirements.

Remember to have a range of management strategies that match the level of behaviour:

Low level or annoying behaviours	Low level responses
Medium level or consistent behaviours	Medium level responses
High level or challenging behaviours	High level responses

And, finally, if there are behaviour problems in your classroom, check first that your teaching and learning strategies aren't the cause of the problem.

PRACTICAL ACTIVITIES

Uni-work

1 This is a group activity. As a small group, consider a regular education classroom at the early childhood, primary, or secondary level in which some students are misbehaving. First, have each person list possible contributing factors to the behaviour problems in the room, using the groupings:

   a the physical environment;
   b the teacher;
   c the curriculum and its teaching; and
   d the students.

   Share the ideas among the group and develop a group list of contributing factors. Now, consider what changes can be made to each grouping to reduce the likelihood of the behaviour problems continuing. How will these changes then come together to improve the teaching–learning environment of the class?

2 This is a library activity. Go to <www.pbis.org> and explore the website. Identify a school at your specialisation level and examine what activities the school is undertaking. How does the school

document the behaviour needs of its students? What activities does the school undertake to support both students and teachers?

3 Select a specific behaviour disorder, such as ADHD, Conduct Disorder, or Oppositional Defiant Disorder, and carry out a brief library search on the topic. Include refereed journals and websites in your list of resources. What are the main recommendations for teaching strategies? From this collection, develop a resource/kit activity that you can share with your student friends that would be useful later during your teaching career.

School-work

Before beginning any of the following activities, speak to your supervising teacher or a member of the school administration to confirm that you can undertake the activity within existing school guidelines and policies.

4 Using the four classroom factors (the physical environment; the teacher; the curriculum and its teaching; and the students), consider the strengths and challenges each brings to the classroom learning and teaching, and management of student behaviour. Consider how your student(s) with special needs alter the four factors and how you manage these within the needs of the whole class. What changes need to be made and how will you achieve this?

5 Using one of the data collection strategies suggested in the CECP FBA Step 3 document to observe a student's behaviour in a classroom or other setting. Make certain that you have permission to do so. Discuss your experiences with others.

6 Take one of the strategies suggested in the chapter for assisting a student with a behaviour problem, such as a social skill strategy, a cognitive strategy, or a reinforcement strategy. Try using it with a student or a group of students as part of a teaching program and evaluate the effectiveness of the strategy.

SUGGESTED READING AND RESOURCES

Books

Ashman, A. F. & Conway, R. N. F. (1997). *Introduction to cognitive education: Theory and applications*. London: Routledge.

Center for Effective Collaboration and Practice (CECP) (1998a). *Addressing student problem behavior Part 1: An IEP team's introduction to functional behavioral assessment and behavior intervention plans*. Washington, DC: Author.

Center for Effective Collaboration and Practice (CECP) (1998b). *Addressing student problem behavior Part 2: Conducting a functional behavioral assessment* (3rd ed.). Washington, DC: Author.

Center for Effective Collaboration and Practice (CECP) (2000). *Addressing student problem behavior Part 3: Creating positive behavioral intervention plans and supports* (2nd ed.). Washington, DC: Author.

Clough, P., Garner, P., Pardeck, J. T., & Yeun, F. (2005). *Handbook of emotional and behavioural difficulties*. London: Sage.

Crone, D. A. & Horner, R. H. (2003). *Building positive behavior support systems in schools: Functional behavior assessment*. New York: The Guilford Press.

Kauffman, J. M. (2005). *Characteristics of emotional and behavioral disorders of children and youth* (8th ed.). Columbus, OH: Merrill Publishing Company.

Porter, L. (2007). *Student behaviour: Theory and practice for teachers* (3rd ed.). Sydney: Allen & Unwin.

Porter, L. (2003). *Young children's behaviour: Practical approaches for caregivers* (2nd ed.). Sydney: MacLennan & Petty.

Journals

Behavioral Disorders

Beyond Behavior

Emotional and Behavioural Difficulties

Journal of Emotional and Behavioral Disorders

Journal of Positive Behavior Interventions

General special education, adolescent and behavioural journals also contain relevant articles.

Websites

<www.cec.sped.org>—Council for Exceptional Children

<www.ccbd.net>—Council for Children with Behaviour Disorders

<www.pbis.org>—Positive Behavioral Support

<www.air.org/cecp>—Center for Effective Collaboration and Practice

<www.cccoe.net/social>—Social skills for schools

<www.racismnoway.com.au>—Racism prevention

<www.beyondblue.com.au>—Depression and OCD

<www.bullyingnoway.com.au>—Anti-bullying

<www.cybersmartkids.com.au>—Cyber bullying issues

<www.kidshelp.com.au>—General support for students

<www.caper.com.au>—CAPER (Child and Adolescent Psychological and Educational Resources)

<www.meceetya.edu.au/pdf/natsafeschool.pdf>—National Safe Schools Framework (NSSF)

REFERENCES

Aboriginal and Torres Strait Islander Commission (2004). *Law and justice: Zero tolerance policing report.* <www.atsic.gov.au/issues/law_and _justice, accessed 11 September 2004.

Achenbach, T. M. (2001). *Child Behavior Checklist/6–18*. Burlington, VT: Research Center for Children, Youth and Families.

Alberto, P. A. & Troutman, A. C. (2006). *Applied behavior analysis for teachers* (7th ed.). Englewood Cliffs, NJ: Merrill/Prentice Hall.

Algozzine, R., Serena L., & Patton, R. (2001). *Childhood behavioural disorders: Applied research and educational practices*. Austin, TX: Pro-Ed.

American Psychiatric Association (2000). *Diagnostic and statistical manual of mental disorders* (DSM-IV-TR). Washington DC: Author.

Ashman, A. F. & Conway, R. N. F. (1993). *Using cognitive strategies in the classroom*. London: Routledge.

Ashman, A. F. & Conway, R. N. F. (1997). *Introduction to cognitive education: Theory and applications*. London: Routledge.

Attwood, T. (1998). *Asperger's syndrome: A guide for parents and professionals*. London: Jessica Kingsley Publications.

Attwood, T. (2000). *Appropriate educational placements for children with Asperger's Syndrome.* <www.tonyattwood.com>, accessed 18 October 2007.

Attwood, T. (2003). *Asperger's syndrome: A guide for parents and professionals* (DVD). Brisbane: Future Horizons.

Attwood, T. (2004). *Asperger's Diagnostic Assessment* (DVD). Brisbane: Future Horizons.

Babkie, A. M. (2006). Be proactive in managing classroom behavior. *Intervention in School and Clinic, 41*, 184–187.

Baird, M. M. (1999). *Legal issues in autism. Proceedings of the 20th National Institute on Legal Issues of Educating Individuals with Disabilities*. Alexandria, VA: LRP Publications, Conference Division.

Beaman, R. & Wheldall, K. (1997). Teacher perceptions of troublesome classroom behaviour: A review of recent research. *Special Education Perspectives*, *6*, 49–56.

Bullard, H. R. (2004). 20 ways to ensure the successful inclusion of a child with Asperger Syndrome in the general education classroom. *Intervention in School and Clinic*, *39*, 176–180.

Bullock, L. M. & Gable, R. A. (2006). Programs for children and adolescents with emotional and behavioral disorders in the United States: A historical overview, current perspectives, and future directions. *Preventing School Failure*, *50*, 7–14.

Canter, L. & Canter, M. (1992). *Assertive discipline: Positive behavior management for today's classroom*. Seal Beach, CA: Canter & Associates.

Carroll, A., Hattie, J., Houghton, S., & Durkin, K. (2001). Goal setting and reputation enhancement among delinquent, at-risk adolescents. *Legal and Criminological Psychology*, *6*, 165–184.

Catholic Education Office, Archdiocese of Sydney (2006). *Individual Positive Behaviour Plan.* Sydney: Author.

Center for Effective Collaboration and Practice (CECP) (1998). *Addressing student problem behavior Part 2: Conducting a functional behavioral assessment* (3rd ed.). Washington DC: Author.

Center for Effective Collaboration and Practice (CECP) (2000). *Addressing student problem behavior—Part 3: Creating positive behavioral intervention plans and supports* (2nd ed.). Washington DC.

Commonwealth of Australia (2000). *Bullying: Information for parents*. Canberra, ACT: Department of Education, Training and Youth Affairs.

Conway, R. N. F. (2003a). *Report of an evaluation of Lake Macquarie District behaviour services*. Newcastle: University of Newcastle, Centre for Special Education and Disability Studies.

Conway, R. N. F. (2003b). *Evaluation of the Tasmanian Department of Education Statewide Behaviour Support Team*. Newcastle: University of Newcastle, Centre for Special Education and Disability Studies.

Conway, R. N. F. (2003c). *Report of a review of the provision of alternative settings in the ACT Government education system*. Canberra, ACT: ACT Department of Education, Youth and Family Services.

Conway, R. N .F. (2006). Students with emotional and behavioral disorders: An Australian perspective. *Preventing School Failure*, *50*, 15–20.

Conway, R. N. F. & Dempsey, I. (2003). *Final report to PMRT Disability Definitions Working Group on development of a common definition of, and approach to, data collection on students with disabilities for the purpose of nationally comparable reporting of their outcomes in the context of the National Goals of Schooling in the Twenty-First Century*. Newcastle: University of Newcastle, Centre for Special Education and Disability Studies.

Cooper, P. (2006). Supporting minority ethnic children and adolescents with social, emotional, and behavioral difficulties in the United Kingdom. *Preventing School Failure*, *50*, 15–21.

Crone, D. A. & Horner, R. H. (2003). *Building positive behavior support systems in schools: Functional behavior assessment*. New York: The Guilford Press.

Daniels, V. I. (1998). *How to manage disruptive behavior in inclusive classrooms*. Teaching Exceptional Children, March/April, 26–31.

Ehlers, S., Gillberg, C., & Wing, L. (1999). A screening questionnaire for Asperger's Syndrome and other high functioning autism spectrum disorders in school age children. *Journal of Autism and Developmental Disorders*, *29*, 129–141.

Elksnin, L. K. & Elksnin, N. (1998). Teaching social skills to students with learning and behavior problems. *Intervention in School and Clinic*, *33*, 131–140.

Feinberg, F. & Vacca, J. (2000). The drama and trauma of creating policies on autism: Critical issues to consider in the new millennium. *Focus on Autism and Other Developmental Disabilities*, *15*, 130–137.

Friend, M. & Bursuck, W. D. (2006). Including students with special needs: A practical guide for classroom teachers (4th ed.). Boston, MA: Pearson.

Garnett, M. S. & Attwood, T. (1994). *Australian Scale for Asperger's Syndrome* (2nd ed.) <www.udel.edu/bkirby/asperger/aspergerscaleAttwood.html>, accessed 15 March 2004.

Garnett, M. S. & Attwood, T. (2000). *The Australian Scale for Asperger's Syndrome* <www.tonyattwood.com>, accessed 15 March 2004.

Gresham, F. M., Cook, C. R., Crews, S. D., & Kern, L. (2004). Social skills training for children and youth with emotional and behavioral disorders: Validity considerations and future directions. *Behavioral Disorders, 30*, 32–47.

Gresham, F. M., Sugai, G., & Horner, R. H. (2001). Interpreting outcomes of social skills training for students with high-incidence disabilities. *Exceptional Children*, *67*, 331–344.

Gresham, F. M., Van, M. B., & Cook, C.R. (2006). Social skills training for teaching replacement behaviors: Remediating acquisition deficits in at-risk students. *Behavioral Disorders*, *31*, 363–378.

Guetzloe, E. (2000). On a positive note: The prerequisites for positive behavior support in the classroom: Conditions, curriculum and consequences. Paper presented at 24th Annual Conference of TECBD, Scottsdale, AZ, November.

Hemphill, S. A. (1996). Characteristics of conduct-disordered children and their families: A review. *Australian Psychologist*, *31*, 109–118.

House of Representatives Standing Committee on Education, Employment and Training (1996). *Truancy and exclusion from school: Report of the inquiry into truancy and exclusion of children and young people from school*. Canberra, ACT: Australian Government Printing Service.

Kanner, I. (1943). Autistic disturbances of affective contact. *Nervous Child*, *2*, 217–250.

Kauffman, J. M. (2005). *Characteristics of emotional and behavioral disorders of children and youth* (8th ed.). Columbus, OH: Merrill Publishing Company.

Lewis, R. (2001). Classroom discipline and student responsibility: The students' view. *Teaching and Teacher Education*, *17*, 307–319.

Lewis, R. (2006). Classroom discipline in Australia. In C. M. Everston & C. S. Weinstein (Eds), *Handbook of classroom management: Research, practice and contemporary issues* (pp. 1193–1214). Mahwah, NJ: Lawrence Erlbaum Associates.

Lewis, T. J. & Sugai, G. (1999). Effective behavior support: A systems approach to proactive schoolwide management. *Focus on Exceptional Children*, *31*, 1–24.

Lovannone, R., Dunlap, G., Huber, H., & Kincaid, D. (2003). Effective educational practices for students with Autism Spectrum Disorder. *Focus on Autism and Other Developmental Disabilities*, *18*, 150–165.

McLoughlin, J. A. & Lewis, R. B. (2005). *Assessing students with special needs* (6th ed.). Upper Saddle River, NJ: Pearson.

Mooney, P., Epstein, M. H., Reid, R., & Nelson, R. (2003). Status of and trends in academic intervention research for students with emotional disturbance. *Remedial and Special Education*, *25*, 273–287.

NSW Department of School Education (1995). Talk time teamwork: Collaborative management of students with ADHD. Sydney: Author.

Porter, L. (2007). *Student behaviour: Theory and practice for teachers* (3rd ed.). Sydney: Allen & Unwin.

Purdie, N., Hattie, J., & Carroll, A. (2001). A review of the research on interventions for children with Attention Deficit Disorder: Which treatment works best? *Review of Educational Research*, *72*, 61–99.

Rigby, K. (2003). *Stop the bullying: A handbook for schools* (Rev. ed.). Camberwell: ACER Press.

Rosenberg, M. S., Wilson, R., Maheady, L., & Sindelar, P. T. (2004a). Standardised instruments for assessment and classification. In M. S. Rosenberg, R. Wilson, L. Maheady, & P. T. Sindelar (Eds), *Educating students with behavioral disorders* (3rd ed.). Needham Heights, MA: Allyn & Bacon, pp. 122–137.

Rosenberg, M. S., Wilson, R., Maheady, L., & Sindelar, P. T. (2004b). Direct and systematic observation. In M. S. Rosenberg, R. Wilson, L. Maheady, & P. T. Sindelar (Eds), *Educating students with behavioural disorders* (3rd ed., pp. 139–176). Needham Heights, MA: Allyn & Bacon.

Ryan, C. A. & Lindgren, S. J. (1999). How to work effectively with girls: Promising practices in gender-specific interventions. *Reaching Today's Youth*, *3*, 55–58.

Salend, S. J. & Sylvestre, S. (2005). Understanding and addressing oppositional and defiant classroom behaviors. *TEACHING Exceptional Children*, *37*(6), 32–39.

Sawyer, M. G., Arney, F. M., Baghurst, P. A., Clark, J. J., Graetz, B. W., Kosky, R. J., Nurcombe, B., Patton, G. C., Prior, M. R., Raphael, B., Rey, J., Whaites, L. C., & Zubrick, S. R. (2000). *The mental health of young people in Australia*. Canberra: Mental Health and Special Programs Branch Commonwealth Department of Health and Aged Care.

South Australian Curriculum Standards and Accountability Framework [CACSA] (2007). <www.sacsa.sa.edu.au>, accessed 20 October 2007.

Stephenson, J., Linfoot, K., & Martin, A. (2000). Behaviors of concern to teachers in the early years of school. *International Journal of Disability, Development and Education*, *47*, 225–235.

Sugai, G. & Evans, D. (1997). Using teacher perceptions to screen for primary students with high risk behaviours. *Australasian Journal of Special Education*, *21*, 18–35.

University of Kansas Medical Center (2000). *Asperger's Syndrome Research Project*. Paper presented at the 24th Annual TECBD National Conference, Scottsdale, AZ.

Vinson, T. (2002). *Inquiry into the Provision of Public Education in NSW*. Sydney: NSW Teachers Federation and Federation of P & C Associations of NSW.

Walker, H. M., Colvin, G., & Ramsey, E. (1995). *Antisocial behavior in school: Strategies and best practices*. Pacific Grove, CA: Brooks/Cole.

Walker, H. M. & Sprague, J. R. (1999). The path to school failure, delinquency, and violence: Causal factors and some potential solutions. *Intervention in School and Clinic*, *37*, 67.

Weatherburn, D. (2003). Turning boys into fine men: The role of economic and social policy. *The Boys in Schools Bulletin*, *6*, 18–26.

Westwood, P. & Graham, L. (2003). Inclusion of students with special needs: Benefits and obstacles perceived by teachers in New South Wales and South Australia. *Australian Journal of Learning Disabilities*, *8*, 3–15.

Doug Bridge and Ruth Croser

6

INFORMATION AND COMMUNICATION TECHNOLOGIES

What you will learn in this chapter

This chapter focuses upon information and communication technologies (ICT), with a particular emphasis on assistive technologies. There is an emphasis on student empowerment and engagement through the use of familiar and unfamiliar technologies. Here, we use the concepts of *inclusive schooling*, *text transformation*, and *universal design* to explain how technologies support students with diverse learning needs or offer alternatives to traditional schooling experiences. As we refer to many websites in this chapter, it would help if you read the chapter at a time when you have easy access to the world wide web. It might also be useful to mark any sites that you find particularly useful.

In this chapter you will learn:

- how technology enables access to the curriculum;
- about assistive and communication technologies;
- how technologies reduce the impact of a disability;
- how technologies support participation;
- how familiar and widely available technologies can support students with diverse abilities;
- about specialised technologies developed to support students with particular disabilities or characteristics;
- where to find information about technologies; and
- about key factors that influence the successful use of information and technologies in the school and classroom.

CASE STUDIES

The case studies illustrate how ICT is engaged in schools and classrooms. In the following cases, one student is enrolled in a special school, while the other is a Year 11 student thinking about tertiary education pathways. As you read these studies, ask yourself:

- How familiar is the technology?
- In what ways does the technology help Sarah and Jack?

How does the technology enable Sarah and Jack to gain access to the curriculum and to achieve educational goals?

SARAH

Eight-year-old Sarah attends a small metropolitan special school and is in a class with nine peers aged between 8 and 11 years. She enjoys school and is an enthusiastic participant within the school community. Sarah has diagnoses of quadriplegic cerebral palsy and moderate intellectual impairment. She finds it hard to articulate words due to difficulty coordinating her tongue and mouth movement. This problem is called dysarthria.

Jelly Bean® switches

Switches that are activated by pressing on the top flat surface. Most are around 60 mm in diameter and are functional for individuals who do not have sophisticated fine motor skills.

Sarah can use her left arm to indicate choices between two objects or to press Jelly Bean® switches positioned on her work tray that usually sits across her lap. She uses these switches in a variety of ways to engage in learning activities at school (see Box 6.2). Connected to a power box, the switches allow her to turn any 240v appliance on or off, so she can use the popcorn maker, blender, or food processor in class cooking sessions, or turn on and off the end-of-lunch music when it is her turn to take this role.

Simple communication devices that look like thicker, angled switches (called BIGmacks® and Step-by-Step™ communicators) can be positioned so that Sarah can play a pre-recorded message or series of messages. In this way she can share news from home (pre-recorded by her older sister) during news time, take a message from her teacher to the office, or present a short report that she has made on a class activity using picture symbols. Sarah pairs up with an older, verbally communicating buddy, who is one of her classmates, who then records the messages that Sarah has compiled in symbols onto the Step-by-Step™ communicator. A teacher aide helps with this process.

A BIGmack® communicator used by Sarah

Sarah has a working vocabulary of about 35 symbols and is using these on low-tech communication boards and on BIGmack® communication devices. She is currently trialling a higher tech communication device with digitised speech using her known symbol vocabulary in 2 x 3 arrays. She is learning to press her switch within the time constraints of an automatic scan, both to gain access to the communication device and to use computer-based software.

Although physically unable to use conventional books independently, Sarah enjoys negotiating her way through books that have been transferred into talking

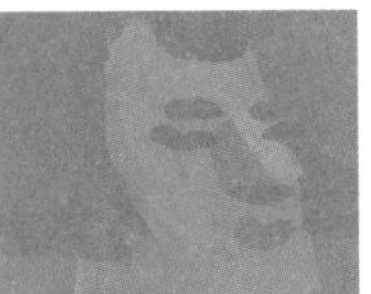

book PowerPoint presentations, with the text for each page linked as a sound file. Pages are turned using a switch-adapted regular mouse. A number of texts have been transformed in this way for Sarah, using PowerPoint and a software package called Clicker 5™ (see Box 6.1).

Sarah's teacher uses Clicker 5™ extensively with all students in the class and has customised a number of symbol matching activities for Sarah, as well as activities where simple sentences including text and symbols are read aloud. Each word/symbol is highlighted and Sarah then inserts a missing word/symbol from a choice of two. Sarah's teacher works closely with a speech pathologist who assists with the introduction of new vocabulary and will discuss key vocabulary choices for units of work the teacher is planning for the class. Clicker 5™ has also been used to make early mathematics texts accessible for Sarah, with matching one-to-one correspondence and early counting activities being generated for both Sarah and other students. The school has also recently acquired a number of products for use with Clicker 5™ that cover a range of curriculum areas, topics, and stages of learning and are accessible via different methods and can be used by all students at the school.

Sarah's occupational therapist and physiotherapist, together with her teacher, the classroom aide, and her family, work out the best computer access methods and the optimal positioning and set-up of devices. Sarah's teacher is currently introducing the class to a new electronic whiteboard and has experimented with ways in which Sarah can use the board by reaching with her left arm while in her standing frame with the tray removed. The teacher is using artRage, a generic art program and the children have really enjoyed this new medium.

physiotherapist

A professional engaged for the treatment of physical disabilities through massage, systematic exercise, manipulation, or the use of heat, light, or water.

BOX 6.1

Word processor Clicker 5™

Clicker 5™, developed and marketed by Crick Software, makes easy-to-use reading and writing software for children, teenagers, and young adults. Many of the company software products are suited to students with diverse learning needs, particularly those with learning disabilities and physical limitations. The software is also appropriate for teaching English as a second language. For a description of Clicker 5™ see <www.cricksoft.com/us/products/clicker>.

Clicker Writer is a talking word processor that can:

- read aloud any text, highlighting each word when spoken;
- show pictures above words; and
- automatically capitalise proper nouns and words at the start of sentences.

You enter text into Clicker Writer using either your keyboard or a Clicker Grid. Clicker Grids enable students to become more independent and confident about constructing their writing. Grids have cells containing words, phrases, or pictures. To write in Clicker Writer, you simply click on a word, phrase, or picture in the Clicker Grid.

The following websites offer information about Clicker 5™, upgrades, and add-ons:

- <www.cwschoolsupportprogramasd.org/application.php?id=9&type=MAC>;
- <www.cricksoft.com/us/products/clicker/upgrade.asp>; and
- <www.inclusive.co.uk/catalogue/acatalog/clicker_essential_addons.html>.

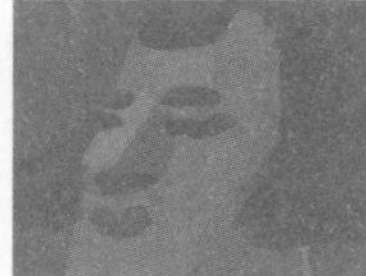

Sarah's teacher regularly meets with her aide to discuss the curriculum plans for the class and how Sarah's technology can best facilitate her full participation. This planning involves consideration of the level of extra physical effort required by Sarah in some activities and how these activities can be positioned within her timetable so that she is not exhausted.

Consultation with music and art teachers also helps ensure that there is time for any additional equipment to be prepared. This includes low technology items such as adapted paintbrush holders, as well as higher technology accommodations such as pre-programming the communication device with lines from a song the class is singing.

Sarah's teacher, her aide, and her family have all had training in the use of technologies, including sessions focusing on the specific devices and software. The training also involved creatively adapting commonly available technologies to facilitate Sarah's learning and provide opportunities for her to interact and communicate about her learning with her teachers, peers, and family.

The importance of technology as a teaching and learning tool is openly acknowledged within the special school that Sarah attends. The school allocates significant resources for technology acquisition and training for staff and students.

JACK

Jack is 17 years old and in Year 11. He intends to undertake a university Bachelor of Law degree. Consequently, he is undertaking courses in legal studies, psychology, English literature, and business studies, among others.

In Year 10 Jack experienced a sudden deterioration in his central vision and was diagnosed with Optic Neuropathy. After his initial diagnosis, Jack went through a time of adjusting to his significant vision loss and the enormous impact of this on many areas of his life. He has very strong and supportive family and peer networks. Jack has touch-typing skills and is very familiar with computer technologies.

Jack was referred to the Department of Education Central Learning Support (Vision) team for assistance with curriculum materials and for advice about the accommodations that might be made by his teachers. A team was set up to support Jack. The team initially concentrated on the use of technologies and text transformations to help Jack gain access to, and participate in, his chosen subjects and school life. The team also supports him developing future learning pathways.

This team includes Jack, his family, Vision Resource teachers, subject teachers, inclusion coordinator, information and technology technicians, and a representative from Guide Dogs Australia. Funding for Jack's technology support was established through Guide Dogs, although resources were garnered from other areas; for example, the school purchased interactive white boards, and his family purchased a new mobile phone <www.guidedogsaustralia.com>.

To maintain and build Jack's self-esteem and sense of control over his future it is critical that he is intimately involved in the selection of, and has the final say about, the technologies used to support him at school. Initial technology priorities for Jack related to maintaining social contact with friends using his mobile phone (reading contact lists), sending and reading text messages, and refining his skills in digital recording of classes using an MP3 player.

Using a program called MobileSpeak on a Nokia phone, Jack can hear text on the phone converted into speech via headphones, allowing much easier access to caller ID, contacts,

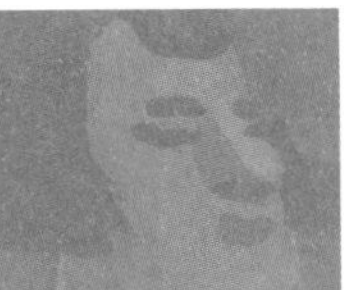

phone settings, and text messaging. After trialling a number of MP3 players, Jack found the Milestone 311 Voice Recorder and MP3 player easiest to use as it was developed specifically for users with low vision or without vision. Jack decided to extend the recording time of this player from two hours to 140 hours. The device is only a little larger than a credit card and is easily carried. Jack likes the layout of the five very clear, large, high-contrast buttons. He is able to transfer recorded teaching sessions to his computer. Find information about the MP3 player at <www.soundbytes.com/page/SB/PROD/757828>.

Jack using the Milestone 311 MP3 Player/Voice Recorder

Once Jack was confidently using phone-based technology, time was taken to look at his computer set-up, and the ways in which this could be modified and enhanced to best meet his vision needs.

Jack was supplied with a new laptop computer with a large screen and two docking stations that can support extra devices such as expansion cards, hard drive bays, optical drive bays, keyboard/mouse connectors and additional USB ports. Having one docking station in his classroom and one in the library allows Jack to carry his laptop between the two. He also has additional (and commercially available) very large digital screens, one for use at home and one set up in the school library.

The vision learning support teacher worked with Jack to set up preferred high-contrast colour settings, large icons, mouse pointers, print size, and auditory cues using the accessibility options built into Jack's computer's Windows-based operating system.

Jack's school administration decided to purchase some new interactive whiteboards for use in the classrooms where Jack is taught. The whiteboards have features to facilitate access for learners with a wide range of abilities. Jack can connect his laptop to the classroom computer and the whiteboard display appears on his computer screen. He can use his screen enlargement software to view notes, diagrams, and illustrations as they are drawn by his teacher on the whiteboard. The school information and technology coordinator was aware of the importance of purchasing whiteboards compatible with Jack's software (JAWS® and Zoomtext).

Jack uses a Quicklook video magnifier that allows him to magnify printed text and graphics. This hand-held system sits on top of the article to be viewed and is moved across the text as Jack reads. Magnification settings were customised to meet Jack's needs and he now uses the magnifier to quickly refer to notes from his peers, as well as his class timetable, bus timetable, and the coffee shop menu.

Currently, Jack thinks that he is managing well with the vision and technology he has, but recognises that his vision may deteriorate further and that in the longer term he may require Braille skills and Braille-based technology, such as the Mountbatten Braille writer/embosser and Braille PDAs.

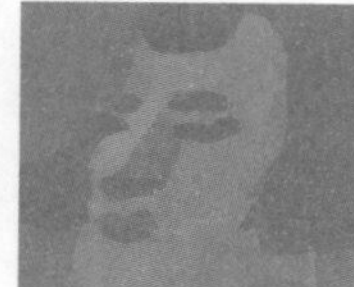

TEACHING–LEARNING CONTEXT

Most schools in Australia are becoming schools for all. Involvement in school and community life for some students is supported through (or dependent upon) the use of a wide range of technologies. These technologies have to be carefully integrated with the school and classroom curricula to ensure that the diverse abilities of students are met and challenged.

The case studies and recent reviews we have conducted into the use of assistive technology in Australian schools suggest that the effective integration of technologies with curricula is influenced by a number of factors:

- excellent leadership;
- good school management and teaching;
- a move to work within multidisciplinary teams;
- commitment to catering for individual learning styles; and
- the use of more complex technology.

Technologies are fundamental to the successful inclusion of students with disabilities in schools.

Jack's story suggests that assistive technology is and will remain important in providing access to post-secondary education for some students with disabilities. It further suggests that principles of universal design for technology should be adopted to ensure that the assistive technology meets the needs of students with disabilities.

The information and technologies world context

Jack's and Sarah's cases are reported against a background of rapid change in the development and use of information and of technologies worldwide, and in most domains of our lives, not just in education.

How we understand the words *information and communication technology* is evolving along with the influence of the world wide web with its power to help us gain access to information along with its associated technologies, hardware, and software.

Keeping abreast of such rapid change is a challenge to all teachers and school systems. This means that the teacher, the information technologist, and the inclusion support teams are aware and responsive, and able to adapt new and evolving technologies rapidly to support students' access to the curriculum. For example, technologies and applications currently being developed specifically for students with diverse learning needs have become synergistic with technologies and applications used by most technology users, and vice-versa. In the words of Sam Palmisano (IBM CEO), "Accessibility—which started out as a philanthropic effort—has now evolved to a business transformation effort for IBM and our clients" <www-03.ibm.com/able/solution_offerings/consulting.html>.

All manner of web-based supports are available. One example comes from IBM that offers Easy Web Browsing software to help people with limited vision, and seniors gain access to web content easily as a simple download. You can download IBM's Accessibility Speech Interfaces from <www-03.ibm.com/able/dwnlds/index.html>.

Information and communication technologies offer students the opportunity to compensate for physical or functional limitations, allowing them access to the curriculum and our communities by enlarging the scope of activities available to them.

Universal design

Universal design principles refer to information and technology infrastructure, hardware, and software that is already in place for the general school population. Universal design involves the development

of a curriculum and classroom usable by all students to the greatest extent possible without the need for adaptation or specialised design. It is underpinned by the following principles which can be directly related to the set-up and use of technologies:

- *Equitable use*—The curriculum and classroom is usable by students with diverse learning abilities. For example, interactive whiteboards are regularly used in the classroom.
- *Flexible use*—The curriculum and classroom accommodates a wide range of student preferences and abilities. For example, a range of alternative communication devices and switches are in regular use in the classroom.
- *Simple and intuitive use*—Students do not need hours of training to use the technology. For example, familiar technologies like the mobile phone and MP3 player are readily available to students.
- *Perceptible information*—There should be a range of processes and tools for interfacing with the computer or technology. For example, a wide library of switching devices is held by the school.
- *Tolerance for error*—The technology should be well matched to the student's abilities. For example, students should be assessed and then matched to particular learning objects.
- *Low physical effort*—Assistive technologies in particular should be easily accessible, easy to activate and easily transportable. A small laptop or small keyboard may help secondary school students move their supportive technologies from class to class.

See Box 6.2 for a quick overview of assistive technology.

BOX 6.2

What is assistive technology?

Assistive technology is any item, piece of equipment, or product system that is used to increase, maintain, or improve functional capacities of people with disabilities. There are two sorts of assistive technology: one enhances a student's strengths and the other compensates for, or circumvents, the effects of disabilities. Jack's use of an MP3 player to record his lessons and Sarah's use of a BIGmack® are examples of compensatory assistive technology. A teacher's use of word banks in Clicker 5™ to extend the work of his or her gifted students is an example of enhancing assistive technology. We learn about these assistive technologies from Sarah and Jack:

- *Jelly Bean®* —The Jelly Bean® is a compact alternative form of switch. It provides Sarah with the power to turn any 240v appliance on or off. See more at <www.inclusive.co.uk/catalogue/acatalog/ablenet_switches.html>.
- *BIGmack®*—This is an augmentative communication device. It offers voice output communication and, in Sarah's case, it offers greetings. It provides Sarah with a channel of communication with the outside world. It gives her the ability to communicate and build meanings, as well as offering her control over her learning environment. (Find out more from <www.acciinc.com/Html/bigmack.htm>.)
- *Step-by-Step™ communicator*—This is a battery-operated device that allows for pre-recording a series of unlimited sequenced messages. This device supports Sarah's communication with her aide and her peers.

- *ArtRage*—This is an easy-to-use painting tool that lets you play with realistic paints on your computer. You can create your own paintings from nothing, load in photos, and recreate them with oil paints, pencils, felt pens, or any of the other tools ArtRage has to offer. (Find more at: <www.ambientdesign.com/artragedown.html>.)
- *ZoomText*—ZoomText is a fully integrated magnification and screen reading program that enlarges, enhances and reads aloud everything on the computer screen. Jack uses ZoomText's dual monitor support that allows him to expand his magnified view across two monitors. (Find out about more features from <www.aisquared.com/Products/zoomtextmrd/index.cfm>.)
- *JAWS® for Windows®*—This is a screen reader that works with your PC to provide access to software applications and the internet. Its internal software speech synthesiser and the computer's sound card allow information from the screen to be read aloud. JAWS also offers Jack refreshable Braille displays. (Find information at <www.freedomscientific.com/fs_products/software_jaws.asp>.)
- *Quicklook*—Quicklook is a hand-held, full colour, electronic magnifier with an integrated visual display. It can magnify text, photos, and maps, or just about anything. It's small enough to fit in Jack's coat pocket. (Find more at <www.quantech.com.au/products/other_products/low_vision/quicklook.htm>.)
- *Braille PDA*—This is a Personal Digital Assistant for blind and visually impaired people with or without knowledge of Braille. It is slim and light, and easily carried. It can function as a notebook, address book, calculator, calendar, and watch. (Find more information at <www.techno-vision.co.uk/nano.htm>.)

6.2

Universal design for learning can be supported through the thoughtful use of universal design. For example, Jack's mobile phone has a universal design element. Universal design is a framework to guide teachers when providing the broadest learning opportunities for increasingly diverse classroom populations. Most software developers already incorporate special accessibility features into their programs. For example, Macintosh® computers and PCs using Windows 95® or later versions include options for enlarged icons and pointers, and almost every model of computer allows for keyboard responses to be tailored to individual needs.

Principles of universal design also underpin good planning for teaching and learning. This involves developing flexible curricula to meet unique learner needs. Some well-designed e-learning materials and learning objects offer flexible access to interesting content and may be built upon universal design principles. Universal design related to information and technologies is underpinned by similar, simple principles:

- technologies are employed to ensure that course content is delivered in a range of formats;
- technologies enable students to demonstrate their application and knowledge through various formats and assessment methods; and
- students can engage with a wide range of technologies (including online technologies) and networks to learn from peers and swap knowledge and ideas.

Inclusive practice involves a move toward universal design principles. Multi-level curriculum design begins at the initial planning stage and is not developed as later additions or modifications for particular students.

The friendly computer

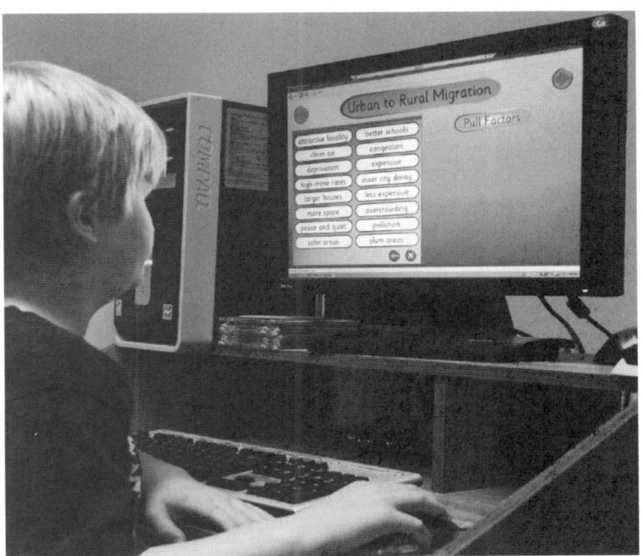

A student using Clicker 5™ to learn about migration

The computer is a powerful information and communication technology that can be readily used to support all learners. Computers are wonderful technological tools that assist students with diverse learning needs and provide a platform from which to develop differentiated curriculum content and teaching activities. A standard computer provides access to many essential tasks that would otherwise be difficult or impossible for a person with a disability to accomplish, for example writing letters and reading the news without the need to handle a pen or turn the pages of a newspaper.

The computer is a primary tool for text transformations. Computer and software programs can offer multiple technological tools in one package, providing an inclusive non-print environment for teaching, studying, and practising skills. Word processors can generate text, edit its content, and alter its physical characteristics. Spellcheckers, speech recognition software, and word prediction software also support (i.e., scaffold) the writing process.

Word processing

The word processor is one of the most widely available technology tools in the 21st century classroom. There has been a great deal of research about the use of word processors in the classroom, and experimental studies have consistently reported a beneficial impact on students' writing or editing through the use of word processors. In a summary of the research undertaken about the effects of the computer, computer programs, and software on learning for students with diverse abilities, Strangman and Hall (2003) claimed that most current research focused on numeracy and literacy, with the greatest emphasis being on reading instruction. In general, this body of research suggests that computer programs and software improve reading for most students. Supplementing reading and writing instruction with computer reading and writing programs can significantly improve achievement in those areas.

Students practising spelling on the computer rather than off the computer tend to spend significantly more time engaged with the work and score significantly higher on spelling tests than students who practise without the use of a computer.

Spellcheckers and word prediction

Investigators who have examined the effects of using spellcheckers on learning outcomes for students with learning difficulties and disabilities support the idea that spellcheckers are beneficial tools. There

is, however, a caution that spellcheckers do not always read for context, so teacher support is essential when students with learning difficulties are using a spellchecker.

Word prediction software is another tool that, when combined with a word processor, can support student writing. There is some research evidence to suggest that word prediction software benefits students with special needs (Hasselbring & Williams Glaser, 2000).

Switches

The idea sounds simple, but switches come in a surprising range of shapes, sizes, and uses. The selection of a switch activation site and method of switching can be a complex process, particularly for students who have neurological conditions such as cerebral palsy. Advice from occupational and physical therapists may be essential to determine the skills a student needs to use a switch interface successfully. These include the following:

- *Motor skills*—Switches can be activated by hand, foot, and head. Even eyebrow or breath-movement switches are available, and motor skills initiate, release, and/or maintain the person's contact with the switch to control the output of the device (the blender in Sarah's case). If the student uses scanning arrays they must undertake the contact/release within a particular time frame.
- *Sensory skills*—These are needed to attend to an activity and switch attention (visual or auditory) from the switch to the activity.
- *Cognitive skills*—The student must have, or be developing, an understanding of cause and effect relationships, that is, that an action elicits a response.
- *Social skills*—The student must have the intention to communicate.

Scanning

You may have digitised images using an optical scanner, but in this context scanning has a different meaning. Scanning involves the student in a more sophisticated interaction with the computer. Software is used to present the student with a sequence of choices known as a *scanning array*. In an automatic scanning pattern, the student can make a choice by activating a switch when the desired choice is identified. Choices can be identified by a sound, by highlighting, or by framing.

The skills a student needs to use this technological strategy are more complex. Resources like Clicker 5™ incorporate scanning options with a dedicated word processor, an onscreen keyboard and a symbol to text capacity (see Box 6.1).

Keyboards

Computers must have an interface with the student/user. Most often this is a standard keyboard and/or mouse. The standard keyboard and mouse, however, may present a barrier to some students, particularly those with physical, sensory, and/or intellectual disabilities. In Jack's case, the computer screen may not be accessible as he has a vision impairment. Some students with learning difficulties also might find the complexity of software and its associated computer environment difficult to negotiate. Sarah's story indicates that there is a wide range of alternatives to keyboards and mice. Some alternatives to the traditional QWERTY keyboard are given below.

STANDARD KEYBOARD WITH GUARD

A guard is available for all standard keyboards. It fits over the keyboard and is suitable for students who need to rest their hands on the keyboard while typing, or who inadvertently hit other keys. You can also get a plastic glove or sleeve for keyboards that colour-codes keys and protects them from fluids.

ON-SCREEN KEYBOARDS

An onscreen keyboard generally appears on the same display used for programs and can remain permanently visible. Computer software and hardware are available to support the use of split screens (using two linked monitors). This allows for two screens to be set up so that the student can view and use the onscreen keyboard and see usual programs and word processing on the second screen.

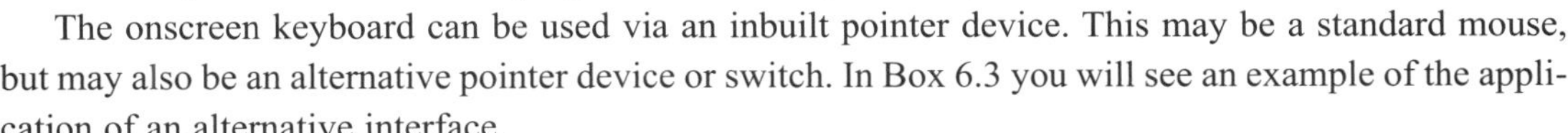

The onscreen keyboard can be used via an inbuilt pointer device. This may be a standard mouse, but may also be an alternative pointer device or switch. In Box 6.3 you will see an example of the application of an alternative interface.

BOX 6.3

Fiona's assistive technology

Fiona is a 10-year-old who attends her local primary school. Two years ago she was involved in a car accident that resulted in quadriplegia. Fiona has paralysis of her legs, her lower body, and her arms. She has a small amount of movement of her thumb and fingers on her right side.

Fiona has an MP3 recorder/player mounted on her wheelchair tray near her right hand to record class sessions. Her teacher, family, resource teacher, and therapists developed a range of strategies to support Fiona's learning. Her teacher provides much of the material used in class in digital format so Fiona can gain access to it on a computer. Fiona's teacher aide is trained in the use of the scanner and text conversion software.

It is surprisingly difficult to use a mouse. In Fiona's case, a regular computer mouse was too hard for her to grasp or manipulate and move around in a controlled fashion. Using an alternative mouse, Fiona can see a mouse cursor on the screen and links its movements to her arm/hand movements. She now uses a Felix MicroPoint mouse with her right thumb and fingers in conjunction with voice input software. MicroPoint functions like a mouse, but it takes up less space than a mouse pad. Manipulating a three-button handle two centimetres in any direction moves the screen cursor. Using the handle Fiona can perform left, right, and double clicks or drag lock. (To find out more about MicroPoint go to <www.infogrip.com/product_view.asp?RecordNumber=922>.)

Fiona also uses Nuance software <www.nuance.com> for text input.

At those times during a busy school day when the background noise in her class is too loud, Fiona uses Penfriend XP's onscreen keyboard and types in words by positioning her mouse over the onscreen keyboard keys and clicking. To speed up this process

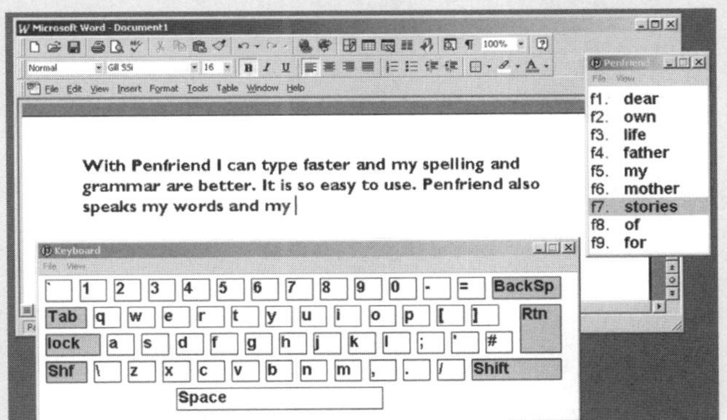

Fiona's onscreen keyboard and predictor

she uses Penfriend's text prediction component of the software so she doesn't have to fully type commonly used words over three letters, as she can select them from a prediction list that pops up on screen. Fiona also has auto text shortcut keys programmed into her computer for common phrases and sentence starters. This is achieved by customising the keyboard part of the tools menu (using Windows®).

6.3

INTELLIKEYS

This is a programmable alternative keyboard that plugs into any computer running Windows. Intellikeys is a membrane keyboard that allows a student to use it applying very little pressure. It can support an endless variety of overlays (an image of a keyboard suited to a particular student's needs). It enables students with physical, vision, or cognitive impairment to type, enter numbers, navigate onscreen displays, and move the mouse. It has input for two switches. Different overlays allow students to use larger or smaller keys, upper/lower case, different colours, and alternative layouts such as ABC instead of QWERTY.

COMPACT KEYBOARD

The compact keyboard is great for those students who have limited arm, hand, or finger movement and it can be positioned to suit the needs of the student rather than the desk. It is small enough to be placed on a wheelchair tray. Because the keyboard does not extend to the right, it also allows right-handed users to operate the mouse or roller ball closer to their body. This usually permits more comfortable and accurate control, as well as reducing the risk of causing pain in the right shoulder. The keys are about the same size as those on a standard keyboard, as its compactness is achieved through omitting some of the usual keys (often the numeric keypad). The keyboard is slim and lightweight, so it can easily be carried around the school.

Activators

There are many alternatives to mice that allow a student to move the computer cursor more easily with his or her hand, or by not using hands at all. These include trackballs, joysticks, touch screens, head pointers, and touch pads. Microsoft and Apple both have utilities that set the keyboard number pad up so that it can control cursor movements. Some voice input systems can also be used to move the curser. Below is a list of some options.

TRACKBALLS

A trackball works like an upside-down mouse. Instead of rolling the ball on the table by sliding the mouse around, the ball is moved directly by the student. The trackball only needs to be gently nudged to move the onscreen curser. A trackball can be set up so that it can be operated with the chin, elbow, foot, or stick held in the mouth.

JOYSTICK

A joystick may be easier for some students to grab and hold than a mouse; it requires a smaller range of motion than a mouse, and it can be operated by chin or mouth movements.

TOUCH WINDOWS/SCREENS

Touch screens let the student point to parts of a monitor/screen to make selections. This technology is particularly supportive of students using alternative communication systems. The touch screen is also

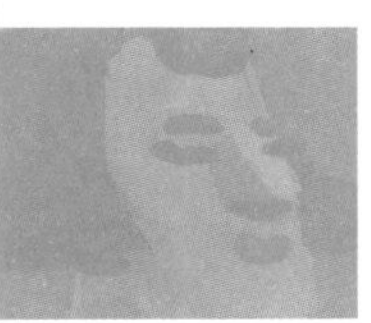

supportive of students with an intellectual disability or cognitive impairment as it can be used for yes/no, stimulus response activities.

DIGITISING TABLET/TOUCH PADS

The student has to move his or her finger, or a stylus, around on a flat tablet to operate a touch pad. The cursor moves in a corresponding pattern on the screen. This is a great alternative to a mouse for students with a physical disability that does not allow them to grasp.

HEAD POINTERS

The original head pointer was a helmet with a long rod attached to it. Now head pointers are electronic and move the computer cursor in response to head movements. The student wears an infrared (Headmaster) or micro-gyroscope (Tracer) sensor on his or her head, or perhaps a reflective dot (Tracker, HeadMouse). The system measures signals from the sensors, or looks at the way light reflects off the dot, to determine whether the user is moving his or her head up or down, right or left. The cursor is moved in the same direction as the user's head movements.

MOUSEKEYS

MouseKeys is a feature built into the Windows and Macintosh operating systems that allows the student to move the cursor with the number pad keys. For example, "8" moves the cursor up, "1" moves the cursor to the lower left. MouseKeys provides a nice cursor control option for people who type with a mouth stick or typing splint. It is slow, but it offers good accuracy for times when a person needs to aim the cursor at a small target.

EYE GAZE AND EYE TRACKING

With this alternative to a mouse, a mounted camera-like device translates eye movements and eye stares (called dwelling) into directing the onscreen mouse. The mouse clicks are achieved by the student with a slow eye blink, an eye dwell, or a hardware switch.

SPEECH TO TEXT AND TEXT TO SPEECH

Speech recognition enables students to use their voice to write on the computer, and/or to have the computer speak the text to the student. This software/hardware is of great use to a wide range of students, including those who have learning disabilities, and physical and sensory disabilities.

Augmentative and alternative communication

In the case studies, Sarah and Jack both use alternative communication technologies as a means of getting their message across to others. Another young person, Mark, uses another piece of technology, the Picture Exchange Communication System (PECS™), which is a specialised form of augmentative and alternative communication. PECS™ is a relatively simple technological resource. Sarah uses a range of communication devices, from simple aids (e.g., single message voice output communication aids) to very sophisticated computer-based systems.

Like most augmentative and alternative communication users, a combination of technology forms is generally used, such as a symbol communication book, voice output communication aids, and computer-based selection arrays.

You might have a student in your classroom that requires alternative or augmentative communication strategies (as Mark does, in Box 6.4 below). Remember that your primary goals are related to teaching and learning, and that information and technology are tools to support student learning. Ideally, a support team will be involved in helping you set up technology appropriate for your student. While the initial introduction of a communication aid may be led by a speech and language therapist, integrating the use of communication aids into classroom learning is your responsibility as teacher.

learning disabilities

Term used in the USA and Canada to describe children with difficulties in language and communication skills generally, but excluding those whose learning problems are primarily due to hearing, vision or motor impairment, emotional difficulties, cultural disadvantage, or intellectual disability.

augmentative and alternative communication

This involves the use of non-speech communication systems such as manual signs or picture-based communication boards.

BOX 6.4

Mark and the Picture Exchange Communication System (PECS™)

Mark, a five-year-old with a diagnosis of Autism Spectrum Disorder (ASD), is using his communication board to choose pictures requesting a drink. Mark loves chocolate drinks and his desire for them is used in his Picture Exchange Communication System (PECS™) training.

Mark's PECS™ training is undertaken at his home and at school. He was an intentional communicator (he exhibited pre-verbal intentional behaviour) when he began his training; he was aware of the need to communicate his message to someone, even if in a limited fashion. Mark's training includes strategies such as chaining, prompting/cuing, modelling, and environmental engineering.

PECS™ is an example of a very simple technology developed to use with young students with ASD. PECS™ is designed to foster spontaneous communicative interactions as the child exchanges visual representations of objects (and/or intentions/feelings) for the object. PECS™ was developed with the intention of teaching the cause and effect of communication. Using this system, a student may develop the understanding that communication is an exchange of information between two or more people.

At the beginning of the program, the student starts by learning to exchange one picture to make a request. As he or she advances through the phases, exchanges become more complex, developing higher-level social communication functions, such as questioning and commenting.

PECS™ is not a set of specific symbols; it is a strategy of communication that involves picking up a symbol and handing it to a partner with whom one is communicating. Symbols and visual supports/cues come in all shapes and sizes and should be set up to suit individual student's needs; some students like photographs, some prefer miniatures of real objects, and others successfully use line drawings, symbols and print. COMPIC symbols might be used within this system.

labelling
The practice of categorising children and adults according to a type of disability or impairment.

modelling
Providing a behavioural example of how a task is to be undertaken so that another can learn by imitation.

Medical or speech and language therapy diagnostic labelling of students can be useful, but might not help you to identify the most effective teaching and learning approaches for each child. Principal approaches (not mutually exclusive) include:

- The remedial approach that involves filling in gaps in knowledge and skill through the provision of structured language learning opportunities, building on the skills the student does have, providing a language-aware environment with plenty of repetition, and modelling.
- The compensatory approach that is engaged where aspects of the language and communication disorder are very severe. This approach bypasses defective channels and tries to use the student's areas of relative strength. Concentrate first on establishing basic functional communication through augmentative and alternative communication technologies, and then use this as the medium for social interaction and the teaching and learning of new skills.
- Specialised approaches. PECS™ is based in behaviourism and is an example of highly specific implementations of a compensatory model of augmentative and alternative communication.

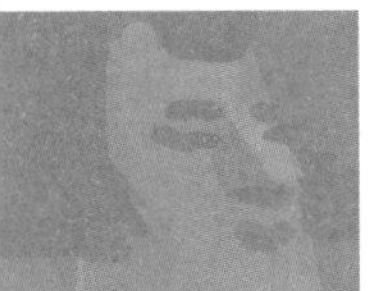

PECS™, in Mark's situation, was taught as a stand-alone package. Other information and technologies can be used alongside PECS™.

ISSUES AND CHALLENGES

Each of the cases reported in this chapter highlight key factors that determine the successful use of information and technology in schools.

Major studies conducted over the past 10 years, including that of Cormack et al. (2000) and key studies from the United States of America (the *Promising Practices in Technology* Report [2000] and the *Synthesis on the Selection and Use of Assistive Technology Report* [2000]), identified common factors determining the successful use of ICT, particularly of assistive technology within schools. The common factors identified in these research papers and reports include:

- school leadership;
- an inclusive and supportive school culture and ethos;
- adequate sector funding and resource management;
- strong technology infrastructure and on-site technical support;
- professional learning and specific training for teachers; and
- effective collaborative practice and teamwork.

School leadership

Our cases suggest that the successful use of ICT in the school and classroom is dependent upon supportive principals, leadership, and administration. In Jack's case, the inclusion support teacher provided information sessions for the principal and other senior staff describing the benefits of Jack's assistive technology. A school culture developed around the principles of equity that facilitated the effective staff use of assistive technologies.

School culture and ethos

Inclusion refers to the acceptance of students who require adjustment to the learning environment so that their experiences are as close as possible to those of the majority of school-aged children. When this happens, participation in these environments leads to learning and skill development appropriate to their age and intellectual capabilities.

All students need the barriers removed that prevent participation in the classroom and in learning activities. Use of technologies may be one powerful strategy to remove barriers to participation. Students with diverse needs, particularly those with disabilities, learning difficulties, or other educational needs, may find it difficult to achieve full inclusion in their communities without the use of technologies. Technologies support both Jack's and Sarah's inclusion in the classroom and community.

Sector funding and resource management

In Jack's case, we can see that his support team ensured that there was strong coordination of resources that supported him at school. Further resource planning would be required to ensure Jack's smooth transition into further education and training or employment when access to assistive technologies available in the school and classroom may be lost.

Funding is a crucial factor influencing the use of ICT (and particularly assistive technology) in schools and classrooms. Reports and research suggest that lack of funding remains the single

greatest barrier to the acquisition of assistive technology (Alameda, 2000; Lazzaro, 2001; Male, 2003).

Some of the strategies used to facilitate the purchase and use of assistive technology in Jack's case included fostering collaboration between the school principal and disability/inclusion support teachers, the school board, and relevant educational sectors and keeping these groups and key individuals informed about Jack's progress. In Sarah's situation, the information and technology support officer was constantly researching new and innovative models for technology initiatives. These could then be adopted, adapted, and implemented to suit Sarah and her classroom situation.

Technology infrastructure and on-site technical support

There are many inconsistencies in development and maintenance of technology infrastructure and on-site technical support between educational sectors and between the schools within them. Constant technological change, individual student abilities and needs, and particular school and classroom contexts make it impractical to endorse a single model for service delivery.

It seems, however, that adopting the principles of universal design is the most sensible approach. In other words, where possible assistive technologies should be sited within, or made part of, the overall school ICT infrastructure. Indeed, we can see that many of the technologies employed in the case studies are appropriate for many if not all students to use.

In Sarah's and Jack's schools, care was taken when planning, purchasing, and using assistive technologies to ensure they were networked within the larger school systems, and that all technologies, hardware and software were compatible.

The school administrations worked collaboratively with state agencies, districts, across education sectors and non-government organisations, to facilitate access to complementary resources and to avoid unnecessary duplication of resources. In Tasmania, for example, the State Department of Education Inclusion Support team personnel worked with the State Department of Health and Human Services to ensure that Sarah's assistive technologies were the same across all therapy sessions.

In the longer term, the most cost-effective approach to the provision of technology and on-site support is to incorporate assistive technologies within a school's broader technology strategy. This would ensure that general technology, such as computers, is accessible to all students.

Professional learning and specific training for teachers

The provision of, and training in, the use of ICT and assistive technologies is a growing issue for schools, teachers and para-professional staff. Ongoing training in effective use of technology is a key factor in successful incorporation of assistive technology into classrooms.

In many schools at present, access by students to assistive technologies depends mainly on knowledge acquired haphazardly from experts outside the school community, perhaps from district officers, or from non-government organisations. Once familiar with the assistive technology tool and reasonably confident in its use, teachers can see its application within the curriculum. Indeed, student learning is best facilitated when teachers are able to create a new blend of computer-based skills and appropriate teaching methodology within the curriculum.

Teachers and teacher assistants initially require basic training in computing skills if these have not already been acquired before training in assistive technology begins. This initial computer training should incorporate work about built-in access features in computer operating systems. Box 6.5 provides some examples of basic training that can be readily implemented in any school situation.

BOX 6.5

Simple examples of basic computer training in school

Cormack et al. (2000) suggested that teachers and teacher assistants initially require basic training in computing skills as well as in the use of assistive technologies. Initial computer training should incorporate built-in access features in computer operating systems, for example control panels, text to speech, and other capabilities.

Here are some suggestions for training staff in the use of assistive technology:

- Develop generic, base-level computer skills if the staff member does not already have them. These sessions need to incorporate awareness of universal design features within operating systems, for example how to reformat and structure keyboards and keys.
- Follow initial technology-specific training with ongoing training to maintain and further develop skills and ensure technology continues to be used. For example, para-professionals might be encouraged to gain TAFE accreditation for computer skills related to their work with students with special needs.
- Link staff within a district in which using specific technology is used via regular meetings or a listserve in which participants can share ideas and solve problems. An initial email from you to all teachers in your local area might invite those interested to share ideas about specific technologies and their use in the classroom or with specific students. Regular processes for sharing online could then be negotiated.
- Offer train-the-trainer sessions with staff experienced in the use of a particular assistive technology. You might have trained in the use of PECS™ (see Box 6.4). You could then organise to support others in the school in basic communication techniques based around the needs of a particular student.
- Identify and/or develop web-based professional learning resources (perhaps centrally maintained) that might be accessed by district and school support staff working with assistive technology. Go to the Le@rning Federation website <www.thelearning federation.edu.au/node1> and see what professional learning might be offered.

Effective collaborative practice and teamwork

Good assistive technology support involves developing effective teams. These would include the student and might involve a teacher assistant, the classroom teacher, on-site disability support teachers, district/regional support teachers, therapists, and parents or carers who work collaboratively to respond to the student's ever changing information and technology needs.

Collaborative technology support teams ensure that there are:

- agreed and effective lines of communication for the team;
- processes in place for information sharing (email, fax, verbal);
- common understanding of the roles of the team members;
- jointly developed processes of assessment, training and review of assistive technology; and
- designated and prioritised meeting times (in person, online, and teleconferences).

See Box 6.6 for some further comments about teamwork.

6.6 Working in teams to build supportive networks

State Departments of Education have branches or units concerned with the support of students with disabilities. While there is considerable variation between states in service structures supporting students using ICT and assistive technologies, at the level of implementation all states aspire to collaborative, school-based teams organised to develop supportive networks for students. Membership of teams may vary according to students' changing needs, but core team members should be parents, the student, the class teacher, and disability and ICT specialists.

Jack's and Sarah's parents contributed to the work of their support teams outlining key educational and life goals for their children, trialling and commenting on the usability of ICT and assistive technologies. They contributed their deep knowledge of their children to the team.

As students, Jack and Sarah contributed to the work of the team as they reviewed and critiqued the usability and effectiveness of their ICT supports and assistive technologies. Jack often spoke about his friends and their expectations; he wanted ICT support that did not make him stand out from his friends and that kept him in contact with friends through technologies they were familiar with (such as the mobile phone).

Support teams include experts in key disability areas. Sarah's team involved experts in physical impairment and in intellectual disability. Both teams included experts in ICT and assistive technologies. These experts contributed new knowledge to the teams, offered strategies to assess the effectiveness of ICT supports, and monitored and reviewed progress in ICT use. They also provided specific professional learning for school staff and teachers.

Teaching staff were key members of the support teams contributing their understandings of curriculum and teaching and learning strategies, ensuring that ICT and assistive technologies were seen as means to an end (learning) rather than ends in themselves.

TEACHING ESSENTIALS

Human beings are always communicating, constructing, and exchanging meanings. We co-construct our sense of self, our shifting identities, and our knowledges though communication with one another. In fact, we seem to be driven to communicate. In Western cultures, control over language and written text seems central to becoming a successful 21st century citizen.

Very importantly, technologies give us control over language and particularly over written texts, which for many students are a primary barrier to participation in school, especially for those who may not have the ability to see, decode, attend to, or comprehend printed text.

Jack's situation gives a good example of a set of text transformations involving text modification and tools. These included changes from the original print format (text-to-speech, for example, as in Jack's case); multimedia, video, and videodiscs hypertext and hypermedia are further examples of modified texts. Technology tools (tools or programs that affect the use of text) included word processors, spellcheckers, word prediction and speech recognition devices.

Riley (see Box 6.7) also uses technologies that help him to read so that he can keep up with essential class work. His case indicates how important it is to see technologies as access to the curriculum, rather than as ends in themselves.

Technologies support us to acquire, store, retrieve, manipulate, and exchange information and data. This often leads to an increase in the quality of life—and the quality of learning experiences—for students with particular learning needs, like Jack and Sarah. Technologies become an extension of a student and so increase their capacity to take control of their learning (and their lives) so that they can achieve personally valued goals through:

- Amplification of their cognitive abilities and self-regulation. For Sarah this is achieved as her language is fostered, and her use of symbols developed, through assistive technologies like her Step-by-Step™ communicator.
- Support for their learning, and social and personal development. This is achieved for Jack through the use of familiar technologies, such as the mobile phone, which are shared with his peers.
- Enhancement of their memory and task performance in ways that do not require reliance on another person. For Sarah, the use of talking books presented on PowerPoint support her independent access to familiar texts.

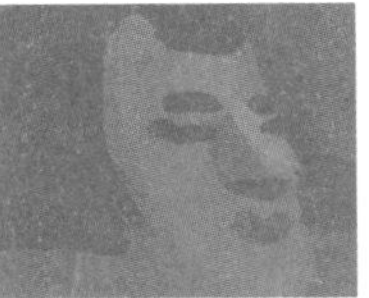

quality of life
The real or perceived status of the life experiences of an individual that satisfy the various levels of need, including shelter, nutrition, friendships, emotional support, purpose, and reason for existence.

BOX 6.7

Riley's technologies

Riley is 13 years old and has just started secondary school. As a result of a brain tumour, Riley has a moderate hemiplegia (i.e., loss of sensation and movement) on the right side of his body and a hemianopia (i.e., loss of half of each visual field), which in Riley's case means that each eye has lost its left visual field.

When he returned to secondary school, Riley was initially issued with a standard-sized laptop that was too heavy to transport from class to class. The laptop carry bag had clasps that were difficult to undo with one hand. Riley now has a much smaller, lightweight laptop with a modified carry bag that will hold both his computer and his schoolbooks.

He also uses a compact keyboard that fits in his new carry bag. He uses one hand to type on his small keyboard. He uses a memory stick at the school desktop machines and saves his work onto the stick to transfer back to his laptop when he gets home.

Riley is learning to view the entire computer screen by turning his head so that he does not miss out on visual information. He needs prompts to do this occasionally. He also uses word prediction software, which speeds up his typing and also helps his sentence structure as it is set to predict grammatically.

Reading is now a tiring task for Riley as he has to concentrate on moving his eyes along a line so he doesn't miss any words. Double spacing text and putting left and right margins on the page help him to visually orient himself on the page and make a big difference to the amount of text Riley is able to read before he needs a break. Any handouts printed for the class and adapted in this manner are much more accessible for him. Riley is also starting to use text-to-speech conversion software to be able to listen to long texts on his MP3 player or computer.

Digital media offer a range of new options for teaching and learning. These technologies allow for multiple representations of the same information: as text, images, and speech. These representations can be redundant, presenting the same information in multiple media, or supplementary, providing background information or alternative perspectives. Simple devices like CD-ROMs make the presentation of multiple media simple and practical.

Technologies can also be used as agents of modelling. The work of researchers like Huang and Wheeler (2006), for example, suggests that the use of video modelling (including self-modelling and peer modelling) can have a great positive impact in the areas of social communication, daily functioning skills, and academic performance on children with various disabilities. Video modelling can be used to teach social skills to children with ASD and to teach them activity schedules. Furthermore, video modelling can be also used to improve other behaviour or skills in students with ASD.

LEARNING ESSENTIALS

The idea that "curriculum leads, technology supports" helps us to keep issues related to information and technology in perspective. This idea suggests that the integration of ICT (particularly assistive technologies) with existing curriculum frameworks is essential if students with diverse learning abilities are to be successful at school. Using the ICT associated with the world wide web illustrates this point.

Teachers and para-professionals working with students who use assistive technology benefit from understanding the universal design features of generic software and operating systems, as well as developing skills in integrating software designed especially for students with disabilities into learning programs for the student population in general.

e-learning and learning objects

Like many areas associated with education and ICT, the use of online learning material and curriculum content (i.e., learning objects) is continually evolving. The Le@rning Federation has developed an exciting and innovative project to support and encourage student learning and to support teachers in Australian and New Zealand in their use of online curriculum content <www.thelearningfederation.edu.au/node1>. Learning objects:

- enable students with diverse needs to work with complex content and ideas in new and dynamic ways; for example, students can manipulate and experiment with variables, explore simulations, design and publish storyboards, prepare exhibitions with authentic artefacts, and explore new concepts in game formats;
- challenge students to question, investigate, analyse, synthesise, solve problems, make decisions, and reflect on their learning; and
- contain teacher-supported (i.e., scaffolded) learning tasks and provide feedback to students on their learning in a variety of supportive and engaging ways.

Learning objects do not have value or utility outside the classroom teaching and learning context. Their value is in their application to classroom settings and to online environments where teachers may or may not be present. As a result, learning objects are designed to help teachers perform these functions:

- introduce new topics and skills;
- provide reinforcement to existing skills;
- extend learning by providing new means for presenting curricular material;
- illustrate concepts that are less easily explained through traditional teaching methods; and
- support new types of learning opportunities not available in a classroom environment.

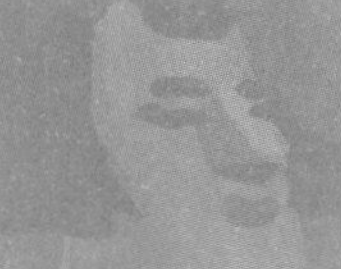

Frances' story in Box 6.8 illustrates how planning for teaching and learning incorporating technology and learning objectives should take place preferably in the context of more detailed individual education plans. This supports her teacher to view the technology as a tool to facilitate learning aims rather than as an end in itself.

BOX 6.8

Working with Frances

Helen Davidson is a lower primary teacher who has been exploring the use of online curriculum content with her students in mathematics and numeracy activities. Her class has been working on number concepts and early addition and subtraction number facts.

The teaching and learning activities involve:

- working with students individually and in small groups with everyday objects and teaching materials, cups, buttons, Lego and fruit;
- drawing attention to the use of mathematics in everyday life within the classroom ("Two people are away from your reading group today? How many are left? Can you draw a picture to help answer this on the whiteboard? How could we show this with numerals?"); and
- exploring different strategies to assist mathematical problem-solving (e.g., counting on from a larger number, breaking numbers into tens and unit sections).

Helen's class includes Frances, a student with cerebral palsy, who has a great deal of difficulty handling manipulatives (like blocks and counters) in mathematical activities. Helen decided to add material from a commercial online product to her range of strategies to promote mathematical understanding for her students.

She chose an interactive media learning sequence called The Number Partner from The Le@rning Federation to use with her numeracy program. Using this online curriculum content, students can explore part–whole relationships of numbers and investigate mathematical strategies. They can choose to create their own addition number facts or explore those facts set within the program. Helen knows that the design of the curriculum content within the software will support Frances to develop numerical understandings.

Students are presented with a bar model to assist with addition (see the picture below). The Number Partner has a tutorial feature as part of the program that Helen uses with the students and parent helpers to introduce them to the activity. "Help" and "Hint" buttons are available throughout the learning sequence and assist students to solve problems themselves. Students can explore the activity in a self-directed manner at their own pace. These features are particularly helpful to Frances. She can also use a trackball with this program and loves being able to work with the on-screen objects to develop her mathematical understanding.

The Le@rning Federation has produced a series of mathematical learning sequences and Helen will use other commercial products that follow on from The Number Partner. Hypertext documents such as The Number Partner offer links within text-to-text-only resources. These documents may have embedded hyperlinks to multimedia supports such as explanatory notes, animated graphics, text-to-speech, definitions, and rereading prompts.

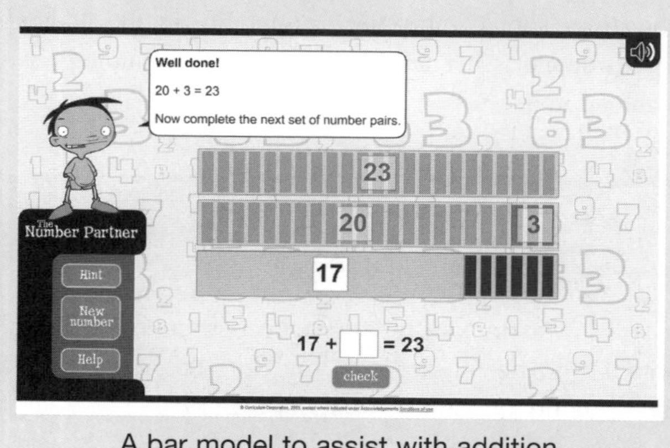

A bar model to assist with addition

BOX 6.8

learning objects
Digital resources that can be used in a range of teaching and learning situations. They have clearly defined aims, are often self-contained, and are structured so that the content and activities are interesting to learners at particular age or grade levels.

The following case illustrates how a teacher, Jim Billings, uses a learning object in his classroom, informed by principles of universal design, to meet the needs of a very wide range of students in his classroom. The learning object supports differentiated curriculum planning. Different students with very different needs require the opportunity to work through the curriculum at a slower (or faster) pace and may need more time than others on basics like literacy and numeracy and for revision. A differentiated curriculum is a program of activities that offers a variety of entry points for students who differ in abilities, knowledge, and skills. Tomlinson and Allan (2000) suggested that in a differentiated curriculum teachers offer different approaches to *what students learn* (content), *how students learn* (process) and *how students demonstrate what they have learned* (product).

The story in Box 6.9 also suggests that curriculum underpinned by principles of universal design is easily linked to, and supported by, technology. A range of approaches to teaching and learning can be engaged based on the learning needs of students, specific content requirements, and teacher style.

The technologies used by Jim Billings are appropriate for students in special education settings and for secondary students with special needs, in both special schools and secondary schools. WebQuest <www.webquest.org/index.php> is another resource offering both learning objects and inquiry topics that can be matched to a wide range of students' needs (primary, secondary, and special school students).

BOX 6.9

Resource for all classrooms: a Year 2 case study

Jim Billings is a Year 2 teacher and has been using Clicker 5™ to scaffold the literacy development of his students. Clicker 5™ includes a word processor that can read aloud text, highlighting each word, and can be set to show pictures above words. Text is entered into the word processor either via the keyboard or by clicking on an onscreen grid (or both). Students are encouraged to listen and then self-correct their work.

Clicker Grids enable Jim's students to become more independent and confident about their writing. Grids have cells containing words, phrases, or pictures (see the picture below). If a student is unsure of the content of any cell on the grid they can right-click to hear the text spoken (without writing it into the word processor).

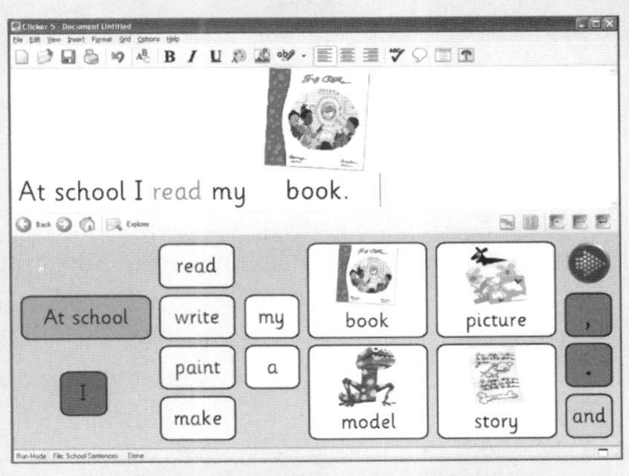

Cells containing words, phrases or pictures

Jim uses a set of linked sentence-building grids included in the software to help a number of students to structure their written work and to build up a piece of writing. Sentence starters, verbs, adjectives, and nouns are colour-coded and sequenced in a left-to-right progression to assist sentence structure.

For some students who are working on left-to-right sequencing of text, the grids can easily be adapted to become force ordered, that is, only some of the cells in the grid are active and it is not until a word in the left-hand column has been selected that the next column to the right then becomes available. This ensures sentences make grammatical sense, even if students choose the wrong word.

For students whose literacy levels are more advanced, Jim uses grids containing word banks relevant to the subject area to help them extend their vocabulary and ideas into new areas. Students can use videos and pictures within their work to create multimedia presentations.

As the school has Clicker™, access is available to hundreds of freely available downloaded grids developed by teachers. Jim edits these to suit the needs of the students in his class. He also uses commercially available Clicker™ resources that the school houses in its Resource Centre. Some of these that have been especially helpful include the Find Out and Write About series (which provides factual information and activities on a range of subject areas from Dinosaurs to the Solar System) and Trackers for Clicker™, which is based on an Oxford University Press structured reading series for struggling readers.

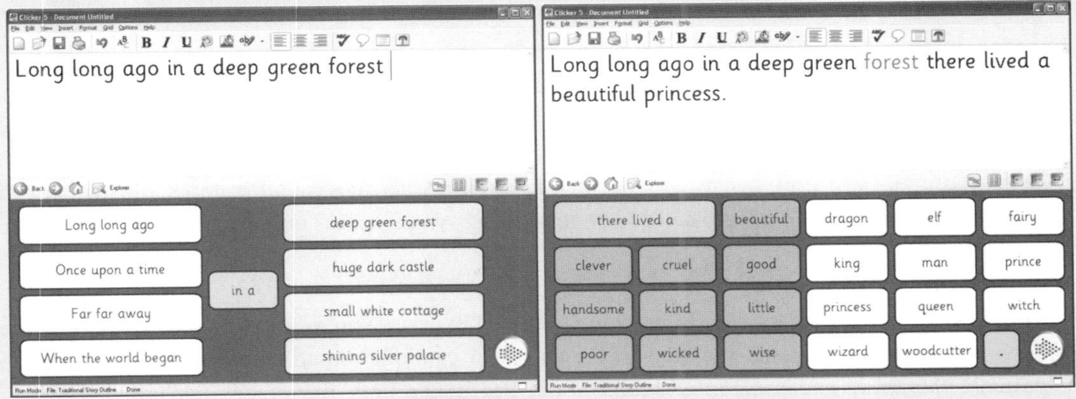

Forced ordered cell in grids

6.9

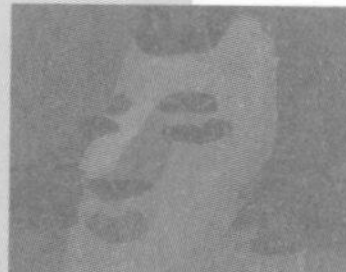

USING THIS CHAPTER IN SCHOOLS

Planning for students' diverse needs

One of the more challenging aspects of addressing diversity in the classroom involves meeting students' very wide range of intellectual and learning needs. Some students may have an intellectual disability that requires curricula responses very different from those of other students. Some students may have extraordinary intellectual abilities, be labelled as gifted, and so also require different responses. Some students with Autism Spectrum Disorder may be both.

Differentiating the curriculum is one way in which you can respond to this diversity. ICT can support curriculum differentiation. Maker (1982) suggested that we make curriculum differentiations in the areas of content, process, product, and learning environment. Technologies play a role in these four areas.

Regardless of the year level at which you will teach, the following should be kept in mind when differentiating the curriculum:

- have high expectations for all students;
- make knowledge and materials accessible;
- vary instructional formats frequently; and
- allow multiple ways for students to show what they have learned.

The case studies in this chapter include examples across the phases of schooling and illustrate how technologies support curriculum differentiation in all these areas. Jim Billing's story shows how learning objects and computer technology can support differentiation in content, process, and student outcomes. In Jack's case, we see how differentiation in process and product, and additional and specialist software and hardware, help with verbal communication and control within the learning environment. It is a similar situation in Sarah's and Fiona's cases.

ICT (particularly assistive technology) can also underpin the physical, emotional, and sensory supports required by students with diverse abilities for their success in classrooms and schooling.

Assessing a student for a new technology

Following is an outline of the steps you might take when assessing a student in your classroom for a suitable technology. When assessing a student's technology needs, selecting augmentative technologies and/or developing teaching and learning sequences for a student, you should establish and involve a professional support team (see Box 6.5) including the students and their parents.

Regularly assess and re-assess

Plan for an intensive initial assessment of the student's needs undertaken in partnership with their support team, and timetable regular reviews of the student's use of their technologies into your program. For example, when Sarah started trialling a communication device that had communication options displayed in a 2×3 grid, her teacher decided to re-assess her movement patterns and switch skills to make sure she was using the most efficient, least tiring switch access option for this new device.

Consult therapists and other experts

The student's support team should include a range of experts. You might also need to consult specific experts who are not regular members of the team; for example, Sarah's teacher talked with her occupational therapist, gathering information about her upper limb movement, including the range of movement in her forearm, wrist, thumb, and fingers, and the impact of arm movement on reflex movement patterns and fatigue levels.

Involve the family and other carers

Ask for observations from the student's family and teacher aide about their manipulative skills, hand preference, and functional use of hands (and limbs and body) in daily tasks. Ask family members to monitor the student's use of technology regularly and to identify difficulties with its use outside the classroom context.

Learn from past experiences

Collect a comprehensive history of your student's successful technology experiences gathered from the family, class teachers, teacher aides, resource teachers, and therapists and from your own careful observations. This history might include information on what technology had been tried in the past, how it had been used by the student, and the type of training that staff had been given.

Consider the options available

Use all the information available to you to match the student to a particular technology. Try a range of technologies to find the one that best meets the student's needs. Consider how the student will gain access to the technology, and what intentions the technology has in the life of the student and of their family. After gathering all this information, ensure that you have considered the technology within the curriculum framework of the classroom. How will it ensure access and participation? Box 6.10 gives some suggestions for setting up a multi-sensory environment that might increase the learning options available to students.

6.10 Setting up a multi-sensory environment

A multi-sensory environment is a way of improving social interaction for students with severe or multiple disabilities. A multi-sensory environment is usually in a separate room or quiet area within the classroom. The space might be darkened, have music, lights, and/or a bubble tube. The space might have simple technologies like a cassette/CD player or special lighting that can be controlled by the student through a switching device. You might include aromatherapy on entry to the room/space to signal the start of the activity.

The objective of setting up a multi-sensory room may be to build trust between the student and teacher (or teacher aide). Carefully observe the pupil when in the environment—do their responses change? Do they become still and attentive? Do they have a favourite type of music—if so, how do you know? Do similar behavioural changes occur when the lighting changes? Note how the multi-sensory environment:

- increases opportunities for interaction between the student and the environment;
- increases opportunities for interaction between the student and the teacher/aide;
- supports the student to understand cause and effect;
- improves the student's abilities to use various switches;
- increases opportunities for the student to make choices, even at a very basic level; and
- reduces the number and frequency of negative behaviours or interruptions.

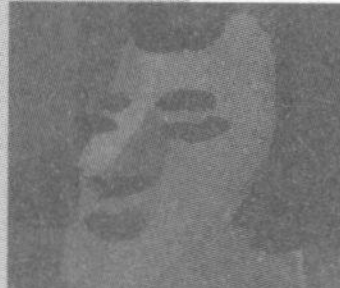

Undertake a trial

Trial new and different technologies with your student before you purchase them. For example, Sarah could use two switches to gain access to her new communication device: one to start/stop the automatic scan and the other to select. Her teacher wondered whether she could release the one switch and re-hit it quickly enough to use a single switch for both tasks. Sarah trialled a variety of different switch types including jelly button switches and wobble (wand) switches before a decision to use two switches was made.

Implement the technology

Once a suitable technology is identified and has been trialled to your satisfaction, and to the satisfaction of the student and their parents or carers, you can introduce it with some confidence. But remember, ongoing reviews of the technology should be timetabled into your program.

Differentiating the curriculum

In this chapter there are a number of examples of how teachers have modified their teaching and learning sequences and materials through the use of technology. In your own teaching practice, think about how you might change the format of materials by using learning objects, communication boards, and/or alternative language symbols such as Compic. This will depend upon the level at which you teach, but adaptation of teaching methods and materials is of benefit to all students, not just those who have particular learning needs. For example, you might convert an assignment from a written essay to a verbal presentation, or to a short video presentation captured by a digital still camera.

You may differentiate the curriculum in the following ways:

- Use visual timetables.
- Use social stories that can be presented via PowerPoint presentations with, for example, photographs of the student that help recall the rules for taking turns in a conversation, or for working cooperatively in a group.
- Ask different questions based on Bloom's taxonomy or on the theory of multiple intelligences (you will find numerous references to Benjamin Bloom's taxonomy on the internet). You might also search for inquiry-oriented lesson formats through WebQuest <www.webquest.org/index.php>, which engage mathematical, musical, and communicative intelligences in problem-solving.
- Provide instructional scaffolding (e.g., background information, graphic organisers, metacognitive strategies). Many learning objects <www.thelearningfederation.edu.au/node1> can be carefully selected to scaffold work you are undertaking with students in your class.
- Provide a one-to-one tutorial or explicit instruction, for example to introduce new learning. This can be supported through online processes and software such as Clicker 5™, which offers individual support to students while allowing you to work with the class or with other groups of students.
- Provide signals, for example visual or auditory cues, for a change of activity. In Sarah's case, a single tone was used to let Sarah know that one activity was coming to completion and that a new one was about to start.

When differentiating the curriculum you might also consider the purposes of schooling, the discipline or domain, the intentions of the particular teaching and learning sequence, the understandings we want to foster, and the outcomes we are working towards. You have to consider how to link teaching, learning, and assessment.

Some learning objects offer multiple assignments within a unit, tailored for students with differing levels of achievement. Students may choose technologies that help them to learn and to demonstrate their learning. You might supplement your classroom materials by adding audio-visual media, for example learning objects, models, or manipulatives. You might also consider oral synopsis of a book or content-related material at a different reading level.

When thinking about differentiation, technology and learning standards and assessment you might:

- allow students to do less work to demonstrate the same standard (e.g., requiring fewer mathematics problems, shorter essays);
- allow students to create a different product to demonstrate the same standard (e.g., a hands-on demonstration instead of a written essay if writing is not the primary learning objective);
- adjust a standard within the same subject-matter area based on the student's individualised educational plan—Jim Billings (see box 6.9) uses commercially available Clicker™ resources to adjust literacy learning standards; and
- develop a personalised grading rubric or contract, based on the student's individualised educational plan (e.g., grade effort, progress, and other dispositions as well as acquisition of content knowledge and skills).

Technology supports students in your classroom by providing physical supports like wheelchair access, visual magnification of texts, or access to particular keyboards and switches. You or a classmate might need to push a student's wheelchair, provide support to an arm as the student types, or take notes for a student. Think also about sensory support that a student might need that can be provided via technologies. For example, you might have to turn down the lights, provide soothing music through headphones, provide a different type of seat, and/or adjust a student's schedule to provide for activity breaks when there have been heavy demands placed upon a student.

Augmentative and alternative communication aims

The following is based on the work of Welcome to the ICTS website, a resource for teachers of students with special educational needs. You can find more supportive materials at <www.inclusive.net/resources/units/units.shtml>.

When planning for individual students, take account of augmentative and alternative communication goals as well as specific curriculum aims. When planning you should consider the following aims:

- *Operational aims*—What are the motor and cognitive skills required by the student to gain access to, and send/signal, a message? (Knowledge of signs, how the student operates the augmentative and alternative communication system or locates the desired message, pointing, scanning, operating switches, controlling cursors, editing).
- *Linguistic aims*—Does the student have adequate receptive and expressive language skills?
- *Social aims*—Is the student competent in the social rules of communication? Does the student make appropriate eye-contact, share the balance of talking, listening, and responding to non-verbal clues like turning gaze away?
- *Strategic aims*—Does the student have the ability to adapt their communication style to suit the listener (know who can understand signs and who will need other clues, change vocabulary to suit peers, older persons or authority figures), or know how to repair and extend the conversation (being able to signal "I don't understand" or "What do you think?")?

You might plan an initial focus on operational and linguistic aims. Once these are established your focus might shift to the social and strategic components that are crucial to the student becoming an efficient and effective communicator. Some other ideas are given in Box 6.11.

6.11 Augmentative and alternative communication

Introducing augmentative and alternative communication strategies (or other information and technologies) to your student should be underpinned by the principles of good teaching and learning. Become aware of the teaching and learning style embodied within the different software you might use. Does this suit the student? Does it suit the intention of the teaching and learning sequences? Structured drills-and-skills type software with fixed content may be good for reinforcing language sub-skills, such as matching and sorting, but ineffective for developing connected language and higher level skills. Creative and exploratory software, such as open-ended frameworks and word/symbol processors that allow you to use your own content, are good for developing understanding of word meanings, discovering new concepts, and sequencing words into sentences and stories. Think about the following when introducing augmentative and alternative communication technologies and/or skills:

- Start from where your student is (or even slightly below) so that success is easily achieved and built upon.
- Gradually phase in the technology (or augmentative and alternative communication processes). Break the tasks/skills down into small steps, give plenty of positive reinforcement, and allow time for consolidation of each stage for the student, family, and staff.
- Introduce voice output communication aids in the natural environments in which specific language and communication needs arise. Teach and practise specific new vocabulary items, language structures, or types of interaction in familiar social contexts linked in a meaningful way to the curriculum.
- Remember that simple augmentative and alternative communication devices can be used as ordinary classroom resources for all students.
- For early learners, choose augmentative and alternative communication devices that are simple and quick to manage in the classroom.
- For students for whom literacy teaching and learning is a primary aim, choose augmentative and alternative communication systems that offer printout (or connection to computer) facilities.
- Always try software out yourself (using the special input method your student will use) before trying it out with the student.
- Choose software that matches the developmental level of the child.
- Think about where the student is now and the many steps they need to negotiate to become an efficient communicator.
- Keep to a small set of software. Don't overwhelm the student (or yourself) with too many different packages at the same time.
- Try to stick to software from the same company, so that presentation and the mode of operation are consistent (especially for scan and switch users), so that the pupil is not distracted from the content of the package by having to master lots of different user interfaces.

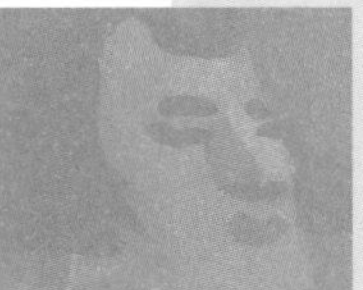

Support between and beyond schools

Support mechanisms for students with disabilities are in place in education departments across Australia. These vary in structure, level of service, and form of service delivery.

All states in recent years have developed comprehensive plans relating to the use of computer-based technology within schools and have provided considerable funding for technology provision; however, with the exception of New South Wales, these plans have not contained specific considerations for students with disabilities. Often, the supply of technology to these students has developed in isolation from the general provision of technology for schools.

When you move to a new school, it is important to seek out networks and professional learning opportunities within and beyond the school. Such networks support:

- the sharing of resources and knowledge across schools, school sectors and districts;
- collaboration and access to a larger personal support base of teachers and professionals working with students using assistive technology;
- greater awareness of available web and company-based resources and information;
- collaborative problem-solving and sharing of specialist expertise and technology support;
- development and delivery of professional learning and training in the use of assistive technologies;
- provision of relevant training for teachers and groups of teachers, which include some who are new to the network and others who have considerable technology experience, that might involve establishing "train the trainer" programs about assistive technologies; and
- the sharing of web-based resources and/or developing a web-based resource specific to your network.

The ideas presented in this chapter are not definitive solutions to the multitude of problems that confront teachers at every level of education. Technologies can provide valuable supports that would otherwise leave students struggling with the curriculum or, in some case, left completely outside of it. Looking at ways in which technologies can assist in the day-to-day delivery of education is the starting point.

PRACTICAL ACTIVITIES

Uni-work

1 Check out the websites listed at the end of this chapter and create your own bookmarks of sites that you consider to be most useful and relevant. Keep a log of the useful information you locate that might be of value for classroom teachers.

2 Locate and visit an education setting where assistive technology is being used so you can see firsthand how learners are using the adaptations described in this chapter. You will need to do some research to find such settings. Brainstorm ideas with some of your friends or study mates or talk to your lecturer about likely locations.

3 Obtain a copy of your national, state, or regional education statement on the uses of technology in the classroom. All of these are specific documents that relate to students with diverse abilities. Make sure you consider children who are gifted and talented, and those with the highest support needs. Jot down where there are overlaps in the statements and some practical examples of where ICT applications can be introduced at the school level at which you will be teaching.

School-work

Remember that school policies may apply that restrict your ability to complete one or more of the activities suggested below. Before beginning any of the following activities, remember to check with your supervising teacher or administration to confirm that you can undertake the activity within existing school guidelines and policies.

4 Spend a few minutes thinking about the students in your class and identify any who might be advantaged by the use of specific technologies that have been mentioned in this chapter. Then, think about and list the resources that are available in your classroom. This list might include mobile phones, televisions or monitors, CD/DVD players, digital still or movie cameras, and/or computers. Make some enquiries among your teacher colleagues about other technical/technological resources available elsewhere in the school (e.g., data projectors, interactive whiteboards). Having read through this chapter, brainstorm ideas that involve the use of the resources to which you have access. Be as creative and innovative as you can. Now, plan a lesson that uses one or more of the resources with the target student(s) in mind. Try out your lesson.

5 Recruit one or more of your teacher colleagues with the objective of joining an online community in a particular education field of interest. This could be a discussion group, newsgroup, or listserv to which you can actively contribute and obtain information. Together, generate a log of the issues and discussions under appropriate headings.

6 You may have a student in your class for whom a curriculum access method has been agreed. Evaluate its effectiveness with a range of curriculum activities. You might review the activities used by the student in terms of the cognitive complexity of the activities and the success of their technological/technical/manipulative skills.

SUGGESTED READING AND RESOURCES

Clough, P. & Corbett, J. (2000). Theories of Inclusive education. A students' guide. London: Paul Chapman Publishing Ltd.

O'Hanlon, C. (2003). Educational inclusion as action research: An interpretative discourse. England: Open University Press.

Websites

<www.ascd.org>—Association for Supervision and Curriculum Development: features many resources related to language and literacy learning.

<www.ataccess.org/rresources/acpanel/0005.html>—Alliance for Technology Access: an organisation that connects children and adults with disabilities to a wide range of technology tools and resources.

<www.cricksoft.com/us/products/clicker>—Clicker 5™: A writing support and multimedia tool, which enables you to write with whole words, phrases or pictures.

<www.dest.gov.au/archive/highered/eippubs/eip99-6/execsum99_6.htm>—The Assistive Technology – Meeting the technology needs of students with disabilities in post-secondary education (1999) report.

<www.dest.gov.au/schools/publications/2000/TechnologyforLearning.pdf>—Technology for Learning: Students with Disabilities: project funded by a grant from the Commonwealth Department of Education, Training and Youth Affairs.

<www.dest.gov.au/sectors/school_education/publications_resources/profiles/technology_learning_students_disabilities.htm>—Technology for Learning: Students with Disabilities (2000).

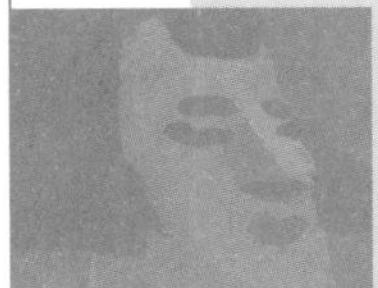

<www.gatewayseducation.com.au/content/view/11/46>—Gateways Education Technologies: offers support related to differentiating the curriculum and access to learning objects that cater specifically to the needs of gifted students.

<www.inclusive.net/resources/units/units.shtml>—Inclusive Consultancy and Training Syndicate (ICTS): free online units with great teaching and learning ideas, as well as online training in the use of different forms of assistive technology. The practical activities presented in this chapter are based on materials from this website.

<www.novitatech.org.au>—NovitaTech: Australian assistive technology provider with research and development division.

<www.scansoft.com>—Nuance: information about products related to speech recognition software.

<www.spectronicsinoz.com>—Australian assistive technology provider with a great resource library.

<www.studyworksonline.com>—Study Works Online: free learning site delivering original approaches that help students develop an understanding of mathematics and science concepts usually taught from grades 7 to 12.

<www.thelearningfederation.edu.au/node>—The Le@rning Federation: information about online learning objects developed for the Australian and New Zealand context.

<www.tifaq.com/speech.html>—Typing injuries frequently asked questions: responds to frequently asked questions about speech recognition software and usage.

<www.webquest.org/index.php>—WebQuest: a range of inquiry-oriented lesson formats in which most or all of the information that learners work with comes from the web.

<www2.edc.org/NCIP/library/wp/toc.htm>—National Center to Improve Practice in Special Education through Technology, Media and Materials (NCIP): information about buying technologies.

REFERENCES

Alameda, C. (2000). *Alliance for technology access. Computer and web resources for people with disabilities: a guide to exploring today's assistive technology* (3rd ed.). Salt Lake City, UT: Hunter House Inc.

Bondy, A. (2002). PECS and verbal behavior. In L. Frost & A. Bondy (Eds), *The Picture Exchange Communication System: Training manual* (2nd ed.). Newark, DE: Pyramid Educational Products.

Cormack, M., Couch, M., & McColl, M. (2000). *Technology for learning: Students with disabilities*. Department of Education, Science and Training <www.dest.gov.au/sectors/school_education/publications_resources/profiles/technology_learning_students_disabilities.htm – publication>.

Hasselbring, T. & Williams Glaser, C. (2000). Use of computer technologies to help students with special needs. *The Future of Children. Children and Computer Technology*, *10*, 102–122.

Huang, A. & Wheeler, J. (2006). Effective interventions for individuals with high-functional autism. *International Journal of Special Education*, *21*, 165–175.

Lahm, E. & Sizemore, L. (2002). Factors that influence assistive technology decision making. *Journal of Special Education Technology*, *17*, 15–26.

Lazzaro, J. (2001). *Adaptive technologies for learning & work environments* (2nd ed.). Chicago: American Library Association.

Leung, P., Owens, J., Lamb, G., Smith, K., Shaw, J., & Hauff, R. (1999). *Assistive technology. Meeting the needs of students with disabilities in post-secondary education.* Evaluations and Investigations Programme, Higher Education Division Department of Education, Training and Youth Affairs © Commonwealth of Australia 1998 ISBN 0 642 23944 4 <www.dest.gov.au/archive/highered/eippubs/eip99-6/execsum99_6.htm>.

Maker, C. J. (1982). *Curriculum development for the gifted.* Austin, TX: PRO-ED.

Male, M. (2003). *Technology for inclusion* (4th ed.). Boston: Allyn and Bacon.

Strangman, N. & Hall, T. (2003). *Text transformations*. CAST Universal Design for Learning <www.cast.org/publications/ncac/ncac_textrans.html>.

Tomlinson, C. A. & Allan, S. (2000). *Leadership for differentiating schools and classrooms.* Alexandria, VA: Association for Supervision and Curriculum Development.

US Department of Education (2000). *Synthesis on the selection and use of assistive technology.* Washington, DC: U.S. Office of Special Education Programs.

US Department of Education (2000). *Promising practices in technology: Supporting access to, and progress in, the general curriculum*. Washington, DC: U.S. Office of Special Education Programs 180U Cross Project Collaboration.

Credits

168 BIGmack®, Step-by-Step, PowerLink2 and Jelly Bean® are manufactured by AbleNet, Inc.; **175, 189** Reproduced with permission from Crick Software <www.cricksoft.com>; **177** © Penfriend Ltd 1999–2002 <www.penfriend.biz>; **187** The Number Partner, The Le@rning Federation learning objective L103. Reproduced with permission from Curriculum Corporation.

SECTION 3

Inclusive Practices

Inclusive Practices 3

Sometimes we sit and reflect on our own school experiences. They are amazingly different. So different that we wonder how our life paths brought us to the same place at the same time. To illustrate this with our personal histories, one of us was a very naughty boy who achieved a childhood goal of expulsion from secondary school with its entire attendant stresses and family complications. The other was the son of a TAFE principal who loved just about everything that school could offer and whose vocational objective was set from a relatively early age on tertiary education, although he too was subject to the vagaries of teachers' attitudes and disciplinary practices.

The reason for mentioning our personal histories is to emphasise the hugely different education demands we presented as children and young adults. It is more important, however, to emphasise that neither of us was located at the furthest limits of the continuum of students' skills and abilities that classroom teachers face today.

Given the current policy of including students with very widely varying needs in regular schools, the authors of the various chapters throughout this book have endeavoured to present a framework for understanding how to accommodate difference rather than emphasising the students' problems. This section begins with a chapter by Robyn Gillies and Paul Pagliano who deal with teaching principles and practices that encourage and support all students in every teaching–learning setting.

Their chapter is followed by one on literacies and numeracy. We talk about *literacies* because literacy is not just about reading but also about writing, spelling, and research skills and, in fact, numeracy. These skill areas are relevant to the early childhood practitioners involved in the early years of schooling and there are many students in secondary schools who need support with reading and writing, even those who will eventually attend university. So, if you're heading for a career teaching secondary school, don't even dream of skipping Christa van Kraayenoord and John Elkins' chapter. Teaching literacies and numeracy is part of your job description as well.

The final two chapters in this section focus on the early phases and the senior phase of schooling. We have included chapters on these areas because there are specific issues relating to inclusion that apply to the early years (preschool, primary, and the middle years) and the secondary years. In the introduction to this book, we urged the reader not to skip over sections that don't seem to be relevant to your intended career (early childhood, primary, middle years, secondary school). There we suggested that it is important for modern teachers to know about education and the process of school generally. It is important for teachers in the early years to know where the students will be going when they move into primary and secondary school, and for secondary teachers to know what experiences their students will have had before they walk into their first high school classroom.

Chapters by Donna Pendergast, Rod Chadbourne, and Susan Dandy on the early years, and by Karen Moni and Ian Hay will provide numerous ideas that can be applied across the school years. Your imagination and creativity should allow you to see the relevance in what each phase has to offer, or learn from, to maximise the learning outcomes of students with whom you work.

Paul Pagliano and Robyn M. Gillies

7

CURRICULUM, ADJUSTMENTS, AND ADAPTATIONS

What you will learn in this chapter

It will come as no surprise to you now you have reached Chapter 7 that schools must provide programs for students that meet their diverse learning needs. In many cases, this means that the curriculum—how it is taught and how students learn—must be adapted to accommodate all students. Here, we describe how this can be achieved in regular classes by devoting considerable attention not only to how the curriculum can be adapted but also to what adjustments may be needed specifically for students with cognitive, sensory, and physical impairments.

After reading this chapter, you will:

- know how to establish learning environments that are inclusive of all students;
- understand the specific learning needs of students with cognitive, sensory, or physical impairments;
- recognise how specific teaching approaches can be used to promote learning for students with specific learning needs; and
- appreciate the key role that teachers play in teaching and facilitating learning in the classroom.

CASE STUDIES

KEVIN

On Jane Hill's first day with her Year 1 class she decided to start with a getting-to-know-you activity. She enthusiastically invited everyone to draw a picture of their favourite food. She walked around the class and encouraged each child to explain what they were drawing. One boy, Kevin, mumbled that he was drawing paper. Jane immediately said loudly, "You *don't* eat paper! I want you to draw something you eat". The other children laughed and Kevin started to fidget and squirm.

Jane assumed that Kevin was off task, maybe even being silly. She had never heard of anyone eating paper before but this spontaneous reaction transformed the teaching–learning context into an uncomfortable place for Kevin, where he did not feel included. Jane, who was more focused on teaching the whole class at the time, was oblivious to the emerging issue.

The next day Kevin missed school and the following day his mother came to see Jane. She explained how Kevin had some unusual behaviours. One of them was chewing pieces of paper and spitting them out. This strategy was used at home to help Kevin settle. He was allowed to chew paper for 10 minutes before and after school as a reward for not doing it at school. This strategy had worked the previous year but the parents had not told Jane about it because they assumed it would continue to be successful. Now, Kevin was very upset, saying that he hated school and was never going back.

Jane thought about where she'd gone wrong. She decided she could have handled the situation much better if she had been more sensitive to context. Regardless of what Kevin claimed he ate, Jane should have treated him with respect, listened attentively to what he had to say, and valued his contribution. He told her his story in a quiet voice because he didn't want the whole class to hear, just her. Jane could have replied softly, "Is that so? What else do you eat? Chicken and chips? Yum! Why don't you draw them on another piece of paper? Soon I'm going to ask everyone to share their drawing".

In future when Jane comes across any unusual student behaviour she will take particular care not to jump to conclusions, she will suspend her judgement until she gathers more information, perhaps from the student's parents, the teacher's aide or other teachers. The next time Kevin came to class he could tell that Jane was interacting with him in a different way—she valued his contribution—he felt much more included!

JASON

Jason was excited about the prospect of following his brother and attending the local high school. He knew many of his brother's friends and he enjoyed playing Gameboy with them or listening as they talked about the football, the mountain bike one of their friends had, or the latest DVD release. Jason felt comfortable with his brother's friends as they were always very prepared to include him in their activities, so it was not surprising that Jason saw starting high school as his way of showing his brother and his friends that he was moving up in the world.

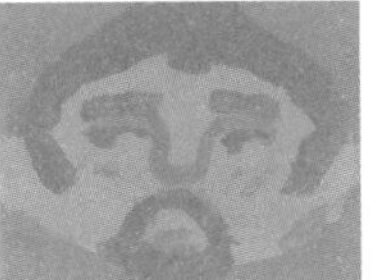

It was not long, however, before the novelty of his new school began to wear off as Jason found he had difficulties moving from classroom to classroom, ensuring he had the right books for each lesson, and reading the timetable. In fact, understanding the timetable became a daily nightmare as he struggled to locate each new room on a rolling seven-day timetable.

Jason had been assessed in primary school as being cognitively impaired and, although he could participate in most classroom activities, he had difficulties organising his routines and following instructions given by his teachers, skills that are critically important for success at high school. It was not long before his teachers realised that Jason needed help, especially if he was to arrive promptly to each lesson and so avoid the teasing that he experienced for arriving late.

Providing Jason with additional and subtle prompts to avoid making his difficulties obvious was the first step. His class teachers did this by providing him with a weekly timetable that provided clear directions on the requirements for each class and where it was located. His teachers also made a point of reminding him before he left his different classes to check his timetable so he would know what to take to his next lesson. Additionally, he was paired with a "buddy" who had initial responsibility of making sure that Jason arrived for his lessons on time. However, as Jason learned to master his timetable and understood what he needed to bring to each class, he relied less and less on his buddy for assistance.

Jason was very sociable and well liked by his peers, so his teachers decided to build on this attribute by setting up small group learning experiences in his various classes where he could work with others to complete specific tasks. The opportunity to work in small groups, either with another student or a group of two or three students, enabled Jason to take risks with his learning that would be too intimidating for him in the larger class group. His group members were very supportive of his efforts and they actively encouraged his contributions by providing prompts and scaffolding his learning when needed.

The opportunity for Jason to contribute to classroom activities in a positive and constructive way improved his status among his class peers and this contributed to Jason's sense of purpose, achievement, and self-confidence as a learner. Jason is now enjoying school. He is working on a differentiated program with adaptations to the regular curriculum that are appropriate for his developing skills and knowledge base and he is fully included in all his classes.

TEACHING–LEARNING CONTEXT

To begin, we have provided a list of key terms that we use throughout this chapter. As you will see in Box 7.1, each form of impairment exists on a continuum. At one end, the impairment may have almost no impact on learning, while at the other it can create considerable difficulties.

The curriculum is the teaching–learning context. It is more than just what is taught and what is learned. It includes:

- how the teaching is delivered;
- what resources are used; and
- how learning success is measured.

BOX 7.1

Key terms

Cognitive, sensory, and physical impairments exist on a continuum of severity from mild (common) to profound (rare). As you will recall from Chapter 3, in education, definitions focus on how these impairments affect student learning. The term *impairment* indicates that the student's difficulty with learning is sufficiently significant to require additional human and material support to that usually provided by the class teacher.

A student with **cognitive impairment** requires assistance with intellectual functioning and ability to cope with the demands of independent living in areas such as communication, self-care, home living, social skills, gaining access to community facilities and resources, self-direction, health and safety, functional academics, leisure, and work. Often students with sensory and physical impairment also require extra assistance to cope with the demands of independent living.

Students with **sensory impairment** fit four categories. After correction they are:

- *hard-of-hearing*—where there is some functional hearing available for learning;
- *educationally deaf*—where there is a total lack of functional hearing available for learning;
- *low-vision*—where there is some functional vision available for learning; and
- *educationally blind*—where there is a total lack of functional vision for learning.

A student with **physical impairment** has functional difficulties with physical skills such as hand use, body control, mobility, strength, or stamina that interfere with school attendance or learning.

functional academics
Skills that allow a person with an intellectual disability to live with some degree of independence in the community. These skills include money handling, sign recognition, arithmetic operations, basic reading, writing, and interpersonal and communication skills.

The curriculum influences, and is influenced by, what society believes its students should be like. It is closely linked to the idea of helping to shape the world we want in the future.

The curriculum also identifies and reflects:

- what society believes students should know;
- what they should be able to understand; and
- what they should be able to do.

The curriculum is much more complicated than just a set of content (i.e., a syllabus) and it is not limited to time spent at school. It is more holistic and far-reaching. This is because we acknowledge the role that the curriculum plays in shaping students' self-identities and their psycho-socio-cultural relationships with others. This complex remit is precisely why we talk about the curriculum as the teaching–learning context.

The curriculum has become a much more flexible, responsive, and demand-led system of skills acquisition. These demands come from legislation, policy, research, socio-cultural expectations, and historical trends. Whether curriculum is for an entire student population, a specific age group, or for an individual, it must ensure that all students receive an appropriate education, one that is accessible, provides equal opportunity, encourages self-sufficiency and guarantees that each student achieves the best outcomes possible.

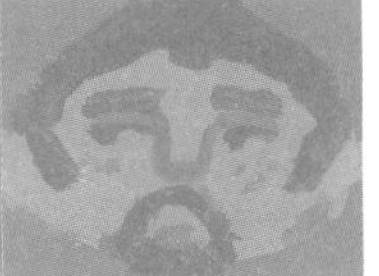

A narrow view of curriculum is unlikely to assist teachers to reach the mandated objectives. Too often, teachers base their teaching on prescribed activities, set texts, and learning outcomes. They feel obliged to prepare students for content-loaded examinations and assessment tasks. This leads them to funnel their efforts and teach to the students who are at or near the age-relevant ability level and capable of performing as desired. Understandably, students who experience diverse learning needs, like those we will consider in this chapter, become frustrated due to lack of support, they feel isolated, and they give up. A narrow, rigid way of defining curriculum will be a barrier to inclusion.

New ways of thinking about the curriculum

The curriculum should not be a barrier. The curriculum can be reframed and reorganised to fit the learning needs of individual students in your class and, in the process, encourage students to take greater responsibility for their own learning. The reframing ultimately makes the curriculum better for all students because teachers greatly expand their repertoire of instructional practices. They become much more effective at tailoring the curriculum to fit the precise learning needs of individual students.

In this chapter, we want to shake up your ideas about the curriculum so you can make the teaching–learning context in your classroom suitable for every student. We want to introduce new ways of thinking about the curriculum that involves the teacher becoming acutely aware that each student has his or her own set of:

- achievements (e.g., what the student already knows);
- learning needs (e.g., support, aids, time);
- learning styles (e.g., how the student learns most effectively);
- interests (e.g., motorbikes, music, books);
- personality (e.g., how the student might respond);
- background (e.g., culture, family circumstances); and
- personal experiences (e.g., what has happened to him or her in the past).

It is vital that every teacher learns how to reflect on his or her own teaching by focusing on what is happening in the learning process for each student. It is equally important that the teacher becomes an expert at making critical assessment decisions about what is working for each student and what is not working. Teaming up with other teachers and specialists can lead to more sophisticated pedagogy being devised if, and when, it is required.

So, how is this new way of thinking different and what is reframing? Reframing means changing the way in which we think about something (see Box 7.2).

The goal with reframing is to find a frame of reference that permits every student in a class to be valued. A good place to start is to focus on students' positive characteristics. In addition, when students are viewed as being more similar than different, this provides an inclusive frame of reference. This frame will immediately create a more optimistic learning environment and a basis for mutual trust and respect. The idea is to provide a safe, flexible learning environment where all students are given sufficient support to reach their potential (i.e., to achieve outcomes that are consistent with their capabilities), become willing and able to take risks, and construct knowledge that is personally relevant and meaningful.

Jane Hill's getting-to-know-you activity with her Year 1 class is an example of reframing in action. Kevin's first response (eating paper) had the potential to exclude him, whereas his second response

BOX 7.2 Reflective thinking about one's own teaching

John Peters decided to reflect on his own teaching. He did this by videotaping one of his lessons and then watching it several times. He also made a tape when he was discussing his teaching with a colleague at the school. During the audio playback of this discussion he noticed that he spoke about his Year 7 class as consisting of "an able group and a special group". When he re-examined the video he realised that in the lesson he had included himself in the able group, thereby creating an "us" and "them" situation. This dichotomy was clearly skewing the context for all classroom interaction and he decided there and then that he needed to do something about it.

As John said, "This insight made an enormous difference. It was such an amazing revelation for me. It was like there was a change in the tide. From then on, I became a very different teacher. Inclusion developed into a key-learning outcome for every lesson. I started reading about inclusion and thinking about what it really meant for my teaching. I wanted to create an inclusive culture in our classroom. I started to see culture as consisting of three parts. First and foremost was the need to have inclusive attitudes. We did this as a class group by developing a values base for our class. Actually, it was quite simple. We started by agreeing that everyone in our class is equal and everybody in our class makes positive contributions."

"Then, we decided that we all expect that everyone in our class will do his or her very best work all the time, and that includes me, the teacher. This meant that the students had high expectations for each other—that was so powerful. Second, we focused on inclusive language. It's our class, our school and everyone is included all the time. If someone does not feel included they need to raise it as an issue, either privately or publicly—that's self-advocacy and it's even more powerful. This led to our third focus, our actions. We needed to understand that our attitudes influence our language and our language influences our actions. Our actions, therefore, also need to be inclusive. And that was the most powerful change of all because we started to become more aware of each person's perspective."

"At this point, the students are operating as a team. Now that it's working so well in our classroom, our next step is to take our ideas outside into the playground. We're on a mission. It's fun!"

(chicken and chips) was much more inclusive. Jane's request that students draw their favourite food provided her with an opportunity to check first that all students were preparing an answer that would be valued. Also, she could privately coach Kevin to choose a valued response before he shared his drawing with the whole class. Consider this for a minute. A student in your class has the potential to engage in behaviour that might set them apart. How would you subtly guide them to share more highly valued responses with their peers? You could start with a probe to find out the student's intention, and then provide one-to-one assistance to help the student refine their answer before asking for the student to share it with the rest of the class.

The teacher carefully avoids the use of pejorative terms, such as slow learner, that might isolate or negatively position a student. Instead of using words that draw attention to a student's impairment, the teacher reframes to focus on each student's learning achievements. In this way the teacher generates a learning environment where each student knows they make worthwhile contributions and differences are accepted with deference. Everybody in this environment is learning how to live and work together, not just the student with diverse learning needs.

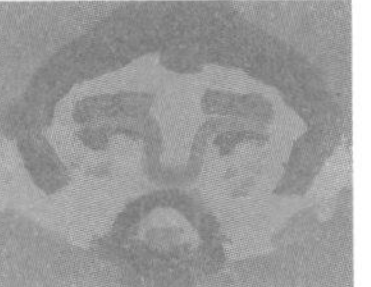

Two short stories will further exemplify this. Cindy is in Year 8. She particularly enjoys practical subjects, especially home economics. Last week Cindy cooked a delicious chocolate cake, which she shared with her classmates. The form teacher was so impressed she asked if she could have a copy of the recipe and then everyone wanted one. Pretty soon a number of the students had used Cindy's recipe to cook their own chocolate cake and were asking her if she had any other good recipes. The second example relates to Alan who is in Year 12. He recently won a prestigious Braille writing competition. With Alan's permission, the school published a print transcription of his essay in the school newsletter and put the actual Braille copy with the award in a display case in the front office. Alan wrote in his diary that, while he was proud of his achievement in winning the competition, he gained more satisfaction from being able to share the experience with his schoolmates. It was like his friends suddenly started to realise that Braille was an important medium. Before that they just seemed to think of it as something he did instead of reading and writing.

self-advocacy

Organisations composed of persons with a disability that are dedicated to improving the opportunities for people to demand the privileges, opportunities, and access to services that are considered to be their rights as members of society. Also, a person asserting the demand for human rights.

Finding out about your students

The better teachers know their students the better they will be at identifying when and how to adapt or refine the curriculum to suit their individual needs. During the first few days with a class—regardless of the level, early childhood through upper secondary—teachers need to start collecting information about what the students already know, what they can do, what they do not know, and what they cannot do. Information about each student is gathered through observation, listening, allowing students to talk, and especially by asking them questions about their work. Another invaluable source of information is the student's parents or guardians, so it is important that teachers pay careful attention during parent interviews and read each student's file thoroughly. This is particularly important when planning to adjust the curriculum to meet the needs of students with cognitive, sensory, and/or physical impairments.

PLOTTING STUDENT ATTRIBUTES

Individual attributes are plotted along a set of continua including central processing and physical capabilities. The idea of using continua establishes the premise that, when learning, students are more similar than different. Each student is making their way along the same continuum but at their own pace and in their own way. There are several continua to be considered. Knowing pertinent information about all the students in a class allows the teacher to decide where to begin teaching. Of course, each student will have a different starting point, so adjustments and adaptations are necessary.

The central processing continuum

This continuum has early cognitive development located at one end and advanced cognitive development at the other. The cognitive attributes of each student in a class are distributed along the line. The continuum makes it clear that students with cognitive impairment follow the same developmental sequence. They just take longer to reach each cognitive milestone and their attainments, although similar, tends not to be as broad. Students with cognitive impairment have early language skills, a developing vocabulary, and emerging social skills commensurate with a particular level of development. As every student fits somewhere along the continuum, there is always going to be another student who is more or less advanced. Each cognitive skill a student acquires helps move that person just a little

BOX 7.3 The cognitive and physical continua

EARLY COGNITIVE DEVELOPMENT	ADVANCED COGNITIVE DEVELOPMENT
Beginning incidental learning	Extensive incidental learning
Check for readiness	Delete mastered material
Teach basic skills slowly step-by-step	Increase pacing for learning
Decrease frustration to achieve success	Increase frustration to achieve success
Concrete real-life learning tasks	Abstract learning tasks
Explicit unambiguous instruction	Original manipulation of information
Structured scaffolds	Open-ended and creative
Ample repetition	Real problems, audiences, deadlines
Generous practice	Freedom of choice
Frequent review	Self-evaluation and audits with authentic criteria
Guide for transfer and generalisation	Independence and personal initiative
EARLY SENSORY PROCESSING	**ADVANCED SENSORY PROCESSING**
No functional vision for learning	Advanced visual functioning
No functional hearing for learning	Advanced auditory functioning
No physical functioning for learning	Advanced physical functioning

Note: This model is only a guideline to assist in curriculum planning. There will be exceptions so each student's functioning must be considered on a case by case basis.

bit further along the continuum (see Box 7.3). Here, the emphasis is on achievement and the continuum helps teachers cater for the central processing learning needs of all students in their class by making them alert to each student's stage of development.

Students with cognitive impairment might be at an earlier stage of cognitive development but they need age-appropriate learning tasks, so they benefit greatly from being with same-aged peers and engaging in the same types of learning tasks. They learn best by doing, and they manage learning tasks with far greater confidence when they have familiar concrete objects to manipulate. These students also profit from explicit instruction, repetition, and supervised practice. A student with cognitive impairment will remember one or two instructions at a time, so the teacher must keep frustration to a minimum by providing generous, pertinent memory aids, and tangible learning scaffolds. For example, a student might benefit from having a card with personal details such as name, age, sex, address, and home phone numbers available in their desk for quick reference. Students also gain support from wall charts of the alphabet, times tables, maps, and other relevant information. It is important that teachers think about their classes and what essential learnings they want their students to master. These goals can then be designed into charts and displayed in the classroom for ongoing reference.

This young person and her classmates are completely engaged in this lesson

Central processing tasks involving memory, reasoning, and critical evaluation are extremely complex skills for students with cognitive impairment to learn. Therefore, overt instruction is needed to help the student learn how to organise information into personally relevant and useful categories. Task analysis allows the learning task to be broken up into small achievable steps and to present the learning task in highly structured, consistent, and unambiguous ways. The focus here is to ensure the student acquires the basic, essential skills and concepts for the next stage of learning. However, the goal must extend beyond just learning the skill. To be of lasting value, the student must understand how they learnt a particular skill and why they might need it in their adult life (this is called *executive control*). This is the teacher's biggest challenge: making the students responsible for their own learning by ensuring education is relevant and applicable to daily life.

The vision, hearing, and physical ability continuum

This is the second set of continua. All three continua start at one end with total lack of functional vision, hearing, or physical ability for learning and stretch to the opposite end with advanced visual, auditory, or physical functioning for learning. The key to reading these continua is to focus on an individual's ability, achievement, and development and to unreservedly reject the idea of deficit. This is because some students with very low functional ability in a particular sensory area can still become extraordinarily proficient in that same area. Think for a moment that Beethoven continued to compose exceptional music when he was deaf, Monet painted with cataracts, and Van Gogh painted with glaucoma. Low physical ability does not preclude a young person winning a gold medal in the paralympics.

Once the student has some functional vision, hearing, or physical capability for learning, encouragement can be provided to make the best possible use of that capability. This occurs in two ways. The first way is through the provision of powerful and enabling prosthetic devices such as low vision aids, glasses, precision lighting, closed circuit television, echo location devices, white canes, cochlear implants, hearing aids, FM radio systems, wheelchairs, walking frames, splints, communication devises, technological and computer aids, and switches. (You were introduced to these in the previous chapter.) The second way involves working with a team of experts who specialise in helping students with these impairments to learn how to make the best use of their residual abilities and to use their prosthetic learning aids. The teacher must be aware how low functional ability in a particular area often makes using those physical or sensory skills extremely tiring, so the student needs to have back-up strategies. For example, a student with low vision might read for a while then listen to a digital recording. Alternatively, one with physical impairment might require different workstations to maintain physical comfort, such as a standing workstation for concrete tasks, a sitting workstation for writing tasks, and a lying down workstation for reading. Each student will have different requirements and these will change over time.

cochlear implant

An electronic device that directly stimulates the remaining hair cells of the cochlea (the organ of hearing) to produce a sensation of sound.

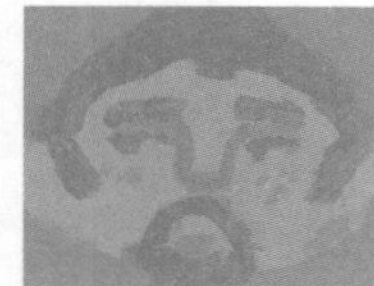

Often a student with a particular learning need will arrive at school having already been comprehensively assessed by the relevant medical and associated specialists. Frequently, parents will also have developed their own expert knowledge relating to the challenges their child faces and will keep the teacher abreast of updates. Teachers still need to be alert to the possibility that some children will not have been assessed or prescribed the most enabling prosthetic devise. This might be due to the young person's condition having only recently surfaced, or through child neglect, abuse, or extenuating family circumstances such as poverty, geographic isolation, religious beliefs, language, or cultural differences. In situations where the teacher believes that additional assessment is necessary, the school guidance officer, psychologist, or social worker can provide skilled assistance and referral. It is important for the teacher to think of the parent or guardian as part of the solution rather than part of the problem. At the same time, however, teachers must be alert to their legal responsibilities about mandatory reporting.

The lower the sensory ability the more likely it is that the student will need to make much greater use of other senses for learning. Many students who are functionally blind, for example, rely heavily on hearing and make extensive use of touch to read Braille and tactually explore the world. Be aware, though, that there are exceptions. For example, vision impairment from diabetes may also be associated with impaired tactual ability. Even thought there is considerable advantage in thinking about students as being more similar than different, overgeneralisation is also dangerous. Class teachers must, therefore, remember that they are part of a team. They must work closely with available experts—such as the advisory visiting teacher—to ensure they are keenly aware of how a unique set of individual differences might affect learning and require specific adjustments and adaptations to the teaching–learning environment.

In situations where a student requires ongoing expert assistance during the day, the school may employ a specialist teacher aide (or education assistant). Teacher aides might be involved in providing support that goes beyond the teacher's main job, such as feeding, toileting, and positioning. Likewise, most students who are functionally deaf make more use of vision to observe and interpret the world, especially through sign and body language. Hearing prosthetics, such as cochlear implants, can help a child who was functionally deaf act as if they were hard of hearing, providing they have the appropriate training that teaches them how to interpret what they hear through their cochlear implant.

Pedagogical strategies for all the physical continua are very similar to those developed for the cognitive continua. Much incidental learning occurs through vision or hearing or by manipulating an object, so an impairment may mean that key learning experiences might have been missed. It is, therefore, essential to start the teaching process by checking for readiness and, if certain basic skills are missing, to teach them explicitly. Similarly, students with impairment generally learn best through concrete learning tasks but their speed of learning will vary according to the level and type of impact that the impairment has on learning.

The impact of impairment on a student's learning is determined by:

- *Degree of impairment*—Impairments range from profound to mild, with the most challenging impact likely to be at the profound end of the continuum. This is not to negate the potentially negative impact that may occur from even mild impairment, especially if the impairment has not been acknowledged and appropriate adjustments made.
- *Presence of other impairments*—The severity of impact is exaggerated when students have more than a single impairment.
- *Age of onset*—The earlier the impairment appears the more severe the impact is likely to be. For example, a hearing impairment acquired before language acquisition is likely to have a bigger impact on learning than if acquired after language acquisition.

- *Early intervention*—The earlier and better the quality of intervention provided, the greater is the likelihood that the negative impact will be reduced.
- *Level of support*—The greater the levels of appropriate material and human support, the greater the likelihood that the impact will be reduced.
- *Personal characteristics*—Personal characteristics such as personality, motivation, and disposition will either positively or negatively influence the impact of the impairment on learning.

ISSUES AND CHALLENGES

A major challenge in education recently has been the design of an inclusive curriculum, one that genuinely caters for the learning needs of all students. The move toward this goal began with the introduction of legislation to support the rights of students with impairments to attend their local community school. Prior to that time, students with impairments mostly attended separate special education facilities where the system of education was largely determined by the type of impairment.

When students with impairment started attending their local school, the initial mainstream response was for class teachers to continue to teach the same curriculum as they always had. They would then "bolt on" specific changes for any student identified as having a deficit that made them eligible for extra assistance. The bolt on approach rested on the preparation of an Individualised Education Plan (IEP) where the extra assistance, both human and material, would be managed by a team of stakeholders who worked together to provide an individualised curriculum specifically designed for this student.

The bolt on approach was heavily criticised as not being authentically inclusive. The procedure used for identifying the student was negative, both for the individual who was labelled as having a deficit and for the system as a whole. The system itself was locked into a divisive method of problem identification in particular individuals rather than allocating resources to developing solutions for the benefit of all students. Sometimes in the course of identification the wrong students were given the wrong labels. For example, those from low socioeconomic backgrounds or minority cultures were sometimes inaccurately categorised as having cognitive impairment. From time to time, deserving individuals fell outside the narrow definitions of impairment being used in the identification process. At other times, young people missed out because service providers changed the definitions for eligibility to cap spending or save money. Students often had to fail before they could be identified, and powerful preventive approaches associated with early intervention were underused. The most serious criticism, however, was of the process of identification that focused on a deficit approach, and the process itself, apart from being unnecessarily harsh, offered little guidance as to how the class teacher might change the curriculum to include all students. Clearly, inclusion was not happening within the deep structure of education systems.

Under the old deficit approach, the class teacher would bolt on limited support for a particular student by creating a three-curricula response:

1. the intended curriculum—what the typical student would be expected to learn;
2. the taught curriculum—what was put into operation for the typical students and those with identified deficits; and
3. the learned curriculum—what students actually gained from the experience, or at least that was the claim.

In reality, students with identified deficits were often excluded from the official benchmarking, which then allowed the system to remain unchallenged.

Class teachers, though well informed about the intended curriculum, often did not have the knowledge necessary to adapt or change it for the diversity of learners in their classes. In addition,

despite learning support and special education teachers being well informed about how to develop and present the curriculum for students with a particular characteristic that complicated their learning, they were much less familiar with the intended curriculum or even how to cater for other students with diverse learning needs outside their area of specialisation. So there was a division within the classroom. The class teacher mostly taught the general curriculum and offered only superficial access to the intended curriculum for students who required extra support. Although students with special learning needs were physically included, that is, they went to the same school, they often were excluded from the intended curriculum.

A new approach had to be found that rejected the need to identify students as having deficits. A systemic change was required where all teachers played a role in educating all students, where an inclusive curriculum ensured that all students received an appropriate education. This new approach came in the form of Response to Instruction (RTI) that provided a holistic and equitable method of resource allocation and support. RTI was originally introduced in the USA to cater for students with learning difficulties (i.e., those experiencing difficulties primarily in literacy and numeracy). It began as a reaction against the negative categorising and labelling of students and focused on early intervention to achieve positive learning outcomes rather than eligibility by identification of deficit or disability.

Because diagnosis concentrated on the need for curriculum adjustment and adaptation rather than student classification, it remained more central to the teaching–learning context of the whole class. RTI, therefore, provided a continuum of instructional support where all educators became responsible for all students in their respective classes. Furthermore, because the process actively included students and their families, it was much more genuinely inclusive.

RTI consists of a three-tiered preventative structure that allows the intensity of instruction to be increased to fit the level of need. Low academic performance and poor response to instruction is initially met with classroom-wide intervention, thought to be sufficient for up to 80% of students. Should that be insufficient, the back-up plan consists of specialised group intervention, thought to suit a further 15% of students. Finally, the third tier offers specialised individualised intervention for the remaining 5%.

The continuum of instructional supports can then be extended to include students with particular impairments that require specialist evaluation and support. The entitlement to extra services is based on intensity of support required to make progress rather than the old idea of identifying a deficit. Determining entitlement comes back to information about educational progress. If the amount of progress made after intervention was insufficient, then additional resources are provided at the whole-of-class level. If there is still a substantial discrepancy between student outcome and that of same-aged peers, then additional support at the group level is provided. Finally, if the student presents with instructional needs that go beyond what can reasonably be offered at the classroom level, then additional support would need to be provided.

Differentiating the curriculum

The inclusive curriculum caters for the learning needs of all students through a procedure called curriculum differentiation. The goal of curriculum differentiation is to improve the curriculum for all students by designing the teaching–learning context so that it provides a neatness of fit for each student while still retaining the locus of control for the curriculum within the classroom. This is achieved by making changes to the:

- learning environment;
- content (what is taught and what is learned);

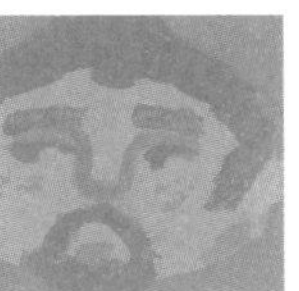

FIGURE 7.1

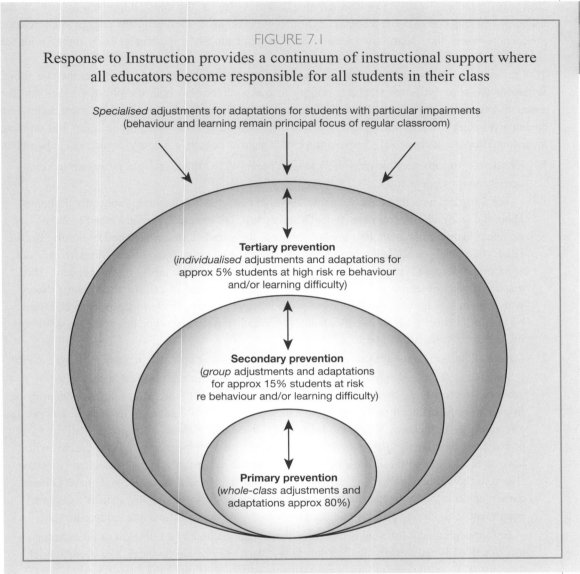

Response to Instruction provides a continuum of instructional support where all educators become responsible for all students in their class

Specialised adjustments for adaptations for students with particular impairments (behaviour and learning remain principal focus of regular classroom)

Tertiary prevention
(*individualised* adjustments and adaptations for approx 5% students at high risk re behaviour and/or learning difficulty)

Secondary prevention
(*group* adjustments and adaptations for approx 15% students at risk re behaviour and/or learning difficulty)

Primary prevention
(*whole-class* adjustments and adaptations approx 80%)

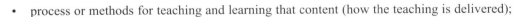

- process or methods for teaching and learning that content (how the teaching is delivered);
- methods for assessment or the products (how learning success is measured); and
- types of human and material assistance required to achieve the adjustments and adaptations (resources).

In the following section, particular attention is given to the learning environment, with less attention given to content, process, methods, assessment, and resources. This is because these topics are discussed in other parts of the chapter.

The learning environment

In the past, many teachers who followed a prescribed curriculum tended to take the learning environment pretty much for granted. This is because they were teaching content rather than students.

Nowadays, teachers realise that the learning environment is the most important feature of the teaching–learning context. The learning environment is the place where students engage in knowledge production, where they learn how to learn. So it is tremendously important to get it right for all the students in the class.

The learning environment could be a sports field or the library, but most often it is the classroom. Wherever the space, it is the teacher's priority to make certain that both the physical space and the emotional space are safe, welcoming, inclusive, and enabling. To do this, teachers must follow six enabling principles. These principles are hierarchical and designed to facilitate learning and promote inclusion. They are fundamentally important for students with cognitive, sensory, or physical impairment.

1 Ensure all students are able physically to gain access to the space and every relevant learning activity in it independently.

   For a student with impairment this will involve considerable planning, especially thinking about the learning task from the student's standpoint. For example, it might mean moving pertinent learning materials into lower cupboards for a student in a wheelchair or putting Braille labels on items for a student who is blind. Allocating a buddy to fetch inaccessible items is not appropriate because it puts the student with the impairment in the position of dependent. This gets in the way of learning flow and creates two groups of students, those who can and those who cannot. It is far better to design the room in ways that emphasise independence and dignity by making it equally accessible for all students right from the start. The better the foundation is, the better the learning will be.

2 Ensure all students have the prerequisite functional skills to participate in each learning activity.

   Functional skills can only be demonstrated once the student has physical access to the necessary materials for the learning activity. Functional skills might be as simple as opening the front door or as challenging as managing a dangerous piece of equipment in science. To operate effectively and efficiently within the learning environment, students must perform all prerequisite functional skills involved in the learning task independently. Many students will have already acquired these skills before they enter the classroom and teachers often pay scant regard to them. Students with a learning disability or impairment, however, may need to have particular skills taught before the learning task begins or they may require specially designed equipment. This can be problematic because learning by doing is fundamental to education.

   Before beginning a learning activity, it is important to conduct a full audit of all essential functional skills and systematically confirm that each student can do them. The occupational therapist (OT) specialises in functional skill acquisition, so if difficulties arise, refer to the OT as soon as possible. For students with vision impairment, the orientation and mobility instructor can provide important guidance, and for students with a physical impairment, a physiotherapist is the person to consult. For students with hearing impairment, the emphasis is on ensuring that the student has the necessary functional communication skills to participate in the learning task, so this will involve the assistance of the speech language pathologist.

orientation and mobility

Knowing one's position in relation to other objects in space (orientation) and being able to safely, independently, and purposefully move about (mobility) are important skills for individuals with vision impairment.

3 Ensure all students have the appropriate social development to participate effectively in the learning activity.

   Once the student is able to function effectively in the learning environment, the student is ready to engage socially. Most learning activities in today's classrooms involve some form of social interaction, so having the requisite social skills are paramount and the earlier the intervention occurs to develop these skills, the better. Appropriate social skills are necessary for learning success in school, for daily living, and for employment.

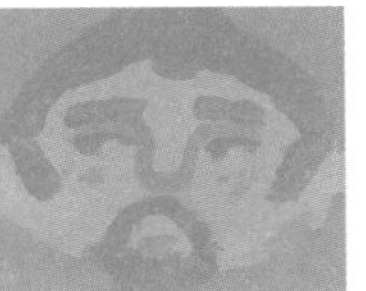

Students should be asked to engage in learning activities requiring social skills only when they possess those skills, otherwise the student is being set up for failure and isolation in the classroom. Pay close attention to each student's social skill development. Valuable questions to ask include the following:

- Does the student understand situations and their rules?
- Does the student have an accurate perception of others?
- Can the student pick up on nonverbal communication of attitudes and emotions?
- Can the student make socially competent judgements that are appropriate to time and place?

These are all necessary skills for learning tasks involving social interaction.

Social skills do not appear automatically. They must be taught and nurtured. You will read more about this in Chapter 11. In the past, it was parents who taught their children social and interpersonal skills, but these days some parents lack the time to teach them, the opportunity, or even the skills themselves. This means that schools must play a more active role.

Students with impairment may not have sufficient social skills to work in small groups, so the skills may need to be explicitly taught to them. This may involve the help of the Speech Language Pathologist. One powerful teaching method is to use direct instruction. This is a four-step process:

- The teacher demonstrates the skill.
- The teacher provides opportunity for the student to practise the skill, first with prompting from the teacher.
- Then, the student practises the skill independently.
- Once the skill has been mastered, the student practises the skill in different settings to promote generalisation.

Direct instruction is particularly valuable as a teaching strategy for students with cognitive impairment. Once students have the necessary social skills, the learning environment can become much more enjoyable for all students.

direct instruction

A teaching method used to teach reading and mathematics, emphasising structured sequences. Lessons sometimes have scripted responses and solution strategies.

4 Ensure all students are able to form personal friendships.

Once students have adequate social skills, they are ready to develop the interpersonal skills to initiate and maintain friendships with students in their class. Teachers need to work closely with parents to encourage friendships. Friendships within the classroom help make the learning environment a rich and welcoming place in which to study.

5 Ensure all students are valued members of the class.

Once students have established friendships they then start to be accepted as valued members of the class. For example, one morning a boy was overheard to say: "Oh great! Matthew's here! We can start our game." This statement clearly told Matthew he was a valued member of the group. Students with impairment may require help to achieve recognition and acceptance within a classroom. In a systematic way, the teacher must provide all students with chances to perform valued roles within the classroom, not just the favoured few. For example, if students are finding it difficult to gain social standing with the class group, they can benefit from being associated with glamorous tasks like being asked to hand out class treats or thanking class guests.

6 Ensure all students are actively involved in the organisation of the classroom.

The highest level of inclusion is the organisational level. This is where students become involved in the planning process of what learning activities are to occur. It involves choice, negotiation,

and the deliberate democratisation of the classroom. It relates to how the space is organised and what activities are conducted within that space. Sometimes students with impairment have a big impact on classroom organisation, but the other students may not think that this was beneficial for the whole class. If changes are to be made to the classroom environment to accommodate a student with impairment, all students in the class must understand why changes are being made, agree they are reasonable, and be explicitly told how they too will benefit from the change (see Box 7.4 for an example).

BOX 7.4 Being part of the decision-making process

This was Jillian Smith's first teaching position. She'd been with her Year 5 class for one term and she was delighted with the way they were progressing. Now, she wanted to increase their level of organisational involvement, reasoning it would help them take more responsibility for their own learning. She began by doing an audit of the ways the students were already involved. "I often give my students choices and they regularly use contracts, but some students are better at taking advantage of these opportunities than others. I'm worried about the students with learning difficulties—how can I better involve them? Perhaps we could form a class association and involve everyone in a more explicit, formal way. We could have weekly meetings where minutes are kept and jobs are allocated. It would make the involvement more concrete."

Jillian put the proposal to the class and they unanimously agreed. At their first meeting, she asked them what they thought about the physical layout of the classroom. Most reported being happy with the class set-up, but Cindy, a student with albinism, said she had problems with glare, especially in the afternoons. Several other students also identified glare as a concern, particularly when they did computer work or watched afternoon television programs. Pretty soon the class had adopted glare-reduction as their class project. They researched solutions on the internet and obtained quotes.

Within a few days they had decided that blinds would be best. They then wrote a letter to the Parents and Citizens Association and within a month the class had new blinds. Spurred on by this success, Steven—a student with a cognitive impairment—proposed at the next class meeting that they buy an aquarium. He had one at home and it was a great hobby. After considerable discussion, the students decided it would make their classroom a better place. They could learn about keeping fish, and they would have to look after the fish and keep the aquarium clean so it would give them more responsibility. A second project began to take shape—one in which Steven was very much involved. Jillian said: "I'm really thrilled! Somehow I don't think it would have had the same impact if it had been my idea."

The content

An inclusive curriculum is not about knowledge reproduction but knowledge production. With knowledge reproduction students learn isolated factual information, whereas with knowledge

production greater emphasis goes toward students understanding key concepts, recognising pertinent relationships between those essential learnings and finding out how they connect to daily life.

Learning is more problem-based where students study how different people react to particular challenging circumstances. Emphasis is also given to understanding methods of inquiry, learning how people learn, not just simply focusing on the what. In many ways, catering to the diverse learning needs of students with cognitive, sensory, and physical impairment provides rich opportunities for a teacher to adjust the curriculum content to make it more relevant and interesting for everyone.

The process or methods for teaching and learning content

It is particularly important for teachers to be aware that students' learning styles and needs must match the learning methods that are being used. Students with hearing impairment, for example, need more opportunities for visual learning, whereas students with vision impairment require more opportunities for auditory and tactual learning.

As mentioned earlier, most students with impairments prefer to learn by doing, that is, by the manipulation of familiar, concrete learning materials. Teachers have many tactics at their disposal to cater for individual students. These include:

- pacing of content presentation;
- providing choice;
- students' self-evaluation and debriefing;
- working in small groups and in teams;
- the use of Bloom's Taxonomy (this is described in Box 7.5);
- creative thinking approaches such as brainstorming; and
- open-ended tasks that encourage risk taking.

THE METHODS FOR ASSESSMENT OR THE PRODUCTS

When designing learning tasks, the key objective is to enable each student to achieve at their own highest potential. Involve students in the initial design process and encourage them to perform tasks that are personally relevant and meaningful. With real problems, which lead to real solutions and the development of real products for real audiences to be completed within real timelines, students must be assisted to become critically engaged from initial planning through to completion and beyond. Students make ideas their own by critically reflecting on them and transforming them to make them relevant to their own circumstance and the circumstances of others. Therefore, students need to engage in self-evaluation and have opportunities to invite representatives from the community, particularly adults with impairments, to become the audience and to provide authentic and challenging feedback.

HUMAN AND MATERIAL RESOURCES

Students with impairments will require additional material or human resources to enable them to have the same educational opportunities as their peers. These additional resources are referred to as the *compensatory curriculum*. Many types of human and material assistance have already been identified in this chapter. They include a wide range of prosthetic devices and stakeholders such as parents, guidance officers, and speech language pathologists.

Another form of assistance is called the *oppositional curriculum*. This applies where a separate curriculum is created especially for students with a particular impairment where those students gather to socialise and possibly learn a specialist skill. A good example here is a five-day Braille maths camp

BOX 7.5 The taxonomy of educational objectives

Bloom (1956) originally proposed the taxonomy of educational objectives for three domains, namely: affective, psychomotor, and cognitive (see below). Each is hierarchical (mastery of higher level skills are dependent on the acquisition of lower ones). This, therefore, makes them valuable tools for teachers when designing learning activities to match individual student ability levels.

COGNITIVE PROCESS	DESCRIPTION	VERB (TASK)	EXAMPLE
Knowledge	To recall information	Name, list, describe, match—Recite a short poem	What materials did the three little pigs use to build their houses?
Comprehension	To demonstrate understanding	Explain—Restate in own words or provide a summary	Tell the story of the three little pigs in your own words.
Application	Use previously learned information in new situation	Apply, change—Retell within new context	What would have happened if one pig had built his house out of steel and glass?
Analysis	Break up into component parts	Separate, select, compare, contrast—How could you classify?	How does the story start? What is the conclusion?
Synthesis	Integrate parts to develop something new	Compile, categorise, devise—Can you predict?	What might have happened if the three little pigs had been good at martial arts?
Evaluation	To judge the value of something and provide a rationale for decision	Assess, rate, appraise, prioritise, reflect—Do you agree with?	What is the take-home message from the story? Is there anything we can learn from the story?

during the school holidays for Year 8 students who are blind. This reminds such young people that they are not the only ones in the world with their particular impairment, and provides opportunities for networking with like-minded individuals.

To sum up, the current overriding issue in education is to design a curriculum that is more genuinely inclusive. The challenge has been to devise a curriculum that appropriately caters to the learning needs

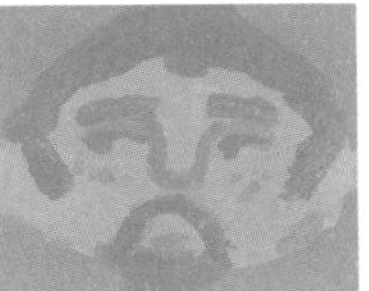

of each student without classifying them as being deficient. To achieve this, a new way of thinking was required. Two key developments have been the emergence of:

1 Response to Instruction (i.e., a three-tiered preventative structure that permits intensity of instruction to be increased to fit level of need, thereby investing in the integrity of the regular class to ensure locus of control remains within the classroom); and
2 curriculum differentiation (i.e., adjustments and accommodations to the learning environment, content, process, methods of assessment, and learning supports to ensure a neatness of fit for each student).

In the above section we have described ways in which the environment can be arranged to accommodate all students in regular classes. What else has been shown is the close connection between the social and intellectual/cognitive domain. These two domains do not operate in isolation. One's cognitive capabilities can affect the interactions that one has with others and one's social competence is a contributing factor to successful learning outcomes. So, how can a teacher take advantage of the symbiotic relationship between the two domains? This is the focus of the next section.

TEACHING ESSENTIALS

Many school communities have deliberately addressed curriculum differentiation as a way of catering for students with a range of learning and adjustments needs. This has come in response to policy initiatives and research that has indicated the benefit of including students with specific learning needs in regular classes because they have opportunities to interact with more able peers than would be the case in special education classes. By interacting in a heterogeneous group, students learn to listen to what others have to say, understand that they may have different perspectives, share information and ideas, and express different points of view in socially acceptable ways. In so doing, they learn to use language to solve problems and reason, explain new experiences and ideas, and construct new ways of thinking and learning (see Box 7.6).

It is now accepted that students benefit considerably by interacting with others in small group settings where they might work in pairs or in small cooperating groups on specific shared tasks. These interactions occur during peer tutoring activities and peer collaborations, and the advantages of these experiences are evident from studies that have examined the use of peer-mediated learning strategies.

In contrast to the interactions that take place between peers in informal situations, the dialogues that occur during cooperative learning are multidirectional, as students must respond to a wider group of peers, negotiate meanings around tasks, contest opposing propositions, and justify their own proposals in ways that others will accept as logical and valid. In so doing, they learn new ways of talking, thinking, and reasoning that they may not have learned previously.

To facilitate the changes in how students learn, teachers have also had to consider changes in how they teach, such as ensuring that the curriculum is more student- than teacher-directed. Teachers have to create opportunities that enable students to be actively involved in their own learning. This means ensuring that they have opportunities to work on tasks that are motivating, embedded in a context that is relevant to the individual, and sufficiently challenging so that solutions are not readily apparent. Students must recognise the need to search for information themselves and work with their peers to solve problems, resolve dilemmas, and construct new understandings.

Explicit teaching

To facilitate this new way of learning, teachers must ensure that they have undertaken the necessary planning so that students know what is expected of them. Teachers need to be *very*

explicit about what students are expected to do and achieve, often pre-teaching the skills that students will need to manage different tasks. This may entail, for example, showing students how to break down tasks so that they work on them step-by-step rather than becoming over-awed by the demands of the larger task. Modelling how to negotiate tasks by using such prompts as: "What is the problem?" "What do I need to do first?" "Do I have the information I need?" These are just some of the questions that students can learn to ask themselves to help them manage the task at hand. These questions (and others) can be printed on cards for students who will be assisted by such additional cues.

Teachers may also need to teach the meanings of specific words that students may encounter, provide background information to help them understand the context of different problems, and help them to link information they have learned in one context to another. Questions such as the following can be useful to build these links: "How does the information we learned today go with what we were learning yesterday?" "Think of what you know about … How can that help you to understand …?" and "How is … similar to … ?"

Additionally, teachers need to:

- monitor students' progress actively;
- encourage their efforts;
- challenge their understanding of ideas and concepts; and
- scaffold their learning.

It is not a case of letting students sink or swim but rather one of creating an environment that is conducive to learning where students feel free to test out ideas among supportive peers. However, if teachers are too directive, students never learn to accept responsibility for their own learning. Instead, they remain dependent on the teacher for direction and assistance. See Box 7.6 for an example of explicit teaching.

BOX 7.6 Example of explicit teaching

Over the last few weeks, the Year 6 students have been investigating the exploits of some of the early Vikings. The teacher helps to prepare the students for the small group discussions they are going to have on what their group would need to take with them if they were Vikings going on a six-day sea voyage, using the following prompts:

- What do you know about the Vikings and the exploits they undertook? (This is a recall questions designed to help the students focus on what information they have learned previously.)
- If they were planning on going on a sea trip, what are the sorts of preparations they would need to undertake? (This question is designed to check the students' understanding or comprehension of the difficulties they would encounter.)
- Think about some of the issues we have discussed previously. How can these help you to think about your own voyage? (The teacher is getting the children to think about how they may use the information they learned previously to help them when they participate in their group discussions.)

- Remember that you will have to justify your choice. (The students have to identify, in order of priority, 10 items that they would need to include on their sea voyage.)
- Remember you can use each other as a resource to help you as you identify what is going to be important in your own trip. (The teacher is reminding the students that other group members will have ideas that they can consider as they work on identifying what is important.)

7.6

Peer-mediated learning

When children work together to help each other learn, they become involved in a process called peer-mediated learning. In peer-mediated learning, students help each other to understand information or master a task they are required to complete. This approach to learning works well for students with a range of attributes, particularly if teachers ensure that the task that students are to undertake has a clear goal and procedures that lead to successful completion (i.e., it is well structured) so they understand what they are expected to do and achieve.

There are two main forms of peer-mediated learning: peer tutoring (sometimes called peer collaboration) and cooperative learning.

PEER TUTORING

Peer tutoring usually involves a more capable student (the tutor) assisting a less able peer (the tutee) to master specific information or skills. It is assumed that the tutor has greater competence and, through the peer tutoring process, can transmit this expertise to the tutee. The tutor acts as a surrogate teacher with control over the information and instructional process. In this sense, the relationship is not equal because the tutor is seen as the expert whose role is to instruct the novice. Despite this lack of equality, there are mutual benefits to the tutor and the tutee from the tutoring experience.

Tutees benefit from peer tutoring because they have one-to-one instruction and extra opportunities to practise, immediate feedback, and the opportunity to build an interpersonal relationship with a high-status tutor. These benefits often provide the additional momentum for the tutee to stay on-task and remain motivated.

Tutors also benefit from the tutoring experience because they have to explain the task clearly. This forces them to organise the material to be taught in their mind so that they can explain it in ways that are readily understood. In so doing, they often develop a good understanding of it themselves.

Peer tutoring can involve same-age and cross-age tutoring; peer collaboration often refers to same-age peers. Same-age tutoring involves a more capable tutor working with a less capable peer, whereas cross-age tutoring involves an older child working with a younger child. For peer tutoring to be effective in both cases, tutors must be taught what and how to teach.

TUTOR TRAINING

While there are many ways in which tutors can guide or mediate learning, they appear to work most effectively when students use the following procedure to help each other master the material.

- The tutor models and gradually fades the directions about the steps needed to complete the task (this is a form of scaffolding).

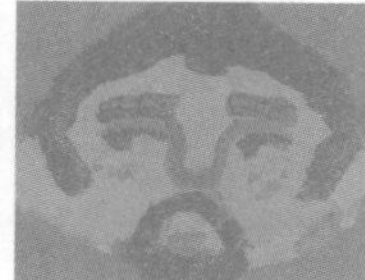

- The tutor provides step-by-step feedback to confirm and praise correct responses and explains and models strategic behaviour when answers are incorrect.
- Both the children engage in regular written interactions together on the problem.
- Both the tutor and tutee reverse roles during each session.

Once the students learn these steps, they then need to learn how to seek elaborated help. Elaborated help includes asking for help and maintaining the request for help until understanding is achieved. Offering elaborated help includes listening to one's partner and giving detailed help as required, and not just giving the answer. We know that understanding is enhanced when students have the opportunity to:

- relate material being learnt with real-life examples that are easy to imagine;
- use visual marks or pictures to represent specific facts;
- use materials that can be manipulated by both partners to represent information being learnt;
- discuss the problem and how to solve it; and
- ask questions that begin with "What", "Where", "When", "How", and "Why".

COLLABORATIVE STRATEGIC READING

Many of the ideas used in peer-mediated learning were adapted from Annemarie Palincsar and Anne Brown's (1988) reciprocal teaching approach to learning (RT) that was designed to teach students to use the strategies that successful readers use to understand text. An adaptation of reciprocal teaching is Collaborative Strategic Reading (CSR) (Vaughn et al., 2001), designed to teach children those strategies that assist their comprehension of written text. The four strategies are:

1. *Preview strategy*—involves making predictions about the passage prior to reading it. For example, students are taught to scan the text and search for clues such as pictures, headings, key words, and phrases that may help them predict what the text is about. This strategy is designed to help students activate background knowledge that may help them to predict what the text is about.
2. *Click and clunk strategy*—involves monitoring reading and learning to enhance vocabulary development. For example, students are taught that when they recognise material that they know then it is a click, whereas when they encounter words, material, or concepts that they are unsure of, they have a clunk. When they identify a clunk they need to find out more about it. Students are encouraged to work together to discuss their clicks and clunks and help each other enhance their understanding of the text.
3. *Get-the-gist strategy*—refers to the identification of main ideas. This strategy is designed to focus on the main idea expressed in a passage, getting students to summarise it in their own words and state what it is in 10 or fewer words. The purpose is to teach students to focus on the most important idea and to exclude unnecessary details. The get-the-gist strategy needs to be practised after every two paragraphs as a way of helping students to monitor their understanding of what they are reading.
4. *Wrap-up strategy*—involves summarising key ideas. At the conclusion of reading the text, students are taught to think of the types of questions that a teacher may ask about the passage they have read. The purpose of this is to help the students focus on the main ideas that were expressed in the text as a way of helping to assist their comprehension.

Each of the strategies is modelled by the teacher and taught one at a time before students practise them in their groups. For example, the *preview* strategy is introduced first and modelled by the teacher before students practise it in their groups. This is followed by the *click and clunk* strategy, which is

again modelled by the teacher and then practised by students in their groups. This process continues until students have learnt all four strategies. Because CSR is conducted in the context of a collaborative learning environment, leadership in the group is rotated so that each member in the group has responsibility for employing the four strategies.

As each section of the text is read, the leader generates a question to which the group members respond. The group members formulate additional questions while reading the material so word meanings and confusing text are clarified. The leader then attempts to summarise the main ideas in the text, giving group members the opportunity to talk about the summary before students predict what might happen in the next paragraph. This process is repeated as each new paragraph is read.

COOPERATIVE LEARNING

This is the second form of peer-mediated learning. Like peer tutoring, cooperative learning involves children working together in small groups to accomplish shared goals. In cooperative learning, however, each student is not only required to complete a task but is also required to ensure that others do likewise. The technical term for this dual responsibility is *positive interdependence* and it is the most important element in cooperative learning.

Positive interdependence exists when students perceive that they cannot succeed unless others do and they must coordinate their efforts to complete the task. When individuals are in a situation in which they have clear, interdependent goals, and in which there is an expectation that they will cooperate, they see themselves as having interdependent goals. As a consequence, if one individual attempts to achieve his or her goal, the others will do likewise. In this way, members influence each other and contribute to the group effort.

Another important element in successful group work is *promotive interaction*. This involves individuals encouraging and facilitating each other's efforts to complete the task and achieve the group's goals. It includes:

- sharing resources;
- providing constructive feedback to each other to improve task performance;
- challenging conclusions to develop greater insights into problems;
- encouraging each other's efforts;
- demonstrating goodwill toward each other;
- striving for mutual benefits; and
- avoiding anxiety and stress.

Individual accountability is the third important element involved in structuring successful group work. It requires group members to accept responsibility for contributing to the group's goal while concurrently facilitating the work of others. It means doing as much as one can to achieve the group's goal.

One way in which students can be helped to be accountable for their efforts is to assign them different roles at the commencement of the project and to rotate them each time the group works together. For example, roles that the children might play in cooperative group work are:

- Motivator—helps to get the group moving with the task.
- Summariser—recaps on points raised in the group.
- Writer—jots down the main points for the group.
- Reporter—reports on the group's progress to the wider class group.

With older students, the teacher may prefer to identify such roles as:

- Publisher—able to design logos, illustrations.
- Media manager—sets up a computer or other equipment for the task.
- Information manager—collects relevant information and shares it with others.
- Editor—summarises ideas of others and helps to organise them for the group project.

When allocating roles, teachers must emphasise students' strengths so that all group members understand that everyone has different skills that will enhance the group's performance. In this way, no child is asked to perform a role that he or she finds difficult. Provided this is managed positively and sensitively, most children accept their roles and participate accordingly.

As mentioned previously, the social skills needed to manage tasks need to be explicitly taught if students are to use them effectively. Placing students in groups and telling them to cooperate does not ensure that they will use the skills required to facilitate communication and to capitalise on the opportunities presented by cooperative learning.

The social skills that facilitate cooperation include:

- listening actively to each member of the group as he or she speaks;
- trying to understand the other person's perspective;
- stating ideas freely without fear of a put down by another group member;
- accepting responsibility for one's own behaviour;
- providing constructive feedback on ideas that are presented;
- taking turns so that each group member has the opportunity to present ideas or share resources;
- sharing tasks so that everyone has a smaller task to complete as part of the larger group task;
- clarifying differences of opinion; and
- making democratic decisions.

Two valuable resources that describe these procedures and provide clear guidelines on how to teach these skills are Gillies (2007) and Johnson and Johnson (2003).

To be motivated to use these skills to achieve mutual goals, group members must get to know each other, learn to trust one another, communicate accurately, accept and support each other, and resolve conflicts positively. Teachers play a critical role in helping students to build trusting and caring relationships with each other by discussing expectations for behaviour with the class before the students commence their group activities.

The final key element in successful cooperating groups is *group processing.* It involves group members reflecting on what the group achieved and, in particular, on recognising which actions are helpful and unhelpful so they can decide what actions to continue or change. Questions such as "What have we done well?", "What could we have done better?" and "What do we still need to do?" are examples of what group members need to ask. Group processing is important not only for the learning that occurs but also for the psychological health of the group because it enables members to:

- maintain good working relationships;
- develop cooperative learning skills;
- receive feedback on their participation;
- think on how they learn effectively and what information is needed; and
- celebrate the success of the group.

Time should be allowed at the end of each group session for feedback and group members need to frame their responses so they provide specific, positive feedback to each other. The wise teacher will ensure that this is handled in a constructive way, either by providing cue cards or response sheets to prompt students' reflections or by debriefing them on their perceptions of how they worked.

Enhancing classroom cooperation

Establishing a cooperative environment was not easy for Jason's teachers (in the second case study at the start of the chapter) because they had to consider how the groups would operate, what their tasks would be, and who would be included. These issues are important because teachers often mistakenly assume that students will cooperate and work together as expected. Additionally, Jason's teachers had to consider issues of group size, composition (ability and gender), and ways to enhance group discussions.

- *Size*—Setting the optimal group size is important. If groups are too large, some students will be overlooked, while others coast along at the expense of the workers. Groups of three or four members are best because they are too small for any member to opt out of the activity or loaf at others' expense. A small group ensures that all members are visible and involved.
- *Group composition*—The ability composition and sex composition of cooperating groups have an effect on the interactions among members and, ultimately, on achievement. In mixed-ability groups, high-ability students give more help to their peers than they do in same-ability groups. Both high-ability and low-ability students are quite active in teacher–learner relationships, whereas medium-ability students tend to be ignored. In contrast, in uniform high-ability groups, students often assume that others know how to solve the problem and make little effort to explain the material, while in uniform low-ability groups, few students understand the problem well enough to explain it to others. However, medium-ability students work well with students of similar ability.

  While the ability composition of groups has been widely investigated, information available on the gender composition of groups is more limited, although there is evidence that the achievement of males and females are nearly identical in gender-balanced groups, whereas in majority male or majority female groups, males outperform females. It appears that in majority male groups, the girl is largely ignored, while in majority female groups, group members direct most of their questions to the boy to the neglect of others in the group and this has a deleterious effect on the achievement of the females (Lou et al., 1996).

Structuring interactions in groups

Group tasks can be designed in a number of ways to ensure participants' interactions. For example, if young children are required to discuss and summarise the main points from the teacher's lesson—so others in their group can understand the concepts taught—they perform better on follow-up achievement tests than do those who only discuss the lesson or those who work by themselves.

Similarly, when children are taught to use a specific, *guided questioning strategy*—designed to help them make links between their own knowledge and the new information they are learning—they outperform their peers who do not use this strategy. Other teachers will script interactions among children as they work in cooperating groups to help them talk about task content. Structuring interactions in small groups promotes achievement among students in primary grades. See Box 7.7 for an example of how children can be taught to ask and answer each other's questions using a guided questioning strategy during cooperative learning.

BOX 7.7

An example of how children can be taught to ask and answer questions

The children have been given a list of questions that they can use to prompt each other as they work on the topic of how to deal with the water crisis that many large cities in Australia are confronting. The children have also been given a problem-solving task sheet that identifies the problem: The water crisis. The group's task is to identify some possible solutions to the problem and a positive and a negative to that solution. The group then have to identify the solution that they think is the best one and give a reason as to why they have chosen that solution. There are four children in the group with each one having an opportunity to take the lead and ask a question:

John: Tell me what you know about the water crisis?

Alisha: We don't have enough water to go around. The dams are nearly empty.

John: So what does that mean for us?

Tony: It means that if we don't get rain soon we'll have to buy our water.

Jen: But that costs money and lots of people won't have any money to buy their water.

John: OK. Let's see if we can work out some possible solutions. OK, what is one possible solution?

(Students then discuss a possible solution)

Tony: Why do you think that? (Student is asked to explain the reason for suggesting that solution.)

Alisha: We could have said that we need more dams to save the water. (Alisha has suggested another solution.)

The group continue to ask questions of each other until they have worked through the task.

LEARNING ESSENTIALS

Explicit teaching plays an important role in helping students to understand what they are learning. With this approach to teaching, the teacher often implements a step-by-step approach to the introduction of new material to ensure that students are able to master the content presented before learning the next step (see Box 7.8).

In the teacher-directed learning approach above, students learn by a process of guided learning where the teacher models the steps, which the students then practise. As the students become more competent, the teacher fades the instructions until the students are able to manage the task independently. Other teacher-directed approaches to teaching include direct instruction where students are provided with all the relevant information they need or teacher-led discussion where the teacher exercises control over the channels of communication (see Box 7.9).

While there is no doubt that explicit teaching is very effective for helping students learn, there are limitations to its use. Students often want to be actively involved in their own learning and, while they will accept direction and guidance on new tasks, they frequently prefer to try out ideas by themselves or in collaboration with their peers. In this sense, peer approaches to learning can be highly motivating because they tap into the need to be connected to others while simultaneously enabling students to exercise autonomy over their own learning.

BOX 7.8

An example of step-by-step instruction

Listen carefully while I go over the steps:

- Make sure you read the instructions carefully. (Teacher checks to see that the students understand what is required before students complete the next step.)
- Read the passage and highlight the key words on the topic. (Teacher checks to see that the students were able to identify the key words.)
- Write down (in a few short words) what the passage is about. (Teacher moves about the class and checks on what students have written.)
- Teacher asks different students in the class to read out what they wrote down.

Peer tutoring approaches such as Reciprocal Teaching (Brown & Palincsar, 1988) and Collaborative Strategic Reading (Vaughan et al., 2001) have been shown to work effectively in regular classrooms to increase both motivation and learning between students. The research points to benefits accruing to all students who are involved from those who are progressing normally through school to those who need support because of a learning difficulty. Although Reciprocal Teaching and Collaborative Strategic Reading are distinct, coherent programs, each relies on training children in specific techniques to make them effective helpers. (See *Using this chapter in schools* for a description of the strategies for teaching Collaborative Strategic Reading.)

BOX 7.9

An example of teacher-directed learning

Before the students begin the task, the teacher reminds them about the steps they will need to follow to complete the task.

- Read the instructions.
- Highlight any key works that you see.
- Write down the key idea in the passage.
- Check for understanding by re-reading the passage to see if it makes sense.

Using children with learning disabilities to support each other

There have been numerous studies conducted over the last two decades that show that children with learning disabilities benefit academically and socially from peer-mediated learning, and that this is true whether they function as tutors or tutees, or both. Academic gains have been recorded in reading, spelling, and mathematics, and social gains have included improved attitudes toward school and other students (Fuchs & Fuchs, 2005). Overall, tutoring can benefit tutors and tutees academically and

socially only if students are appropriately selected and trained in their roles, if the content of the tutoring is appropriate to both the tutor and the tutee, and if progress toward specified goals is continuously monitored.

To optimise on the benefits that can be derived from tutoring, the following guidelines are suggested for establishing tutoring behaviour in tutors and tutees:

- Be nice to your partner and sit facing each other.
- Decide who will be the tutor first, then take turns asking and answering questions in an orderly fashion, and reverse roles when all questions have been answered correctly.
- Speak in a pleasant tone when answering questions or responding.
- Encourage your partner by using statements such as "Great job" or "Good answer" or "Not quite. Can you think of something else?"
- Record the correct and incorrect responses.
- Review any incorrect question several times.

Just as you will find examples in the literature about how students with learning difficulties have benefited from peer tutoring, there are also reports about the social and academic benefits that children with learning difficulties derive from cooperative learning (e.g, Shachar, 2003). These benefits include increased friendships and enhanced positive relationships between students with learning difficulties and their non-disabled peers, improved achievement, and increased motivation to learn. Moreover, the results of these studies demonstrate that not only do students with disabilities benefit from cooperative learning experiences, but benefits also accrue to their peers who do not have a limiting impairment or disability. This is important because teachers can be reluctant to promote cooperative activities if they believe that there are minimal benefits to students with disabilities or their non-disabled peers.

However, if students with learning difficulties are to be effectively integrated into cooperative group activities, there are a number of guidelines to be followed. These include:

- Explain the procedures the cooperative group will follow.
- Train non-disabled children in helping, tutoring, teaching, and sharing skills. The use of prompts and praise are easily taught and will encourage students with learning difficulties to remain engaged with the task.
- Make the academic requirements for the children with disabilities reasonable. Requirements for different tasks can be adapted so the students with different achievement levels can participate in the same cooperative group through: (a) the use of different criteria for success for each group member; (b) varying the amount each group member is expected to master; (c) giving group members different subtasks to complete and then using the average percentage worked correctly as the group's score; and (d) using improvement scores as a measure of success, especially for students with learning difficulties.
- Ensure the children with learning difficulties have the academic skills that they will need to complete the group's work.
- Train the children with learning difficulties in collaboration skills in advance of their involvement in peer-mediated learning activities. Use a special education teacher or aide to teach these skills to the children with learning difficulties.
- Give the children with learning difficulties a role that they are able to manage in the group (e.g., if they cannot read, they might be able to facilitate the group's work by organising materials and by offering encouragement to other members).

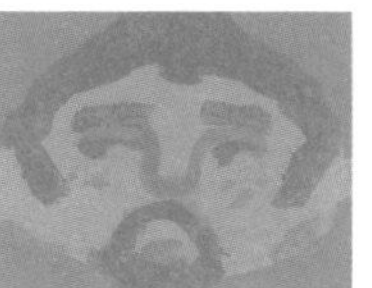

- Give bonus points to groups that have students with disabilities. This will create a situation in which the non-disabled students will want to work with their less-able peers to receive bonus points. For example, each group member may receive 5 points if they contribute to completing the group task (giving a total of 20 points in a four-person group) with the possibility of receiving an additional 10 points if they include a student with diverse learning needs. This provides an incentive to ensure that this student is included in the group.

Characteristics of peer-mediated learning models include:

- a clear goal relating to the promotion of positive self-concept and attitudes;
- students working in pairs or small groups;
- children working in situations that are typical of the class (e.g., same-age or cross-age groupings);
- each student having a specific role (e.g., expert, tutor or novice);
- the activity being of short duration (usually only a few weeks);
- skills-based activities in which students learn an explicit teaching strategy to assist learning (e.g., collaborative strategic reading);
- encouraging positive social interactions among students;
- teaching interpersonal skills that help to reduce classroom behaviour problems; and
- providing time for practice.

Assessing group and individual learning

There are a number of ways that the learning from a cooperative learning experience can be assessed. The first often involves the group generating a group product that is the outcome of their group experience. These products may include a group report or the presentation of a group construction (e.g., diorama), play, debate, or the development of a group portfolio. In assessing these products, teachers should ensure that students understand the basis for assessment, that is, how the product will be evaluated and how each student's contribution will be assessed.

Assessing individual students' contributions is also important because it sends a clear message that there will be no social loafing or students relying on more competent or willing peers to complete their task, and it ensures that all students, irrespective of ability level, are required to contribute. The tendency of more capable peers to dominate is often apparent when groups have to produce a single group product. The following ideas can be used to help overcome this problem:

- Tell the students that the task requires multiple abilities or talents possessed by different group members (e.g., artistic skills to assist in layout; computer skills to assist with retrieving information; personal skills to promote harmony).
- Assign competence to low-status students because of their particular skills and link them to task requirements. Make it clear that these children have unique skills and talents that the group will need to use if they are to complete the task successfully.
- Train low-ability students in particular skills that they will need prior to the group activity to ensure their participation (e.g., how to ask questions, find information, participate in discussions, provide constructive feedback to their peers, and demonstrate appropriate social behaviours).
- Ensure that each group is awarded points on the basis of each individual's contribution and these are totalled and group bonus points added.

The second way of evaluating learning focuses on assessing individual outcomes as a result of the group experience. The following generic question stems can be used to asses how children use different

problem-solving skills and make connections between information presented during their small group activities. Some question stems require children to integrate content, whereas others require them to integrate new information into previous understandings and knowledge. (These are based on *Bloom's Taxonomy of Educational Objectives* reported first in 1956, and still used widely.) The advantage of these questions is that they are transferable and can be used with different content. For children with cognitive, sensory, or physical impairments, the following questions can be posted on cueing cards:

- Recall—"What is …?", "List as many ways as you can to …", "List as many names as you can …"
- Comprehension—"What do you think …?", "Explain how …"
- Application—"Examine the …"
- Analysis—"Compare … with …", "Give an alternative ending to …"
- Synthesis—"Imagine you're …", "What would you need to focus on?", "What planning would you need to do?"
- Evaluation—"Discuss the pros and cons of …", "Select and justify…"

USING THIS CHAPTER IN SCHOOLS

In this chapter, we have introduced you to the idea of curriculum differentiation as a way of establishing learning environments that are inclusive of all students, including those with cognitive, sensory, and physical impairments. In developing curricula activities for these students, we have suggested that you consider plotting their strengths on a range of continua so you can clearly see how students are more similar than different to their same age peers.

The Response to Instruction (RTI) initiative with its three-tiered approach to providing instruction at the student's level has helped teachers to realise that up to 80% of students with diverse learning needs can be accommodated in the regular classroom, while others with more intense needs can be included with various levels of support. We have also provided you with a range of pedagogical practices that teachers can explicitly teach through to those that can be implemented by peers in small group settings which are effective for helping students to learn. This includes such peer-mediated learning strategies as Collaborative Strategic Reading (CSR) and cooperative learning.

What might you do when/if you discovered that there is a student with a hearing/speech/vision problem in your class? If you find that there is such a student in your class, you start by learning about the child and organising assistance. Meet with the parents and ask them about the child's condition. Ensure that families have had their child's suspected problem formally identified and treated, and a report of this information has been made available to the school so that educational implications can be taken into account (this information would normally flow through the guidance officer or school counsellor to specialist teacher[s], then to the class teacher). If educational provisions have been made already, the student must have access to them. Check with other teachers if this is the case. The key point here is to become a member of a specialist team that works together to ensure that the student is provided with the best and most appropriate support available. The particular problem that the young person is experiencing will determine what information is required.

For example, if a visual problem is suspected then the student would need to see an ophthalmologist (a surgeon who specialises in diagnosing and treating eye conditions) to have the health of the eyes examined and an optometrist (a non-medical practitioner who assesses vision) to prescribe lenses and/or visual therapy. Educational implications may include determining the extent and quality of vision available for learning and possible compensatory measures.

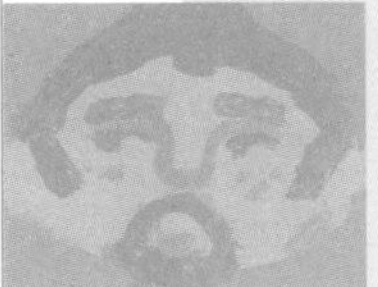

If a young person has a suspected hearing problem and/or communication problem, it would be important for parents to arrange for a consultation with an otorhinolaryngologist (yes, this is really a word, it's a surgeon who specialises in diagnosing and treating ear, nose, and throat conditions) for a health examination, an audiologist (a non-medical practitioner who assesses hearing, and prescribes hearing aids and/or auditory therapy), and a speech language pathologist (a non-medical practitioner who accesses and/or prescribes speech language therapy). Educational implications would include determining the extent and quality of hearing available for learning and possible compensatory measures and/or determining the extent and quality of communicative ability available for learning and possible compensatory measures.

As a newly qualified class teacher, you would use the above information to develop the most effective educational strategies for the young person, particularly those that relate to curriculum differentiation. Involving other professionals and parents/guardians in the planning process would be essential.

Reading and writing problems are not limited to young people in the early or middle years of schooling. These are issues that affect young adults in secondary school as well. Collaborative Strategic Reading is one way of assisting students across the school years if they are having problems in reading. Here are some guidelines that you might follow when implementing CSR:

- Ask the children to look at the text and predict what the story is about (look at pictures, key words).
- Words they know will CLICK but words they do not know are CLUNKS. Students work on the CLUNKS.
- State in 10 words or less what the text is about (state the gist of the text).
- Summarise the main ideas in the text (wrap-up).

As we mentioned above, peer-mediated learning has been shown to be an effective teaching–learning approach across age and capability dimensions. Peer mediation can work well in the primary years but it is also successful for achieving positive learning outcome in the secondary school as well. Here are some guidelines for implementing cooperative learning:

- Tell the students they will be working in four-person groups on a learning task.
- Allocate the students to groups so there is a balance of boys and girls and all groups have a student with diverse learning needs.
- Teach the social skills (discussed previously) to manage group discussions.
- Ensure that all group members have a specific role or task (e.g., scribe, information gatherer, reporter, timer) and that everyone must contribute to successfully complete the work task.
- Monitor the groups as they work on their tasks and intervene to ensure that they understand what they are doing and that all are contributing.
- Arrange for the groups to report back at the end of the lesson on what their group has achieved and what they still need to do to complete the task.

The practical activities below will further assist you in becoming more familiar with the topics and issues presented in this chapter.

PRACTICAL ACTIVITIES
Uni-work

1 It is important to understand that students with cognitive, sensory, and physical impairment experience the world in different ways. The following activities will help you to recognise the

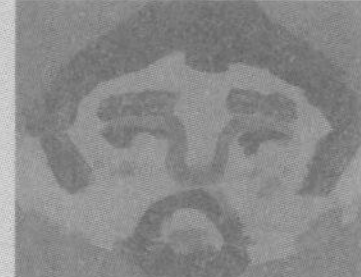

effects that these impairments may have on the student's conception of the world. Choose two of these as your activity.

a Wear a blindfold while doing a range of everyday activities like eating breakfast, cleaning your teeth, or walking around the house. Note five things you have learnt from the experience. Note five ways your simulated vision impairment might be different to actually having a vision impairment.

b Watch a DVD with which you are unfamiliar (perhaps borrowed from a friend) with the volume turned off. Write down what you think happened in the DVD. Re-watch the DVD with the volume turned up and compare your observations. Note five things you have learnt from the experience. Note five ways your simulated hearing impairment might be different to actually having a hearing impairment.

c Rent a wheelchair from your local chemist (or borrow one if you can) and use the wheelchair to do your weekly shopping at your local supermarket (doing this doesn't qualify you to park in a spot reserved for people with a disability). This will give you one of the most amazing experiences of your life. Note five things you have learnt from the experience. Note five ways your simulated physical impairment might be different to actually having a physical impairment.

d Attend a lecture on a topic that is completely outside your area of expertise. Note five things you have learnt from the experience. Note five ways your simulated cognitive impairment might be different to actually having a cognitive impairment.

2 Arrange to have some of your friends or student colleagues work together in small groups (of three to four members) to construct the highest geometric shape they can make that will stand unsupported for one minute. Give each group a bundle of 30 plastic straws and some Blu-Tack and tell them that they have five minutes to complete their construction. Stand back and watch. How did the group members decide what they would do? Was everyone involved? How did they support each other's efforts while they were constructing the geometric shape? How did the group members react to the task? What have you learnt from this activity that you could apply to other group activities?

3 Arrange to visit a primary or high school in your local area. Meet with the principal or a senior teacher and ask if you can observe students working in peer tutoring dyads or small cooperative groups. You might find this easier in a primary school setting. It doesn't matter if you are studying to be a secondary school teacher; the principles will be the same in both settings. Make a note of the following: age of the students, numbers in the group, type of activity the students are working on together, and time spent on the activity. Watch for student involvement in the group, and the type of help provided (e.g., sharing materials, sharing information, explaining difficult ideas).

School-work

Remember that school policies may apply that restrict your ability to complete one or more of the activities suggested below. Before beginning any of the following activities, speak to your supervising teacher or a member of the school administration to confirm that you can undertake the activity within existing school guidelines and policies.

4 When you are on a practicum placement, identify a child with learning difficulties. Watch how he or she is included in the group activities. Is the task explained clearly so this child can

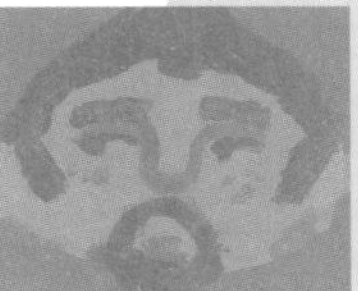

understand what he or she has to do? How do the other children provide help (e.g., point to the answer, explain how to do it)? Does this child have a role in the group? How is this help provided (e.g., explanations, or prompts and cues, or through put-downs)?

5 Make contact with a teaching colleague who has used peer tutoring and/or cooperative learning. Ask what they think of these strategies for helping students to learn. Frame your questions so you can obtain information on how frequently they use these approaches, the type of activity students are required to do, the behaviour of the students during small group activities, the levels of student motivation they have observed, and how they monitor the activity. Having read through this chapter and referring to one of the books mentioned in the *Suggested reading and resources* section (below), reconcile the practices with the theory. Which practices are consistent with theory, and which aren't?

6 Take a stroll around your school. Look for examples of architecture, resources, spaces that might affect students with physical, sensory, and learning problems (e.g., stairs, lack of large print books in the school library, places where equipment or furniture are moved and left regularly). How might you change some of the practices around your school to make it easier for these students?

SUGGESTED READING AND RESOURCES

Gillies, R. (2007). *Cooperative learning: Integrating theory and practice*. Thousand Oaks, CA: Sage.

Gillies, R. & Ashman, A. (Eds) (2003). *Cooperative learning: The social and intellectual outcomes of learning in groups*. London: RoutledgeFalmer.

Westwood, P. (2003). *Commonsense methods for children with special educational needs: Strategies for the regular classroom* (4th ed.). London: RoutledgeFalmer.

REFERENCES

Bloom B. S. (1956). *Taxonomy of educational objectives, Handbook I: The cognitive domain*. New York: David McKay Co Inc.

Brown, A. & Palincsar, A. (1988). *Guided, cooperative learning and individual knowledge acquisition*. In L. Resnick (Ed.), *Cognition and instruction: Issues and agendas* (pp. 393–439). Hillsdale, NJ: Lawrence Erlbaum.

Fuchs, D. & Fuchs, L. (2005). Peer-assisted learning strategies: Promoting word recognition, fluency, and reading comprehension in young children. *The Journal of Special Education*, *39*, 34–44.

Gillies, R. (2007). *Cooperative learning: Integrating theory and practice*. Thousand Oaks, CA: Sage.

Giorcelli, L. (1996). An impulse to soar: Sanitisation, silencing and special education. *The Australasian Journal of Special Education*, *20*, 5–11.

Johnson, D. & Johnson, F. (2003). *Joining together: Group theory and group skills* (8th ed.). Boston: Allyn and Bacon.

Lou, Y., Abrami, P., Spence, J., Poulsen, C., Chambers, B., & d'Apollonia, S. (1996). Within-class grouping: A meta-analysis. *Review of Educational Research*, *66*, 423–458.

Shachar, H. (2003). Who gains what from cooperative learning: An overview of eight studies. In R. Gillies & A. Ashman (Eds), *Cooperative learning: The social and intellectual outcomes of learning in groups* (pp. 103–118). London: RoutledgeFalmer.

Vaughn, S., Klingner, J., & Bryant, D. (2001). Collaborative strategic reading as a means to enhance peer-mediated instruction for reading comprehension and content-area learning. *Remedial and Special Education*, *22*, 66–74.

Westwood, P. (2003). *Commonsense methods for children with special educational needs: Strategies for the regular classroom* (4th ed.). London: RoutledgeFalmer.

Christina E. van Kraayenoord and John Elkins

8 LITERACIES AND NUMERACY

What you will learn in this chapter

In a world where messages are sent and received through cyberspace, where communication is digital, where the population is diverse with many cultures and languages, the development of literacy and numeracy competencies are essential. Indeed, individuals learn about, with, and through literacy and numeracy. Literacy and numeracy learning is one way in which students are able to gain the knowledge and skills that they need to be able to interact with and participate with their family, community, and the world. Teachers have a very important role in assisting students to learn about, with, and through literacy and numeracy by planning for and using appropriate and responsive teaching approaches and strategies. Teachers have a particularly important role to play in those situations where students find the learning of literacy and numeracy difficult. In this chapter you will learn:

- how literacy(ies) and numeracy are understood;
- that literacy and numeracy are crucial aspects of the curriculum for all students;
- about student diversity and various influences on literacy and numeracy achievement;
- about a number of challenges teachers face in improving students' literacy and numeracy achievement;
- how to assess literacy and numeracy and diagnose the nature of students' difficulties;
- aspects of planning lessons in literacy and numeracy;
- ways of helping students acquire useful knowledge, skills, and strategies in literacy and numeracy; and
- how learners respond to teaching.

CASE STUDIES

PETER

Peter is in Year 9 and has difficulty with several aspects of literacy. On entry to high school Peter was identified as a student who would have problems with reading and writing in most of his subjects. Indeed, Peter's difficulties have been obvious since his earliest years at school, and although he has had various types of support since Year 4, his difficulties have persisted. Specifically, although Peter has adequate decoding skills (i.e., can recognise and work out what the visual and non-visual information in a text says), he has poor comprehension of what he reads. To develop his comprehension skills his classroom teachers and the support teacher are collaborating to ensure that he is prepared for new material by understanding the purpose of reading and how this influences how text is read. Peter's teachers are also providing strategy instruction focusing on teaching him how to predict, visualise, and summarise.

When writing, Peter also has difficulty organising his ideas on paper, and what he writes has many grammatical errors. The teachers are encouraging Peter to use computer software that will help him to organise his ideas and generate outlines for his written work. In addition, he is reminded to use the software's checking features to alert him to where changes are needed in spelling and syntax. Peter is a good listener and speaker. The teachers encourage him to use these skills by ensuring that there are options in class assignments that allow him and his peers to respond via these means. Peter particularly enjoys role-plays and group activities where he can share his ideas verbally, and he often prepares elaborate graphics to illustrate what he has learned. Peter loves using his mobile phone to text his friends and, despite his difficulties with literacy, he has connections with his friends in a chat group on the internet.

syntax
The structures of language, sometimes synonymous with grammar. Terms such as "clause" and "phrase" belong here.

MARY

Mary is in Year 4 and managing most of the topics that her teacher introduces, but she finds arithmetic very difficult. She makes many simple and careless errors, and she has developed a dislike of mathematics lessons. Indeed, she has begun to think of herself as a hopeless student in mathematics, especially when she needs to ask her teacher for help or when she is trying to complete her homework.

Mary's parents and her teacher have discussed whether she should use a calculator and she has started doing this to check her homework. As she is an average reader, she doesn't find the reading of word problems difficult. However, she often finds it hard to work out the relevant mathematical aspects so she can write down number sentences and then move forward to a solution.

Mary wishes that she didn't have to study mathematics at school. She doesn't enjoy it or find the work relevant. "After all," she complains, "when I go to the supermarket, the machine adds up and makes the change." Even doing maths games on a computer can become boring after a while.

Mary might not receive special help with mathematics since support teachers give priority to students who have literacy difficulties. Her parents and teacher wonder what mathematical tasks she will need if she is to live effectively as she grows up and progresses through school. What will numeracy be for Mary in the coming decades?

TEACHING–LEARNING CONTEXT

Proficiency in literacy and numeracy has been associated with the development of personal identity and sense of agency by contributing to one's own life and to the lives of those in the family and local community. In addition, knowledge and skills in literacy and numeracy provide other opportunities related to work, leisure, recreation, and citizenship. Being competent in literacy and numeracy opens up possibilities for problem-solving, decision-making, and transforming one's life, as well as affecting our global community.

Literacy and numeracy achievement are considered to be essential in school and have been recognised as important goals of Australian education for all students, irrespective of ability or circumstances. Many Commonwealth and state government initiatives in recent years have focused on the development of these two essential skills. For example, one of the goals related to the curriculum in The Adelaide Declaration on National Goals of Schooling in the Twenty-first Century (Australian Government Department of Education, Science and Training, 1999) states that students should have "… attained the skills of numeracy and English literacy; such that, every student should be numerate, able to read, write, spell, and communicate at an appropriate level".

Understandings of literacy(ies) and numeracy

There are many meanings of the terms *literacy* and *numeracy* and, therefore, we have used the word "understandings" to reflect this. Understandings of literacy and numeracy have changed over past decades, but increasingly our understandings have broadened, with the suggestion that literacy and numeracy involves comprehensive and complex knowledge, skills, strategies, and motivations. For example, literacy has been described as a set of situated, social, and cultural practices that involve symbols (e.g., letters, words, pictures, graphs, Braille) developed through interactions with others. It results from practices prescribed by the symbols themselves, social situations, the cultural contexts, and personal factors such as gender and age. Today, the term *literacies* is often used (hence, the title of this chapter) to indicate the many ways people are literate and to accurately reflect the range of practices that are needed to engage with text. These literacies include: reading, writing, speaking, listening, viewing, and shaping. The term *multiliteracies* refers both to being literate using various media of communication (oral, print, and multimedia) and being able to use literacies in various contexts. The word *text* in this chapter refers to oral or written modes delivered on paper, electronic, or live platforms (Anstey & Bull, 2006).

literacy

A set of situated, social, and cultural practices that involves symbols such as letters, words, pictures, graphs, and Braille that are developed through interactions with others.

Numeracy has become the term for those aspects of mathematics that are related to functioning in society and, therefore, it comprises a facility with mathematics for the purposes of daily living. As such, it varies with cultural contexts and among individuals. Numeracy encompasses more than number sense and involves data, spatial, and formula sense as well as being able to communicate effectively with others through the language of mathematics, to interpret everyday quantitative information, and to have a repertoire of strategies to deal with problems that may arise.

Diversity in classrooms

The diversity of students in classrooms means that students today have a range of knowledge, skills, and attitudes toward literacy and numeracy. For example, some students will be very able and engage in higher order thinking and use literacy and numeracy in innovative, creative, and evaluative ways. A student who is gifted might write elaborate fantasy texts that describe the injustices in an imagined society. Some other students will have problems with literacy and numeracy. Some of these students may have disabilities, such as students with cerebral palsy or Autism Spectrum Disorder (ASD), which

affect their ability to learn, while others may have difficulties in acquiring literacy and numeracy skills related to intrinsic, social, cultural, and/or environmental factors that you will recall from Chapter 1. Frequently these factors occur together.

Typically, students who experience difficulties in literacy have problems with literacy knowledge and skills in interaction with texts and tasks in both school and out-of-school settings. Students who experience difficulties in numeracy may have limited understanding of basic number, as well as difficulty with critical and analytical thinking associated with mathematics tasks and everyday numeracy activities. For example, a student with learning difficulties may not understand the concept of place value in addition problems.

Because literacy and numeracy operate across the curricula, they are found in other subjects or Key Learning Areas such as the sciences, geography, art, and creative industries. Therefore, students who have problems with literacy and numeracy may have difficulties in these subjects as well. Difficulties in comprehending material on websites and in textbooks might affect the learning of history. Difficulties with calculations may affect learning in science, and the use of spatial information and statistical data in geography.

Literacy and numeracy achievement and the achievement gap

Louden (2000) reported that about 16% of Australian children experience learning difficulties in literacy. American researchers suggest that about 6% of students experience marked difficulties in learning mathematics (Rourke & Conway, 1997). Studies such as *Program for International Student Assessment* (PISA), which compares the reading performance of Australian and New Zealand 15-year-olds with the performance of 15-year-olds in 31 countries (including the United States, Canada, and Japan), show wide differences in Australian students' performance in literacy and numeracy. For example, results of the PISA 2000 study revealed marked differences in Australian students' performance in literacy and numeracy in terms of socioeconomic background and gender (Lokan, Greenwood, & Cresswell, 2001), and Australia's Indigenous students performed at a lower level in both literacy and numeracy than non-Indigenous students in the same study (de Bortoli & Cresswell, 2004).

Other studies have also revealed differences in performance in mathematics. The *Trends in International Mathematics and Science Study* (TIMSS), involving Australian students in Years 4 and 8 and conducted in 2002/2003, revealed that students in Year 4 achieved significantly higher than the international average in the areas of measurement, geometry, and data, and lower than the international average for number. Students in Year 8 performed above the international average in all the content areas assessed. It is of interest, however, that there were no significant gender differences in overall mathematics achievement at either year level (Thomson & Fleming, 2004). The TIMMS 2003 data again showed the gap between Indigenous and non-Indigenous students in mathematics achievement (Thomson, McKelvie, & Murane, 2006).

ISSUES AND CHALLENGES

There are a number of issues and challenges faced by schools and teachers. Some of these challenges are related to the diversity of students in classrooms, namely language and culture, gender differences, and engagement and motivation, especially self-efficacy. Another challenge that has gained prominence for teachers in recent years is that of assessment and testing. And, finally, there is the challenge for teachers of meeting professional standards.

Language and culture

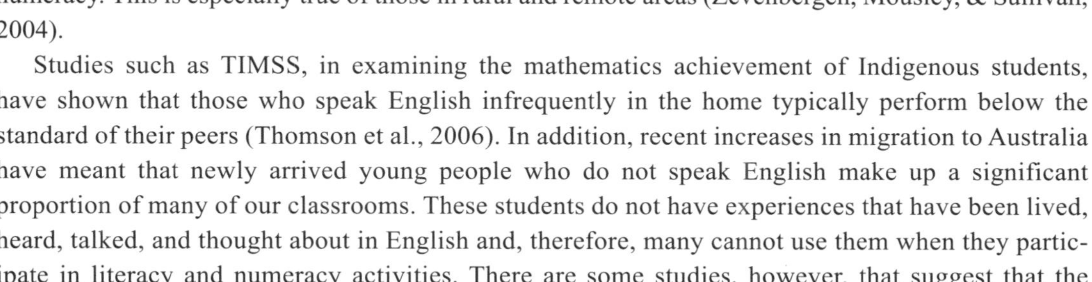

Students in our classrooms who do not have English as their first language or do not speak Standard Australian English do not have the English or Standard Australian English language experiences on which they can draw for literacy and numeracy activities in schools. For example, the ability to use Standard Australian English is a factor that affects Indigenous students' performance in literacy and numeracy. This is especially true of those in rural and remote areas (Zevenbergen, Mousley, & Sullivan, 2004).

Studies such as TIMSS, in examining the mathematics achievement of Indigenous students, have shown that those who speak English infrequently in the home typically perform below the standard of their peers (Thomson et al., 2006). In addition, recent increases in migration to Australia have meant that newly arrived young people who do not speak English make up a significant proportion of many of our classrooms. These students do not have experiences that have been lived, heard, talked, and thought about in English and, therefore, many cannot use them when they participate in literacy and numeracy activities. There are some studies, however, that suggest that the relationship between mathematics achievement and language background is far from clear (see, e.g., Thomson & Fleming, 2004).

When students are from non-English-speaking backgrounds or other cultures it is possible that parents and other community members have different views about learning. For example, with respect to mathematics, some Asian people believe (with justification) that the abacus is a very good tool for computation. Hatano (1997) explained very clearly how to learn to use an abacus, noting that it improves written computation skills, but not the place value concept. Nelson, Joseph, and Williams (1993) have described how teachers can introduce mathematical ideas that were developed in other parts of the world and provided examples of how common curriculum elements such as percentages, measurement, and proportion have been handled by other cultures.

There may be subtle cultural differences with respect to Indigenous students also, such as the use of subsitising (the word means "knowing by looking", which is not guessing), rather than counting, in early out-of-school mathematical activities. Difficulties may then arise if teachers assume that one-to-one correspondence is the only way to approach counting and devalue culturally-based learning (Willis, 1990).

Gender differences

Australian research findings comparing boys' and girls' school literacy and numeracy achievement have not always been consistent with respect to the common belief that girls do better in literacy than boys, and girls do more poorly than boys in numeracy (Cresswell, Rowe, & Withers, 2003; Thomson & Fleming, 2004). In recent years, any differences between the achievements of the boys and girls seem trivial. It would appear that presenting literacy and numeracy as a social practice might enable both boys and girls to acquire the literacy and numeracy that society expects. A number of authors have suggested that instructional practices that are personally relevant, engaging, culturally responsive, and capitalise on the resources that students bring to the classroom are essential when teaching both boys and girls (issues that were raised in Chapter 3).

Engagement and motivation

Literacy and numeracy achievement are strongly influenced by engagement and motivation. While motivation is intrinsic to learners, it is also strongly influenced by school and classroom factors that contribute to poor student engagement and motivation. Such factors include:

- the nature of teachers' instruction;
- the level of difficulty of classroom tasks and texts;
- shifts in expectations about literacy and numeracy as students progress through the year levels; and
- a lack of connection between the instructional activities and students' lives.

There are a number of motivational constructs that influence performance in literacy and numeracy. Self-efficacy is one that affects the way in which students respond to tasks, for example whether they persist with tasks, especially when the tasks are challenging (Folkman & Moskowitz, 2004).

Self-efficacy refers to an individual's expectations and beliefs about their competence. Because self-efficacy varies across academic domains, a student's self-efficacy in literacy may be different to that in numeracy. The research has indicated that students with learning difficulties have reported lower academic self-efficacy than their normally achieving peers (e.g., Linnenbrink & Pintrich, 2003). One of the debilitating aspects of low self-efficacy is that negative school-related attitudes persist into adolescence and therefore, often, they are barriers to learning in secondary school. Instructional approaches are recommended that:

zone of proximal development (ZPD)
The point at which an individual is ready to progress to the next stage in learning through scaffolding and interactions with more capable peers. Participation in shared problem-solving within the ZPD can lead to a gain in understanding and skills that will prepare the learner to perform tasks independently.

- use tasks just beyond the student's current skill or knowledge level (sometimes called the "zone of proximal development" after Vygotsky, 1978);
- are challenging but ensure success;
- allow the student to feel competent and in control;
- use a range of tasks, materials and texts related to the student's interests and everyday experiences; and
- have a social dimension (see Wilhem & Smith, 2007).

In addition, approaches that build positive attitudes and feelings of competence alongside students' learning of skills and strategies appear to be effective (Montague, 2006).

Assessment and testing

Assessment to determine the nature of student learning to inform instruction and diagnose students' strengths and weaknesses is an important and very useful practice for teachers (Afflerbach, 2007). Within the classroom, literacy and numeracy assessment involves the collection of information with a variety of tools from multiple sources to establish students' knowledge, skills, and attitudes. Teachers use such assessment information about individual students' progress and needs to make pedagogical changes in their literacy and numeracy teaching.

BOX 8.1 Literacy and numeracy assessment practices

To establish students' progress and diagnose their strengths and weaknesses a range of assessment practices should be used. Here is a list of some formal and teacher-developed assessment practices:

- observational techniques, including anecdotal records, checklists, rating scales;
- interviews, which might include interviews with the parents as well as the student;
- testing, including standardised tests, and criterion-referenced tests;

- direct assessment, including curriculum-based assessment (CBA);
- dynamic assessment;
- outcomes-based assessment;
- learning logs;
- journals and diaries;
- students' work samples and the use of assessment matrices and rubrics;
- self-assessment, including self-observation and self-report;
- inventories used to assess literacy behaviour, interests, and habits;
- error analyses; and
- portfolio assessment.

BOX 8.1

Assessment for accountability purposes—a purpose of assessment often sought by system and school administrators and politicians—is increasingly becoming more common in Australia. Assessment for accountability involves the use of standardised tests conducted at state, territory, and federal levels. Students' achievement, as indicated on these tests, is examined against benchmarks and then school, sector, state, and territory comparisons are made and reported. Since 1999, assessment against national benchmarks in literacy (reading, writing, spelling) and numeracy have progressively been introduced. In 2001, all students in Years 3 and 5 were assessed against the national benchmarks. Since then, all states and territories have also tested Year 7 students and compared their performance against benchmarks (Australian Government Department of Education, Science and Training, 2007a).

This practice continued in 2008 in Years 3, 5, 7 and 9 in state schools as the first national tests in literacy and numeracy. The literacy tests will comprise tests of reading, writing, spelling, and language conventions (that is, grammar and punctuation) (New South Wales Government Department of Education and Training, 2007a). In addition, for the first time in Australia the test results will be reported to parents using a common reporting scale (New South Wales Government Department of Education and Training, 2007a).

The growth of these mandatory high-stakes tests in literacy and numeracy for accountability purposes has meant that teachers and students have had to adopt new roles that do not always have positive consequences. Reports from the United States and other countries have revealed that such changes in teachers' roles have included changes in curriculum pacing, curriculum alignment, data-related tasks such as managing, interpreting, and using large data sets, and instructional responses to test data. These changes in turn have positively and negatively affected pedagogy (although more the latter) and teacher–student relationships, and have increased teacher stress (Valli & Buese, 2007).

Reports on the influence of high-stakes tests on students have also shown that they may be harmful to students' self-esteem and motivation. In particular, such tests are often used to label individuals and groups of students. These labels may lead to many related consequences such as lowered expectations and differential treatment by teachers and others in classrooms, and for those identified as low achieving as an outcome of the testing, decreased perseverance in literacy and numeracy activities (Afflerbach, 2005; 2007).

In an example of the negative consequences of mandated testing in Australia, with reference to migrant students who have English as a second language, Hammond (1999) indicated that when these students are assessed on state-wide tests designed for students whose first language is English, and

criterion-referenced tests
Assessment of student performance in relation to set standards, not in comparison to the performance of others. (See also norm-referenced assessment.)

curriculum-based assessment
Measurement that uses direct observation and recording of a student's performance on curriculum tasks (or academic skills) to inform decisions about how instruction should be delivered.

dynamic assessment
An interactive form of assessment that embeds aspects of intervention to prompt correct replies, in the form of structured hints, to gauge whether the student has the potential to learn.

portfolio assessment
A selected collection of a student's work used to evaluate learning progress.

when their achievement is reported against national benchmarks, their performance is often perceived to be poor. She argued, however, "… it would be inaccurate to suggest that these students are 'failing' in literacy development. It would also be inaccurate to portray the needs of such students as 'problems'" (p. 127). This is because many (often older) migrant students on arrival in the Australian school system are likely to be fluent speakers of their first language. Thus, an English test is inappropriate for judging the literacy achievement of recently arrived non- or limited-English speakers.

Professional standards

The main professional organisations for literacy and mathematics teaching in Australia have created statements of professional standards. Standards for Teachers of English Language and Literacy in Australia (STELLA) refer to standards of Professional Knowledge, Professional Practice, and Professional Engagement (see Australian Association for the Teaching of English & Australian Literacy Educators' Association, 2002).

Similarly, the Standards for Excellence in Teaching Mathematics in Australian Schools, originally produced in 2002 by the Australian Association of Mathematics Teachers (2006), referred to standards related to Professional Knowledge, Professional Attributes, and Professional Practice. Both statements of standards serve as goals toward which teachers can work in developing as teachers in these domains. More recently Teaching Australia, The Institute for Teaching and School Leadership (2007), developed a consultation paper that proposes a model of national professional standards for advanced teaching and school leadership.

One of the main purposes of developing these national standards is to assist teachers in shaping their professional learning at an advanced level. Along with Teaching Reading, the National Inquiry into the Teaching of Literacy (Australian Government Department of Education, Science and Training, 2005a), which has made a number of recommendations related to the teaching of reading, these standards are likely to have profound consequences for the teaching of literacy and numeracy to diverse students in our schools.

TEACHING ESSENTIALS

Teaching is concerned with what and how. In this section, we describe those aspects of teaching in relationship to literacy and numeracy. To begin, see Box 8.2.

The what of teaching literacy

The most common model of literacy and literacies in Australia is the Four Resources Model (Luke & Freebody, 1999). This model suggests that there is a repertoire of practices in which individuals engage when interacting with print, oral language, or multimedia. The practices are related to four roles:

1 *Code-breaker* (how do I crack this text?);
2 *Text-participant* (what does this mean?);
3 *Text-user* (what do I do with this text?); and
4 *Text-analyst* (what is this text trying to do to me?).

Being a code-breaker refers to decoding, while being a text-participant focuses on making meaning of the text. Text-user refers to establishing a purpose for the text and thinking about other possible purposes. Text-analyst involves thinking analytically about the content of the text and considering its underlying and implicit assumptions. The four practices are not hierarchical by age or ability. All are necessary and should be used in a flexible manner according to the nature of the text being used and the literacy activity being undertaken.

Elements of literacy

8.2

The elements of literacy comprise the knowledge, skills, and attitudes students develop as they become competent in literacy:

- awareness of environmental media;
- prior knowledge;
- vocabulary, including subject-specific vocabulary;
- letter knowledge;
- concepts about print;
- phonemic awareness (hearing, identifying, and manipulating phonemes);
- the alphabetic principle;
- word recognition and identification;
- decoding;
- automaticity and fluency of reading;
- handwriting;
- automaticity in handwriting;
- spelling conventions;
- comprehension of material read;
- metacognitive knowledge;
- knowledge of the writing process and skills necessary for its execution (e.g., planning, drafting, editing, revising and production);
- writing conventions (e.g., elements such as directionality of written text—written English versus written Hebrew—punctuation, and formats for different text types—list versus TV script versus newspaper article);
- strategies, especially in reading and writing;
- knowledge and understanding of a variety of genres (including the purposes and textual features of the genres) in written, visual, and spoken forms;
- awareness of audience and purpose in written, visual, and spoken forms;
- composition of written, visual, and spoken text;
- knowledge of use of words, colour images, sound, and video;
- communicative intent and skills;
- generation, organisation, elaboration, integration, and analysis of ideas;
- keyboard skills;
- awareness of context and history and their influence on text, creator, and user;
- awareness of social organisation and power relations on text, creator, and user;
- evaluation of sources and evidence;
- developing an analytical and critical perspective;
- creating and designing information; and
- transforming information.

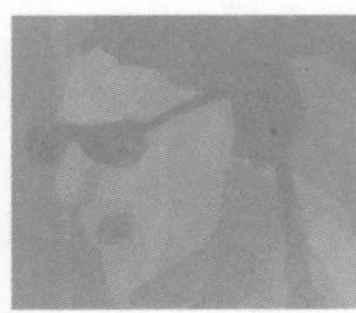

Teaching strategies for literacy

Applications of the Four Resources Model can be seen in many of Australia's classrooms. Spinks and Kilham (2006) and Shaddock (2006) have documented a number of action research projects that applied the Four Resources Model with a wide range of students, including those with learning difficulties and disabilities. An examination of the strategies that teachers used in applying the Model revealed use of the following:

communicative intent
The assumption of motivation in behaviour interpreted as being communicative. (See also speech acts.*)*

- explicit teaching through direct teacher explication and use of commercial materials in Direct Instruction;
- cooperative reading groups;
- guided reading (when the teacher guides the reading of grouped students);
- shared reading (when the teacher reads aloud);
- modelling (when the teacher reads or writes with students);
- discussions;
- sentence construction activities for reading and writing;
- production of text on the computer;
- phonemic awareness training;
- brainstorming to generate ideas or topics;
- Cloze activities in which words are missing to prompt prediction;
- before, during, and after literacy activities;
- phonics programs that teach symbols of print and their sounds;
- resources such as Big Books, picture books, custom-made, personalised books, and listening posts; and
- multimedia materials, including videos, DVDs, and the web.

The what of teaching numeracy

Mathematics comprises several content areas, plus problem-solving, meaning making, and communication (Booker, Bond, Sparrow, & Swan, 2004). The content areas that are used in mathematics curriculum and syllabus documents are:

- number;
- space;
- measurement; and
- chance and data (e.g., Goos, Stillman, & Vale; 2007; Zevenbergen, Dole, & Wright, 2004).

Some authors also refer to algebra and working mathematically as content areas (e.g., Zevenbergen et al., 2004). Often at the secondary school level, in relation to space, reference is also made to geometry, in measurement—trigonometry, with calculus being presented as a separate content area (Goos et al., 2007).

NUMBER

Number refers to the concept of number and patterning. It has been suggested that number sense (feeling at ease with numbers and counting) is the foundation of early numeracy. For example, an understanding of what numbers mean, and some ability to handle numbers mentally, are essential for numeracy. Although most students develop number sense through everyday experiences, others need opportunities to develop it in school. It is likely that attempts to teach formal mathematics can be hindered if students do not have adequate number sense.

Mental computation

Mental computation requires number sense. Examples of operations that might be handled mentally are the basic facts about the four operations (e.g., 7 plus 8, 45 divided by 9). Next are basic facts with numbers involving place value (e.g., 125 – 20). More demanding are the sorts of operations met in daily life, such as 145 + 17 (although some students might be able to handle even more demanding computations, such as 819 divided by 7, without recourse to paper and pencil or a calculator). The goal of numeracy ought to include these three types.

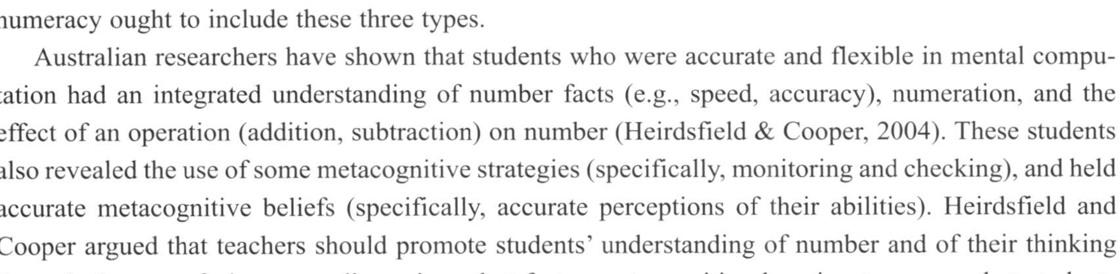

Australian researchers have shown that students who were accurate and flexible in mental computation had an integrated understanding of number facts (e.g., speed, accuracy), numeration, and the effect of an operation (addition, subtraction) on number (Heirdsfield & Cooper, 2004). These students also revealed the use of some metacognitive strategies (specifically, monitoring and checking), and held accurate metacognitive beliefs (specifically, accurate perceptions of their abilities). Heirdsfield and Cooper argued that teachers should promote students' understanding of number and of their thinking through the use of classroom discussions that foster metacognitive learning to ensure that students develop competency in mental strategies (see also Montague, 2006).

SPACE AND SHAPE

The central focus of teaching about space is about developing students' understanding of how space is filled and described, and how ideas about space (and shape) are used. In secondary schools, teachers build on these understandings to teach geometry, and for students in the senior school (Year 12), calculus and trigonometry. Again, the application of information about space and shape in everyday contexts is a focus of much teaching in this content area. For example, students may be asked to use higher order thinking skills with perceptual skills, for instance to determine what shape will result when a 3-D figure is rotated.

The difficulties that students may have with space and shape are often signalled by misconceptions that include limited conceptualisations of particular shapes, limited orientations, difficulties with describing the mathematical attributes of objects, symmetry, tessellations, and position (that is, conventions related to coordinates) (Booker et al., 2004). In teaching about space and shape, many authors refer to the work of Dina and Pierre van Hiele who suggested that students must be assisted to move through five levels of geometric thinking: visualisation, analysis, abstraction or informal deduction, formal deduction, and rigour. The teaching approaches that should be used include visualisation, communication, drawing and modelling, and the application of geometric concepts and knowledge (see Zevenbergen et al., 2004).

MEASUREMENT

Measurement deals with the measurement of objects and the assignment of numerical values to attributes of objects (National Council of Teachers of Mathematics, 2000). It comprises estimating and measuring geometric measures such as area, length, volume, and capacity, as well as angles, physical measures such as mass and time, and other measures such as value and money (Booker et al., 2004). It should be noted here that some authors consider the latter as related to the content area of number.

At the secondary level, teachers help students acquire strategies related to measurement that allow them to become problem-solvers in real contexts. Based on findings from the TIMSS study (Lokan, Ford, & Greenwood, 1996), it is clear that Australian secondary students often have difficulties with measurement, with particular problems in distinguishing capacity and volume.

CHANCE AND DATA

Chance refers to constructs such as randomness and the prediction of outcomes or probability. The word *data* here refers to data handling such as collecting, recording, presenting, and making mathematical inferences. Acquisition of statistical literacy (that is, the understanding and use of data, especially in everyday contexts) is regarded as an important aspect of data. Ideas such as measures of central tendency (that is, mean, median, mode) are part of statistical literacy that students learn about in this domain.

Booker et al. (2004) argued that chance and data should be taught concurrently, and not separately or in isolation. These authors suggested that the teaching of chance and data could be integrated into other curriculum areas such as science, health and physical education. Common problems of secondary students in the area of chance and data include the notion of randomness, difficulties with various aspects of statistical literacy, and difficulties with graph interpretation.

There are a number of strategies that have been proposed for the teaching of mathematics. These include:

- scaffolding;
- problem-based learning;
- direct instruction;
- the use of questioning;
- student self-assessment and reflection;
- the modelling of problem-solving—moving from concrete to representational to abstract levels;
- tackling faulty or confused mathematical thinking by clarifying confusions and assisting students to reconstruct their thinking;
- using inquiry-based approaches comprising exploration, explanation, reflection, and recording;
- using mathematical talk;
- teaching of strategies (i.e., conscious and systematic ways of interpreting information);
- using technology;
- making connections across lessons and content areas;
- small cooperative group work;
- using texts (e.g., narratives that address mathematical ideas, biographies of mathematicians);
- undertaking investigations;
- assisting students to develop new ways of thinking in situations where they make errors; and
- providing opportunities for success.

One project involving the Victorian Department of Education and Training, the Catholic Education Commission of Victoria, and the Association of Independent Schools of Victoria in conjunction with RMIT (Australian Government Department of Education, Science and Training, 2004) identified 12 scaffolding practices that contributed to improved student learning outcomes. These were:

1 excavating—uncovering what is known and making it transparent;
2 modelling—demonstrating, naming, and explaining;
3 collaborating—acting as a co-learner and problem-solver;
4 guiding—cuing and prompting;
5 convince me—seeking explanation and justification;
6 noticing—highlighting, drawing something to attention, and valuing;

7 focusing—coaching, tutoring, and redirecting;
8 probing—clarifying, monitoring, and checking;
9 orienting—setting the scene;
10 reflecting/reviewing—sharing, reflecting, summarising, and reinforcing;
11 extending—challenging; and
12 apprenticing—inviting peer assistance and peer teaching.

Another project conducted by the NSW Department of Education and Training, the Catholic Education Commission NSW, and the Association of Independent Schools of NSW (Australian Government Department of Education and Training, 2005b) identified outstanding numeracy practices and strategies in 25 high-performing schools. These practices were then trialled in 10 low-performing schools across New South Wales and the results compared against 10 other reference schools that were performing at or slightly above the average in numeracy.

The outcomes of the trial revealed that teachers' knowledge of the strategies led to improvements in students' numeracy achievement. The within-classroom factors and some of the related strategies included:

- Language as a focus for learning—learners used talk to scaffold their learning, expert others (peers, adults) scaffolded tasks involving the manipulation of resources or a problem-solving activity, students were expected to use oral or written language in explanations, teachers and students created questions, and frequent connections were made between numeracy and literacy.
- Assessment to identify and accommodate difference—individual students' abilities were identified and monitored, management structures such as ability grouping or individualised learning were used, and teachers built on and responded with awareness to students' cultural knowledge.
- Purposeful pedagogy—specific outcomes and associated indicators were identified, structured explicit teaching was used, resources such as concrete manipulatives were used, and fun drill and practice activities were used to develop automaticity of basic skills.

Inclusive, responsive teaching

The notion of inclusive and responsive teaching should be one of three concepts (the others are discussed below) to be foregrounded in all considerations of curricula (content), instruction, and assessment related to literacy and numeracy. Inclusive teaching has been variously defined although commonly it involves the ideas of access to, and participation by all students in, classroom teaching and learning experiences, plus the development of a sense of belonging to a classroom community.

An inclusive, responsive classroom is one in which all learners have access to a planned curriculum and in which a range of teaching and assessment approaches and practices are used to meet the knowledge, skills, cultural, and linguistic backgrounds, and needs of the students. A variety of teaching approaches and strategies are used with the key requirement that they are inclusive and responsive to the students. Technology may be incorporated into the instruction—for example, an audio-recording of text could be used alongside print, or a speech synthesiser might accompany material appearing on a computer screen. Feedback involving praise should be given frequently and be based on performance toward the required learning outcomes (see also Giangreco, 2007).

Universal Design for Learning

Another concept that is used at the point of teachers' planning is Universal Design for Learning (UDL). (You will recall the same concept being used in Chapter 6 in regard to the design and use of

technology.) Originating in the field of architecture, the central tenet of Universal Design is "the design of products and environments to be usable by all people to the greatest extent possible without the need for adaptation or specialized design" (Center for Universal Design, 2008). When applied to education, Universal Design for Learning has been suggested as a response that meets the needs of students because it promotes access, participation and progress in regular education for all learners (Center for Applied Special Technology (CAST), 2006). Bauer and Kroeger (2004, p. 22) also stated:

> *Universal design attempts to create a curriculum without adaptation or retrofitting by providing equal access to information, [and] ... allows the student to control the method of accessing information. The teacher monitors the process and initiates new methods. Through Universal design, the teacher encourages students' self-sufficiency, and imparts knowledge and facilitates learning. Universal design does not remove challenges—it removes barriers to access.*

Universal Design for Learning involves the conscious and deliberate planning of lessons and outcomes that allow all students access to and participation in the same curricula (i.e., content). According to the National Center on Accessing the General Curriculum 2007), when curricula, instruction and assessment are designed and specified in a lesson plan using UDL, students are offered various means of:

- presentation—multiple, flexible means of presentation such as allowing students alternative ways of recognising essential concepts (e.g., notes placed on the web as well as being delivered verbally);
- expression—multiple, flexible means of expression to allow students to demonstrate mastery (e.g., using oral, written, multimedia systems); and
- engagement—multiple, flexible options for engagement such as offering various skill levels, preferences and interests (e.g., texts at different reading levels or mathematics problems at different levels).

UDL was originally conceptualised to involve seven principles that should be considered during planning. Scott, McGuire, and Shaw (2001) then developed the term Universal Design for Instruction© (UDI) that refers to nine principles. Although UDI was developed for the post-secondary sector, the nine principles are comprehensive and helpful when planning in all phases of learning from preschool through secondary school. The principles and associated meanings are:

- equitable use—identical (or when not equivalent) instruction;
- flexibility in use—variety of instructional approaches and teaching strategies, offering options;
- simple and intuitive—predictable and easily understood instruction, with no unnecessary complexity;
- perceptible information—effective communication of information regardless of ambient conditions or students' sensory abilities;
- tolerance for error—responds to variety in students' pace of learning and prerequisite skills;
- low physical effort—nonessential physical effort minimised, attention maximised;
- size and space for approach and use—appropriate space and size, regardless of a student's physical condition and communication needs;
- a community of learners—school and classroom environments that promote interaction and communication among peers, between students and teachers, and among all other classroom participants (e.g., teacher aides and volunteers); and

- instructional climate—welcoming and inclusive with high expectations (see McGuire, Scott & Shaw, 2006).

Many authors have described UDL, with some directly addressing literacy and providing suggestions for making textbooks more accessible. Studies reporting the effects of training in UDL on lesson plans, and other evidence-based studies, are emerging (e.g., Spooner, Baker, Harris, Ahlgrim-Delzell, & Browder, 2007).

Differentiated instruction

To minimise the need for accommodations and modifications, teachers should first design and plan inclusive curricula, and teaching and assessment activities based on UDL. Nevertheless, modification using differentiated instruction may still be necessary for some students (see Box 8.3).

As you will recall from the previous chapter, differentiated instruction refers to changes to curricula, instruction, and assessment based on students' abilities, interests, and preferences. It allows teachers to respond to the needs of each student and ensure that learning progress is successful. Content, processes, and products can be differentiated. Differentiated instruction involves knowing, affirming, and using students' histories, experiences, and contributions to create learning experiences that have a better learning-fit for students. There are several principles that underlie differentiated instruction. They are:

- Using diversity—recognition and use of the student's abilities, culture, languages, motivations, and interests to promote learning in their classrooms.
- Creating a community of learners—providing opportunities for social transaction. For example, expert-others (the teacher, volunteer, aide, or peers) scaffold the learning of the not-so-expert learner through modelling, thinking aloud, and sharing strategies and routines in a supportive and collaborative way.
- Responding to the student as a learner—responding to the student's existing knowledge and capabilities by adapting the outcomes, tasks, and teaching structures.
- Developing continuity—making connections between past learning and past life events and current learning and experiences. For example, students should be encouraged to see what is common about the content they are learning, and about the cognitive and metacognitive thinking processes that they are using across the curriculum.

Lawrence-Brown (2004) identified a number of supports for students who may require assistance in the regular classroom curriculum. These included:

- the use of taped books and mathematics media that illustrate authentic life applications;
- resources that lend themselves to developing student independence (e.g., manipulatives, visual aids, outlines, and summaries);
- emphasising the big ideas and the most important skills;
- providing clear expectations and examples (e.g., giving students the instructions necessary to complete the task in the form of a checklist);
- breaking down and sequencing the skills and strategies to be learned;
- making connections with prior knowledge; and
- fading assistance so that independence is developed.

For students with more severe disabilities the accommodations and modifications that may be made as part of differentiated instruction are referred to as a *prioritised curriculum*. This refers to the use of targeted and individually tailored curriculum, instruction, and assessment.

Box 8.3 A summary of classroom pedagogies for effective literacy and numeracy teaching

When teachers use inclusive teaching, Universal Design for Learning, and differentiated instruction, they create learning environments that have important features and they use a range of pedagogies.

- Create a positive learning environment that values students' contributions and accepts error.
- Create a media-rich environment and use the artefacts around the classroom during teaching; encourage students to use the artefacts when they are working in groups or independently.
- Make connections between what is to be learned and students' interests, motivation, and real-life experiences and challenges.
- Ensure active engagement, for example through investigations or problem-based learning.
- Explicitly tell students the purpose and goals of the lesson.
- Provide an outline or overview of what will be taught in the lesson.
- Provide information and allow students to respond orally, in print and through multimedia.
- Use a combination of direct teaching by the teacher only, teaching involving a gradual release of responsibility through supported learning, and individual student learning.
- Scaffold instruction using modelling, questioning, and the use of aids (e.g., concrete materials and manipulatives, visual prompts, cognitive and mnemonic strategies).
- Provide examples.
- Focus on the process of learning.
- Teach strategies explicitly—that is, teach students how to learn. Focus on both cognitive and metacognitive strategies.
- Model, demonstrate, and encourage students to think aloud the strategies they are using.
- Use homogeneous or heterogeneous group and pair approaches. When students are working in groups, make sure they are aware of the purpose of the group. When groups are organised for collaboration, ensure students have the skills to promote each other's learning and socialisation.
- Provide individual instructional support when necessary.
- Provide opportunities for students to use technology such as software, programs, the internet, e-books, audio players, digital cameras, modems, laser disk players, video players, whiteboards, graphics calculators, and CD-ROMs.
- Ensure there are frequent opportunities for students to respond.
- Actively monitor progress.
- Provide frequent, targeted, and explicit feedback that focuses on achievement and motivation.

Literacy and numeracy programs

Sometimes particular content and pedagogies are organised as programs. Both literacy and numeracy programs can be categorised as:

- first wave, referring to early years' classroom-based teaching with the focus on preventing literacy and numeracy problems;
- second wave, referring to early intervention programs; and
- third wave, referring to subsequent interventions, typically involving older primary or middle school students.

Some examples of second and third wave programs follow.

SECOND WAVE PROGRAMS

Reading Recovery

Clay (1993) developed this program for children who have the poorest performance in reading after one year of instruction. The program provides accelerated learning so that students can catch up with their peers who are performing at the average of their class. Typically, this takes 12–20 weeks. If students do not achieve satisfactorily in the program, they are removed and offered alternative support. The program is intensive with short lessons of 30 minutes daily.

Opinions about the efficacy of Reading Recovery are strongly polarised and the results of the studies are ambiguous (see Reynolds & Wheldall, 2007). In their recent Queensland study, Wyatt-Smith, Elkins, Colbert, Gunn, and Muspratt (2007) found that students who had Reading Recovery "… are, on average, well below their classmates in reading and writing at Years 3, 5 and 7, but they are comparable to those who received other interventions, and better than those who were referred for different ongoing support" (pp. 35–36). The authors also noted that in their study all the groups gained "at approximately the same rate … which is encouraging, and perhaps better than might be expected if the Matthew Effect [Stanovich, 1986] was powerful (the latter suggesting that rates of progress would diverge)" (p. 36).

To deliver greater efficacy, some researchers (e.g., Chapman, Tunmer, & Prochnow, 2001) called for explicit instruction to develop phonological skills within Reading Recovery, while others (Wyatt-Smith et al., 2007) have suggested that given other and broader conceptualisations of literacy learning, additional language opportunities and/or sociocultural foundations for engaging in literacy learning for some groups of students are warranted.

phonological
Processes or rules about the ways in which the sound patterns of a language are simplified.

Mathematics Recovery

Developed in 1992, Mathematics Recovery (Wright, 1991; 2003) is an early years, short-term intervention for students who achieve poorly in mathematics. It involves three central elements: counting, grouping and number words, and numerals. Some key features of Mathematics Recovery are:

- intensive, individualised teaching of low-attaining six- to eight-year-old children by specialist teachers for teaching cycles of 10–15 weeks in length;
- an extensive professional development course to prepare the specialist teachers, and ongoing collegial and leader support for these teachers;
- use of a strong underpinning theory of young children's mathematical learning;
- use of a learning framework to guide assessment and teaching; and
- use of a specially developed instructional approach, and distinctive instructional activities and assessment procedures.

Assessment is interview-based and seeks to identify both student knowledge and the strategies used. The assessment can be profiled over time, and linked to teaching via the Learning Framework in Number. The approach to instruction conforms to the zone of proximal development (to which we referred earlier). Mathematics Recovery has led to an inservice program in New South Wales called Count Me in Too (New South Wales Government Department of Education and Training, 2003). Building on the work in Mathematics Recovery, Wright, Stanger, Stafford, and Martland (2006a, b) have described their inquiry-based approach to teaching early number concepts and provided numerous examples of teaching activities and described teaching strategies for the development of students' more sophisticated knowledge of number.

THIRD WAVE PROGRAMS

The task of developing effective literacy and numeracy interventions for students beyond the early years and into middle and high school has been more difficult than in the second wave. Many authors have argued that students with difficulties (still) need to have intensive, explicit, and systematic instruction. However, it is important that older students are supported to develop skills and strategies to tackle the content area texts that dominate the middle and secondary years of schooling. In some cases, programs have been created for special populations of students. Some of these programs are used in out-of-school or withdrawal settings, but others have been developed for use in the regular classroom.

WriteIdeas

WriteIdeas was explicitly developed to be used by regular classroom teachers at the middle-school level. The program was created to assist teachers to develop and improve the writing of students with developmental disabilities and learning difficulties in regular classrooms. However, it was quickly adopted as a whole class program to teach writing (Moni, Jobling, van Kraayenoord, Elkins, Miller, & Koppenhaver, 2007; van Kraayenorrd, Moni, Jobling, Koppenhaver, & Elkins, 2003, 2004).

The program involves professional learning during which teachers develop knowledge, skills, and attitudes related to writing and the writing process, an awareness of the learner characteristics of students with developmental disabilities and learning difficulties, the principles of planning instructional support, and knowledge of teaching practices, learning activities, and tools for developing writing.

Teachers also learn about technology that can be used to support writing. Research related to the program has shown that the teachers involved in a year-long implementation of writing instruction based on the professional learning program developed knowledge of the writing process and a repertoire of teaching practices around the WriteIdeas Model. Students' metacognitive knowledge of the self-as-a-writer changed after the instruction they received, while changes in students' writing achievement is currently being investigated.

Literacy and Technology—Hands On (Latch-On)

Latch-On is a two-year post-school literacy program for young adults with intellectual disabilities. The program draws on over 30 years of research on children and young adults with intellectual disabilities and has been developed and researched by a team from the University of Queensland (Moni & Jobling, 2001; Lloyd, Moni, & Jobling, 2006).

Latch-On is framed by philosophical underpinnings connected to socio-cultural theories of literacy learning. Latch-On recognises the importance of multi-literacies and provides a structured approach to help students engage with print, oral, and multimedia domains in a wide range of contexts so that they better understand and participate in the world in which they live. The program is sequenced over two

years, with students attending two days a week. The four semesters of work in the program have been designed using the Four Resources Model to ensure a balanced approach.

Counting On

Counting On is a New South Wales program developed to support numeracy learning in middle years students. By about Year 7, many students have become confused about mathematical processes and may benefit from systematic teaching of concepts and problem-solving strategies. Its focus is professional development of teachers so that they can assess students' difficulties and provide instruction that targets the specific learning needs of the students. The Counting On website (New South Wales Government Department of Education and Training, 2007b) lists a number of elements for teachers to consider (see <www.curriculumsupport.education.nsw.gov.au/counting_on/Pages/Home.html>). These include:

- counting by ones;
- numbers within numbers;
- unitary procedures;
- place value;
- linguistic or conceptual place value;
- partitioning and decomposition;
- jump or split;
- mental computation; and
- imagery.

Working Out What Works (WOWW)

Working Out What Works (WOWW) is a professional development program that was created to support teachers to improve literacy and numeracy outcomes for students with learning difficulties in Years 4, 5, and 6 (Australian Government Department of Education, Science and Training 2007c). Based on research into effective intervention approaches, the program recommends that teachers use a Combined Direct Instruction and Strategy Instruction approach.

With the aim of mastery learning, Direct Instruction in this combined approach refers to the direct or explicit teaching of skills, including the use of drill and practice at a fast pace, and structured and systematic corrective feedback for errors. Direct Instruction is mostly teacher-controlled and often scripted, and most often involves small group teaching. Some researchers have suggested that the teaching of strategies involves small concrete steps, while others have suggested the use of teacher or peer modelling; guided student practice through the use of techniques such as overt verbalisations or thinking aloud and feedback are also used.

In the research that the Australian Council for Educational Research conducted on WOWW, a published Direct Instruction program, Corrective Reading (Englemann, Meyer, Carnine, Becker, & Johnson, 2001), was used, while the Strategy Instruction was based on teachers selecting strategies related to the needs of the students in their classrooms and using their knowledge of Strategy Instruction developed in the professional development program. This knowledge comprised teacher explanation, modelling, and creating opportunities for guided and independent practice.

Programs for Indigenous students

Of the factors influencing the literacy and numeracy achievement of Indigenous students, the most important are poverty and poor health conditions. For example, middle-ear disease is a particular problem that leads to hearing disabilities and affects students' abilities to hear and perceive speech. There are a number of promising initiatives for these students. One well-known initiative to support Indigenous students' literacy achievement is reported here.

The National Accelerated Literacy Program (NALP) (2007) operates in remote communities in the Northern Territory, northern Western Australia, South Australia, and one school in Queensland. This program was originally known as Scaffolding Literacy™. Created by Brian Gray and Wendy Cowey, it initially provides students with an orientation to books following the elements of the Four Resources Model (code-breaker, text-participant, text-user, text-analyst). It includes discussions using preformulation (drawing students' attention to aspects of text), focus questions, and reformulations (accepting students' responses and expanding on them). Students then undertake independent reading before moving to writing texts. NALP is being used and evaluated in the Northern Territory from 2004 to 2008.

Other resources related to teaching Indigenous students are *Building bridges: Literacy development in young Indigenous children*, written by Fleer and Williams-Kennedy (2002), and *Aboriginal voices: Activities and resources for English*, produced by the Department of Education, Training and Employment (2000).

LEARNING ESSENTIALS

In this section we focus on how students respond to the teaching they receive, and examine some of the reasons for these responses. We also identify several abilities that are fundamental to the development of literacy and numeracy and that we believe underlie acquisition and progress in literacy and numeracy. We have selected abilities that appear to be common to both literacy and numeracy. We also explore aspects of students' environments that promote learning.

The individuality of learners

While it is obvious that learning is, at least in part, governed by innate abilities (Olson, 2006), the role of the brain and its relationship to learning of literacy and numeracy and education is a contested area (see, e.g., Hall, 2007; Willis, 2007). There is, however, some research in the cognitive neurosciences that has provided insights into individual differences in some areas of learning. For example, there is evidence that severe reading difficulties (sometimes referred to as *dyslexia*) are often related to problems with phonological awareness (the ability to recognise and manipulate component sounds in words). In turn, this awareness focuses on the temporo-parietal junction of the brain. In addition, neuroimaging investigations in which evoked response potentials (ERPs) are measured of the basic auditory processing of children with dyslexia suggest that the phonological system is immature, that is, shows delayed development.

dyscalculia

A severe learning difficulty in mathematics.

The origin of severe learning difficulties in mathematics (sometime referred to as having dyscalculia) is also uncertain. Evidence of the relationship between problems in reading and problems in mathematics is clearer in that most students with severe reading problems will have some degree of difficulty in numeracy. However, most of these students respond to specific assistance in those aspects of numeracy in which they need help. In other words, their mathematical difficulties are more tractable than their literacy problems.

Goswami stated (2004, pp. 8–9) that:

> *if dyslexia has a phonological basis, then it seems likely that the mathematical system affected in these children should be the verbal system underpinning counting and calculation. Dyslexic children with mathematical difficulties may show neural anomalies in the activation of this system ... [and] children with dyscalculia who do not have reading difficulties may show different patterns of impairment.*

It is important to note that while many of the neurocognitive studies are providing exciting findings, they are mostly still preliminary investigations. Furthermore, the implications of these studies for learning to become literate (and numerate) and for what and how teachers should teach are at best speculative.

While there may be groups of literacy and numeracy learners who have similar problems, not all students have problems in all literacies (i.e., strands of literacy) or all the elements of literacy knowledge and skill (e.g., decoding and comprehension). The same is true in numeracy. Those with difficulties will not necessarily have difficulties in all the content areas of mathematics. Students can be at different levels of proficiency for different basic facts. For example, a student might be able to retrieve doubles up to 9 plus 9 from memory, add one by verbal counting on, and yet need to manipulate blocks for 8 plus 4. Although students might understand mathematics problems such as adding two 2-digit numbers, they lose confidence if they obtain incorrect solutions because of a weakness in underlying skills such as mental addition.

Furthermore, not all strands and/or content areas in mathematics are necessary to be competent literacy and mathematics learners. Students with vision impairment, for example, may use colour in different ways from sighted students, and handwriting may be redundant for students with a physical impairment who use computers for word-processing. This suggests that attention must given to students' individual needs. For students with physical disabilities, alternative or augmentative communication systems are important for many students' development in literacy and numeracy. You will have discovered these in Chapter 6 (e.g., communication boards, which comprise pictures, photos, and illustrations to which the student points to communicate; talking keyboards).

Common abilities in both literacy and numeracy

ACCURACY AND SPEED

Many aspects of literacy and all aspects of mathematics require accuracy. Reading and spelling in literacy and computation in mathematics require the learner to be accurate. In computation, both accuracy and speed are necessary in basic fact retrieval since these enable cognitive resources to be allocated to more complex tasks. One difference between literacy and numeracy with respect to accuracy is that mathematics requires accuracy at all steps and, thus, can be more difficult than literacy since there is usually some redundancy in language. Nevertheless, accurate decoding in reading allows cognitive resources to be allocated to the more complex task of comprehension.

While speed may be important, students who have problems with numeracy make slow progress in replacing physical counting strategies (using fingers or objects to count) with verbal counting and, in turn, with accurate and quick retrieval from memory. Where the problems appear to stem from slow or inaccurate computation, intervention should focus on teaching students to use appropriate strategies that ensure that their understanding is given priority, although at some point it will be necessary to increase their speed of use of strategies or the use of recall from memory. Spelling difficulties that reflect problems with accuracy may be tackled by focusing on developing students' strategies through explicit teacher-directed training in strategy use and encouraging self-monitoring of spelling errors.

FLUENCY/AUTOMATICITY

Fluency in reading refers to the ability to recognise words and comprehend at the same time. Most understandings of fluency in reading are based on theories of automaticity (performing cognitive tasks without having to think about them) and information processing (using ways of storing and retrieving information). Suggestions made to improve students' fluency in reading include:

- repeated reading (i.e., multiple reading of the same text);
- using simple practice in reading (e.g., through Sustained Silent Reading); and
- ensuring that instruction is given in the elements of reading, specifically letter knowledge, phonemic awareness, decoding and word recognition.

While there is research to indicate the efficacy of repeated reading, the effect of simple practice is unclear, and intervention programs that emphasise that fluency should be embedded in the teaching of all the elements listed above have yet to be evaluated. In mathematics, automaticity is predominantly linked with mathematics facts. Researchers have suggested that automaticity in the basic facts might be best developed using a combined approach of strategy instruction and timed practice drills (see Woodward, 2006). With respect to populations such as those with intellectual disabilities, efforts should be made to have these students acquire fluency with addition and multiplication facts so that they can apply these in daily tasks, such as measurement and understanding information provided in numerical form.

COMPREHENSION

Comprehension involves extracting and assigning meaning through interaction with text. Traditional views have suggested that comprehension in literacy involves identifying the main ideas and the theme, the author's purpose, finding supporting details, making inferences and being able to summarise texts.

More recent views of comprehension in literacy include critical and evaluative comprehension processes. These are used when students, for example, evaluate and negotiate meanings, explore multiple perspectives, and understand how the text language reflects power relationships in society.

Comprehension or understanding in mathematics has been described as knowing that, knowing how, knowing why, and knowing to. According to Goos et al. (2007), mathematical understanding is a "continual process of negotiating meaning, or of attempting to make sense of what one is learning" (p. 24).

Comprehension difficulties often emerge in the upper primary grades (Year 4 and above). This is found not just in English but also in mathematics. For example, students may have difficulties comprehending mathematical word problems.

There are three common forms of assistance provided to students with difficulties in comprehension in both literacy and mathematics. These are:

- teaching of basic skills to develop fluency, vocabulary, and a knowledge base;
- assisting students to use text enhancements to highlight or organise information and improve understanding of it, such as using visual representations (e.g., symbols, graphs, charts); and
- metacognitive approaches that teach awareness of task demands and strategies such as prediction, monitoring, and correction procedures.

STUDENTS' LANGUAGE AND THE SPECIAL LANGUAGE OF THE CURRICULUM AREA

A number of difficulties in both literacy and numeracy appear to be language-related. These difficulties can appear as problems with metalinguistic abilities (i.e., awareness of how language works, syntax, and the structure of language, such as word order); phonological processing skills (e.g., associating letters in words with their respective sounds through blending, segmenting and sequencing sounds); and metacognition—knowledge and regulation of thinking when using literacy skills. Knowing the sounds and blends (phonemic awareness) also has implications for spelling, when spoken words must be analysed into component parts and the sounds matched to combinations of letters. If students are not aware of this connection, they often have difficulties with spelling.

metacognition

Knowledge of self, of tasks and of strategy characteristics that influence learning and self-regulation of that knowledge during learning and problem-solving activities.

One of the most pervasive problems in mathematics is associated with the language of mathematics. Young children can find the vocabulary to be a stumbling block, as teachers might assume that concepts such as more, less, more than, less than, first, next, and last are familiar to students. Later, students might have trouble remembering the meaning of specifically mathematical words or symbols. It is useful to teach mathematical symbol-reading explicitly. Also, in English the number words between 11 and 19 represent their magnitude less clearly than larger numbers (21, 22, and so on). Students can, therefore, have difficulty recognising the structure of numbers from 11 and 19 if these are expressed only in words.

Allen (2007) argued that vocabulary instruction should make words relevant, memorable, and useful. She suggested that these three attributes are best developed in discussions around text and within tasks.

In a traditional classroom, the teacher asks the questions and knows the answers. If questions are repeated, this signals to students that they have not supplied the right answer. In contrast, it is possible to use language as a scaffold for learning about mathematics. For example, if students find it hard to understand word problems, teachers can engage in discussion with students about the real-life situation that the word problem refers to, asking students to express their ideas and responding to them, so that the students are engaged in deep thinking, not trying to guess what the teacher wants them to say.

One of the main reasons for the difficulties of students with hearing impairments in literacy and numeracy is their delayed development in speech and language. There has been relatively little research on numeracy among students with hearing impairments and this contrasts sharply with the considerable attention to their literacy. Obviously, their problems with language affect learning in other areas. This includes numeracy—which has a complex language that requires precise interpretation.

COGNITION AND METACOGNITION

cognition

The process of thinking, that is, knowing, perceiving, reasoning, and problem-solving.

Reasoning can be a limiting factor for students who have intellectual disabilities, but, for most students experiencing difficulties in literacy and numeracy, poor reasoning ability is usually not the cause. For example, many students demonstrate quite capable reasoning outside mathematics classes and in their daily activities outside school. If problems with applying mathematical reasoning are found, students should use both cognitive and metacognitive strategies, just as is true for reading comprehension.

Metacognition refers to students' knowledge of themselves as learners, of the task, and of strategy characteristics that influence learning, as well as the self-regulation of that knowledge. The strategies used in self-regulation include planning, monitoring, revising or self-correcting, and evaluating and apply to both literacy and numeracy learning. Several groups of students have difficulties with metacognition and strategy use.

The teaching of strategies is one of the most important and effective ways in which metacognition can be generated in literacy and numeracy. However, it appears that strategy instruction that is deeply embedded in curriculum content learning is the most powerful. Programs like Reciprocal Teaching that teach reading strategies were considered in Robyn Gillies and Paul Pagliano's chapter.

PROVIDING SUPPORT THAT RESPONDS TO STUDENTS

As schools increasingly use a three-wave model of instruction, the types of support offered in literacy and numeracy are altering. The need for second and third wave intervention can be minimised by improving the quality of the classroom program. In particular, this requires the application of research-based teaching approaches and strategies, and the use of assessment that identifies students' needs (Wyatt-Smith et al., 2007).

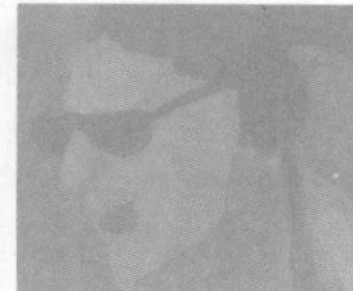

Some students, however, will experience difficulties that require greater support than might be provided by their teachers. Thus, other professionals (e.g., speech-language pathologists) and specialist teachers (e.g., support teachers, teacher-librarians), teacher aides and volunteers often provide help to these students individually or in small groups.

One concern is that if this support is provided in class time, the students may miss class instruction. Help provided out of class time, at school or elsewhere, increases instructional time, though it may also involve additional expense. Another concern is that the students most needing help may be assisted by less expert persons than their teacher (Wyatt-Smith et al., 2007). Furthermore, when students are withdrawn from the regular classroom for special or intensive instruction, the assumption is that the students will receive more effective instruction than is available in the regular classroom. However, often there is little congruency or consistency between practices used in withdrawal settings and those used in the regular classroom. More importantly, there is little transfer from one setting to the other. Often what students learn in the withdrawal setting is not applied when they return to the regular classroom (Wyatt-Smith et al., 2007).

Another perspective on the role of other professionals and specialist teachers is that they should be used to increase the skills of classrooms teachers, such as by collaborating in the classroom, helping them carry out action research or offering them professional development. To ensure that other professionals and specialist teachers can work together with classroom teachers and vice versa, both groups need to be skilled at working collaboratively. Collaboration skills include sharing of common goals, understanding each other's professional language, having the same expectations and demands of the students, using each other's respective specialist knowledge and skills for curriculum planning, teaching and assessment, and providing feedback to each other on the effectiveness of their work together.

SUMMARY

In this chapter, the many ways in which literacy(ies) and numeracy have been understood have been described. You have also learned about some of the difficulties that students have in literacy and numeracy. It is an ongoing challenge to understand the differences of students, and to see them not as problems but as opportunities that allow teachers to incorporate various approaches and teaching strategies. It is also helpful to draw upon basic psychological principles of learning and motivation, and to understand the social and cultural forces that influence learning.

Education systems and schools have implemented instructional support and intervention programs that can be used with groups or individual students. Notwithstanding this, teachers still need to understand the individual literacy and numeracy needs of their students and plan curricula, instruction, and assessment that will develop their students' competencies and meet these needs. In order to do so, teachers need to be ready to use a range of teaching approaches and strategies. Working together collaboratively with colleagues means that teachers can share their challenges and successes.

USING THIS CHAPTER IN SCHOOLS

At the start of this chapter we pointed to the importance for all students of developing competencies in literacy(ies) and numeracy. We suggested that such competencies contribute to personal and social growth and help individuals transform their own lives, as well as enhance their participation with their family, community and the world. As a teacher, therefore, you have a crucial role in ensuring students acquire and develop these competencies.

All teachers are teachers of literacy and numeracy, and although middle and secondary schools teachers may be specialists in teaching particular school subjects (e.g., science or history), they also have a responsibility to plan and provide instruction in literacy and numeracy alongside their content area.

The teacher

In the classroom, you will see and experience the various understandings of literacy and numeracy, and the theories and models of literacy and numeracy in practice. The elements of literacy that we have identified are consistent with using the Four Resources Model, and it is important for you to ask if these elements are those considered most relevant in your school. Some (e.g., phonemic awareness, word recognition skills, and comprehension) might be emphasised more in the early years of schooling. The content of the mathematics curriculum will be common across Australia classrooms, although it is necessary to establish if specific areas are dominant at particular year levels in your school.

You will notice considerable diversity among the students you teach. Such diversity means that you will have to assess your students' strengths and needs in regard to their knowledge, skills, strategies, and motivation in literacy and numeracy. Appropriate assessment practices are essential here. You need to be critical of assessment and testing practices employed in your state or territory, in your school and in your classroom to ensure that they suit the audience(s) and purpose(s) of assessment. Remember here that "being critical" does not necessarily mean "being negative".

You may also notice students who are having trouble in learning literacy and numeracy. To address these difficulties you will need to plan curricula and instruction based on the assessment information you have collected and analysed. Such planning involves thinking about how the knowledge and experiences that the students possess will be used in the selection of curricula and in your teaching.

We have called for teachers to plan for the use of inclusive, responsive approaches and teaching strategies involving the principles of Universal Design for Learning (UDL) and the practices of differentiated instruction. We suspect that few teachers use UDL *first* in their planning and, therefore, must make modifications as part of differentiated instruction that could be avoided if UDL were used first. Worse still, sometimes teachers make no modifications in response to the failure of their students to learn particular literacy or numeracy concepts, or to use particular skills and strategies.

It would be interesting for you to reflect on and evaluate how much retrofitting occurs in the instruction you observe or in which you participate, and to record the modifications that are made during, and subsequent to, the delivery of instruction. What implications can you draw from your reflection and investigation?

You will also need to know and use a range of teaching approaches and strategies. Those suggested in this chapter have emerged from the research literature and from findings of Australian studies of classroom practices. There is efficacy data on the majority of these approaches and strategies but this is not the case for many others used in literacy and numeracy lessons in schools.

Become aware of the various literacy and numeracy programs that are available. Some have been designed for particular student populations. As you learned in the chapter, there are some programs that are responses to the achievement gap between Indigenous students and other students. Although you may have only a few Indigenous students in your classroom, if any, it is important to be aware of government initiatives and to support your colleagues who are working with these students.

Schools employ various professionals, besides teachers, who may have specialist knowledge about learning and supporting students, such as support teachers and teacher librarians. Make an effort to get to know these very important colleagues when you are planning programs and lessons. Do you have the skills necessary to undertake such collaborations? Who in the school can assist you develop these skills?

The students

In the first part of this chapter we identified the relationship between engagement, motivation, and students' desire to learn and improve their literacy and numeracy. And we also suggested that teachers focus on developing students' self-efficacy. Activities where choice and challenge are provided and tasks based on students' interests and preferences are generally very successful for engaging interest and maintaining persistence.

Similarly, instruction that includes praise and provides supportive feedback about performance will also build students' feelings of self-worth and enhance their efforts to learn. Talk with the students in your classroom. Learn about what motivates them. What tasks and texts do they like? You will also find that many of your students like to work with their peers. As we indicated in the chapter, because learning is a social practice, students enjoy learning from, and with, each other. What activities can you design that increase students' opportunities to learn from and with each other?

Accuracy and speed, fluency/automaticity, comprehension, students' language, and cognition and metacognition are regarded as building blocks of literacy and numeracy achievement. Be aware of these variables and create opportunities to develop these abilities and processes through direct teaching and classroom activities.

When your students are having difficulties, it is imperative that you provide timely and intensive instruction. Talk to the other professionals in your school and get their views about ways in which they provide support for students.

Finally, your students cannot make progress in any area without your strong support and effective teaching. Remember also that you can get valuable support from the community, your education system, and your school. Success for your students and for you will come about from honouring the rights of your students and valuing your own.

PRACTICAL ACTIVITIES

Uni-work

1 As a group activity, visit a workplace in your university (e.g., the student union offices, the refectory, a foyer located near one of the faculty or departmental offices, the sports or recreation centre). During your visit, gather information about the use or applications of literacy and numeracy in that workplace. Look for information about the range of tasks, the purposes and audience for each task, and the nature of the literacy and numeracy practices employed by various types of workers. Make a note if technology is used in any of the tasks. Make sure you also examine the physical environment, and collect or, if appropriate, digitally record relevant artefacts.

   Following the visit, compile a list of literacy and numeracy knowledge, skills, and strategies that the workers were using. Identify any overlap between literacy and numeracy. Categorise the tasks and artefacts with respect to whether they are literacy-only, numeracy-only, or integrated literacy and numeracy.

   Present your findings using both numeracy and literacy. What conclusions can you draw from your analyses of the information? What implications do your findings have for the teaching and learning of literacy and numeracy in schools in terms of preparation for the use of literacy and numeracy in the workplace?

2 Visit your local library. Select two sections of the library (e.g., adult crime novels, play materials for infants and toddlers, self-help books about maths learning, health magazines, audiobooks).

Examine the resources for indications of inclusion. Make comparisons between the two sections. Detail how the materials in each section you have chosen contribute to inclusion or exclusion. Also consider the factors of language and cultural background, including those of Indigenous students, of gender, and of motivation that you have read about in this chapter.

What recommendations would you make to the library based on your findings? What recommendations would you make to various groups of library users?

3 Go to cast.org or other internet sites about Universal Design for Learning. Develop a set of three or four interactive and engaging activities linked to the development of one particular skill in numeracy or literacy (e.g., in literacy the skill might be inferential comprehension of written material). Make sure that each activity incorporates the nine principles of Universal Design for Learning that you have learned about in this chapter.

School-work

Remember that school policies may apply that restrict your ability to complete one or more of the activities suggested below. Before beginning any of the following activities, speak to your supervising teacher or a member of the school administration to confirm that you can undertake the activity within existing school guidelines and policies.

4 Interview one of your colleagues at school who teaches a student with a disability (e.g., ASD, intellectual disability). Ask the teacher what the student can do well in literacy or numeracy. Also ask about the student's needs in literacy or numeracy.

Ask the teacher to comment on how the school is meeting the literacy or numeracy needs of the student. Specifically, what program(s) is(are) being used? What teaching approaches and strategies are being used? Apart from this teacher, who else in the school is providing support? What conclusions can you draw about the nature of the support provided at school with respect to the student's needs?

5 Identify a second- or third-wave intervention program in literacy or numeracy that is being used in your school. This may be more relevant to preschool through middle years, although it is possible that you might find an intervention like this in secondary schools.

Talk to the teacher who coordinates this program and pose the following questions:

- What is the purpose of the intervention with respect to literacy or numeracy?
- What strands of the relevant syllabus are addressed?
- What specific knowledge, skills and attitudes are addressed?
- What characteristics of the program make it an intervention program?
- In what ways are students asked to respond to the program?
- In the teacher's view, what are the strengths of the program and what are the weaknesses?
- With respect to the weaknesses, how would the teacher address these in an ideal situation?

Following your interview with the teacher, undertake a literature search to establish the research evidence related to this program. To organise your thinking, respond to the following questions:

- What evidence in the literature suggests that the program is effective or not effective?
- What constraints does the literature identify with respect to the program?
- According to the literature, what needs to be done to improve the intervention?
- What further studies need to be undertaken?

Share the outcomes of your investigation with your teacher. If you discover there is poor efficacy or no research evidence related to the program, what are your conclusions?

6 Parents can assist their children in both literacy and numeracy in the home. Select a year/grade level relevant to the students you are teaching. With the help of the material in the teachers' professional library in the school, create a brochure for the parents of these students focusing on a particular aspect of literacy or numeracy. There may also be DVDs or CDs in the teachers' library that might be useful.

The brochure should comprise suggestions, tips, or activities in a particular aspect of literacy or numeracy that will help the parents support their child at home. For example, "Tips for listening to your child read aloud", "Helping your children with writing in project work" or "Tips for practising mental computation at home".

SUGGESTED READING AND RESOURCES

Books

Konza, D. (2003). *Teaching children with reading difficulties*. Tuggerah, NSW: Social Science Press.

Shaddock, A., Giorcelli, L., & Smith, S. (2007). *Students with disabilities in mainstream classrooms: A resource for teachers*. Canberra: Australian Government Department of Education, Science and Training.

Westwood, P. (2000). *Numeracy and learning difficulties: Approaches to teaching and assessment*. Camberwell, Vic: ACER Press.

Westwood, P. (2006). *Teaching and learning difficulties.* Camberwell, Vic: Australian Council for Educational Research.

Websites

<www.alea.edu.au>—Australian Literacy Educators' Association.

<www.literacyandnumeracy.gov.au/forteachers/default.htm>—Australian Government site for literacy and numeracy.

<www.aate.org.au>—Australian Association for the Teaching of English.

<www.aamt.edu.au>—Australian Association of Mathematics Teachers.

<www.nctm.org>—National Council of Teachers of Mathematics.

<http://CAST.org>—Universal Design for Learning.

REFERENCES

Afflerbach, P. (2005). *National Reading Conference Policy Brief: High stakes testing and reading assessment: Journal of Literacy Research*, *37*, 151–162.

Afflerbach, P. (2007). *Understanding and using reading assessment, K–12.* Newark, DE: International Reading Association.

Allen, J. (2007). Mastering the art of effective vocabulary instruction. In K. Beers, R. E. Probst, & L. Rief (Eds), *Adolescent literacy: Turning promise into practice* (pp. 87–104). Portsmouth, NH: Heinemann.

Allington, R., Guice, S., Michelson, N., Baker, K., & Li, S. (1996). Literature-based curricula in high poverty schools. In M. M. Graves, P. van den Broek, & B. M. Taylor (Eds), *The first R: Every child's right to read* (pp. 73–95). Newark, NJ: International Reading Association.

Alloway, N. & Gilbert, P. (2002). Gender and literacy in early childhood contexts: Boys on the side? In L. Makin & C. Jones Diaz (Eds), *Literacies in early childhood* (pp. 251–269). Sydney: MacLellan & Petty.

Alloway, N., Freebody, P., Gilbert, P., & Muspratt, S. (2002). *Boys' literacy and schooling: Expanding the repertoires of practice.* Melbourne: Curriculum Corporation <www.dest.gov.au/sectors/school_education/publications_resources/profiles/boys_ literacy_schooling.htm>, accessed 1 December 2007.

Anstey, M. & Bull, G. (2006). *Teaching and learning multiliteracies: Changing times, changing literacies.* Kensington Gardens, SA: Australian Literacy Educators' Association and Newark, DE: International Reading Association.

Australian Association for the Teaching of English (AATE) & Australian Literacy Educators' Association (ALEA) (2002). *Standards for Teachers of English Language and Literacy in Australia: STELLA Standards Framework* <www.stella.org.au/statements.html>, accessed 1 December 2007.

Australian Association of Mathematics Teachers (2006). *Standards for Excellence in Teaching Mathematics in Australian schools* <www.aamt.edu.au>, accessed 30 November 2007.

Australian Government, Department of Education, Science and Training (1999). *The Adelaide Declaration on National Goals for Schooling in the Twenty-first Century* <www.dest.gov.au/sectors/school_education/policy_initiatives_reviews/national_goals_for_schooling_in_the_twenty_first_century.htm>, accessed 1 December 2007.

Australian Government, Department of Education, Science and Training (2004). *Researching numeracy teaching approaches in primary schools* <www.dest.gov.au/NR/rdonlyres/603355E5-3EDE-4F00-9A37-C45DAEB CC4C7/4550/Full_document.pdf>, accessed 23 November 2007.

Australian Government, Department of Education, Science and Training (2005a). *Teaching reading: Reports and recommendations. National inquiry into the teaching of literacy* <www.dest.gov.au/nitl/report.htm>, accessed 12 December 2005.

Australian Government, Department of Education, Science and Training (2005b). *Building mathematical understanding in the classroom: A constructivist teaching approach* <www.dest.gov.au/sectors/school_education/ publications_resources/profiles/building_mathematical_understanding.htm>, accessed 1 December 2007.

Australian Government, Department of Education, Science and Training (2007a). *Your child's future—Literacy and numeracy in Australia's schools* <www.dest.gov.au/sectors/school_education/publications_ resources/summaries_brochures/your_childs_future.htm>, accessed 23 November 2007.

Australian Government, Department of Education, Science and Training (2007b). *Reading Assistance Voucher Programme* www.dest.gov.au/NR/rdonlyres/AF3A8DBE-5FCE-4B4B-8EAD-56E51CEF1D71/14019/RAV Brochure.pdf>, accessed 23 November 2007.

Australian Government, Department of Education, Science and Training (2007c). *Working Out What Works (WOWW) Training and Resource Manual: A teacher professional development program designed to support teachers to improve literacy and numeracy outcomes for students with learning difficulties in Years 4, 5 and 6* (2nd ed.). Camberwell, Vic: Author.

Bartolini Bussi, M. G. (1998). Joint activity in mathematics classrooms: A Vygotskyian analysis. In F. Seeger, J. Voigt, & U. Waschescio (Eds), *The culture of the mathematics classroom* (pp. 13–49). Cambridge: Cambridge University Press.

Bauer, A. M. & Kroeger, S. (2004). *Inclusive classroom: Video cases on CD-Rom–Activity and learning guide.* Upper Saddle, NJ: Pearson.

Benjamin, A. & Shermer, M. B. (1991). *Teach your child math.* Los Angeles: Lowell Press.

Bishop, J. (2006, May 6). *Help for children struggling with reading skills.* Media release <www.dest.gov.au/ministers/bishop/ budget06/bud0606.htm>, accessed 23 November 2007.

Booker, G., Bond, D., Sparrow, L., & Swan, P. (2004). *Teaching primary mathematics* (2nd ed.). Frenchs Forest, NSW: Pearson Education.

Borasi, R. & Siegel, M. (2000). *Reading counts: Expanding the role of reading in mathematics classrooms*. New York: Teachers College Press.

Brownwell, M. T. & Walther-Thomas, C. (2000). An interview with Dr Michael Pressley. *Intervention in School and Clinic*, *36*, 105–108.

Burgstahler, S. (2007). *Universal design of instruction (UDI): Definition, principles, and examples*. Seattle, WA: University of Washington <www.washington.edu/doit/Brochures/PDF/instruction.pdf>, accessed 16 November 2007.

Center for Applied Special Technology (CAST) (2007). *Teaching every student* <www.cast.org/teachingeverystudent/toolkits/%20tk_introduction.%20cfm?tk_id=21>, accessed 30 November 2007.

Center for Universal Design (2008). *About UD.* Raleigh, North Carolina State University, Center for Universal Design <www.design.ncsu.edu/about_ud/about_ud.htm>, accessed 30 January 2008.

Chapman, J. W. & Tunmer, W. (2003). Reading difficulties, reading-related self-perceptions, and strategies for overcoming negative self-beliefs. *Reading & Writing Quarterly*, *19*, 357–365.

Chapman, J. W., Tunmer, W. E., & Prochnow, J. E. (2001). Does success in the Reading Recovery program depend on developing proficiency in phonological processing skills? A longitudinal study in a whole language instructional context. *Scientific Studies of Reading*, *5*, 141–176.

Christopherson, S. (1997). Math: New teaching for an old challenge. *Perspectives in Education and Deafness*, *15*(3), 4–6.

Clay, M. (1993). *Reading Recovery: A guide book for teachers in training.* Portsmouth, NH: Heinemann.

Coles, G. (2004). Danger in the classroom: 'Brain Glitch' research and learning to read. *Phi Delta Kappan*, *85*, 344–351.

Cresswell, J., Rowe, K. J., & Withers, G. (2003). *Boys in school and society.* Camberwell, Vic: Australian Council for Educational Research.

Cumming, J. J. & Elkins, J. (1996). Stability of strategy use for addition facts: A training study and implications for instruction. *Journal of Cognitive Education*, *5*, 101–116.

de Bortoli, L. & Cresswell, J. (2004). *Australia's Indigenous students in PISA 2000: Results from an international study.* Camberwell, Vic: ACER Press.

Department of Education, Training and Employment (2000). *Aboriginal voices: Activities and resources for English*. Canberra, ACT: Author.

Deshler, D. D. & Schumaker, J. B. (1986). Learning strategies: An instructional alternative for low-achieving adolescents. *Exceptional Children*, *52*, 583–590.

Elbaum, B., Vaughn, S., Tejero-Hughes, M., & Watson-Moody, S. (2000). How effective are one-to-one tutoring programs in reading for elementary students at-risk for reading failure? A meta-analysis of the intervention research. *Journal of Educational Psychology*, *92*, 605–619.

Englemann, S., Meyer, L., Carnine, L., Becker, W., Eisele, J., & Johnson, G. (2001). *Corrective Reading: Decoding and Comprehension Trainer's Guide*. Columbus, OH: SRA/McGraw-Hill South East Region.

Fleer, M. & Williams-Kennedy, D. (2002). *Building bridges*: *Literacy development in young Indigenous children*. Watson, ACT: Australian Early Childhood Association.

Folkman, S. & Moskowitz, J. T. (2004). Coping: Pitfalls and promise. *Annual Review of Psychology*, *55*, 745–774.

Franklin, J. (2003). *Unlocking mathematics for minority students* <www.ascd.org/publications/curr_update/2003fall/franklin.html>, accessed 30 January 2007.

Frederickson, N. & Jacobs, S. (2001). Controllability attributions for academic performance and the perceived scholastic competence, global self-worth and achievement of children with dyslexia. *School Psychology International*, *22*, 401–416.

García, J. & de Caso, A. M. (2004). Effects of a motivational intervention for improving the writing of children with learning disabilities. *Learning Disability Quarterly*, *27*, 141–159.

García, S. & Sobel, D. (2007). Preparing highly qualified teachers for increasingly diverse schools. *Intervention in School and Clinic*, *42*, 310–317.

Geary, D. C. (1993). Mathematical disabilities: Cognitive, neuropsychological and genetic components. *Psychological Bulletin*, *114*, 345–362.

Gersten, R. & Chard, D. (1999). Number sense: Rethinking arithmetic instruction for students with mathematical disabilities. *Journal of Special Education*, *33*, 18–28.

Giangreco, M. F. (2007). Extending inclusive opportunities: How can students with disabilities meaningfully participate in class if they work many levels below classroom peers? *Educational Leadership*, *64*, 34–37.

Goos, M., Stillman, G., & Vale, C. (2007). *Teaching secondary school mathematics: Research and practice for the 21st century*. Crows Nest, NSW: Allen & Unwin.

Goswami, U. (2004). Neuroscience and education. *British Journal of Educational Psychology*, *74*, 1–14.

Graves, M. F. (2000). A vocabulary program to complement and bolster a middle-grade comprehension program. In B. M. Taylor, M. F. Graves, & P. van den Broek (Eds), *Reading for meaning: Fostering comprehension in the middle grades* (pp. 116–135). Newark, DE: International Reading Association.

Guthrie, J. T. & Wigfield, A. (2000). Engagement and motivation in reading. In M. L. Kamil, P. V. Mosenthal, P. D. Pearson, & R. Barr (Eds), *Handbook of reading research* (Vol. 3, pp. 403–422). New York: Erlbaum.

Guthrie, J. T., Wigfield, A., & Perencevich, K. C. (Eds) (2004). *Motivating reading comprehension: Concept-orientated reading instruction*. Mahwah, NJ: Erlbaum.

Hall, J. (2007). *Neuroscience and education: What can brain science contribute to teaching and learning?* <www.scre.ac.uk/spotlight/%20spotlight92.html>, accessed 1 December 2007.

Hammond, J. (1999). Literacy crisis and ESL education. *The Australian Journal of Language and Literacy*, *22*, 120–134.

Hanbury, L. (2000). Student problems inhibiting the successful answering of geometrical questions. In J. Wakefield (Ed.), *Mathematics: Shaping the future* (pp. 340–347). Melbourne: MAV.

Harris, C. R., Kaff, M. S., Anderson, M. J., & Knackendoffel, A. (2007). Designing flexible instruction. *Principal Leadership*, *7*, 31–39.

Hatano, G. (1997). Learning arithmetic with an abacus. In T. Nunes & P. Bryant (Eds), *Learning and teaching mathematics: An international perspective* (pp. 209–232). Hove, UK: Psychology Press.

Heirdsfield, A. M. & Cooper, T. J. (2004). Factors affecting the process of proficient mental addition and subtraction: Case studies of flexible and inflexible computers. *Journal of Mathematical Behavior*, *23*, 443–463.

Hill, P. W. (1997, October). *The literacy challenge in Australian primary schools.* Paper presented at the APPA/ACPPA National Conference, Sydney, Australia.

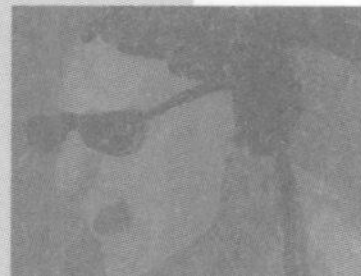

Hitchcock, C., Meyer, A., Rose, D., & Jackson, R. (2002). Providing new access to the general curriculum: Universal design for learning. *Teaching Exceptional Children*, *35*, 8–17.

Hughes, C. A., Ruhl, K. L., Schumaker, J. B., & Deshler, D. D. (2002). Effects of instruction in an assignment completion strategy on the homework performance of students with learning disabilities in general education classes. *Learning Disabilities: Research and Practice*, *17*, 1–18.

Keddie, A. & Mills, M. (2007). *Teaching boys: Developing classroom practices that work.* Crows Nest, NSW: Allen & Unwin.

LaBerge, D. & Samuels S. J. (1974). Toward a theory of automatic information processing in reading. *Cognitive Psychology*, *6*, 293–323.

Lawrence-Brown, D. (2004). Differentiated instruction: Inclusive strategies for standards-based learning that benefit the whole class. *American Secondary Education*, *32*, 34–62.

Linnenbrink, E. A. & Pintrich, P. R. (2003). The role of self-efficacy beliefs in student engagement and learning in the classroom. *Reading and Writing Quarterly: Overcoming Learning Difficulties*, *19*, 199–138.

Lloyd, J., Moni, K.B., & Jobling, A. (2006). Breaking the hype cycle: Using the computer effectively with learners with intellectual disabilities. *Down Syndrome Research and Practice*, *9*, 68–74.

Lokan, J., Ford, P., & Greenwood, L. (1996). *Mathematics and science on the line: Australian junior secondary students' performance in the Third International Mathematics and Science Study*. Melbourne: ACER.

Lokan, J., Greenwood, L., & Cresswell, J. (2001). *15-up and counting, reading, writing, reasoning: How literate are Australian students? The PISA 2000 survey of students' reading, mathematical and scientific literacy skills.* Camberwell, Vic: ACER Press.

Louden, W. (2000). Mapping the territory. In W. Louden, L. K. S. Chan, J. Elkins, D. Greaves, H. House, M. Milton, S. Nichols, M. Rohl, J. Rivalland, & C. van Kraayenoord (Eds), *Mapping the territory. Primary students with learning difficulties: Literacy and numeracy* (Vol. 1, pp. 1–27). Canberra, ACT: Department of Education, Training and Youth Affairs.

Louden, W., Chan, L. K. S., Elkins, J., Greaves, D., House, H., Milton, M., Nichols, S., Rohl, M., Rivalland, J., & van Kraayenoord, C. (2000). *Mapping the territory. Primary students with learning difficulties: Literacy and numeracy* (Vols 1–3). Canberra, ACT: Department of Education, Training and Youth Affairs.

Luke, A. & Freebody, P. (1999). A map of possible practices: Further notes on the Four Resources Model. *Practically Primary*, *4*, 5–8.

Martino, W. & Kehler, M. (2007). Gender-based literacy reform: A question of challenging or recuperating gender binaries. *Canadian Journal of Education*, *30*, 406–431.

Mason, J. & Spence, M. (1998). Toward a psychology of knowing-to. In C. Kane, M. Goos, & E. Warren (Eds), *Teaching mathematics in new times.* Proceeding of the 21st Annual Conference of the Mathematics Education Research Group of Australasia (pp. 342–349). Brisbane, Qld: MERGA.

Mawdsley, R. D. & Cumming, J. J. (2004). High stakes testing and demand for school district accountability: A dilemma for special education students in the United States and Australia. *Australia & New Zealand Journal of Law & Education*, *9*, 19–36.

McGuire, J. M., Scott, S. S., & Shaw, S. F. (2006). Universal design and its applications in educational environments. *Remedial and Special Education*, *27*, 166–175.

Miles, T. R. & Miles, E. (Eds) (1992). *Dyslexia and mathematics*. London: Routledge.

Mochon, S. & Roman, J. V. (1998). Strategies of mental computation used by elementary and secondary school children. *Focus on Learning Problems in Mathematics*, *20*, 35–49.

Moni, K. B. & Jobling, A. (2000). LATCH-ON: A program to develop literacy in young adults with Down syndrome. *Journal of Adolescent and Adult Literacy*, *44*, 40–49.

Moni, K. B. & Jobling, A. (2001). Reading-related literacy learning of young adults with Down syndrome: Findings from a three year teaching and research program. *International Journal of Disability, Development and Education*, *48*, 377–394.

Moni. K. M., Jobling, A., van Kraayenoord, C. E., Miller, R., & Koppenhaver, D. (2007). Teachers' knowledge, attitude, and the implementation of practices around the teaching of writing in inclusive middle years' classrooms: No quick fix. *Educational and Child Psychology*, *24*, 18–36.

Montague, M. (2006). Teaching self-regulation strategies for better math performance in middle school. In M. Montague & A. Jitendra (Eds), *Middle school students with mathematics difficulties* (pp. 89–107). New York: Guilford Press.

Morgan, M., Moni, K.B., & Jobling, A. (2004). What's it all about? Investigating reading comprehension strategies in young adults with Down syndrome. *Down Syndrome Research and Practice*, *9*, 37–44.

National Accelerated Literacy Program (NALP) (2007). *National Accelerated Literacy Program* <www.nalp.edu.au>, accessed 30 November 2007.

National Center on Accessing the General Curriculum (NCAC) (2007). *Differentiated instruction and implications for UDL implementation: Effective classroom practices report.* Washington, DC: US Office of Special Education Programs.

National Council of Teachers and Mathematics (2000). *Principles and standards for school mathematics*. Reston, VA: Author.

National Institute of Child Health and Human Development (2000). *Report of the National Reading Panel. Teaching children to read: An evidence-based assessment of the scientific research literature on reading and its implications for reading instruction.* (NIH Publication No. 00-4769.) Washington, DC: US Government Printing Office.

Nelson, D., Joseph, G. G., & Williams, J. (Eds) (1993) *Multicultural mathematics: Teaching mathematics from a global perspective*. Oxford: Oxford University Press.

New South Wales Government Department of Education and Training (2003). *Count Me In Too. Professional development package.* Ryde, NSW: Author.

New South Wales Government Department of Education and Training (2007a). *National assessment program for literacy and numeracy in 2008: Fact sheet* <www.det.nsw.edu.au/media/downloads/dethome/yr2007/nafl_fact.pdf>, accessed 23 November 2007.

New South Wales Government Department of Education and Training (2007b). *Counting on* <www.curriculumsupport.education.nsw.gov.au/counting_on/Pages/Home.html>, accessed 5 December 2007.

Olson, R. K. (2006). Genes, environment, and dyslexia: The 2005 Norman Geschwind Memorial Lecture. *Annals of Dyslexia*, *5*, 205–238.

Palincsar, A. S. (1986). The role of dialogue in providing scaffolded instruction. *Educational Psychologist*, *21*, 73–98.

Palincsar, A. S. (2007). Reciprocal teaching 1982 to 2006: The role of research, theory and representation in the transformation of instructional research. In D. W. Rowe, R. T. Jiménez, D. L. Compton, D. K. Dickinson, Y. Kim, K. M. Leander, & V. J. Risko (Eds), *56th Yearbook of the National Reading Conference* (pp. 41–52). Oak Creek, WI: National Reading Conference Inc.

Palincsar, A. S. & Brown, A. I. (1984). Reciprocal teaching of comprehension-fostering and comprehension-monitoring activities. *Cognition and Instruction*, *1*, 117–175.

Pisha, B. & Coyne, P. (2001). Smart from the start: The promise of universal design for learning. *Remedial and Special Education*, *22*, 197–203.

Pressley, M. (2002). *Reading instruction that works: The case for balanced teaching* (2nd ed.). New York: The Guilford Press.

Queensland Studies Authority (2007). *Testing: Overview Queensland Years 3, 5 and 7 tests* <www.qsa.qld.edu.au/testing/357tests/ overview.html>, retrieved 16 November 2007.

RAND Reading Study Group (2002). *Reading for understanding: Toward an R&D program in reading comprehension.* Santa Monica, CA: Author.

Reynolds, M. & Wheldall, K. (2007). Reading Recovery 20 years down the track: Looking forward, looking back. *International Journal of Disability, Development and Education*, *54*, 199–223.

Rose, D. H. & Meyer, A. (2002). *Teaching every student in the digital age: Universal design for learning.* Alexandria, VA: Association for Supervision and Curriculum Development.

Rose, D., Gray, B., & Cowey, W. (1999). Scaffolding reading and writing for Indigenous children in school. In P. Wignell (Ed.), *Double power: English literacy and Indigenous education* (pp. 23–60). Melbourne: Language Australia.

Rourke, B. P. & Conway, J. A. (1997). Disabilities of arithmetic and mathematical reasoning: Perspectives from neurology and neuropsychology. *Journal of Learning Disabilities*, *30*, 34–46.

Samuels, S. J. (1994). Toward a theory of automatic information processing in reading, revisited. In R. Ruddell, M. R. Ruddell, & H. Singer (Eds), *Theoretical models and processes of reading* (4th ed., pp. 816–837). Newark, DE: International Reading Association.

Samuels, S. J. (2007). The Dibels Tests: Is speed of barking at print what we mean by reading fluency? *Reading Research Quarterly*, *42*, 563–566.

Schunk, D. H. (2003). Self-efficacy for reading and writing: Influence of modelling, goal-setting, and self-evaluation. *Reading & Writing Quarterly*, *19*, 159–172.

Scott, S. S., McGuire, J. M., & Shaw, S. F. (2001). *Principles for universal design for instruction.* Storrs, CT: University of Connecticut, Center on Postsecondary Education and Disability <www.ahead.org/members/jped/articles/Volume17/17_1/jped171mcguireuniversal.doc>, accessed 18 August 2007.

Scruggs, T. E. & Mastropieri, M. A. (1993). Special education for the twenty-first century: Integrating learning strategies and thinking skills. *Journal of Learning Disabilities*, *26*, 392–398.

Shaddock, T. (2006). *Researching effective teaching and learning practices for students with learning difficulties and disabilities in the Australian Capital Territory: Final research report.* Canberra: Australian Government Department of Education, Science and Training.

Spinks, T. & Kilham, C. (Eds) (2006). *A resource book: Teaching and learning strategies for students with learning difficulties.* Canberra, ACT: Australian Government Department of Education, Science and Training.

Spooner, F., Baker, J. N., Harris, A. A., Ahlgrim-Delzell, L., & Browder, D. M. (2007). Effects of training in universal design for learning on lesson plan development. *Remedial and Special Education*, *28*, 108–116.

Stanovich, K. E. (1986). Matthew effects in reading: Some consequences of individual differences in the acquisition of literacy. *Reading Research Quarterly*, *19,* 278–303.

Stewart, R., Wright, R., & Gould, P. (1998). Kindergarten students' progress in the Count Me In Too project. In C. Kanes, M. Goos, & E. Warren (Eds), *Teaching mathematics in new times* (pp. 556–563). Brisbane: Mathematics Education Research Group of Australasia.

Swanson, H. L. (2001). Searching for the best model for instructing students with learning disabilities. *Focus on Exceptional Children, 34*, 1–15.

Teaching Australia, Australian Institute for Teaching and School Leadership (2007, March). *National professional standards for advanced teaching and school leadership: A consultant paper* <www.teachingaustralia. edu.au/ta/webdav/site/tasite/users/ldeluca/public/National%20professional%20 standards%20for%20advanced%20teaching%20and%20school%20leadership%20-%20A%20consultation% 20paper>, accessed 29 November 2007.

Thomson, S. & Fleming, N. (2004). *Summing it up: Mathematics achievement in Australian schools in TIMSS 2002. TIMSS Australia Monograph No. 6.* Camberwell, Vic: Australian Council for Educational Research.

Thomson, S., McKelvie, P., & Murnane, H. (2006). *Achievement of Australia's early secondary Indigenous students: Findings from TIMSS 2003. TIMSS Australia Monograph No. 10.* Camberwell, Vic: Australian Council for Educational Research.

Tomlinson, C A. (2001). *How to differentiate instruction in mixed-ability classrooms* (2nd ed.). Alexandria, VA: ASCD.

Valli, L. & Buese, D. (2007). The changing roles of teachers in an era of high-stakes accountability. *American Educational Research Journal, 44*, 519–558.

van Kraayenoord, C. E. (1997, September). *Differentiated instruction for all students.* Paper presented at the 21st National Conference of the Australian Association of Special Education Inc., Brisbane, Queensland, Australia.

van Kraayenoord, C. E. (2003). Literacy assessment. In G. Bull & M. Anstey (Eds), *The literacy lexicon* (2nd ed., pp. 273–287). Frenchs Forest, NSW: Prentice Hall.

van Kraayenoord, C. E. (2004). Teaching strategies for reading: How can we assist students with learning difficulties? In B. A. Knight & W. Scott (Eds), *Learning difficulties: Multiple perspectives* (pp. 67–84). Frenchs Forest, NSW: Pearson SprintPrint.

van Kraayenoord, C. E. (2006). Students with disabilities and learning difficulties—assessment is pivotal. *Independent Education, 36*, 24–25.

van Kraayenoord, C. E. (2007). School and classroom practices in inclusive education in Australia. *Childhood Education, 83*, 390–394.

van Kraayenoord, C. E., Moni, K. B., Jobling, A., Koppenhaver, D., & Elkins, J. (2004). Developing the writing of middle school students with developmental disabilities: The WriteIdeas Model of Writing. *Literacy Learning: The Middle Years, 12*, 36–46.

van Kraayenoord, C. E., Moni, K. B., Jobling, A., Koppenhaver, D., & Elkins, J. (2003). *WriteIdeas: Enhancing writing—Teaching students in the middle phase of learning with developmental disabilities in regular classrooms. The manual.* Brisbane, Qld: School of Education, University of Queensland.

van Kraayenoord, C. E., Moni, K. B., Jobling, A., Miller, R., & Koppenhaver, D. (2006, July). *Metacognitive knowledge of writing: Students and individual differences.* Paper presented at the SIG 16 Metacognition at the biennial conference of the European Association for Research on Learning and Instruction, Cambridge, UK.

Vaughn, S., Gersten, R., & Chard, D. J. (2000). The underlying message in LD intervention research: Findings from research syntheses. *Exceptional Children, 67*, 99–114.

Vygostsky, L. S. (1978). *Mind in society: The development of higher psychological processes*. Cambridge: Harvard University Press.

Wilhem, J. F. (1997). *"You gotta be the book": Teaching engaged and reflective reading with adolescents.* New York: Teacher College Press.

Wilhem, J. F. & Smith, M. W. (2007). Making it matter through the power of inquiry. In K. Beers, R. E. Probst, & L. Rief (Eds), *Adolescent literacy: Turning promise into practice* (pp. 231–242). Portsmouth, NH: Heinemann.

Willis, J. (2007). Which brain research can educators trust? *Phi Delta Kappan*, *88*, 697–699.

Willis, S. (Ed.) (1990). *Being numerate: What counts?* Hawthorn, Vic: Australian Council for Educational Research.

Wong, B. Y. L. & Wong, R. (1986). Study behaviour as a function of metacognitive knowledge about critical task variables: An investigation of above average, average and learning disabled readers. *Learning Disabilities Research*, *1*, 101–111.

Woodward, J. (2006). Developing automaticity in multiplication facts: Integration strategy instruction with timed practice drills. *Learning Disability Quarterly*, *29*, 269–289.

Wright, R. J. (1991). What number knowledge is possessed by children entering the kindergarten year of school? *Mathematics Education Research Journal*, *3*, 1–16.

Wright, R. J. (2003). Mathematics Recovery: A program of intervention in early number learning. *Australian Journal of Learning Disabilities*, *8*, 6–11.

Wright, R. J., Martland, J., & Stafford, A. (2000). *Early numeracy: Assessment for teaching and intervention.* London: Paul Chapman.

Wright, R. J., Stanger, G., Stafford, A. K., & Martland, J. (2006a). *Teaching number in the classroom with 4–8 year olds.* Thousand Oaks, CA: Sage.

Wright, R. J., Stanger, G., Stafford, A. K., & Martland, J. G. (2006b). *Teaching number: Advancing children's skills and strategies.* London: Paul Chapman.

Wyatt-Smith, C., Elkins, J., Colbert, P., Gunn, S. J., & Muspratt, A. (2007). *Changing the nature of support provision—Students with learning difficulties: Interventions in literacy and numeracy project (InLaN).* Canberra: Department of Education, Science and Training.

Zevenbergen, R., Dole, S., & Wright, R. (2004). *Teaching mathematics in primary schools.* Crows Nest, NSW: Allen & Unwin.

Zevenbergen, R., Mousley, J., & Sullivan, P. (2004). Making the pedagogic relay inclusive for Indigenous Australian students. *International Journal of Inclusive Education*, *8*, 391–405.

Donna Pendergast, Rod Chadbourne, and Susan Danby

9

EARLY AND MIDDLE YEARS OF SCHOOLING

What you will learn in this chapter

From P to 12, students move through a series of developmental phases. This chapter focuses on inclusion for students from the early years of schooling through to early adolescence, because there have been significant changes that have occurred recently across all Australian education systems catering for those students. Although there are some national and state differences, early childhood education typically encompasses the preschool years and the first years of formal schooling, including the preparatory year and Years 1–3. Middle childhood usually aligns with Years 4 and 5, and in Years 6 to 9 young people enter the phase of early adolescence, which has been popularly named the middle years of schooling.

Early years and middle years' programs can contribute significantly to children and young people's cognitive, social, and health development and to the social support for families. Education is particularly effective for developing networks for supporting children and families with children with physical, cognitive, and sensory disabilities and for children experiencing additional learning needs arising from socioeconomic disadvantage, and because of linguistic, ethnic, and cultural diversity (OECD, 2006).

In this chapter you will learn about:

- how inclusion for the early and middle years offers a set of unique challenges;
- how school communities can promote inclusion for children and young adolescents;
- strategies that teachers can use to build and maintain community in early and middle years' settings;
- factors that influence the success of teachers working with children and young adolescents in inclusive schools;
- practical measures that teachers can take, in light of these factors, to promote the success of inclusion; and
- the different responses that children in the early and middle years have to inclusion, how teachers can identify those responses, and what they can do to ensure that they are positive.

If you are reading this chapter and you are studying to be a secondary school teacher, much of the material contained here will still be relevant to you. At least some of the students you will have, or have already had, in your class will be operating cognitively, socially, or emotionally at levels that will not be significantly different from the young people who are the focus of this chapter. The important point is to look for the general principles that underlie teaching practices, not just specific examples that relate to your work context.

CASE STUDIES

JAMES

I met James several years ago when he was having difficulties settling into Year 1. When he began school, he was extremely articulate and interested in science and learning, but he battled with reading and writing. He loved books and having books read to him, but struggled with reading aloud and copying down words and sentences from the whiteboard. His fine motor coordination was such that he had trouble holding his pencil for long periods.

James had trouble keeping up with his peers educationally, and beyond that, he was overweight and had troubles playing physical games. This meant that he began to avoid outdoor sports and physical education activities.

At home and with adults, he engaged in elaborated conversations, but at school with his peers he had trouble developing friendships and participating in peer culture. He was always the last child to be chosen to belong to a team and he usually ate his lunch alone and did not join in the playground activities of playing soccer and other ball games. He began to dislike going to school and started to refuse to attend, complaining of being sick.

After several months, his class teacher advised his parents that James would be better off if he moved to a school catering for children with learning difficulties. She suggested that this would provide additional support for his learning and motor coordination, and to cope with James' increased anxiety about attending school. His parents were upset to hear this news as they believed that, while James had learning and peer troubles, he still belonged in a regular classroom and with his peers.

His mother, Marian, an early childhood teacher, who had worked with children over many years, believed that this recommendation was inappropriate. She met several times with the teacher, the principal of the school, and the school distant education department. Marian found out that the teacher did not know how to support James fully and had suggested a specialist classroom without really being aware of the criteria for such an enrolment. The teacher also made this decision without consultation. James had not been assessed by any other educator. Rather than seeking support for appropriate teaching strategies, the teacher had made the decision that moving the child somewhere else best solved the problem.

After much advocacy work by James' mother, he and his teacher were each provided with support and guidance and James remained in the same class. This support included finding out that James required glasses for both short- and long-distance work. This made an immediate

difference to his participation in a wide range of activities, including copying from the board, reading, and playing sports.

Recently, after 18 years, I met James and his family. He is now in his second year of his PhD studies, having achieved excellence all through his secondary schooling and undergraduate and postgraduate studies. He is a charming, socially skilled, and confident young person. I think about what the outcomes might have been if he had been moved to a special school for children with learning difficulties. The power of the mother's advocacy is very evident in this case study. Without her involvement, the outcome might have been very different.

This vignette shows that teachers, while acting in what they might see as the best interests of the children, but working in isolation from their community of educators, may be more prone to make decisions about children that will have serious long-term consequences. The mother, by taking this concern more broadly into the school community, was able to broker decisions that supported both James and his teacher within his neighbourhood educational community.

AMALFI COLLEGE

Anne took up her first teaching position as a Year 7 teacher at Amalfi P–12 College. Her room was in a block that housed two Year 6 classes and two Year 7 classes, all staffed by generalist teachers. Anne's initiation into teaching began badly, and then got worse. Within a month she was on the verge of a nervous breakdown. Her class of 32 students included three children on ADHD medication, two in foster care, five others considered to be at risk, and Jason, a boy with multiple and severe disabilities. Jason's parents had organised a roster of 10 voluntary teaching aides (TAs) but Anne found this unsatisfactory because the TAs were untrained, unreliable in attendance, inconsistent with their approach to Jason, in some cases countered Anne's instructions, and talked publicly about what they did not like in the classroom.

Jason was a late inclusion at Amalfi and the College had not made adequate adjustments to its human and physical resources to accommodate his special support needs. To make matters worse, during her one-year Graduate Diploma teacher preparation program at university, Anne received no information on inclusion and teaching students with special support needs.

Anne's three teacher colleagues in the Year 6–7 block became deeply concerned about her. They realised that she was out of her depth and in a situation that set her up to fail, and that without their intervention she would go under. So, they invited her to meet with them and together they worked out the following proposal to take to the principal. Each of them would teach each of the four classes. Rather than work as generalists, each of them would teach only two subjects, which meant that between them they would cover most of the curriculum. They would spend one week of the first term vacation with resource consultants to in-service themselves on the principles and practices of inclusion and prepare for the delivery of the Year 6 and 7 program under the new collaborative arrangement. They would meet as a team for an hour a week after school for the rest of the year for ongoing program and professional development. Individually, and throughout the year, they would each undertake a course of study that deepened their content knowledge and pedagogical content knowledge of the two subjects they would teach. And rather than take time off in lieu for all this extra work, they would each receive a one-off additional payment of $3,000 for the year, a feasible request given Amalfi's budgetary flexibility as

an independent school. Furthermore, they proposed that one full-time, paid TA should replace the system of unpaid voluntary TAs, and that to meet Jason's particular needs, a range of equipment and facilities would be installed.

When they met with the principal he quickly agreed with some aspects of the proposal. Along with other staff he had been thinking and talking for some time about restructuring the Year 6 and 7 classes into a sub-school. So he was glad that Anne's situation had brought the matter to the stage of a formal decision. At first, he contested the resource aspects of the proposal but the four teachers had prepared their case thoroughly and after hours of discussion he accepted their plan.

The principal and teachers then organised four meetings with parents, one for each of the Year 6 and 7 classes, to seek their support. At these meetings they presented the proposal as being in the best interests of all students. For example, they pointed out the Year 6 and 7 students were at or rapidly approaching the phase of early adolescence and thus required a more developmentally appropriate sub-school structure, more specialist teaching, a more seamless transition from primary to secondary schooling, and a more collaborative system of pastoral care. These reasons, the sincerity and commitment of the teachers, and the leadership of the principal resulted in most parents supporting the proposal on a three-year trial basis. Armed with endorsement from the parents, the principal took the proposal to the College Council and after long debate gained approval for the requested expenditure.

Anne's colleagues were right. Without their collegiality, professionalism, and intervention she would not have survived more than one term of teaching. Under the new arrangements, she thrived, as did Jason, the other Year 6 and 7 students, and the three other teachers in the block.

TEACHING–LEARNING CONTEXT

Early years

The past 15 years in Australia have seen the growth of early childhood services for children aged up to eight years and separate middle schools or sub-schools for young adolescents. In regard to the early years, government support for working families has resulted in a burgeoning number of long day care classrooms for children aged up to five years, aimed primarily at providing an educational environment for young children whose parents may be working or studying. As well, in Queensland, the introduction in 2007 of the preparatory year for children aged five to six years has meant that children in that state have an extra year of schooling and will graduate from high school at approximately the same age as their peers in the other Australian states. Recent research shows that the early years are a critical period for young children's cognitive and social development. In this period, acquisition of language is a major developmental task, as are the cognitive tasks of achieving literacy and numeracy. Just as important is the development of social skills required for participating in social activities.

Middle years

The unique developmental needs of young adolescents are well known. They spring from a range of far-reaching physical, cognitive, emotional, social, and moral changes that often commence from age 10–11 years for girls and age 11–12 years for boys. During puberty, young adolescents experience more

rapid and dramatic hormonal and structural changes than at any other period in their life. The sequence of physical change is generally similar from one person to another, although the onset, rate, and timing of these changes are highly individual, often creating stress and feelings of insecurity for the adolescent. Likewise, changes to brain and cognitive development peak during this period. Recent research (e.g., Giedd et al., 1999) suggests that, apart from the first five years of life, at no other time does the capacity and functioning of the brain undergo such an overhaul. This affects the learning ability of young adolescents and their success in managing the emotional, social, and moral changes connected with this stage. Disengagement, alienation, and boredom in school often peak in the middle years and this leads to a decline in achievement. Recent initiatives to address this pattern have included the introduction of middle schooling principles into the teaching of middle year students, ranging in age from 10 to 15 years. Chadbourne (2001) prepared a statement for the Australian Education Union that defined middle schooling in the following way:

Middle schooling refers to formal education that is responsive and appropriate to the developmental needs of young adolescents. This education is characterised by a philosophy, curriculum, and pedagogy based on constructivism. In practice, this involves elements such as:

- higher order thinking, holistic learning, critical thinking, problem-solving and lifelong learning;
- students taking charge of their own learning and constructing their own learnings;
- integrated and disciplinary curricula that are negotiated, relevant, and challenging;
- cooperative learning and collaborative teaching;
- authentic, reflective, and outcomes-based assessment;
- heterogeneous and flexible student groupings;
- success for every student;
- small learning communities that provide students with sustained individual attention in a safe, healthy school environment;
- emphasis on strong teacher–student relationships through extended contact with a small number of teachers and a consistent student cohort;
- democratic governance and shared leadership; and
- parental and community involvement in student learning (pp. 2–3).

pedagogy
The style and strategies used by a teacher, sometimes called the art or science of being a teacher.

constructivism
A theoretical framework that guides teaching and learning practices. The emphasis is on developmentally appropriate learning that is guided by a supportive facilitator but initiated and directed by the learner.

This definition is generally accepted as capturing the intent of middle schooling in the Australian context and is built on many of the influential national and international literatures informing this emergent field of educational research. The principles of middle schooling are incorporated in traditional primary and secondary contexts, along with P–12 structures and purposely organised middle schooling environments. Importantly, like the early years, literacy and numeracy feature in the middle years, with research indicating that students who fail to master acceptable literacy and numeracy proficiency find the transition into secondary schooling contexts particularly challenging, leading to disengagement and failure to meet their potential in the school environment.

Societal contexts

In addition to the developmental changes typifying the early to middle years, understandings of changes in society and how students experience life in today's communities form an important component of the teaching and learning context. Today's students live in a society that is known as both the Age of Terrorism and the Information Age. Characteristics of this contemporary society include digital culture, globalisation, the rapid production of knowledge and information, along with a focus on risk control and safety (Bahr & Pendergast, 2007).

From a teaching and learning perspective there are many lessons to be learned about the educational needs of these children. As the first generation born into the Information Age, they are known as digital natives (Prensky, 2005/6). Most of their teachers are digital immigrants. Today's students are a new breed; they are technologically competent, prefer visual learning to written language, and think in a non-linear way. Today's students also consider their community to be global rather than local. They often engage in complex game play, developing sophisticated strategic and leadership online skills. They use computers for interactive activities rather than simple transmission of information. They build wikis and blogs, create multiple identities and share intimate information with strangers on relatively unsupervised internet sites.

What enables schools to be responsive to the unique developmental characteristics of children and young adolescents in this contemporary societal situation? In a nutshell, we believe this is possible through the building of small learning communities. In the early years this usually happens within classrooms or centres with young children and consistent teaching and support staff, and for the middle years this usually comprises an interdisciplinary team of around four to six staff with varying content expertise and 100–150 young adolescents. The structure and culture of these small communities mandate and facilitate reforms that in the past have often evaded schools. A list of these reforms is given in Box 9.1.

BOX 9.1 School-based education reforms

The initiatives listed below support the development of an inclusive education environment. These include general principles and specific teaching strategies that can have positive influences on all students and at all levels of schooling.

- Interdisciplinary team-teaching and collaboration—when teachers with expertise in subject areas come together to form teaching teams.
- Integrated, negotiated, and exploratory studies—when subject matter is presented as cohesive and linked, and where students have a voice in making curriculum choices.
- Teaching for understanding and higher order thinking and problem-solving across subjects—when there is a focus on challenge and high expectations.
- Program-wide philosophy and overarching learning outcomes—when there is an agreed approach to teaching and learning in a school context.
- Child- and adolescent-centred, developmentally appropriate education—when teachers have specialist knowledge about the capabilities of their students.
- Differentiated and small group teaching and learning—when classrooms are flexible enough to enable interest groups to be constructed for teaching and learning.
- Authentic, developmental, non-competitive assessment—when real assessment strategies are employed that enable students to demonstrate what they know and can do.
- Flexible teaching spaces and timetable—when structures enable change.
- Seamless transition from early years to primary schooling, and from primary to secondary schooling—when attention is paid to the causes of transitional issues and when clusters of typically primary and secondary schools collaborate.

- Heterogeneous, mixed-ability grouping of students—when groups of students are formed around interests, topics, and relevance rather than ability groupings.
- Multi-age classrooms—where groups of students such as Years 1/2/3 or Years 4/5/6 occur, rather than discrete year-level classes, which enables opportunities for peer mentoring, peer modelling, and leadership.
- Advisories, an adult advocate for each student, collaborative pastoral care—when a mentor program is in place.
- Parent and community involvement—when schools are open to the wider community and encourage their involvement and participation.
- Small learning communities that provide students with sustained individual attention and a safe, healthy school environment—when a focus on the learner and their needs is prioritised.

BOX 9.1

In recent times, considerable reform has occurred in terms of school contexts, particularly in the models of delivery for the middle years that incorporate these features. For instance, middle schools have been set up with a range of structures to implement the reforms listed above. Brown Hill College and Challenge State High School, described in Box 9.2, are two examples of middle school models currently operating in Australia.

BOX 9.2

Two schools in Australia

Brown Hill College is organised into three precincts: Junior (P–6, around 1,070 students); Middle (Years 7–9, around 600 students); Senior (Years 10–12, around 600 students). The college operates a split shift for these precincts, enabling better use of facilities and greater access to technology for all students. Within the framework of an overall college and associate principal, each precinct has its own principal and separate identity. Students within each precinct belong to a pod. Each pod has a purpose-built facility with access to computers, wet and dry areas, and flexible teaching spaces. Also each pod has a coordinator, four teachers, two specialist teachers known as integrating facilitators, and, in some cases, learning support teachers. Each pod operates according to planning decisions made at weekly team meetings. These meetings, which run for 90–180 minutes, determine all aspects of curriculum implementation, including timetabling, student groupings within the pod, and whether class sessions are optional or essential.

The staff team in each pod develop integrated studies programs that include deep understandings, a concept map of learning experiences and resources, models for learning groups and delivery, and the culminating activity. These programs run for approximately a term and, where possible, include negotiation of topics between the students and teachers.

Challenge State High School provides a range of offerings for young adolescents in Years 7 and 8 that prepare them to take their place in society and meet the challenges of a rapidly changing world. The school overtly acknowledges that each child has a preferred learning style and it makes every effort to accommodate the requirements of each style. Significant emphasis is placed on the skills of multiple literacies, communication, cooperative learning, reasoning, problem-solving and research.

The school encourages adaptability, flexibility, and effective application of knowledge and skills to a given situation. Students are required to be involved actively in their learning by making decisions, assuming responsibility, evaluating, analysing and taking action. All Year 7 and 8 students undertake a program of core subjects, which include English, mathematics, science, history/geography, art, LOTE (French and Japanese), music, physical education, health, ICT, religious and values education (RAVE), and pastoral care and sport.

At each Year level the students are placed in six homerooms. For English and maths they break into five groups and then into four academic groups for all other subjects, except art, which takes place in homeroom groups. At Year 8 level there is one all-boys class. This was established to focus more specifically on the learning needs of boys, as identified by research showing that their learning in English and maths can be optimised in a single-sex classroom. Across the Year 7 and 8 curriculum, course content is designed to meet individual needs. For example, there are several remedial and enrichment programs for special needs in literacy and numeracy. Also, students with exceptional academic ability are extended in programs which focus on developing the higher-order thinking skills and exploring challenging concepts.

9.2

ISSUES AND CHALLENGES

Teachers face a number of issues and challenges when attempting to implement inclusion across the early and middle years. These arise from the nature of children and young adolescents and from variable models of schooling, along with the developmental changes unique to these periods. Although many of the issues are the same from early childhood through to adolescence, some specific issues related to effective inclusion arise and are noted below.

Early years

EARLY IDENTIFICATION

Children with special learning needs are typically identified as requiring specialised support. In the early years the issue of effective early screening to support the children and their families and the effective provision of services is extremely important.

LABELLING

Identifying children as having particular learning needs may disadvantage the child over time. A student may never be able to escape from the labelling and the effects of this naming of a disability or learning challenge, which might be compounded by ability streaming or other structural arrangements. A child may have their entire educational experience affected by a misdiagnosis or inappropriate labelling, or simply by being labelled.

STRUCTURES

There are a number of challenges in the early years of schooling. These include the organisation of classrooms to meet the needs of all children, the provision of specialist support staff, the availability of teacher aides, and even fairly basic issues like accessible toileting facilities.

STRATEGIES

Teachers need to be flexible when developing strategies related to curriculum differentiation and individualisation of pedagogy so that each child has the opportunity to achieve at their optimal level.

Middle years

WIDENING ABILITY GAP

As students grow older and move from childhood to early adolescence, the gap between those with and without special support needs generally widens academically, socially, physically, and emotionally.

GROWING AWARENESS

Young adolescents without special support needs are more aware of this gap than are younger students, sometimes leading to resistance, embarrassment, and failure to participate in support programs.

PEER PERCEPTIONS

Young adolescents without special support needs are likely to have a more fully formed and fixed position on the gap than younger students. In some cases, this position may be negative, discriminatory, and resistant to change.

IDENTITY FORMATION

Young adolescents with special support needs may feel threatened by inclusion. For instance, they may worry about what inclusion will mean for their personal and social identity and their acceptance by their peers.

PARENTAL CONCERN

Parents of young adolescents with special support needs may be less supportive or enthusiastic about inclusion for their children at this stage of their development as they see their child as vulnerable to possible criticism and negative peer group messages.

ACADEMIC CONCERNS

The subject-centred structure and university-entrance-dominated culture of secondary schools may increase staff opposition to the inclusion of young adolescents with special support needs.

TRADITIONAL SECONDARY STRUCTURES

Secondary school teachers typically teach 150 or more students per week and change classes every 40 minutes. Students change teachers, and sometimes classrooms, every 40 minutes. These structures provide challenges for inclusion and the development of community.

RISK

Secondary schools have more dangerous equipment and activities (e.g., machine shop, kitchens) than preschool and primary schools, providing a potentially riskier learning environment.

Teacher competence

To the extent that inclusion is difficult for teachers, some face a greater prospect of being unsuccessful with inclusion. Some teachers positively respond to inclusion, accepting it as an integral part of their

job, take it in their stride and maintain a can-do perspective. Others experience difficulty coming to terms with the challenges of inclusion, find it unproductively stressful, and develop deep-seated reservations. Generally, the early years are regarded are being inhabited with young, inquisitive minds keen to learn, so inclusion is accepted as a specific challenge. The picture changes dramatically for the middle years and for middle-years teachers where, irrespective of inclusion, young adolescents are broadly regarded as the group of students who are most unteachable and unmanageable and as the group teachers might least want to teach across all the years of schooling. Further difficulties arise when beginning teachers receive inadequate preparation for inclusion during their preservice course, minimal induction during their first year of teaching, and no ongoing professional development throughout their probationary years.

Several other factors affecting success warrant mention. Unsatisfactory work conditions in some classrooms set teachers up to fail. For example, some teachers find the intensification of work generated by inclusion to be insurmountable. And some teachers find that students with special support needs make slow progress when compared with the other students in the class, in some cases too slow and too small to give the teachers any sense of achievement. Put in a sightly different way, because teachers see these students every day, the gains seem to be imperceptible. At times, the perceived lack of progress leads teachers to experience frustration, failure, and even guilt. For some teachers, these feelings can be underpinned by a strong sense of professionalism to teach effectively, to get results, to make a difference, and not let down any of the students in the class.

Ability streaming

A strategy that teachers and administrators might consider as a possible strategy to deal with differentiated ability students is ability streaming or levelling students as a basis for forming classes. This has particular significance for inclusion. Should ability be used as the major determinant to allocate students to classes, pods, or other communities, so that they can receive ongoing specialised attention? In many ways this directly contradicts the principles of inclusion. Earlier, we identified heterogeneous, mixed-ability grouping of students as a key feature of inclusive schooling. In principle, we believe that schools should not countenance ability streaming. In practice, however, some schools do set up classes based on student ability. Research into the effects of ability streaming are clear—those students in the lower ability streams are unlikely to achieve their potential, while those in the higher ability groupings are likely to benefit most from the strategy (Ireson, Hallam, & Hurley, 2005). Since ability grouping and system-wide stratification do not raise the attainment of students overall but do increase inequity between students, it would seem unwise to be tempted to use ability grouping.

Fortune Community College, described in Box 9.3, provides a case in point around the question of ability grouping and raises the question, "How can tension between principle and practice on this matter be resolved?". One option is to insist on mixed-ability classes but allow selective sub-groups within those classes for individualised work.

TEACHING ESSENTIALS

For early and middle-years students in school, inclusion best takes place within the structure and culture of small communities. In many respects, school communities are models of society and this empowers them to be agents of social change. It also empowers them to help teachers successfully face the challenges outlined above.

In our view, inclusion is not an add-on component to schooling. It is not a special program to be set up when a child or young adolescent with special support needs arrives at the school, and dismantled

BOX 9.3

Schools and streaming

Fortune Community College is a small P–12 school located in a rural community, one-hour drive from a major city. It enrols approximately 350 students, 10% of whom come from an Indigenous background. The year levels are combined (multi-age) with students streamed into one of three groups, named "Boat," "Aeroplane," and "Truck" based on performance in literacy and numeracy tests. Students complete their integrated studies in these groupings.

A review of the school that included interviews with students and parents revealed that students knew what it meant to be allocated to either the Boat, Aeroplane, or Truck class and had constructed a whole range of perceptions about streaming. For example, the Truck group was seen to be home for the smart kids who, on the negative side, were regarded as having no fun and having to copy too many notes from the blackboard. The Aeroplane group was seen to be the special class where students, mainly Indigenous, were regarded as less smart but as having more fun. Apparently, this perception motivated one non-Indigenous student in the Aeroplane group to work hard to move out of this class. Another perception was that some students intentionally performed poorly on the leveling test so they could stay with friends who were not expected to perform well. According to the review, these types of perceptions of the levelling process led some parents to move their children to a different school.

when that student leaves school. On the contrary, we argue that inclusion should be an integral, non-negotiable, and permanent element of schooling philosophy. This means that a particular school cannot say, "Although inclusion has not worked here, we are a highly successful school." Success for schools means success for all students, not just most students. Similarly, the principle of developmentally responsive and appropriate curriculum and pedagogy applies to each student, not just to those who have special support needs. It is a principle that, in a broad and fundamental sense, helps make differences seamless between students with special support strengths and needs.

Successful inclusion in schools depends largely on teachers understanding the connections between community and inclusion. When school communities operate properly, they promote inclusion on two broad levels. First, the overall structure and culture of the community makes an impact; the medium is the message; that is, transition from preschool to primary or primary to secondary schooling is made seamless by the structure and culture of a school community. Second, particular elements of the overall structure and culture of a community can be used by teachers to resolve the issues and challenges that inclusion can present. The final chapter of this book provides details about establishing community in the senior years of schooling. In this chapter, we focus on developing community in the early years through to the middle years.

School communities in the early and middle years

By itself, developing the structure and culture of community can go a long way towards strengthening inclusion. Structurally, and where possible, a school community is larger than a single school class because children and young adolescents need more academic challenge, independence, risk taking,

freedom, and choice of peers for friendship groups. But it has to be smaller than large school age-graded cohorts to prevent children in the early and middle years feeling anonymous, unsupported, and uncared for. For example, in practice, this means that a small school community might have a membership of about 80–120 students and 4–6 staff who together have their own building, resources, facilities, name and identity. A middle school with 500 students could set up five small communities, each organised along the lines outlined above. In the early years, groups are ideally somewhat smaller, but the same principles apply.

However, structure by itself does not guarantee the existence of community. To become a community, all members must in effect be able to say: "Within this community I feel that my needs, interests, values, and experiences are known, understood, accepted, and valued. I identify myself, and others accept me, as a respected member of this community. I feel I belong to it. I'm pleased and proud to belong to it. It's part of who I am." But even that is not enough. To become a community, all members must sign on to and work hard to establish and maintain:

- a climate of trust, openness, care, friendliness, high morale, non-judgemental atmosphere, and can-do optimism rather than a climate of suspicion, secrecy, indifference, cynicism, hostility, condemnation and defeatism; and
- a culture that values diversity, inclusion, sharing, equity, support, cooperation, challenge, success, shared power, and facilitative leadership rather than a culture of intolerance, segregation, hoarding, elitism, put-downs, rivalry, neglect, rejection, isolation, domination, and power-based leadership.

Stated in those terms, communities can claim to be powerful vehicles for delivering inclusion. The climate and culture of communities does not automatically or inevitably rise from the initial setting-up of a community. Teachers must actively build and continually maintain the structure of community. This won't occur unless they are convinced of the need to do so. Nor will it occur unless teachers have developed a wide repertoire of community-building knowledge and skill. What can teachers within a school community do to extend such a repertoire? The list in Box 9.4 contains some measures for consideration. Where possible, within any one community, all teachers should collaborate to jointly consider, plan, implement, and take responsibility for the outcomes of these measures.

BOX 9.4 Tips for building community in the early and middle years

- Model the ethos and values of community.
- Involve students in decisions on a continuous basis.
- Conduct class meetings and community forums.
- Establish lines of open and regular communication—for example, daily or weekly broad-sheets, posters, notices, in-house radio, emails, website discussion boards.
- Organise festivals, parties, socials, camps, basket lunches, special breakfasts.
- Make judicious use of emblems, mottos, symbols, rituals, assemblies, and ceremonies.
- Commemorate important events.
- Celebrate success, exhibit students' work, applaud performances.
- Advocate for a play-based curriculum in the preschool and preparatory years of schooling.

- Develop a repertoire of active friendship strategies to support friendship formations.
- Design group-building exercises and consensus-building activities.
- Use conflict resolution, peer support and pastoral care programs.
- Build resilience.
- Insist on mixed-ability classes, inclusive curriculum, non-competitive assessment.
- Set activities that require cooperative learning, teamwork, joint work, class discussions, workshops, group assignments, and assessment.
- Rotate positions of student leadership and responsibility.
- Make classrooms feel like home—for example, add music, aquariums, pets, photos, paintings, furnishings, gardens.
- Establish policies and programs to combat bullying, violence, prejudice, discrimination, and the development of harmful cliques, rejection and isolation.
- Where appropriate, make the concept, importance, and building of community a teaching point.
- Conduct friendly intercommunity competitions such as chess, rock, science, and sporting activities.
- As a community, sponsor worthy causes and participate in worthy projects in the broader world.
- Place community maintenance as a standing item on staff meeting agendas.
- Gain further ideas from the literature—see, for example, Moss (2006), Strahan, Smith, McElrath, and Toole (2001), and Bauer and Brown (2001).

9.4

It is worth emphasising that community is like a battery. When it's fully charged it has the power to deliver, but unless continually recharged it goes flat.

Other factors affecting the success of teachers

So far, we have discussed one critical factor affecting the success of inclusion in schools, namely, the commitment and capacity of teachers (and students) to build and maintain community. We now outline briefly some other factors that affect inclusion. Some of these factors arise from schooling in general. Others arise from inclusion in particular. All of them are influenced by community. Each has the potential to derail inclusion or to help take it down the right track. An important theme running across these factors is that all teachers in a school community teach all students and that, in so doing, all teachers have equal responsibility for all students with special support needs.

RESPONDING TO SMALL STEPS AND SLOW PROGRESS

As mentioned earlier, young children and young adolescents with special support needs often progress slowly and in small steps and, in some cases, to the point where progress seems imperceptible. If not prepared for this, teachers can become frustrated and demoralised and adopt a minimalist approach to inclusion. This leads to a vicious circle where they do not have success with inclusion because they are negative toward it, and they are negative toward it because they do not have success.

While this factor applies to teachers across the P–12 years, it is more crucial for middle-years teachers than primary teachers, for several reasons. First, the performance gap between students with and without special support needs increases as they get older. Second, teachers in the higher grades come under pressure to be subject-centred rather than child-centred.

When faced with this factor, teachers can be encouraged to develop expectations that are positive and realistic, to be patient but persistent, and to maintain a long-range view of what can be achieved, take satisfaction from the tiny steps that students might make toward those distant goals, and accept that those steps are a major cause for celebration in themselves. Of course, this is easier said than done. However, being a member of a school community offers support in several ways. It provides a teacher with a group of colleagues who work in a climate of high morale and can-do optimism, who are committed to not giving up on young children and young adolescents, and who immerse themselves in stories of hope and success. It offers a structure in which all teachers teach all students and, therefore, share responsibility for student outcomes.

Teachers working in such a professional community are more likely to be encouraged to develop a deep understanding of students with special support needs and empathy with them. They are more likely to receive affirmation that helping students with special support needs to make small gains gives cause for a greater sense of achievement than working with high-achieving students who sometimes succeed in spite of, rather than because of, the teacher.

An overarching implication underlies what we have said so far. Teachers must do more than build community. They must also create a professional community among themselves. At times, though, not even professional community can carry the day—at least not in the short term—as exemplified by the vignette in Box 9.5.

BOX 9.5 Bill's education

Bill began his teaching career at Newtown School. Despite the collegiality and pro-inclusion stance of the other staff, he could not come to terms with having to teach Adam, a young adolescent with Down syndrome, in one of his classes. So, at the beginning of third term, he went to the principal and explained that, after spending two terms trying to make inclusion work, he still could not bring himself to develop a positive relationship, let alone empathy, with Adam and thus considered himself personally unsuited to teach in inclusive settings. Bill went on to ask if he could be shifted to another part of the school where there were no students with disabilities.

In response, the principal thanked Bill for his openness but said that, in his view, teachers who declared themselves to be personally unwilling, unable, or unsuited to teach students with special support needs were basically declaring themselves unqualified to teach. So, he could not consider moving Bill to a different part of the school. However, he said he would support any program that might help Bill develop the interest, empathy, and capacity for the positive relationships he felt he lacked. More specifically, with the blessing of Bill's professional community colleagues, he would allow Bill to use two student-free days for activities that could deepen his understanding of Adam and Down syndrome. For example, during these days Bill could do the following things: undertake volunteer work at the Down Syndrome Association; read a selection of books and articles, and watch inspirational films recommended by this Association; have a substantial conversation with Adam's parents about the history and nature of his particular needs and the support he benefits from; and discuss with the parents their hopes and fears for Adam. In return, the principal asked Bill to share what he learned from this program with his team colleagues and seek additional avenues for developing a positive relationship with Adam.

Bill agreed to take this opportunity and spent some time doing a range of these activities. Importantly, he met with Adam's parents and realised that he had been seeing Adam first as a student with Down syndrome and second as a person. By opening his mind and focusing on the person, not the special needs, Bill found a closer connection with Adam. He also realised he had made assumptions and had limited knowledge about the potential Adam had as a learner, and about his interests and ways of connecting learning opportunities with these interests. Bill decided he should gain a wider understanding of inclusive education practices and has subsequently found that he incorporates a range of teaching practices that benefit all of his students.

9.5

CONSTRUCTING INDIVIDUALISED PLANS FOR LEARNING

As a philosophy, schools advocate that students should be provided with an education plan that is responsive and appropriate to their strengths and concerns, and their family priorities. These plans are known most usually as individual education plans (IEPs), although they can also be known as family support plans (for home settings), inclusion support plans, and education support plans, to name just a few. Constructing an education program has to take into account the student's strengths as well as diversity across the student cohort and within individual students.

Inclusion adds another layer of complexity because it requires teachers to identify not only developmental needs but also the special support needs for students with particular differences. Successful inclusion depends partly on teachers correctly identifying these needs, and setting appropriate goals, priorities, and targets that help make up the individualised plan. In carrying out this task, teachers receive support from a variety of sources. Often, they can call on the services of psychologists, physiotherapists, and occupational therapists, as well as specialist advisory teachers with expertise in inclusive schooling. Another powerful resource is the parents of the students with special support needs. These parents have unique information and insights about the nature of their child's support needs and often have acquired a wide range of material and ideas on inclusion from journals, conferences, private consultants, visiting scholars, and the internet. Also, a needs analysis for each student should be conducted collegially, as part of developing an individual plan. The same applies to setting goals, priorities and targets, or outcomes for each student. The end result is a collective plan constructed in large measure by the interdisciplinary team of teachers who will implement it.

When constructing developmentally appropriate individual plans, teachers should keep in mind that students with special support needs are children first. That is, as they develop, these students experience the same physical, social, emotional and intellectual changes as students without special support needs. They want the same things from life as other students. They are characterised by the same degree of diversity as other students.

The belief that children with special support needs are children first has implications for the curriculum and pedagogy used to implement their individual plans for learning. To be responsive to the nature of early childhood and adolescence, a curriculum must be challenging, exploratory, integrative, grounded in standards, and relevant to children's concerns. This applies equally to children with and without special support needs.

The National Research Council has identified three principles for best practices in curriculum planning and implementation (Dempsey & Arthur-Kelly, 2007, p. 65):

- curriculum should build on students' prior knowledge;
- curriculum should provide factual knowledge to support curriculum learning; and
- students should have opportunities to think about, and take more control of, their learning.

This means that curriculum should be both responsive to children's experiences and also be sufficiently flexible to support students' strengths, interests and requirements. It is the responsibility of the teacher to consider these principles when planning and implementing curriculum for children of diverse abilities. For example, each student in an inclusive classroom does not have to master the same amount of work on the same level. Schaffner and Buswell (1996, pp. 23–24) provide several examples of what it does mean:

> *One of the ... biology units (in Mrs Madsen's class) is on frog dissection. During the unit, Josh had an adapted vocabulary list which included words like "stomach," "lungs," "front," "back," and "blood" (which are words and concepts important for him to learn). Josh's worksheets and homework papers were customised to provide independent activities at his own reading and writing levels to help him learn these concepts and apply them to his daily life. Mrs Madsen kept a copy of Josh's vocabulary list and learning goals at her desk, and each day during class discussions included several questions based on Josh's learning needs that he could respond to. During the frog dissection lab, Josh participated with his lab partners in a cooperative group where he had a key role in the dissection. His learning goals were to set up and put away materials, learn to use a knife, and learn to work with other students. The verbal interaction that naturally occurred around the dissection activity allowed Josh to practice important language skills as well.*
>
> *Maria is in a pre-algebra class in which she works on her own [individualised learning] goals while participating with classmates in common activities. Her primary learning objectives in math this year are addressed through various activities. To build number skills, she counts out the papers her teacher needs for the class and then hands them out when requested. Maria also serves as time-keeper for the class, reminding them when activities are to be completed. When students are working in small problem-solving groups, Maria participates, and her specialty is addition and subtraction facts under ten ... Another task Maria works on in pre-algebra class is reading her classmates' names since it is her responsibility to hand back graded papers. Maria is a proud and successful student in pre-algebra.*

To prepare appropriate curricula for students, teachers must be double-adapters. That is, they have to adapt broad curricula so that it is responsive to the nature, strengths and needs of students. Then, they have to adapt this curriculum to make it responsive to the particular requirements of the student requiring special support (see Box 9.6). To make these adaptations, lesson after lesson, week after week, takes time and is challenging work. Buying a book with 1,000 lessons that have already been adapted might seem useful, but teachers still have to make further adaptations to these lessons to ensure they fit particular individual learning plans, which would constitute a third level of adaptation. That is, teachers need to be curriculum-makers rather than curriculum-takers.

BOX 9.6 Early childhood teachers as double-adapters: Guiding principles and associated practices

PLANNING FOR INCLUSION

- Is the activity embedded in classroom activities and routines?
- Is the activity representing general concepts and processes and not an isolated skill?
- Is the activity promoting active engagement and involvement at each child's level of competence?
- Is the classroom curriculum and pedagogy reflecting a mixture of informal and directed teaching approaches?
- Is the teacher intervention focused on increasing the likelihood that the child will acquire skills and competencies in ways that encourage maximum child participation and interaction with peers and the teacher and, at the same time, is minimally intrusive?

ACTIVITY ADAPTED FOR INCLUSION

1 A painting/collage activity:
   - child with developmental language delay: discuss the differing textures of the materials; and
   - child with fine motor difficulties: provide appropriately sized paint/glue brush.

2 Matching and sorting game:
   - have a mixture of materials of differing sizes and complexity for children to engage with in different ways;
   - reaching and grasping the different shapes; and
   - categorising and counting.

3 Teacher-read story:
   - have small groups so that children with hearing and visual impairment sit close to the teacher; and
   - have small books that individual children can hold.

4 Routines:
   - for child with limited expressive language skills, take photographs of frequently-used classroom items and place on chart; and
   - change song words for children with movement impairment (blink not run).

Source: Adapted from Talay-Ongan, 2004 (pp. 128, 332 and 337–338).

Teachers also need to be double-adapters when adopting pedagogy to deliver the curriculum they have developed. They have to adapt their pedagogy to make it responsive to the developmental needs and learning styles of their students. Then they have to adapt student-focused pedagogy to make it responsive to the particular needs of the students requiring special support—for example, by giving them shorter assignments, less written and more oral assessment, less silent reading and more listening to audiotapes. At a general level, the two types of adaptation involve teaching and learning practices that are compatible and mutually reinforcing. For example, Manning and Bucher (2005, p. 169)

recommend 10 practices for teachers working with students with special support needs. Most of these practices, listed below, also apply in classrooms that have no students with special support needs:

1. Learn about the student as a person.
2. Adapt instructional materials and procedures to meet individual needs.
3. Work from the concrete to the abstract.
4. Break complex learning into simpler components.
5. Check for understanding of procedures and instructions.
6. Provide sufficient drill and practice.
7. Help students maintain a record of assignments.
8. Plan questions and their sequences carefully.
9. Encourage and provide peer support and peer tutoring.
10. Provide opportunities and experiences for some degree of success.

Manning and Bucher (2005) also recommend that teachers develop a wide repertoire of teaching practices. Many of these practices, listed alphabetically in Box 9.7, are appropriate for all students, and not just those with special support needs. You will have already encountered several of these as you've been working your way through this textbook.

BOX 9.7 A repertoire of teaching strategies

Cooperative learning	Field trips	Mastery learning
Debates	Homework	Peer-tutoring
Demonstrations	Individualised instruction	Projects
Drill and practice	Inductive discovery	Role-playing
Exploratory activities	Learning centres	Simulations
Expository teaching	Lecture	Service learning

Source: Manning & Bucher, 2005, pp. 164–66. Adapted with permission of Pearson Education, Inc., Upper Saddle River, N.J.

The curriculum and pedagogy practices referred to above apply to students of all ages, stages, and abilities. Yet, certain teaching repertoires—namely, teacher exposition and drill and practice—typically dominate in many classrooms. What is required instead is moderation, variety, and a balance of the full range of strategies. This caters for the range of learning styles, makes the learning process less predictable and potentially less boring, and encourages students to take responsible roles as learners. Teaching within school communities makes the difficulty and demands of double-adaptation less daunting because teachers can provide each other with substantial support.

Individual learning plans attract criticism if they single out students with special support needs for separate activities within the classroom or withdrawal from the classroom. When that occurs, they are likely to create a feeling of being excluded rather than included. This can be minimised in several ways:

- by consistently including differentiated instruction as a class norm to make teaching inclusive of all students;

- ensuring that all students are provided with support, not just those with special needs;
- by being flexible with the presentation of curriculum content and by negotiating the curriculum when possible, as this allows for students to undertake separate projects; and
- using non-competitive assessment based on Howard Gardner's notion of multiple intelligences.

All of these features of schooling reduce the prospect of students feeling singled out and excluded.

ESTABLISHING PRODUCTIVE TEACHER–PARENT PARTNERSHIPS

For inclusion to succeed, teachers and parents of students with special support needs must be partners working together in agreement rather than rivals engaged in unhealthy contestation. Conflicts of interests and ideology on the implementation of inclusion can lead to teacher–parent tension. Teachers are likely to resist parents who place unreasonable pressures on them by, for example, insisting on unrealistic goals in the individualised learning plan; making teachers feel constantly under surveillance; vetoing the teacher's professional judgements on issues such as withdrawal from the classroom; pushing an inflexible version of inclusion; monopolising the teacher's time before and after school; and imposing on the teacher's non-teaching or preparation time. Parents are likely to object if they feel teachers dilute inclusion by, for example, setting individualised learning goals that are not age appropriate; allowing their children to be withdrawn too often from the classroom; excluding the parents from meetings with advisers; making inappropriate use of the teacher aide; dismissing the parent's knowledge on inclusion as inconsequential; and writing uninformative reports on their child's school work.

One of the eight design elements outlined in *Turning Points 2000* requires teachers to "involve parents and communities in supporting student learning and healthy development" (Jackson & Davis, 2000, p. 25). This means that teachers and parents must work towards consensus on matters such as: what counts as inclusion; what the students with special support needs should learn; how classroom learning should be structured to enable these students to achieve their individualised learning goals; and where the line should be drawn between parents' and teachers' rights and responsibilities.

The early years of schooling traditionally attract strong involvement from parents. However, by the time children reach their middle years, schools typically encounter difficulty attracting and retaining parent involvement. As children get older, they often actively discourage their parents from coming to school. However, school communities are well placed to break down these barriers by enhancing opportunities for teachers to work collaboratively as well as individually with parents on establishing relations of mutual trust, respect, and cooperation.

Teachers can keep the lines of communication between them and parents open through a variety of measures. For example, they could:

- invite parents once a term to meet with the entire teaching team of the school community to which their child belongs;
- set up a communication book for entries to be written by the parents, teachers, and teacher aide; and
- phone and/or email the parents on a fortnightly basis, and ask the teacher aide to do likewise.

In the process of doing those things, teachers are likely to gain a better understanding of the other person's point of view.

FINDING POSITIVES IN THE INTENSIFICATION OF WORK

Students with special support needs sometimes require assistance with matters such as medication, toileting, moving around the room, anxiety attacks, and frustration management. Much of this

assistance comes from the teacher aide and visiting professional staff. Even so, inclusion can increase the intensity and complexity of teachers' work by requiring them, for example, to:

- meet with and oversee the work of the teacher aide and relief teacher aides;
- develop individual learning plans at case conferences and team meetings;
- maintain lines of communication and regularly consult with parents;
- brief preparation-time relief staff on inclusion matters;
- help manage the micro-politics of inclusion in the school and local community; and
- coordinate the acquisition and use of special equipment, materials and facilities.

This situation affects teachers in different ways; and some teachers respond to this situation in ways different to others. Some teachers find the situation stressful and develop a negative view of inclusion. For example, they see it as spreading their work too thinly and reducing professional effectiveness and they cope with it by taking a minimalist approach in order to survive. Other teachers respond positively to the demands and difficulties of inclusion by seeing it as an opportunity to improve their professional development, job satisfaction, and career advancement. For example, some teachers find that inclusion helps them:

- become aware of how to teach students with special support needs;
- discover resources and services available for these students;
- adapt special education strategies to the teaching of other students;
- learn how to work closely with teacher aides and manage their work;
- become more tolerant, patient, understanding, persistent, and positive;
- interact with a wider range of professional people outside the school; and
- gain permanency and promotion by showing an extra side of themselves that otherwise may have been inactive.

Teachers do not have to rely on the goodwill of their colleagues to help them cope with the intensification of work; the structure and culture of a professional community helps all members share any extra work, difficulties, and concerns arising from inclusion. Also, the autonomy enjoyed by school communities allows members opportunities to deploy staff and funding flexibly to assist teachers cope with particularly demanding situations that may arise from time to time.

INCLUDING THE TEACHER AIDE AS AN INTEGRAL PART OF THE TEAM

Cost-neutral, naturally occurring supports or resources for inclusion sometimes operate effectively to remove the imperative for a teacher aide (TA) or outside money-based resources. Natural resources include the students without special support needs, experienced teachers, and community volunteers. Throughout this chapter, we have emphasised that early and middle teachers have an additional and particularly powerful natural support or resource—namely community. There are situations, however, that make a TA necessary. In these cases, a number of important principles apply.

First, the TA is a member of the team and works as a TA for the whole community, not just one class or one teacher. Second, the TA is an aide for all students in the community, not exclusively an aide for students with special support needs. Third, although the TA reports to the team and is accountable to the team, the more the team can build a collegial, rather than line management, relationship with the TA and work together collaboratively with the TA, the more successful the teachers, the TA and the team will be. Many things can be done to develop a productive professional relationship with the TA. For example, teachers can individually and collectively:

- invite the TA to attend and participate in team meetings and social events;
- involve the TA in planning, not just implementing individual learning plans;
- show the TA the daily work pad each morning or evening;
- consult the TA on student behaviour management;
- use the TA as a critical friend, a person to bounce ideas off;
- ensure that the TA receives adequate induction and professional development;
- ensure that the TA does not become bored due to the lack of meaningful work;
- ask the TA to supervise small groups and the class when appropriate; and
- avoid taking the laissez-faire approach of providing TAs with little direction on the nature of their work or leaving them with almost complete responsibility for students with special support needs.

USING PROFESSIONAL COMMUNITY FOR INDUCTION AND PROFESSIONAL DEVELOPMENT

Ideally, teachers new to a school receive notification of their teaching job the year or term before they take up the position. This allows time for induction into the school community in which they will be working and its approach to inclusion. It also allows time for induction into the philosophy, principles, and practices of inclusion and the specific elements of schooling (e.g., the philosophy of multi-age or middle school contexts) if preservice teacher preparation has not covered them. For example, teachers beginning in a new early or middle-years situation could make a two- or three-day visit to the school of their appointment to:

- be introduced to the classes in which they will be working;
- meet the parents of any students with special support needs;
- become familiar with the structure, climate, and culture of the school community;
- identify how many of the measures for building and maintaining community, outlined earlier in this chapter, are used at the school;
- attend a meeting of the staff team and be briefed on the community's inclusion programs and resources and the school's philosophy and plan for inclusion;
- discuss ways of gaining knowledge about the support needs of particular students;
- discuss with the team ways of preparing individual learning plans ready for implementation when teaching begins;
- unobtrusively shadow a student with special support needs;
- gain their ideas on how to determine what can be reasonably expected of the student in terms of learning outcomes, and how to develop and implement an individual learning plan; and
- see if the outgoing teacher will share files that contains the teacher's strategies, programs, work samples, school reports, individual learning plans, resources, and a list of where to go to get help with phone numbers and addresses.

Good teaching in the early and middle years is complex, sophisticated work. It is a job that practitioners can never stop at getting better. Successful inclusion requires teachers not to equate coping with success; that is, not to accept that if things come easily, there is no real need for ongoing professional development. To ensure continuous and inclusion-effective professional development, teachers in the early and middle years could, for example, engage in the following activities.

- Undergo professional development specific to understanding the support needs of students in their classes—professional development on special support needs in general is necessary but not often sufficiently refined.

- Value, and make use of, the parents of students with special support needs as an important source of professional development—as previously noted, as students move from the early to the middle years, parental involvement in the school often declines so specific strategies to harness their ongoing involvement is required.
- Visit schools with long-standing and successful experience of inclusion in the early and/or middle years and spend a day observing and discussing what happens.
- Initiate and support moves to strengthen the professional community among colleagues so that it becomes possible to engage in effective joint classroom-based work with them. This work includes team teaching, peer coaching, mentoring, and collaborative action learning.

The last of these suggestions identifies the most powerful form of teacher collaboration. Traditionally, however, it has been the least practised by teachers, probably because it is more difficult than other types of teacher collaboration, such as social, industrial, political, technical, and academic collaboration. Fortunately, for the success of inclusion, a symbiotic relationship exists between community and collaboration. The structure, climate and culture of school communities activate teachers to practise joint classroom-based work, and joint classroom-based work strengthens professional community among teachers. This is particularly important for the transitional stages as students move from the early to the middle and the middle to later years of schooling. Often the ease of this transition, particularly for students with special needs, can be enhanced through effective teacher sharing of knowledge and insights. The potential looping of teachers—where a teacher moves through the year levels with a group of students—is a way of building community over an extended period of time.

LEARNING ESSENTIALS

So far, we have discussed what teachers can do for community and what community can do for teachers. In this section, we look at the impact of community on student responses to inclusive schooling.

Students' responses to school

The school years mark a number of transitions as children move from one educational setting to another. Traditionally, school transitions were seen as lasting only a few days or, at most, a couple of weeks. Now, transitions are understood to happen long-term, anywhere from six months to two years. There is growing recognition of the long-term impact of transitions for all children upon life outcomes, such as employment and incarceration. Increasingly, atypical children are being targeted as requiring specialised support in transitions (Petriwskyj, Thorpe, & Taylor, 2005).

EARLY YEARS

The early years mark the entry to school as a process of transition from home and informal contexts to formal schooling. Many children make the transition from home to preschool settings before they begin formal schooling. Typically, children have already participated in child care and preschool contexts.

The early work around children's entry into schooling has been traditionally described as school readiness. In this understanding, children were assessed against a set of criteria that determined how ready they were to engage in the activities of learning. Thus, a child was measured against a set of abilities involving visual and auditory cues, and behaviour management. If children were deemed not ready for school, they were told that they required an extra year to mature before beginning school. Similarly, children were retained from year level to year level because they were deemed not sufficiently ready for the next grade level. Sometimes labelled as a "gift of time", others have more recently

argued that children have been denied access to school literacies and knowledge because of delayed entry (Graue, Kroeger, & Brown, 2002). In many cases, the delay of the school year meant that any developmental concerns went undetected for yet another year.

This maturational view of children being ready for school has been replaced in recent years. This is largely in response to the incompatibility of school readiness views with emerging views of inclusion. Key concerns were:

- readiness assessments were not reliable indicators of children's abilities;
- grade retention was found to be detrimental for children's development of emotional, social, and academic learning; and
- delayed school entry further disadvantaged those children with increased vulnerability in certain home contexts (Petriwskyj et al., 2005).

The term *school readiness* has been replaced largely with the term *transition to school*. School transition has been defined as "an ongoing process of mutual adaptation by children, families and schools to facilitate children moving successfully from home and early childhood education and care (ECEC) settings into the early years of school" (Petriwskyj et al., 2005, p. 56). Recent developments focus on the importance of parents and children having continuity of experiences (including language acquisition) as they transition from one setting to the next. A core aspect is valuing partnerships with families and communities.

Successful transition programs to school go beyond a focus on the initial first few weeks of school to consider long-term outcomes for students. An increasingly recognised critical element of transition programs is the consideration of the diversity of the learners, family, and home contexts, and a flexible educational provision to increase opportunities for young children with social, cultural, and developmental differences. Children with developmental delays are particularly affected when discontinuities occur between home and school settings, and between mainstream and specialist services differences. Consequentially, there is a call for all children to be involved in programs that provide support within and across educational communities.

Core qualities of successful transition programs in the early years include:

- universal access to preschool settings for all children;
- access to high-quality early childhood programs;
- flexibility in curriculum and teaching approaches;
- the recognition of educational climates that accommodate children's social, cultural, and developmental differences; and
- facilitation of positive relationships among children and between teachers and children.

The early years are critical for maintaining engagement in school and yet, even at this age, young children are opting out of the school experience because of its alienating character.

MIDDLE YEARS

The relatively recent introduction of middle schooling has introduced another transition for students as they move from the early years of schooling. The middle schooling initiative came partly from concern about the high level of alienation and disengagement displayed by young adolescents in traditional secondary schools. While a few students thrived in these schools, many just survived or made little progress, and a worrying number became either active or passive dissenters (see Box 9.8). These schools could not claim to be inclusive because alienation and disengagement made many students feel excluded. As a result, often these students decided to exclude themselves.

BOX 9.8 Young adolescents' responses to school

ACTIVE OPPONENTS	PASSIVE DISSENTERS	NEGOTIATORS	ACTIVE SUPPORTERS
Anti school	Anti school	Partly pro school	Pro school
Resistance fighters	Passive resistance	Selective resistance	No resistance
Open and guerrilla warfare	Indifferent, withdrawn	Make and extract concessions, bargain	Compliant, conform

How can we account for the different responses by middle years students described in Box 9.8? Students respond not to the objective school situation but to their subjective interpretation of it. That is, they respond to their definition of the situation and different definitions result in different responses. For example, the way *active supporters* see the situation is that their interests and goals will be best met by cooperating with the school. They think that conformity will lead to success; that conformity will make them winners at school and in society. They believe that school values them and, therefore, they value school. Conversely, the way *active opponents* see the situation is that school offers them nothing but failure. They consider that school regards them as losers, treats them as losers, and no amount of cooperation and conformity on their part will change that. In their eyes, school does not value them so why should they value schools, and the only way to defend themselves against oppression is to destroy school before it destroys them.

Passive dissenters share some aspects of the active opponents' definition of the situation but they see their interests best met by adopting the stance of passive resisters rather than guerrilla warfare fighters. The fourth response of students to school is that of *negotiator.* Most of the time, most students regard school as a place where their interests are best met by adopting a policy of give and take, extracting concessions from the school and, in the process, making compromises.

To explain the differences documented in Box 9.8 by saying that different student definitions of the situation result in different student responses to school invites a further question: "Why do different students construct different definitions of the same school situation?" For example, isn't it the case that, in any one school, all students may be confronted with compulsion, coercion, unfair competition, institutionalised failure, curriculum irrelevance, regimentation, uniformity, authoritarianism, and social injustice. If so, why do some students find these elements to be palatable while others take deep exception to them? Is the answer to be found in personality differences among students or in subtle differences in the ways that schools treat different students, or both? A lack of hard data means that these questions are often answered on the grounds of ideology and reasoned speculation rather than conclusive research findings.

From what has been said so far in this section, we would put forward the following propositions for consideration. Students who are disengaged at school are unlikely to make significant academic progress; and if they do make progress, it will be in spite of the school, not because of it. Students who construct an active opponent or passive dissenter definition of the school situation will become disengaged at school. Teachers attempting to change young adolescent student responses to schooling

from a position of alienation to one of engagement need to identify the students' definition of the school situation and the bases for these definitions.

Students with special support needs are young adolescents first. As such, their responses to school will cover the range indicated in Box 9.8. A few will be active supporters and active opponents, some will be passive dissenters, and most will be negotiators. This point needs to be made explicit because some people may implicitly assume that resistance at school by students with special support needs is a function of their disabilities rather than a function of their definition of the school situation. Some people may even believe that students with special support needs are incapable of constructing a definition of the school situation. The paucity of research on this matter allows such beliefs to flourish, as does the difficulty of identifying the students' feelings or views about school (see Box 9.9).

BOX 9.9

From alienation to engagement

"I don't want to go to school today." That's what Chris, an eighth grader at Bigaton College, told his mother every morning. When he did go to school, he sat alone during lessons, sometimes worked on separate tasks with his TA, and for the rest of the time stared out the window. Occasionally, teachers invited Chris to join in whole classroom work but their questions, suggestions, and requests were treated with sullen indifference. At recess and lunchtime, Chris ate by himself and took no part in playground activities. He also consistently resisted any participation in school sporting events, assemblies, socials, and drama productions.

Chris' teachers characterised his behaviour as irrational and dysfunctional. They attributed it to a combination of low self-esteem, other personality deficiencies, and the side-effects of his medication—on his tenth birthday Chris sustained head and spinal injuries from a car crash.

Chris, himself, however, would have described his behaviour as sensible and effective. From day one at Bigaton College, he felt excluded. The students politely ignored him and the teachers quickly abandoned him to the TA. Other aspects of the classroom added to his sense of alienation: competitive assessment, the formal arrangement of desks in rows, the teachers' bookish chalk-and-talk approach to teaching, and the university-entrance-dominated curriculum. The way Chris saw the situation, Bigaton College comprised a world he was forced to live in but denied citizenship of, a world that invited him to step forward but would cut him down if he did. So, for him, the most sensible course of action was clear: make a small target of himself, refuse to run the race, and drop out.

In Year 9, Chris' definition of the situation changed completely when he moved to a different school. It was a school that included him in everything. A school where the basketball team made him a player, even though they knew it reduced their chance of winning matches. A school where he performed in the choir's annual concert, even though they knew he would sing badly and out of tune. A school that gave him a place on the student council, a regular job in the school canteen, and an active role in classroom learning workshops. A school that gave him a reason to arrive each day with a smile on his face.

How can teachers get inside the minds of students with special support needs (or any student) to identify their view or definition of the school situation? One approach involves direct verbal communication with the student. Where this is not possible, teachers can turn to nonverbal indicators, that is, make inferences about how students regard school based on observations of their behaviour. Other indirect sources of information include the parents and friends of the student, along with discussion with colleagues within the school community in which they work. Teachers can also use these approaches and sources to identify the bases on which students construct their definitions of the school situation. Once this information is gathered, teachers are in a better position to customise, on a case-by-case basis, ways to reduce negative responses and resistance to schooling.

As a general principle, school communities aim to maximise student engagement at school by minimising active and passive dissent and negotiating a working agreement with them to gain a productive level of consensus. Much of this consensus building occurs within the process of developing community and making all students feel equally respected, accepted and valued. The less students feel this way, the less schools can claim to have built community. When considering how to build community, schools confront the question: "What makes many students alienated from schooling and resistant to it?" As indicated in our discussion of students' definitions of the school situation, there is no one answer to this question that applies to all students. The reasons vary from group to group and individual to individual. However, as also intimated above, some themes that are likely to recur within students' definitions of the situation include: compulsion, coercion, unfair competition, institutionalised failure, curriculum irrelevance, regimentation, uniformity, authoritarianism, and social injustice. Given these themes, teachers in the middle years could claim that a number of their practices help make all students feel equally respected, accepted and valued. For example, middle years teachers could:

- offer students choice, for example by using curriculum exploratories, differentiated curriculum, integrated studies, multiple intelligences, and ways to adjust teaching styles to fit students' learning styles;
- make the curriculum relevant to the strengths, needs, and interests of middle-years students, for example by adopting or adapting an integrated approach to curriculum based on students' concerns about themselves and the world;
- remove institutionalised failure, for example by making structural adjustments to student grouping and assessment practices that produce losers; and
- value diversity, for example by removing any cultural bias from curriculum, assessment, pedagogy, school organisation, and staffing.

ACADEMIC AND SOCIAL OUTCOMES

At an overarching level, schools for students in the early and middle years of learning should be attempting to be inclusive by building communities that break down the barriers that lead anti-schoolers to exclude themselves from the life and work of the school. Some critics claim that the emphasis on community privileges social relationships at the expense of academic rigour. When extended to inclusion, this claim implies that, at best, for students with special support needs the social gains will outweigh the educational gains. Supporters make the counterclaim that community raises the intellectual quality of all students' work, not just the traditional high-flyers, because it strengthens social relationships at school. And "all students" here includes students with special support needs. How does community do this? Research by Beck and Kosnik (2006) has suggested that community encourages and enables students to engage in:

- whole class and small group discussions; and higher quality discussions;
- risk-taking activities, for example by asking questions, voicing opinions, voicing doubts, accepting criticism, questioning each other's opinions and providing honest critiques of others' work;
- personal growth activities—for example, students develop self-acceptance, self-confidence, and resilience;
- inclusive behaviours—for example, students work to eschew prejudice, discrimination, and violence (verbal, social, psychological, physical); and
- activities that are group-oriented—for example, they show patience, interest in the work of other students and willingness to share resources; they also offer support when personal problems arise, and seek help and resources from their fellow students.

These processes or elements provide teachers with one set of indicators that community and inclusion are alive and well in the schools. These principles apply equally for the early and middle years.

CULTURAL CAPITAL AND STUDENTS' RESPONSES TO SCHOOL

The question "Why do different students construct different definitions of the same school situation?" can be approached from another direction, namely, the concept of cultural capital. Bourdieu (1986) explained the concept of cultural capital as the knowledge, skills, education, and any advantages a person has that gives them a higher status in society, including high expectations. In the school context, parents provide children with cultural capital, the attitudes and knowledge that makes the educational system a comfortable familiar place in which they can succeed easily. According to this concept, different types of schooling require students to possess different prerequisites for success. For example, success in traditional schools for early and middle-years students requires students to be competitive, individualistic, future oriented, and able to spend most of their time sitting, listening, reading and writing (see Box 9.10). Without these qualities, which constitute a form of cultural capital, students experience school as a foreign place and often withdraw from or become antagonistic to it. Such responses indicate that not all students do feel equally accepted, valued, included, supported and able to achieve.

The structure, culture, climate, curriculum, and pedagogy of schools should present students with a different set of prerequisites for success (see Box 9.10). Students without these prerequisites could find schools alienating and not the kind of community presented in this chapter. In such cases, supporters would be reluctant to change their small communities to fit the students. This leaves them with the challenge, in the interests of inclusion, of changing the student to fit the school.

9.10

Cultural capital required for student success

STUDENTS NEED TO BE	DUE TO
Accepting of difference	Mixed-ability classes, non-selective entry
Flexible	Give and take of small group work, often daily adjustments to timetable, interdisciplinary team of teachers

Cooperative	Less competition, less individualism, more collaborative work, cooperative learning
Interdependent	Joint work, shared assessment
Self-regulating	Open classroom, curriculum exploratories and projects, classroom as workshop, differentiated instruction
Assertive	Democratic decision making, negotiated curriculum
Self-confident	Exhibitions of work, speaking in public, workshops
Open	Disclosure of concerns about self and society, public critique of their work
Problem-solvers	Less rote learning and instruction, more constructivism

9.10

USING THIS CHAPTER IN SCHOOLS

Inclusive practices in the early and middle years in Australia involve reforms to traditional ways of schooling. A set of philosophical principles underpins this approach, for example success for each and every student, and making schools responsive to the learning that students have reached. Inclusion of all students underpins this approach. To use the information in this chapter in schools, you need to think about the major overarching theme underlying the chapter. That is, a two-way relationship exists between community and inclusive practices. The community strengthens inclusive practices and inclusion strengthens the community.

Throughout the chapter, we have also either explicitly or implicitly emphasised other themes, and each of these contribute to enhancing community and inclusion practices in the early and middle years. When you first join the staff of a school in either a practicum placement or as a full-time teacher, we recommend you use the principles outlined in Table 9.1. The principles are accompanied by an example for each of the early and middle years contexts.

TABLE 9.1 PRINCIPLES THAT ENHANCE COMMUNITY AND INCLUSION IN THE EARLY AND MIDDLE YEARS OF SCHOOLING

Principles	Example 1 Early years	Example 2 Middle years
The structure, climate, and culture of school communities should make them models of an inclusive	Demonstrate a classroom climate where students and teachers respect each other, by responding to	Explain to a group of parents the distinguishing features of an inclusive society. Suggest ways in

TABLE 9.1 PRINCIPLES THAT ENHANCE COMMUNITY AND INCLUSION IN THE EARLY AND MIDDLE YEARS OF SCHOOLING continued

Principles	Example 1 Early years	Example 2 Middle years
society. Inclusion is an integral part of these communities, not an add-on.	children's questions and comments with care and thought.	which parents can help their middle school make our society more inclusive.
Schools should be student-centred.	Use resources to help children understand that diversity is valued, such as providing song cards for children to point to when choosing a song in a classroom where they may be bilingual or language-delayed children.	Understand the unique developmental needs of middle-years students.
Students with special support needs are children and adolescents first; they require the same responsive schooling as students without special support needs.	Provide a diverse range of materials and activities for all children's engagement and meaning-making, and make opportunities for children to share their meanings to others.	Get to know students by exploring their interests and engaging with parents. Recognise their need for peer acceptance.
School communities should provide teachers with a natural resource that goes a long way towards helping them successfully meet the challenges of inclusion.	Feel comfortable in answering children's questions. Questions such as "Why can't Sally climb the fort by herself?" could be answered with "Sally's arms and legs are not strong enough to climb without help" (MacNaughton & Williams, 1998).	Answer a question, from a job selection panel, about how the challenges of inclusion faced by teachers of young adolescents differ from the challenges faced by teachers of young children. Explain to the panel how a small middle-school community will empower you to successfully meet those challenges.

TABLE 9.1 PRINCIPLES THAT ENHANCE COMMUNITY AND INCLUSION IN THE EARLY AND MIDDLE YEARS OF SCHOOLING continued

Principles	Example 1 Early years	Example 2 Middle years
School communities offer an antidote for preventing the development of an anti-school subculture among students. They foster student responses to schooling that lead to higher levels of student engagement and achievement.	Promote children's thinking skills by encouraging them to explain their reasoning, collaborate with others, and explore ideas in a safe and stimulating environment.	Help colleagues develop ways to map young adolescents' definitions of their school situation. Help colleagues identify the bases on which different definitions get constructed.
Successful teachers in inclusive schools are committed to the philosophy of inclusion, have a deep understanding of students with and without special support needs, relate positively to all these students, build community in and across classrooms, and work collaboratively with their colleagues.	Model understandings that recognise children's differing abilities and provide experiences for children to develop positive and non-discriminatory attitudes. This can be accomplished through conversations, literature, puppets, posters, and photographs.	At your annual performance-management meeting outline tangible indicators of your contribution so far to community building in the middle school. You can nominate steps for increasing that contribution.
The curriculum pedagogy and work organisation of schools must be responsive, relevant and appropriate to the experiences of students.	Provide curriculum experiences where children can express their own individual experiences, such as the opportunity to paint themselves as they are, including their disability, and not an idealised version.	Bring a middle-schooling perspective to course planning and program review sessions at your school. Determine whether all educational experiences provided by these courses and programs are inclusive and reflect young adolescent development.

TABLE 9.1 **PRINCIPLES THAT ENHANCE COMMUNITY AND INCLUSION IN THE EARLY AND MIDDLE YEARS OF SCHOOLING continued**

Principles	Example 1 Early years	Example 2 Middle years
Teachers working in inclusive schools need to be double-adapters. They have to adapt the curriculum and their teaching so that is becomes student-centred and then adapt that to make it appropriate for students with special support needs.	Scaffold the learning experiences that both support and challenge the child. The balance may be different for each child in different contexts.	Write programs for young adolescents that are responsive to their developmental needs. Adapt these programs and write them as IEPs for young adolescents with special support needs.
The curriculum and pedagogical practices adapted for inclusion are both generic and specific. They apply to inclusion of students with special support needs at all stages of schooling.	Ongoing discussions are important for helping children understand how to interact with others of differing abilities. This means ongoing conversations and special planning times.	Outline, at PD days for P–12 staff, how your middle-years teaching and curriculum practices are similar to and different from those used by teachers of young children and young adults.

PRACTICAL ACTIVITIES

Uni-work

1 In a group of five, draft, rehearse, and perform an 8–10 minute impromptu play based on the following brief. Your group is an ad hoc grievance committee convened and chaired by the principal of a school. The other four members of the group are two teachers and two parents. Your committee meets in the principal's office to discuss a complaint from the parents of a student with special support needs about a particular incident at the school, or a particular aspect of the school's inclusion program, that has impacted badly on their child. Half of your committee adopts a supportive position on the complaint; the other half is unsympathetic.

2 Survey the editions of three education journals that have been published over an extended period of time:

a How many articles focus on inclusion and the schooling of students with special support needs?

b Are the articles predominantly practical or theoretical, research-based or anecdotal, school-specific or generic?

c Is there an explicit or implicit editorial position on inclusion and the schooling of early years students or young adolescents with special support needs?

If your library does not have three education journals, use journals that focus on childhood or adolescence to make up the required number. Select one article that you consider to be of most interest and use to you and discuss the reasons for your choice.

3 Conduct an internet search on one of the following topics:
- How to build community in classrooms.
- Ability streaming as a solution to differentiated classrooms.
- How to use Information and Communication Technologies (ICT) to increase engagement in middle-years classrooms.

School-work

Remember that school policies may apply that restrict your ability to complete one or more of the activities suggested below. Before beginning any of the activities, speak to your supervising teacher or a member of the school administration to confirm that you can undertake the activity within existing school guidelines and policies.

4 Design a small problem-based learning (PBL) module (say 2–4 lessons) for your class, paying particular attention to the needs of students who are working below grade expectations. Before you begin, select a particular model of PBL, for example a model developed by Savery and Duffy (1995) or Stepien, Gallagher, and Workman (1993). (Both references are given in the *References* below.) When designing the module ensure that it is:
- faithful to the principles of PBL;
- adapted to meet the experiences, developmental needs, interests, and characteristics of your students; and
- contains adaptations that make it responsive to the needs, interests and characteristics of all of your students.

5 Interview a teacher in your school who has had experience teaching students with special support needs. Ask the teacher what he or she considers to be the characteristics of teachers who successfully implement inclusion, from observation and experience. Alternatively, conduct a similar interview with a parent who has a child with special support needs attending school. Remember that there are likely to be school policies about when and how you would set up interviews with parents. Check this out with a supervising teacher before you start, or with the school administration. Before conducting the interview, compile a list of 10–20 prompts that will help ensure the interview covers a wide range of relevant issues that will help you understand the student's background and current educational needs.

6 Select a student with special inclusion needs in a class you are teaching. Imagine you are about to hand over the teaching of this student to a new teacher. The new teacher has no experience of inclusion and received no preparation for it at university. The principal has given you time to compile a handover inclusion kit. Nominate the specific disability that the student has and compile an induction kit for the new teacher that is customised in terms of their situation. In addition to the suggestions made earlier in this chapter, include details of any relevant films, DVDs, novels, etc. that you consider helpful.

SUGGESTED READING AND RESOURCES

Chadbourne, R. (1997). *Including children with intellectual disabilities in regular classrooms: A review of the Western Australian project.* Report of a study for the Disabilities Services Commission and the Education Department of Western Australia. Perth: Western Australia.

Chadbourne, R. (2004). A typology of teacher collaboration in middle schools. *Australian Journal of Middle Schooling, 4*, 9–15.

Hines, R. & Johnston, J. (1997). Inclusion (pp.109–120). In J. L. Irvin (Ed.), *What current research says to the middle level practitioner*. Columbus, OH: National Middle School Association.

Kennedy, C.H. & Fisher, D. (2001). *Inclusive middle schools.* Baltimore: Brooks Publishing.

Manning, M. Lee & Bucher, K. (2005). *Teaching in the middle school.* Upper Saddle River, NJ: Pearson/Prentice Hall.

Organisation for Economic Co-operation and Development (OECD) (2006). *Starting Strong II: Early Childhood Education and Care.* Paris: Author.

Pendergast, D. & Bahr, N. (2005). *Teaching middle years. Rethinking curriculum, pedagogy and assessment.* Crows Nest, NSW: Allen & Unwin.

Tomlinson, C. A, Moon, T. R. & Callahan, C. M. (1998). How well are we addressing academic diversity in the middle school? *Middle School Journal, 29*, 3–11.

REFERENCES

Bahr, N. & Pendergast, D. (2007). *The millennial adolescent.* Canberra: Australian Council for Educational Research.

Bauer, A. M. & Brown, G. M. (2001). *Adolescents and inclusion: Transforming secondary schools.* Baltimore: Brooks Publishing.

Beane, J. (1997). *Curriculum integration: Designing the core of democratic education.* New York: Teachers College Press.

Beck, C. & Kosnik, C. (2006). *Innovations in teacher education: A social constructivist approach.* State University of New York Press.

Bourdieu, P. (1986). Forms of capital. In J. G. Richardson (Ed.). *Handbook of theory and research for the sociology of education* (pp. 241–258). New York: Greenwood Press.

Chadbourne, R. (2001). *Middle schooling for the middle years: What might the jury be considering?.* Victoria: Australian Education Union.

Demsey, I. & Arthur-Kelly, M. (2007). *Maximising learning outcomes in diverse classrooms.* South Melbourne, Vic: Thomson.

Ireson, J., Hallam, S., & Hurley, C. (2005). What are the effects of ability grouping on GCSE attainment? *British Educational Research Journal, 31*, 443–458.

Jackson, A. W. & Davis, G. A. (2000). *Turning points 2000: Educating adolescents in the 21st century.* New York: Teachers College Press.

Luke, A., Elkins, J., Weir, K., Land, R., Carrington, V., Dole, S., Pendergast, D., Kapitzke, C., van Kraayenoord, C., Moni, K., McIntosh, A., Mayer, D., Bahr, M., Hunter, L., Chadbourne, R., Bean, T., Alverman, D., & Stevens, L. (2003). *Beyond the middle: A report about literacy and numeracy development of target group students in the middle years of schooling, Volume 1.* Brisbane: JS McMillan Printing Group.

MacNaughton, G. & Williams, G. (1998). *Techniques for teaching young children: Choices in theory and practice*. Frenchs Forest, NSW: Longman.

Manning, M. Lee (2002). *Developmentally appropriate middle level schools.* Olney, MD: Association for Childhood Education International.

Manning, M. Lee & Bucher, K. (2005). *Teaching in the middle school*. Upper Saddle River, NJ: Pearson/Prentice Hall.

Moss, J. (2006). *How to succeed with making schools inclusive*. Carlton South, Vic: Curriculum Corporation.

Organisation for Economic Co-operation and Development (OECD). (2006). *Starting Strong II: Early Childhood Education and Care.* Paris: Author.

Petriwskyj, A., Thorpe, K., & Tayler, C. (2005). Trends in construction of transition to school in three western regions, 1990–2004, *International Journal of Early Years Education*, *13*, 55–69.

Prensky. M. (2005/6). Listen to the natives. *Educational Leadership*, *63*, 8–13.

Savery, J. & Duffy, T. (1995). Problem based learning: An instructional model and its constructivist framework. *Educational Technology*, *35*, 31–38.

Schaffner, C. B. & Buswell, B. E. (1991). *Opening doors: Strategies for including all students in regular education*. Colorado Springs, CO: Peak Parent Center, Inc.

Stepien, W. J., Gallagher, S. A., & Workman, D. (1993). Problem-based learning for traditional and interdisciplinary classrooms. *Journal for the Education of the Gifted*, *16*, 338–345.

Strahan, D., Smith, T., McElrath, M., & Toole, C. (2001). Connecting, caring and action: Teachers who create learning communities in their classrooms. In T. Dickinson (Ed.), *Reinventing the middle school* (pp. 96–115). New York: RoutledgeFalmer.

Talay-Ongan, A. (2004). *Early development risk and disability: Relational contexts*. Frenchs Forest, NSW: Pearson.

Acknowledgement

Thank you to Anne Petriwskyj for her valuable suggestions in relation to the early childhood context.

Credit

Quote on page 286 reproduced with permission from Schaffner, C. B. & Buswell, B. E. (1991). *Opening doors: Strategies for including all students in regular education* (pp. 23–24). Colorado Springs, CO: Peak Parent Center, Inc.

Karen B. Moni and Ian Hay

10

SECONDARY SCHOOL AND TRANSITIONS

What you will learn in this chapter

This chapter focuses on students with diverse needs in adolescence and young adulthood (ages 14–18 years). If you are training to work at a level that is not the upper secondary, this chapter still has considerable relevance for you for at least two reasons. First, many of the issues that challenge students in the senior years of high school can be reduced, if not eliminated, by good teaching practice and support in the earlier years of school, even from preschool. For example, establishing effective social skills in the early years will lead to fewer interpersonal traumas in the later years of schooling. Second, this book is about inclusive practices that advantage all students, those who experience difficulties in school because of learning problems or other complicating circumstances, and those who are gifted and talented. Knowing what happens in the secondary school is important for teachers who must plan acceleration and enrichment activities for the brighter students or recognise some of the challenges that any student might face in the future in secondary school. So, there is much of relevance in this chapter for new teachers regardless of the phase of schooling you are studying.

As adolescents move further into their teenage years and connect to the adult world, they face unfamiliar territory. There are issues relating to independence, sexuality, identity, and, for a small minority, homelessness and drugs. All of these issues, those that are traumatic and not-so-traumatic, affect their learning. The impact of these influences is easily hidden in the context of large, anonymous secondary schools. Thus, while there is some overlap in this chapter with issues that arise for students during the middle years of schooling, here we focus on inclusion in traditional high school settings, and in the later years of high school, as students move toward certification and the world of work or tertiary study.

In this chapter, then, you will learn about:

- the context of high schools and the challenges faced by students with diverse needs;
- the interactions between adolescence and diversity;
- transitions from school to training, work, and further study;
- issues and challenges for students;
- getting to know the learner;
- planning for diversity; and
- key teaching strategies, including the language of instruction, explicit teaching, and task analysis.

CASE STUDIES

AT THE EDGE

Josh is 16 years old. He spent much of his primary school years travelling around New South Wales with his parents, who were itinerant fruit pickers. During this time, he attended five schools. In some years when there wasn't much work, the family travelled a lot and Josh didn't attend school regularly. The family moved to the city mid-way through Year 9 and Josh was enrolled in a large urban high school. It was soon apparent to teachers that he had large gaps in his knowledge and skills, and was finding it hard to socialise with other students. Although he finished Year 9 with the other students, the school recommended that he not be promoted to Year 10.

During his repeat year, Josh's home circumstances deteriorated. His father left home, and Josh did not get on well with his mother's new partner who found it difficult to deal with him. He was pretty much left to his own devices. In addition, school was not going well. He was bored with the same subjects and content. He was a year older than his classmates and thought that they should be deferring to him in the classroom. However, he still found the subjects difficult and struggled to cope with basic reading and writing tasks. His response to this was to misbehave, disrupting the class to get the attention he wanted and to avoid any school work. He was withdrawn from some classes for extra support in literacy, but he was resistant to this as well, often disappearing out of the school when he was supposed to be in class. By the end of Year 9 when he was 15, Josh had a reputation in the school as a student who was performing poorly and engaging in disruptive behaviour. He was a regular truant and beyond the control of his mother.

An ugly incident with his mother's partner left him virtually homeless and he left school following a series of episodes in which he was involved in fights with other students and in confrontations with teachers. After being arrested and charged with breaking and entering a convenience store to steal food and cigarettes, his probation officer suggested he should try *The Edge*, a flexi-school in the centre of the city.

The Edge was established in the year 2000 to provide an alternative education for students, such as Josh, who didn't fit into the mainstream. The school offers a range of subjects and support for literacy and numeracy. *The Edge* also runs a breakfast club, and there are showers, washing machines, and access to support services. Although it took a while for Josh to settle in, he attended the school regularly and completed Year 10. He still lives in shelters around the city, but has made contact with his mother again. He is thinking of joining the army when he turns seventeen.

ENGLISH IS GAY

Joe Wilton had always wanted to be an English teacher. He came from a solid middle-class background, attended a boys school, and completed his degree in English Literature with an excellent grade point average. After completing his DipEd in which both practicums were undertaken in a private single-sex boys school, Joe applied for a job in the state education system and ended up in a rural high school. The community was badly affected by drought, there were few job opportunities for young people as the rural sector was collapsing, and the tourist season lasted only during the winter months.

As a beginning teacher, Joe was given classes where there were low-achieving students and students with challenging behaviours. Joe was innovative and creative and designed a range of units that he thought would engage students in the poetry and novels they were required to read. He designed drama activities, brought music into the classroom, and focused on teaching his students to appreciate and love literature in the same way he did. He exhorted his senior students to see education as a way they could escape the local social and economic situation and was met with passive resistance, stony silence, and homophobic taunts.

By the end of the first semester, after several confrontations over homework and non-completion of assessment tasks, he was angry and frustrated. He could see that he wasn't developing positive relationships with his students that were allowing them to learn. He felt the students were apathetic, unappreciative, and had either limited abilities or no interest in learning in English, or both.

During a parent–teacher interview, in a conversation with a parent who was an elder from the local Indigenous community, Joe commented about the child's lack of interest in school. Much to his consternation, the parent challenged Joe by asking him what interest *he* had shown in the local community. During the next few days Joe did a lot of thinking and decided he needed to change his course of action.

In the third term holidays, instead of returning to the city and his friends, as he usually did, he spent the first week in town. By the end of that week he'd learned that a couple of his senior students were working to keep family businesses running in town. He also learned that one girl was the sole carer for her three younger siblings, and another was being cared for by her aunt as her mother was dying of cancer. Other students from local properties were taking a major role in mustering. He also received invitations to two barbecues, and an evening of pig shooting from families of students he taught. Other things he learned:

- Some of his Year 12 boys frequented the only café in town where there was internet access to play networked internet games.
- There was a rodeo in spring which was a "big deal" in town.
- The community was raising money to repair the swimming pool.
- There were strong softball and football leagues.
- The local river was a popular spot for water skiing and swimming.

Joe decided to use some of the things he'd learned about the students and the community in

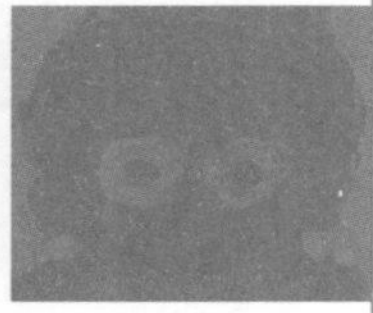

his teaching. For example, when his Year 10s were studying *Romeo and Juliet*, he planned activities to transform the play into a rodeo setting. He taught expository and persuasive writing through projects focusing on raising money for the pool and writing submissions to protect the river. Joe also invited community members into the class, and, with his senior students, he developed digistories about the town, which were used by the local library and museum on their websites. He also watched his students playing sport and used footage from games to teach students about media representations.

digistories
Short narratives about a personal event or life experience made using simple multi-media software such as Adobe Photoshop or iMovie and posted on the internet.

By the end of the year, Joe was exhausted but felt that he had made some headway. His students were friendlier, and were more willing to undertake work when they saw connections to their own interests and community. He wasn't sure about the Year 11 boys, who remained resistant, until he spoke to a mother in the supermarket, who told him her son was always talking about what he was doing in English, and how she had even caught him reading the set novel at the weekend.

TEACHING–LEARNING CONTEXT

Educational policies that focus on a non-categorical, full-inclusion model of educational services have resulted in more diversity in Australian secondary classrooms (Department of Education, Science, and Training, 2002). In secondary schools the recurrent challenge is how to accommodate and value educational diversity and achieve curriculum flexibility within a structure that is increasingly focused on competitiveness, standardisation of accreditation, and hierarchically organised content knowledge linked to specific subjects, such as Science, Mathematics, and History.

When considering secondary classrooms the temptation is to perceive the issues only from the teachers' perspective. And, yet, there are other key stakeholders whose contributions can enhance the learning outcomes of students with a very wide range of learning needs. These are the students themselves, their parents, and support staff. These stakeholders can perceive the same classroom situation from very different perspectives. There is also significant diversity of responses to students with special learning needs from one secondary school to another, even in the same district. For example, in one school a curriculum department may adopt a whole department or subject approach to accommodating students' abilities and interests but this approach may not be consistent across other subjects in the same school or the next secondary school in the same town. In reality, it is often the attitudes, values, and educational philosophies of the leaders in a school that are the most significant determining factor on how students with diversity are accommodated in secondary education and how state and system policies on students with diversity are interpreted and enacted within that school (Waite, Lawson, & Robertson, 2006).

The transition from primary/middle to secondary school can be challenging for all students, but the challenges for students with particular learning needs are exacerbated by the complex interactions and changes to relationships, routines, expectations of teachers, and the needs of each learner.

Secondary school students have to develop relationships with more teachers and more students than in any education period up to this point. In their primary and middle schools, students typically spend the day, and indeed the school year, with one cohort of students and with one teacher or a small group of teachers. In secondary schools, students may change classes for subjects and may have five or six teachers during the one school day. In addition, secondary schools tend to have a broader student base than primary schools. Students have to develop relationships with peers from a range of ethnic and language backgrounds, cultures, and socioeconomic groups.

In general, secondary schools are larger, less organic settings than primary schools. Students move from an integrated day, where subjects are often combined, to a more fragmented day where a broader curriculum comprising up to eight disciplines or Key Learning Areas is taught in shorter sessions and across the week. This traditional organisation is efficient in terms of dealing with large numbers of students who can move from class to class independently. It makes it harder, however, for schools to introduce accommodations to routines for groups or individual students. Furthermore, this level of movement between classrooms, the associated increase in noise, the changing teachers and their expectations, and even student groups can be very confusing and frustrating to students with special education needs (see, e.g., Ivey, 2004; Prior, 2003).

It should be remembered that teachers in secondary schools on a full teaching load often have five or more class groups each week. This means that they need to establish and maintain relationships with more than 150 students during a school year. Purely from a logistical perspective, this means that teachers may not have the same amount of time to spend with students and there are expectations that students will become independent in the secondary setting very quickly.

BOX 10.1

Supporting students to make the transition to high school

The following suggestions and strategies provide a useful starting point for teachers and schools in addressing some of the issues around transition.

- Develop a program of orientation for all new students, not just for those starting at the beginning of the year.
- Recognise that students need time to adjust to the level of work and to develop good relationships with teachers.
- A new student who starts mid-year or who has transferred from another location or school may not have a peer support network to fall back on. Using a buddy system with peers or a mentoring system with an older student may help new students to establish friendships more quickly.
- Students moving into high school may become stressed because their self-concept of who they are as a learner is now under more pressure. The "big fish little pond effect" enhances academic and general self-concept; the opposite reduces self-concept, which encourages fight or flight responses within the student.
- Teachers also need to be encouraging and supportive of parents/caregivers because effective communication between the home and the school is important.

Adolescence

Adolescence is a period of transition characterised by accelerated processes of change in cognition and social and psychological functioning, as well as the marked physical restructuring of puberty. Adolescent learners with developmental disabilities, learning difficulties, and those at risk have to cope

with the complications arising from their particular circumstances and also with the personal challenges of typical adolescent development.

Teachers have become more conscious of the challenges that adolescence presents with the development of the middle-years movement (see previous chapter) that has responded to the needs of early adolescents through a re-thinking of educational philosophies around learning, a restructuring of educational settings and practices, and a renewal of curriculum, pedagogy and assessment. However, adolescence continues beyond Year 9 and issues around adolescence become increasingly complex as students progress though secondary school.

A number of common psychological problems, such as low self-concept, depression, anxiety, and psychosis typically have their peak onset during adolescence, particularly if there is evidence that the young person is involved with substance abuse (Frey, Nolen, Van Schoiack-Edstrom, & Hirschstein, 2005). There is also an increase in the identification and rates of mental health problems and these are estimated to be between 14% and 25% of individuals aged 12 to 17 years (Campbell, 2004). It has been argued that there is a reciprocal relationship between low self-concept, low academic skills, low coping skills, and a lack of social relationships (Flook, Repetti, & Ullman, 2005; Resnick et al., 1997).

Social relationships

Major changes to social relationships are common in the adolescent years. Peers and peer groups have more influence on the actions and behaviours of individuals as they extend their networks outside of the family unit as part of developing autonomy, and there are new connections established beyond the family into the broader community.

Adolescents' perceptions of their friendships and social standing are important to their levels of psychological adjustment and, indirectly, their academic and social progress (Demir & Urberg, 2004). Friendships and social skills are, thus, seen to be protective factors that help adolescents to cope and advance as individuals (Hay & Ashman, 2003; Rutter & Maughan, 2002).

Friends provide emotional support, a sense of belonging, and comfort in the knowledge that someone else may be going through similar challenges and that there is someone to talk to and be with. However, for students with learning and other difficulties, friendships can be difficult to form and maintain due to the interactions between their personal circumstances and perceived difficulties or deficits (in vocabulary and language, for instance). For example, students with behavioural disorders or from different cultural backgrounds may react to social situations in ways that are different to their peers and subsequently these students may be more isolated from social groups. Some students with significant intellectual disabilities may be marginalised because they have difficulty maintaining a fast-paced conversation or lack the skills to maintain and extend a social interaction. Students from homes where there is a high level of poverty, disadvantage, or even violence in the home may feel unable to take friends home, or avoid socialising through fear of exposing their problems.

Young people with disabilities also find secondary schools to be unfriendly environments. A recurring theme in secondary school research is the problem of teasing and bullying. This is dealt with in some detail in Chapter 5 and will be considered further in Chapter 11. Perhaps all that need be said here is that anti-bullying programs need to be encouraged and systematically maintained across the total school environment. The psychological wellbeing of students who are bullied is important and both the bullies and their victims need to be encouraged to use school and community counselling services when such incidents occur. Students with special needs also benefit from training in assertiveness, anger management, and social skills, and most guidance officers or school counsellors can advise school personnel on these types of activities (see Prior, 2003).

There are a number of programs that can be of assistance. They include FRIENDS (Barratt, Webster, & Turner, 2000), ABLE (Mason, 1993), and Exploring Self-concept (Hay, 2005). Also within the secondary school environment more attention could be given to providing semi-organised activities before school, at break times, and after school for students with special needs. These might include board games, computer-based activities, or sporting activities with peers.

ISSUES AND CHALLENGES

For teachers

At some point in time both preservice and experienced teachers doubt their abilities to teach students who require support beyond that provided by the regular program (Watson & Bond, 2007). Although many teachers believe that support through withdrawal programs has more to offer than inclusion, the reality is that most of the students with special needs spend much of their time in regular classrooms and are the responsibility of classroom teachers. Thus, catering for students with particular educational needs is a daily challenge and dilemma for most classroom teachers.

Secondary teachers work in school settings where there are strong disciplinary cultures that affect how teachers feel about inclusion and implementing inclusive practices. Teachers also hold strong views about the effectiveness or otherwise of streaming students into groups according to their abilities, about how to provide support for students, for example whether this should be in class or through withdrawal, and about the levels of service or access that schools should offer.

In addition, there are long-held perceptions that adolescent students with cognitive impairments and other intellectual disabilities, for example, reach a plateau in their learning that means that they can no longer learn academic skills. Although there is a great deal of research that refutes these beliefs, they are hard to change and there is considerable resistance to including these students fully in mainstream classrooms.

Certainly, just placing a student with additional needs in a general education classroom is not enough to ensure that the student will succeed academically, develop socially appropriate behaviours, or be socially accepted. Teachers need to develop their own resources and also to be aware of other support systems they can access or establish to support all students.

WORKING COLLABORATIVELY TO SUPPORT STUDENTS WITH DIVERSE NEEDS

There are five key groups of individuals that can be of significant assistance to teachers who are working with students with diverse special needs in secondary classrooms. These are:

1 other teachers;
2 support staff and teacher aides;
3 tutors and mentors;
4 specialist teachers and services; and
5 parents and caregivers.

Working with other teachers

In part, teaching is a problem-solving activity and it is a case of considering the students' learning within its social and curriculum environment. Teachers need to review and reflect on how they teach

and how students learn and ask themselves questions about when the student is on-task or off-task and why. Talking to other teachers about the students and the activities that engage the students helps facilitate the notion of the teacher as the reflective practitioner.

Working with teacher aides

Teacher aides are the second key resource that teachers can use to support students with diverse needs in their classrooms. However, just because a teacher aide is allocated to a student with special needs it is incorrect to assume that the teacher aide has the skills to work appropriately and independently with the curriculum content or the students in the classroom.

Teacher aides need information about the expectations of the teacher in a particular classroom and the preferred method of instruction and assessment. Secondary school teachers also need to clarify the roles and responsibilities of the teacher aides working within their classroom as well as provide more systematic feedback and evaluation information to the aides about their performance with the students with special education needs (Howard & Ford, 2007). It is not recommended that the teacher aide always work with the students with difficulties. Instead, the opposite can be more effective, where the classroom teacher spends time and energy interacting with these students, while the teacher aide works with other groups in the class.

Tutors and mentors

The third resource is tutors and mentors. These can be peer tutors, cross-grade tutors, parents, or other volunteers. In any case, the tutors need instruction about when, how, and for how long to work with the target students. While tutors can be used across all curriculum areas, they are most often used in literacy programs. This is because secondary school readers who have struggled for years and have developed a resistance to reading need an intervention framework that focuses on their personalised response to reading. A relationship-based approach combined with interesting texts and student choice of material is the most effective way of facilitating improved reading and literacy (Woolley & Hay, 2007).

It is important that tutors understand ways in which they can promote productive interactions that encourage learning. Effective questioning is important and tutors are encouraged to advance students learning using the "wh" questions ("who", "what", "where", "when", and "why") to focus the reader's attention on relevant features of the narrative texts. "Who", "what", "where", and "when" develop explicit inferential comprehension, while "why" questions go beyond the surface features of the text to elicit links with the reader's prior knowledge. This generates deep understanding of the narrative. The goal in asking "wh" questions is to promote students' self-questioning by relating information from their knowledge base to make inferences and predictions that deepen their understanding of the reading/learning process and lead to further knowledge acquisition.

Mentoring programs are often associated with tutoring. These programs involve volunteers who have specific skills, empathy, knowledge, and the time to work and interact with particular students. Mentoring programs have been used with a variety of secondary students considered at risk, and research has found that one-on-one intervention programs can enhance students' motivation and self-confidence, and increase their desire to be positively engaged or re-engaged with learning (Worthy et al., 2002).

Working with specialist teachers and services

In many schools, the learning support teachers are a crucial link across the school in terms of programs and strategies, and can coordinate the more effective use of teacher aides, parent support, and peers. Some

schools have the services of visiting teachers and guidance officers. However, while these services can provide advice and support to the teachers, parents, and students, the main responsibility for teaching the student remains with the teacher who has that student in his or her classroom. Special education staff can, however, play a significant role in coordinating services and linking the school to the home and the community. While this is an important role, there is an increasing recognition that government and non-government agencies need to be better integrated so that social workers and psychologists can work across traditional school, home, and community boundaries to deliver programs to vulnerable and at-risk students and their families (Homel, Elias, & Hay, 2001).

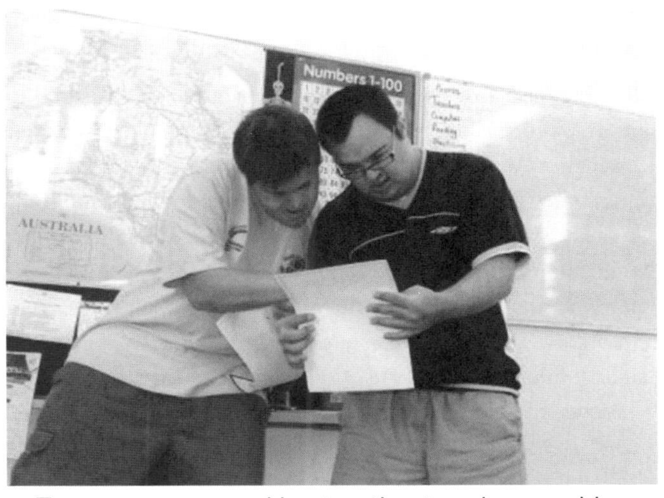

Two young men working together to solve a problem

Working with parents and caregivers

Parents of children with special education needs often experience greater levels of stress, anxiety, and depression when compared with parents of children without a special education need (Bitsika & Sharpley, 2004). While there are multiple causes of this heightened distress, it is often considered to be a consequence of their children's social and communication behaviour, the parents' need to understand their child's disability or condition more fully, and the negative effect on family members. Parents of children with special education needs commonly report home and school misunderstandings, receiving infrequent and inconsistent communication from the school, and regularly describe being disappointed with their child's educational progress (Ivey, 2004).

While home and school links are important, much of the communication between teachers and parents of children with special education needs often pertains only to homework issues, and parents/caregivers are unsure of the teacher's expectations (Hay & Winn, 2005). The issue is more complicated when home culture and ethnicity are considered; for example, in New South Wales, 17% of all school students from the ages of 5 to 17 years speak a language other than English in the home (Clark, 2005). Secondary teachers, therefore, must consider procedures for improving home–school links and reducing students' and parents' homework anxieties. This might involve monitoring the amount of homework required (if any), providing assistance to the students and parents, providing alternative assignment topics and procedures, and developing other ways of communicating with parents of adolescents with special learning needs. (Refer back to the case study about St Rose's College in Chapter 1.)

For students

In the past, the community perspective of learners with particular educational needs has focused on their limitations rather than their strengths and needs. Like all learners, they have characteristics, behaviours, and needs and are as diverse as other groups of learners in terms of their interests, previous learning experiences, and aspirations. There are, however, several general areas where their learning may be affected and these are outlined below.

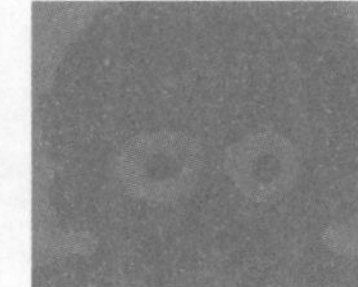

COMMUNICATION

Language and literacy abilities and skills vary greatly across all students regardless of the phase of schooling. For example, students with intellectual disabilities may have difficulties in auditory and cognitive processing, which affect their ability to answer questions or follow instructions. For instance, a teacher may assume that the student with a mild learning difficulty can deal with issues requiring higher order thinking and then be confronted with a situation where a student cannot answer a question in a discussion about the "Tyranny of distance shaping Australian's history" because they do not know the meaning of the word "tyranny", or because they only think of the word "shaping" as what artists do when making a piece of pottery, or because their experience of "distance" is only within their local community. Thus, teachers should adjust their language of instruction to a suitable level of complexity that accommodates students' oral language processing (Catts & Kamhi, 2005).

Some students who have a chronic medical condition, or whose families move around, may have missed parts of their education, and thus have gaps in their content knowledge and literacy and numeracy skills. In terms of literacy difficulties, these students may need additional support to address the following:

- trouble comparing or contrasting events, or in connecting events in texts to personal experience or real-life events;
- difficulties in spelling and using dictionaries and a word processor;
- difficulties in organising thoughts when writing;
- difficulties in remembering main ideas or recalling events from the text in the correct sequence;
- inability to use the structure and features of the text, such as headings, charts, overviews, bold print or italics, to help them navigate through the text; and
- task engagement and time on task.

SELF-CARE AND DAILY LIVING

These are aspects of life associated with home circumstances, independent travel, personal care, and/or accessing community facilities. Students who are from disadvantaged backgrounds may arrive at school without having eaten. Some schools have breakfast clubs where all students can go regardless of their backgrounds. Such clubs often provide cereal, toast, and fruit for students. Other students may be homeless and need assistance with clothing, showering or accessing health services. If these basic needs are not addressed then learning can be compromised.

SOCIAL INTERACTION

This involves the development of social skills and social networks appropriate to their community contexts. For some individuals with intellectual disabilities, teachers and teacher aides may be the students' main "friends" in the school (Hay & Winn, 2005). Because of the communication and social problems often associated with many students with special education needs, developing long-term friendships is a challenge (Frey et al., 2005). Thus, for many of these young people, their families remain their central social network.

Over time, however, the home situation changes (i.e., parents grow older and perhaps die, siblings move out of home and form new families). Therefore, it is important to encourage all youth with any form of disability to develop their communication skills as well as their community, social, and life skills. Part of this community and social engagement is developing their travelling and mobility skills. In particular, young people with sensory, physical, or intellectual disabilities need to be able to travel independently to participate in social events, such as going to the movies with friends or to parties.

Loneliness is a particular aspect of life for a growing number of young people with disabilities, after they leave school, especially if support services are reduced (Waite et al., 2006).

SELF-REGULATION AND SELF-DIRECTION

These are aspects of learning that involve an individual taking responsibility for his or her own learning and actions. Educational programs can either foster the development of these aspects or, with the provision of non-specific and ongoing support and care, smother their development. For example, in many secondary contexts, young people receive support from teacher aides whose role is to assist students in the classroom. In the worst case scenarios, some teacher aides end up completing tasks for the students and taking any decision-making out of the students' hands. These students can become passive learners who rely on others to make choices for them (Pressley, 2006). They become accustomed to being helped and develop a learned helplessness that is difficult for teachers to counteract.

learned helplessness
Beliefs held by individuals that they have no control over the outcome of events.

ASSESSMENT

Assessment is an issue of significant concern for teachers and parents as well as stress to students. For many secondary students with special learning needs, the main adaptation occurs during times of assessment, where students are given extra time to complete the assessment tasks, and they may have access to a reader who can help with the comprehension of the written examination and/or a scribe who can write down the students' examination responses (Clark, 2005).

As students progress through their schooling and enter the senior years, issues around assessment become greater as students move toward certification with the impact of externally mandated assessment, particularly in states where there are external examinations at senior level. This culmination at the end of Year 12 on examinations and the formal accreditation procedures is aimed at ranking each student in the different discipline domains in terms of their ability to progress onto further study. Homework is a recurring source of stress for parents, and the common theme is the lack of understanding about expectations associated with homework and the need for teachers to demonstrate more flexibility is designing assessment tasks and not overly rely on essays and workbook activities.

TEACHING ESSENTIALS

As students progress through the secondary school, learning activities become more complex and sophisticated. This is made more challenging for students with diverse needs by the traditional focus in high schools on content and the transmission of curriculum, so that catering for the needs of diverse groups of students has not been a high priority.

What a teacher believes a student can accomplish can influence the teacher–learner partnership (Thomas & Vaughan, 2004). Historically, deficit models have constructed failure to learn as a result of faults in the learner with the teacher's role being to fix these faults. Teachers need to work from a perspective that constructs all students as learners. This involves having high expectations for participation and performance, facilitating and supporting active involvement by all learners in all activities, and being responsive to learners' needs. This can be achieved though careful planning and the development of a broad repertoire of effective teaching strategies.

Planning for diversity

Once teachers become aware of students' needs, the challenge is how to plan to meet these needs in daily learning and teaching activities. One strategy that can help is mapping the needs of each student in a class to develop a class overview (see Box 10.2). These are needs in terms of organisation and management, needs that require particular teaching strategies, and needs around learning. Once these needs are mapped, it is possible to identify several key strategies that can help all students. These strategies can then be incorporated into unit and lesson plans.

10.2 Developing a class overview

The overview below is that of a composite Year 10 English class in a large urban secondary school. It was created by a group of preservice English teachers after they had completed their first practicum.

STEP 1: WRITE A BRIEF INTRODUCTION TO THE CLASS

Write a short paragraph (2–3 sentences) about the class as a whole.

10J comprises 17 boys and 10 girls. It is a lively class with some boys who are keen on comics and graphic novels, and a group of assertive girls. They enjoy working collaboratively in friendship groups, but sometimes find it difficult to stay on task. In their previous unit, it was clear that they needed to work on their writing in paragraphs and on using more formal language.

STEP 2

Complete Column 1 by answering the following questions about each of the students you have identified as needing support beyond that provided by the regular program.

1. What does this student already know?
2. What can this student do? What are his/her strengths that I can build on?
3. What is this student interested in?
4. What support do they need to learn?
5. What will be the indicators of their success in learning?

You should now be able to write a short paragraph about your student(s) to go in Column 1.

STEP 3

Complete Columns 2–4 identifying some of the management, learning and teaching strategies that will be useful in helping these students to learn in your classroom.

STEP 4

Identify 3 to 5 key strategies that seem to be common across all of the students you have identified as needing support; for example, in the table below these would be:

1. scaffolding;
2. breaking the task down; and
3. modelling.

STEP 5

Highlight these in your table or list them underneath your table. These strategies are the ones that you should be using to guide the development of your unit and to plan the detailed lessons.

Who are your students? What do you know about them? What are their needs?	What does this mean for management?	What does this mean for learning? How can they demonstrate their learning?	What does this mean for teaching?
1 boy with learning difficulties, good artist, a comics fan. Organisation problems.	• Technology aids such as Inspiration for planning essays. • Use advanced organisers. • Develop checklists for tasks.	• Incorporate visual elements into tasks. • Storyboard may help with organisation of ideas. Use cards with ideas on them to help him physically put arguments together.	• Scaffolding. • Modelling expected behaviour. • Task analysis—breaking down tasks.
1 boy excellent social skills, good sportsman but with poor self-concept—difficulties in handling failure or criticism.	• Use advanced organisers. • Pair work with a supportive partner.	• Develop tasks with small achievable goals.	• Scaffolding. • Modelling expected behaviour.
1 girl good orally, writing difficulties, limited comprehension but enjoys reading with other students, good listening skills.	• Technology, Co-writer, Inspiration software. • Use advanced organisers. • Use group work to structure reading.		• Scaffolding. • Modelling expected behaviour. • Modify writing tasks.

Who are your students? What do you know about them? What are their needs?	What does this mean for management?	What does this mean for learning? How can they demonstrate their learning?	What does this mean for teaching?
Girl from non-English-speaking background—reserved, limited participation in class, reluctant to ask for help, cultural differences re appropriate behaviour.	• Use advanced organisers. • Pair work so talking is not so threatening.	• Use books on tape.	• Scaffolding. • Modelling expected behaviour.

10.2

Key teaching strategies

Differentiated instruction has often been the most recommended approach to assist all students to learn more effectively, but this has often proved hard to achieve in secondary schools (Watson & Bond, 2007; Prior, 2003). Since differentiating instruction requires teachers to shift from focusing on content instruction to focusing more on individual students' needs, the challenge for secondary teachers is how to meet the individual needs of their students, while at the same time meeting set curriculum content and assessment requirements.

Developing a repertoire of teaching strategies is important for all teachers in every curriculum area. While it is not possible to provide specific teaching strategies for each subject that is taught in secondary school, there is a range of key strategies that have been shown to be effective across different subject areas. The most well-known of these are described below.

SPACING AND PACING

Spacing and pacing are important elements in quality teaching for students with diverse needs. Spacing is linked to the design of the lesson or set of activities. It means that there is time to engage students with the learning activity according to the sequential parts or phases of the lesson. These include:

- the orientation of the students to the task;
- a review of the previous content;
- a preview of what is to be learnt in this lesson;
- the sequence of learning tasks often with some practice activity; and
- a conclusion and summary of the learnt material.

Within the learning activity, the pacing, flow, and delivery of the content needs to be such that there is time to explore and explain the vocabulary and concepts. Rushing through the content and failing to explain or demonstrate the information is poor teaching for all students, but it has a special impact on students who may have difficulty in following directions or who may lack the confidence or the skills to work independently on the task (Cooney & Hay, 2005). For example, secondary students may understand the word "energy" in the English class context, such as, "The youth displayed high energy on the dance floor." However, in a science context, energy has a different meaning and is linked to concepts such as force and acceleration. Teachers in both of these situations have to spend time explaining and talking about the vocabulary and the concepts linked to those words in a relevant and context-driven way (Wagner, Muse, & Tannenbaum 2007).

SCAFFOLDING TASKS

Scaffolding is a common metaphor used to describe how teachers or peers can support students to learn new concepts, skills, knowledge, and practices. Through scaffolding, the teacher helps the student master a task or concept that in the first instance the student is unable to learn independently. Students are expected to make mistakes during their learning, but the teacher provides support and feedback until the student is able to achieve the task (Gambrell et al., 2007; Hattie & Timperley, 2007). As the student starts to master the task, the teacher fades out. This involves gradually removing support to allow the student to work more independently.

Scaffolding can be provided to assist students to undertake any written, reading or speaking task in the classroom. Typical scaffolding in secondary schools may include:

- Teaching students the generic features and structures of different types of text. For example, in Science, students learn IMRAD, that is, Introduction, Materials and methods, Results, and Discussion when writing their Science laboratory reports.
- Teachers and students jointly construct written texts either as a whole class or in small groups. Joint construction of text involves the teacher and students in the process of creating texts together by using the relevant writing skills and strategies for particular genres. The teaching/learning cycle involves modelling and joint negotiation, leading to the independent creation of text (Literacy and Education Research Network and Studies Directorate, 1989). For example, in teaching the IMRAD structure, described above, groups of students write one section of the complete laboratory report in groups, and then pool their sections to make one complete laboratory report.
- Reading tasks can be scaffolded by pre-teaching key vocabulary, annotating the text to highlight important ideas, or adding visual cues, diagrams, and prompts

EXPLICIT TEACHING

This refers to teaching specific knowledge, skills, and practices through a sequence of guided activities. You may recall reading about explicit teaching in Chapter 7. Each major topic is broken down into smaller units or steps. Each unit/step is then taught sequentially by the teacher who explains, demonstrates, and guides students through activities where they practise the task. As they practise, the teaching cycle may be repeated and extended as students gain more confidence and experience. Ownership and control of the task moves from the teacher to the students until the students are ready to take over responsibility for the task, with minimum teacher involvement.

There are many descriptions of explicit teaching. Some of these are summarised in Table 10.1.

TABLE 10.1 STRATEGIES USED IN EXPLICIT TEACHING

Explicit teaching	Suggested strategies (and examples from secondary school subject areas)
Setting a context and purpose for learning	• Giving students a graphic organiser to guide them through a unit of work. • Establishing a genuine audience for completed written tasks. • Showing an excerpt from a documentary about Hitler at the start of a unit on the Second World War in history. • Students write short stories and these are collated and published by the school library.
Telling students what to do	• Providing step by-step instructions. • Breaking the task down into short achievable steps. • Using WebQuests.
Showing them how to do it	• Modelling. • Teacher models how to write a lab report from an experiment he or she has demonstrated in a science class.
Providing multiple opportunities for practice under teacher guidance.	• Teachers and students jointly construct key aspects of texts (e.g., the introduction for an essay in history). • Solving a complex mathematical problem in groups. • Students undertake a sequence of short tasks exploring Shakespearean language in a play. • Students in groups create a wiki about an issue (e.g, drugs in sport).
Independent practice	• Students apply their knowledge and skills to a new task. • Students create mathematical problems for each other. • Students develop a portfolio of their own poems to demonstrate their understanding of poetic forms.

TASK ANALYSIS

This is often used to identify the sequence of activities for explicit teaching contexts. First, a task or part of a task is broken down into component parts; for example, in reading and summarising a chapter from a textbook or a magazine article, students must do the following:

- read and construct meaning from the text;
- understand the main generic features of a textbook chapter or magazine article;
- identify those features in the text they have been reading;
- relate content to their prior knowledge, other reading, and personal experience;
- evaluate the content based on their prior knowledge, other reading, and personal experience; and
- understand the main generic features of summaries and transpose their evaluation to a written summary.

The teacher then establishes small achievable goals to ensure students develop these skills, designs appropriate learning activities that support students with each part, and develops checklists to help students monitor their own progress. This type of task analysis is also useful in analysing assessment tasks as it allows teachers to check that these skills have been taught in a particular unit prior to assessment.

USING ICT IN CLASSROOMS

There has been considerable advocacy for the use of technology to support adolescents with diverse needs, as there has been in all other phases of schooling, as you will already be aware from Chapter 6. The following list, then, is merely a summary of some of the main advantages.

- Technology is highly motivating. Learners with limited literacy and numeracy can produce professional products. Animations and graphics make information attractive and catch users' attention.
- Technology is largely interactive. Learners are engaged, as there are choices to be made in terms of links within and across internet sites.
- Computers, software, and internet sites are multimodal, containing visual and auditory as well as text-based elements. This means that students who learn in different ways can be supported by symbols and sound. For example, students can use software programs for word processing that will read their work back to them or give them spoken instructions to help them complete tasks.
- Many educational programs are structured so that they give immediate progress reports and feedback to the user and so align with models of just-in-time learning. Just-in-time learning means learning something at the point at which you need to know it so that you can use the information (e.g., learning how to create a table in Word because you have some data for a paper that needs to go in a table). The opposite is just-in-case learning where, for example, you do a course in how to use Word because some day you'll buy a computer. The idea is that the more you need to use the concept or skill, the more likely you are to really remember it.
- Computers allow for repetition, so the user can repeat tasks or parts of a program as often as they like until a particular skill is mastered. In addition, work can be saved and returned to, amended, and changed at any time with ease.

10.3 Supporting the YouTube generation

Jasmine was working on a unit in ICT with her Year 10 class. The focus of the project was the role that the internet plays in allowing individuals to create a public and social group identity. One of the outcomes was to develop individual profiles to be uploaded to a group site on 'SchoolTube'. Jasmine had two students in her class with mild intellectual disabilities (one has a diagnosis of Down syndrome). Jasmine wanted to plan the unit so these students could be included fully and would be just as engaged as other students in learning about using technology to create a social identity.

She decided that the important elements of this for her students with intellectual disabilities would be to develop their understanding of the internet as a public space, and the creation of an individual identity that was suitable to upload on this space. To achieve this, Jasmine drew on models of *explicit teaching*.

First, she used *task analysis* to identify the sequence of steps involved in creating an online profile. She then converted these steps into a sequence of specific short tasks, which the students could do either independently or with support from another student.

Understanding that she needed to make the abstract concept of "public" more concrete for her students, she involved parents in the unit. After uploading the first part of the group profile onto the internet, students took a note home asking parents and family members to look at the site from home and to share their excitement about being able to review student work from home. This worked particularly well with Lucy, the student with Down syndrome, as her brother was working in London at the time, and he was able to open the site from there.

The second core concept that Jasmine wanted to teach was that web profiles are created using particular kinds of language and discourses. She created two different *scaffolds*, one related to creating a personal profile for a job interview and a second related to creating a profile for friends. Using these scaffolds, the students were able to see the differences in content and language, and the students with intellectual disabilities were able to join in whole-class discussions about appropriate public content and language use.

Using the sequence of short steps and the scaffolds developed by Jasmine, all of the students could develop and upload their profiles. At the end of the unit, Jasmine felt confident that the students had developed their skills in using technology and understanding the nature of information on the internet. She had been surprised by the level of understanding shown by her students with intellectual disabilities and their well-developed sense of social identity. She felt that she had learned more about her students on both a personal and an educational level. More importantly, she felt that her approach had enabled the other students in the class to see the two, often marginalised, students as equal partners in the project with their own experiences to offer.

It is important, however, for teachers to avoid the hype around technology (Gambrell et al., 2007). Research has shown that there are challenges for teachers in terms of the cost of software, the development of expertise necessary to both set up and implement software appropriately, and the limited availability of software that is appropriate for adolescents with high support needs. Software may be appropriate at one skill level, but content is often not age-appropriate, students are unable to reach the goals advocated, and independence is not encouraged. For example, some of the problems learners with intellectual disabilities have with software designed to develop literacy skills include:

- students making random choices of games and levels which may lead to learning skills out of sequence;
- students being rewarded with graphics and prompts even though they make random wrong guesses;
- being unable to read written on-screen instructions;
- having insufficient time to think through options before answering questions, which means that the program moves on regardless; and
- assumptions made about prior knowledge of letters and phonemic awareness.

The focus for teachers, therefore, should be on the powerful use of technologies for learning, rather than on powerful technologies. This requires careful planning, as the vignette in Box 10.4 shows.

BOX 10.4

Teaching 21st century students

Kai is a Year 11 student at St Matthews College. He has childhood leukemia, which means that he is often confined to bed for long periods and occasionally has long hospital stays. Although his attendance in Year 11 has been intermittent, he is doing well in all his subjects, and wants to go to university to study engineering. He has told his teachers that, apart from playing games on the internet and sending emails, doing schoolwork keeps him sane during the long periods of inactivity and he is keen to keep up with his assignments.

On a pupil-free day at the start of Term 3 when Kai's difficulties had become very evident, the principal organised a meeting with Kai's teachers to see if they could develop strategies to help him. Prior to the meeting, the principal checked with the state education department about policies for special consideration for assessment tasks. The response from the department was that the school could make its own decisions about varying the conditions under which Kai completed assessment tasks, as long as his performance in those tasks was assessed using the same standards as those used for other students. After discussing the issue during the meeting, the teachers came up with the following strategies that teachers could integrate into their planning to give Kai opportunities to maintain his schoolwork and social contact with his peers:

- Teachers divided units and assessment tasks into modules so that Kai could complete sections of a task and return to them later, if his illness prevented him from completing all of the task at once. This required teachers to make submission dates flexible.

- Using and developing structured WebQuests (see the URL after *Practical activities* at the end of the chapter) for units meant that Kai could undertake relevant independent research at home.
- Teachers established blogs around novels/plays/issues so that students could discuss their responses online and Kai could participate.
- Kai developed PowerPoint presentations and recorded a podcast of any oral activities that could be sent electronically to teachers. Similarly, teachers recorded important lessons and these could be downloaded by Kai.
- All handouts, teaching supports, and instructions were placed on the school intranet so Kai could download them.
- Where appropriate, group work assignments were adapted so that students could work together to develop a wiki*. As they developed the wiki, teachers were able to trace Kai's contributions.
- Where appropriate, online tests and quizzes were developed so that Kai could respond under supervision at home and submit electronically.

*A wiki is a webpage that allows a group of users to add and edit content collectively to create a group page. Wikis can be restricted so that only specific users can edit entries. Each member of the group's contributions can be traced online. Entries in Wikipedia are created using this process.

10.4

LEARNING ESSENTIALS

Everyone is and can be a learner. Learning for us all is a lifelong process that takes place in social and cultural contexts. In these contexts individuals can learn independently, cooperatively and through interaction with others. With this approach there is no deficit model of learning. Learning is a process of making meaning out of experiences and is affected by the learner's abilities or expertise in a specific domain, their prior knowledge of topics, concepts and experiences, their diverse strengths and needs, and their learning preferences and interests.

Many secondary schools work on a mixed model of withdrawing students with special needs for certain lessons or subjects, usually academic subjects such as English or mathematics, and including the students in other subjects that have a more functional component, such as drama, art, or home economics. There is, however, no one correct model of support, and there are advantages and disadvantages in using a withdrawal compared with a full inclusion model. One argument is that in a withdrawal model young adults maybe be marginalised by completing a separate program that does not have high enough expectations for the students' academically; this is the notion of "dumbing down" the curriculum. An example of this is the withdrawal of students with literacy difficulties from English classes to enable them to get extra support, when it may be more appropriate to include them in units dealing with popular culture, film, or oral presentations.

Again, the critical issue is having some level of curriculum flexibility where the support and differentiation of the content is on a continuum that reflects the students' overall needs (Hay et al., 2007; Watson & Bond, 2007). It is possible to accommodate many students with different educational needs by varying across groups the assessment expectations, the homework tasks, the amount of time to

complete the tasks, and the level of support. As already mentioned, to facilitate inclusion, some students with special education needs are supported by teacher aides within the regular classroom, and again there are advantages and disadvantages to this practice.

In the upper secondary school most of the syllabuses require students to master an increasingly sophisticated level of knowledge and for the students to recall and independently adapt this knowledge. For many young adults with a disability, this may be translated as the need to shift toward more of a life-skills curriculum and a functional approach to learning. The issue is that many students with a learning or social problem can have strengths in particular domains. For example, a student with Asperger's syndrome may find the social interactions of a senior drama class demanding, but may cope to a very high standard in the Year 12 technology or mathematics class. Students and, indeed, their parents need to be kept well informed with regular meetings and discussions about their child's progress and subject selection, because in Australia the legal responsibility about the student's education belongs with the parent/caregivers and not with the provider school. There is evidence that indicates that professions too easily dominate the selection of educational and life-focused goals of students with special needs, overly controlling the parents' and students' aspirations by taking a narrow view of the possibilities and the way in which support services and teachers can work toward those aspirations and possibilities (Waite et al., 2006).

Parents of children with special needs may also lack the confidence to disagree with the school's recommendations or lack knowledge about the long-term consequences of doing a particular program or subject (Hay & Winn, 2005). Often students with special needs in the upper secondary school may take fewer subjects so that the student can concentrate more on core subjects but still take enough subjects to meet the admission requirements of a particular tertiary course of study. Making this decision requires parents and the student to be fully aware of this strategy and have a plan worked out as to how the student will use the extra time in the school day to work on the core subjects.

Some parents and their adolescent children may not be given any useful advice or choice about whether or not the student should stay within the regular program or move into an alternative curriculum. For example, a school may recommend that the student do a program of activities for students with behaviour problems, but the consequence is that the student moves away from a program of study that has an academic focus and so this option may reduce the student's future career opportunities. It should be recognised that in terms of developing agency and autonomy, there has to be a stronger recognition by teachers that it is the individual student receiving the education who has to be at the centre of the decision-making process, and that education is done *with* and not *to* students. Where possible, high expectations and a focus on academics skills are important for teachers to maintain for students from diverse backgrounds and with diverse skill levels rather than default to a functional curriculum that concentrates on life skills only (such as using public transport, cooking and other household duties, and budgeting). While a functional curriculum is often prioritised for some students with particular needs as they approach the end of their secondary school years, it is important, where possible, that academic skills are also maintained and developed, and that students with special needs are also introduced to higher-order thinking and problem-solving activities.

Leaving school is not the end of learning, and students with diverse needs should be enculturated into lifelong learning as much as their peers. This is because, for many of these students, late adolescence and young adulthood is a time when, cognitively, they are more ready to learn and, socially, they are even more aware of the need to be able to communicate in the community in order to develop social networks beyond those of the family (Hay & Ashman, 2003).

Experiential learning programs

Some secondary schools conduct experiential learning programs that focus on outdoor activities such as camping, canoeing, high ropes, hiking, and overnight excursions. These programs can be included in an alternative or extension program for secondary students with special learning needs. Secondary schools often justify including these activities in the students' educational program on the expectation that these programs improve the students' self-confidence, social skills, motivation, and self-concept (Hay & Dempster, 2004).

It is important, however, to be aware that if an adolescent is having academic difficulties, this individual may not want to engage in adventure-based learning activities, or have the physical endurance, fine and gross motor skills, or interpersonal and social skills to cope with them. It is also incorrect to assume that these programs alone are going to improve students' academic schoolwork, unless the two programs come together in some way. It is important that teachers are aware of the school's risk management procedures associated with taking students on excursions and trips away from the school and, as part of the risk management procedure, understand all of the students' medication needs and the required ratio of adult supervision to students, depending on the activity being undertaken.

Experiential learning activities can be incorporated into the students' secondary program

Transition to post-compulsory education, work-training, and work

The larger numbers and diversity of students in Years 11 and 12 have caused tensions between government calls for higher academic achievement and policies of inclusion in terms of schools and teachers' ability to cater for this broader student population. Florian and Rouse (2001) referred to this as a tension between equity and excellence. Teachers in secondary education must work toward helping at-risk students, because completing school still provides the best chance for succeeding in later life. Therefore, catering for diversity becomes increasingly complex and problematic.

For individuals with a disability, work-related learning is an attempt to insert greater relevance and flexibility into the students' individual learning and transition plans (Waite et al., 2006). Generally, it involves four elements, some of which occur in the secondary school context and over a long period of time, and some in an off-campus location and for a specific duration. The four main elements are:

1 Learning *for* work (developing key skills, such as communication, numeracy, use of technology, functional literacy, travel training, and developing social relationships and problem-solving).
2 Learning *about* work (career education, doing applications, handling money, time management, and understanding the links between vocational course and outcomes).
3 Learning *at* work (doing in-context work programs, engaging in simulations and interviews, participating in community programs and visits).
4 Learning *through* work citizenship, social participation, values, and aspirations.

INDIVIDUAL TRANSITION PLANS

Work experience and Vocational Education and Training (VET) programs are often considered to be parts of a student's Individual Transition Plan (ITP). Like IEPs, these plans must be agreed to by the parents/caregivers, the school and the student, with regular review periods and specified and measurable objectives. Such plans usually start about two years before the student is expected to complete high school, although many of the skills associated with transition from school are introduced well before this point. The six dimensions usually associated with an ITP are:

- continuing secondary education needs and adjustments;
- Vocational Education and Training and preparation (including the use of technology, starting VET program or prerequisites, school-based traineeships, school VET course);
- personal management (including health care, risk assessment, behaviour plan, communication, and social skills);
- community living skills (such as independent living skills, and time and money management);
- leisure and social and sporting activities; and
- transport and mobility training.

Work experience and Vocational Education Training programs conducted by TAFE or similar providers are often developed as parts of a student's Individual Transition Plan.

WORK EXPERIENCE

Work experience programs focus on facilitating the transition from school to the world of work by broadening the students' experience of work opportunities and developing associated skills and knowledge associated with work. For many older secondary students with special education needs, work experience or work shadowing becomes a part of an alternative educational program or an extension program (Eagar et al., 2006). While there are significant benefits from such activities to the students, such programs need to be very well planned, closely monitored, and well resourced. Just doing a work experience activity for its own sake without considering the implications of the student's ability, interest, and skill levels may be putting the individual in an "at risk" situation.

TRANSITION TO TERTIARY EDUCATION, WORK-TRAINING, AND WORK

As students progress through high school they are faced with another major transition, to tertiary education, work-training, and the workforce. The Australian National Centre for Vocational Education Research (2007) found that the most disadvantaged individuals in terms of vocational transition belonged to one or more of the following groups:

- those living with a disability;
- those living in a rural or remote location;
- those living in low socioeconomic communities; and
- those who drop out of school or are early secondary school leavers.

Furthermore, what school leavers do in their first year out of school is especially important, such that involvement with employment, education, and training soon after leaving secondary school greatly increases the long-term chances of moving into full-time work or study, and improves the person's level of wellbeing. In contrast, being out of the labour market and education decreases the likelihood of future employment and this has a negative affect on wellbeing (Marks, 2006). This means that those individuals who make a poor transition from school to work and who belong to a disadvantaged sector in the community are more likely to remain out of the full-time workforce.

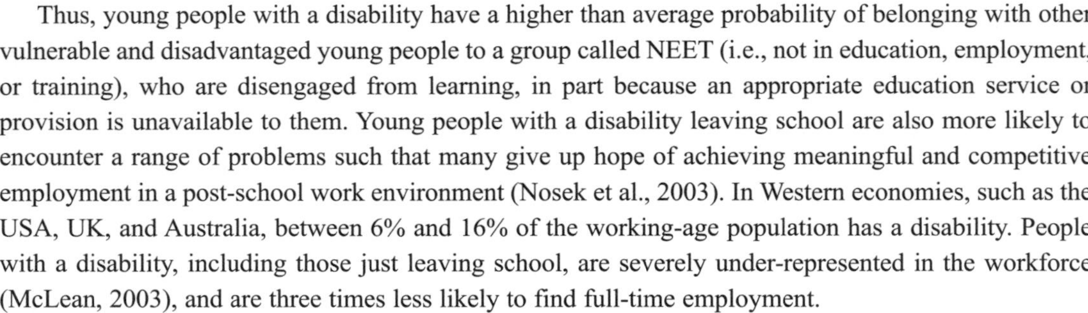

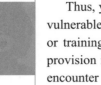

Thus, young people with a disability have a higher than average probability of belonging with other vulnerable and disadvantaged young people to a group called NEET (i.e., not in education, employment, or training), who are disengaged from learning, in part because an appropriate education service or provision is unavailable to them. Young people with a disability leaving school are also more likely to encounter a range of problems such that many give up hope of achieving meaningful and competitive employment in a post-school work environment (Nosek et al., 2003). In Western economies, such as the USA, UK, and Australia, between 6% and 16% of the working-age population has a disability. People with a disability, including those just leaving school, are severely under-represented in the workforce (McLean, 2003), and are three times less likely to find full-time employment.

In terms of young adults without a significant disability, the following results of the Australian national longitudinal study of school leavers (Marks, 2006) are relevant. This four-year study identified that around 70% of school leavers go into employment or study straight after leaving school and spend the first four years after school in full-time work or study (see Table 10.2). This group of school leavers is more likely to have the following characteristics:

- male;
- living in a large city;
- non-Indigenous;
- without a disability;
- from an English-speaking language background;
- have parents who have university or other post-school qualifications;
- are in the second quartile of literacy achievement or above (in other words, they have good literacy skills);
- have completed Year 12;
- have undertaken Vocational Training Education in Schools; and
- have worked part-time while at school.

TABLE 10.2 DESTINATION SUMMARY FOR THE LONGITUDINAL SURVEYS OF AUSTRALIAN YOUTH

Percentage	Destination
40%	Full-time education and training or work
30%	Higher education
24%	Mixed employment experience (i.e., a mixture of work and unemployment)
6%	Little/no work or study since leaving school

Source: Adapted from Marks (2006).

POST-SCHOOL EDUCATION OPPORTUNITIES

Within the context of the provision of post-school services for individuals with intellectual disability, the issue of providing continuity in education is rarely discussed. For example, adult learning has seldom been considered an option for those with an intellectual disability. Primarily, post-schooling options have focused on the development of employment and life skills, which might enable these adults to move into the community and live independently.

Furthermore, of the post-school options that do exist, few encompass opportunities for ongoing education development. Generally, there are three main training and employment options for adults with an intellectual disability post-school. These include: competitive employment, supported employment, and employment opportunities within sheltered workshops/activity centres.

sheltered workshops/activity centres
Work setting for persons with disabilities in which low productivity and low wages predominate.

Unfortunately, competitive employment opportunities serve only a small number of young adults with an intellectual disability unless there is a significant level of support and appropriate post-school vocational training opportunities (Gilbert & Hay, 2004). Therefore, while further continuing education may be incorporated into employment/training, access to these is often limited. Many young adults who participate in mainstream literacy courses operating through the VET and TAFE systems find that the instructors and teachers will adapt their pace of instruction and allow students to take longer to complete each module compared to adults without a disability. Even so, many VET and TAFE courses do not always accommodate the specific needs of individuals with a disability.

In general terms, the main factors associated with successful transition from school to vocational programs and subsequent employment for individuals with a disability, and in part being more successful in the school context, include having:

- fewer hospitalisations and reduced time spent in the last hospitalisation;
- more of the prerequisite skills for that selected industry;
- a less severe disability;
- the cognitive and intellectual capacity to acquire and retain instruction;
- a positive attitude about the importance of work and education; and
- a supportive family and social relationships.

USING THIS CHAPTER IN SCHOOLS

This chapter has concentrated on the notion that the secondary school teacher is a reflective practitioner able to monitor the students' progress within his or her classroom and to adjust the delivery of the content of their teaching. Inclusion is not a one-size-fits-all model, but rather a dynamic, complex network of individuals, including teachers, students, support staff, school leaders, and parents who often have different demands and expectations, who have to work together to make opportunities occur for students. While secondary school teachers may have the responsibility of delivering more specific content to the students in their care, the pedagogy and instruction associated with that content is still very important.

Overwhelming evidence in the professional literature supports the importance of explaining the vocabulary, engaging in an interactive dialogue with students, demonstrating, and providing feedback to the students. When these conditions exist, students will achieve and learn the content being presented. In secondary education, there is a tension between the needs associated with the accreditation process and the student learning needs. While there is no simple answer, the two

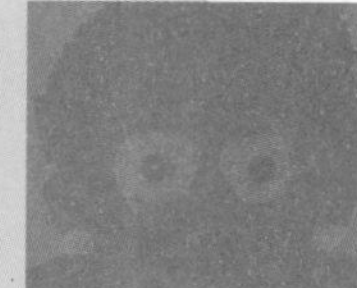

needs can be better accommodated within secondary education through curriculum and assessment flexibility.

Increasingly, the successful transition of students from secondary school to work, training, or future education is being seen as a responsibility of the secondary school system, and for this to occur, parents, teachers, and the students involved have to collaborate. When secondary students with learning and special needs were asked to describe "good" secondary school teachers, the follow list was generated (Hay, 2000). They:

- give good explanations;
- modify programs to suit understanding;
- do not cover advanced work too quickly;
- give realistic practice and homework tasks;
- spend extra time in explaining or in explanations;
- know their content and make it interesting;
- do not get angry with students;
- treat the students in a pleasant manner;
- give hands-on tasks; and
- help students gain a feeling of achievement.

It is interesting that this list is very similar to other research findings about what all students want and regard as good teaching, regardless of their ability (see Hattie & Timperley, 2007). In the end, it is how secondary school teachers approach the task of teaching that is important.

Four imperatives are raised in this chapter that relate to teaching students with diverse learning needs in secondary contexts. These are:

- the need to understand the culture and context of secondary schools;
- the importance of knowing and understanding the needs of learners;
- the development of a broad repertoire of teaching strategies; and
- the establishment and sustaining of collaborative partnerships with students, parents and caregivers, and other professionals.

In this section, we suggest some practical strategies that build on ideas that we have discussed which might help you address some of these imperatives in the early years of teaching.

Understanding the culture

Starting as a teacher at a new school is a daunting process for everyone, as there is so much to learn in the first few weeks. Obviously, your priorities will be focused on the students and getting to know each class. However, during your first six months at the school it is important to develop an understanding of the culture of the school and how it addresses inclusion and diversity. Schools have policy documents and handbooks that can provide you with useful information reasonably quickly. Below is a list of some of the policies and materials that might be useful for you to find out about. Some of these policies may be mandated at a system or state level and you may also find up-to-date information on departmental websites, as well as in the school:

- staff handbook;
- school's behaviour management policy and plans;
- policies and processes for communicating with parents;
- policies about medication and health issues;

- workplace health and safety procedures—these also include reporting of accidents and other incidents involving students;
- inclusion policies;
- policies and procedures for supporting students with diverse needs (e.g., withdrawal procedures, requests for support, or diagnostic assessments);
- policies and processes for assessment and submitting assignments;
- availability of resources such as interactive whiteboards, data projectors, computers, assistive technologies;
- access to counselling and guidance services; and
- access to specialist support services.

Knowing and understanding the needs of learners

One crucial aspect of getting to know your class when you first meet them is to find out who they are, and what they do. Here are some ways in which you can do this.

- Share personal information in the form of writing students a letter at the start of the school year telling them a little bit about yourself (remember that you don't have to reveal too much about your private life). Then ask them to respond, outlining their goals for the year, the kinds of activities they like doing, and how they think they learn.
- Talk to your teacher colleagues, the guidance officer, and other support staff about the needs of students in each class you're taking. Your colleagues may have strategies for working with some specific students that might be useful.
- When you have the opportunity, make contact with families/caregivers regularly about positives as well as questions and problems. One successful way is to start a communication book for students who are finding school challenging. Other teachers and family members can write comments or provide information that may impact on learning. Some teachers prepare a small newsletter every month that students take home to their parents, which informs them about the positive things that have happened since the last newsletter. This doesn't need to be a burden and can be jointly prepared and written by members of the class.
- Allow learners to demonstrate skills with materials with which they are familiar and confident in using. For example, students can find magazine and online articles about issues covered in textbooks and compare them.
- Undertake classroom activities that focus on finding out about the learner's interests to provide useful information to inform planning. For example, over the first few weeks of a new year, play "Hot Seat" where each student in turn sits in the Hot Chair and other students ask questions about their lives and interests. Model this by going first.
- Use photos and other technologies to document students' achievements during the year.

Use the information these strategies generate to inform your planning, resource selection and teaching and learning activities. In the practical activities below we suggest an activity that you can do to get you started on this.

Some schools assess students' skills in literacy and maths at the start of their secondary school careers using standardised tests, and use the results to group students for particular subjects. However, be aware that this information provides only a starting point for working with students. Students' circumstances, attitudes and skills will change as the year progresses and you need to constantly update

and add to your knowledge. You will also need to be aware of issues of confidentiality and ethics in accessing students' records and acting on any information they provide about medical conditions, mental health concerns, or home circumstances. This is where it's also important to be familiar with the relevant school and Education Department policies about your responsibilities for reporting suspected child abuse, for example.

Developing a broad repertoire of teaching strategies

One of the key strategies here is to find a teaching buddy, mentor, or partner. Some schools formally assign a more experienced teaching mentor to beginning teachers for their first year to help them develop professional skills. If this doesn't happen at your school, then it's a good idea to find one yourself. The relationship does not have to be onerous or formal. Look for someone who is teaching in your subject area and year levels who is sympathetic to students, who is creative and innovative in their teaching, and who is willing to share their ideas with you. Take opportunities, if possible, to observe your buddy in action, to jointly plan and even teach a unit together.

Another excellent idea is to join your state subject area professional association. There is one for Science, Mathematics, English, and so on. This gives you access to professional journals that are often full of useful practical suggestions and units, and access to regular in-service and professional learning activities through seminars and state conferences. Membership in a professional association provides you with a state-wide network of colleagues who can help you.

Developing collaborative partnerships

This will be a long-term goal, but it begins as soon as you walk into a school and meet colleagues, support staff, students, and parents for the first time. Every meeting you have is an opportunity to find out more about your students, to learn about a new strategy, or to find a partner or help in supporting a particular student.

When you first begin teaching, working out the kind of partnerships that are most useful can be difficult. Some beginning teachers feel that asking for help from colleagues or the learning support teacher could be a sign that they are not coping in the classroom. This is not the case; all teachers need to build collaborative partnerships to support their professional development and, as we have seen, many teachers with years of experience lack confidence in supporting students with diverse needs and are themselves looking for ideas and strategies in this area.

However, as mentioned in this chapter, having a positive attitude and high expectations means that it is important to be proactive in accessing support to enhance learning outcomes for all of your students. One useful strategy is to use the class overview model referred to earlier. Using the guidelines provided, develop an overview for a class that has several students with diverse needs and where you feel that you need some support in developing strategies for more inclusive teaching. Share your overview with the learning support teacher and use the overview to discuss the needs of the class in terms of management, teaching and learning, identifying key strategies that you could integrate into units that would support these students. As you plan the unit, this then becomes useful in talking to teacher aides about the roles that they might play in your classroom, and in developing individual plans for students that allow them to participate in activities associated with a unit of work.

PRACTICAL ACTIVITIES

Uni-work

1 Choose a short extract or chapter from a textbook, literary text, newspaper article, or other text relevant to your subject area. Brainstorm a range of strategies you could use in a lesson following

the "before reading", "during reading", and "after reading" phases to assist all learners to understand the text. Develop a lesson plan around reading this text using some of these strategies.

2 In subject area groups, undertake a literature search for recent research and professional articles focusing on strategies for inclusive practices in your subject area. Each group member then chooses a strategy and develops a practical activity employing that strategy to deliver to the rest of the class as part of a group presentation.

3 You will recall Josh from the first case study at the beginning of the chapter. Assume that Josh has successfully completed Year 10 at an alternative school. He has asked to return to St Matthews High School to complete his senior years. Discuss the kind of support and infrastructure that would be needed to facilitate Josh's return. Do some background research about the availability of support for students like Josh in your state. Then role-play a meeting between the principal, a head of department, a classroom teacher, and Josh's support worker in which the participants discuss plans to support Josh's return.

School-work

Remember that school policies may apply that restrict your ability to complete one or more of the activities suggested below.

4 Refer to the section *Knowing and understanding the needs of learners* (page 331). Prepare a letter that you would give to each of your classes at the start of the school year, sharing the kinds of personal information about yourself that you think it is important for them to know so that they might understand you as a teacher. Include in your letter an invitation for the students to respond, outlining their goals for the year, the kinds of activities they like doing, and how they think they learn.

5 Choose a software program/DVD suitable for supporting learning in your subject area. Undertake a task analysis of the steps needed for one of your students to learn how to use the program independently. (If this is too complex, focus on one task within the program, for example establishing a personal setting/records). Chunk your steps into a series of short activities that would enable this student to learn how to complete this task successfully. Evaluate your steps by giving them to a teaching colleague and ask them to work through the steps.

6 Identify a unit that you are going to teach next term that you want to improve so that it meets the needs of your students more effectively. Collect all of the resources (e.g., worksheets) that you generally use for that unit and arrange a time to meet with your learning support teacher at the school to discuss how the unit could be improved.

SUGGESTED READING AND RESOURCES

Books

Hay, I. & Winn, S. (2005). Students with Asperger's Syndrome in an inclusive secondary school environment: Teachers', parents', and students' perspectives. *Australasian Journal of Special Education*, *29*, 140–154.

Jobling, A. & Moni, K. B. (2004). I never imagined I'd have to teach these children: Providing authentic learning experiences for secondary pre-service teachers in teaching students with special needs. *Asia-Pacific Journal of Teacher Education*, *32*, 5–22.

Lloyd, J., Moni, K, B., & Jobling, A. (2006). Breaking the hype cycle: Using computers in a literacy program for young adults with Down syndrome. *Down Syndrome Research and Practice*, *9*, 68–74.

Moni, K. B. (2006). Beyond the comfort zone: Developing effective strategies for supporting beginning English teachers to cater for diversity. In W. Sawyer and B. Doecke (Eds), *Only connect: English teaching, schooling and community* (pp. 356–369). Adelaide, SA: Wakefield Press.

Morgan, M., Moni, K. B., & Jobling, A. (2006). Code breaker: Developing phonics with a young adult with an intellectual disability. *Journal of Adolescent and Adult Literacy*, *50*, 52–65.

Websites

<www.webquest.org/index.php>—WebQuests originated at the San Diego State University Department of Educational Technology. It is a structured inquiry-oriented lesson format in which most or all the information that learners work with comes from the web. The WebQuest site has a searchable database of webquests for all subject areas and across all grade levels. Even if you don't use the actual WebQuest in your classroom, the example given can direct you to a range of relevant websites in many subject areas. There is also an excellent tutorial that includes templates to enable you to develop your own webquests.

<www.digistories.co.uk and www.photobus.co.uk>—The Digital Storytelling and Photobus sites provide very useful information and background on digital stories and how to create them, plus some great examples and models. At the simplest level, digital stories are short, personal, multimedia narratives. They lend themselves particularly to humanities and social science topics. They have quite strict rules for their construction, which makes them both ideal and challenging for classroom use. These rules include a script of 250 words, a dozen or so pictures, images, or movie footage, and a length of approximately two minutes. Teaching students how to create them doesn't take long and both websites have tutorials. The main strategy is through collaborative workshops and peer teaching where the teacher works as a collaborator and facilitator rather than a technical expert.

REFERENCES

Australian Government Attorney-General's Department (2005). *Disability Standards for Education* <http://ag.gov.au.agd/WWW/agedHome.nsf/AllDocs/1821B>, accessed 3 November 2007.

Barrett, P., Webster, H., & Turner, C. (2000). *FRIENDS: Group leader's manual for children* (3rd ed.). Brisbane, Australian Academic Press.

Beavis, A. (2006). On track? Students choosing a career. *Professional Educator*, *5*, 21–23.

Bitsika, V. & Sharpley, C. F. (2004). Stress, anxiety and depression among parents of children with Autism Spectrum Disorder. *Australian Journal of Guidance and Counselling*, *14*, 151–161.

Bond, G. R. (1992). Vocational rehabilitation. In R. P. Liberman (Ed.), *Handbook of psychiatric rehabilitation* (pp. 244–275). New York: Macmillan.

Campbell, M. A. (2004). Identification of "at-risk" students for prevention and early intervention programs in secondary schools. *Australian Journal of Guidance and Counselling*, *14*, 65–77.

Catts, H. W. & Kamhi, A. G. (2005). *The connection between language and reading disabilities*. Mahwah, NJ: Erlbaum.

Clark, L. (2005). *All I want is what's best for my child.* Harris Park: NSW, Multicultural Disability Advocacy Association of New South Wales.

Cooney, C. & Hay, I. (2005). Internet-based literacy development for middle school students with reading difficulties. *Literacy Learning: The Middle Years*, *13*, 36–44.

Demir, M. & Urberg, K .A. (2004). Friendship and adjustment among adolescents. *Journal of Experimental Child Psychology*, *88*, 68–82.

Department of Education, Science, and Training. (2002). *Senate inquiry into the education of students with disabilities*. Canberra, ACT: Department of Education, Science, and Training.

Doyle, M. B. (1997). *The paraprofessional's guide to the inclusive classroom*. Baltimore, MD: Brookes.

Eagar, K., Green, J., Gordon, R., Owen, A., Masso, M., & Williams, K. (2006). Functional assessment to predict capacity for work in a population of school-leavers with disabilities. *International Journal of Disability, Development and Education*, *53*, 331–349.

Ellison, M. A., Danley, K. S., Bromberg, C., & Palmer-Erbs, V. (1999). Longitudinal outcome of young adults who participated in a psychiatric vocational rehabilitation program. *Psychiatric Rehabilitation Journal*, *22*, 337–341.

Flook, L., Repetti, R. L., & Ullman, J. B. (2005). Classroom social experiences as predictors of academic performance. *Developmental Psychology*, *41*, 319–327.

Frey, K. S., Nolen, S. B., Van Schoiack-Edstrom, L., & Hirschstein, M. K. (2005). Effects of a school-based social–emotional competence program: Linking children's goals, attributions, and behavior. *Applied Developmental Psychology*, *26*, 171–200.

Gambrell, L., Morrow, L. M., & Pressley, M. (2007). *Best practices in literacy instruction* (3rd ed.). New York: Guilford Press.

Gilbert, C. & Hay, I. (2004). Wellbeing and competitive employment for adults with an acquired physical or psychological disability. *Australian Journal of Rehabilitation Counselling*, *10*, 27–35.

Hattie, J. & Timperley, H. (2007). The power of feedback. *Review of Educational Research*, *77*, 81–112.

Hay, I. (2000). Cognitive strategies in the secondary school: Investigating process based instruction and students' perceptions of effective teaching strategies. *Journal of Cognitive Education and Psychology*, *1*, 164–176.

Hay, I. (2005). Facilitating children's self-concept: A rationale and evaluative study. *Australian Journal of Guidance and Counselling*, *15*, 60–67.

Hay, I. & Ashman, A. F. (2003). The development of adolescents' emotional stability and general self-concept: The interplay of parents, peers and gender. *International Journal of Disability, Development and Education*, *50*, 79–93.

Hay, I. & Booker, G. (2006). Teachers' perceptions and classroom application of mathematical computer software. *Journal of Cognitive Education and Psychology*, *6*, 61–71.

Hay, I. & Dempster, N. (2004) Student leadership development through general classroom activities, In B. Bartlett, F. Bryer, & D. Roebuck (Eds), *Education: Weaving research into practice* (Vol. 2, pp. 141–150), *2nd International Language, Cognition, and Special Education Conference*, Gold Coast (December).

Hay, I., Elias, G., Fielding-Barnsley, R., Homel, R., & Frieberg, K. (2007). Language delays, reading delays and learning difficulties: Interactive elements requiring multidimensional programming, *Journal of Learning Disabilities*, *40*, 400–409.

Homel, R., Elias, G., & Hay, I. (2001). Developmental prevention in a disadvantaged community. In J. Dixon & G. Vimpani (Eds), *Social origins of health and wellbeing* (pp. 269–279). Cambridge, UK: Cambridge University Press.

Howard, R. & Ford, J. (2007). The roles and responsibilities of teacher aides supporting students with special needs in secondary school settings. *Australasian Journal of Special Education*, *31*, 25–43.

Ivey, J. K. (2004). What do parents expect? A study of the likelihood and importance of issues for children with Autism Spectrum Disorders. *Focus on Autism and Other Developmental Disabilities*, *19*, 27–34.

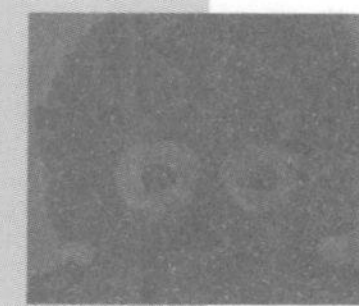

Kavale, K. A. (2002). Mainstreaming to full inclusion: From orthogenesis to pathogenesis of an idea. *International Journal of Disability, Development, and Education*, *49*, 201–214.

Kidd, M. P., Sloane, P. J., & Ferko, I. (2000). Disability and the labour market: An analysis of British males. *Journal of Health Economics*, *19*, 6, 961–981.

Lloyd, J. M. (2006). *An investigation to teach word processing skills to young adults with intellectual disabilities*. Unpublished Master of Philosophy thesis, University of Queensland, St Lucia.

Marks, G. N. (2006). *The transition to full-time work of young people who do not go to university: Longitudinal Surveys of Australian Youth—Research report 49*. Camberwell, Vic: Australian Council for Educational Research.

Mason, E. (1993). *ABLE: A programme for adolescents*. Cheltenham, Vic: Hawker Brown Education.

McLean, J. (2003). Employees with long-term illness or disabilities in the UK social service workforce. *Disability and Society*, *18*, 51–70.

Mowbray, C. T., Bybee, D., Harris, S. N., & McCrohan, N. (1995). Predictors of work status and future work orientation in people with a psychiatric disability. *Psychiatric Rehabilitation Journal*, *19*, 17–28.

Nosek, M. A., Hughes, R. B., Swedlund, N., Taylor, H. B., & Swank, P. (2003). Self-esteem and women with disability. *Social Science and Medicine*, *56*, 1737–1747.

Pressley, M. (2006). *Reading instruction that works: The case for balanced teaching* (3rd ed.). New York: Guilford Press.

Prior, M. (2003). *Learning and behavior problems in Asperger syndrome*. London: Guilford Press.

Resnick, M. D., Bearman, P., Blum, R. W., Bauman, K. E., Harris, K., Jones, J., Tabor, J., Beuhring, T., Sieving, R. E., Skew, M., Ireland, M., Bearinger, L., & Udry, R. (1997). Protecting adolescents from harm: Findings from the national longitudinal study of adolescent health. *Journal of American Medical Association*, *278*, 823–832.

Rigby, K. (2002). *New perspectives on bullying*. London: Jessica Kingsley.

Rutter, M. & Maughan, B. (2002). School effectiveness findings 1979–2002. *Journal of School Psychology*, *40*, 451–475.

Thomas, G. & Vaughan, M. (2004). *Inclusive education: Readings and reflections*. Maidenhead, UK: Open University Press.

Wagner, R., Muse, A., & Tannenbaum, K. R. (2007). *Vocabulary acquisition: Implications for reading comprehension*. New York: Guilford.

Waite, S., Lawson, H. & Robertson, C. (2006). Work-related learning for students with learning difficulties: Relevance and reality. *Cambridge Journal of Education*, *36*, 579–595.

Watson, J. & Bond, T. G. (2007). Walking the walk: Rasch analysis of an exploratory survey of secondary teachers' attitudes and understanding of students with learning difficulties. *Australian Journal of Learning Disabilities*, *12*, 1–9.

Woolley, G. E. & Hay, I. (2007). Reading intervention: The benefits of using trained tutors. *Australian Journal of Language and Literacy*, *30*(1), 9–20.

Worthy, J., Patterson, E., Salas, R., Prater, S., & Turner, M. (2002). More than just reading: The human factor in reaching resistant readers. *Reading Research and Instruction*, *41*, 177–202.

SECTION

4

Inclusive Outcomes

Inclusive Outcomes 4

In each of the chapters up to this point, the authors have dealt with issues that affect the interpersonal and intellectual growth of young people. Education is a process of acculturation and how an individual fits into the society in which they live has important implications for their future happiness and wellbeing.

In several chapters, authors have drawn attention to the social aspects of learning and education (e.g., Chapters 1, 3, 4, 5, 9, and 10). In this section, the authors bring many of the issues already raised into sharper focus.

Heather Jenkins deals comprehensively with social and interpersonal development, taking the position that one of the primary foci of inclusive education is the development of social interactions among students and there is substantial research evidence to show that inclusion promotes improved interactions. She provides a wealth of ideas that will help new and experienced teachers improve the teaching–learning environment and the learning outcomes for students in their classes, and encourage responsive and positive interactions inside and outside the classroom.

It has often been said that the success of education comes through collaborations between the school, the home, and the community. In the final chapter, Suzanne Carrington focuses on consultation, collaboration, communication, and collegiality among all stakeholders within a school community. If there is one ideal outcome for education, it is facilitating changes within and beyond the boundaries of the school campus. These can become a reality when there is respect for the contributions that all parties make to achieve positive and productive outcomes for all students.

Heather Jenkins

11

SOCIAL AND INTERPERSONAL DEVELOPMENT

What you will learn in this chapter

The social and interpersonal development of students is a very important aspect of their involvement inside and outside the classroom. The inclusion of students with diverse abilities in regular classrooms also contributes in important ways to the social and interpersonal development of the other students. Teachers who can develop positive classroom environments will also discover that all students benefit from their confident and responsive involvement in classroom activities that promote positive interactions.

In this chapter, you will learn:

- strategies to promote a socially responsive, inclusive, and supportive classroom;
- characteristics of students that interfere with their capacity to engage in positive social interactions and be included in the social groupings of the classroom;
- strategies to develop friendships among students;
- strategies that will assist teacher aides to facilitate social interactions among students; and
- whole-school programs that support the social and interpersonal development of all students from kindergarten through to secondary schooling.

CASE STUDIES

JACOB

Jacob is a student with Autism Spectrum Disorder (ASD) and Attention Deficit Hyperactivity Disorder (ADHD) attending a mainstream Year 5 class in a metropolitan government school. He was observed by a student teacher on teaching placement to be very noncompliant with directions and suggestions, and would not join in the class activities. For example, if the class group were asked to sit together, Jacob would sit underneath a desk about three metres away from the other children. The teacher frequently said that he was being silly, and when she asked him to move to the front, he kicked three students on his way through the group before kneeling in front of the teacher and placing his hands on her shoe and leg. Eventually, the teacher asked the teacher aide to sit with Jacob separately and work through the required task with him on a one-to-one basis.

Following these observations, the student teacher got permission from her supervising teacher to devise a program that focused on Jacob's attention, improving his compliance with instructions, and rewarded him for appropriate participation and social interaction with other children. Jacob was then able to collect the necessary equipment, repeat the instructions to the student teacher, and work systematically with other members of a small group in which he had been placed. This group worked together on a selected activity in a harmonious way and finished first. Jacob's successful participation in this activity ensured that he mastered the task and was more accepted by his class peers than in the past. It also improved his participation in small group work, which was a significant step in improving his social relationships with other children in the class. Some of the children commented that they were pleased to have Jacob in their group because he could work with them in a friendly and cooperative manner.

MATTHEW

Matthew has learning and behavioural difficulties and is in Year 9 at a regional secondary school. He was observed in English and mathematics classes. He is a slow reader and needs extra time to complete work, and the work that he submits is generally below the class average. Matthew is frequently disruptive. When he calls out in class, the teacher reprimands him, and then Matthew argues with the teacher. He has a few friends in the English class. They rarely get into trouble, while Matthew's behaviour is a regular source of irritation. Matthew's behaviour often leads to laughter among the other students, and, although it is directed toward Matthew, he appears to enjoy the attention and has commented that he would like to be a stand-up comedian. Matthew's classmates also resent his disruptions to the lessons, and as a consequence he has few friends.

The English teacher has found that the only successful strategy to improve Matthew's interactions within class is to contact his father—a local agricultural contractor. Matthew's behaviour improves for about two weeks but then it deteriorates again. Similar problems were observed within the mathematics class, which is more formal and requires a higher level of achievement than Matthew can demonstrate. The mathematics teacher found that the only way he could effectively deal with Matthew was to remove him from the classroom. The teacher admits that this is not especially successful as it results in slowing Matthew's progress in mathematics, isolates him more from other students, and enhances his sense of social isolation. The social inclusion of Matthew was finally resolved when the mathematics teacher noticed that Matthew was struggling to master an

assignment that involved working on computers. The teacher assigned Matthew a peer mentor, David, who is a competent student and was willing to demonstrate how Matthew could engage in each step of the assignment. Matthew seemed very pleased to receive this support and the teacher noticed that his disruptive behaviour declined, especially when other students praised him for his completion of the work, in partnership with David. This strategy led to Matthew improving his relationships with his peers and demonstrating more friendly behaviours toward other boys in the class.

TEACHING–LEARNING CONTEXT

By the time Jacob completes primary school, he will have spent approximately 7,000 hours in classrooms. When Matthew completes secondary school, he will have spent about 15,000 hours in classrooms. It is evident that, for both of these students, some of this time will be unhappy and may not lead to friendships and social skills that should be among the positive outcomes of schooling.

Students who lack appropriate social skills and cannot develop cooperative social interactions are disadvantaged in many ways, since they lack friends and are often excluded from many activities that make school so enjoyable and memorable for the majority of students. By introducing strategies to improve Jacob's and Matthew's social skills, their teachers made a positive contribution to their inclusion. The activities outlined in this chapter are intended to support teachers in their efforts to understand students who lack social skills and friendships and to provide strategies to promote the positive development of friendships and social inclusion.

Effective teaching and learning cannot take place in classrooms that are chaotic, threatening, punishing, or provoke students' or teachers' anxiety. There are many practices that are supported by research evidence that are available to teachers to promote safe, harmonious, positive classroom learning environments. Naturally, this requires a dedicated approach and a teacher's willingness to reflect on practices that are unsuccessful, and to learn from those experiences. For students who have disabilities or other challenges to their learning (such as English as a foreign language, or traumatic refugee experiences), the importance of a positive classroom environment should not be underestimated, since these students are less likely to experience success in the normal course of events. They may also struggle to establish the types of friendships that sustain other students through tough times in school.

It should also be noted that teachers and schools are obliged to fulfil the requirements of the Disability Standards in Education, which accompany the Commonwealth *Disability Discrimination Act 1992*. Included is the requirement that educational providers ensure the development and implementation of strategies and programs to prevent harassment and victimisation. These strategies and programs are most successful if undertaken as a whole-of-school approach, meaning that all teachers, students, and classrooms reflect positive social interactions that value every member of the school community.

There are at least three essential social skills that all students require, and teachers may have to work intensively with students with diverse abilities to develop them, namely:

- joining or entering a social group;
- establishing and maintaining friendships; and
- responding to social cues.

All students benefit from these basic social skills and teachers will improve the social development of every student within their class if they allocate time toward these three social priorities. They are important because:

- every child needs at least one good friend;
- diversity within regular classrooms has been found to enhance the positive self-concept of these children;
- children who lack social skills face a bleak future with respect to their future success, happiness, and acceptance;
- children who lack social skills cannot overcome their difficulties without significant support from their teachers and parents;
- it is a normal parental expectation that their children will participate in, and benefit from, the social life of their school; and
- when children complete their schooling, all of them should have the social skills to participate effectively in the life of the communities to which they will belong.

In this chapter, therefore, I outline strategies that teachers can implement in classrooms to assist students to achieve these three important social and interpersonal outcomes.

It cannot be assumed that the social inclusion will occur automatically, and practical strategies are needed, especially with students who are experiencing learning difficulties. Before addressing these issues with any student, teachers need to establish that the classroom is already an appropriate positive social environment, and they may also wish to establish the social status of the student who is isolated, excluded, or lonely. Some useful strategies that will help achieve this include:

- assessing the learning environment;
- interviewing the target student; and
- asking students to identify safe and unsafe parts of the school.

Let's now look at these three strategies.

Assessing the learning environment

There are many ways of assessing the learning environment, but most importantly these assessments must involve feedback from the students themselves. There is little point in a teacher feeling proud of a beautiful classroom when behind her back there is a bully sending vicious SMS messages about one student to her peers.

Classroom environment rating scales can be helpful as most contain statements about what happens in the classroom, and the students are asked to indicate whether the events occur never, seldom, sometimes, often, or always. It is preferable if students complete these scales anonymously, as this is more likely to encourage honest responses. For example, if a student reads an item "Members of the class are my friends" and genuinely believes that they have no friends in the class, the student is more likely to select "Never" if the response is anonymous. The following factors have been found to be important in students' perceptions of what is happening in their learning environment (Aldridge, Fraser, & Huang, 1999):

- student cohesiveness (e.g., "In this class, I get help from other students");
- teacher support (e.g., "The teacher helps me when I have trouble with work");
- involvement (e.g., "My ideas and suggestions are used during classroom discussions");
- investigation (e.g., "I find out answers to questions by doing investigations");
- task orientation (e.g., "I know the goals for this class");
- cooperation (e.g., "When I work in groups in this class, there is teamwork"); and
- equity (e.g., "My work receives as much praise as other students' work").

In the full version of the Aldridge et al. questionnaire (What Is Happening in the Classroom), there are eight items under each of the seven factors listed above. However, for students who are experiencing learning difficulties, this may be too complex and a simplified version has been created in which the student selects and colours in a smiling, neutral, or frowning face in response to one item that expresses each factor in a short form. See Box 11.1 for an example of a simplified rating scale.

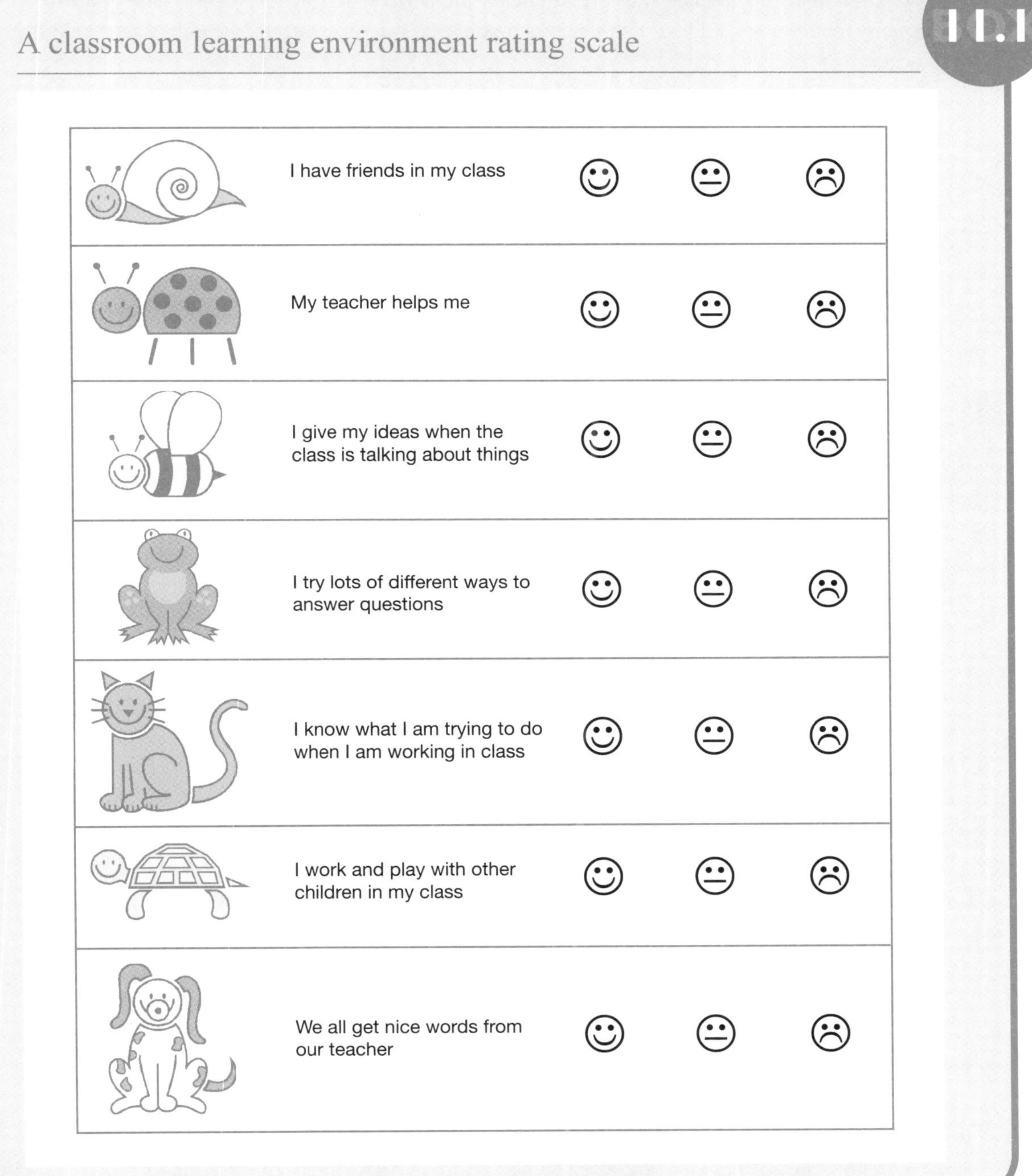

BOX 11.1

A classroom learning environment rating scale

I have friends in my class
My teacher helps me
I give my ideas when the class is talking about things
I try lots of different ways to answer questions
I know what I am trying to do when I am working in class
I work and play with other children in my class
We all get nice words from our teacher

These items can be read in private to a student who lacks the necessary reading skills, and sometimes this creates the opportunity and the language for discussion of matters that the student may not have been able to raise independently. For example, a student who does not believe they have any friends may signal this by selecting the neutral or frowning face, and this creates an opportunity for discussion. Alternatively, the discussion may reveal some unintentional outcomes, such as the five-year-old preschool boy who assured the interviewer that the teacher never helped him. The interviewer, who knew that the teacher was a particularly supportive person, expressed some surprise at this response, and the boy told her that this was because he was so smart that he didn't need help from the teacher.

Another learning environment scale to assess students' perceptions of the science classroom is the Constructivist Learning Environment Survey. This is suitable for secondary students, and an online version is available at <http://surveylearning.moodle.com/cles>. The survey can be completed online or the items can be printed, depending on the resources available to the teacher.

Interviews with students

Confidential interviews with students are an excellent way to gain insights about a student's perspectives on aspects of the classroom, playground, and school. The points listed in Box 11.2 should be taken into consideration when interviewing children, especially those who are vulnerable due to limited cognitive capacities.

11.2 Considerations when interviewing vulnerable children

1. Before the interview, make a list of the topics that you want to cover, but be prepared to be flexible.
2. Consider the reasonable attention span of the child.
3. Allow the child time to process the question and to respond and do not interrupt them once they start responding.
4. Make the questions open-ended (e.g., "Tell me how you feel about what is happening at lunch-time").
5. Ask simple questions that contain only one part that requires a single response.
6. Ensure that you are sitting so that you can easily keep eye-contact, but if the child looks away when responding, don't insist on eye-contact.
7. Be attentive to your body language. If you are taking notes, explain that this helps you to remember the important things that the child will say, and that you won't be showing them to anyone else.
8. If something arises that you think should be discussed with the parent, ask the child if it is alright to discuss this with their mother or father, and respect their wishes if they indicate that one parent is preferred, or neither.
9. If you are asking the child to recollect events, use time markers (e.g., before the holidays, last week when we had music lessons, on Monday afternoon).
10. Respect the child's confidential disclosures, if there are any. Self-disclosure is a sign that the child feels comfortable with the listener, and this trust must not be abused.

11 The responsibility for clear communication lies with you.
12 If the child has English as a second or alternative language, then it may be appropriate to have a translator present. This was illustrated effectively in the case of a 12-year-old girl from a Chinese background who was making no progress in her English reading lessons. When a Chinese language translator spoke with her, she said that she was offended because the teacher kept showing her reading books that were for very young children. When age-appropriate reading material was provided, with themes that reflected 12-year-old girls' interests, her improvement in reading was significant.
13 Close the interview by thanking the child for their time and discussion, and remind the child that you will not discuss the interview with anyone else, unless this has been agreed upon during the course of the interview. Try to summarise the actions that you will take that will result from what you have learned.

11.2

Safe and unsafe parts of the school

The availability of cheap disposable cameras and small digital cameras means that students can easily collect visual images of their school to represent safe and unsafe areas. A group of British teachers used this approach and discovered that the children's photographs provided many insights about their views of the school classrooms, playgrounds, toilets, bike sheds, and eating areas (Kaplan & Howes, 2004). Some areas, such as the bike sheds, were perceived as safe by some students but were seen as unsafe by others. A picture of the empty sports field reminded one student of the games and fun that he had enjoyed there, while another's response to the image was to make him feel lonely. Such visual techniques provide original and insightful ways through which students can communicate their social and interpersonal thoughts and feelings about the school in which they spend so much time each week. There have also been some interesting photographs taken by Australian secondary students of aspects of their school that assisted staff in developing an inclusive school environment (Carrington, Allen, & Osmolowski, 2007).

Observation checklists

Teachers may determine the frequency of cooperation, sharing, inclusion, and exclusion or rejection that occurs with respect to the students and their peers when they observe students in a variety of social contexts, in learning groups, at lunch time, and during sport and drama activities. This is quite valuable because it provides effective evidence for the skills that are lacking and highlights classroom and individual strategies that may need improvement in response to observed problems.

It is an advantage to seek student feedback about the learning environment at the beginning of term, as this provides an opportunity for the teacher to get to know the students and provides a basis for evaluating the effectiveness of changes to classroom practice again at the end of a term. Changes that are intended to improve the quality of the learning environment should be reflected in changes in assessment practices. For example, one mathematics secondary teacher observed that his Year 8 students were not motivated to complete their mathematics lessons and their disengagement was leading to lower achievement. He changed his methods of teaching to incorporate a variety of approaches to mathematics' topics, such as observing patterns in nature, rather than just in number sequences. By the end of the term, the students in this class reported that they thought that the mathematics' lessons were more interesting and they were engaged for longer periods in their mathematics' work, which led to higher levels of task completion.

The cognitive advantages of social inclusion

It is important to note here that students with diverse learning needs who are included in the social relationships within the classroom also benefit cognitively. This is because children's cognitive development improves through social interaction, and the work of Vygotsky is helpful in understanding how this happens. First, Vygotsky emphasised the importance of language as the first tool for initiating interactions with others, and it is apparent that children who lack effective means of communication are severely limited in their opportunities to develop social interaction skills. Second, when children interact with one another, one frequently provides support to the other and then both children progress in their understanding. Sometimes this support, or scaffolding as Vygotsky called it, may be provided by an adult, when neither child is sufficiently advanced to support the other (Krause, Bochner, & Duchesne, 2003). In Box 11.3, some examples are given of ways in which teachers at the different levels of schooling have paired students who need support with more capable others.

BOX 11.3 Examples of scaffolding

PRESCHOOL

Teacher: "It's time for lunch. Everyone go to your bags and take out your lunchbox, sit down and start eating lunch."

Mary: (aged four years, gets her lunchbox, but struggles to unfasten the clips to open it) "I can't open my lunchbox!"

Jean: (aged five years, who knows about tricky lunchboxes) "Here. You put your finger under this clip, like this, and it pops up! (demonstrates successfully) Now you try it on this other side."

Mary: "If I put my finger there, then pull it up. Yes! I've done it! Thanks, Jean."

(At this level, Jean is teaching Mary a motor task. She is supporting or scaffolding Mary in her efforts to complete the response by showing first, then getting Mary to try the same action. By the time Jean has supported Mary in this way, Mary has acquired a new skill that ensures she can sit down and eat her lunch with her new friend Jean.)

PRIMARY SCHOOL

Teacher: "Today we're going to write some acrostic poems and then draw some pictures to illustrate our acrostic poems. Does everyone remember how to write an acrostic poem?"

Tom: "That's when you take the letters in a word and use them to start each line in the poem."

Teacher: "Excellent, Tom! Now I want you to work in pairs to develop an acrostic poem based on the word 'snake', since we have been studying reptiles in science this week."

Sam: (who has a low level of vocabulary is working with Sam) "How do we start?"

Tom: "Okay. I'll show you. Let's write it out here, and then think of words about snakes to put onto each line. How about thinking about the noise a snake makes?"

Sam: "Sssssssssss. That could be our first line."

Tom: "Are snakes nice or nasty, Sam?"

Sam: "Nasty! Now we have the second line."

Tom: "Well, they're not all nasty. Should we stay close or far away from a snake?"

Sam: "Away! That's our third line."

Tom: "What happens when a kookaburra sees a snake?"

Sam: "The kookaburra kills the snake! That could be our fourth line."

Tom: "And then what does the kookaburra do?"

Sam: "It eats it. That's the fifth line. Let's read it.
S sssssssssssssss is the sound of a snake
N asty are snakes when they are poisonous
A way from snakes we should stay
K ookaburra likes to catch snakes and then the kookaburra
E ats the snake."

At this level, the teacher deliberately paired Tom with Sam because she knew that Tom would support Sam to help him understand how to construct the acrostic poem. Sam's willingness to accept guidance from Tom means that the two boys are learning together. Sam benefits from this social interaction.

SECONDARY

Teacher: "Today we are going to develop a poster about the Ningaloo Reef. I want everyone to work in pairs and develop a poster that explains all about the value of the Ningaloo Reef on the West Coast of Australia. Natalie, I'd like you to work with Jane, please."

Natalie: "What'll we put on our poster? I don't know anything about Ningaloo Reef."

Jane: "I know lots about it because we went on a holiday to Coral Bay, where the reef comes into the bay, and we went on a boat tour of the reef."

Natalie: "What does it look like?"

Jane: "The coral's blue, purple, and white. Some of it looks like cabbages. Some of it looks like a big brain."

Natalie: "Wow, that sounds cool! Are there fish?"

Jane: "Yeah. The fish are the best part because no one can fish in the Ningaloo Marine Park, so you see hundreds of fish and turtles. The fish are gorgeous colours, electric blue, yellow and black. The turtles are lovely too."

Natalie: "Are there sharks?"

Jane: "No, only whale sharks, but you have to go out in a boat to see them, and it's only from July to September."

Natalie: "We've got lots to put on a poster. Can we go onto the internet and see if we can find some pictures for the poster?"

The teacher deliberately paired Natalie with Jane because she knew that Jane had been to the Reef and could explain the most interesting parts to Natalie in language and ways that Natalie would understand. In that way, Natalie would be motivated to work on the poster, and at the same time she'd be developing a friendship with Jane, based on the shared knowledge about Jane's holiday.

11.3

ISSUES AND CHALLENGES

As indicated earlier, the aim of this chapter is to provide insights into the characteristics of some students that cause them to struggle in their efforts to develop effective interpersonal relationships, and to assist teachers in establishing strategies that will promote positive and socially accepting classrooms. Some of the issues and challenges associated with developing social interactions inside and outside the classroom are as follows:

- Some students with special learning needs lack the ability to understand the other child's point of view, and do not reciprocate in their social activities, establish eye-contact, or demonstrate the nonverbal and verbal cues that signal the desire for friendship and acceptance.
- Some students can't engage in imaginary or pretend play, and this means they are excluded from the many games that are enjoyed by young children.
- Some students may be impulsive in their actions, and lash out or lose their temper very quickly in social situations, which causes other children to be very wary of close contact with them.
- Some students may have poor perceptual motor skills, they may be clumsy or poorly coordinated, and this means that they cannot join in the climbing, chasing, ball games, and other sporting activities that are common in Australian school playgrounds and that often form the basis for friendship groups to be established.
- Some students may be accompanied by an education assistant so intensively that it is impossible for other children to befriend them and teachers need to manage this with sensitivity—as one boy remarked, "It's like having your mother with you all the time."

TEACHING ESSENTIALS

The teaching strategies required to assist students with special learning needs to achieve the three essential social skills of joining a social group, making friendships, and responding to social cues are outlined in the following sections.

Joining a social group

If a teacher is aware that a new student with special learning needs is joining the class (or group at the early childhood level), or if this is the situation at the beginning of the new school year, then one of the most important strategies is to ensure that the class is prepared for the inclusion of that young person. The idea of creating welcoming communities has been promoted very effectively by the Curriculum Support Package entitled "Open Your Mind. Count Us In", which outlines teaching strategies for early childhood, middle childhood, early and late adolescent classes that enable all students to understand the challenges faced by students with diverse abilities and accept each student for the unique individual

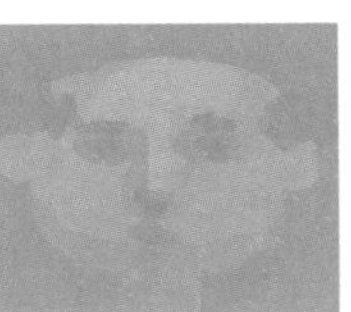

contribution that they make to the classroom. This resource is available at <www.countusin.com.au> and provides a wide range of age-appropriate activities to enable students to understand the challenges of accepting students into their friendship and peer groups.

EARLY CHILDHOOD

At the early childhood level, young children in regular classrooms need simple guidelines to assist them to understand and welcome children with diverse abilities. The "Open Your Mind. Count Us In" package identifies three themes, as outlined below.

Let's communicate

Everyone communicates, sometimes in different ways and for different purposes. This enables young children to understand that a nonverbal child may need pictures or symbols to assist in their communication, and will also help in discussions about what we need to communicate and for what purposes. The activities encourage children to attempt to communicate with drawings, finger spellings, and gestures.

Let's go

Everyone moves about, some unaided, some with assistance, and some more slowly than others. The activities encourage children to think about moving to get the things we need, to get from one place to another, to go to places in the community, and to play games.

Let's learn

Everyone learns, sometimes in different ways, and this may require changes to the learning environment, but it ensures that everyone is able to participate. The activities include learning by touching, listening, watching, and experimenting.

The program *Stop, Think, Do:* Social Skills Training, *Early years of Schooling Ages 4–8 years* (Petersen, 2002) also teaches young children to develop social skills by encouraging them, through games and activities, to use the traffic light symbols of STOP (red), THINK (orange), and DO (green) as a strategy for developing appropriate relationships. For example, if there is a problem between two children, the teacher encourages them to:

> social skills training
> *Instructional techniques involving description, modelling, rehearsal, and feedback to assist individuals achieve social competence.*

- STOP: Don't react impulsively to the situation, clarify the problem.
- THINK: Consider solutions to the problem, and think about the consequences.
- DO: Choose the best solution and then act on it.

This sequence may need practice to assist young children to develop an effective strategy, supported by the visual chart of the traffic stoplight, and to develop the skills necessary to maintain a position within a social group. The charts are available in large sizes for the whole classroom, and smaller sizes for the child's desk to use as a cue to assist him or her in managing personal behaviour.

MIDDLE CHILDHOOD

The development of social skills that enable children to join a social group is more challenging in the middle years of childhood. Developing an understanding of the similarities and differences among children is an important strategy and may be helped by encouraging children to share their interests and preferences. At this age, children with special learning needs (including gifted and talented students) may need assistance to get to know people, and to understand how to join groups and behave in acceptable ways. The *Stop, Think, Do: Social Skills Training, Primary Years of Schooling Ages 8–12* (Peterson, 2002) contains a wide range of activities to support children as they master these essential skills.

EARLY ADOLESCENCE

The onset of puberty, from around 11 to 15 years, is a testing time for young people, their parents, and their teachers. The challenges of belonging to a peer group are very important, and for children with diverse abilities this may be a time when they feel particularly alone and vulnerable. To assist those students who lack the social skills to maintain their membership of a social group, teachers must address several factors that may be inhibiting the student. There are at least three faulty assumptions that need to be reversed (Balson, 1995):

- I am a failure (negative self-concept).
- Life holds nothing for me (pessimism).
- It is futile starting anything (low risk-taking).

The teacher needs to work with the student to assist them to believe:

- I can cope with the problems of living (positive self-concept).
- Eventually things will turn out for the best (optimism).
- I will take a chance (risk-taking).

These goals can be achieved by helping adolescents focus on the positive aspects of their personality and talents, through personal affirmation, encouraging a more positive view of the world, and encouraging students to take risks. In these circumstances, it is essential that the teacher establishes a positive relationship with the students, and speaks to them privately if there are issues that need to be addressed. A short Self-Concept Test devised by Cambra and Silvestre (2003) is suitable for adolescents and provides some useful practical insights for teachers to work with adolescents who have a poor self-concept.

If a student has been rejected by classmates due to unacceptable behaviour, then other strategies are needed to help the student to become socially included again. The 'Circle of Friends' strategy is one approach that enables a young person to receive the support of his or her peers in developing acceptable interpersonal and social skills.

Circle of friends

This strategy was developed to enhance the social inclusion of a child (known as the focus child) who is experiencing difficulties at school due to their challenging behaviours (Newton, Taylor, & Wilson, 1999). 'Circle of Friends' is a systematic approach to establishing a small group of generally primary-school-aged peers, led by a teacher, which assists the focus child to understand the problems that their behaviour is causing, and to mobilise the child's peers to support and engage them in problem-solving. It is described in more detail at <www.inclusive-solutions.com/circlesoffriends.asp>. The key stages of this approach include identifying the child with the social problem and then developing a peer group led by an adult to assist the child to make friends and understand why their current behaviour is causing their exclusion.

At the first meeting of the Circle, a small group of children from the child's class are introduced and the aims of the group are established. The importance of trust and confidentiality are emphasised, and the group brainstorms strategies to assist the focus child. For example, if John is the focus child, then the group may identify the unfriendly behaviours, such as shouting, swearing, pushing, and bullying that have isolated John from his peers. The group then develops strategies to help John develop alternative responses to situations that lead to the unfriendly behaviour inside and outside the classroom. For example, a group might develop a tapping code so that when John starts annoying someone in class the Friend would tap on the desk or the floor as a cue to stop being annoying. If John

is getting angry with the canteen lady, then a Friend would walk up to him and start talking to him and help him walk away from the problem.

The outcomes of this approach have led to focus children reducing their problem behaviours and developing a friendship network, and it has also been shown to develop empathy, skills in problem-solving, listening skills, and improved capacity to express feelings (Frederickson & Turner, 2003). Teachers and parents also report that they feel more supported and can see the improvements in children like John as their inclusion in social groups is improved.

Establishing and maintaining friendships

Children with special learning needs, in particular, often struggle to maintain friendships, usually because they do not understand what needs to be done in a friendly relationship, and because they may unintentionally damage the potential for a relationship because of inappropriate responses. For these children to develop friendships with others, at least two conditions must be present to ensure that the friendships are generated and sustained. There must be: (a) the opportunity to get to know other children through interaction, and (b) these opportunities must be sustained over a reasonable length of time.

The role of peer groups in school and classrooms is very important for the academic, social, and emotional health of students. Ways that teachers manage peer groups has significant implications for the quality and inclusiveness of the classroom. Peer relationships serve many important functions (McDevitt & Ormrod, 2004), not just in school but throughout our lives:

- Peers serve as partners for practising social skills.
- Peers socialise one another.
- Peers contribute to a sense of identity.
- Peers help one another make sense of their lives.
- Peers provide emotional and social support.

There is a wide range of strategies recommended for developing effective peer relationships and good social skills. However, before these strategies are implemented, it is important to consider how to estimate the social status of the students in a class, to identify those who are most at risk of alienation and rejection by other members of the class.

ESTIMATION OF SOCIAL STATUS AND SOCIAL SKILLS

Five social groups of children have been identified within school (McDevitt & Ormrod, 2004), and these are:

1. *Popular children*—These children have good social and communication skills and show leadership potential.
2. *Average children*—These children have an average level of social awareness with respect to their age and are generally able to find a social group with whom they feel comfortable.
3. *Controversial children*—These children may be aggressive in some situations, and then helpful and cooperative in other situations. Their unpredictability means they do not have many friends.
4. *Neglected children*—These children may be shy and withdrawn and have some anxiety about interacting with other children.
5. *Rejected children*—These children may be aggressive, immature, anxious, or impulsive, and other children will not enjoy playing with them.

Students may be asked to draw maps of their friendship circles and social networks and this can also

be a revealing exercise, although care must be taken to manage the results with sensitivity. For example, teachers must judge whether the best interests of all students are served by asking the students to engage in activities that may have the opposite effect to that intended, by drawing attention to those children who are friendless within the classroom. A strategy to determine the groups of children who fall within the five social categories is the construction of a sociogram. The procedure for constructing a sociogram begins with a questionnaire-based sociometric test, which asks each class member the following:

- Write down the two or three peers you like the most, like working with, or are your best friends.
- Write down the two or three peers you least like, dislike working with, or that you reject as friends.
- Rate every member of the class in terms of like or dislike on a 5-point scale.
- Do not discuss your answers with anyone else.

After the mean ratings are collated, the teacher draws up a sociogram depicting groups, inter-relationships among the groups, and those children who are rejected. An example of a sociogram is given in Box 11.4. In this sociogram, it can be seen that children 11 and 14 are rejected completely by the group, while child 24 receives no reciprocal nominations. These outcomes assist the teacher to identify the children who require support to gain entry to the social groups within the class. The teacher should not show this sociogram to the class, because it would not be in the best interests of the children who are isolated in the diagram.

Teacher observation and rating scales can also help identify young people who are not fitting into a teaching–learning environment. There are two ways in which teachers may estimate the social status of students within their classrooms. The Strengths and Difficulties Questionnaire (SDQ) is a rating scale that includes aspects of peer relationships and prosocial behaviour. It is located at <www.sdqinfo.com>, and the website offers many versions. The instructions for scoring must be followed carefully. The SDQ is useful for assessing whether a planned intervention to improve outcomes for certain students has been effective. A second way is to construct a sociogram that shows the relationships among students (see Box 11.4).

BOX 11.4 Example of a sociogram

The sociogram below was generated from students' nomination of the three classmates with whom they most liked to spend free time (positive nominations), and the three classmates with whom they least liked to spend free time (negative nominations). The sociogram shows that students 11 and 14 are completely rejected and student 24 receives no reciprocal choices.

Sociogram like this are helpful in enabling a teacher to develop strategies to include those students who are clearly rejected by others in the class. This may first require careful observation of the class to determine why the students are so isolated, and it may be necessary to teach them the appropriate social skills and friendship strategies before they will be accepted by their classmates.

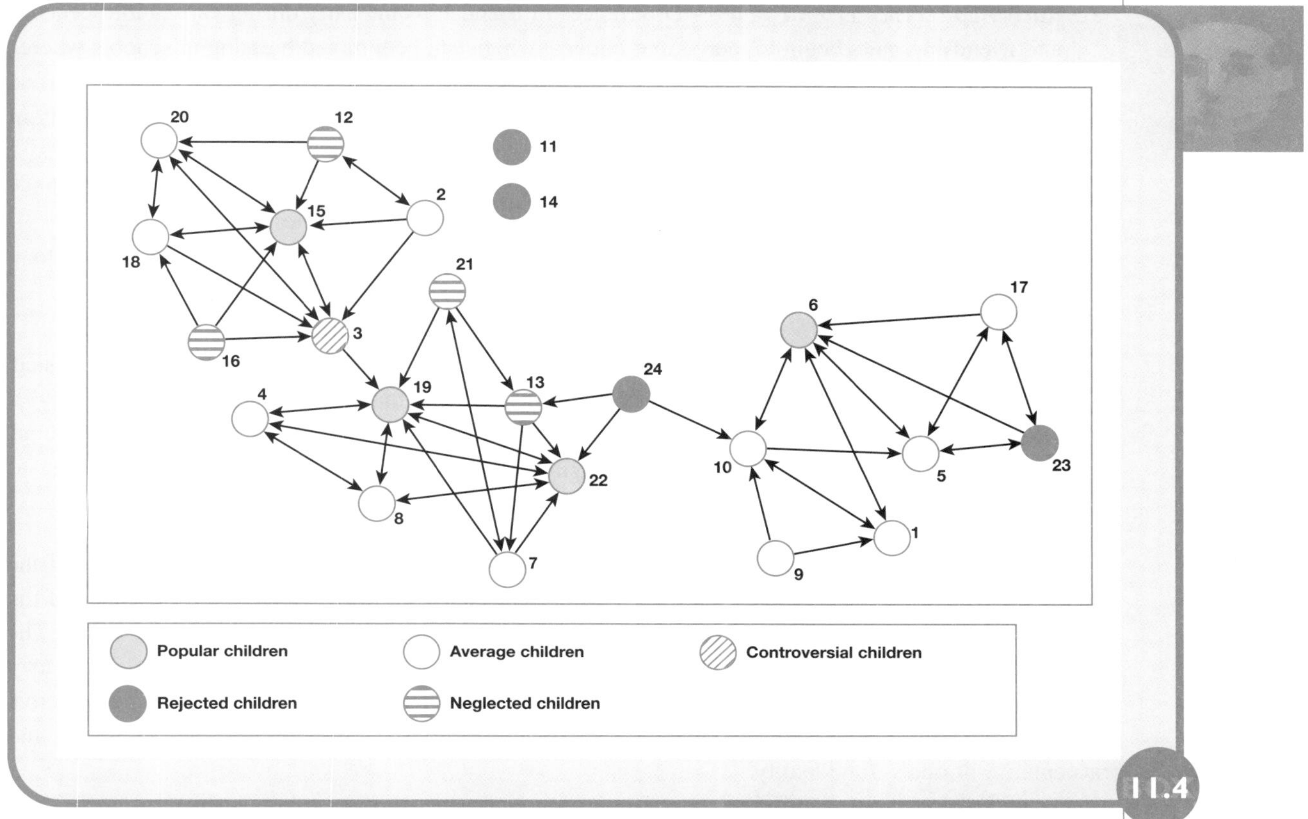

FRIENDSHIP STRATEGIES

Friendships differ from other types of peer relationships in three ways (McDevitt & Ormrod, 2004):

- Friendships are voluntary relationships; in other words, we choose our friends.
- Friendships are powered by shared routines and customs.
- Friendships are reciprocal.

Children understand friendship in different ways at different ages and it is important to note that, for children whose cognitive development may be delayed, their understanding of friendship will correspond to their developmental level, as below, which may not be the same as their chronological age and class placement.

- *Infancy (0–2 years)*—Infants smile, babble, gesture, and play with other children, especially siblings, and even without language they are clearly engaging in "friendly" behaviour.
- *Early childhood (2–6 years)*—Young children develop their social interactions with language, play, and games of make-believe. They understand friendship at relatively superficial levels, as friends are for sharing toys and games. An important skill developed at this age is to assert themselves while maintaining productive relationships.
- *Middle childhood (6–10 years)*—Friendships become more deliberate and stable in the middle-childhood years. Friends develop a sense of loyalty and start to use self-disclosure as a friendship strategy, especially girls. Children seek friends with similar interests, and for this reason friendships are more likely to be with same-sex peers, although this is not always the case.

- *Early Adolescence (10–14 years)*—Differences in friendships intensify during early adolescence and friendship pairs begin to merge into cliques, which can be a mixed blessing in schools where some children are popular and others are rejected. Feelings of possessiveness and jealousy start to emerge, and the maturity differences between boys and girls (due to the earlier onset of puberty in the majority of girls) may also have an impact. Middle-school students in mixed-gender classes may be quite disruptive, and there are a number of solutions to these conflicts. Some schools have chosen to develop same-sex classes for mathematics and science and these appear to have increased participation in these learning areas, although segregation does not necessarily lead to improved outcomes.
- *Late adolescence (14–18 years)*—Older adolescents are quite selective and friendships are an important aspect of establishing one's identity, and of beginning to establish intimacy with trusted others. The beginning of boyfriends/girlfriends emerges, and this may sometimes disrupt same-sex friendship patterns. At this age, friends are often the source of personal and emotional support, and friends made at this time are often sustained over our lifetimes.

SAME-SEX-ATTRACTED YOUTH

During adolescence, about 10% of students become aware that they are attracted to members of the same sex. This awareness is often not discussed or acknowledged in the first instance because of the fear and anxiety associated with the consequences of identifying as a same-sex-attracted youth. The awareness of same-sex attraction may be acknowledged by the young person, although he or she may continue to act in a way that does not identify a sexual preference. There may be some selective disclosure to close friends, and then beyond school, active identification with the gay community and acceptance of one's true identity.

There is a high rate of bullying and victimisation of youths who identify as lesbian or gay in their sexual orientation, and up to 50% of same-sex-attracted young people report homophobic bullying or harassment. Given that same-sex-attracted youth are at increased risk of substance abuse, self-harm, and depression, it is very important that schools acknowledge that same-sex-attracted students are present within the school, and adopt strategies to combat homophobia, since every student has the right to be free from bullying and harassment.

Strategies that are recommended to prevent homophobic bullying in schools include:

- encouraging pupils to reflect on issues of social justice and their own sexuality- and gender-related values and how best to prevent and respond to homophobic incidents;
- videos and drama activities that increase the students' understanding of sexual orientation;
- challenging unhelpful stereotypes of same-sex-attracted people, and discussing the contributions of same-sex-attracted adults to art, culture and literature; and
- discussing the value of diversity and individual differences among adolescent boys and girls.

Teachers must feel comfortable about discussing sexual identity with students of all ages, and it may also be appropriate to indicate to parents that the issue will be discussed at school. Some parents may worry that discussing homosexuality in an open way may be encouraging homosexuality, but this is not the case.

Schools that permit the harassment and victimisation of same-sex-attracted students are failing in their legal and ethical duty of care to provide a safe environment for all students. A very useful booklet, *Safety in our schools: Strategies for responding to homophobia*, has been developed by a research group at Latrobe University, Victoria, and more details about this publication, which is available online at <www.latrobe.edu.au/ssay/assets/downloads/safety_in_our_schools.pdf>.

An example of an activity that may enable teachers to discuss sexual identity at a distance is to identify a popular artist or musician who is same-sex-attracted, and discuss whether or not this makes any difference to the value of their work. For example, Elton John is a well-known musician who has campaigned effectively for the rights of gay men. A secondary class could discuss whether this has any impact at all on the popularity and quality of his song writing, his performances, and the public attitudes toward him.

Teachers engaging with their classes in discussions about personal issues such as sexual identity may have to implement a strategy called "Protective Interrupting", to prevent a student from self-disclosing a personal matter that may subsequently cause embarrassment or shame. If the teacher believes a student is about to disclose something personal, then the teacher must interrupt with the assurance that, "I'd like to hear about that, but it can wait until you and I can talk without being interrupted", while referring the class back to the original discussion point. The teacher then needs to set aside time when the student and teacher can engage in a private, uninterrupted discussion. Similarly, if it appears that a student is about to repeat some gossip or rumour about another student, the teacher must interrupt and ensure that the sensitive material is not revealed to the whole class.

FRIENDSHIP FACILITATION

All children need friendships, but some struggle more than others to make friends, especially if they are different in some obvious way. The role of teachers in helping children make friends can have its advantages and disadvantages. No one is helped if the children resent the artificial insincerity of friendships that teachers attempt to create through seating plans and small group work. One research team asked middle-school students what they considered to be the best strategies for facilitating friendships and the students described a wide range of strategies that seem more student-friendly than adult versions (Chadsey & Han, 2005).These are some of the strategies that the students recommended:

- Include students with disabilities in our classrooms, and if they need extra help, provide it to them; don't put them in separate classes.
- Teachers should talk to us and give us information about students with disabilities, and explain why they might act differently or have trouble learning, and also how they are the same as us in some ways.
- Don't let students make fun of students with disabilities. Give us a reason to be nice to them. Praise students with disabilities in the classroom so we know you think they are doing a good job.
- Create programs where students with and without disabilities can hang out with each other. Don't have programs where we're teaching them. Make programs that are fun for all of us.
- Use volunteer peer buddies and make sure that the buddies are positive and suited to the role.
- Group students with disabilities into our social networks so they are included among a group of students who consider each other to be friends.
- Have students with disabilities tell us about their disabilities, so that we understand more about them, and how they manage their daily lives, and what they like us to do and what they don't want us to do.
- Clubs and after-school activities should include students with disabilities and have suitable activities such as board games, when you could talk to the students with disabilities and get to know them better.
- Students who have friends with disabilities can explain to others that they are not very different to other students, and can answer our questions and help us make friends with students with disabilities.

LONELINESS

Loneliness is one of the consequence of social exclusion but it may also result from health factors. Some students with the following characteristics have been shown to be more vulnerable to loneliness:

- students with learning disabilities;
- children with Attention Deficit Hyperactivity Disorder (ADHD);
- victimised adolescent females;
- adolescents with hearing impairments;
- students with Developmental Coordination Disorder;
- rural adolescents who feel disconnected to their community and school environments;
- immigrant children; and
- same-sex-attracted youth.

The following strategies may assist students to overcome their feelings of loneliness:

- Listen carefully and observe with insight the challenges faced by unhappy or lonely children (e.g., playing alone at recess; lack of familiarity with games such as marbles; eating lunch alone; other children mocking the contents of the lunch box; one boy was sent to school every day with cold curry in his lunch box, and eventually the teacher needed to speak to his mother about the appropriate lunchbox contents in an Australian context).
- Develop communication strategies (e.g., teach lonely children how to approach other children and what to say or do in order to join in their games; one boy was included by others when the teacher spoke to his mother and he brought a small toy truck to school, which was fun to play with in the sandpit).
- Arrange the physical space in the classroom appropriately (e.g., seat the lonely child next to another child who is friendly and willing to include the other child in their working groups).
- Provide relevant social interactions (e.g., develop art or craft activities where lonely children are placed in small groups with other children and the group works together on a shared art or craft project).
- Use nonverbal communication effectively (e.g., direct and frequent eye-contact from the teacher can improve attention, intensify participation and boost the self-esteem of students; however, be alert to cultural differences in which direct eye-contact may not always be appropriate; in these cases, find culturally appropriate ways to signal teacher approval of the child's work and participation, which also models inclusion to the other children).
- Respect the identity and individuality of the child and try to use this as a strength to build on within the classroom activities (e.g., speak privately with the lonely child and discuss interests or strengths and then try to develop a classroom theme that builds on this strength; one lonely boy was fascinated by frogs and since the presence of frogs is an important indicator of environmental health, his astonishing breadth of knowledge about frogs became a class resource and the children developed excellent projects about the importance of preserving frog habitats in the bushland close to the school).
- Respect the identity and individuality of the child, and try to use this as a strength to build on within the classroom activities.

SOCIAL SKILL AUTOPSY

Some young people may not appreciate the impact that they have on peers and adults (including the school staff). The social skill autopsy has been developed by Richard Lavoie (2005) to assist students

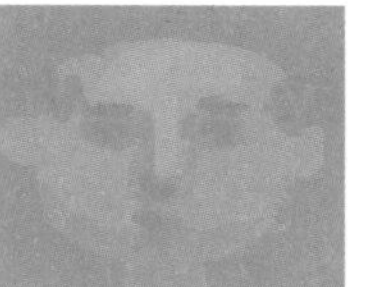

with special learning needs who genuinely do not understand why their peers have rejected them. This strategy is based on three basic ideas:

- Most social skill errors are unintentional. Every child wants to have friends and be accepted, and if the child is unable to maintain friendships, then the reasons for this are due to his or her lack of social insights and skills.
- If the error is unintentional, then it is unreasonable to punish the child for their social errors.
- Traditional approaches to social skills training will not be effective unless they give the child insights into how to manage and control their behaviour more effectively in a wide variety of situations.

The social skill autopsy has five stages:

1 Ask the child to explain what happened in a particular situation, and let them give you the full story.
2 Ask the child to identify the mistake he or she made. Some children will be unable to do this, and this is helpful in understanding why it is that they are so unsuccessful in the efforts to make friends.
3 Assist the child in determining the actual social error that he or she made.
4 Create a scenario similar to the previous situation and ask the child to provide an appropriate response to it.
5 Set some social homework; for example, ask the child to use the target skill in another situation and report back to the adult when that has happened.

The social skill autopsy provides the child with a problem-solving approach to a social problem. It allows the child to participate actively and it is most effective when conducted immediately after the social error has occurred. Here's an example of the use of the social skill autopsy.

Two boys, Alex and Harry, are arguing loudly on the school verandah. Mrs Jenkins, their teacher, walks up to them and wants to know why the two boys are arguing so intensely.

Alex shouts at Mrs Jenkins, "Harry stole my cricket ball out of my school bag and now no one knows where it is!"

Harry immediately replies, "I did not! Just because I was standing near your bag doesn't mean I took it!"

Mrs Jenkins asks the other students standing nearby if they know what has happened to Alex's cricket ball. Mary points to the school oval where Mrs Jenkins, Alex, and Harry can see Michael and his friends playing cricket.

"Let's go and talk to Michael," says Mrs Jenkins.

The three walk toward Michael who sees them approaching and frowns.

"Michael, do you have Alex's cricket ball?" asks Mrs Jenkins.

"Yes."

Mrs Jenkins decides that this is an appropriate time to undertake a social skill autopsy. [Seek an explanation from the child]

"Michael, can you explain how you have Alex's cricket ball?"

"I'm sorry, Mrs Jenkins. I really wanted to play cricket and we couldn't find a ball in the classroom sports bag, and then I remembered that Alex showed me his, so I borrowed it."

[Ask the child to identify the social mistake]

Mrs Jenkins says, "Okay, I understand what happened. What was your mistake, Michael?"

"I should have asked Alex if I could borrow it, and if he wanted to play cricket with us."

[Assist the child to recognise the social error]

"Good, our social lesson is that you should have asked first. Is that right?"

"Yes, I should have asked first."

[Create a similar scenario and ask the child to respond]

"Now let's just check that you understand the lesson. Suppose Harry comes to school tomorrow and you see that he's got a new football. And you and Alex want to play football, but you can't find a spare football anywhere. What should you do?"

"I should ask Harry if we can play football together, because he's got a nice new football."

[Set some social homework]

"That's good, Michael. Now here's some social homework. I want you to use the social skill of asking to borrow something from another boy this week, and then tell me on Friday how you did it."

"Alright, Mrs Jenkins. Alex, I'm sorry I borrowed your cricket ball without asking you. I won't do it again."

In this example, we can see that the teacher's actions could help all the boys involved in this incident to understand what happened, and how to stay friends with one another.

Responding to social cues

Many students with special learning needs lack the skills necessary to respond appropriately to social cues. They are unable to notice the facial and body language signs that signal that the other person in the conversation is bored or wants to move on to another group or conversational topic. Their ability to recognise the basic human emotions of love, joy, surprise, anger, sadness, and fear in the faces of others and also within their own bodies is sometimes severely limited. Teachers may sometimes need to teach these skills generally to all children. One preschool teacher who found that her students did not recognise her feelings, found pictures of faces that expressed the five basic emotions, stuck them onto paper plates with an icy-pole stick handle attached, and then taught the children to recognise the different emotions. Later, when she was angry or sad or surprised, she would pick up the picture of the face and the children would understand her feelings, which she could then discuss with the group. She also found that some of the children would borrow the faces (which were kept on an accessible shelf in the playroom) if they wanted to talk about their feelings with her.

LEARNING ESSENTIALS

The strategies that are used with students having different types of disabilities vary because each type has its own implications for the development of social skills. Appropriate considerations and strategies for several of the more common difficulties that students experience are outlined in the following sections. It should also be noted that many of these strategies will be effective with a wide range of students, but they have been developed with particular student needs in mind.

Students with Asperger's syndrome and Autism Spectrum Disorder

Students with Autism Spectrum Disorder (ASD) have difficulties with "theory of mind" as one of their core cognitive deficits (Tager-Flusberg, 1999). Theory of mind relates to the understanding of emotions and the mental states of others. The following list of challenges has been identified as

problems that accompany theory of mind deficits commonly found among students with special learning needs:

- difficulty explaining their own behaviours;
- difficulty understanding emotions—both their own and others;
- difficulty predicting the behaviour or emotional state of others;
- problems understanding the perspectives of others;
- problems inferring the intentions of others;
- lack of understanding of how behaviour affects the way others think or feel;
- problems with attention and other social conventions; and
- problems differentiating fact from fiction.

ASSISTING STUDENTS WITH ASD IMPROVE THEORY OF MIND DEFICITS

Teachers who have worked with students with ASD have recommended the following strategies.

Power Cards

Power Cards (Gagnon, 2004) are single cards that draw on the child's special interest to help guide their behaviour. For example, Megan is an eight-year-old with ASD, who loves drawing but often draws on her body and the table, and then leaves the tops off the marker pens. She has a special interest in her Barbie doll, so her Power Card reads:

Barbie loves to draw with her colourful markers. Barbie wants you to remember these three things:

1. *Take the cap off the end of your marker before you draw.*
2. *Be careful to draw only on the paper.*
3. *Put the cap back on the marker when you are finished.*

Try your best to remember these three things so you can draw just like Barbie!

Teaching the hidden curriculum

Many young people with ASD are genuinely puzzled about social situations and don't understand why they upset other people when they eat or go to the public toilet, for example. Myles, Trautman, and Schelvan (2004) list many of the hidden social rules and explain them so that the social rules are clear and can be practised (e.g., bathroom rules: for boys, "Don't talk to others around you when using the urinal"; for girls: "Avoid complaining to the person who came out of the stall that she made it stink.").

The incredible 5-point scale

In a book by Buron and Curtis (2003), the authors explain how to develop 5-point scales that teach young people with ASD how to modulate their behaviour. There is a range of problems and associated graduated scales to accompany them, which are illustrated in the book. There is also an accompanying children's book that incorporates the 5-point scale, called *When My Autism Gets Too Big!* (Buron, 2003).

An example of a 5-point scale that teaches how to modulate one's voice is found in Table 11.1.

Practical solutions for tantrums, rage, and meltdowns

Asperger Syndrome and Difficult Moments: Practical solutions for tantrums, rage, and meltdowns by Myles and Southwick (2005) describes the Rage Cycle and explains how to intervene early and what adult behaviours can be used to avoid escalating the problem. The stages are identified as the:

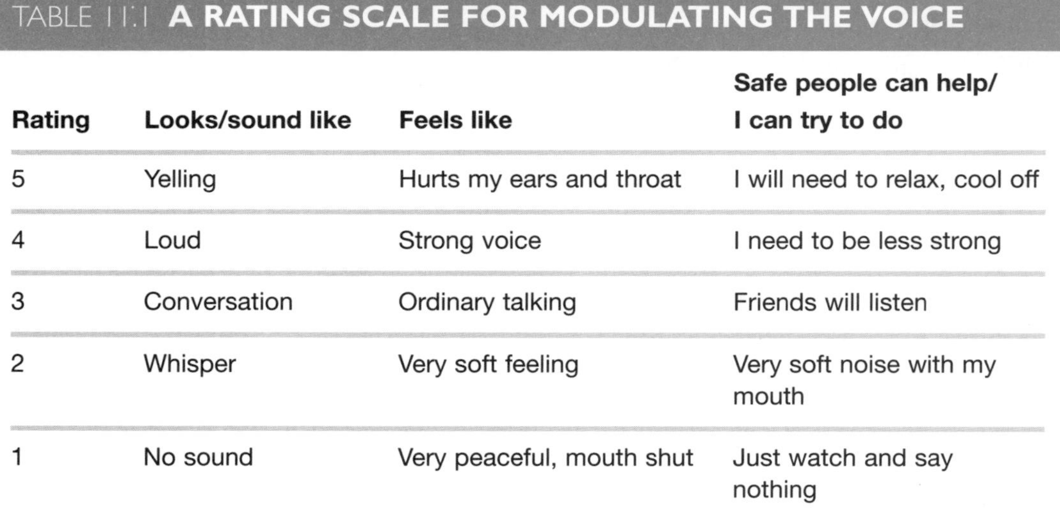

TABLE 11.1 A RATING SCALE FOR MODULATING THE VOICE

Rating	Looks/sound like	Feels like	Safe people can help/ I can try to do
5	Yelling	Hurts my ears and throat	I will need to relax, cool off
4	Loud	Strong voice	I need to be less strong
3	Conversation	Ordinary talking	Friends will listen
2	Whisper	Very soft feeling	Very soft noise with my mouth
1	No sound	Very peaceful, mouth shut	Just watch and say nothing

- Rumbling Stage (signs of stress);
- Rage Stage (explosive, impulsive emotional behaviours); and
- Recovery Stage (needs relaxation, sleep, quiet).

The book contains a range of valuable strategies to teach teachers how to manage students with ASD when these students have severe emotional problems. Box 11.5 gives a case study in which a boy with ASD was helped to manage his anger and as a consequence was accepted by other children, who previously had been afraid of his volatile temper.

BOX 11.5 Case study of a boy with autism overcoming his anger and becoming more socially accepted

Chad was a nine-year-old with Autism Spectrum Disorder attending Year 4 in a small independent school located in a country town of Western Australia. Although he was in the mainstream class, his social participation was restricted by various social problems. These included insensitive remarks to others, screaming at people, showing anger through growling and head shaking, not sitting in his seat and shaking his head and moving the chair around, getting annoyed at different sounds and then totally out of control and screaming. The school identified that there were five situations in school that often triggered Chad's anger. They included being given special attention in class, noise, people touching his belongings, difficult situations in the playground, and other students telling him what to do.

To help Chad manage his anger, a program was put in place to help him manage the rumbling, rage, and recovery stages of his anger. This was achieved by helping him recognise his body sensations that were associated with angry feelings, and providing a numerical five-point scale, which ranged from calm, happy, grumpy, and angry to very angry. He also identified his feelings at visual points on an emotional thermometer chart.

The visual cues of a red light (STOP) were introduced to assist Chad to recognise when his anger was getting out of control. The orange light (THINK) was a visual cue for problem-solving, and trying to be assertive or calmer. When he was calmer, then the green light (DO) was introduced to enable Chad to act when he felt calmer. The visual cues were important as Chad, like many children with Autism, learned more effectively with visual materials. A reward system was also implemented, since Chad was saving for an air mattress, and he was rewarded with 20 cents each time he demonstrated a skill taught within the program.

The program was implemented for the whole school year, with the support of Chad's parents and his psychologist (Pauline Pannell) who designed the program. By the end of the year, the school noted four areas of improvement that led to improvements in his relationships with his peers inside and outside the classroom. The improvements included more effective participation in the playground during recess and lunchtime; frustrations more effectively expressed through verbal expressions than by kicking and screaming; participation in class discussions, and the ability to take turns and listen to others; and a more positive attitude towards his daily life. As a consequence of these changes, Chad was accepted and included more by his peers in their daily games and the school staff were better able to manage his inclusion within the classroom.

Source: This case study is adapted from the work undertaken by Pauline Pannell for her Master of Education thesis at Curtin University of Technology.

11.5

Developing social skills

Effective inclusion is impossible to achieve if any member of the class demonstrates unacceptable behaviours such as disruption, defiance, swearing, aggression, property destruction, or self-injury. Young people with special learning needs are more likely to displaying these behaviours, sometimes as a direct consequence of their circumstances and other times as an indirect consequence (e.g., if they are unable to communicate their needs and get very frustrated as a consequence).

self-injury
The infliction of a physical injury upon one's self (e.g., head banging, hair pulling, eye gouging). This is a characteristic of some people with severe and profound intellectual disabilities or of those exhibiting autistic behaviour.

Children with ASD are particularly in need of support because a lack of effective communication and social skills are a part of the defining characteristics of the disorder. To assist these children learn social skills, the technique of Social Stories is employed, and these are an effective strategy for many different types of children within the early childhood and primary settings. A Social Story uses four types of sentences, in the following order:

1. *Descriptive* sentences—can be used to describe what people do in particular social situations, and they can also be used to describe a social setting or the procedure for completing a social activity.
2. *Directive* sentences—direct a person to an appropriate and desired social response. They are used to state clearly and positively what type of behaviour is required.
3. *Perspective* sentences—are used to present other people's reactions to the social situation. These sentences aim to teach the individual how others perceive events.
4. *Control* sentence—identifies to the individual ways in which the Social Story can be remembered and understood.

An example of a Social Story is described in Box 11.6.

11.6 Social Story: seeking help when lost

Children with Autism Spectrum Disorder are particularly vulnerable to confusion, and the following Social Story was constructed, with supporting pictures in a storybook style, to help four children to understand what to do if they were to get lost in the local supermarket. Each statement was placed on one page with a photograph of the child, their parent, and the store manager in the local supermarket to assist the comprehension of the story. The story could be adapted to suit other occasions, such as getting lost on a school excursion.

A DESCRIPTIVE SENTENCES

1 I'm out with my mum in the shop when all of a sudden I can't see her anymore.

2 I'm lost.

B DIRECTIVE SENTENCES

3 I remember to stay calm, she probably isn't too far away.

4 I walk slowly around the area near to me, I try hard to look for my mum.

5 If I am in a shop, I know that I must not leave the shop.

6 I know that I must not wander too far away because Mum is looking for me too.

7 If I can't find my mum by myself, I know that somebody will help me.

8 I can ask the shop worker for help. Shop workers wear a uniform and a badge.

9 If I am not in a shop, I can ask someone behind a counter or desk to help me.

10 Another mum can help me too. I can ask them to help me look for my mum.

11 I tell the helper my mum's name and try to remember what she was wearing.

12 I can tell the helper my mum's mobile phone number.

C PERSPECTIVE SENTENCES

15 The helper finds Mum for me and I say thank you very much.

16 Mum is very pleased to find me and she is happy that I remembered how to ask for help.

17 The helper is proud to help me.

D CONTROL SENTENCES

18 I remember to ask someone to help when I am lost by thinking of a game of hide and seek.

19 Not being able to find Mum is like she's hiding. When this happens it means ask someone to help me look for her.

This story was presented to four children with ASD with the photographs in each story book containing pictures of each child with their respective mothers. All four children improved in their capacity to ask for help as a result of reading the story several times, with Clare Clayton.

Source: This Social Story was constructed by Clare Clayton for her B.Ed (Honours) project at Curtin University of Technology. The cooperation of the local supermarket was very helpful in the development of the pictures and enacting of the Social Story for the four children with Autism who benefited from this story.

Some students with certain types of impairments related to vision and hearing, attention, language, and motor coordination will have particular needs in regard to the development of their social and interpersonal skills that contribute to the development of their social inclusion and friendships. It is important for teachers to understand these needs and to provide the support and strategies that are required to assist them to make friendships at school. The issues associated with these sensory and physical impairments are discussed in the following sections.

Students with vision impairment

From the earliest stages of infancy, the social and emotional development of children with vision impairment (VI) is absolutely critical to their wellbeing. Infants with VI do not smile in reciprocation when you approach the crib, they do not know to reach out to touch, and consequently issues of bonding, trust, and intimacy may remain underdeveloped unless their family and friends appreciate the importance of holding babies, talking to them, and touching them in affectionate and gentle ways. The isolation and lack of reciprocity that may be experienced by such children may even predispose some to develop autistic-like features, particularly in regard to social emotional responsiveness.

It is extremely important that teachers help students with VI to develop social relationships, friendships, and a strong sense of self-efficacy and personal confidence. Strategies that have been employed to do this include the development of personal portfolios and teaching these students how to express themselves with body language and to place appropriate emphasis in their voice. This may take some instruction and practice, such as learning how to shake hands, how to wave, how to express surprise and interest, and how to introduce emphasis when this is appropriate. Sitting with legs crossed, appropriate posture, leaning forward to indicate interest in the speaker, and making eye-contact, even if you can't see the speaker, are important social strategies that will assist the child with vision impairment to maintain their membership of social groups.

Some children with VI develop "blindisms", which are stereotypical behaviours that provide stimulation for the child but are not socially appropriate and may alienate other children. Common blindisms include eye pressing, rocking and bouncing, spinning, and head banging. Eye pressing is generally considered socially unacceptable although most children do it when they are tired or upset. Training children who engage in eye pressing with the cue "hands down" can be helpful in reducing the frequency of this habit. Rocking and bouncing may occur because the child is bored, or lacks exercise, due to over-protection and the inability to use appropriate exercise routines. Teachers need to identify safe exercises for children who engage in this behaviour. For example, one teacher installed a rocking chair in her classroom that was to be used only when a set amount of work was completed.

Spinning is another activity enjoyed by many young children, and the provision of a safe means of spinning, perhaps on a swing made from a tire, a merry-go-round, or other form of circular activity, is helpful. This will enable a child with vision impairment to join in with other children, as they enjoy the sensation of spinning and the wind rushing past.

Head banging is of greater concern as it can lead to serious damage. Head banging in students with vision impairment may be a response to frustration, and is the equivalent of a tantrum. Teachers and parents have found that the most effective response to this behaviour is to recognise it as frustration and to provide the child with an effective way to ask for what they want or need.

Students with hearing impairment

Feelings of social isolation are common among students with hearing impairment and it is important for teachers to develop strategies that assist in the acceptance of those students. In a study in which

students with hearing impairment were interviewed, they identified the following factors that facilitated their inclusion, and also the barriers that impeded their inclusion within the regular classroom (Eriks-Brophy, Durieux-Smith, Olds, Fitzpatrick et al., 2006).

FACTORS RELATED TO TEACHERS AND SCHOOL ADMINISTRATORS

Facilitators included high-quality visiting teachers, supportive attitudes from school principals, positive classroom teachers who organised the classroom effectively and provided supports for communication, good technology devices, and used FM microphones. *Barriers* included teachers with negative attitudes, inflexible in their teaching and assessment and poor collaborators with parents; teachers with reduced expectations of students with hearing loss, or who drew unnecessary attention to the students with hearing loss; outdated technology; inflexible visiting teachers who did not give choices to adolescents with hearing loss; principals and school councils who gave lip service to inclusion but did not support it in their budgeting or school management strategies.

FACTORS RELATED TO THE PARENTS OF STUDENTS WITH HEARING LOSS

Facilitators included parents with assertive attitudes and active advocacy skills; membership of school committees; building strong relationships with classroom and visiting teachers; persisting with home–school communication and managing transitions; and support for homework and extra-curricular activities. *Barriers* included parents who lacked appropriate advocacy skills, were unfamiliar with the educational system, or lacked the time, skills, or knowledge to assist them at home; financial barriers also meant that both parents were unavailable for meetings or to attend therapy sessions.

FACTORS RELATED TO HEARING PEERS

Facilitators included peers who acted as notetakers, "buddies", and interpreted academic and social situations in inconspicuous ways; peers who were long-term classmates and who also knew the student's siblings; early acceptance and unspoken understandings about when it was appropriate to intervene, explain, or not. SMS text messages on mobile phones were also very helpful. *Barriers* included negative, apathetic, or insensitive attitudes; deliberately not using clear speech or communication strategies, teasing (experienced as more hurtful as the students with hearing loss got older); loneliness due to inability to receive phone calls or follow the latest movie or get the latest joke; resentment from peers due to perceptions of reduced expectations or favouritism.

FACTORS RELATED TO THE STUDENTS WITH HEARING LOSS THEMSELVES

Facilitators included participation in preschool early intervention programs, which usually led to adequate speech intelligibility, communication abilities, auditory skills, and good organisational skills. Students who were independent, well organised, willing to ask for help when needed, and planning ahead with new topics (e.g., in learning new vocabulary) had a sense of humour and willingness to engage in problem-solving. *Barriers* included shyness, a lack of assertiveness, and an unwillingness to participate or seek help. The absence of other hearing-impaired peers in an inclusive community school was also cited as a difficulty for some students.

Students with Attention Deficit Hyperactivity Disorder

symptom

An event, behavioural response, or sign that is indicative of a disease or disorder.

Students with Attention Deficit Hyperactivity Disorder (ADHD) constitute 4–8% of the student population and are characterised behaviourally with major symptoms of distractibility, impulsivity, and inattentiveness exhibited persistently across different contexts such as home and school, and at levels that are developmentally inappropriate for their age. Current explanations propose that ADHD is much

more than a behavioural dysfunction and emphasise the contributory role of neuropsychological dysfunction. ADHD has been characterised by a neurological deficit of response inhibition, which in turn restricts the development of four executive functions:

- nonverbal working memory;
- verbal working memory;
- self-regulation of emotion and motivation; and
- reconstitution (problem-solving) (Barkley, 2000).

Strategies to promote the self-regulation of emotions are essential in supporting students with ADHD.

SELF-REGULATION OF EMOTIONS

Everyone feels happiness, surprise, fear, sadness, disgust, and anger at some time. These are six of our most basic emotions. There are over 600 words in English to describe them and we use 42 muscles in our faces to express them. Some children, however, do not recognise emotions in themselves or other people. Other children have such chaotic home lives that they bring their fragile emotions to school, and teachers often experience the brunt of these emotions when a child reaches an angry or frustrated point in the day.

STRATEGIES TO PROMOTE THE SELF-REGULATION OF EMOTIONS

- Take note of what appears to produce the emotional outburst.
- Redirect the child's attention away from the problem.
- Model appropriate emotional modulation by talking aloud through situations that provoke anger or sadness and explain how you deal with your feelings.
- Teach children to talk to themselves to help control their behaviour.
- Allow children to assume the perspectives of others in role-play situations and pretend play. For example, they may consider how someone else may feel or respond in a given situation.
- Allow children the time to practise appropriate emotional reactions.
- Provide a quiet space in or near the classroom where children can take a short break or cool off.

STRATEGIES TO PROMOTE BETTER RESPONSE INHIBITION

- Explain to children how their behaviour affects others—actions and consequences.
- Teach children how to "Do turtle" and retreat to their shells—Turtle is a motoric response to keep hands and feet to self: crossing your arms, putting your hands by your sides and/or locking your hands together.
- Teach child STOP, THINK, DO or similar control strategies.
- Use the inevitable social problems that arise when children work and play together to discuss "feelings" with your students. For example, "When you snatched the toy off Michelle, it made her feel …"
- Reinforce positive behaviour as children learn socially acceptable responses as a result of reinforcement either by adults or peers.

A case study of a student with ADHD who learned to self-regulate his behaviour with the assistance of a structured worksheet is outlined in Box 11.7.

BOX 11.7 Jack's self-regulation

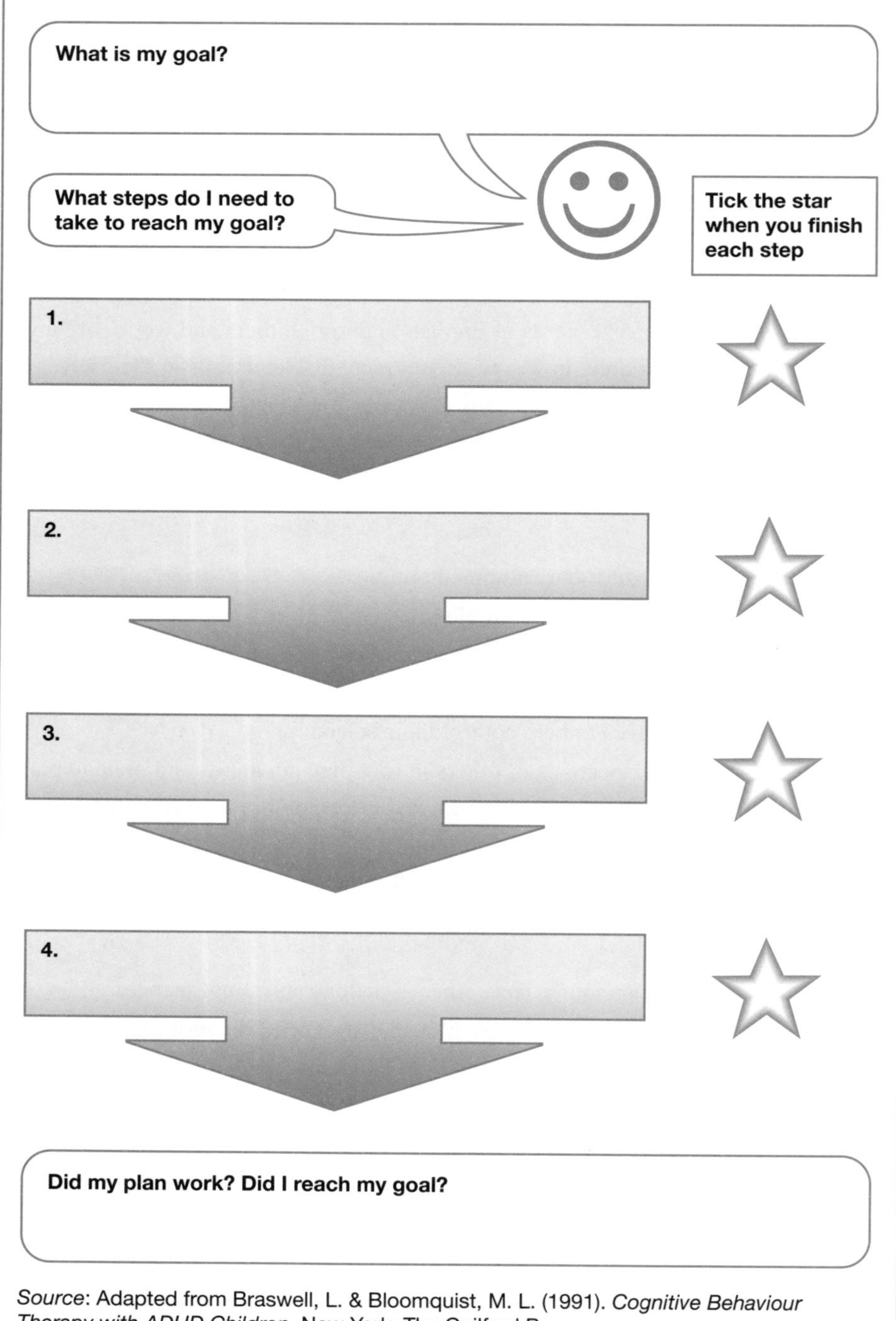

What is my goal?
What steps do I need to take to reach my goal?
Tick the star when you finish each step
1.
2.
3.
4.
Did my plan work? Did I reach my goal?

Source: Adapted from Braswell, L. & Bloomquist, M. L. (1991). *Cognitive Behaviour Therapy with ADHD Children*, New York: The Guilford Press.

Jack is a 10-year-old with ADHD and an intellectual disability. He attends his local primary school and receives special support for numeracy and literacy. There is one education assistant who works in the afternoons with Jack and three other students with intellectual disabilities. Jack rarely completed any of his set work in the regular classroom and the student teacher, Kim, developed this structured worksheet to help Jack manage his own learning more effectively, and to complete the set work.

Jack was shown how to set goals and discuss them with Kim to work out the steps needed to achieve them. As each step was completed he ticked a star on the worksheet. After three weeks of supervised practice, the support was withdrawn and he was able to carry out the planning steps for simple tasks independently. This meant that Jack was completing the set work, which meant that his off-task behaviour was reduced because he could now engage effectively in the task.

The other students noticed that Jack was now participating more effectively in their class activities, and were very pleased about this. When Jack was asked, "What is goal-setting?" at the end of the term, he said, "It's for finishing my work and then I can play on the computer." Then he was asked, "What is goal-setting for?" and he answered, "So I know what to do." Finally, he was asked, "How do you reach your goals?" and he responded, "By figuring out what to do."

These responses showed that Jack was taking control of his own work and recognising the importance of his own actions in completing his work. The class teacher said, "It makes life easier for me when he can work independently and Jack seems more confident in tackling the tasks when he uses his planning guide ... Anything that gets Jack to finish some work is definitely worthwhile." The strategy, therefore, improved Jack's opportunities for learning, and also his social participation within the class.

Source: This case study is based on work undertaken by Kim Bailey, who completed this case study for her Honours project in the Bachelor of Education program at Curtin University of Technology.

11.7

Students with specific language impairments

Students with specific language impairments experience many difficulties due to their challenges in receptive and expressive language. These include problems with social interactions, including initiating conversations, responding to the conversational bids of others, and participating in group discussions. It has also been found that these students are often not able to hide their emotions when it is socially appropriate to do so (Brintom, Spackman, Fujiki, & Ricks, 2007). For example, in one hypothetical situation:

> *[DISGUST]: Chris's mum always cooks something good for dinner. One day, Chris's mum is sick. She has to stay in bed. The next-door neighbour, Mrs Smith, brings dinner for Chris's family. Mrs Smith brings tuna casserole. Chris thinks the tuna casserole is very yucky and he said so to Mrs Smith.*

Children with specific language impairment often do not understand that it would be socially inappropriate to display disgust in this situation, and require assistance to understand that the appropriate emotion would be to express gratitude for the neighbour's kind gesture. This could be practised through role modelling in the classroom, and might lead to improved understanding of the appropriate social behaviour.

Students with developmental coordination disorder

Approximately 5–6% of children in the school population have developmental coordination disorders, which are associated with clumsy motor skills, poor levels of successful participation in physical activity, and sometimes hyperactivity. Due to their inability to participate in games and sporting activities successfully, students with developmental coordination disorders are more likely to experience social rejection and to be excluded from team sports and social games, such as playing with marbles or throwing and catching balls. In these circumstances, it is important to assess the specific limitations of the student and then adapt the physical education program to suit the student and enable them to participate. For example, a student with limited strength, power, or endurance may be allowed to participate for a shorter distance, or time, than the other students. For students with limited balancing ability, it may be appropriate to use carpeted surfaces and ensure that the student knows how to fall in a safe way. For students with limited coordination and accuracy, it may be appropriate to use larger, lighter, softer balls.

Some students with Down syndrome have motor coordination problems, and in one school, all of the students were aware that Andrew, a 10-year-old with Down syndrome, participated in physical education and sport classes with certain modifications. For example, in the long running races, he had special sections marked out around the school oval where he was expected to walk and other sections where he was expected to run. This track was laid out specifically for Andrew and he was encouraged by other students, who would call out to him as they jogged past. In addition, he was allowed to stand closer to the target for throwing games, and some other students also needed to stand closer to use the correct overhand throw. Such modifications ensured that Andrew was a part of the annual sports day, and that the other students in his class could include him in the weekly physical activity classes. This ensured that Andrew felt socially included in physical games and it was also important for him to maintain his fitness, rather than becoming overweight, which is a common problem among students with motor coordination disorders who lack an appropriate amount of daily physical activity.

Another recreational activity that is valued by students with diverse abilities is the opportunity to go on a residential camp. These camps also provide an important source of respite for the families of children with diverse abilities. The camps create many opportunities to develop social skills and friendships, and an account of one camp is given in Box 11.8.

11.8 A residential camp for social skills development

Children who have learning problems are challenged in the development of their social skills. Kids' Camp provides a residential six-day camp where children with diverse learning abilities are given the opportunity to grow socially and emotionally, and develop confidence in themselves. Through the course of the week the children are given opportunities to learn about themselves and to develop friendships and relationships. The growth that takes place in these children is seen on a personal level and in their social interactions.

A RESIDENTIAL CAMP FOR SOCIAL SKILLS DEVELOPMENT

On Kids' Camp the children are exposed to a wide variety of activities, interactions, and social settings. The leaders are there to model the expected social behaviour and help modify any maladaptive social behaviour. Because the staff and students go into public settings in the community, the children's behaviour needed to be socially appropriate. For example, one child with Autism Spectrum Disorder had a tendency to undress himself and this needed to be prevented through distraction techniques. Another child's desire to hug everyone needed to be addressed by camp leaders so that the child understood personal space limits. The problem for many children with diverse learning needs is to find ways of communicating with others socially. For the nonverbal children, the leaders modelled communication with the communication board and basic Maketon signs. In this case, other campers became interested and joined in communicating using the communication board. This allowed the nonverbal children to talk, and become socially close, with the verbal campers.

PEER RELATIONSHIPS

There are opportunities for peer relationships to develop at camp. The children are allocated to cabins and because they go to sleep and wake together this gives them a common ground to build peer relationships. The girls keep each other company, share jobs, tell stories, give approval on clothing options, and learn to tolerate each other when they are tired or annoyed. In their free time, children are given further opportunities to develop or extend these peer relationships. Through cricket, the children mix in different social combinations. They are very open to understanding the diversity of skill level of their peers. The score becomes unimportant. It's the game and the friendship of their peers that are rewarding. The students do not feel isolated, which is more common among children with learning problems. In fact, they feel very much included by their peers and accepted by the social group.

Children with diverse learning needs may experience difficulty in making friends and gaining acceptance, particularly if they have irritating or challenging behaviours. They may experience rejection and teasing from other children. When these situations arise on camp, the leaders try to diffuse the situation by giving the camper feedback to correct their antisocial behaviour, or strategies for dealing with unfair discrimination. The leaders try to help the children develop coping skills or social skills depending on the situation. This social learning is resilience building and it is very real and relevant for the children.

CHILD/ADULT RELATIONSHIPS

Children are typically dependent on their parents or carers before they develop a sense of independence. Children move toward independence through relative dependency, which is when the child fluctuates between stages of dependency and independency. It is important as a camp leader to know the times it is necessary to support the child's dependency, and when to pull back and encourage independence. The leaders are given something a classroom teacher rarely gets—an excellent child-to-adult ratio and time to build a strong emotional attachment. The camp leaders interact with their campers to form sensitive, secure, and positive attachments. In a short period, the leaders' attachments extends to other campers outside of their specific responsibility. Communication between leaders is crucial to develop consistency. The nightly meetings, after the children have gone to bed, are opportunities to communicate the frustrations and joys of the day. They also allow time to exchange ideas and encourage each other with observations of success seen through the course of the day.

PARTICIPATION IN GROUP ACTIVITIES

The children on Kids' Camp are encouraged to participate in all group activities. It is all about doing rather than watching from the sidelines, as these children are often forced to sit on the sidelines because of their learning limitations. In addition, normal everyday activities also require full participation. For example, meals are eaten as a group, bingo and videos are group activities. The bingo night is an example of where a group activity creates a sense of bonding and cooperation. Lastly, the children are allocated jobs to do while on camp. These responsibilities are taken seriously and performed to the children's ability. There is always a real sense of unity between the campers and the leaders.

FRIENDSHIPS

Friends provide a valuable form of support. Children who experience physical barriers to friendship, such as the need for special transportation, a wheelchair or a ramp for mobility, can become isolated socially. These physical barriers reduce the ability to gain access to friends' homes and spontaneously participate in peer activities. On camp there is a serious endeavour to remove all physical barriers and encourage friendships. By removing the physical supports, such as wheelchairs and splints, these children are able to move amongst each other and this allows friendships to be established more readily. If students with diverse learning abilities are to make friends and be accepted into the peer group, social skills must be given a high priority. The occasional inappropriate response, such as aggression or shouting, makes it difficult for a few children to be socially accepted. Intervention is necessary to eliminate the negative behaviours and help the children replace them with pro-social behaviours.

Kids' Camp promotes the rights of children with diverse learning abilities and, in particular, the right to participate in and enjoy recreational activities. Through Kids' Camp, the leaders get to know the children as children who just want to have fun. Camps greatly enrich the lives of those children who attend.

Source: This brief report is based on a longer report written by Jayne Kaiko, a teacher who is studying at Curtin University and who attended the camp as one of her practical units within the course. The photographs are from the Kids' Camp webpage, <www.kidscamps.org.au>. Reproduced with permission.

11.8

Social and emotional problems as a consequence of trauma

The terrorist attacks that occurred in New York and Washington on 11 September 2001 have led to a greater awareness of the impact of traumatic events on the social and emotional behaviour of young people. Some do not understand the events that have affected them, and these misunderstandings can generate fear and anxiety that lead to antisocial and aggressive behaviour. The extent of misunderstanding can be judged, for example, by the reaction of one child with an intellectual impairment who was greatly distressed when his father said he was flying on an aeroplane several months after September 11. It transpired that the child had seen the pictures of the planes flying into the Twin Towers repeatedly but did not realise that the television pictures were being replayed. He thought that each event was a new plane crash. His parents resolved this by demonstrating the extent of misunderstanding that can occur.

It has been found that boys tend to be more antisocial and have more violent and aggressive behaviours than girls, while girls tend to have more anxiety and mood disorders than boys. However, girls are more expressive about their emotions than boys, and teachers may be among the first professionals to recognise the impact of a traumatic event on a child. For example, a group of Dutch children were exposed to a massive disaster when a fireworks factory exploded in the Netherlands in May 2000. Three years later, it was found that the boys who were most directly affected by the disaster were displaying considerable aggressive and assertive behaviour, while the girls were impaired in their play behaviour when compared with children who did not witness the disaster (Doel, Smit, & Bosch, 2005). In these circumstances, teachers need to be careful in their observations of children who are unusually disturbed, and school-based interventions such as small group activities, play, artwork, story-telling, and role-playing may be helpful in assisting the children to understand what has happened and regain their normal perspective on their world.

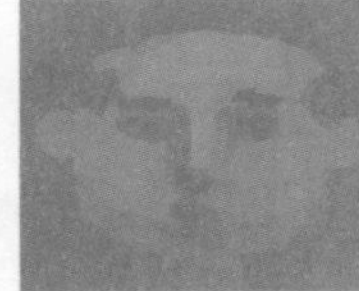

BEREAVED CHILDREN

The loss of a family member through an unanticipated accident or illness can also have a major impact on a child's social and interpersonal behaviour. In children with intellectual or severe learning abilities, there may be little understanding of the finality of death and this may leave a child feeling angry and abandoned.

One school responded very effectively to Marcus, a six-year-old and only child, whose father died suddenly. In the weeks after the death, Marcus became quite aggressive and began to disturb other children, even to the extent of removing all his clothes. The principal, school counsellor, and Marcus's teacher met with the mother and grandmother and it was decided to develop a special pastoral care program for Marcus. The school was fortunate to have a male teaching assistant who met with the family to discuss what Marcus had been told about his father (was he in heaven, in the sky, under the ground?) and then proceeded to give Marcus individual attention. He also assisted Marcus to make a memory box, in which he put some of his favourite photographs, thoughts, and mementos. Marcus needed lots of hugs, which the staff discussed, and they were also sensitive to occasions such as Christmas and Fathers' Day and advised his teacher in the following year of the anniversary of his father's death. These strategies helped Marcus to adjust and he gradually understood that his father was never coming back. His behaviour and social relationships with the other children in the class improved, and he slowly regained his confidence (Burnham, 2007).

The role of education assistants

The role of education assistants (or teacher aides) and volunteers in the classroom is an important human resource in supporting teachers and assisting students. The appropriate management of these adults by the teacher is vital to ensure that they are used in ways that promote the learning of all students, and that they do not infringe on the social development of the students inappropriately.

Giangreco, Yuan, McKenzie, Cameron, and Fialka (2005) suggested that education assistants can assist the classroom teacher by:

- doing clerical tasks that free up the teacher's time;
- engaging in follow-up activities to support student learning and homework;
- providing supervision in group settings (e.g., at the cafeteria, school bus queues);
- assisting students with personal care needs (e.g., eating, toileting, dressing for physical education or swimming lessons); and
- facilitating social skills, positive behaviour, and peer interactions.

Accompanying these benefits are some concerns associated with the inappropriate assignment of education assistants to individual students without proper management and guidance.

- The least-qualified staff members may be teaching the students with the most-complex learning needs.
- The support and close proximity offered by education assistants may have unintentional detrimental effects, such as generating unnecessary dependence, excluding peers and preventing friendships from developing, feeling stigmatised, and reducing the sense of locus of control for the student, which is so important in developing self-efficacy.
- Individual education assistant support is often linked to low levels of teacher involvement with students with particular learning needs.

- Teachers, parents, and students may not be getting exactly what they expect, due to a lack of preparation or training for the education assistant.

The presence of education assistants may disguise underlying problems within the school that should be addressed (e.g., teachers may be resistant to inclusion unless an education assistant is employed, and fail to develop the skills that are appropriate for adapting the curriculum and other inclusive strategies).

If we listen to students with special learning needs we may learn a great deal about how they feel about the presence of the education assistant (EA). Interviews with 16 young adults with intellectual disabilities revealed four thematic roles and each of these four roles had both advantages and disadvantages (see Broer, Doyle, & Giangreco, 2005).

Hence, there are both positive and negative aspects to these roles (see Table 11.2), and training for education assistants is essential to enable them to fulfil their important role of supporting the classroom teacher. In one study, Malmgren, Causton-Theoharis, and Trezek (2005) provided training for the education assistants working with students with behavioural disorders. The training focused on providing:

- Self-reflection on personal connection and disconnection to social groups, and then how to relate that to the experiences of their students.
- Completion of a circle of friendship map, first for themselves and then for their students.
- A discussion of "Why social relationships are important".
- A long session on how the education assistants might facilitate the building of bridges between their students and their peers, including:
  —modelling interaction skills;
  —highlighting similarities between students with diverse abilities and their peers;
  —interpreting peer behaviours for their student; and
  —moving students to work in closer physical proximity.

The researchers demonstrated that, after the intervention:

- rates of student interaction increased;
- rates of education assistant facilitation of social interaction increased;
- the education assistant faded their assistance more frequently; and
- the education assistant spent less time in close proximity to their students.

There is an important role for teachers in managing education assistants to ensure that they maximise the learning of children with diverse abilities, but that they do not do this in ways which stifle the development of the child's self-concept and limit the child's capacity to make friends and socialise with other children.

Whole-of-school strategies

It is apparent that if school leaders, teachers, education assistants, and students are to thrive within a safe and inclusive learning environment that fosters social relationships and friendships, there must be a consistent theme developed that is supported at all levels of the school and classroom. Four whole-of-school programs that develop social, emotional, and friendship skills across primary and secondary schools have been shown to be very effective. These include:

- *Promoting Alternative Thinking Strategies (PATHS)*—This program is suitable for primary school children and develops emotional and social competencies.

TABLE 11.2 SOME POSITIVE AND NEGATIVE ASPECTS OF EA INVOLVEMENT

EA role	Advantages	Disadvantages
Mother	• Some girls and boys felt that this woman was kind to them.	• Embarrassing. • Wanted someone younger. • Boys wanted a male. • Interfered with the development of friendships. • Perpetuated stereotypes of the students as "helpless" or "childlike".
Friend	• Source of companionship in a lonely situation.	• Inappropriate conversations with peers. • Hindered development of peer-related friendship skills.
Protector from bullying	• Students were rarely bullied when in the company of the EA. • EA acted as an advocate for the student if they witnessed unpleasant events.	• Students were bullied when the EA was not around. • Presence of the EA was a stigma that attracted teasing comments. • If the EA shielded the student, the school failed to acknowledge that bullying was a problem and needed attention.
Primary teacher	• EA often taught the students, who credited them with supporting them through the most challenging subjects. • The fading of EA support was a cause for celebration.	• Reduced teacher knowledge of, and interaction with, the students. • EA needed to know when to "back off". • Feelings of having a babysitter were not appreciated. • EA intervenes while the student is trying to complete the work. • EA completes the work instead of the student.

- *Tribes Learning Communities*—This program is useful in all school communities and focuses on attentive listening, appreciation and mutual respect, participation, collaboration and problem-solving, and community celebrations of achievements.
- *Friendly Schools, Friendly Families*—This Australian program is designed to assist schools and classrooms reduce bullying and build resilience and social responsibility.
- *Developing social, emotional, and behavioural skills in secondary students*—This British program focuses on self-awareness, managing feelings, motivation, empathy and social skills, and has been shown to lead to significant changes in teachers' approaches to their students, who in turn worked better in teams and showed greater respect for each other's differences and strengths.

Further information on how to access these programs is given in the *Practical activities* section of the chapter.

USING THIS CHAPTER IN SCHOOLS

The social and personal development of children with special learning needs is an essential aspect of their social inclusion in school. To assist in this development, you can apply a number of ideas that have been presented in this chapter. Here are three very basic points.

First, make certain that your classroom is a safe, secure, and positive learning environment. Plan carefully to ensure that all children are welcomed within the classroom. For example, if you are working in the early and middle phase of schooling, you might sit with your new class at the beginning of the school year and discuss how important it is to have friends, to be kind and to show respect to one another, and to tell you if there are any problems that you should know about. Asking the children to give examples, and then discussing how you would respond to particular examples, would help them to understand your approach.

Second, establish systematic class routines. These are also helpful in creating a safe and secure classroom, as predictability that arises from a known routine is very reassuring for students of all ages.

Third, always deal with your students in a calm manner. Certainly, there will be frustrating times but this is very important as the teacher who shouts or startles students with an unpredictable response can generate fear and anxiety that is difficult to dispel. This is as important in the secondary school as in the earlier phases of schooling.

Skills needed for joining a group

Building basic social skills is essential for students who have learning or behavioural difficulties. This is particularly important for joining social groups. Think about using the *Stop Think Do!* programs, and also *Circle of Friends* activities. You could introduce the *Stop Think Do!* program with a *Getting to know you and me* activity, in which the rules of social interaction are introduced that are relevant at every level of education:

STOP: We listen to each other.

THINK: We do not put others down.

DO: Everyone has a turn to speak and everyone can join in.

A *Getting to know you and me* activity can involve mini-interviews with the students in pairs, asking a range of question, such as:

- What is your favourite movie?
- What is your favourite food?
- What is your favourite sport?

- What did you do in the holidays?
- Do you have a pet?

The roles of interviewer and interviewee can then be swapped, and the information shared at the end of the activity with the rest of the class. Students will often identify the same favourite movies and this creates an opportunity for you to discuss why we like similar things, and how this often helps create long-lasting friendships. It may also serve as a way of enabling new or shy children to listen carefully and to identify peers with whom they may wish to make friends. You need to monitor the activity carefully while students are working in pairs to ensure that the rules of the interview are being followed, and that the *Stop Think Do* sequence is respected.

This type of activity could be introduced effectively as a research or survey tool in secondary school.

Skills needed to establish and maintain friendships

Students with particular learning needs (including gifted and talented young people) often struggle to initiate friendships and require support to initiate conversations and develop appropriate strategies to make and keep friends. Often, they will not understand why other children reject them and, in these situations, you can try a social skill autopsy to help them understand the problem and work with them to develop new and more appropriate social skills.

To this end, you could implement a *Similarities and differences* activity that enables you to discuss how important it is that we share our similarities and celebrate our differences. Depending on the age level of the class, this could be achieved through a variety of activities:

- *For younger children*—In pairs, the students lie down on butcher's paper and draw around their partner's body profile. Then the partner draws their profile. They write their names on each sheet and then search through magazines for pictures of food, colour, movies, sports teams, and television characters that reflect their interests. They then paste these onto their body shapes and present them to the class.
- *For older children*—The class sits in a circle, and one student sits in the middle, and identifies something they have in common with another student, such as same eye or hair colour, similar t-shirt, similar shoes, similar favourite popular singer. The students then move into different seats, and the person left without a seat then sits in the middle and the game continues until everyone has had a turn. Activities like these are commonly used as warm-up excises in training workshops and professional development sessions. They are not as clichéd or corny as you might think.

By the end of these activities, all of the students in the class should have identified a common interest with at least one other person, and you will have a deeper understanding of their preferences, which will be helpful in deciding how to generate themes for lessons in the future.

Skills needed to respond to social cues

Students with special learning needs sometimes lack the perceptiveness and sensitivity to respond to social cues, facial and nonverbal cues, and the basic signs of the fundamental emotions of love, joy, surprise, anger, sadness, and fear. They will need support to overcome their frustrations, to develop appropriate social skills, and to implement them in practice.

An activity that you could use to assist these students would be to pair each student with a special learning need with another student who does not have a particular learning need (see Table 11.3), and ask them to discuss the basic emotions with respect to the questions. Explain to all students that they may have to think about this, and that if they think of something they don't want to discuss, then that is appropriate. It may be helpful to provide examples on the board before the activity commences.

Children with different disabilities are often challenged in different ways by their circumstances. For example, students with ASD are most severely challenged due to their inability to understand the hidden social curriculum, their own emotions and the emotions of others, and their need for routines. Strategies such as Power Cards, social stories, and 5-point scale cards are all helpful in assisting children with ASD to manage their social and emotional reactions more effectively within the classroom and playground.

An activity that you could use to assist these children to be more socially accepted would involve the whole class in the development and production of Power Cards. For example, you would first discuss with the parents of the child with ASD what their child's particular preferences are, and having established this preference, start from that point to develop pairs of children with similar preferences. Together, they would then develop Power Cards to emphasise, for example, the classroom rules. If Mary (who has ASD) loves the Bratz doll Sasha, it is likely that at least one other girl will also like that doll, and then the two can be paired to develop a Power Card about what to do at lunch-time:

Sasha wants to eat her lunch with the other girls. To do this, Sasha must remember these things:

- Take her lunch out of her school bag.
- Walk over to the group of girls with whom she would like to eat lunch.
- Ask if she can eat her lunch with the girls.
- Listen carefully to the girls.
- Sit down and eat lunch with the girls.

Students with vision and hearing impairments also require assistance to avoid feelings of isolation and difficulties in communication and this may often be achieved by active advocacy and support by the

TABLE 11.3 **HOW DO YOU EXPRESS YOUR EMOTIONS?**

Emotions	What makes me feel like this?	What does it look like, in my voice and face, and the way I use my arms and hands?
Love		
Joy		
Surprise		
Anger		
Sadness		
Fear		

teacher. These students often, but not always, enjoy musical activities more than many people appreciate, and the opportunity for them to play instruments and join in some musical activities with their peers is very helpful. Students with hearing impairment might respond best to percussion instruments. They may, for example, provide the sound effects for an assembly item or class drama production.

One teacher managed to include all her children in the annual Christmas nativity play by having one group of children shake bells every time an angel appeared, and another group played the "clip-clop" sound effects on the percussion instruments to convey the sound of the donkey carrying Mary into Bethlehem and the horses bearing the three wise men, while a third group provided animal noises for the shepherds watching over their flocks and the animals inside the barn where Jesus was born. This took some practice. It was, however, thrilling for the children to be included and for their parents to see them alongside their classmates in the class production.

Children with Attention Deficit Hyperactivity Disorder are challenged by their impulsive nature and inability to self-regulate their own emotions. They require support in regulating their emotions and developing response inhibition and emotional control. The *Stop Think Do!* programs are an effective way to encourage this development.

Students with language impairments experience many difficulties with social interactions and may also not understand the inappropriateness of blurting out their initial responses to social situations.

Young people who respond inappropriately to social situations can be helped by the development of scenarios that could be written by other children in the class. For example, you might lead a discussion with the class about social situations that have generated a range of emotions, such as fear, anger, disgust, sadness, and happiness, and then ask the class to write about these, and to write about appropriate responses to each situation. These could then be developed into short plays by groups of children who then present them to the class and discuss how they chose the appropriateness of the response. For example, what happens when we get a birthday present that we don't like? How should we react?

Students with special learning needs may work with an education assistant in some activities and these students might tell about how the presence of this adult can be a significant barrier to the development of friendships and social interactions. You will need to think carefully about how to manage an education assistant to ensure that the appropriate support is given within the teaching and learning context, but this support is withdrawn when the students are engaged in leisure and social activities with their peers.

The promotion of whole-school strategies can lead to significant improvements in the social and emotional wellbeing of students and staff as a consequence of improved collaboration, friendships, and respect for the individual differences that exist within the school community. When you join a school, it is important to have discussions with the principal, deputy principal, learning support coordinator, or other staff in leadership positions about whole-school strategies that are used to support students with special learning needs, and, if so, how you can be mentored by an experienced colleague to understand how these strategies are implemented.

When a school becomes socially inclusive, the difference that this makes to all students is very powerful. It is you who can initiate changes within your classroom and ensure that every young person feels included and has a friend. The acceptance of all students has a profound effect on everyone, and the joy of students with special learning needs in particular at being included is articulated very effectively in two poems, written by two students with diverse abilities (see Box 11.9). Your success with respect to the social and interpersonal development of your students will be judged by those who remember that they were included in the social and friendship activities within your class.

11.9

Poetry written by students with diverse abilities

The 2007 annual poetry competition conducted by the British National Association for Special Educational Needs (NASEN) in conjunction with Emap Education was based on the theme of inclusion. The winning and highly commended entries were published in a book entitled, *Even though … a collection of poems on 'inclusion'*, published in 2007 by Rising Stars UK Ltd. The publishers have kindly granted permission to reprint the following poems from this collection, which express, in the children's own words, the importance of social inclusion and friendship.

Inclusion

Sitting in my wheelchair,
I can't do anything at all.
Everyone just laughs at me,
They won't even pass me the ball.

I feel so excluded,
I really want to change,
I want people to smile at me,
And not think that I am strange.

I'm suddenly turning round and round,
I look behind me,
My heart begins to pound.
I see Sophie spinning me on the ground.

People now smile at me,
And Sophie is my best friend,
Everyone passes me the ball,
I hope this friendship never ends.

Jessica Browne-Swinburne, Finton House School

My friend and me

My friend is kind and good to me.
She is an angel as you will see.
Sometimes she seems quite sad
And then I feel bad.
I try to find time to be kind
And then I give her a hug.
That will make her feel good.

My head sometimes gets in a muddle,
And then I don't know what to do,
I have sensitive hearing too,
I get worried when I have to do something new,
I make noises when I shouldn't
I think I struggle, don't you?
My friend helps me when I struggle,
She sometimes gives me a cuddle,
She lets me join in at Playtime,
And I have a great time.
My friend looks after me as you can all see.

Ben Redfearn, St John the Baptist Catholic Primary School

Source: © nasen <www.nasen.org.uk>.

11.9

PRACTICAL ACTIVITIES
Uni-work

1 One of the challenges for students with disabilities is to be accepted by other children. The Disability Awareness Resource "Open Your Mind. Count Us In" Curriculum Support Package has been designed to enable teachers to work with all students, to enhance their knowledge and understanding of disability at age-appropriate levels and provide them with the skills to create an inclusive and welcoming classroom. Using the "Open Your Mind. Count Us In" resource <www.countusin.com.au>, construct a group activity in which your group is preparing a class of students at early childhood, middle childhood, or in the secondary school to welcome a student with a nominated disability. The presentation should include four parts:

   1 An introduction about the uniqueness of every individual.
   2 An activity that helps all students to understand the nominated disability. This may be drawn from the "Open Your Mind. Count Us In" package or it could be based on a book, movie, game, or other learning source that is appropriate.
   3 An activity that includes the student with the disability and focuses on building positive social relationships.
   4 A reflection on the insights you have gained as a consequence of developing the activity.

2 Locate a journal article that explores the social and personal consequences of a disability, and discuss:

   a the strategies that would be appropriate to assist a gifted and talented student, or one with the nominated disability, improve their self-concept and their social relationships; and
   b strategies for whole-class adoption to ensure that the student is included in the social activities. Two examples of suitable articles are:

- Singer, E. (2005). The strategies adopted by Dutch children with dyslexia to maintain their self-esteem when teased at school. *Journal of Learning Disabilities*, *38*, 411–423.
- Konza, D. (2005). Secondary school success for students with Asperger's syndrome. *Australasian Journal of Special Education*, *29*, 128–139.

3 When students reach secondary school, we expect them to be more independent. This can be challenging for students with special learning needs. One approach to enable them to manage effectively is to develop a self-advocacy portfolio. As an activity, develop a portfolio in partnership with another student, who may need to imagine that they have a disability, which reflects the following sections:

- What I know about my disability.
- My learning strengths and needs.
- A letter written to my class teacher, explaining how I learn best and what I need to be successful in the classroom.

School-work

Remember that school policies may apply that restrict your ability to complete one or more of the activities suggested below. Before beginning any of the following activities, speak to your supervising teacher or a member of the school administration to confirm that you can undertake the activity within existing school guidelines and policies.

4 In association with a practicum placement in a classroom, complete the Strengths and Difficulties Questionnaire (SDQ) for one child within the class who appears to be having social, personal, and behavioural difficulties. The SDQ is a brief screening questionnaire that is available for teachers and parents of students aged 4–10 years and 11–17 years. It assesses five dimensions:

   1 emotional problems;
   2 conduct problems;
   3 hyperactivity/inattention;
   4 peer relationship problems; and
   5 pro-social behaviour.

   The SDQ and the scoring instructions are available for downloading from the website <www.sdqinfo.com>. Instructions for scoring must be followed carefully and the child's identity must remain confidential, unless you are discussing the outcomes with the student's teacher. As a consequence of the outcomes of your administration of the SDQ, develop a set of strategies that will affirm the child's strengths and address the child's difficulties in age-appropriate ways.

5 Social Stories are very usful in assisting young people who need to develop a social or personal skills. Some examples of situations that may benefit from a Social Story include:

- being a poor loser and learning how to respond to disappointment;
- listening to a person without interrupting them;
- starting a sensible conversation; and
- calming down when I get angry.

   Use the key aspects of the Social Story to develop a story that focuses on a particular social or interpersonal issue. Remember, use the four types of sentences, in the following sequence:

- Descriptive sentences can be used to describe what people do in particular social situations, and they can also be used to describe a social setting or the procedure for completing a social activity.
- Directive sentences direct a person to an appropriate and desired social response. They are used to state clearly and positively what type of behaviour is required.
- Perspective sentences are used to present other people's reactions to the social situation. These sentences aim to teach the individual how others perceive events.
- Control sentences identify to the individual ways in which the Social Story can be remembered and understood.

6 This activity involves developing a teaching strategy or curriculum activity about social interactions. Select an age-appropriate book that is related to working with young people who have diverse abilities, and develop a lesson plan in which you assist the class to analyse the key themes and to understand the book or movie plot from the perspective of the child, youth, or adult who is depicted in the book or movie. Some examples of suitable books drawn from Appendix 4 of the Teacher Information Book associated with the "Open Your Mind. Count Us In" package are:

- *Early childhood*—Leers. L. (1998). *Ian's walk: A story about autism*. Morton grove, Il: Albert Whitman & Co.
- *Middle childhood*—Piper, D. (1996). *Jake's the name, sixth grade's the game*. Unionville, NY: Royal Fireworks Press.
- *Early and late adolescence*—Haddon, M. (2003). *The curious incident of the dog in the nighttime*. London: Jonathan Cape.

The Social Story may be accompanied by pictures of the relevant child in the school context, if you have permission to do this. A simple way to construct a Social Story is to use PowerPoint, embed digital photographs in the story and then print the slides in colour as book pages. Most students with diverse abilities are thrilled to see themselves as the "star" of the book, and consequently identify quickly with the strategies that are depicted.

SUGGESTED READING AND RESOURCES

Books and articles

Balson, M. (1995). *Understanding classroom behaviour* (3rd ed.). Melbourne: ACER Press.

Buron, K. D. (2003). *When my autism gets too big! A relaxation book for children with ASD*. Shawnee Mission, KS: Autism Asperger Publishing.

Buron, K. D. & Curtis, M. (2003). *The incredible 5-point scale: Assisting students with ASD in understanding social interactions and controlling their emotional responses*. Shawnee Mission, KS: Autism Asperger Publishing.

Gagnon, E. (2004). *Power Cards: Using special interests to motivate children and youth with Asperger Syndrome and Autism*. Shawnee Mission, KS: Autism Asperger Publishing Co.

Lavoie, R. (2005). *It's so much work to be your friend: Helping the child with learning disabilities find social success*. New York: Touchstone.

Myles, B. S. & Southwick, J. (2005). *Asperger syndrome and difficult moments: Practical solutions for tantrums, rage and meltdowns*. Shawnee Mission, KS: Autism Asperger Publishing.

Myles, B. S., Trautman, M. L., & Schelvan, R. L. (2004). *The hidden curriculum: Practical solutions for understanding unstated rules in social situations*. Shawnee Mission, KS: Autism Asperger Publishing.

Newton, C., Taylor, G., & Wilson, D. (1999). *Circles of friends*. Dunstable, UK: Folens.

Petersen, L. (2002a). *Stop, think, do: social skills training: Primary years of schooling ages 4–8*. Melbourne: ACER Press.

Peterson, L. (2002b). *Stop, think, do: social skills training: Primary years of schooling ages 8–12*. Melbourne: ACER Press.

Questionnaires

Aldridge, J. M., Fraser, B. J., & Huang, T. C. (1999). Investigating classroom environments in Taiwan and Australia with multiple research methods. *The Journal of Educational Research*, *93*, 48.

Websites

<www.countusin.com.au>—"Open Your Mind. Count Us In" Disability Awareness package.

<www.sdqinfo.com>—Strength & Difficulties Questionnaire.

<www.inclusive-solutions.com/circlesoffriends.asp>—Circle of Friends.

<www.glhv.org.au/?q=taxonomy/term/100,55>—Strategies for responding to Homophobia.

PATHS: <www.colorado.edu/cspv/blueprints/model/programs/PATHS.html>—Whole-school strategies.

<www.tribes.com>—TRIBES.

<http://chpru.ecu.edu.au/fsaf>—Friendly Schools and Families.

<www.ofsted.gov.uk>—Developing social, emotional and behavioural skills in secondary schools.

<www.latrobe.edu.au/cleu/resources_teachers.html>—Community Liaison and Education Unit, LaTrobe University has useful resources about sexuality.

REFERENCES

Aldridge, J. M., Fraser, B. J., & Huang, T. C. (1999). Investigating classroom environments in Taiwan and Australia with multiple research methods. *The Journal of Educational Research*, *93*, 48.

Balson, M. (1995). *Understanding classroom behaviour* (3rd ed.). Melbourne: ACER Press.

Barkley, R. A. (2000). Genetics of childhood disorders: XVII. ADHD, part 1: The executive functions and ADHD. *Journal of the American Academy of Child and Adolescent Psychiatry*, *39*, 1064.

Brintom, B., Spackman, M. P., Fujiki, M., & Ricks, J. (2007). What should Chris say? The ability of children with specific language impairment to recognise the need to dissemble emotions in social situations. *Journal of Speech, Language and Hearing Research*, *50*, 798–811.

Broer, S. M., Doyle, M. B., & Giangreco, M. F. (2005). Perspectives of students with intellectual disabilities about their experiences with paraprofessional support. *Exceptional Children*, *71*, 415.

Burnham, L. (2007). Loss adjustment for a bereaved child. *Special*, *July*, 34–35.

Buron, K. D. (2003). *When my autism gets too big! A relaxation book for children with ASD*. Shawnee Mission, KS Kansas: Autism Asperger Publishing.

Buron, K. D. & Curtis, M. (2003). *The incredible 5-point scale: Assisting students with ASD in understanding social interactions and controlling their emotional responses*. Shawnee Mission, KS: Autism Asperger Publishing.

Cambra, C. & Silvestre, N. (2003). Students with special educational needs in the inclusive classroom: social integration and self-concept. *European Journal of Special Needs Education*, *18*, 197–208.

Carrington, S., Allen, K., & Osmolowski, D. (2007). Visual narrative: A technique to enhance secondary students' contribution to the development of inclusive, socially just school environments lessons from a box of crayons. *Journal of Research in Special Education Needs*, *7*, 8–15.

Chadsey, J. & Han, K. G. (2005). Friendship-facilitation strategies: What do students in middle school tell us? *Teaching Exceptional Children*, *38*, 52.

Doel, D. A., Smit, C., & Bosch, J. H. (2005). School performance and social-emotional behaviour of primary school children before and after a disaster. *Pediatrics*, *118*, 1311–1320.

Eriks-Brophy, A., Durieux-Smith, A., Olds, J., Fitzpatrick, E., & Duquette, C., & Wittingham, J. (2006). Facilitators and barriers to the inclusion of orally educated children and youth with hearing loss in schools: Promoting partnerships to support inclusion. *The Volta Review*, *106*, 53–88.

Frederickson, N. & Turner, J. (2003). Utilising the classroom peer group to address children's social needs: An evaluation of the Circle of Friends intervention approach. *Journal of Special Education*, *36*, 234–245.

Gagnon, E. (2004). *Power Cards: Using special interests to motivate children and youth with Asperger Syndrome and Autism*. Kansas: Autism Asperger Publishing Co.

Giangreco, M. F., Yuan, S., McKenzie, B., Cameron, P., & Fialka, J. (2005). "Be careful what you wish for ...". five reasons to be concerned about the assignment of individual paraprofessionals. *Teaching Exceptional Children*, *37*, 28.

Kaplan, I. & Howes, A. (2004). "Seeing through different eyes": Exploring the value of participative research using images in schools. *Cambridge Journal of Education*, *34*, 143–155.

Krause, K., Bochner, S., & Duchesne, S. (2003). *Educational psychology for learning and teaching*. Melbourne: Thomson.

Malmgren, K. W., Causton-Theoharis, J. N., & Trezek, B. J. (2005). Increasing peer interactions for students with behavioral disorders via paraprofessional training. *Behavioral Disorders*, *31*, 95.

McDevitt, T. M. & Ormrod, J. E. (2004). *Child development: Educating and working with children and adolescents* (2nd ed.). New Jersey: Pearson Education.

Myles, B. S. & Southwick, J. (2005). *Asperger syndrome and difficult moments: Practical solutions for tantrums, rage and meltdowns*. Shawnee Mission, KS: Autism Asperger Publishing.

Myles, B. S., Trautman, M. L., & Schelvan, R. L. (2004). *The hidden curriculum: Practical solutions for understanding unstated rules in social situations*. Shawnee Mission, KS: Autism Asperger Publishing.

Newton, C., Taylor, G., & Wilson, D. (1999). *Circles of friends*. Dunstable, UK: Folens.

Petersen, L. (2002a). *Stop, think, do: Social skills training: Primary years of schooling ages 4–8*. Melbourne: ACER Press.

Peterson, L. (2002b). *Stop, think, do: Social skills training: Primary years of schooling ages 8–12*. Melbourne: ACER Press.

Tager-Flusberg, H. (1999). A psychological approach to understanding the social and language impairments in autism. *International Review of Psychiatry*, *11*, 325–334.

Suzanne Carrington

12

HOME, SCHOOL, AND COMMUNITY RELATIONSHIPS

What you will learn in this chapter

This chapter focuses on the development of inclusive relationships between homes, schools, and communities. Collaboration, team work, and good communication have long been recognised as important qualities for teachers and a characteristic of high-performing schools. We know that when teachers collaborate and solve problems, they develop new knowledge together that can lead to curriculum reform and transformation of teaching for social change. More recently, schools are described as communities made up of teachers, students, parents, specialists, and support staff that are embedded within the culture of the people in the neighbourhood. Business groups and community organisations are often involved in various ways in the life of the school to provide direct support to the students and parents, and to benefit the greater community as a whole. Shared decision-making involving members of the school community can empower and transform students' lives. Communities that value and respect members and provide a safe learning environment for everyone to express their views, build awareness and develop capabilities together are more likely to be inclusive.

In this chapter, you will learn about:

- developing inclusive relationships between teachers, students and parents;
- ideas that encourage students to have a voice and be represented in processes of school review and development;
- processes that facilitate engagement with parents and communities; and
- how teams of specialist staff can be involved in school activities.

Two case studies are presented to support the development of a set of ideas and strategies that can be incorporated across the school sector. The case studies illustrate how parents, students, and teachers can work together to achieve shared outcomes for more inclusive schooling.

Before reading the case studies, it is necessary to know a little about The *Index for Inclusion* (Booth & Ainscow, 2002). This resource is designed to support schools in a process of inclusive school development and was developed in the United Kingdom at the Centre for Studies in Inclusive Education (CSIE) in collaboration with the University of Manchester and University of Christ Church College Canterbury. The *Index* provides a framework for school review and development on three dimensions: school culture, policy, and practice. A school culture includes beliefs, values, habits, and assumed ways of doing things among the school community. Culture is the heart and soul of an organisation and can develop by osmosis or can be influenced by purposeful leadership. Policy can include written expectations about how people work together, use resources, and provide educational programs for students in the school. Policy is usually informed by school and education organisation priorities and plans. The dimension of practice includes areas such as classroom ways of orchestrating learning and roles and duties of staff in the school. You were introduced to the *Index* in Chapter 4.

The three dimensions overlap because developments in school culture require the formulation of policies and the implementation of practice. Each dimension of the Index is divided into a number of indicators that can be considered as goals for achieving more inclusive schooling. Each indicator suggests a number of questions that can be used to encourage thinking about various issues related to inclusive education. The detailed questions ensure that the materials can provoke thought on school issues, whatever its current state of development. While the questions do not provide solutions for schools, they prompt people to think differently and to consider how the school could be improved to meet the needs of the school community. The intent is threefold: to establish existing knowledge and community understandings about culture, policy and practice in the school; to consider priority areas for school and teacher development; and to manage and document the process of change. There are five phases in the *Index* process:

- Phase 1—Starting the *Index* process;
- Phase 2—Finding out about the school;
- Phase 3—Producing an inclusive development plan;
- Phase 4—Implementing developments; and
- Phase 5—Reviewing the Index process.

The *Index for Inclusion* was used in the following two case studies.

CASE STUDIES

GUM TREE STATE SCHOOL

Gum Tree State School is an inner-city primary school with approximately 250 students participating in a P–7 (primary, preschool, and special education) multi-age program. This program means that students have access to a flexible, supportive learning environment and have the opportunity to progress at their own rate of development. The school principal wanted to explore structures, policies, and practices so that the inclusion policy for the school would address key priorities.

A working party comprising the head of special education services, a class teacher, a behaviour support services representative, the principal, parent representatives, and the education advisor (Inclusive Education) from the school district was formed. Opportunities at school staff meetings were planned for all staff, including teacher aides, teachers, administrators, and specialists, to discuss their beliefs and understandings about inclusive education. This process is important because shared beliefs of members of the school community affect actions, which in turn affects the school culture. Open communication is fostered and members are encouraged to feel comfortable and express opinions and thoughts on issues. The *Index for Inclusion* assisted in this process. Use of the *Index* encourages collaborative enquiry and assumes that all schools are at different points in the journey toward more inclusive school development.

A particular issue was identified during one of the staff meetings that became an early focus for the working party. Some staff believed that teacher aide support did not focus sufficiently on student learning and development. These staff thought that the support model met the needs of some adults and also caused many students with disabilities to become support-dependent. The education advisor (Inclusive Education) facilitated a workshop specifically for teacher aides. Activities and conversations, underpinned by the *Index*, challenged assumptions about the learning and participation of students with disabilities and led to an acknowledgment that disability is one aspect only of human difference. Teacher aides recognised that current support options had the potential to impede the learning and independence of students. Ongoing discussions with support staff extended and strengthened these views and provided opportunities to share and extend individual understandings of inclusive education that supported future student aspirations.

In addition to the meeting with the teacher aides, layers of data were collected from members of the school community. Initially, a staff survey created from the culture and policy dimensions of the *Index* identified priority areas. The following areas were considered by the working party to be of the highest priority because 12–25% of staff respondents disagreed with the statement.

- Staff professional development activities help staff to respond to student diversity.
- Staff treat each other with respect irrespective of their roles in the school.
- Staff feel valued and supported (50% of teacher aides disagreed with this compared with 15% of teaching staff).
- The staff's belief in meeting diverse needs reduces the barriers to learning and participation for all students (teachers and others groups disagreed more strongly than teacher aides).
- Meetings involving staff, students, parents/carers, and others attempt to deal with problems flexibly before they escalate (teacher aides and others disagreed most strongly).

At Gum Tree State School, priorities and issues were also identified through parent and student questionnaires that were informed by the *Index for Inclusion*. The parent questionnaire was sent to every family in the school and deeper levels of understanding were developed through Parent Forums. These forums were advertised through the school newsletters and internet site to consider specific issues such as communication between home and school and reporting on children's progress. At the school, every student in Years 6 and 7 undertakes training at the beginning of the school year to become a peer support leader. Peer support groups involve

12.1 A student survey

☐ I am a girl

☐ I am a boy

I am in year ____________

	Most of the time	Some of the time	None of the time
I like being at this school.			
My friends help me with my class work when I need help.			
I help my friends with their work when they need help.			
My teacher likes to help me with my work.			
My teacher lets me know how I am doing with my work.			
I like to help my teacher when she or he has jobs that need doing.			
My teacher likes to listen to my ideas.			
There is a choice of activities in my room.			
Teachers don't mind if I make mistakes as long as I try my best.			
The children in my class call others by unkind names.			
Kids are mean to me in the playground.			
If I feel unhappy at school I can talk to my teacher or another adult about my problems.			

	I agree	Not sure	I do not agree
At this school, when children fight or argue the teacher sorts it out fairly.			
We help make the rules of our classroom.			
I feel comfortable with most of the children at this school.			
The staff at this school are friendly to me.			
I am learning a lot at this school.			
At lunchtimes there are places in the school I can go to be comfortable.			

The three things I like best about my school are:

____

____

____

The three things I would change about this school are:

____

____

____

vertical groupings of the whole school, with older students teaching and mentoring a multi-age group of younger children, for a 30-minute lesson every week. Students from across all year levels were surveyed using the Student Survey (Box 12.1) and the following issues were identified as concerns:

- The children in my class call others by unkind names.
- Kids are mean to me in the playground.
- At this school, when children fight or argue the teacher sorts it out fairly.

After the survey, the peer support groups discussed significant issues identified in the student survey. Peer support leaders facilitated conversations with their multi-age groups about each issue and recorded suggestions for improvement. These were later considered in a combined peer support group meeting. The collection of layers of data provided a deep understanding of issues from a range of perspectives and information gathered provided useful feedback to the school.

The surveys confirmed that all groups felt a high degree of satisfaction about issues such as:

- Everyone is made to and feels welcome.
- Students enjoy being at the school.
- There is a partnership between staff and parents/carers with opportunities for parents/carers to be involved in school decision-making.
- All local communities are involved in the school and those who volunteer at the school are valued.
- Staff work hard to help students.

The following were identified as issues to be improved:

- Communication between groups in the school.
- Sharing of resources between groups.
- Staff collaboration.
- Staff planning to meet needs of all students.

The school principal reported that the *Index* process assisted in the review of support services to students and provided a focus for professional conversations with staff. An inclusion policy was developed addressing key priorities as identified by staff, students, and parents. The working party identified that further professional conversations needed to occur for staff to reflect on classroom practices. The implementation plan for the new inclusion policy needed to be sensitive to staff feelings and perceptions, as well as facilitating professional development. The staff, in particular, required a supportive, participatory process that would lead them to question the taken-for-granted assumptions linked to culture, policy, and practice in the school community. Ensuring the process was owned and driven from within the school increased sustainability. Staff, students, parents, and administration need to be actively involved in a successful school development process. The *Index for Inclusion* did not provide a solution; it gave insiders permission to think differently, to take away the usual restraints, and to look at all possibilities for moving forward.

COTTON TREE SECONDARY SCHOOL

Cotton Tree Secondary School has about 500 students from a diversity of backgrounds. The school has a special education unit supporting 33 students who have a range of disabilities, including intellectual disability, Autism Spectrum Disorder, physical impairment, and speech language impairment. Aboriginals and Torres Strait Islanders comprise 3.5% of the student population and 3.4% of families indicate that they speak a language other than English in their home (e.g., Filipino, Portuguese, Russian, Spanish, and Indian). The principal was keen to involve students in a process of review and future planning for the school. She believed that student views frequently are lost in the business of school improvement and noted that they are rarely thought of as active participants in school review processes.

A Student Management Team, consisting of approximately 35 students from Years 9 to 12, had been involved in decision-making about school matters such as uniforms and school special events. The principal was keen to extend opportunities for this group of students to be more involved in developing and refining school policies and procedures. In general, the students represented the diversity in the student population. The Student Management Team met with teachers from the school to discuss student response to a number of statements:

- In most lessons, students and teachers behave well toward each other.
- Opinions of students are sought about how the school might be improved.
- Students are confident that their difficulties will be dealt with effectively.
- Students share responsibility for helping to overcome the difficulties experienced by some students in lessons.
- When you first joined this school you were helped to feel settled.
- Students worry about being bullied at this school.
- Students are taught to appreciate people who have different backgrounds to their own.
- Teachers try to help all students do their best.
- At lunchtime, there are places in the school where students can go to be comfortable.
- When students have problems with their work they ask the teacher for help.

The 10 statements were drawn from the culture, policy, and practice dimensions of the Index for Inclusion. The students were asked to discuss each statement and record an answer: “Yes, we agree”; “We are not sure”; or “No, we do not agree” on a recording chart for each statement posted on a wall. Students could also make any comments from their discussion on sticky notes posted on the recording charts. Once the information was collated, students were asked to consider future actions (see Box 12.2).

Representatives from the Student Management Team presented the issues and the range of actions to a school committee (school principal, teaching staff representatives, students, and members of the school community, including parents of students attending the school). Staff and parents were impressed with the insights and actions proposed by the students. For example, the Student Management Team suggested a number of student-driven ways to welcome new students: the office could liaise with the Student Team in the organisation of a welcome committee and peer buddy system, and provide information about processes and policies at the school. The school principal, teachers, and parents were supportive of the recommended actions.

12.2

Student management team forum, data and planning

Statements	Strength/ Concern	Action
In most lessons, students and teachers behave well toward each other.	Concern	• We need to learn to interact with each other. • Reinforce teacher–student relationship. • Revisit code of behaviour (Student Management Team to review and rewrite).
Opinions of students are sought about how the school might be improved.	Concern	• Representatives to go to Teacher Management Meeting to make sure the right information is getting told. • Participate in a range of meetings—Parents and Citizens and Triennial School Review.
Students are confident that their difficulties will be dealt with effectively.	Concern	• Students should be made aware of their options, where they can go for help. • Set time in class for students to raise concerns.
Students share responsibility for helping to overcome the difficulties experienced by some students in lessons.	Strength	• No action needed here.
When you first joined this school you were helped to feel settled.	Concern	• Extend workshop and camps to form stronger support groups and friendships. • Older grades have friendship-building activities. • Students volunteer to help new students. • A book of hints made by Student Management Team to give to students in Year 7 (e.g., have information on peer mediation process).

Statements	Strength/ Concern	Action
		• Buddy system but do not force people.
Students worry about being bullied at this school.	Concern	• Continue peer mediation, raise awareness about what they do—needs publicity about this. • Give students information book in Year 8. • Focus on teaching about bullying in Years 8 and 9. • Acknowledge the issues—bullying still exists in upper school but it is subtle.
Students are taught to appreciate people who have different back-grounds to their own.	Concern and Strength	• Treat everyone as equals—needs to be more embedded in teaching. • School expectation is a strength and needs to continue.
Teachers try to help all students do their best.	Strength and Concern	• Included in Action for Statement 1.
At lunchtime there are places in the school where students can go to be comfortable.	Concern	• More seating (all year levels). • Year 12s need a place to eat lunch so younger grades do not feel intimidated near the tuckshop.
When students have problems with their work they ask the teacher for help.	Strength and Concern	• Most teachers do their best to help. • Students tease other students for asking questions. • Sometimes students are embarrassed to ask questions. • This needs to be addressed.

12.2

Empowering the students to contribute to school review and planning helped the development of pride in showcasing the school to future students and the community. One student said, "It's just an awesome achievement for us to be able to be involved." The process demonstrates how students can raise awareness of issues of importance to them and provide feedback on positive school cultural characteristics that lead to a higher level of respect for students and their views about the environment and culture of the school.

TEACHING–LEARNING CONTEXT

Before progressing with a discussion about how home, school, and community relationships can be developed, it is important to consider the key assumptions that underlie inclusive education that influence the development of these relationships. In Australia, our understandings about inclusive education have evolved from the notion of integrating students with disabilities into regular schools. Currently, the terms *integration* and *inclusion* are still confused. With integration, there is a focus on helping students with disabilities to fit in to the regular classroom. This focus emphasises teaching the normal curriculum with teachers considering what modifications may be needed to meet the needs of students who have a disability. Therefore, integration neither necessarily challenges the organisation and provision of curriculum for students nor considers the development of respectful relationships among students, parents, and the community. There is little recognition of the social and cultural differences that exist in the range of communities. In contrast, an inclusive approach to schooling focuses on diversity and difference in our society. For schools to cater for diverse populations of students, questions are raised about personal assumptions and beliefs that inform views about schools, teachers, students, teaching and learning, and the interconnectedness between individuals, education, and society. In an inclusive approach, teachers listen to their students and their families and build a curriculum that is appropriate and respectful for those needs.

A preservice teacher recently commented to me:

> *I realised that inclusion begins with everyday actions—the way you treat people and the language you use to talk about different groups of people can reinforce or tear down inclusion and acceptance ... An inclusive society can only be created when people look beyond another person's skin colour, religion, sex, or social status to see a real person who deserves respect and the same chances in life as anyone else.*

In formal terms, schools are now being asked to move away from a deficit model where a problem, such as a learning difficulty, is essentially located within the individual, to a social model that recognises that difference can be created through social institutions that have oppressive, discriminatory, and disabling practices.

In the past, if students had problems with learning or had a disability, the students were usually removed from the regular classroom and identified and labelled in some way. Remedial programs and special interventions were designed to fix their problem. Some students with disabilities were not included in regular school programs. Inclusive education strives to achieve a way of life in schools where people are valued and treated with respect for their varied knowledge and experiences. Inclusive education demands that schools listen to the needs of the students and parents/carers to inform the planning of flexible curriculum and pedagogy that is learner-focused, rather than content-driven. This inclusive way of thinking means that teachers consider the social and cultural backgrounds of the families and students when planning their classroom programs. It is their responsibility to meet the needs of the students in their classroom.

ISSUES AND CHALLENGES
Working in school communities

If teachers are to embrace the strengths and needs of students and parents in their school community, they need to invest time and energy to listen to students and understand the diverse backgrounds from which they come. Working with students who have a disability or who come from different cultural backgrounds can be daunting for teachers. Many teachers have not had a broad experience with a range of people in society. Teachers working in some areas need to work with a number of government agencies that provide support services to families who are disadvantaged. These matters have been raised in a number of chapters in this textbook. As a teacher, you can recognise that every individual, family, or community member can contribute to your learning and understanding to achieve a successful school program. Education departments, governments, and community organisations have a variety of support services and specialists to assist teachers to support the diversity of student needs. You will find a list of several at the end of Chapter 4.

Developing sustainable school communities

Many school communities have made good progress in developing an inclusive culture, inclusive policies, and inclusive practices. Progress can be driven by key personnel in the school such as a school principal. Yet, with a change of leadership, priorities can be altered and a school might slip back into authoritarian and traditional ways of working. If the value of working in inclusive ways is not embedded in the work practices of the people in the school, then a new school principal can direct the focus to other priorities that may not value and support all students and families. To avoid this lack of sustainability of inclusive school development, school principals and school leaders need to develop democratic and shared leadership that encourages a commitment to shared goals. "Beige teachers" cannot achieve inclusive schools.

The concept of beige teachers was presented by Linda Graham in her doctoral studies where she drew on the ideas of the Scottish comedian "Billy Connolly, who wages a self-confessed war against the 'beige army'—all those who wear beige, are beige and seek to make others beige as well" (Graham, 2006, p. 198). In contrast, beginning teachers need to be passionate and creative about engaging with the broader community in democratic ways, where difference and diversity are valued, and the problem of injustice and exclusion in education can be addressed and shared. Enthusiastic teachers who are committed to achieving inclusive schooling can become active participants and drivers of school change. A strong inclusive school culture can be achieved and sustained when students, parents, teachers, and the school administration work at various levels to achieve common goals. Later in this chapter you will be asked to consider how you could plan for sustainable change in a school community.

Students with diverse abilities work here in an inclusive school setting

Inclusive schooling versus standards agenda

There is tension between an inclusive approach in schools and the focus on raising standards. It is evident that there are many non-inclusive aspects of the current national focus on testing, raising standards, and the education department resourcing models based on categories of disability and difference. The range of ever-changing external policy agendas create pressures within schools to lift standards and this may create negative views about some children and some family backgrounds, and lead to exclusion of students. In a positive way, these external agendas can also prompt schools leaders to consider students who are not achieving well and prompt problem-solving for students' outcomes. Therefore, the focus on standards can be interpreted in several ways at the school level, each being informed by the school culture and priorities.

Pressure in some schools to cover the set curriculum may not allow teachers to differentiate instruction depending upon students' abilities because of the need to teach a sequence of curriculum content in a specified period of time. This situation is a common problem for secondary school teachers. A focus on covering the content combined with pressure about raising standards usually means that teachers are rarely able to address the needs of individual students in the classroom. Teachers may perceive that the structure of the curriculum and associated high academic expectations are barriers to the development of an inclusive approach to teaching. Where withdrawal (or pull out) programs exist for students who are experiencing learning difficulties, the responsibility for the student shifts to someone outside of the regular classroom. In some schools with a culture of high achievement expectations, students who have difficulties with learning the standard curriculum were thought to "weigh down" the regular students. This type of thinking implies that students have a deficit because they are not meeting the demands of the curriculum.

A close focus on academic achievement and traditional teaching practices provides few opportunities for teaching staff, special educators, and school administrators to meet, reflect, and discuss key issues about meeting the needs of students, especially those who are in secondary schools. In such schools, staff operate from within the perspective of an existing structure and this makes it difficult to think about an alternative school organisation and teaching of the curriculum.

Inclusion is more than placement

Inclusive education is about much more than the location where learning takes place. A student who has a disability may be sitting in a Year 5 or a Year 9 classroom but may be ostracised by their peers and may not have their learning needs met by the teacher. Even when special assistance is available, it may not mean that the student is truly included in the regular class. For example, in one secondary school, in-class support was provided for students who have learning difficulties. The support was provided by regular class teachers who were not engaged in a class for that period. This idea seems innovative but after observing the initiative in practice and discussing the process with staff, it became clear that this practice was not inclusive. In a science class, for example, a supporting class teacher was timetabled to assist three students with learning difficulties. These students were seated at the back of the class and worked on a science task with the supporting class teacher. The regular class teacher did not include the three students when she was teaching the regular lesson to the remainder of the class. The students with difficulties were still very much segregated from the class because the class teacher was not encouraged to modify her teaching or the curriculum to cater for individual differences. Some teachers want to carry on with their regular teaching for the "normal" students with as little disruption as possible to their usual routines and do not take responsibility for all learners in their classroom. Leadership and cultural change, as identified earlier, can assist teachers to be more inclusive in their classroom practice.

Support to develop inclusive practices

Teachers need in-school support when planning and differentiating instruction and for motivating and monitoring learning in the classroom. There must be recognition of the time needed for teachers to collaborate and work with teams that include teachers, specialists, and parents. The principal and school leaders can assist by providing teachers with formalised release time for these activities if inclusive education is a priority in the school. Professional development is necessary to ensure that teachers feel confident in planning and teaching all students in their classroom.

Thus, we can see that the traditional ways in which teachers have been encouraged to work need to be critiqued and challenged to facilitate the introduction of inclusive practices into classroom practice. As beginning teachers you can actively reflect on your teaching and model inclusive ways of interacting with students in your classroom. Teachers resisting the trend toward sameness and working actively to alter a school culture are important factors for embedding inclusive practices into a school community.

From this section of this chapter we can see that:

- an inclusive teacher listens to students to develop relevant curriculum that caters for all students;
- sustainable cultural change in the school is required for teachers to adopt inclusive practices;
- this sort of change requires leadership from the principal, who can model inclusive values to staff;
- an inclusive teacher needs to be innovative and work collaboratively to solve teaching and learning problems;
- standardised testing and the pressure to cover a set curriculum are two key factors that sustain a traditional approach to teaching;
- inclusive education is about the curriculum rather than just the location of students; and
- leadership and professional development are needed to engender cultural change so that teachers will adopt inclusive culture and practice in their classrooms.

TEACHING ESSENTIALS

This section focuses on principles that teachers can develop to inform an ethical and inclusive approach in schools.

Collaboration and team-work

Teachers must work together, share ideas, and plan to achieve agreed missions and goals. A class of students in early childhood, primary, and secondary schools usually contains a broad range of student abilities and family backgrounds, so the teacher needs support from specialists available inside and outside the school. A support network can include members of the school administration, team teachers, teacher aides, parents, community volunteers, and specialist teaching support such as special education teachers and counsellors. Additional support from state or regional-based advisory teams is usually available, as you will recall from Chapter 4. These support networks can assist teachers in sharing ideas on creating a flexible curriculum and in addressing students' individual learning and social needs.

The opportunity to discuss programs, assessment practices, resources, and activities with supporting personnel ensures the sharing of good ideas and increases the probability that solutions are found to difficult problems. Collaboration is essential because the invention of new ideas requires reflective problem-solving that will develop inclusive practices. These practices, in turn, ensure that student needs

are met within the education and wider community. One of the most effective ways of achieving organisational change and an inclusive school is to provide time and opportunities for collaboration and problem-solving between general, special, and other educational and community-based staff (Carrington & Robinson, 2006).

Many school programs have classroom-based support staff, such as teacher aides or teacher assistants. Their employment and deployment are usually managed by principals and they are assigned to a variety of roles. In addition, support teachers, special education teachers, English as a second language (ESL) teachers, guidance officers, and advisory visiting specialists all work collaboratively with teachers to provide students with quality learning experiences. Due to the intense nature of teaching, a challenge for these teams is to ensure there is adequate time to work together. Effective collaboration and teamwork in schools frequently occurs on the run. That is, teachers and teacher aides catch up informally to discuss student progress or share successes and problems while passing in the school corridors or while on playground duty. These ongoing communications can compliment more formally arranged meetings.

In some schools there are weekly meetings where student support needs are identified and addressed, and specialist services can then be organised. In the past, teachers have identified a lack of knowledge and skills in meeting the pedagogical needs of diverse student populations, especially for students with disabilities (Forlin, Douglas, & Hattie, 1996). There is a need for ongoing commitment to professional development and learning from individual teachers, schools, and education systems. Collaboration and teamwork provide support for teachers to work and learn together to develop more inclusive ways of working (Barton, 2003; Skrtic, Sailor, & Gee, 1996).

In traditional schools, teachers have usually worked in isolation and generally have not had the opportunity to observe how their colleagues deal with the challenges of classroom teaching. Because of this, many teachers have not been exposed to a range of practices and, therefore, have not critically reflected on their own. Staff working together to solve problems can provide effective ways of working with students because there is ongoing evaluation of teaching styles and strategies and the school organisation to inform the development and refinement of inclusive policies and practice (Ainscow, 2007). An example of this can be found in Box 12.3. The combination of professional knowledge gained from working and learning in a team provides a varied and interesting approach to teaching and usually enhances the job satisfaction for all involved.

An excursion to the zoo

12.3

Classroom teachers and special education teachers often work together in inclusive schools. The following story illustrates the benefits for a whole class when teachers share their knowledge and skills.

A group of children in Year 2 were planning a school excursion to the local zoo. The Year 2 teacher was particularly worried about how a child who had Autism Spectrum Disorder (ASD) was going to cope with the demands of the excursion. The young boy did not cope well with change from the general classroom routine and could become very anxious, which could result in tantrums and difficult behaviour. The class teacher discussed her concerns with the special education teacher from the Special Education Unit, and the special education teacher planned

a Social Story for the child. A Social Story is a teaching strategy that builds on natural social skills and behaviours based on a concept developed by Carol Gray (2000). It is presented as a short story that describes a situation, a concept, or social skills so that the child has improved awareness and understanding of a social experience. It is read with, or by, the child a number of times. Sometimes photographs are used to support the story.

The Special Education Teacher wrote the following Social Story:

Next week on Friday our class is going to the zoo for the day.
My teacher, teacher aides, and some parent helpers will come too.
I will meet my friends at the front of the school on Friday.
I will have my hat and my backpack with my lunch inside.
My friends and I will walk onto the bus and find a seat.
We can talk quietly in the bus on the way to the zoo.
When we get off the bus, I will stay with my group.
We will walk together and listen to our group leader when she is talking.
We will see lots of animals at the zoo. Some animals will smell funny.
All of the animals are in cages or enclosures and cannot hurt me.
After we have lunch at the zoo, we will come back to the school on the bus.

Once the classroom teacher received the Social Story, she decided to use it with the whole Year 2 class. The story was presented in large print on a flip chart and the teacher and the class read the story together every day in the week leading up to the excursion. The strategy was excellent in preparing all students for the excursion so the students knew how they were expected to behave and what they would do on the day of the excursion. The Social Story was developed initially to enhance the social skills of one child but was used to prepare all students for the excursion, and also promoted literacy skills.

12.3

Critical engagement with inclusive ideals and practices

There are many historical and structural factors that have informed teaching practice, but these days teachers are encouraged to work with students in ways that suit the local context and community. This change demands a series of deconstructions and reconstructions of beliefs, knowledge, and language rather than transformations of traditional beliefs, knowledge, and practices. This means there is a need to expose and dismantle stereotyped views and then consider new ways of thinking about what is possible in schools for certain groups of students.

A common language develops when teachers learn to work together with a range of professionals and community members. When critical engagement with issues occurs it can provoke deep reflection on taken-for-granted assumptions about, for example, particular groups of pupils or parents. Language usually reflects preconceptions and beliefs about many issues and this is exemplified in Box 12.4. Through critical reflection on views and actions, teachers gain an awareness of their assumptions, beliefs, and how these relate to practice (Crebbin, 2004). Through this process, teachers develop coherent rationales for their beliefs and classroom practices and may even become more aware of appropriate alternatives rather than proceeding on impulse and intuition.

BOX 12.4

Teachers' language

A teacher's use of language can reflect and maintain dominant power relationships. Read the following story and consider how this teacher's language revealed her beliefs.

A specialist teacher who was working in a secondary school to support refugee students in the school community stated in exasperation, "These girls! They have such limited life experiences!"

The question is, however: Did these girls have *limited* life experiences or *different* life experiences? The teacher may not have realised that her white middle-class beliefs about difference and her expectations about schooling were influencing (in a destructive sense) her plans for an inclusive approach in the school. This anecdote about the specialist teacher may be an example of someone who is unknowingly emphasising the beliefs valued by the dominant group to which she belongs (white middle-class), while advocating an inclusive approach in her work in schools.

In a discussion of how to brainstorm for good ideas for essay writing in a secondary school English class, a teacher was discussing imagination and stated, "Some of you have it and some of you don't. That's the nicest way of saying it." This statement would not contribute to the development of a healthy self-esteem for many students in the class. As you might expect, even the brighter students would be questioning whether they have it or don't. Reluctance by students to take a risk in the classroom was evident when the teacher asked a question after this comment and only one student raised a hand to answer.

This anecdote demonstrates the way language can communicate the value placed on natural ability and inadvertently reinforce the negative view of a student who is not achieving.

Development of an inclusive culture

Traditionally and historically, schools have been hierarchical and based on authoritarian models of governance that alienate and marginalise rather than respect, care for, and include members of the school community. The culture of a school organisation affects the way in which schools operate and the ways that problems are solved. In an organisation there is collective social action that is based on relationships that are informed by collective understandings among members that are related to roles. The individuals' perspectives direct their behaviour.

School culture can be influenced by beliefs, values, and knowledge relating to the following issues:

- social justice and equity issues;
- disability and learning problems;
- barriers to inclusive schooling;
- the nature of knowledge;
- teaching and learning;
- the goals of education;

- organisation and management of student behaviour;
- the nature and delivery of the curriculum;
- leadership within the school;
- the needs of teachers; and
- the needs of the students.

An inclusive school culture assumes that the principal and staff of the school will accept the responsibility for the progress of all students. The ways of organising a classroom and a school, the construction of the role of teaching, and the delivery of the curriculum influence the way students are taught. An inclusive approach requires an organisational philosophy that is committed to the improvement of strategies, programs, and the use of available resources. Although a school organisation is influenced by social structures, it has properties of its own and will develop in response to its internal dynamic, as the example in Box 12.5 shows.

BOX 12.5 A case of withdrawal

This story is about a school principal of a large secondary school who indicated in an interview that he was supportive of inclusive schooling. In practice, however, he continued to emphasise high achievement and standards for each year level in his school. This meant that, if students were not able to meet the high expectations, then opportunities were provided for them to complete modified work or complete the set work with specialist special education support.

In his school, staff time and effort were frequently devoted to the development of alternative resources and modified teaching programs that were often taught away from the usual teaching program for that year. Students were separated from their peers and received a watered-down version of the curriculum. Teachers in these programs viewed the learners in these withdrawal programs differently to their age peers. Consequently, the students in withdrawal programs often could not meet the requirements of a traditional content-focused curriculum. By ignoring their responsibility to provide active and successful learning experiences for the learners in each class, the teachers continued to reinforce the deficit perception of learners who were not responding appropriately to the set curricula.

It is possible for staff to reconstruct the organisation of a school to meet the needs of the students within it. This requires staff to:

- communicate;
- solve problems;
- demonstrate respect for each other, their students, and families;
- develop a shared vision or philosophy that will enable them to move out of the boundaries of traditional school organisation and practice;
- learn about the limitations in current practice; and
- create new knowledge and skills that are needed to include all students.

The story in Box 12.5 highlights the deep change in thinking that is required to facilitate the change toward an inclusive approach in schools. The difficulty comes from not looking deeply inside us to question beliefs and practice about teaching young people from diverse backgrounds and with diverse abilities. The experience of questioning these unspoken truths can be uncomfortable, but it can also be an exciting process as new possibilities and perspectives are considered. The following ideas may be useful for teachers who wish to be inclusive:

- be reflective and critical about what you observe and experience in schools;
- seek out and use a critical friend;
- be open to constructive critique and be ready to engage in debate and discussion that might be uncomfortable; and
- be committed to pursuing ongoing development and learning.

The beliefs and understandings that you uncover can be personal but can also be shared views in a social context. Many traditional school routines based on unquestioned beliefs and assumptions can support ongoing patterns of behaviour that block progress to a more inclusive approach to schooling. However, it is very complex. We have all been immersed in our own experiences of schooling and built our own understandings around those experiences. To move toward inclusive practices, we must recognise the impact of our own beliefs and cultural backgrounds on limitations and barriers that exist to inclusive schooling.

Development of inclusive policy

The beliefs held within education organisations generated policies that led to practices. These policies also identify a process. Read through School A's and School B's behaviour policies in Box 12.6 and think about how each policy may contribute to different practices and expectations. Also, consider the underlying values and ideals for each policy.

BOX 12.6

School behaviour policies

School A behaviour policy	School B behaviour policy
Students will: • attend school regularly, on time, ready to learn and participate in school activities • work hard and comply with requests or directions from all staff • abide by school rules, meet homework and assessment requirements • be well presented and wear the school's uniform as prescribed • behave in a responsible manner that does not infringe on others' rights to learn	Through the understanding of student's needs and by giving them some control and ownership of the curriculum and learning activities in their classrooms, we not only minimise behaviour issues and develop important social outcomes but also strive to provide the highest quality education that makes a positive difference to the lives of all young people in our school community.

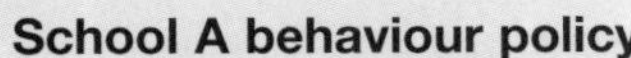

School A behaviour policy

- respect the property of the school and others
- maintain a clean and safe environment.

Parents will:

- take an active role in my child's academic and social development by attending school activities, parent evenings and interviews
- inform the school if there are any problems that may affect my child's ability to learn
- inform the school of the reason for any absence prior to or within 48 hours of the absence
- make arrangements to enable my child to arrive at school on time
- treat school staff with respect and tolerance
- support the authority and discipline of the school.

School B behaviour policy

At the core of our plan is also a focus upon the individual student and their responsibilities in the learning/behaviour relationship.

We believe that each individual:

1 makes choices about how they act and treat each other
2 is responsible for their behaviour and the choices they make
3 should accept the consequences of their actions and understand the importance of making amends
4 can choose to change their behaviour.

All members of the school community are expected to conduct themselves in a lawful, ethical, safe and responsible manner that recognises and respects the rights of others. Four key elements underpin the creation of a positive climate across the school community:

- **RESPECT**: For self, for others and natural/built environments
- **RESPONSIBILITY**: Cooperation, courtesy and consideration for all
- **RIGHTS**: Every student has the right to learn unhindered
- **REPUTATION**: Promote and enhance the good name of the school.

12.6

In reading these behaviour management policies you will note the difference in their language. For example, notice the words used in School A's behaviour policy and then compare this with the language in School B's behaviour policy. School A has a focus on rules with an expectation of compliance for both students and parents. School B has a focus on a shared responsibility to ensure positive outcomes for all in the school community. You can see that behaviour policy A articulates traditional power relations, whereas behaviour policy B is empowering for students. Policy B involves the school recognising and valuing each student. The School A behaviour policy, by contrast, constructs students as a homogenous group. It is alienating rather than inviting parental involvement.

Learning about the community and developing partnerships

Here, the focus is on community partnerships that promote active connections, trust, mutual understanding, and shared values and behaviours. It is the shared commitment that binds the community and makes cooperative action possible. Some schools are adopting values-based planning to achieve whole-school teamwork that involves parents and the community in shared decision-making. The key focus is on developing a sense of belonging for all members of the school community alongside coordinated review, planning, and action. This approach was reflected in the case studies earlier in the chapter.

Values-based planning involving parents and the community can be used to develop:

- a school's vision (i.e., a dream about what could be);
- the school's mission (i.e., the fundamental reason for the school's existence); and
- strategic planning processes (how we are going to get there).

This planning requires an understanding of the value platform for a school culture through developing relationships among staff, between staff and students, and between staff and parents/community. In particular, as noted above, there is a need for respect for the full range of contributions made by parents and the community in contrast to the traditional notions of parent help or community sponsorship. Schools frequently refer to parents as partners in the educative process, but the nature of the involvement of families is superficial in many schools. Indeed, while it is generally accepted that parents play a vital role in children's education, in some schools parents are seen to be more part of the problem than part of the solution, a matter that was also raised in Chapter 1. With the structure and make-up of families changing, there is a need for a variety of ways in which parents and carers can contribute in a valuable way to schools.

Teachers can consider ways in which parents and other community members can be engaged in and contribute to a school. The important issue is to value a broad range of contributions from parents and provide ongoing opportunities for parent feedback and consultation. Here are some suggestions that might help.

- Listen to parents and make them feel welcome in the school.
- Roster teachers to attend and address Parents and Citizens' meetings.
- Distribute newsletters for parents about key projects and activities in the school.
- Survey parents to gather information and feedback on a range of topics.
- Invite parents to contribute and comment on special project proposals and school review and planning.
- Invite community members, organisations, and business to address staff and students.
- Consider the representation of stakeholders in the school community.

In a school where there is genuine respect for all family groups, opportunities exist for a variety of contributions that are valued. Irrespective of socioeconomic status, education level, cultural background, or family structure, parents usually want their children to do well in school. If learning is accepted as a social process originating in the meaning-based relationship that begins in the home, valuing the full range of contributions is not only an obligation but a means of tapping into a rich resource. Listening to parents can lead to meaningful participation in resolving collective problems. This connectedness between school and families is a positive factor for educational success and further constitutes social capital that facilitates achieving goals linked to education reform.

In some school communities, key and valued representatives of the cultural community work in partnership with the school principal and teachers. For example, in many Indigenous communities, it is

important to speak with the Elders. Taking the time to visit with and talk (or "yarn with") the senior and respected members of a community can ensure that key issues are shared and discussed. These conversations build respect and understanding and facilitate a shared vision for the children and community. More recently, community involvement has moved beyond the token support roles influenced by the traditional hierarchies of power. In some Indigenous school communities, for example, Elders and community people work collaboratively to enhance student attendance and relevance and connection of the school curriculum to the local context, with the aim of increasing student achievement and progression through the school years (Sarra, 2007). Issues such as language, cultural history, community relationships and protocols, and appreciation for the land are embedded in the school culture, policy, and practice.

When contemplating the contribution of families to a school, it is valuable to consider an inward and outward perspective to transform a school to a school community. For example, inclusive education can be described as inward-directed participation in an education system that includes a focus on changing school culture through reconstructed curriculum and pedagogy. This could mean changing teaching and the curriculum to meet the needs of the learners in the school. However, inclusive education can also promote and direct social inclusion in society. This change means that education is viewed as a form of citizenship, rather than learning about citizenship. Through being socially connected to people from diverse backgrounds, awareness can be raised about power dynamics in our society. Students learn to work and support each other and develop awareness that some people in society need more help in some ways than others. Students learn to become citizens in a community. This learning may influence teachers' beliefs and values, but could also inform relationships with students and their families and a more inclusive approach to pedagogy and curriculum.

Critical friends

The final principle for the development of more inclusive practices involves the use of a critical friend. For example, most schools have access to an education advisor (Inclusive Education) or an equivalent person or specialist from a District office who can become involved as a consultant in a school renewal process. Some schools have academic partners from outside the university. A critical friend from outside the school can provide focus and guidance and encourage processes that uncover the deeper aspects of thinking needed for reform. The role of this outsider is to facilitate, observe, and challenge interactions between stakeholders. For example, a critical friend can:

- confront oppressive and exclusionary behaviour and language in a constructive manner; and
- act as an interrogator to challenge school policy and practice.

Through such a process, teachers and administrators have time and ongoing support to consider new ideas and implement new practices. The stakeholders in a school community, with help from a critical friend, might consider how students are grouped in classes. It may become apparent, for example, that a group of children in Year 1 are not ready for traditional teaching of academic literacy and need to spend more time on play-based use of language. Students in a secondary school may be missing too many classes due to outside paid work commitments and the school may consider staggered timetabling to allow for flexibility in school hours. Examples of these types of changes can be found in many early childhood, primary, and secondary schools and demonstrate how school communities work to address students' needs.

LEARNING ESSENTIALS

How can a teacher develop a classroom culture that has a student focus and treats young people as citizens and not as tourists drifting through the classroom with no sense of belonging? To answer this question, I draw from Freiberg's work (1996) where it was suggested that classroom-management systems should be built on trust and support.

Freiberg's model, Consistency Management and Cooperative Discipline, is a research-based, classroom-tested program that combines instructional effectiveness (through consistent classroom organisation) with student self-discipline developed cooperatively with teachers. Students are encouraged to contribute in useful ways to the school community so that cooperation, participation, and support are key factors. In this model, there is a focus on student roles and responsibilities in the classroom so that students feel that they belong to a class. For example, students might perform jobs in the classroom such as organise paper and supplies for the classroom computers, ensure work stations are stocked with appropriate resources, or even take responsibility for briefing supply or relief teachers about the class and the current unit of work. Students work with the teacher to develop shared expectations for behaviour in the classroom so there is a sense of ownership and pride about the activities and performance of the class. This type of approach prevents or minimises discipline problems. The underlying assumption is that students can be more valued and respected as citizens in a school community and able to participate in school review, planning, and action.

Consistency Management and Cooperative Discipline

An American model developed by Freiberg (1996) that combines instructional effectiveness with student self-discipline, developed cooperatively with teachers.

To enable this respectful culture in schools, we need to overcome the traditional power relationships between teachers and students that create barriers to achieving inclusive classrooms. Power relationships and hierarchies in education systems usually reinforce authoritarian teacher–student relationships that alienate many students. These traditional power relationships can even lead to student disengagement from school.

Peer-supported learning can help re-engage students who have lost interest in the education process. Here, as students participate in active ways, there is little need for dominating strategies. Students might work together to solve problems or work on a group project or experiment. With peer-supported learning, students can bring their own knowledge, experiences and interests to bear on their learning. Thus, teachers can invite them to be co-constructors and co-creators of their learning experiences rather than students being merely passive consumers of the curriculum (Smyth, 2000) or disengaging from it. This altered relationship means those students' perspectives, cultures, and experiences come into the centre of the curriculum because there is communication between the teacher and students. If the teacher has a better understanding of the students' ongoing experience in the classroom, they can monitor how students are learning. A pedagogy that gives students a sense of belonging can only enhance classroom relationships and opportunities to achieve positive learning outcomes as students have a greater desire to learn. Box 12.7 provides an example of how students were involved as citizens in a secondary school community process for school review and development. The comments illustrate the sense of respect for students' ideas and suggestions in the process.

To create a learner-centred classroom that is informed by the students' needs and background, teachers may provide choice in content focus areas or in assessment tasks. Students may be encouraged to choose assessment options that provide the best opportunity for them to demonstrate their strengths and learning. Students are encouraged to be more involved in constructing the learning process. An inclusive program assumes that different students will be doing different activities and learning in different ways.

Treating students with respect and involving them more in decision-making about their learning provides opportunities for them to take the initiative and develop responsibility and commitment to

12.7 The school review

A secondary school community was invited to participate in a school review and development process by the principal. This process established collaboration and teamwork in a culture where students were treated as citizens and not tourists.

One student explained that when she first began her schooling at Cotton Tree State High School, she thought, "You just come to school, you learn, you have a great time while you were here and then you go" in the same way that tourists pass through a town. The word "involvement" was mentioned a number of times by students and captured the change to becoming citizens in their school community. Another student said:

We get involved now. We've looked at a lot of stuff that could be improved in our school. It makes us feel like we belong to the school and that we are part of it, and that we have something to say that can get across and be listened to … It makes us feel like that we are, like the school principal has told us since we first came, family. And the more she involves us in decisions that get made, the more we feel like we are part of a family.

Thus, as the school leaders involved students as active participants in decision-making about their school, the traditional power relationships between teachers and students were altered to relationships that were more akin to those of citizenship.

meet goals. Generally, students want to participate actively in learning at school. Teachers can dismantle some of the traditional hierarchies and relationships that prevent teachers and students working together in respectful ways. These strategies are not complex. The tools of collaboration, teamwork and communication based on the inclusive values of care and respect that have been discussed in this chapter can also inform teaching strategies in the classroom. Consideration of student feedback and involvement in problem-solving can open opportunities for more activity-based and peer-supported learning that students find more engaging. Teachers are constantly faced with the challenge of teaching students who have a wide variety of ability levels and come from different backgrounds. In order to be inclusive, teachers need to believe that it is their responsibility to cater for the needs of the students in their classroom.

student voice

The thoughts as expressed by students; the concept urges the reception of these ideas by the teacher.

Conceptual support for the principle of student voice and participation is particularly evident in the extensive literature on the middle years of schooling (Beane 1990; Hill & Crevola 1997; Russell, Mackay, & Jane, 2003). Further to this, a recent Australian report (Lamb, Walstab, Teese, Vickers, & Rumberger, 2004), which includes a review of international literature relating to factors in retention and early school leaving, highlights the need to examine the student perspective on what is valuable in school. Student involvement has been shown to be a powerful and effective force for school improvement (Carrington & Holm, 2005; Flutter & Rudduck 2004; Levin, 1994; Raymond, 2001; Rudduck & Flutter, 1996; Silva, 2001; SooHoo, 1993).

By listening to students' voices and seeing them as active participants in classroom learning, teachers can cater to students' diverse needs and interests better. Thus, we have seen that:

- actively involving students in decision-making about their schools enhances their sense of belonging;
- an inclusive school is one in which traditional power structures have been replaced by those of citizenship; and
- listening to students' voices enhances classroom teaching because teachers are more aware of the diverse backgrounds, needs, and interests of their students.

USING THIS CHAPTER IN SCHOOLS

After reading this chapter, you should have some practical ideas about how to develop inclusive relationships with partners in the community, school, and home. The importance of ongoing development of communication, collaboration, and teamwork skills has been stressed and you have read about some cases in schools where people have worked together to solve problems. You should have a good understanding of the dimensions of culture, policy, and practice that inform the *Index for Inclusion* and understand how these dimensions influence the development of inclusive schools. The case studies at the start of the chapter and the boxes throughout the chapter illustrate how the dimensions overlap and inform each other.

The teacher

When you are in schools as a preservice teacher and as a beginning teacher, it is important to observe the way staff, students, and parents interact. Look for examples of inclusive ways of working where teachers, parents, and students are respected and valued for their strengths. Be conscious of judgemental language and sarcasm that may indicate beliefs and values that are not inclusive. Watch what happens in the school office when parents and visitors are welcomed or not welcomed into the school. As you become more aware and reflective, you will develop your own philosophy about teaching and have clear thoughts on what you value in future relationships with teacher colleagues, students, and their parents or carers. It is important to realise that you may not be able to change policy and whole-of-school practice as a beginning teacher, but you can follow your own ideals and values in your classroom and model your behaviour for others. Gradually, you may become confident to take on leadership roles in the school and influence more inclusive ways of working. You will learn to evaluate how school policy may or may not address the needs of all members of the school community in respectful ways.

Reflection on the observations you make of practices inside and outside of classrooms will also assist your learning and understanding of how schools operate. For example, as a teacher you will need to question and challenge the ways in which school communities work when you see that the needs of students, teachers, and parents are compromised. You can use a critical friend such as an education advisor or you might have access to an advisor within your education system who could help you to challenge and alter traditional practices. Academics can also help, as can specialists from government and non-government organisations. Chapter 4 provides information about a range of organisations that provide support to schools, students and families. It is your responsibility as a teacher to develop the knowledge, understanding, and skills to support the students in your classroom.

The students' environment

A teacher who values and respects students is well placed to develop an inclusive classroom. Beginning teachers needs to be confident and have clear expectations about how people will work together. Consider how you would describe your classroom culture and list the key principles that will inform

how you operate. By modelling and discussing your expectations in the classroom and by inviting input from your students, you will develop a shared sense of ownership that will allow students to develop as citizens. Motivation and engagement in learning are improved when students have a sense of belonging and commitment. Consider how you will plan to achieve this in your classroom.

A classroom and a school that are welcoming for parents and carers invite community participation. Each school community context will be different; therefore it is important for beginning teachers to invest time in getting to know the local people. As a teacher, you also need to take the time to get to know your students. Discuss the teaching focus areas and establish what students know, and identify what they need to know to be successful in the school year. Providing opportunity for class discussion and some choice in the class activities will ensure a shared commitment and will help you as the teacher get to know your class. Some schools plan a function to enable parents to meet with new teachers. The important key to success is to be open and respectful of students and their families and be willing to learn and listen.

Summary

The inevitable presence of difference among students means that schools must become comfortable about building links to the broader community and valuing diversity. The school community should foster respect for different views, collaboration, cooperation, and problem-solving among the various stakeholders: students, teachers, and parents. There is also a need to develop partnerships among a range of government and non-government agencies.

These partnerships assist schools to meet the needs of their students, and to ensure that all students are valued and treated equitably. Indeed, it is only when traditional power relationships between teachers and students are altered that an inclusive school culture can be developed and sustained.

PRACTICAL ACTIVITIES

Uni-work

1 View a range of school prospectus documents from the internet. Critically analyse the documents for evidence of inclusive and exclusive school policies taking into consideration the content of this chapter. Consider the values and assumptions that inform the various policies. Whose interests are considered or not considered? How is this inclusive or exclusive?

2 Visit the CSIE website <http://inclusion.uwe.ac.uk/csie> and find out how you can use the *Index for Inclusion* to assist you in the development of an inclusive school classroom. Develop you own student survey to focus on review and development of how well your teaching approach meets all students' needs in your classroom.

3 In a group with a number of your student colleagues, assume that a school principal has asked you to generate a long-term goal that the school community might develop to achieve a more inclusive approach to schooling. Brainstorm the important considerations that might ensure the achievement and sustainability of the goal. What recommendation would you make to the principal that would lead to joint school–community ownership and commitment?

School-work

Remember that school policies may apply that restrict your ability to complete one or more of the activities suggested below. Before beginning any of the activities, speak to your supervising teacher or a member of the school administration to confirm that you can undertake the activity within existing school guidelines and policies.

4 Observe how teachers, parents, students and members of the school community interact and work together. What are some of the common workplace practices and approaches that you can identify from your observations? What are the model beliefs, values, and behaviours that might guide your future teaching approach?

5 Take notice of and critique the language that teachers use in the staff room to describe students and their families. Make a list of common words and phrases that are used for students who are complying with the expectations of the teacher, and the words and phrases that are used for those who are seen as "difficult students". Looking at your list, jot down words or phrases that you can substitute for those that have negative connotations that would reflect an inclusive teacher's disposition?

6 This is a tough one. Make a list of the characteristics of the school culture that you admire and aspire to. Then, make a list of any resources that are available in the school to support the positive school culture. How might the community outside of the school enhance the current school culture? Consider how your school can develop into a more inclusive environment than it is now. What changes can be sustained easily and which might be harder to sustain? You could make a summary of notes and observations that might inform your developing role and character as a teacher.

SUGGESTED READING AND RESOURCES

Allen, J. (Ed.) (2003). *Inclusion, participation, and democracy: What is the purpose?* London: Kluwer Academic Publishers.

Booth, T., & Ainscow, M. (2002). *The Index for Inclusion*. Bristol, England: Centre for Studies on Inclusive Education.

Keeffe, M. & Carrington, S. (Eds) (2007). *Schools and diversity* (2nd ed.). Sydney: Pearson Education Australia.

Ruddock, J. & Flutter, J. (2004). *How to improve your school*. London: Continuum.

REFERENCES

Ainscow, M. (2007). Taking an inclusive turn. *Journal of Research in Special Education Needs*, *7*, 3–7.

Barton, L. (2003). *Inclusive education and teacher education: A basis of hope or a discourse of delusion*. London: Institute of Education, University of London.

Beane, J. (1990). *A middle school curriculum: From rhetoric to reality.* Columbus, OH: National Middle School Association.

Booth, T. & Ainscow, M. (2002). *Index for Inclusion. Developing learning and participation in schools.* Bristol, UK: Centre for Studies on Inclusive Education.

Carrington, S. & Holm, K. (2005). Students direct inclusive school development: A secondary school case study. *The Australasian Journal of Special Education*, *29*, 155–171.

Carrington, S. & Robinson, S. (2006). Inclusive school community: Why is it so complex? *The International Journal of Inclusive Education*, *10*, 323–334.

Crebbin, W. (2004). *Quality teaching and learning: Challenging orthodoxies.* New York: Peter Lang Publishing.

Flutter, J. & Rudduck, J. (2004). *Consulting pupils: What's in it for schools?*. London: RoutledgeFalmer.

Forlin, C., Douglas, G., & Hattie, J. (1996). Inclusive practices: How accepting are teachers? *International Journal of Disability, Development and Education*, *43*, 119–133.

Freiberg, H. J. (1996). From tourists to citizens in the classroom. *Educational leadership*, *54*, 32–36.

Graham, L. (2006). Done in by discourse ... or the problem/s with labeling. In M. Keeffe & S. Carrington (Eds), *Schools and diversity* (pp. 46–64). Sydney: Pearson Education Australia.

Gray, C. (2000). *The new social story book: Illustrated edition*. Arlington, TX: Future Horizons.

Hill, P. & Crevola, C. (1997), Whole school design for school improvement. In V. J. Russell (Ed.), *Messages from MYRAD: Improving the middle years of schooling.* Melbourne, Vic: Incorporated Association of Registered Teachers of Victoria.

Lamb, S., Walstab, A., Teese, R., Vickers, M., & Rumberger, R. (2004). *Staying on at school: Improving student retention in Australia—Summary Report, Queensland.* Department of Education and the Arts <http://education.qld.gov.au/publication/production/reports/retention/studentretention.pdf>, accessed 16 November 2006.

Levin, B. (1994). Educational reform and the treatment of students in schools. *Journal of Educational Thought*, *28*, 89–101.

Raymond, L. (2001). Student involvement in school improvement: From data source to significant voice. *Forum*, *43*, 58–61.

Rudduck, J. & Flutter, J. (1996). *Consulting young people in schools*. Cambridge: University of Cambridge, Economic and Social Research Council.

Russell, J., Mackay, T., & Jane, G. (2003). *Messages from MYRAD: Improving the middle years of schooling.* Melbourne, Vic: Incorporated Association of Registered Teachers of Victoria.

Sarra, C. (2007). Young and black and deadly: Strategies for improving outcomes for Indigenous students. In M. O'Keeffe & S. Carrington (Eds), *Schools and diversity.* Sydney: Pearson Education Australia.

Skrtic, T. M., Sailor, W., & Gee, K. (1996). Voice, collaboration, and inclusion. *Remedial and Special Education*, *17*, 142–157.

Smyth, J. (2000). Reclaiming social capital through critical teaching. *The Elementary School Journal*, *100*, 491–511.

SooHoo, S. (1993). Students as partners in research and restructuring schools. *Educational Reform*, *57*, 386–393.

Acknowledgement

Special thanks to Robyn Robinson for her work on the development of the first case study.

Appendix

Children with a disability and mental illness

NON-GOVERNMENT ORGANISATIONS

Australian Government, Australian Institute for Family Studies. Communities and Families Clearing House Australia <www.aifs.gov.au/cafca/resources/disabilities/disabilities.html>.

Scope (Victoria) <www.scopevic.org.au/therapy_schoolage.html>.

Learning Links <www.learninglinks.org.au>.

Specific Learning Difficulties Association of NSW <www.speldnsw.org.au>.

SPELD NSW Teachers Training Package <www.auspeld.org.au/tsp>.

Royal Institute for Deaf and Blind Children <www.ridbc.org.au>.

GOVERNMENT AND OTHER PUBLIC SECTOR SERVICES

Australian Capital Territory Department of Education and Training, Special Education Section <www.decs.act.gov.au/services/SpecEd.htm>.

Australian Disability Clearinghouse on Education and Training <www.adcet.edu.au/default.aspx>.

New South Wales Government, Department of Education and Training, Programs and Services Supporting Students in Public Schools 2005, People with disabilities <www.schools.nsw.edu.au/media/downloads/schoolsweb/studentsupport/programs/lrngdificulties/whoteach.pdf>, pp. 17–23.

Government of South Australia, Department of Education and Children's Services, Special Education Resource Unit <http://web.seru.sa.edu.au>.

New South Wales, Department of Education and Training, Disability Access—Whole of Life–All of Life <www.det.nsw.edu.au/communityed/disabilityacces/da_edtraining.htm>; <www.schools.nsw.edu.au/studentsupport/programs/lrngdifficulty.php>.

Western Australia, The Disability Services Commission <www.countusin.com.au/2/178/67/School_Years.pm>.

Mental Health Victoria Department of Human Services <www.health.vic.gov.au/mentalhealth/search.htm>.

Department of Education and Training, Public Schooling in WA: Students with disabilities and learning needs <www.det.wa.edu.au/schoolinginwa/specialist-services.html>.

Queensland, Department of Education, Training and the Arts, 2007, Supporting students with additional education needs <http://education.qld.gov.au/schools/about/support.html>.

Northern Territory Government, Department of Health and Community Services, Children's Development Team <www.nt.gov.au/health/comm_health/primaryhc_coordcare/allied_health/school_therapy.shtml>.

Northern Territory Government, Department of Employment, Education and Training, Students With Special Needs <www.deet.nt.gov.au/education/students_with_special_needs>.

Government of Tasmania, Department of Education <www.education.tas.gov.au/school/educators/support/disabilities>.

Indigenous people

NON-GOVERNMENT ORGANISATIONS

ACOSS <www.acoss.org.au/Default.aspx>.

National Council of Churches—Make Indigenous Poverty History <www.ncca.org.au/natsiec/indigenous_poverty>.

GOVERNMENT

Queensland Government, Department of Education, Training and the Arts, Remote Indigenous Students Tuition <http://education.qld.gov.au/finance/grants/fund/garp/html/ris.html>.

Queensland Government, Department of Education, Training and the Arts, 2007 <http://education.qld.gov.au/schools/about/support.html#aboriginal>; <http://education.qld.gov.au/schools/indigenous>.

Queensland Government, Department of Education and Training—Schools and Educators, Indigenous Education <http://education.qld.gov.au/schools/indigenous/educators/index.html>.

Government of Tasmania, Department of Education <www.education.tas.gov.au/school/educators/support/aboriginal_education>.

Immigrants and refugees

NON-GOVERNMENT ORGANISATIONS

FECCA—Partnerships—The Australian Collaboration. A Collaboration of National Community Organisations (FECAA, Choice, ACOSS, ACF, National Council of Churches in Australia, Trust for Young Australians) <www.fecca.org.au/Partnerships_AC.cfm>; <www.australiancollaboration.com.au>.

GOVERNMENT

Queensland, Department of Education, Training and the Arts, 2007, Supporting students with additional education needs <http://education.qld.gov.au/schools/about/support.html>.

Government of Victoria, Department of Education and Early Childhood Development—Programs—English as a Second Language <www.education.vic.gov.au/studentlearning/programs/esl/eslschools.htm>.

Safe and supportive whole school environment <www.education.vic.gov.au/studentlearning/programs/esl/refugees/default.htm>.

Queensland, Department of Education, Training and the Arts <http://education.qld.gov.au/library/resource/tesol/refugee-bk.html>.

New South Wales Government, Department of Education and Training, Programs and Services Supporting Students in Public Schools <www.schools.nsw.edu.au/studentsupport/programs/esl.php>.

Government of Tasmania, Department of Education <www.education.tas.gov.au/school/educators/support/esl>.

Rural and remote students

GOVERNMENT

Queensland, Department of Education, Training and the Arts, 2007 <http://education.qld.gov.au/schools/about/support.html#rural>.

Government of Tasmania, Department of Education <www.education.tas.gov.au/school/educators/support/rural_and_remote_education>.

Department of Education and Training, Public Schooling in WA: Students with disabilities and learning needs, Schools of Isolated and Distance and Education (SIDE) <www.side.wa.edu.au>.

Gifted and talented children

GOVERNMENT

Queensland, Department of Education, Training and the Arts, 2007 <http://education.qld.gov.au/schools/about/support.html#gifted>.

Government of Tasmania, Department of Education <www.education.tas.gov.au/school/educators/support/extendedlearning>.

Government of Victoria, Department of Education, Gifted Education <www.sofweb.vic.edu.au/gifted/index.htm>.

aptitude A capacity or potential ability to perform an as yet unlearned skill or task.

ascertainment The process of determining the most suitable educational placement for a student with a disability or impairment.

ASD *See* Autism Spectrum Disorder.

Asperger's syndrome A form of Autism Spectrum Disorder (ASD) characterised by difficulties in social interaction, and by restricted, stereotyped interests and activities. People with Asperger's syndrome generally have no delays in language or cognitive development.

assistive technology Any item, piece of equipment, or product system that is used to increase, maintain, or improve functional capabilities of individuals with disabilities.

at-risk This refers to children who have been identified by school personnel as being vulnerable to an educational or learning difficulty. The cause may be social, behavioural, intellectual or medical.

Attention Deficit Hyperactivity Disorder (ADHD) Excessive motor activity and restlessness. Frequently associated with poor attention and chronic distractability.

attitudes Learned predispositions to react consistently in a particular way toward certain persons, events, objects, or concepts. Attitudes have cognitive, emotional, and behavioural components.

attributes Qualities or characteristics that are either fundamental or inherent parts of someone or something.

audiologist A non-medical practitioner who evaluates the degree of hearing impairment and prescribes hearing aids.

augmentative and alternative communication This involves the use of non-speech communication systems such as manual signs or picture-based communication boards.

Auslan *See* Australian Sign Language.

Australian sign language (Auslan) The language of the Australian Deaf community.

autism *See* Autism Spectrum Disorder.

Autism Spectrum Disorder (ASD) The symptoms and characteristics of autism can present themselves in a wide variety of combinations, from mild to severe. Although autism is defined by a certain set of behaviors, children and adults can exhibit any combination of the behaviors in any degree of severity. This is characterised by impairments in social interaction, communication, and stereotyped behaviours, interests, and activities.

behaviour disorders Although there is no agreed definition of behaviour disorders, most educators agree that behaviours that disrupt other students and teachers to a marked degree are disordered. Students with severe behaviour disorders have often been called emotionally disturbed.

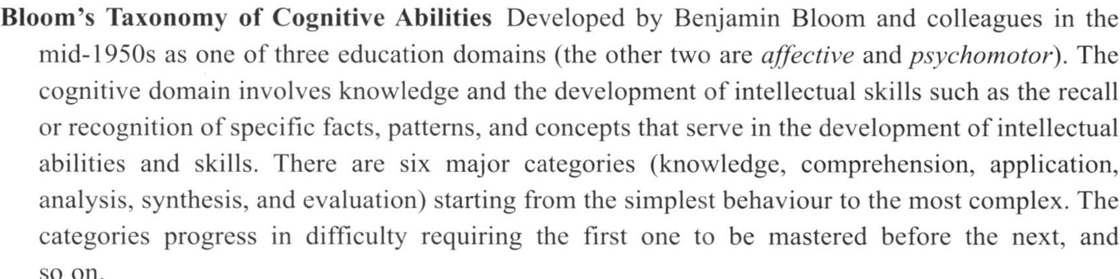

Bloom's Taxonomy of Cognitive Abilities Developed by Benjamin Bloom and colleagues in the mid-1950s as one of three education domains (the other two are *affective* and *psychomotor*). The cognitive domain involves knowledge and the development of intellectual skills such as the recall or recognition of specific facts, patterns, and concepts that serve in the development of intellectual abilities and skills. There are six major categories (knowledge, comprehension, application, analysis, synthesis, and evaluation) starting from the simplest behaviour to the most complex. The categories progress in difficulty requiring the first one to be mastered before the next, and so on.

Braille A tactual language system based on a cell of six potential raised dot positions, arranged in two columns and three rows. Various combinations of these six dots then form the basis for all Braille symbols.

cascade of services model A concept, introduced by Deno, that ranked educational placements from least to most integrated. Also referred to as a continuum of services from least to most restrictive.

cerebral palsy A general term for a group of diseases that cause physical disability in human development by affecting areas of the brain. Cerebral palsy damages the motor control centres of a developing brain and this can occur during pregnancy, childbirth, or after birth up to about age three.

cochlear implant An electronic device that directly stimulates the remaining hair cells of the cochlea (the organ of hearing) to produce a sensation of sound.

cognition The process of thinking, that is, knowing, perceiving, reasoning, and problem-solving.

communicative intent The assumption of motivation in behaviour interpreted as being communicative. (*See also* speech acts.)

consistency management and cooperative discipline An American model developed by Freiberg (1996) that combines instructional effectiveness with student self-discipline, developed cooperatively with teachers.

constructivism A theoretical framework that guides teaching and learning practices. The emphasis is on developmentally appropriate learning that is guided by a supportive facilitator but initiated and directed by the learner.

cooperative learning A form of peer-mediated learning that involves children working together in small groups to accomplish shared goals. In cooperative learning, each student is not only required to complete a task but is also required to ensure that those with whom s/he is working do likewise; in other words, students are dependent on one another.

creativity A process in which a person creates a new idea (thinking) or a new product (outcome), or changes existing ideas or outcomes, which results in something new for the individual.

criterion-referenced tests Assessment of student performance in relation to set standards, not in comparison to the performance of others. (*See also* norm-referenced assessment.)

curriculum Structured content of schooling, often used to include all planned experiences of students.

curriculum differentiation The need to arrange teaching–learning environments and practices so that they are appropriate for the different learning styles and characteristics of different students. This might involve deleting already mastered material from the curriculum, adding content, processes, or expectations, extending existing curriculum through enrichment activities, providing work for able students at an earlier age than typical, and including new units or courses that meet the needs of specific students.

curriculum-based assessment Measurement that uses direct observation and recording of a student's performance on curriculum tasks (or academic skills) to inform decisions about how instruction should be delivered.

Deaf community It is characterised by its own language (sign language) and its own pattern of beliefs, values, customs, arts, institutions, social forms, and knowledges.

developmental disability A disability that arises or is manifested early in a person's life and that persists (most often refers to an intellectual disability).

didactic instruction Teaching approaches that are in lecture form designed to tell in contrast to other approaches that promote discovery or shared learning.

digistories Short narratives about a personal event or life experience made using simple multi-media software such as Adobe Photoshop or iMovie and posted on the internet.

direct instruction A teaching method used to teach reading and mathematics, emphasising structured sequences. Lessons sometimes have scripted responses and solution strategies.

discourse Units of language above single sentences. Includes conversation and storytelling (narrative).

discrimination The unfair treatment of a person or group of people on the basis of prejudice to the extent that the person or group is disadvantaged because of, for example, age, colour, handicap, marital status, national origin, race, religion, sex, or sexual preference.

dissociative disorder Problems with memory, awareness, perception, and may include aspects of identity.

distributed leadership A situation in which all staff members are considered experts in their own right with important sources of knowledge and experience. All staff members are considered to be responsible and accountable for leadership within their areas, and everyone feels free to develop and share ideas.

Down syndrome A condition resulting from a chromosomal abnormality. There are three types: Trisomy 21, mosaicism, and translocation.

dynamic assessment An interactive form of assessment that embeds aspects of intervention to prompt correct replies, in the form of structured hints, to gauge whether the student has the potential to learn.

dyscalculia A severe learning difficulty in mathematics.

dyslexia An impairment of the ability to read. This is a controversial term more often used by medical practitioners.

early intervention A program provided for young children with a disability or impairment to optimise their chances of enrolment in regular education programs. Typically, early interventions focus on management of bodily functions and on preacademic skills, such as concept development.

***Education of All Handicapped Children Act* (PL 94-142)** This is the US legislation that prescribes education for all children. The legislation contains a mandatory provision that states that school systems must provide free public education for every child 3–21 years of age, regardless of disability, unless state laws do not provide for education between ages 3 and 5 years, or over 18 years. A supplementary law (PL 99-457) extended PL 94-142 to remove the exception clause (for children aged 3–5 years) and to encourage early intervention incentives.

emotional disorder/disturbance A condition where emotional reactions are inappropriate or deficient. Emotional disturbance has often referred to extreme acting out or withdrawn behaviour. It is now being replaced by the term "severe behaviour disorders".

fine and gross motor skills Those skills associated with the use of small muscles (e.g., finger movement) and large muscles (e.g., arms, legs, trunk).

FM transmitters and receivers A hearing aid that uses FM radio waves to broadcast directly to a hearing aid from a miniature transmitter worn by a teacher. Also known as a *radio aid*.

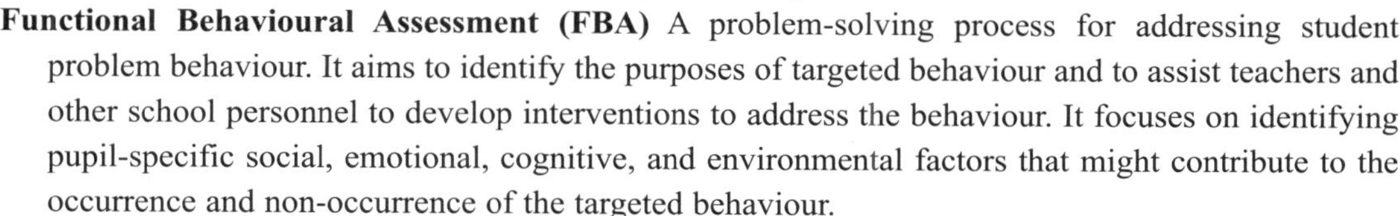

functional academics Skills that allow a person with an intellectual disability to live with some degree of independence in the community. These skills include money handling, sign recognition, arithmetic operations, basic reading, writing, and interpersonal and communication skills.

Functional Behavioural Assessment (FBA) A problem-solving process for addressing student problem behaviour. It aims to identify the purposes of targeted behaviour and to assist teachers and other school personnel to develop interventions to address the behaviour. It focuses on identifying pupil-specific social, emotional, cognitive, and environmental factors that might contribute to the occurrence and non-occurrence of the targeted behaviour.

human rights A convention prescribing opportunities for all individuals to gain access to the social, educational, vocational, legal, and political structures of the society. In Australia, there is no legal basis to guarantee human rights or access to the services provided in the community.

IEP *See* Individual Education Program.

incidence The relative frequency of an occurrence given as a number per 1,000 or a percentage (e.g., the occurrence of Down syndrome per 1,000 live births).

Index for Inclusion A resource designed to support schools in a process of inclusive school development. It was developed in the United Kingdom at the Centre for Studies in Inclusive Education.

individual differences The various personal qualities (intellectual, personality, social-emotional) that constitute the differences between individuals.

individual education plan (IEP) A written document that is intended to aid in the provision of educational programs for students with special needs. It includes a statement of the student's present performance, instructional objectives and goals (sometimes called the individual education plan), services required by the student, and evaluation procedures to be used.

information and communication technology Refers to the range of technologies that are being integrated into school environments as part of the infrastructure for learning. This definition encompasses the broad range of technologies used for accessing, gathering, manipulation, and presentation or communication of information.

integration The process of moving children from special education settings into regular classrooms where they undertake most, if not all, of their schooling. Also called *desegregation*.

intellectual disabilities *See* developmental disability.

IQ A figure determined as a results of the administration of one of the many tests of intelligence. The IQ represents the position of a person relative to others of similar age on the same test. An IQ of 100 is the convention that represents the average score of those taking the test. If an individual is given two different tests of intelligence, two different IQs are likely to result.

Jelly Bean® switches Switches that are activated by pressing on the top flat surface. Most are around 60 mm in diameter and are functional for individuals who do not have sophisticated fine motor skills. See <www.inclusive.co.uk/catalogue/acatalog/ablenet_switches.html>.

Key Learning Areas (KLAs) The main subject areas identified by the Australian Education Council, and developed by the Australian Education Council's Curriculum and Assessment Committee, in response to a formal initiative to develop national collaborative curriculum projects. The KLAs are the Arts, English, Health and physical education, Languages other than English, Mathematics, Science, Studies of society and environment, and Technology. Various Australian states use slightly different labels for their KLAs.

labelling The practice of categorising children and adults according to a type of disability or impairment.

learned helplessness Beliefs held by individuals that they have no control over the outcome of events.

learning difficulties Term used in Australia and New Zealand to describe individuals who experience marked difficulties with achieving in school. These problems, however, may continue in adolescence and adulthood.

learning disabilities Term used in the USA and Canada to describe children with difficulties in language and communication skills generally, but excluding those whose learning problems are primarily due to hearing, vision or motor impairment, emotional difficulties, cultural disadvantage, or intellectual disability.

learning objects Digital resources that can be used in a range of teaching and learning situations. They have clearly defined aims, are often self-contained, and are structured so that the content and activities are interesting to learners at particular age or grade levels.

least restrictive environment The educational setting in which a child with a disability or impairment can succeed and which is as close as possible to the regular classroom (which is considered to be the ideal).

literacy A set of situated, social, and cultural practices that involves symbols such as letters, words, pictures, graphs, and Braille that are developed through interactions with others.

mainstream An early US term that referred to the general education stream in which students with special needs may be placed. Mainstreaming is the US term for integration of students with special needs into the ordinary education system.

metacognition Knowledge of self, of tasks and of strategy characteristics that influence learning and self-regulation of that knowledge during learning and problem-solving activities.

modelling Providing a behavioural example of how a task is to be undertaken so that another can learn by imitation.

multiple disabilities Usually refers to more than two disabilities.

narrative A monologue, either fictitious or a recounting of real events. (*See also* discourse.)

National Curriculum Movement within the UK that has been emulated in Australia seeking to standardise curricula and monitor student progress using achievement tests.

normalisation A belief that people with a disability or impairment should enjoy the same rights, privileges, opportunities, and access to services and facilities as those who do not have a disability or impairment.

obsessive-compulsive disorder (OCD) A psychiatric disorder most commonly characterised by anxiety, and by obsessive, distressing, and intrusive thoughts that lead to compulsions or rituals designed to neutralise the obsessions.

occupational therapist A paramedicist or rehabilitation professional who works to improve the patient's muscular control, often through the use of handicrafts or other creative art activities. Occupational therapists are most commonly employed in hospitals and facilities for aged people and for those with an intellectual disability.

oppositional defiant disorder An ongoing pattern of disobedience, hostility, and defiance directed toward authority figures.

oral communication A method to teach deaf children where the emphasis is placed on student talk using amplification, speech reading, cued speech, auditory training, and state-of-the-art technological aids to assist with auditory, tactile, and visual information input.

orientation and mobility Knowing one's position in relation to other objects in space (orientation) and being able to safely, independently, and purposefully move about (mobility) are important skills for individuals with vision impairment.

otitis media An inflammation of the middle ear and one cause of conductive hearing loss.

pedagogy The style and strategies used by a teacher, sometimes called the art or science of being a teacher.

peer tutoring A method of teaching whereby one individual in a pair takes on the role of the teacher while the other individual is the learner.

phonological Processes or rules about the ways in which the sound patterns of a language are simplified.

physiotherapist A professional engaged for the treatment of physical disabilities through massage, systematic exercise, manipulation, or the use of heat, light, or water.

portfolio assessment A selected collection of a student's work used to evaluate learning progress.

prejudice An opinion or belief that is not based on accurate knowledge, actual experience, or logical reasoning.

prevalence The number of cases existing within the population at any given time (e.g., the percentage of the total school population having a learning difficulty).

quality of life The real or perceived status of the life experiences of an individual that satisfy the various levels of need, including shelter, nutrition, friendships, emotional support, purpose, and reason for existence.

Reading Recovery Developed in New Zealand by Professor Marie Clay, this program selects the children at age six who have the poorest performance in reading and writing and tries to bring them to average levels of performance. Tuition is individualised and lasts about 12–20 weeks.

reciprocal teaching A teaching approach that was designed to teach students to use the strategies that successful readers use to understand text. There are four main strategies: previewing, monitoring reading and learning, focusing on the main idea, and summarising.

scaffolding A term that refers to the gradual withdrawal of teacher support given during an educational intervention as the learner become more capable and is, thus, able to work independently. In language development, scaffolding refers to the way a competent communicator builds conversation using the less adequate utterances of a partner.

school culture A term used to describe the beliefs, values, habits, and assumed ways of doing things in a school community.

school phobia A symptom of a childhood anxiety disorder similar to separation anxiety. Children who develop school phobia become terrified and try every tactic possible to stay away from school.

self-advocacy Organisations composed of persons with a disability that are dedicated to improving the opportunities for people to demand the privileges, opportunities, and access to services that are considered to be their rights as members of society. Also, a person asserting the demand for human rights.

self-concept The perception or image that people have of themselves.

self-efficacy The developing sense of personal effectiveness as a learner, and an enhanced awareness of one's own capacity to learn and perform tasks.

self-esteem The value that people place on the data of their self-concept. It refers to the positive and negative judgements of the characteristics people attribute to themselves.

self-injury The infliction of a physical injury upon one's self (e.g., head banging, hair pulling, eye gouging). This is a characteristic of some people with severe and profound intellectual disabilities or of those exhibiting autistic behaviour.

self-perception A general term that refers to how we view ourselves in terms of the way we think others see us or how we appear to others. That is, it is our view of other people's evaluation of us and our internal positive or negative reaction to it.

self-system The dynamic interaction between self-awareness and self-regulation (metacognition), intellectual and academic performance (cognition), and a positive feeling state about learning (motivation).

sensory impairment The loss or degradation or absence of a sense organ (e.g., vision, hearing), which leads to a learning problem.

service delivery The provision of an educational, training, therapeutic, medical, vocational, or other program or treatment to an individual, group, or organisation.

sheltered workshops/activity centres Work setting for persons with disabilities in which low productivity and low wages predominate.

sign language A language in its own right. It has its own grammar, morphology, syntax, location, semantics, and pragmatics. Meaning is achieved through the combination of hand shape, location, movement pattern, and intensity, as well as facial and bodily expression. In both Australia and New Zealand, the language of the Deaf community is recognised as a legitimate national language.

skill An acquired aptitude or learned act (e.g., reading, riding a bicycle).

social justice The concept of a society in which justice is achieved in every aspect, in which individuals and groups receive fair treatment and an impartial share of the benefits of society.

social role valorisation A re-formulation of the normalisation principle.

social skills Skills that relate to human interactions (e.g., waiting for a turn, asking questions politely, responding when spoken to, shaking hands when appropriate).

social skills training Instructional techniques involving description, modelling, rehearsal, and feedback to assist individuals achieve social competence.

socialisation The process of learning the behaviours, beliefs, values, and norms of a culture.

socioeconomic status (SES) An individual's standing in society, generally related to occupation. High SES is generally attributed to professional occupations, with low SES being attributed to semi-skilled and unskilled jobs.

speech therapy The diagnosis and treatment of speech and language problems by a trained professional. Speech therapists work in schools, hospitals, and other settings where children and adults may attend or be referred.

spina bifida A group of congenital defects in which one or a number of spinal vertebrae do not fuse, leaving a gap. In some instances, the spinal cord or its surrounding membrane may protrude through the gap.

student voice The thoughts as expressed by students; the concept urges the reception of these ideas by the teacher.

symptom An event, behavioural response, or sign that is indicative of a disease or disorder.

syntax The structures of language, sometimes synonymous with grammar. Terms such as "clause" and "phrase" belong here.

talent Distinctly above-average performance on systematically developed skills in a field of human endeavour, such as academic, technical, artistic, interpersonal, and athletic.

teaching strategies Any of the numerous ways in which a teacher can present curriculum content or information to students.

topography of behaviour The patterns of the behaviour including when it occurs, where it occurs, how it presents, and its consequences. It is a mapping of the behaviour as would occur through a Functional Behaviour Assessment (FBA).

values The principles or standards of behaviour that reflect judgements about what is held to be important in life. They are affected by cultural influences and personal preferences and beliefs.

vocational training A program designed to teach the knowledge, skills, and attitudes required for success on a particular employment position or a specific work task. Vocational training for students with an intellectual disability commonly occurs after leaving school. There are two philosophies in vocational training: one prescribes training before placing the individual in a work setting; the other prescribes placing the individual and training on the job for the specific job.

zone of proximal development (ZPD) The point at which an individual is ready to progress to the next stage in learning through scaffolding and interactions with more capable peers. Participation in shared problem-solving within the ZPD can lead to a gain in understanding and skills that will prepare the learner to perform tasks independently.

Cross-reference table

Topic	Chapter number	Page number
Acquired brain injury	Chapter 1	23, CD
Attention deficits	Chapter 1	20, 23
	Chapter 2	44, 46
	Chapter 3	67, 75
	Chapter 4	94
	Chapter 5	125, 129, 144, 153–154
	Chapter 11	340, 356, 364–367, 378, CD
ASD	Chapter 1	4
	Chapter 3	75
	Chapter 4	95, 111, 112, 114, 115, 116
	Chapter 5	129, 134, 153, 156–157
	Chapter 6	169, 180, 186
	Chapter 8	237, 261
	Chapter 11	340, 358–363, 377
	Chapter 12	397, CD
Asperger's syndrome	Chapter 3	58, 67, 68
	Chapter 4	107, 112
	Chapter 5	129, 134, 153, 156, 157–159
	Chapter 10	325
	Chapter 11	358–363, CD
Behaviour disorders/ Challenging behaviour	Chapter 1	12, 23
	Chapter 3	67, 68, 72, 80, 81
	Chapter 4	112

Topic	Chapter number	Page number
	Chapter 5	123–161
	Chapter 10	307
	Chapter 11	350, 369, CD
Communication/language skills	Chapter 1	4, 9, 11
	Chapter 2	37, 40, 44, 45
	Chapter 3	58
	Chapter 4	98, 101, 103, 115
	Chapter 5	139, 148, 156, 157, 158
	Chapter 6	180, 193, 194
	Chapter 7	204, 207, 214, 231
	Chapter 9	286, 287
	Chapter 10	314
	Chapter 11	346, 349, 351, 356, 361 364, 369, 377, CD
Cultural minorities	Chapter 1	11, 16, 20, 27, 28, 29
	Chapter 2	70, 76
	Chapter 5	128, 129, 137, 139
	Chapter 6	179
	Chapter 9	296
	Chapter 10	310, 318
	Chapter 11	356
	Chapter 12	393
Early childhood	Chapter 5	145
	Chapter 9	271–301
	Chapter 11	348, 349, 353, 361
	Chapter 12	396, 404, CD
Early intervention	Chapter 2	36, 38
	Chapter 4	111
	Chapter 5	145
	Chapter 7	211, 212
	Chapter 8	251
	Chapter 11	364, CD
Gifted and talented	Chapter 2	45, 51
	Chapter 3	60, 62, 65–77, 79
	Chapter 4	94, 102, 103, 104, 107
	Chapter 6	173, 190
	Chapter 8	237

Topic	Chapter number	Page number
	Chapter 11	349, 376, CD
Hearing impairment	Chapter 1	23
	Chapter 2	40, 41
	Chapter 3	60, 67, 79, 80
	Chapter 4	103, 112
	Chapter 7	210, 214, 217
	Chapter 8	257
	Chapter 11	356, 363–364, 377, 378, CD
Indigenous students	Chapter 1	10, 11, 23
	Chapter 3	80
	Chapter 4	94, 102, 114
	Chapter 5	129
	Chapter 8	238, 239, 253, 259, 261
	Chapter 9	281
Intellectual disability	Chapter 1	11, 13, 21, 23
	Chapter 3	59, 61, 64, 65, 73, 75, 79, 80, 81
	Chapter 4	102, 112
	Chapter 5	129, 158
	Chapter 6	179, 184, 190
	Chapter 7	204
	Chapter 10	329
	Chapter 11	367
	Chapter 12	390, CD
Learning difficulties	Chapter 1	10, 11, 20
	Chapter 2	46
	Chapter 3	62, 63, 67, 68, 69, 73, 75, 78, 86
	Chapter 4	101, 104, 107, 111, 112, 114, 115–116
	Chapter 5	124, 126, 133, 147
	Chapter 6	175–176, 181
	Chapter 7	212–213, 216, 227–228
	Chapter 8	238, 240, 244, 252, 253, 254
	Chapter 9	272–273
	Chapter 10	309, 314, 317
	Chapter 11	342, 343
	Chapter 12	393, 395, CD
Parents	Chapter 1	4, 11, 13–22, 26, 28–31
	Chapter 2	36–44, 46, 49, 52

Topic	Chapter number	Page number
	Chapter 3	58–59, 62, 71–74, 80–82, 87
	Chapter 4	96, 99, 101–103, 107, 110, 113, 114–117
	Chapter 5	124–126, 129, 136–139, 143–144, 155–160
	Chapter 6	183–184, 190, 192
	Chapter 7	202, 207, 210, 215, 216–217, 230, 231
	Chapter 9	274, 289
	Chapter 10	306, 308, 312, 313, 315, 330, 331
	Chapter 11	350, 373
	Chapter 12	386–391, 393–396, 402, 403, 407–408
Physical impairment	Chapter 1	11, 13, 21, 22, 23, 27
	Chapter 2	44, 46, 47
	Chapter 3	61, 64, 72
	Chapter 4	107
	Chapter 5	128
	Chapter 6	168, 169, 172, 176, 178, 179, 184
	Chapter 7	204, 207–209, 214, 217, 230
	Chapter 8	255
	Chapter 10	314
	Chapter 11	363, CD
Poverty	Chapter 1	5, 10, 12, 23, 26
	Chapter 2	41, 50
	Chapter 5	138, 139
	Chapter 7	210
	Chapter 8	253
	Chapter 10	310
Severe impairment	Chapter 1	10, 23, CD
Vision impairment	Chapter 2	41
	Chapter 3	60, 67, 73, 75, 79, 80
	Chapter 6	176
	Chapter 7	210, 214, 217
	Chapter 8	255
	Chapter 11	363, CD

Index

Page numbers followed by *t* and *f* denote tables and figures, respectively.

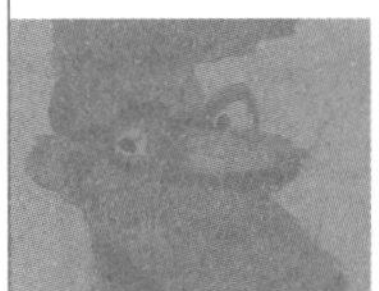

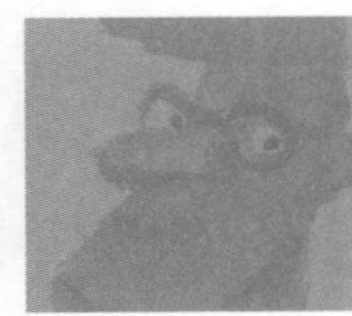